Black nationalism in America

THE AMERICAN HERITAGE SERIES

The American Heritage Series

UNDER THE GENERAL EDITORSHIP OF
Leonard W. Levy and Alfred F. Young

Black nationalism in America

Edited by

JOHN H. BRACEY, JR.
Northern Illinois University

AUGUST MEIER
Kent State University

ELLIOTT RUDWICK
Kent State University

THE BOBBS-MERRILL COMPANY, INC.
Indianapolis and New York

To three Black Queens
Helen, my mother
Connie, my sister
Jessica, my wife
J.H.B.

To Harold and Esther Wilson
A.M.

For Jo Ann Bogle and
Patrick W. Riddleberger
E.R.

Foreword

The fact that the phrase "the past illuminates the present" is abused should not prevent us from using it where it deserves to be used. Few, we believe, will turn away from this pioneering study of black nationalism without a deepened understanding of the movements that seemingly have burst upon the battle-scarred American racial scene since the mid-1960s.

This is the first collection of documents devoted exclusively to black nationalism, and the introduction is one of the few essays that attempt to lay out a pattern for black nationalism over the sweep of American history.

The editors, two of them historians, one a sociologist, have illuminated their subject in at least three ways. First, they have documented the persistence of black nationalism in American life. Simply put, the ideas that inform the current slogans of "Black Power" and "Black is Beautiful" have a long lineage. Doubtless it will amaze many to learn that in 1787 free Negroes named their separate church, the African Methodist Episcopal Church; and that in 1885 Francis J. Grimké advocated black teachers in black schools; and in 1898 Bishop Henry M. Turner preached "God is Black."

Second, the editors have defined the varieties of black nationalism which range, as they see it, from racial solidarity, cultural nationalism and religious nationalism, through economic nationalism (bourgeois and socialist) and political nationalism (both reform and revolutionary), to territorial separatism and Pan-Africanism. By illustrating each type of nationalism in successive phases called "Origins," "Maturation,"

"Flowering," and "Eclipse," they lay a basis for seeing both the parallels and unique features of the current "Revival."

Third, they have chosen selections not only from the few well-known nationalists—Marcus Garvey, Malcolm X, Eldridge Cleaver—but they have illustrated the subtle nationalist strain that twines through such central figures as Frederick Douglass, Booker T. Washington, and W. E. B. Du Bois. At the same time they have ferreted out the forgotten manifestos, speeches, leaflets, and letters that express nationalism at such root sources as Afro-American newspapers, Negro businessmen's leagues, and colored peoples' conventions.

It should not be surprising that the editors disagree in interpreting the history they document. They bring to their task diverse experiences as scholars and diverse points of view as participants in contemporary movements. It may establish a healthy precedent among collaborators, however, that they have set down their disagreement in the introduction. August Meier and Elliott Rudwick, on the one hand—and John Bracey, on the other—disagree as to how to conceptualize the status of the black man in America, whether the emphasis belongs on the essential continuity or on the ebb and flow of black nationalism, and on how varied nationalisms relate to social class. Their book is thus an invitation to thought; its spirit manifests neither special pleading nor condemnation. And for this reason it is an outstanding demonstration of the contribution skillful scholars with a rich command of the sources can make toward clarifying present-day alternatives.

This book is one of a series created to provide the essential primary sources of the American experience, especially of American thought. The series, when completed, will constitute a documentary library of American history, filling a need long felt among scholars, students, libraries, and general readers for authoritative collections of original materials. Some volumes will illuminate the thought of significant individuals, such as James Madison or Louis Brandeis; some will deal with movements, such as the Antifederalists or the Populists; others will be organized around special themes, such as Puritan political thought, or American Catholic thought on social questions. Many volumes will take up the large number of subjects traditionally studied in American history for which surprisingly there are no documentary anthologies; others will pioneer in introducing new subjects of increasing importance to scholars and to the contemporary world. The series aspires to maintain the high standards demanded of contemporary editing, providing authentic texts, intelligently and unobtrusively edited. It will also have the distinction of presenting pieces of substantial length which give the full character and flavor of the original. The series will be the most comprehensive and authoritative of its kind.

Alfred F. Young
Leonard W. Levy

Contents

PART ONE

Origins

PART TWO

Maturation

PART THREE

Flowering

PART FIVE

Revival

Introduction

Black men, throughout their history in America, have manifested nationalist sentiment. Some have always leaned toward separatist ideology and solutions. Even essentially integrationist and assimilationist thinkers have often had nationalist strains in their social philosophies. Thus, in 1897, W. E. B. Du Bois wrote:

> . . . One ever feels his two-ness—an American, a Negro; two souls, two thoughts, two unreconciled strivings; two warring ideals in one dark body, whose dogged strength alone keeps it from being torn asunder.
> The history of the American Negro is the history of this strife,— this longing to attain self-conscious manhood, to merge his double self into a better and truer self. In this merging he wishes neither of the older selves to be lost. He does not wish to Africanize America, for America has too much to teach the world and Africa. He does not wish to bleach his Negro blood in a flood of white Americanism, for he believes . . . that Negro blood has yet a message for the world. He simply wishes to make it possible for a man to be both a Negro and an American without being cursed and spit upon. . . .[1]

Nationalist ideologies have been in the ascendant only at certain historical periods; in others, the major emphasis has been on racial integration and assimilation. During four periods, nationalist sentiment in various forms has been prominent in Negro thought: the turn of the eighteenth century, roughly

---

[1] W. E. B. Du Bois, "Strivings of the Negro People," *Atlantic Monthly,* LXXX (August 1897), 194–195.

from 1790 to 1820; the late 1840s and especially the 1850s; the nearly half-century stretching approximately from the 1880s into the 1920s; and since the middle 1960s. In general, nationalist sentiment, although present throughout the black man's experience in America, tends to be most pronounced when the Negroes' status has declined, or when they have experienced intense disillusionment following a period of heightened but unfulfilled expectations.

This introductory essay will describe the chief recurring varieties of black nationalism and trace black nationalism as a whole in the main periods of black history in the United States. In a concluding section the three editors will present their differing interpretations of the nature and pattern of the phenomena they first describe.

I.

The term "black nationalism" has been used in American history to describe a body of social thought, attitudes, and actions ranging from the simplest expressions of ethnocentrism and racial solidarity to the comprehensive and sophisticated ideologies of Pan-Negroism or Pan-Africanism. Between these extremes lie many varieties of black nationalism, of varying degrees of intensity.

The simplest expression of racial feeling that can be called a form of black nationalism is *racial solidarity*. It generally has no ideological or programmatic implications beyond the desire that black people organize themselves on the basis of their common color and oppressed condition to move in some way to alleviate their situation. The concept of racial solidarity is essential to all forms of black nationalism. The establishment of mutual aid societies and separatist churches in the late eighteenth century had little ideological justification beyond that of racial solidarity.

A more pronounced form of black nationalism is *cultural nationalism*. Cultural nationalism contends that black people— in the United States or throughout the world—have a culture, style of life, cosmology, approach to the problems of existence, and aesthetic values distinct from that of white Americans in particular and white Europeans or Westerners in general. Mild forms of cultural nationalism say merely that the Afro-American subculture is one of many subcultures that make up a pluralistic American society. The most militant cultural nationalists assert the superiority of Afro-American culture—usually on moral and aesthetic grounds—to Western civilization. Programmatic or institutional manifestations of cultural nationalism include the development of a body of social-science literature—history, philosophy, political science, and the like—written from the Afro-American point of view; the unearthing and publicizing of all the past glories of the race; the development of a distinct Afro-American literature, art, and music; the formation of appropriate vehicles for the transmission of Afro-American culture—newspapers, journals, theaters, artistic workshops, musical groups; the assertion of a distinct life-style and world view in such ways as assuming African or Arabic names, wearing African clothes, and speaking African languages.

Closely linked in forms and function to cultural nationalism is *religious nationalism*. Within the theological boundaries of Christianity are such nationalist assertions as that blacks should establish and run churches of their own, for their own people; that God, or Jesus, or both were black (the "Black Messiah" theme); that Afro-Americans are the chosen people. Religious nationalism has also taken non-Christian forms, as can be seen in such twentieth-century groups as the Nation of Islam, the Moorish Science Temple, the several varieties of black Jews, and the Yoruba Temple. A milder expression of religious nationalist feeling is manifested in the recent formation of black caucuses within the major Christian denominations. In Chicago in 1968 black Catholic priests conducted a "Black Unity Mass" to the beat of conga drums; they wore vestments of colorful African cloth and shared the altar with, among others, a Baptist preacher.

Economic nationalism includes both capitalist and socialist outlooks. The capitalist wing, or the bourgeois nationalists, advocates either controlling the black segment of the market-place by attempting to establish black businesses and by "buy-black" campaigns, or establishing a black capitalist economy parallel to the economy of the dominant society. Slightly to the left of the bourgeois nationalists are those who contend that formation of producer and consumer cooperatives is necessary. Further to the left are black nationalist socialists who feel that abolition of private property is a prerequisite for the liberation of the Negro people. (Such socialists should be distinguished from black integrationist socialists like A. Philip Randolph and Bayard Rustin.) At the opposite extreme are those who call for the reinstatement of preindustrial communalism. Black nation-alist socialists tend to coincide with revolutionary nationalists who apply Marxian theory to the experience of Afro-Ameri-cans, whereas those who favor preindustrial African economic forms tend also to be militant cultural nationalists. Negro capitalists tend to be bourgeois in their political and cultural outlooks as well.

In the area of *politics*, black nationalism at its mildest is *bourgeois reformism*, a view which assumes that the United States is politically pluralistic and that liberal values concern-ing democracy and the political process are operative. Program-matic examples of such a view are the slating and supporting of Negro candidates for political office; the drive for black political and administrative control of local and county areas where Negroes predominate; and the formation of all-black political parties. In contrast, *revolutionary black nationalism* views the overthrow of existing political and economic insti-tutions as a prerequisite for the liberation of black Americans, and does not exclude the use of violence.

A most significant variety of black nationalism is *emigra-tionism*. From the earliest attempts of slaves to capture the ships bearing them to the New World in order to steer them back to Africa, a substantial number of black people have wanted to return to the ancestral homeland. However, to emi-grationists for whom Africa was too far away in time and space, or unacceptable for other reasons, the West Indies, South America, Mexico, Canada, and even the island of Cyprus have been touted as potential homelands.

Related to emigration is what we may call *territorial separatism,* a term best applied to the view of those blacks who wanted a share of the country that their labor had made so prosperous but who had no illusions about living in peace and equality with white Americans. Territorial separatists advocated the establishment of all-black towns, especially in the South and Southwest, all-black states, or a black nation comprising several states. Recent and milder forms of territorial separatism are often linked to the concept of political pluralism and advocacy of "black control of the black community."

Implicit in many of these varieties of black nationalism is the international extension of racial solidarity in the doctrines of *Pan-Negroism,* or *Pan-Africanism.* Both foster the belief that people of African descent throughout the world have common cultural characteristics and share common problems as a result of their African origins, the similarity of their political oppression and economic exploitation by Western civilization, and the persistence and virulence of racist theories, attitudes, and behavior characterizing Western contact with people of African descent. Afro-American advocates of Pan-Negroism historically assumed that Afro-Americans would provide the leadership for any worldwide movement. Only recently, with the political independence of African nations, have Afro-Americans conceded that Africans themselves might form the vanguard in the liberation of all peoples of African descent.

The varieties of black nationalism are often not sharply delineated, nor are they mutually exclusive categories. Any one individual may assume any number of combinations of black nationalism. Moreover, nationalism and racial integration as ideologies or as programs have often coexisted in organizations, in theories, and in the minds of individual Negro Americans. To deal exclusively with the varieties of black nationalism in American history is not to suggest that only black nationalism existed. In fact, a book of documents on black nationalism is needed to correct the generally held view that integration and assimilation had an undisputed reign in the minds of black Americans. This book can serve to remind the reader that the problems of the complexities of human behavior are no less formidable where black folk are concerned.

II.

The era of the American Revolution was a pinnacle of anti-slavery sentiment and racial equalitarianism. Largely influenced by the equalitarian ideology of the Revolution, northern states took steps to free their slaves. State legislatures usually provided for gradual emancipation during and shortly after the war, and Negroes enjoyed the same voting rights as whites in the original northern states for a generation after the Revolution. Even in the upper South, Virginia and North Carolina passed laws encouraging owners to emancipate their slaves. Moreover, during the eighteenth century the Methodists and Baptists, appealing to the poor and downtrodden, sometimes accepted Negroes and whites on a relatively equal basis, even in the South. Here and there Negroes ministered to white or mixed Baptist congregations, and early in the nineteenth century a Negro Baptist minister was elected first moderator of the Louisiana Baptist Association, which, except for himself, was composed of white clergymen.

Toward the end of the eighteenth century, prospects for black men changed markedly. The Constitution of 1787, with its explicit recognition of slavery, symbolized the shift; six years later, in 1793, Congress passed the first fugitive slave law to implement the Constitutional clause on slavery. The invention of the cotton gin that same year presaged even more certainly the deteriorating future of Negroes in this country. In the North, although New York and New Jersey finally passed gradual emancipation laws (in 1799 and 1804 respectively), the equalitarian enthusiasm of the Revolutionary years was clearly on the wane—a trend best symbolized by the growing segregation and exclusion of Negroes in the hitherto often interracial and relatively equalitarian Methodist and Baptist churches. In the context of worsening conditions and declining status the first clear tendencies toward black nationalism in America developed.

Negroes had always experienced a sense of alienation, of differentness, of separateness in American society, and during the Revolutionary era this was exemplified by the formation of the first Negro Baptist church in America, founded at Silver Bluff, South Carolina, in the 1770s. But separatism did not become a serious movement until black mutual benefit societies and churches were formed during the period beginning with adoption of the Constitution. Negro Masons in Boston and the Free African Society in Philadelphia appeared in 1787, and the A.M.E., A.M.E. Zion, and Baptist churches of the North appeared between the 1790s and 1820s, as a series of secessions from the increasing discriminatory white churches. In the late 1820s, the third major institution of the Afro-American community appeared: the press (Documents 1–6).

The turn of the century also reveals the earliest evidence of emigrationist sentiment. In 1789 the Free African Society of Newport sent a proposal to the Free African Society of Philadelphia, making a plea for return to Africa as a means for Negroes to escape from conditions in the United States. No results of this proposal are recorded, and actual emigration had to wait another quarter-century until in 1815 Paul Cuffe, a New Bedford shipowner, took 38 free Negroes at his own expense to Sierra Leone.

Several factors lay behind Cuffe's interest in colonizing Africa. For one thing, like so many after him, he hoped to Christianize Africa and to export Western civilization; for another, he hoped that this process could stop the slave trade and replace it by other forms of commerce between Africa and the United States. A number of Negroes wanted to go to Africa; by 1816 so many applications had come across his desk that Cuffe wrote "he believed he might have colonized the greater part of Boston and vicinity." And there are glimmerings of nationalist sentiment in a letter written by some of the migrants to Liberia in 1818: "Be not fearful to come to Africa, which is your country by right . . . Though you are free, that is your country, Africa, not America is your country and your home"[2] (Documents 9–12).

The documents from this early period are few, and those that survive do not show a full-blown nationalist ideology. Nationalism at the end of the eighteenth century was just emerging in the Western world as a popular ideology, and besides, black leaders in the United States were largely bent on adjusting to practical realities. The documents from this period reveal an incipient group consciousness rather than a detailed argument for group separatism. Nevertheless, they do show how the gap between American democratic values and American racial practices encouraged both identification with Africa and belief in the need for separate racial institutions in this country. The very names of the early churches—African Methodist Episcopal and African Methodist Episcopal Zion churches, the Abyssinian Baptist church—and the Free African societies epitomize these nationalistic tendencies.

Documents of the 1820s give only the sketchiest information about Negro thought. Evidently the majority of articulate Negroes denounced emigration and feared the American Colonization Society, many of whose members were interested in deporting the free black population rather than in ending slavery. Some Negroes, however, especially in Maryland where the strongest white state colonization society existed, were interested in emigration (Document 11). Later in the decade John B. Russwurm, co-editor of *Freedom's Journal,* the first black newspaper in the United States, became a supporter of the American Colonization Society. After Russwurm broke with his anticolonizationist co-editor, Samuel Cornish, he turned the paper into an emigrationist organ. In the March 7, 1829, issue of *Freedom's Journal,* Russwurm wrote an editorial entitled, "Our Rightful Place Is in Africa." Not long after,

[2] Henry N. Sherwood, "Paul Cuffe and His Contribution to the American Colonization Society," *Proceedings of the Mississippi Valley Historical Association,* VI (1912–1913), 391–392.

he himself went to Liberia, having been appointed superin-
tendent of schools there by the American Colonization Society.

On the whole, however, articulate black men of the late
twenties advocated collective action to advance the race and
achieve equality within the United States (Documents 7 and
8). One of these was David Walker, whose *Appeal* urged
slaves to break their "infernal chains" by armed rebellion.
Walker also had a vigorous race pride:

I would wish, candidly, however, before the Lord, to be understood,
that I would not give a *pinch of snuff* to be married to any white
person I ever saw in all the days of my life. And I do say it, that the
black man, or man of colour, who will leave his own colour (provided he can get one, who is good for anything) and marry a white
woman, to be a double slave to her, just because she is *white*, ought
to be treated by her as he surely will be, viz: as a NIGGER ! ! !³

III.

The 1830s were years of renewed optimism on the part of
Negro leadership, probably because the militant white anti-
slavery movement had sprung to life, denouncing not only
slavery but colonization and the "sins of caste." More typical
than David Walker's viewpoint was the action of Negro leaders
who in 1830 called for a national Negro convention. This
gathering and the Negro conventions of the next five years
were clearly a form of collective action based upon consciousness of the problems of black men as an oppressed minority in
American society. Yet, the colored leaders debated the propriety and consistency of holding separate all-Negro conclaves
as a means of fighting segregation and discrimination, and these
early conventions did not themselves overtly express an ideology of nationalism (Documents 13 and 15).

The convention movement petered out in the middle of the
decade, and some of its leaders organized the American Moral

³ David Walker, *Appeal in Four Articles*, originally published in 1829
(New York: Hill & Wang, 1965), p. 9.

Reform Society, an all-Negro group which hopefully, but unsuccessfully, opened its doors to whites and discountenanced separate action by black men. A New York minister and editor, Samuel E. Cornish, denounced the Moral Reformers for showing that they lacked race pride by shunning such terms as "Negro," "colored," and "African," and identifying themselves instead as "oppressed Americans." "Oppressed Americans! *who are they?*" Cornish asked. "Nonsense, brethren! ! You are COLORED AMERICANS. The Indians are RED AMERICANS, and the white people are WHITE AMERICANS and *you are good as they, and they are no better than you.*"[4] Although separatist tendencies were a decidedly minor theme during the thirties, in pressing for a stronger racial consciousness and solidarity Cornish helped to lay the groundwork for the revival of the national Negro convention movement in 1843.

In the forties and fifties Negroes in the North and West continued to protest and agitate, campaigning against disfranchisement, discrimination in the courts, exclusion from public schools, and segregation in public accommodations. In New York and Pennsylvania, for instance, they fought unsuccessfully to stem the tide of disfranchisement, although in 1841 Rhode Island blacks helped to defeat a new constitution that provided for universal white male suffrage. Negroes in the Northeast protested vigorously against jim crowism in transportation, but without much success except in Massachusetts. Some boycotted local omnibuses, while others tried to occupy seats reserved for whites. In the early forties, blacks like Frederick Douglass were forcibly dragged from white coaches for defying segregation on the Massachusetts railroads. Aided by leading white abolitionists, they agitated for remedies, and in 1843 the railroads in the state abolished separate coaches.

Blacks also protested inadequate public education; and although most Negroes helplessly accepted separate and inferior schools, some insisted on attacking school segregation directly.

---

[4] Quoted in Leon Litwack, *North of Slavery: The Negro in the Free States,* 1790–1860 (Chicago: University of Chicago Press, 1961), p. 238.

For example, during the 1850s Douglass led a victorious fight against the separate school system in Rochester, New York. The most notable desegregation campaign took place in Boston, where in 1849 Benjamin Roberts unsuccessfully sued the school board for excluding his daughter from a nearby white school. In 1855, however, the Massachusetts legislature, under pressure from blacks and whites, outlawed school segregation.

In the 1840s a number of converging developments turned Negro ideologies in more nationalist directions: the essential failure of the antislavery movement to liberate the slaves; the evidences of racism among many white abolitionists who failed to accord Negroes positions of real influence in the antislavery societies, usually avoided social contact with black men, and often discriminated against them in employment; increasing trends toward disfranchisement and segregation in public accommodations in many of the northeastern states, combined with the continuing pattern of discrimination in the Old Northwest that made the black man's condition there similar to that in the South; and the growing hopelessness of the economic situation, which was exacerbated by the rising tide of Irish immigrants vying with Negroes for their traditional jobs in domestic service and on the waterfront. At the same time, the Compromise in 1850, with its new and more rigorous fugitive slave law, the Kansas-Nebraska Act, and the Dred Scott Decision all made the outlook bleaker than ever.

In the face of these conditions, many Negroes concluded that black men must band together and help themselves. The new spirit was manifested in several ways. One was the revival, in 1843, of the convention movement. A second was the serious debate over the advocacy of violence and slave rebellions. There were proposals for organizing the race, particularly for promoting economic cooperation along racial lines. There was growing interest in the history of the race's achievements in Africa and the United States (Document 21). There was even an experiment with an independent black political party. Finally, there was a dramatic upsurge of support for emigration.

The National Convention Movement was revived in 1843

with a conference at Buffalo, and it continued an active life through the rest of the antebellum period. Those who pressed for separate meetings denied any desire to eliminate joint activity with whites in the antislavery societies or in political organizations like the Liberty Party (Document 13). The 1843 convention was famous for the heated controversy aroused by the Reverend Henry Highland Garnet's speech, "An Address to the slaves of the United States of America." Garnet, a Presbyterian minister to a white congregation at Troy, New York, urged the bondsmen to kill any master who refused to liberate them (Document 16). Frederick Douglass, Charles L. Remond, and others argued that approval of Garnet's address would create further hardship for free Negroes in the slave and border states. A resolution endorsing the speech failed by only one vote, the convention declaring instead that "a righteous government" would destroy slavery. At the next convention, four years later, when Garnet's address was discussed again, it aroused far less disapproval. Indeed, during the late forties the use of violence to destroy slavery was widely discussed by black men in the North.

For the vast majority of articulate Negroes, the doctrine of racial unity and cooperation became a major theme. Douglass, as consistent an integrationist as any black leader in the history of the United States, during this period regarded black men as "my oppressed people," "a nation within a nation,"[5] and urged the organization of a National League (Document 14). All the major national conventions of the forties and fifties called for racial solidarity. The 1853 convention took a more nationalist position than any of the earlier ones and sought to tighten the bonds of racial unity by creating a national council to supervise a highly organized social system of racial uplift (Document 15).

[5] Douglass, "The Present Condition and Future Prospects of the Negro People," speech at annual meeting of the American and Foreign Anti-Slavery Society, New York, May 1853, reprinted in Philip S. Foner, *The Life and Writings of Frederick Douglass,* II (New York: International Publishers, 1950).

The ideology of racial self-help and unity was applied to the political scene. In 1855, some New York Negroes, despairing of any effective action on their behalf from the Republican party, which merely called for the exclusion of slavery from the territories and remained silent on the voting rights of Negroes, formed a New York State Suffrage Association. This group intended to act as a political party and to serve as a balance of power in close elections. Although it did not run candidates of its own and reluctantly threw its limited weight behind the Republicans, it symbolized the Negroes' estrangement from the mainstream of American politics.

Finally, during the 1850s, a growing group supported colonization. Some leaders embraced this ideology, only to spurn it later, but a greater number, including some of the most prominent—Alexander Crummell, Samuel Ringgold Ward, Henry Highland Garnet, and Martin R. Delany—rejected their earlier emphasis upon struggling for equality in the United States and remained consistent colonizationists until the Civil War. Of the views of the mass of black freedmen we have no evidence; even of the elite we cannot say with precision what proportion espoused colonization—but the leading authority on the subject maintains that in the late 1850s the majority of prominent black men had become supporters of emigration and colonization[6]—although they were divided on the issue of whether Africa, Central America, the West Indies, or the far western frontier of the United States would be the best place in which to establish separate black communities.

Black colonizationists held their own national conventions in 1854, 1856, and 1858. As the most practical site for colonization some chose the Caribbean, especially Haiti, whose ruler encouraged their aspirations. Several preferred Baja California and the far West of the United States. But the most popular place was Africa. A few leaders, most notably Crummell, even made their peace with the American Colonization Society. All

[6] Howard H. Bell, "A Survey of the Negro Convention Movement, 1830–1861" (unpublished Ph.D. dissertation, Northwestern University, 1953).

agreed that it was hopeless to continue agitating for equal rights in the United States. They agreed, too, in articulating a nationalist ideology which insisted that Negroes had contributed to world civilization in the past, and that by destroying the slave trade and redeeming and Christianizing Africa, they were to make such a contribution in the future. Crummell, an Episcopal clergyman who had received a degree from Cambridge University before going to Africa on behalf of the American Colonization Society, summed it up best when he described Liberia as "this spot dedicated to nationality, consecrated to freedom, and sacred to religion." (Documents 17–20).

IV.

The Civil War and Reconstruction brought about a marked shift in black ideologies. Emancipation, congressional legislation, the Constitutional amendments, and the perceptible increase in white support for the black man's rights produced an overwhelmingly non-nationalist outlook in the overtly expressed ideologies of Negro leaders and spokesmen.

Nationalist sentiments and tendencies did not, of course, entirely disappear. During the Reconstruction conventions the generations-old issue whether Negroes were justified in holding separate conclaves was debated. For instance, the national convention in 1865 declared that united action was needed for racial elevation; that "the want of union among us . . . is so palpable, the lack of thorough combination and organized effort so manifest" that equal-rights leagues should be formed in every community.[7] The self-help and racial solidarity doctrines of the fifties survived in attenuated form, most notably in some statements of Frederick Douglass, as one aspect of his multifaceted approach toward achieving acceptance in American society. Evidence of pro-emigration sentiment cropped up sporadically, though much research will be needed in order to

---

[7] *First Annual Meeting of the National Equal Rights League, . . . 1865* (Philadelphia, 1865), p. 14.

estimate its true extent. Finally, and most important, the widely expressed and dominant philosophy of participation in the "body politic" did not entirely replace the desire for a separate group life. In fact there were marked tendencies toward institutional separatism, especially in the South. Thus the black members of Congress and of the South Carolina Constitutional Convention of 1868 opposed legal school segregation, but assumed that most Negroes and whites would want their children to attend schools peopled by members of their own race. Especially significant was the rapid spread of Negro churches and fraternal societies in the South, where they had been permitted only a sharply restricted existence before the war. The major black denominations actively proselytized among ex-slaves, and new connections like the Colored Methodist Episcopal Church appeared as black people withdrew from the white-dominated churches in which they had been raised. The fraternal orders based in the North—the Masons, the Oddfellows, the Good Samaritans—spread widely in the South; at the same time numerous local mutual-benefit societies spontaneously appeared among the freedmen.

All these developments need careful study and analysis— and research about them has scarcely begun. Yet it cannot be overemphasized that the prevailing articulated thought during Reconstruction was characterized by a broad program for the integration and assimilation of black men into American society.

V.

After the collapse of Reconstruction, the Negro's position in American society deteriorated steadily. By the turn of the century, disfranchisement, lynching, jim crow laws, and farm tenancy were the Negro's lot in the South. Throughout the country labor unions excluded him from the skilled trades. After 1900 race riots became commonplace in the North.

In this context of changing race relations, with black men deserted by their erstwhile white allies, two trends became prominent in Negro ideologies. One was the ascendancy, for nearly a generation beginning in the 1890s of a philosophy of accommodation. Booker T. Washington and other spokesmen for this viewpoint blamed Negroes themselves for their subordinate position in American society and for white prejudice against them. They flattered southern whites and northern philanthropists, advised acceptance of segregation and disfranchisement, and urged blacks to earn the respect of whites by cultivating thrift, industry, and Christian character, by acquiring property, and by leading lives of middle-class respectability. In the early years of the twentieth century a tiny but articulate minority of Negro intellectuals agitated against this philosophy of accommodation; in 1905, under the leadership of W. E. B. Du Bois, they formed the Niagara Movement, and in 1909 they joined with a small band of concerned white progressives and socialists to found the National Association for the Advancement of Colored People (NAACP). By the end of World War I protest had in large measure regained the ascendancy among leading spokesmen for the race.

Secondly, during the entire period from the 1880s to the 1920s, with Negroes forced back upon themselves as contemporaries put it, various kinds of nationalist ideology moved to the forefront. Colonization during the late nineteenth and early twentieth centuries did not enjoy the vogue it earlier claimed, but belief in the importance and value of racial self-help and solidarity was the most widely held ideology among blacks in all sections of the country during the half-century beginning around 1880. (Frederick Douglass, who died in 1895, was exceptional in his clear-cut rejection of these doctrines in the last decade of his life.) Appeals to race pride and race unity became commonplace, and separate educational, religious, and economic institutions were more and more widely advocated (Documents 2, 3, 22, 23, 25, 26). These ideas pervaded the spectrum of black social thought in the nineties and after the turn of the century, although, in general, they characterized the thinking of accommodators like Booker T. Washington more than that of protest leaders. The emphasis shifted with the rise of the NAACP, whose interracial leadership symbolized the renewed concern of an influential minority of whites for the black man's citizenship rights; and in the post-World War I years ideologies of integration and of separatism were both prominent in Negro thought. In fact, these postwar years produced the largest and most dramatic colonization movement in the black man's history in the United States. Finally, there was a direct connection between the separatist and nationalist tendencies of the prewar generation and those of the 1920s.

The ambiguous way in which nationalism has functioned in Negro thought was never more apparent than during this period. Almost always, except in the case of out-and-out colonization movements, separatism was advocated as a means of paving the way for full acceptance in American society. At the turn of the century doctrines of racial solidarity, self-help, group pride, and collective action were integral parts both of the philosophy of protest, as exemplified in the Afro-American League and Council (Document 33) and of the philosophy of accommodation epitomized by Booker T. Washington (Documents 34 and 35). Washington's nationalism was especially related to his ideology of economic advancement—of urging Negroes to work hard, save their money, and support black businessmen—as the best way to improve the race and achieve recognition of Constitutional rights (Documents 36–39). Yet protest leaders like Du Bois also advocated economic nationalism, along lines very similar to those of Washington (Document 41), although early in the twentieth century Du Bois personally took the exceptional step of becoming a socialist and an advocate of the consumers' cooperatives (Document 42). Moreover, unlike Washington, who stressed industrial education and working with the hands, Du Bois believed passionately in the necessity of higher education for what he called a "Talented Tenth" who would be a black elite, the leadership cadre of a united race, uplifting their brethren and advancing the race's welfare and status. For this doctrine of the "Talented Tenth" Du Bois owed a great deal to Alexander Crummell (Documents 24, 43).

Of all the black intellectuals Du Bois was the one who most deeply identified with Africa. At the time, most American Negroes felt ambivalent, at best, toward the ancestral continent, accepting prevailing white views about the barbarism and idolatrousness of its inhabitants (even while they glorified its ancient civilizations), and yet holding that Negro churches had a special responsibility for Christianizing the continent. Du Bois—two generations ahead of his contemporaries—expressed a view of Africa that did not become widely accepted until the middle of the twentieth century. He combined a sophisticated appreciation for the history and cultures of West Africa with a deep emotional commitment to Africa and to people of color throughout the world. Du Bois was probably the first American Negro to express the idea of Pan-Africanism: the belief that all people of African descent had common interests and should work together in the struggle for their freedom (Documents 40 and 43). No matter where Negroes lived, they owed a special attachment to Africa as the race's "greater Fatherland."

Upon the initiative of a group of West Indian intellectuals, the first Pan-African Conference was held in London in 1900. Du Bois wrote the conclave's "Address to the Nations of the World," urging self-government for Africans and West Indians and the creation in Africa of "a great central Negro State of the world." Although he envisioned no back-to-Africa movement, Du Bois believed that the formation and growth of such an African state would raise the status of Negroes everywhere. Between 1919 and 1927 Du Bois convened four Pan-African congresses in Europe and the United States. Like the original London conference, these conclaves, dominated by Du Bois's personality, ceaselessly condemned racism and imperialist exploitation of Africa. Two decades later, after World War II, Du Bois pursued his interest in Pan-Africanism by attending the Fifth Pan-African Congress in Manchester, England, and publishing *Color and Democracy: Colonies and Peace,* which called for the liquidation of the British and French colonial empires.

The cause of African emigration or colonization was pressed

during the late nineteenth and early twentieth century by a handful of prominent clerics and a larger group of obscure and humble individuals. After World War I the teeming ghettos, swelled by the great northern migration, produced Marcus Garvey's Universal Negro Improvement Association, the emigrationist movement that had the largest popular following. The U.N.I.A. provided a compensatory escape for Negroes to whom the urban promised land had turned out to be a hopeless ghetto. It is significant, however, that the relationship between Negro migration within the United States and nationalist ideologies was not a new one. Since the Civil War the peaks of interest in African colonization among Negroes had coincided with peaks of domestic migration—in the late 1870s, around 1890, and again on the eve of World War I. In many cases, in fact, spokesmen for the migrants regarded African colonization as an alternative to seeking better opportunities elsewhere in the United States. Economic misery seems to have been the chief stimulus both for Negro migration and for the upsurges in colonization sentiment; but colonization attempts ordinarily had a strongly nationalist emphasis, as, to a lesser extent, did internal migration. This was particularly true of the all-Negro towns—the most famous of which was Mound Bayou, Mississippi—and of the even more ambitious attempt to found an all-black state in Oklahoma in the nineties. Later, when their dream collapsed, many Oklahoma emigrants became intensely interested in the prospect of going to Africa. Thus, though it existed in a ghetto setting, the Garvey ideology and movement were part of a larger pattern associated with migration tendencies among southern Negroes (Documents 27–32).

The Garvey movement came at a time when nationalistic tendencies of other kinds were exceedingly popular in the cities, especially in the North. St. Clair Drake and Horace Cayton have described the "Dream of a Black Metropolis," cherished by many black Chicagoans: the dream of a self-contained black community, with black capitalists and professionals supported by the patronage of the black masses, who would elect black men to office—a vision based upon the values of race pride and racial solidarity.[8] It was popularly believed that unity and cooperation among the various black organizations and advancement movements would be essential in solving the problems facing the race (Document 53). The doctrine of economic nationalism was widely held by all social classes, though it was aggressively pushed by the small but growing business elite, which depended upon the Negro market (Document 39).

Best known, however, during the 1920s, was the maturing of a cultural nationalism. If economic and political nationalism were especially characteristic of Chicago, cultural nationalism centered in New York, where the literary and artistic movement known as the Harlem Renaissance developed. The advocates of cultural nationalism ranged from those who felt that Negroes had a peculiar genius for the arts to those who asserted that a cultural renaissance was an essential stage in the awakening of any people. Rooted in the prewar period, the cultural nationalism of the twenties expressed pride in the race's past, celebrated the black man's unique cultural achievements and contributions, called for specifically black literature, art, and theater that would reflect the life, interests, and needs of the Negro people of America, and explored with equal verve and sensitivity the experience of both the Negro elite and the black masses (Documents 44, 46–52).

Together, the developments of the war and postwar eras produced what contemporaries called a New Negro. The New Negro was described as proud of his race, advocating racial self-help and solidarity, and urging blacks to depend upon themselves; he was militant, self-assertive; he was no meek accommodator, but a vigorous protester, claiming his rightful place in American society. It is true that the Garvey movement, which can be regarded as the lower-class counterpart of the middle- and upper-class New Negro, reflecting the bitter al-

[8] St. Clair Drake and Horace Cayton, *Black Metropolis* (New York: Harcourt, Brace & World, Inc., 1945), pp. 80–82.

ienation of the slum dwellers who had so hopefully migrated to the northern cities in search of better conditions, advocated expatriation to Africa. But as Alain Locke indicates (Document 52), and James Weldon Johnson's song, which became known as the Negro National Anthem (Document 54) shows, nationalist expression in broad sectors of the Afro-American community was characterized by ethnic ambivalence and by a distinct optimism about the future of the black man in American society.

VI.

The proliferation of nationalist ideologies and organizations that reached a climax during the 1920s was followed by a thirty-year period in which nationalism as a significant theme in black thought was virtually nonexistent. From the thirties until the sixties, with few exceptions, leading Negro organizations stressed interracial cooperation, civil rights, and racial integration. Among the chief reasons for the temporary demise of nationalism were the effects of the Depression and the consequent necessity of relying on the New Deal for survival, and the influx of trade unionists and Communists into the black community preaching and practicing racial equality and brotherhood. The principal ideological concerns of articulate blacks during the Depression decade focused on very practical aspects of the Negro's relationship to New Deal agencies and the Roosevelt administration, on the role of industrial unions in the advancement of the race, and on the relevance of Marxist doctrines to the Negro's problems.

The depression ended all effective support for the Garvey movement, which was already in decline. Only a few fringe sects represented territorial and emigrationist nationalism: the emigrationist Ethiopian Peace Movement was formed in Chicago in 1932, and the National Movement for the Establishment of a Forty-Ninth State was founded there two years later. Religious nationalism was represented by Noble Drew Ali's Moorish-American Science Temple, founded in Newark, New

Jersey, in 1913, and by the Nation of Islam, established in 1930 by W. D. Fard, leader of one faction in the Moorish Temple. Many ex-Garveyites found their way into the sects of Daddy Grace and Father Divine and into the new industrial labor unions. Some of the cultural nationalists of the Harlem Renaissance responded sympathetically to the propaganda of the Communists and submerged their nationalism in the class struggle.

The Communist party during the period 1928–1935 advocated the formation of a black Soviet Republic in the southern part of the United States under the slogan "Self-Determination in the Black Belt." This rather mechanical application of Soviet nationality theory to Black America attracted few adherents and is mentioned only in passing since it was not a projection of the Negro community. The party played down the idea in the period of the "United Front"; Benjamin J. Davis' pamphlet of 1947 (Document 57) represents a return to this earlier theme.

During the Depression nationalist tendencies were chiefly evident in the economic realm. The bourgeois economic nationalism of the black business advocates retained considerable popularity (Document 55). A new departure was the "Don't-Buy-Where-You-Can't-Work" campaign, which utilized the methods of boycott and picketing to get jobs for Negroes in white-owned stores located in black communities. At times, elements of cultural nationalism were present—for example, in the case of Sufi Abdul Hamid, an American black who adopted a Muslim name and Oriental clothing and led demonstrations in Chicago and Harlem. These campaigns occurred in many cities of the North and upper South; in some places they were led by NAACP and Urban League officials, in others by purely local groups (Document 56).

The major ideological debate over nationalism during the 1930s occurred when W. E. B. Du Bois resigned his post with the NAACP in an argument over his proposal for a separate all-black cooperative economy to solve the economic problems of the Negro masses. Though the issue arose because Du Bois felt that the NAACP was middle-class in orientation and failed to come to grips with the problem of poverty, the argument centered on the separatist aspects of his proposal. In the course of the discussion Du Bois made a searching exploration of the question of segregation, foreshadowing the distinction between segregation and separation that was to become widely held in the 1960s (Document 45).

Like Du Bois, A. Philip Randolph throughout his career has championed the interests of the black working class. His concern took a nationalist turn in the March on Washington Movement, which Randolph established in 1941. He threatened a mass Negro convergence on the capital if President Roosevelt failed to secure greater employment for Negroes in the defense industries. Roosevelt forestalled the march by creating a Fair Employment Practices Committee. The March on Washington Movement, though its career was brief, prefigured things to come. An avowedly all-Negro protest movement, it consciously drew on the power of the black masses (Document 58).

VII.

From World War II through the early sixties, integration continued to be the overwhelmingly dominant ideology, though the Nation of Islam (Documents 60, 61, 62) and the small groups that succeeded Garvey's U.N.I.A., such as the African Nationalist Pioneer Movement in Harlem persisted (Document 70). In the mid-fifties the Montgomery bus boycott initiated an era of nonviolent, direct-action protest. On the world scene Ghana's independence in 1957 and the continuing dissolution of the British and French empires in Africa sparked a growing interest in and identification with Africa among an increasingly large segment of Afro-Americans. W. E. B. Du Bois's move to Ghana in 1961 was a return to the motherland for Afro-America's leading intellectual; for others it was a symbol of the revived place of Africa in their thinking (Document 59).

The civil-rights protest, despite the dominance of an integrationist ideology, produced a growing strand of nationalism at its fringes. In the late 1950s revolutionary nationalism was

prominent in the actions and rhetoric of Robert F. Williams
and Malcolm X. Williams, who headed the NAACP chapter in
Monroe, North Carolina, advocated armed retaliation against
Ku Klux Klan violence, and organized the black community for
self-defense. Later, charged with kidnaping a white couple, he
fled first to Cuba and then to China where he continued to publish his newsletter, *The Crusader*. Williams developed an ideology of revolutionary nationalism and armed struggle which had
a growing influence, inspiring such later groups as the Revolutionary Action Movement (RAM) and the Republic of New
Africa.

Malcolm X rose to national prominence by candidly criti-
cizing the integration movement. A minister of the Nation of
Islam, undoubtedly the largest nationalist organization of the
early sixties (see Document 62), he was the most effective
spokesman for the Black Muslim program of separatism, self-
defense, and liberation "by any means necessary." Most Muslim
adherents were lower-class blacks, and the group was particularly effective in organizing prison inmates. Malcolm left the
Nation in 1964 because of differences with Elijah Muhammad
and broadened his approach beyond that of the Muslims'
bourgeois economic nationalism and territorial separatism. At
the time of his assassination in 1965 he was formulating a
revolutionary nationalist viewpoint (Document 63).

The intensity of the integration struggle unleashed a number
of social forces which produced a striking ideological convergence of older nationalist groups, such as the Muslims and
the surviving Garveyite groups, and militant civil-rights activists of the Student Nonviolent Coordinating Committee
(SNCC) and the Congress of Racial Equality (CORE). This
eventually manifested itself in the black power and black nationalist movement so prominent after 1966. A group anticipating this convergence was RAM, formed in 1963, whose members involved themselves in integration-oriented civil-rights
activities, but at the same time expressed an ideology that
would fall "somewhere between the Nation of Islam and
SNCC" (Document 73).

Interest in Africa had been rising throughout the sixties; even more important, it was reciprocated by Africans who spoke out in the United Nations about the plight of their Afro-American brothers. African leaders invited civil-rights workers to visit Africa, and some Africans went into the American South to bear witness to the black struggle there.

The expectations of black America were on the rise after the early successes of the boycotts and sit-ins, and defeats became harder to take. New methods and solutions were being sought for the most recalcitrant areas of the deep South, and for the economic and social plight of the urban and rural poor. Bourgeois political nationalist movements, such as the short-lived Freedom Now Party and ACT, were attempts to give direction to a movement that was meeting increasingly stiff resistance as it shifted attention from the rural and small-town South to the ghettos of the urban North and West. The Freedom Now Party, launched in 1963 at the time of the March on Washington, advocated independent black political action. ACT, a confederation of black groups and individuals in the militant wing of the civil-rights movement, bridged the gap between civil-rights protest and nationalism by projecting an all-black organization as a necessary instrument for attaining equal rights.

Negro reaction to the bombing of a church in Birmingham, after the optimism of the March on Washington in 1963, epitomized the increasing doubt in the minds of many civil-rights workers about the adequacy of the nonviolent, direct-action approach. The rejection of the claims of the Mississippi Freedom Democratic Party delegation by the Democratic party convention in 1964, coupled with racial uprisings in Harlem that same summer, were further stimuli for growing militancy and the painful reevaluation of nonviolence and integration as meaningful methods and goals.

The racial disturbances in the Watts section of Los Angeles in August 1965 signaled the end of the interracial nonviolent, direct-action movement. Within the year CORE moved to oust whites from positions of leadership, SNCC elected Stokely

Carmichael chairman as it converted to an all-black group, formed the Lowndes County, Alabama, Freedom Democratic Organization, or Black Panther party, as the initial step looking toward a political takeover of areas in the South where blacks constituted a majority of the population, and "Black Power" had become a national slogan (Documents 67 and 68). Ignored in the uproar were previous uses of the phrase, such as Richard Wright's book about Africa, *Black Power* (1954); C. E. Wilson's article in *Liberator* (March 1964), "Towards Black Community Power"; the conference called to establish an Organization of Black Power in the summer of 1965; and Adam Clayton Powell's speech before Congress and Howard University baccalaureate address in the spring of 1966.

Since 1966 a wide spectrum of black nationalist ideologies and organizations has developed, reminiscent of the ferment of the 1890s and 1920s. Cultural nationalism has flourished in such small journals as *Black Dialogue* and *Journal of Black Poetry,* and even in such mass-distribution black publications as *Negro Digest* and *Ebony.* Le Roi Jones's Spirit House Movers in Newark and the Chicago-based Organization for Black American Culture are but two of many cultural organizations. Black poetry, art, and literature are currently enjoying a renaissance comparable to that of the 1920s (Documents 64–66). And the African theme has never been more pronounced in cultural nationalism: the adopting of African names, the wearing of African-styled clothes, and the speaking of African languages.

Territorial separatism has a host of advocates: Robert S. Browne, an economics professor at Fairleigh-Dickinson University; the Republic of New Africa, a group that has declared its independence of the United States and seeks five southern states and reparations to form a black nation (Document 74); and Max Stanford, field chairman of the Revolutionary Action Movement (Document 73). Emigration has had a minor revival; for example, the Al-Beta Israel Temple, a group of black Jews based in Chicago, has recently acquired land and founded a community in Liberia.

An intensification of religious nationalism is apparent in such theological works as Elijah Muhammad's *Message to the Blackman* (1965, Document 61), and the Reverend Albert Cleage's *The Black Messiah* (1969). Cleage, in keeping with his beliefs, has changed the name of his church in Detroit to the Shrine of the Black Madonna, and the building interior is highlighted by a wall-filling portrait of a black Madonna and Child in the tradition of Garvey's African Orthodox Church.

Militant black student groups are now commonplace on the nation's campuses, north and south. Asserting their claim to an education relevant to the needs and expression of black people, they have been demanding and obtaining courses in black studies, admission of more black students, employment of more black faculty (often with a voice in the hiring), and at times separate living and extracurricular facilities (Document 69).

The two earlier forms of economic nationalism are being reasserted. CORE, the Nation of Islam, and numerous local groups are imitating and implementing bourgeois nationalist programs in the hope of developing black capitalism (Documents 70 and 71). In Mississippi and Alabama, black cooperative movements have been started.

Most striking, revolutionary nationalism has been revived by an increasing number of groups with ghetto constituencies: RAM, which endorsed the ideas of armed struggle for a separate nation (Document 73); the Republic of New Africa, which named Robert F. Williams its president (Document 74); and the Black Panther Party, which, borrowing its name from SNCC's political experiment in Alabama, was founded in Oakland, California, in 1966. The Black Panthers soon emerged as the leading nationalist organization among black youth. By 1969, the Black Panthers were deemphasizing their nationalism, and were working more closely with such white left groups as S.D.S. and the Communist Party (Document 76). A significant variety of revolutionary nationalism has recently appeared among young black industrial workers such as those who formed the Dodge Revolutionary Union Movement (DRUM). They are challenging both the traditional trade-union movement as well as management (Document 77). Older working-class theoreticians such as James Boggs, disillusioned with the failures of Marxist integrationism, are now directing their attention to the tactics and strategies of the new movements (Document 75).

Racial solidarity or black consciousness has pervaded all strata of Afro-America. Black caucuses have been organized by such groups as teachers, social workers, priests, lawyers, scholars, and athletes. Paradoxically, this increasingly effective display of racial solidarity has actually produced more integration than the advocates of separatism perhaps realize. Black politicians are gaining in number and influence within the two-party system. Blacks are more highly visible in government, private industry, and the mass media than ever before. In the trade-union movement, black caucuses are gaining more representation in leadership positions.

The attainment of any of the ultimate nationalist goals—whether black capitalism or a separate nation—is in the future, if it occurs at all. In terms of ideology, rhetoric, and programs, most features of the black nationalism of the 1960s have been seen before: cultural nationalism, territorial separatism, emigrationism, religious nationalism, economic nationalism, and revolutionary nationalism. What appears to be distinctive about the current trend is the depth and intensity of black nationalist feeling; the widespread acceptance of black consciousness, at least at the rhetorical level, among all classes of Afro-America; the willingness of the nation's business and government leaders to recognize some varieties of militant black separatism and black power as a legitimate and respectable ideology; the sharing of ideologies with independent African nations; the tendency of some blacks to reject completely the legitimacy of American values and institutions; and the widespread advocacy of armed self-defense and retaliation.

VIII.

In distinguishing the varieties of black nationalism and in selecting the representative expressions that make up this anthology, the editors are in essential agreement. In interpreting black nationalism they disagree, and they sketch here the broad outline of their differences. The areas of their disagreement are threefold: first, the status of the black man in America—whether it is that of colonial nation or of minority group; second, the pattern of black nationalism in American history—whether one should emphasize an essential continuity or an ebb and flow; and third, how the various kinds of nationalism may be related to social class.

First, August Meier and Elliott Rudwick interpret black nationalism:

Black nationalism in the United States must be viewed as an example of the nationalist tendencies characteristic of ethnic minorities in modern nation-states. Its history has especially striking parallels in the ideologies of European Jews and of groups that have migrated to the United States from Europe, Latin America, and Asia. The experience of black men in the United States is, of course, hardly identical with that of the other minority groups. Of all the national and racial minorities in this country, Negroes and American Indians have suffered the most oppression and discrimination and have had least access to the larger society. Nevertheless, the ethnic dualism discussed earlier in this essay makes it necessary to place American black nationalism in a category quite distinct from that of colonial peoples. The spectrum of Negro ideologies is remarkably similar to that of American Jews, ranging from assimilation through cultural pluralism to emigrationism (for the Jews, Zionism).

We hold that this ethnic dualism, this ethnic ambivalence—this identity both with the larger American society and with the black minority—is central to an understanding of black nationalism in America. Like the various immigrant groups in the United States, Negroes for the most part have, as Du Bois expressed it, wanted to maintain their group identity yet be full-fledged Americans. Even today, most black power spokesmen privately would say, as Booker T. Washington and others put it quite explicitly, that black separatism and black con-

sciousness are the prerequisites for developing the power Negroes must have if they are to secure integration into American
society on a truly equal footing. It is our thesis that throughout
American history—and today as well (as the most recent public
opinion polls demonstrate)—the dominant thrust of black ideologies has been the desire for inclusion in the broader American
society. It would be unfortunate if that fact were obscured by
current popular excitement over separatist tendencies, or by
the focus and emphasis of this volume.

In this introduction and in the headnotes preceding the documents, are a number of references to the relationship between
certain nationalist ideologies and the different social classes in
the black community. We agree that by and large, as with other
minority groups in American society, the thrust toward integration and assimilation has been strongest among the black
middle and upper classes, while separatist tendencies have
probably been strongest among the lower class, whose members
are most alienated from the larger society. However, such a
generalization oversimplifies the complexity of historical reality,
as the widespread interest in African emigration among the
black elite before the Civil War, the presence during the 1930s
of many lower-class ex-Garveyites in the ostentatiously inter-
racial sect of Father Divine, and in the 1960s the thrust for
separatism from certain articulate spokesmen of middle- and
upper-class origins all demonstrate.

Indeed, the analysis of the whole relationship of social class
to nationalist ideology is complicated by several factors. Not all
members of a particular social class share the same outlook.
Moreover, the attitudes that are ascendant in a particular social
class have varied sharply from one period to another. Finally,
adequate sources of information, especially about the thinking
of the lower classes—and often that of the middle and upper
classes as well—are sadly lacking. Extensive research will have
to be done before even an approximate picture of the relative
extent of nationalist tendencies in the different social classes
in various historical periods can be drawn, and in view of the
nature of the evidence, it may be impossible to produce any-

thing more than a series of challenging and conflicting interpretations.

Nevertheless, the evidence clearly indicates an instability in black ideologies, and an ebb and flow in the popularity of nationalist doctrines among all social classes. Negro thinking has varied under the impact of changing social conditions. Noting that to a large degree black Americans have been "denied identification with the nation or with national groups," Gunnar Myrdal perceptively observed more than a quarter-century ago:

[T]o them social speculation, therefore, moves in a sphere of unreality and futility. Instead of organized popular theories or ideas, the observer finds in the Negro world, for the most part, only a *fluid and amorphous mass of all sorts of embryos of thoughts. Negroes seem to be held in a state of eternal preparedness for a great number of contradictory opinions*—ready to accept one type or another depending on how they are driven by pressures or where they see an opportunity. Under such circumstances, the masses of American Negroes might, for example, rally around a violently anti-American, anti-Western, anti-White, black chauvinism of the Garvey type, centered around the idea of Africa as the mother country. But they might just as likely, if only a slight change of stimulus is provided, join in an all-out effort to fight for their native country . . . for the Western Civilization to which they belong, and for the tenets of democracy in the entire world. . . . Or they might develop a passive cynicism toward it all.[9]

Basically, nationalist tendencies and ethnic ambivalence have always been present in all classes of the black community. On the other hand, the rise and decline of nationalist sentiment, and of particular varieties of nationalist ideology, must be regarded as caused by the changing conditions which Negroes as a whole—and the different classes within the black community—faced, and by their changing perceptions of those conditions. Only in this way can we account for such phenomena as the dramatic drop in colonization interest among the black elite

[9] Gunnar Myrdal, *An American Dilemma* (New York: Harper & Brothers, 1944), p. 782.

during the Civil War and Reconstruction or among the black masses during the economic depression of the 1930s, or the current thrust toward black separatism, based upon a feeling that social conditions are worsening, when in fact many indices demonstrate that in a number of respects the status of black men in America has actually improved.

John Bracey sketches his interpretation of black nationalism:

First, Black America exists in a state of colonial subordination to White America. Black America is a Colony.[10] It is and has always been subjected to political, economic, social, and cultural exploitation by White America. These circumstances define Black America's "underdevelopment" as a nation. Political decisions are made by whites outside the black community; no black bourgeoisie with any meaningful economic power has been allowed to develop, and the major vehicles for cultural expression such as schools, radio, television, and the printed media are under white control.

Second, black nationalism is a variety of the nationalisms of non-Western peoples in general, and of the black peoples of Africa and the West Indies in particular. Years ago in his study of this question for the Carnegie-Myrdal volume, *An American Dilemma,* Ralph Bunche noted that the same historical conditions that produced nationalism throughout the Western and

[10] The colonial approach has been discussed more extensively in recent articles such as Robert Blauner's "Internal Colonialism and Ghetto Revolt," *Social Problems,* XVI (Spring 1969), 393–408; Charles V. Hamilton's "Conflict, Race and System-Transformation in the United States," *Journal of International Affairs,* XXIII, No. 1 (1969), 106–118; and Albert and Roberta Wohlsetters " 'Third Worlds' Abroad and at Home," *The Public Interest,* No. 14 (Winter 1969), 88–107. Among other relevant discussions are Stokely Carmichael and Charles V. Hamilton, *Black Power: The Politics of Liberation in America* (New York: Vintage Books, 1967); Kenneth Clark, *Dark Ghetto: Dilemmas of Social Power* (New York: Harper Torchbooks, 1967); Harold Cruse, *Rebellion or Revolution* (New York: William Morrow, 1968); and Harry Haywood, *Negro Liberation* (New York: International Publishers, 1948). Of interest also is "Colonialism and Liberation in America" special issue *Viet-Report,* Vol. 3, Nos. 8 and 9 (Summer 1968).

non-Western worlds were operative in the United States among black Americans.[11]

Third, the development of black nationalism has been slow and winding, but persistent and intensifying, from 1787, if not earlier, to the present. The documents in this volume testify to the persistence of nationalist ideologies and institutions. To even consider the idea of "integrating" black churches and social clubs requires tremendous effort. To compare the experience of Black America to that of immigrant groups who came to the United States voluntarily is to distort the reality that for the vast majority of black people most of the time they have spent in this country has been as slaves. And few slaves, if any, were ever concerned with joining the "mainstream" of American society. The documents in Part Five of this book certainly indicate the intensification and pervasiveness of nationalism today.

Fourth, the different social strata of Black America exhibit nationalism in varying degrees. The intensity or strength of black nationalist sentiment and institutions can *generally* be related both to the colonial status of Black America and to the socioeconomic status of black Americans. Black nationalism has shown greater strength and persistency in the minds and institutions of lower-class blacks than among the black upper classes and intelligentsia. Historic factors account for this, as they account for the slow and uneven development of black nationalism, but there is no justification for the view that nationalism is of little importance among blacks or no more than an "extremist" ideology.

In antebellum United States, north and south, free Negroes, because they were few, beleaguered, and cut off from meaningful contact with the enslaved black masses, were limited in the development of nationalist alternatives to mutual-aid and fraternal societies, separatist churches, conventions, and emigration schemes. The enslaved masses developed the "invisible

[11] Ralph Bunche, "Conceptions and Ideologies of the Negro Problem" (unpublished memorandum for the Carnegie-Myrdal Study of The Negro in America, 1940), pp. 149–150.

church," as E. Franklin Frazier so aptly put it, as their chief nationalist expression.

After the Civil War the nationalism of the masses of freedom asserted itself in aspirations for "40 acres and a mule" and for emigration to Africa and elsewhere. But black political leaders who tended to be middle and upper class opted for the limited but tangible benefits of assimilation, and the masses, left without leadership, channeled their nationalistic impulses into their churches and into further development of their folk culture. The nationalist stance of some black church leaders at the turn of the century is not surprising, given such impulses among their constituents.

In the next generation Booker T. Washington and W. E. B. Du Bois, whose contrasting ideologies are paralleled among black leaders in colonial Africa and the West Indies, symbolized the bourgeois nationalisms of the masses and of the western-trained elites during this period. Du Bois was too ambivalent, Washington set the price for the development of an economic base for nationhood too high: a broad multiclass nationalist movement failed to develop. Given the strident racism and imperialism, perhaps such a nationalist movement could not develop at this time in Black America any more than it could in colonial Africa or the West Indies.

After World War I Garvey tapped the latent nationalism of the masses, but he failed for a number of reasons to come to grips with the bourgeois nationalism manifested in Du Bois's Pan-Africanism, or the Harlem Renaissance. Consequently, through the 1920s the black masses remained separate from their potential leaders and thinkers. The jobs movements of the Depression demonstrated that the masses still harbored nationalist feelings. So did the thrust from local black communities in the South to secure the "equal" side of the Supreme Court's "separate but equal" formula. In the fifties and sixties the integration movement was middle-class run and oriented: no one can contend that the pressure of the black masses produced the *Brown* vs. *Board of Education* decision in 1954, or that there was then any great rush of lower-class blacks to get their children into white schools.

In the sixties with the combination of successes and failures of the civil-rights movement, some younger middle-class blacks turned more and more to a nationalist rhetoric in an attempt to gain wide support for their essentially assimilationist goals and to maximize any gains from the annual summer rebellions of the lower-class blacks. Since then, the unstructured rebellions of the black lower classes have been linked to the articulate rhetoric and ideologies of the black middle-classes and intelligentsia. For the first time in the history of the United States, there is a full-blown black nationalist movement with nationalist leadership and a nationalist ideology which is accepted and openly espoused through all strata of the black population. Bourgeois and cultural nationalism predominate, but such groups as the League of Revolutionary Black Workers suggest the prospect of a strong, continuing revolutionary wing of nationalism.

This interpretation of the sources and nature of black nationalism will, of course, be subjected to the charge of insufficient monographic evidence. But this is more an indication of the antilower-class and antinationalist bias of most historians—black or white—of the black experience—than it is of overinterpretation on my part. It is true that scholars have written little on the subject; but I would argue that one of the few detailed studies we have of black nationalism, written by one of my co-editors, supports my contention that today's black nationalism results from a long historical development and is not merely a specific response to immediate conditions.[12] More research is needed. But for scholars to ignore the actions of the black masses and the many manifestations of black nationalism, and then to decry the lack of evidence on which to base any conclusions, is to have one's cake and eat it too.

[12] August Meier, "The Emergence of Negro Nationalism: A Study in Ideologies from the American Revolution to the First World War" (unpublished M.A. thesis, Columbia University, 1949).

Our disagreement as scholars mirrors a larger disagreement in American society. The future of the black man is still very much undecided. We think our readers will agree that the centuries-old conflict between White America's rhetoric of equality and the reality of oppression will continue, as will the conflict between Black America's blackness and its "Americanness."

JOHN H. BRACEY, JR.
Evanston, Illinois

AUGUST MEIER
Layton, New Jersey

ELLIOTT RUDWICK
Layton, New Jersey

July 1969

Selected bibliography

With the exception of several documentary collections and a few works which combine documents and analysis, this bibliography consists of the more important and more accessible secondary sources on black nationalism. The editors made no attempt to be comprehensive, but merely to guide the reader to the most relevant literature.

Documentary collections with varying degrees of attention to the theme of nationalism are Herbert Aptheker's *A Documentary History of the Negro People in the United States*, 2 vols. (New York: Citadel Press, 1951); Francis L. Broderick and August Meier's *Negro Protest Thought in the Twentieth Century* (Indianapolis: Bobbs-Merrill, 1965); Carter G. Woodson's old but still valuable *The Mind of the Negro as Reflected in Letters Written During the Crisis, 1800–1860* (Washington, D.C.: Association for the Study of Negro Life and History, 1926); and Howard Brotz's *Negro Social and Political Thought, 1850–1920: Representative Texts* (New York: Basic Books, 1966).

An early analysis of black nationalism in the nineteenth and twentieth centuries is August Meier's unpublished master's thesis, "The Emergence of Negro Nationalism: A Study in Ideologies from the American Revolution to the First World War" (Columbia University, 1949), a condensed version of which was later published in *Midwest Journal* as "The Emergence of Negro Nationalism (A Study in Ideologies)" *Midwest Journal,* IV (Winter 1951–52), 96–104 and (Summer 1952), 95–111. This treatment reflected the influence of Ralph Bunche's memoranda prepared for the Carnegie Foundation-Gunnar Myrdal Study, *An American Dilemma:* "Conceptions and Ideologies of the Negro Problem" and "The Programs, Ideologies, Tactics and Achievements of Negro Betterment and Interracial Organizations." Typescript copies of these two memoranda are in the Schomburg Collection of the Countee Cullen Branch of the New York Public Library. Microfilm copies can be ordered.

Other article-length discussions of the historical development of black nationalism are Herbert Aptheker's "Consciousness of Negro Nationality in 1900," in *Toward Negro Freedom* (New York: New Century, 1956), pp. 104–111; St. Clair Drake's "Hide My Face," in Herbert Hill (ed.), *Soon One Morning* (New York: Alfred A. Knopf, 1963), pp. 78–105, and "Negro Americans and the African Interest," in John P. Davis (ed.), *American Negro Reference Book* (Englewood Cliffs: Prentice-Hall, 1965), pp. 662–705; E. U. Essien-Udom's "The Relationships of Afro-Americans to African Nationalism: An Historical Interpretation," *Freedomways*, II (Fall 1962), 391–407; Hollis R. Lynch's "Pan-Negro Nationalism in the New World, Before 1862," in *Boston University Papers on Africa, II, African History*, Jeffrey Butler (ed.), (1966), 149–179; and George Shepperson's "Notes on Negro-American Influences on the Emergence of African Nationalism," *Journal of African History*, I (No. 2, 1960), 299–312. George Padmore's *Pan-Africanism or Communism?* (New York: Roy Publishers, 1956), is both an analysis and an important document itself by a significant West Indian Pan-Africanist. For a recent controversial discussion see the proceedings of the 1966 Socialist Scholars Conference panel published as "The Legacy of Slavery and the Roots of Black Nationalism," *Studies on the Left*, VI (November–December 1966), 3–65. The participants were Eugene Genovese, Herbert Aptheker, C. Vann Woodward, and Frank Kofsky.

The literature on the "Origins" of nationalism is skimpy. Leon Litwack in *North of Slavery: The Negro in the Free States, 1790–1860* (Chicago: University of Chicago Press, 1961) treats the institutional developments in a larger context. Charles H. Wesley's *Richard Allen, Apostle of Freedom* (Washington, D.C.: Association for the Study of Negro Life and History, 1935) is a study of the founder of the A.M.E. Church. An early essay on Paul Cuffe is H. N. Sherwood, "Paul Cuffe," *Journal of Negro History* (hereafter cited as *J.N.H.*), VIII (April 1923), 153–232. Bella Gross has done pioneering work on the early conventions and the first black newspapers: "*Freedoms Journal* and the Rights of All," *J.N.H.*, XVII (July 1932), 241–286; "The First National Negro Convention," *J.N.H.*, XXXI (October 1946), 435–443; and *Clarion Call: The History and Development of the Negro People's Convention Movement in the United States from 1817–1840* (New York: Bella Gross, 1947). William M. Brewer did a brief study of one colonizationist in "John B. Russwurm," *J.N.H.*, XIII (January 1928), 413–422. Charles I. Foster treats the Liberian experience in "The Colonization of Free Negroes in Liberia, 1816–1835," *J. N. H.*, XXXVIII (January 1953), 41–66.

The major work done on the period of "maturation" is that of Howard Bell. Bell has produced a doctoral dissertation: A Survey of the Negro Convention Movement: 1830–1861" (Northwestern University, 1953) and a number of articles including: "National Negro Conventions of the Middle 1840s: Moral Suasion vs. Political Action," *J.N.H.*, XLII (October 1957), 247–260; "The Negro Emigration Movement, 1849–1854: A Phase of Negro Nationalism," *Phylon*, XX (Summer 1959), 132–142; "Expressions of Negro Militancy in the North, 1840–1860," *J.N.H.*, XLV (January 1960), 11–20; and "Negro Nationalism: A Factor in Emigration Projects, 1858–1861," *J.N.H.*, XLVII (January 1962), 42–53. Kathleen O'Mara Wahle gives a sympathetic treatment of an important figure in her "Alexander Crummell: Black Evangelist and Pan-Negro Nationalist," *Phylon*, XXIX (Winter 1968), 388–395. Louis R. Mehlinger's "The Attitude of the Free Negro toward African Colonization," *J.N.H.*, I (July 1916), 276–301, and William M. Brewer's "Henry Highland Garnet," *J.N.H.*, XIII (January 1928), 36–52, play down the nationalist sentiments of their subjects. A. H. M. Kirk-Greene, "America in the Niger Valley: A Colonization Centenary," *Phylon*, XXII (3rd Quarter, 1962), 225–239, is a brief account of the travels of Martin Delaney and Robert Campbell. Bill McAdoo's "Pre-Civil War Black Nationalism," *P.L.*, IV (June–July 1966) is a provocative interpretation.

The ideas of Booker T. Washington, W. E. B. Du Bois and other major and minor figures are dealt with in August Meier's *Negro Thought in America, 1880–1915* (Ann Arbor: University of Michigan Press, 1963). Louis Harlan's "Booker T. Washington and the White Man's Burden," *American Historical Review,* LXXI (January 1966) takes up Washington's interest in Africa. George Shepperson's "Pan-Africanism and 'Pan-Africanism': Some Historical Notes," *Phylon,* XXIII (4th Quarter, 1962), 346–358, is a brief but insightful discussion of the Pan-Africanism of the period. The Kansas exodus is discussed in the following articles: Walter L. Fleming, " 'Pap' Singleton, the Moses of the Colored Exodus," *American Journal of Sociology,* XV (July 1909), 61–82; John G. Van Deusen, "The Exodus of 1879," *J.N.H.,* XXI (April 1936), 111–129; Roy Garvin, "Benjamin 'Pap' Singleton and His Followers," *J.N.H.,* XXXIII (January 1948), 7–23; and Glen Schwedemann, "St. Louis and the 'Exodusters' of 1879," *J.N.H.,* XLVI (January 1961), 32–46. The black settlements in Oklahoma are analyzed in depth by Mozell Hill in his doctoral dissertation: "The All-Negro Society in Oklahoma" (University of Chicago, 1946) and more succinctly in "The All-Negro Communities of Oklahoma: The Natural History of a Social Movement," *J.N.H.,* XXXI (July 1946), 254–268. William Bittle and Gilbert Geis deal with both internal and external migratory impulses in "Racial Self-fulfillment and the Rise of an All-Negro Community in Oklahoma," *Phylon,* XVII (3rd Quarter, 1957), 247–260; "Alfred Charles Sam and an African Return: A Case Study in Negro Despair," *Phylon,* XXIII (2nd Quarter, 1962), 178–194; and *The Longest Way Home: Chief Alfred Sam's Back to Africa Movement* (Detroit: Wayne State University Press, 1964). Two interesting migration attempts are described in George B. Tindall, "The Liberian Exodus of 1878," *South Carolina Historical Magazine,* LII (July 1952), 133–145, and in J. Fred Rippy, "A Negro Colonization Project in Mexico, 1895," *Journal of Negro*

History, VI (January 1921), 60–73. Edwin Redkey's "Bishop Turner's African Dream," *Journal of American History*, LIV (September 1967), 271–290, treats of one aspect of the thought of a complex figure.

The ambivalences of W. E. B. Du Bois are treated by Francis Broderick in *W. E. B. Du Bois: Negro Leader in a Time of Crisis* (Stanford: Stanford University Press, 1959) and Elliott Rudwick in *W. E. B. Du Bois: A Study in Minority Group Leadership* (Philadelphia: University of Pennsylvania Press, 1960). The standard study of Marcus Garvey is E. David Cronon's *Black Moses: The Story of Marcus Garvey and the Universal Negro Improvement Association* (Madison: University of Wisconsin Press, 1955). To get the feel of the Garvey movement and of the man, one should also read Amy J. Garvey's *Garvey and Garveyism* (Kingston, Jamaica: United Printers Ltd., 1963). Elliott Rudwick details the ideological and personal differences between Du Bois and Garvey in "Du Bois vs. Garvey: Racial Propagandists at War," *Journal of Negro Education*, XXVII (Fall 1959), 421–429. Sterling Stuckey discusses the great interest that Du Bois and Carter G. Woodson had in Africa in his "Du Bois, Woodson and the Spell of Africa," *Negro Digest*, XVI (February 1967). Charles H. Wesley's "Carter G. Woodson-As a Scholar," *J.N.H.*, XXXVI (January 1951), 12–24, is a sympathetic portrayal of the pioneering efforts of the founder of the Association for the Study of Negro Life and History.

Alain Locke's *The New Negro* (New York: Albert and Charles Boni, 1925) is indispensable for an understanding of the cultural nationalism of the 1920s. Charles S. Johnson's *Ebony and Topaz* (New York: National Urban League, 1927) also contains articles of value. Parts I and II of Harold Cruse's *The Crisis of the Negro Intellectual* (New York: William Morrow, 1967) offer a controversial interpretation and analysis of all aspects of black nationalism in Harlem in the 1920s. The entire period from the 1880s through the 1920s has to be subjected to detailed scholarly treatment; research here has just begun.

The paucity of secondary literature on the "eclipse" period parallels that of the documents. The definitive work on Randolph's March-On-Washington Movement is Herbert Garfinkel's *When Negroes March* (Glencoe, Ill.: The Free Press, 1959). Harry Haywood's *Negro Liberation* (New York: International Publishers, 1948) is a lengthy analysis and advocacy of nationalism from the Communist point of view. Wilson Record's *The Negro and the Communist Party* (Chapel Hill: University of North Carolina Press, 1951) details the Communist Party's varying postures towards black nationalism from 1919 through the 1940s. Arthur Fauset's *Black Gods of the Metropolis: Negro Religious Cults in the Urban North* (Philadelphia: University of Pennsylvania Press, 1944) and Howard Brotz's *The Black Jews of Harlem: Negro Nationalism and the Dilemmas of Negro Leadership* (New York: The Free Press of Glencoe, 1964) provided some data on religious nationalism. The outstanding sources for this period are the Bunche memoranda mentioned earlier.

Analyses of the "revival" of nationalism in the 1960s include John Henrik Clarke's "The New Afro-American Nationalism," *Freedomways,* I (Fall 1961), 285–295; E. U. Essien-Udom's "The Nationalist Movements of Harlem," *Freedomways,* III (Summer 1963), 335–342; Richard B. Moore's "Africa Conscious Harlem," *Freedomways,* III (Summer 1963), 315–334. Harold Cruse's *The Crisis of the Negro Intellectual,* cited earlier, and his *Rebellion or Revolution?* (New York: William Morrow, 1968) are provocative and controversial. Ernest Kaiser's review of Cruse's work in *Freedomways,* IX (Winter 1969), 24–41 should also be consulted. A. James Gregor's "Black Nationalism: A Preliminary Analysis of Negro Radicalism," *Science and Society,* XXVI (Fall 1963), 415–432 is a well argued discussion of nationalist sentiment among the black lower classes.

The standard studies of the Nation of Islam are C. Eric Lincoln's *The Black Muslims in America* (Boston: Beacon Press, 1961), and E. U. Essien-Udom's *Black Nationalism: The Search for Identity in America* (Chicago: University of Chicago

Press, 1962). Louis Lomax's *When the Word Is Given* (Cleveland: World Publishers, 1963) captures some of the flavor of the Muslim rhetoric. *Autobiography of Malcolm X* (New York: Grove Press, 1965) is a classic and with George Breitman's *Malcolm X Speaks* (New York: Merit Publishers, 1965) is a useful introduction to an understanding of Malcolm's tremendous impact on Black America.

The literature on black power is legion. Floyd Barbour (ed.), *The Black Power Revolt* (Boston: Porter-Sargent, 1968) has many representative documents from the current period. Howard Dratch in "The Emergence of Black Power," *International Socialist Journal,* No. 26–27 (July 1968), pp. 321–365, gives an analysis of both the literature and the movement itself. Claude Lightfoot's *Ghetto Rebellion to Black Liberation* (New York: International Publishers, 1968) provides the Communist viewpoint on black power and the new nationalism.

Separatism in education is discussed at length in two special issues of *Negro Digest*: "The Black University," XVII (March 1968), and "Toward a Black University," XVIII (March 1969). LeRoi Jones's (now Ameer Baraka) and Larry Neal's *Black Fire: An Anthology of Afro-American Writing* (New York: William Morrow, 1968) is a compendium of some of the literary output of the cultural nationalists. Of the many journals and magazines now being published, three of the most important are: *Negro Digest* (Chicago), *Liberator* (New York), and *Journal of Black Poetry* (San Francisco).

Two useful bibliographical essays that analyze and discuss the deluge of new works on black history and culture, and the literature of nationalism are Ernest Kaiser's "The History of Negro History," *Negro Digest,* XVII (February 1968), and "Recent Literature on Black Liberation Struggles and the Ghetto Crisis (A Bibliographical Survey)," *Science and Society,* XXXIII (Spring 1969), 168–196. The latter article is particularly useful in putting the literature of nationalism in its historical and historiographical context.

Editors' note and acknowledgments

The many selections included in this volume have been printed as in the original in each case, even with variant spellings and grammatical usages. However, it has been necessary to abridge several selections in order to present a wide spectrum of black nationalist thought. Wherever this has occurred, ellipses mark the abridgement, but the reader may be sure that no passage has been pruned of its central thought.

We wish to acknowledge the helpfulness of the following libraries: Northwestern University, Kent State University, Princeton University, the Beinecke Library at Yale University, New Bedford Public Library, the Library of Congress, The Schomburg Collection of the New York Public Library and the New York Public Library's main collection at 42nd Street, and the Moorland Foundation Room of the Howard University Library. We would like to express a special note of thanks to Mrs. Dorothy Porter of the Moorland Room, for opening the collection to us at a time when it would have otherwise been closed.

We are indebted to Professor James M. McPherson of Princeton University for calling our attention to the document by Francis J. Grimké, to Professor Donald M. Jacobs of Bridgewater State College for suggesting the document by David Walker, and to Professors Otto H. Olsen of Northern Illinois University and Edwin S. Redkey of the University of Tennessee for informing us of the existence of the *Voice of Missions*.

Messrs. Meier and Rudwick wish to acknowledge with appreciation the assistance of Gerald and Melinda Martin, Miss Betsy Cox, Miss Linda Van Keuren, Miss Eileen Petric, Mrs. Carol Toncar and Mrs. Barbara Hostetler in typing and other chores connected with the preparation of the manuscript. They are also grateful for the support provided by the Kent State University Center for Urban Regionalism and its director, Professor James G. Coke.

Finally, we are indebted most of all to Alfred F. Young, general editor in charge of this volume, who gave us invaluable editorial assistance and friendly encouragement through every phase of preparation and publication. This book owes more than we can say to his constructive suggestions and perceptive criticism.

John H. Bracey, Jr.
August Meier
Elliott Rudwick

PART ONE

Foundations
of the black community:
the church

The institutional organization of the Negro community is
historically rooted in the church and the fraternal or mutual
benefit orders. The origins of both go back to the late
eighteenth century.

The independent church movement arose because of racial
prejudice in the white-dominated churches. The origins of the
African Methodist Episcopal (A.M.E.) Church exemplify
Negro response to this treatment. Its leading founder and first
consecrated bishop was Richard Allen, a former slave from
Maryland who had been converted to Methodism. He later
became a Methodist circuit preacher, and moving to
Philadelphia began attending the predominantly white
St. George's Methodist Episcopal Church in 1786. Perceiving
that blacks were unable to achieve positions of true leadership
at St. George's, Allen urged the creation of a separate place
of worship. The response of most Negro parishioners was
cool. But Allen's magnetic personality was drawing ever larger
numbers of colored people to St. George's, much to the
annoyance of the trustees, who stopped his prayer service and
ordered Negro communicants to sit in the rear of the gallery.
Facing such galling treatment, Allen and his friend Absolom
Jones departed from St. George's with their followers.*
Ultimately, despite opposition from Methodist elders, Allen
succeeded in establishing his own church, while Jones founded
the first black Episcopal church in America.

Parallel developments were occurring elsewhere. Finally in

* Jones's first name has been spelled in differing ways. However, he used
the spelling Absolom.

1816 representatives of African Methodist churches in
Pennsylvania, New Jersey, Delaware, and Maryland met
in Philadelphia and formed a separate Methodist connection,
the African Methodist Episcopal Church.

In the documents that follow, A.M.E. leaders explain the
origins and justify the existence of a separate African or Negro
Methodist church. The selection from Richard Allen's
autobiography recounts his experiences as a Methodist preacher
and the events that led to the establishment of the A.M.E.
church. The other two selections, one by a layman named L. H.
Reynolds and the other by the distinguished bishop, Daniel
Alexander Payne, are both defenses of religious separatism. The
excerpt from Payne's *History of the African Methodist
Episcopal Church,* published in 1891, is representative of the
thinking of leaders in the black churches for more than a
hundred years. Reynolds, despite his use of late-nineteenth-
century terms such as "race instincts," also expressed a
viewpoint that was widespread among black churchmen.

1. RICHARD ALLEN DESCRIBES
THE FOUNDING OF THE AFRICAN METHODIST
EPISCOPAL CHURCH

December 1784, General Conference sat in Baltimore, the first
General Conference ever held in America. The English preach-
ers just arrived from Europe were, Rev. Dr. Coke, Richard
Whatcoat and Thomas Vassey. This was the beginning of the
Episcopal Church amongst the Methodists. Many of the min-
isters were set apart in holy orders at this conference, and were

From Richard Allen, THE LIFE, EXPERIENCE
AND GOSPEL LABORS OF THE RT. REV. RICHARD ALLEN
(Philadelphia: Lee & Yocum, 1888), pp. 11–17, 23–24.

said to be entitled to the gown; and I have thought religion has been declining in the church ever since. There was a pamphlet published by some person, which stated, that when the Methodists were no people, then they were a people; and now they have become a people they were no people; which had often serious weight upon my mind.

In 1785 the Rev. Richard Whatcoat was appointed on Baltimore circuit. He was, I believe, a man of God. I found great strength in travelling with him—a father in Israel. In his advice he was fatherly and friendly. He was of a mild and serene disposition. My lot was cast in Baltimore, in a small meeting-house called Methodist Alley. I stopped at Richard Mould's, and was sent to my lodgings, and lodged at Mr. McCannon's. I had some happy meetings in Baltimore. I was introduced to Richard Russell, who was very kind and affectionate to me, and attended several meetings. Rev. Bishop Asbury sent for me to meet him at Henry Gaff's. I did so. He told me he wished me to travel with him. He told me that in the slave countries, Carolina and other places, I must not intermix with the slaves, and I would frequently have to sleep in his carriage, and he would allow me my victuals and clothes. I told him I would not travel with him on these conditions. He asked me my reason. I told him if I was taken sick, who was to support me? and that I thought people ought to lay up something while they were able, to support themselves in time of sickness or old age. He said that was as much as he got, his victuals and clothes. I told him he would be taken care of, let his afflictions be as they were, or let him be taken sick where he would, he would be taken care of; but I doubted whether it would be the case with myself. He smiled, and told me he would give me from then until he returned from the eastward to make up my mind, which would be about three months. But I made up my mind that I would not accept of his proposals. Shortly after I left Hartford Circuit, and came to Pennsylvania, on Lancaster circuit. I travelled several months on Lancaster circuit with the Rev. Peter Morratte and Irie Ellis. They were very kind and affectionate to me in building me up; for I had many trials to pass through, and I received nothing from the Methodist connection. My usual method was, when I would get bare of clothes, to stop travelling and go to work, so that no man could say I was chargeable to the connection. My hands administered to my necessities. The autumn of 1785 I returned again to Radnor. I stopped at George Giger's, a man of God, and went to work. His family were all kind and affectionate to me. I killed seven beeves, and supplied the neighbors with meat; got myself pretty well clad through my own industry—thank God—and preached occasionally. The elder in charge in Philadelphia frequently sent for me to come to the city. February, 1786, I came to Philadelphia. Preaching was given out for me at five o'clock in the morning at St. George church. I strove to preach as well as I could, but it was a great cross to me; but the Lord was with me. We had a good time, and several souls were awakened, and were earnestly seeking redemption in the blood of Christ. I thought I would stop in Philadelphia a week or two. I preached at different places in the city. My labor was much blessed. I soon saw a large field open in seeking and instructing my African brethren, who had been a long forgotten people and few of them attended public worship. I preached in the commons, in Southwark, Northern Liberties, and wherever I could find an opening. I frequently preached twice a day, at 5 o'clock in the morning and in the evening, and it was not uncommon for me to preach from four to five times a day. I established prayer meetings; I raised a society in 1786 for forty-two members. I saw the necessity of erecting a place of worship for the colored people. I proposed it to the most respectable people of color in this city; but here I met with opposition. I had but three colored brethren that united with me in erecting a place of worship—the Rev. Absalom Jones, William White and Dorus Ginnings. These united with me as soon as it became public and known by the elder who was stationed in the city. The Rev. C—— B—— opposed the plan, and would not submit to any argument we could raise; but he was shortly removed from the charge. The Rev. Mr. W—— took the charge, and the Rev. L—— G——. Mr. W—— was much opposed to an African church, and used very degrad-

ing and insulting language to us, to try and prevent us from
going on. We all belonged to St. George's church—Rev. Absalom Jones, William White and Dorus Ginnings. We felt ourselves much cramped; but my dear Lord was with us, and we
believed, if it was his will, the work would go on, and that we
would be able to succeed in building the house of the Lord. We
established prayer meetings and meetings of exhortation, and
the Lord blessed our endeavors, and many souls were awakened; but the elder soon forbid us holding any such meetings;
but we viewed the forlorn state of our colored brethren, and
that they were destitute of a place of worship. They were considered as a nuisance.

A number of us usually attended St. George's church in
Fourth street; and when the colored people began to get numerous in attending the church, they moved us from the seats
we usually sat on, and placed us around the wall, and on
Sabbath morning we went to church and the sexton stood at
the door, and told us to go in the gallery. He told us to go, and
we would see where to sit. We expected to take the seats
over the ones we formerly occupied below, not knowing any
better. We took those seats. Meeting had begun, and they were
nearly done singing, and just as we got to the seats, the elder
said, "Let us pray." We had not been long upon our knees
before I heard considerable scuffling and low talking. I raised
my head up and saw one of the trustees, H—— M——, having
hold of the Rev. Absalom Jones, pulling him up off of his
knees, and saying, "You must get up—you must not kneel
here." Mr. Jones replied, "Wait until prayer is over." Mr. H——
M—— said "No, you must get up now, or I will call for aid
and force you away." Mr. Jones said, "Wait until prayer is over,
and I will get up and trouble you no more." With that he
beckoned to one of the other trustees, Mr. L—— S—— to come
to his assistance. He came, and went to William White to pull
him up. By this time prayer was over, and we all went out of
the church in a body, and they were no more plagued with us
in the church. This raised a great excitement and inquiry among
the citizens, in so much that I believe they were ashamed of

their conduct. But my dear Lord was with us, and we were filled with fresh vigor to get a house erected to worship God in. Seeing our forlorn and distressed situation, many of the hearts of our citizens were moved to urge us forward; notwithstanding we had subscribed largely towards finishing St. George's church, in building the gallery and laying new floors, and just as the house was made comfortable, we were turned out from enjoying the comforts of worshipping therein. We then hired a store-room, and held worship by ourselves. Here we were pursued with threats of being disowned, and read publicly out of meeting if we did continue worship in the place we had hired; but we believed the Lord would be our friend. We got subscription papers out to raise money to build the house of the Lord. By this time we had waited on Dr. Rush and Mr. Robert Ralston, and told them of our distressing situation. We considered it a blessing that the Lord had put it into our hearts to wait upon those gentlemen. They pitied our situation, and subscribed largely towards the church, and were very friendly towards us, and advised us how to go on. We appointed Mr. Ralston our treasurer. Dr. Rush did much for us in public by his influence. I hope the name of Dr. Benjamin Rush and Robert Ralston will never be forgotten among us. They were the first two gentlemen who espoused the cause of the oppressed, and aided us in building the house of the Lord for the poor Africans to worship in. Here was the beginning and rise of the first African church in America. But the elder of the Methodist Church still pursued us. Mr. J—— M—— called upon us and told us if we did not erase our names from the subscription paper, and give up the paper, we would be publicly turned out of meeting. We asked him if we had violated any rules of discipline by so doing. He replied, "I have the charge given to me by the Conference, and unless you submit I will read you publicly out of meeting." We told him we were willing to abide by the discipline of the Methodist Church, "And if you will show us where we have violated any law of discipline of the Methodist Church, we will submit; and if there is no rule violated in the discipline we will proceed on." He replied, "We will read you all out." We told him if he turned us out contrary to rule of discipline, we should seek further redress. We told him we were dragged off of our knees in St. George's church, and treated worse than heathens; and we were determined to seek out for ourselves, the Lord being our helper. He told us we were not Methodists, and left us. Finding we would go on in raising money to build the church, he called upon us again, and wished to see us all together. We met him. He told us that he wished us well, that he was a friend to us, and used many arguments to convince us that we were wrong in building a church. We told him we had no place of worship; and we did not mean to go to St. George's church any more, as we were so scandalously treated in the presence of all the congregation present; "and if you deny us your name, you cannot seal up the scriptures from us, and deny us a name in heaven. We believe heaven is free for all who worship in spirit and truth." And he said, "So you are determined to go on." We told him "Yes, God being our helper." He then replied, "We will disown you all from the Methodist connection." We believed if we put our trust in the Lord, he would stand by us. This was a trial that I never had to pass through before. I was confident that the great head of the church would support us. My dear Lord was with us. . . . Robert R. Roberts, the resident elder, came to Bethel, insisted on preaching to us and taking the spiritual charge of the congregation, for we were Methodists he was told he should come on some terms with the trustees; his answer was, that "He did not come to consult with Richard Allen or other trustees, but to inform the congregation, that on next Sunday afternoon, he would come and take the spiritual charge." We told him he could not preach for us under existing circumstances. However, at the appointed time he came, but having taken previous advice we had our preacher in the pulpit when he came, and the house was so fixed that he could not get but more than half way to the pulpit. Finding himself disappointed he appealed to those who came with him as witnesses, that "That man (meaning the preacher), had taken his appointment." Several respectable white citizens who knew the colored people had been ill-used, were present, and told us not to fear, for they would see us righted, and not suffer Roberts to preach in a forcible manner, after which Roberts went away.

The next elder stationed in Philadelphia was Robert Birch, who, following the example of his predecessor, came and published a meeting for himself. But the method just mentioned was adopted and he had to go away disappointed. In consequence of this, he applied to the Supreme Court for a writ of mandamus, to know why the pulpit was denied him. Being elder, this brought on a lawsuit, which ended in our favor. Thus by the Providence of God we were delivered from a long, distressing and expensive suit, which could not be resumed, being determined by the Supreme Court. For this mercy we desire to be unfeignedly thankful.

About this time, our colored friends in Baltimore were treated in a similar manner by the white preachers and trustees, and many of them driven away who were disposed to seek a place of worship, rather than go to law.

Many of the colored people in other places were in a situation nearly like those of Philadelphia and Baltimore, which induced us, in April 1816, to call a general meeting, by way of Conference. Delegates from Baltimore and other places which met those of Philadelphia, and taking into consideration their grievances, and in order to secure the privileges, promote union and harmony among themselves, it was resolved: "That the people of Philadelphia, Baltimore, etc., etc., should become one body, under the name of the African Methodist Episcopal Church." We deemed it expedient to have a form of discipline, whereby we may guide our people in the fear of God, in the unity of the Spirit, and in the bonds of peace, and preserve us from that spiritual despotism which we have so recently experienced—remembering that we are not to lord it over God's heritage, as greedy dogs that can never have enough. But with long suffering and bowels of compassion, to bear each other's burdens, and so fulfill the Law of Christ, praying that our mutual striving together for the promulgation of the Gospel may be crowned with abundant success. . . .

2. BISHOP DANIEL ALEXANDER PAYNE
REVIEWS THE CONTRIBUTION
OF THE NEGRO CHURCH

As to the result of this separation from the Methodist Episcopal
Church, permit us to remark that it has been really beneficial
to the man of color. First: It has thrown us upon our own resources and made us tax our own mental powers both for
government and support: For government—viewed in the light
of official responsibility—when we were under the control of
the M. E. Church we were dependent upon them for our ministerial instructions. They supplied our pulpits with preachers,
deacons and elders, and these in the vast majority of instances
were white men. Hence if the instructions given were of the
right kind, the merit was the white man's and his alone; so
also, if the manner of instruction was pleasing, the merit was
the white man's and his alone. The colored man was a mere
hearer.

Again: we were dependent upon them for government. Not
only were the presiding elders and preachers in charge all white
men, but in a multitude of instances the very class leaders were
also white. So then, if the churches among the colored people
were well governed, the merit was the white man's and his
alone. The colored man was a mere subject.

But, again: Although the colored members of the M. E.
Church always supported to their utmost ability the institutions
of the Connection, yet because their white brethren were so
vastly in the majority, that support which was so cheerfully and
cordially given could not be felt. This was not only true of us
when we formed a constituent element of the M. E. Church, but
it is equally true to-day of our colored brethren who still con-

From Daniel A. Payne, HISTORY OF THE AFRICAN METHODIST
EPISCOPAL CHURCH (Nashville, Tenn.: Publishing House of the A.M.E.
Sunday School Union, 1891), pp. 9–12.

tinue in connection with it. . . . The existence of the colored man as a factor of the M. E. Church, always was, still is, and ever must be a mere cipher. The tendency of all this was to prove that the colored man was incapable of self-government and self-support and thereby confirm the oft repeated assertions of his enemies, that he really is incapable of self-government and self-support. But is not the existence of the African Methodist Episcopal Church a flat contradiction and triumphant refutation of this slander, so foul in itself and so degrading in its influence? For the last seventy years a period of more than seven-tenths of a century, it has been governing itself and supporting itself. Being compelled to teach others, its ministry has been constrained to teach itself. This has caused them to seek knowledge on the right hand and on the left. It has forced them to implore and explore earth and heaven for information that they might be able to lead the erring souls of men from the one to the other. Compelled to govern others, its ministry has been constrained to read and investigate church history for models of government. They have also been led to cogitate for themselves; to discriminate between laws which were just, and those which were unjust; to expunge from the statutes of the Church those which were unequal in their bearings and to substitute those of a more equable character, so that the blood-washed flock of Christ might walk before him in all peace and quietness, feeling that the ecclesiastical yoke and burdens are both easy and light. . . .

Compelled to support their own institutions, our members have learned to economize and to forecast as they never could or would, had they remained in connection with their white brethren. Does any man require the proofs of these assertions? Let him go to all these cities, to New York, to St. Louis, to Nashville, and others as well. There he will see the commodious and beautiful edifices which have been constructed and dedicated by ourselves to the worship of Almighty God—edifices varying in their costs from $3,000 to $60,000. Let him go to Philadelphia and see our Book Concern, where our hymn books, disciplines and weekly papers are published, which,

though in a very imperfect and infant state, give every evidence
of an intellect that is at work for itself, and for its own development. Let him go to our Sunday-School Publishing House in
Nashville, where our own Sabbath-school literature is issued
and publications brought forth. Let him go to our several seats
of learning—to Wilberforce, near Xenia, O., to Allen University
at Columbia, S.C., to Paul Quinn College at Waco, Texas, to
Morris Brown College at Atlanta, Ga.—there he will see our
children and our youth under the culture of educated men and
women giving the pledge of minds that will in the development
of mature powers, cause the world to know that they lived and
lived to good purpose. Let him visit our churches where he
may often hear preachers, who by their native talents or literary acquirements (and sometimes both) demonstrate to the
most prejudiced hearer that the man of color can think for
himself and guide the sacramental host into the fullness of the
blessings of the Gospel of Christ.

Secondly and lastly: The separation of our Church from the
M. E. Church, which was brought about by the agency of our
venerated fathers, the Rev. Richard Allen of Philadelphia and
Rev. Daniel Coker of Baltimore, has been beneficial to the man
of color by giving him an independence of character which he
could neither hope for nor attain unto, if he had remained as
the ecclesiastical vassal of his white brethren. This is evident
from the training which the force of circumstances has given us.
These circumstances have been such as to produce independent
thought; this has resulted in independent action; this independent action has resulted in the extension of our ecclesiastical
organization over nearly all of the States and also into Canada;
this ecclesiastical organization has given us an independent
hierarchy, and this independent hierarchy has made us feel and
recognize our individuality and our heaven-created manhood.

3. A LAYMAN EXPLAINS
"WHY NEGRO CHURCHES ARE A NECESSITY"

In discussing this subject we shall lay down four propositions as embodying the principles underlying and governing in all cases where churches are organized on color or race lines:

1. There is in every race certain characteristics, temperaments, peculiarities, habits and customs varying from those of other races and marking its distinctive racial character. The fact of the existence of mental, moral and social differences in the various races of the human family, as marked as any physical differences, is universally admitted. That they are in the most part artificial or acquired, not natural differences, has no weight in this discussion, neither has the question, What produced them? With the fact of their existence alone we have to do. For instance, the Scotch are a steady, industrious people, intensely practical, with a large share of obstinacy, and he who undertakes to deal with them without taking into consideration these traits need blame no one but himself if he fails to obtain results commensurate to his efforts. The average American is an astute, inquisitive individual, eager to accomplish results but impatient of methods. The Italian is nervous, irritable and vengeful. In laboring with these various peoples, all branches of the same race, the intelligent worker will modify his methods to suit the peculiar temperaments and habits of each. If the different subdivisions of the same race, whose character, modes of thought and customs have been formed under similar social and climatic conditions, and who are products of the same civilization, present as marked differences of race-traits as is observable in the examples just cited, may we not expect to find greater differences between radically distinct races, whose characters have been formed under entirely different influences? Nor are we disappointed, as a glance at the Chinese and their habits, the

From L. H. Reynolds, "Why Negro Churches Are a Necessity,"
A.M.E. CHURCH REVIEW, IV (October 1887), 154–157.

Japanese and their customs will convince the most superficial observer.

2. These peculiarities, often combined with social and historical accidents, form the basis of race repulsions more or less intense. There is no other way by which we can rationally account for race-antagonisms than upon this hypothesis. That there are race-antagonisms so deep-seated, so intense and so aggressive as to be the source of continual annoyance to individuals, to organizations, to communities and to the commonwealth our every experience attests and the history of all ages confirms. My neighbor Hans is a sturdy, methodical individual, with an eye to dollars and cents, not much of an enthusiast, and a firm believer in the doctrine of every man attending to his own business, hence he has the most profound contempt for boisterous, impulsive, generous Pat. The latter reciprocates the feeling most heartily. So with the Frenchman and the German, the Italian and the Spaniard, and I may safely say it is the same with all nationalities. Each has its own prominently distinctive traits, are proud of them, and in the rub of continual contact there is often much friction. It is useless to say these things ought not to be so; facts are facts, and theorize as we may they ever prove stubborn things. "The movements that grow out of race instincts," says Dr. Haygood, "do not wait upon the conclusions of philosophy, nor do they for a long time take counsel of policy." Take any town in Minnesota or Iowa (I cite these two States because the color line is less tensely drawn therein than in any other State, save, perhaps, Michigan and Wisconsin) with a dozen colored families and they want a colored church. It matters not how cordially they are invited to attend the white churches, how kindly they may be treated therein, nor with what faithfulness the white pastors may seek them out, they are not fully satisfied till they have a church of their own. The whites also, from the pulpit to door, prefer to have them take such a course. The fault doubtless lies in both parties. The whites, conscious of their superior general intelligence, believing also that their color is better than that of their darker-hued brother, and fully aware of the past social, political and moral degradation of that same brother, either chill him with a

cold, haughty, repellant manner, irritate him with sneers and contemptuous looks, or bestow upon him a lofty patronage infinitely more galling to a sensitive nature than even mistreatment. On the other hand, the black man goes looking for these things. Painfully conscious of the disadvantages under which he labors, he is morbidly sensitive to every look and move of the entire congregation. Feeling thus it is exceedingly easy to see or hear something unpleasant. Every colored church in the States mentioned, of whatsoever denomination, is an example of the truth of this proposition. Repelled from the white churches by the subtile influence of race-antagonism, they are drawn together by a law of race-affiliation more potent than the ties of years of association or the bonds of denominational preference. There is, I believe, paradoxical as it may appear in the light of the present reasoning, a higher law of race-assimilation, based upon a residence in the same country with a common language, common training, common pursuits and identity of interests, that must eventually form a composite race in our country essentially and distinctively American; but subordinate to this higher law, and may I not add, preparatory therefor, comes this law of race-affiliation which draws colored communicants into colored churches, and demands for their pulpits colored preachers. . . .

3. Each race is best reached through agencies and by methods least calculated to aggravate this latent hostility. This proposition is almost self-evident. To successfully communicate truth requires the most favorable conditions attainable. Anything tending to embarrass either party is an impediment to such communication. Perfection in the art of teaching is the bringing of both teacher and taught into such a simple, natural and unstrained relation as will not distract the mind of either from the subject-matter. This is the ideal of successful teaching, and in proportion as we recede from it by allowing the introduction of other conditions, be they lingual, social or racial, we hinder instruction. A difficulty often met is difference of tongue. Not only should the teacher use the language of the taught, but he should use it so perfectly as not to attract attention to the manner of his delivery to the detriment of the matter. Hence the

necessity of churches on the lingual line, Swedes into Swedish churches, and Germans into German churches. But it is not lingual differences alone that make such churches a necessity, but that same law of race-affiliation before mentioned. I am confident that a German pastor, though well versed in the Swedish language, would not succeed so well in charge of a Swedish congregation as would one of their own nationality. Why? The German pastor, it matters not how fully Swedenized, would arouse race-antipathies, if not intense, at least sufficient to retard his success. Missionaries in foreign fields recognize this fact and direct their earliest and most persistent efforts toward getting native help to work, organizing for this purpose schools for the training of native youth that they may be evangelists among their own people.

4. It is wise to recognize these differences, and to adjust our labor so as to avoid as much friction as possible. The wisdom of such a course is found in the general principles already laid down and in the specific, and in many ways peculiar, relations the white and Negro races sustain toward each other in this country. Unfortunately their intercourse has not been of such a character as to inspire confidence in the minds of the Negroes in the honesty, honor or justice of the white race in dealing with them. To the ordinary race-antipathies common all over the world there is, in this case, superadded the bitter remembrance of the wrongs, indignities and persecutions of the last two and a-half centuries on the one hand, and contempt for ignorance, improvidence and lack of energy on the other. It may be said that good men on both sides will lay down their prejudices, forgive and forget. Granted, but you must remember that the mission of the Church is not to good men, but to men wrapped in sin and ruled by folly; men to whom the Church must go if they will not come to the Church. Then the true course is for each race to have its separate churches to the intent of, as nearly as possible, reaching all; in order also to avoid such friction as arises from a commingling of the races before they are fully prepared for it, and last, but by no means least in vital importance, that all which is best in the methods of each may be utilized.

Foundations
of the black community:
the mutual benefit societies

In their origins the church and the fraternal or mutual benefit
society were closely interrelated. During the late eighteenth
century the distinction between the sacred and the secular was
not sharply drawn. In a period when there were scarcely
any ordained ministers, it was natural for the mutual aid
society to perform both religious and secular functions—as
did the Free African Society founded by Richard Allen and
Absolom Jones a few months before they left St. George's
Methodist Church. One of the principal functions of these
societies was the quasi-religious one of providing a decent
burial for its deceased members. In Newport, Rhode Island,
for example, the mutual benefit societies preceded by many
years the creation of the first Negro church there, which was
founded under the auspices of the African Benevolent
Society in 1824.

In 1787 appeared the first mutual benefit societies—the Free
African Societies of Philadelphia and Newport—and the
first Negro secret fraternal order, the Masons. They served
similar functions: both offered their members companionship,
recreation, recognition, and prestige that to some degree
compensated for the racial proscriptions facing them. Both
offered economic protection in case of sickness or death and
sought to encourage thrift, industry, and morality, thus
providing a method for upward mobility. The economic
functions of these societies would become very clear in the late
nineteenth century, when they provided the basis for most
of the early black banks and insurance companies. Finally,
these societies were an example of race unity and solidarity

that offered a feeling of worth and dignity to their members.

The first document in this section relates to the Free African Society of Philadelphia, one of the first mutual benefit societies formed among Negroes in this country. It illustrates the interest of the early leaders both in mutual aid, for protection in the face of life's catastrophes, and also in inculcating middle-class respectability. As early as 1787, the Free African Societies of Philadelphia and Newport exhibited a concern for uplifting Africa. This theme is illustrated by the second document, a letter from a Boston group formed expressly for the purpose of assisting the fatherland, written to Paul Cuffe, a Massachusetts Negro shipowner noted for his concern about Africa.

4. THE FREE AFRICAN SOCIETY OF PHILADELPHIA

Preamble of the Free African Society

Philadelphia
12th, 4th mo., 1787

Whereas, Absalom Jones and Richard Allen, two men of the African race, who, for their religious life and conversation have obtained a good report among men, these persons, from a love to the people of their complexion whom they beheld with sorrow, because of their irreligious and uncivilized state, often communed together upon this painful and important subject in order to form some kind of religious society, but there being too few to be found under like concern, and those who were,

From W. E. B. Du Bois (ed.), ECONOMIC CO-OPERATION AMONG NEGRO AMERICANS (Atlanta, Ga.: Atlanta University Studies, No. 12, 1907), pp. 21–22.

differed in their religious sentiments; with these circumstances they labored for some time, till it was proposed, after a serious communication of sentiments, that a society should be formed, without regard to religious tenets, provided the persons lived an orderly and sober life, in order to support one another in sickness, and for the benefit of their widows and fatherless children.

The following persons were the charter members: Absalom Jones, Richard Allen, Samuel Boston, Joseph Johnson, Cato Freeman, Caesar Cranchell, James Potter and William White.

Articles

17th, 5th Mo. 1787

We, the free Africans and their descendants of the City of Philadelphia, in the state of Pennsylvania, or elsewhere, do unanimously agree, for the benefit of each other, to advance one shilling in Pennsylvania silver currency, a month; and after one year's subscription from the date thereof, then to hand forth to the needy of this society, if any should require, the sum of three shillings and nine pence per week of the said money; provided, this necessity is not brought on them by their own imprudence.

And it is further agreed, that no drunkard nor disorderly person be admitted as a member, and if any should prove disorderly after having been received, the said disorderly person shall be disjoined from us if there is not an amendment, by being informed by two of the members, without having any of his subscription returned.

And if any one should neglect paying his subscription for three months, and after having been informed of the same by two of the members, and no sufficient reason appearing for such neglect, if he do not pay the whole the next ensuing meeting, he shall be disjoined from us by being informed by two of the members as an offender, without having any of his subscription money returned.

Also, if any person neglect meeting every month, for every

omission he shall have to pay three pence, except in case of sickness or any other complaint that should require the assistance of the society, then and in such case, he shall be exempt from the fines and subscription during said sickness.

Also, we apprehend it to be just and reasonable, that the surviving widow of the deceased member should enjoy the benefit of this society so long as she remains his widow, complying with the rules thereof, excepting the subscriptions.

And we apprehend it to be necessary that the children of our deceased members be under the care of the society, so far as to pay for the education of their children, if they can not attend the free school; also to put them out as apprentices to suitable trades and places, if required.

Also, that no member shall convene the society together; but it shall be the sole business of the committee, and that only on special occasions, and to dispose of the money in hand to the best advantage for the use of the society, after they are granted the liberty at a monthly meeting, and to transact all other business whatsoever, except that of clerk and treasurer.

And we unanimously agree to choose Joseph Clarke to be our clerk and treasurer; and whenever another should succeed him, it is always understood, that one of the people called Quakers, belonging to one of the three monthly meetings in Philadelphia, is to be chosen to act as clerk and treasurer of this useful institution.

The following persons met, viz: Absalom Jones, Richard Allen, Samuel Boston, Joseph Johnson, Cato Freeman, Caesar Cranchell and James Potter, and also William White, whose early assistance and useful remarks were found truly profitable. This evening the articles were read, and after some beneficial remarks were made, they were agreed unto.

5. THE AFRICAN INSTITUTION
OF BOSTON

Boston,
August 3rd, 1812

Dear Sir—

I received yours of the 10th of last month in due season &
think we ought most cheerfully to sacrifice ease & many other
privileges & comforts, for the purpose of diffusing light, &
civilisation & knowledge in Africa. There are several men in
this place who calculate to go on to Africa with you, when ever
there is an opening; as you observed in your last, the passage to
Africa was undoubtedly now closed. An attempt was made to
call a general meeting of the people of colour in this town that,
they might consult upon the best method of organising a society, & committee of correspondence with the other societies
which are formed for the purpose of making arrangements for
going to Africa. But it appeared that there was likely to be a
diversity of opinions on political ground the democratic party
are opposed to the plan of going on account of its being under
British government. And say that those who go, are going for
the purpose of speculation & trading in slaves; from such op-
probrious insinuations & on some other accounts, it was thought
best by those who are desireous to go that the society or committee should consist of those persons who wish to go. They
have accordingly chosen a committee &c, from those who
calculate to go to that country we should be glad to see you
here as soon as you can make it convenient. . . .

Prince Sanders, secy
Thomas Jarvis, chairman
Perry Locks, president

**From a letter of Prince Sanders, Thomas Jarvis, and Perry Locks
to Paul Cuffe, August 3, 1812, Paul Cuffe Papers,
New Bedford, Mass. Public Library.**

Foundations
of the black community:
the press

At first, protest activity among the free people of color was confined to local mass meetings and the irregular publication of pamphlets. Then, at the close of the third decade of the nineteenth century, race protest achieved an institutionalized form with the establishment of the first black newspaper, *Freedom's Journal*, in 1827.

The publishers of colored newspapers viewed their function as advancing the cause of the race. They implicitly, and at times explicitly, called for support from free blacks by appealing for race unity and race solidarity. Colored people, they maintained, must unite behind race newspapers if they were to achieve their rights and overcome oppression. Among others, Frederick Douglass, the most famous and influential Negro editor during the antebellum period and Reconstruction, articulated this philosophy. The following document is a lucid expression of this viewpoint, from the first issue of *Freedom's Journal*.

6. THE FIRST NEGRO PAPER: "TOO LONG HAVE OTHERS SPOKEN FOR US"

To our patrons

In presenting our first number to our Patrons, we feel all the diffidence of persons entering upon a new and untried line of business. But a moment's reflection upon the noble objects, which we have in view by the publication of this Journal; the expediency of its appearance at this time, when so many schemes are in action concerning our people—encourage us to come boldly before an enlightened publick. For we believe, that a paper devoted to the dissemination of useful knowledge among our brethren, and to their moral and religious improvement, must meet with the cordial approbation of every friend to humanity.

The peculiarities of this Journal, render it important that we should advertise to the world the motives by which we are actuated, and the objects which we contemplate.

We wish to plead our own cause. Too long have others spoken for us. Too long has the publick been deceived by misrepresentations, in things which concern us dearly, though in the estimation of some mere trifles; for though there are many in society who exercise towards us benevolent feelings; still (with sorrow we confess it) there are others who make it their business to enlarge upon the least trifle, which tends to the discredit of any person of colour; and pronounce anathemas and denounce our whole body for the misconduct of this guilty one. We are aware that there [are] many instances of vice among us, but we avow that it is because no one has taught its subjects to be virtuous; many instances of poverty, because no sufficient efforts accommodated to minds contracted by slavery,

From FREEDOM'S JOURNAL (New York, N. Y.), March 16, 1827.

and deprived of early education have been made, to teach them how to husband their hard earnings, and to secure to themselves comforts.

Education being an object of the highest importance to the welfare of society, we shall endeavour to present just and adequate views of it, and to urge upon our brethren the necessity and expediency of training their children, while young, to habits of industry, and thus forming them for becoming useful members of society. It is surely time that we should awake from this lethargy of years, and make a concentrated effort for the education of our youth. We form a spoke in the human wheel, and it is necessary that we should understand our [de]pendence on the different parts, and theirs on us, in order to perform our part with propriety.

Though not desirous of dictating, we shall feel it our incombent duty to dwell occasionally upon the general principles and rules of economy. The world has grown too enlightened, to estimate any man's character by his personal appearance. Though all men acknowledge the excellency of Franklin's maxims, yet comparatively few practise upon them. We may deplore when it is too late, the neglect of these self-evident truths, but it avails little to mourn. Ours will be the task of admonishing our brethren on these points.

The civil rights of a people being of the greatest value, it shall ever be our duty to vindicate our brethren, when oppressed, and to lay the cure before the publick. We also urge upon our brethren, (who are qualified by the laws of the different states) the expediency of using their elective franchise; and of making an independent use of the same. We wish them not to become the tools of party.

And as much time is frequently lost, and wrong principles instilled, by the perusal of works of trivial importance, we shall consider it a part of our duty to recommend to our young readers, such authors as will not only enlarge their stock of useful knowledge, but such as will also serve to stimulate them to higher attainments in science.

We trust also that through the columns of the FREEDOM's

JOURNAL, many practical pieces, having for their bases, the improvement of our brethren, will be presented to them, from the pens of many of our respected friends, who have kindly promised their assistance.

It is our earnest wish to make our Journal a medium of intercourse between our brethren in the different states of this great confederacy; that through the columns an expression of our sentiments, on many interesting subjects which concern us, may be offered to the publick; that plans which apparently are beneficial may be candidly discussed and properly weighed; if worthy, receive our cordial approbation; if not, our marked disapprobation.

Useful knowledge of every kind, and every thing that relates to Africa, shall find a ready admission into our columns; and as that vast continent becomes daily more known, we trust that many things will come to light, proving that the natives of it are neither so ignorant nor stupid as they have generally been supposed to be.

And while these important subjects shall occupy the columns of the FREEDOM'S JOURNAL, we would not be unmindful of our brethren who are still in the iron fetters of bondage. They are our kindred by all the ties of nature; and though but little can be effected by us, still let our sympathies be poured forth, and our prayers in their behalf, ascend to Him who is able to succour them.

From the press and the pulpit we have suffered much by being incorrectly represented. Men, whom we equally love and admire have not hesitated to represent us disadvantageously, without becoming personally acquainted with the true state of things, nor discerning between virtue and vice among us. The virtuous part of our people feel themselves sorely aggrieved under the existing state of things—they are not appreciated.

Our vices and our degradation are ever arrayed against us, but our virtues are passed by unnoticed. And what is still more lamentable, our friends, to whom we concede all the principles of humanity and religion, from these very causes seem to have fallen into the current of popular feeling and are imperceptibly

floating on the stream—actually living in the practice of prejudice, while they abjure it in theory, and feel it not in their
hearts. Is it not very desirable that such should know more of
our actual condition, and of our efforts and feelings, that in
forming or advocating plans for our amelioration, they may do
it more understandingly? In the spirit of candor and humility
we intend by a simple representation of facts to lay our case
before the publick, with a view to arrest the progress of prejudice, and to shield ourselves against the consequent evils. We
wish to conciliate all and to irritate none, yet we must be firm
and unwavering in our principles, and persevering in our
efforts.

If ignorance, poverty and degradation have hitherto been
our unhappy lot; has the Eternal decree gone forth, that our
race alone, are to remain in this state, while knowledge and
civilization are shedding their enlivening rays over the rest of
the human family? The recent travels of Denham and Clapper-
ton in the interior of Africa, and the interesting narrative which
they have published; the establishment of the republic of Hayti
after years of sanguinary warfare; its subsequent progress in
all the arts of civilization; and the advancement of liberal
ideas in South America, where despotism has given place to free
governments, and where many of our brethren now fill important civil and military stations, prove the contrary.

The interesting fact that there are FIVE HUNDRED THOUSAND
free persons of colour, one half of whom might peruse, and the
whole be benefitted by the publication of the Journal; that no
publication, as yet, has been devoted exclusively to their improvement—that many selections from approved standard authors, which are within the reach of few, may occasionally be
made—and more important still, that this large body of our
citizens have no public channel—all serve to prove the real
necessity, at present, for the appearance of the FREEDOM's
JOURNAL.

It shall ever be our desire so as to conduct the editorial department of our paper as to give offence to none of our patrons;
as nothing is farther from us than to make it the advocate of

any partial views, either in politics or religion. What few days we can number, have been devoted to the improvement of our brethren; and it is our earnest wish that the remainder may be spent in the same delightful service.

In conclusion, whatever concerns us as a people, will ever find a ready admission into the FREEDOM'S JOURNAL, interwoven with all the principal news of the day.

And while every thing in our power shall be performed to support the character of our Journal, we would respectfully invite our numerous friends to assist by their communications, and our coloured brethren to strengthen our hands by their subscriptions, as our labour is one of common cause, and worthy of their consideration and support. And we do most earnestly solicit the latter, that if at any time we should seem to be zealous, or too pointed in the inculcation of any important lesson, they will remember, that they are equally interested in the cause in which we are engaged, and attribute our zeal to the peculiarities of our situation, and our earnest engagedness in their well-being.

The Editors

Pleas for racial unity

The spirit of racial unity and self-help early in the nineteenth century was exhibited in the development of community institutions among free blacks from the Atlantic to the Mississippi. We present here two addresses that exemplify this trend, one by a Bostonian, the other by a Midwesterner.

The first is an address to the General Colored Association of Boston by David Walker, who is well-known for his *Appeal in Four Articles* (1829), in which he advocated slave rebellion. The second, by the Reverend David Nickens of Chillicothe, Ohio, describes the evolution of a local social organization. It is also significant as an early expression of pride in the contribution of Africa to world civilization.

7. DAVID WALKER: "TO UNITE THE COLORED PEOPLE"

Mr. President,—I cannot but congratulate you, together with my brethren on this highly interesting occasion, the first semi-annual meeting of this Society. When I reflect upon the many impediments through which we have had to conduct its affairs, and see, with emotions of delight, the present degree of eminency to which it has arisen, I cannot, sir, but be of the opinion, that an invisible arm must have been stretched out in our

David Walker, "Address Delivered Before the General Colored Association at Boston," FREEDOM'S JOURNAL, December 19, 1828.

behalf. From the very second conference, which was by us convened, to agitate the proposition respecting this society, to its final consolidation, we were by some, opposed, with an avidity and zeal, which, had it been on the opposite side, would have done great honor to themselves. And, sir, but for the undeviating, and truly patriotic exertions of those who were favorable to the formation of this institution, it might have been this day, in a yet unorganized condition. Did I say in an unorganized condition? Yea, had our opponents their way, the very notion of such an institution might have been obliterated from our minds. How strange it is, to see men of sound sense, and of tolerably good judgment, act so diametrically in opposition to their interest; but I forbear making any further comments on this subject, and return to that for which we are convened.

First then, Mr. President, it is necessary to remark here, at once, that the primary object of this institution, is, to unite the colored population, so far, through the United States of America, as may be practicable and expedient; forming societies, opening, extending, and keeping up correspondences, and not withholding anything which may have the least tendency to meliorate *our* miserable condition—with the restrictions, however, of not infringing on the articles of its constitution, or that of the United States of America. Now, that we are disunited, is a fact, that no one of common sense will deny; and, that the cause of which, is a powerful auxiliary in keeping us from rising to the scale of reasonable and thinking beings, none but those who delight in our degradation will attempt to contradict. Did I say those who delight in our degradation? Yea, sir, glory in keeping us ignorant and miserable, that we might be the better and the longer slaves. I was credibly informed by a gentleman of unquestionable veracity, that a slaveholder upon finding one of his young slaves with a small spelling book in his hand (not opened) fell upon and beat him almost to death, exclaiming, at the same time, to the child, you will acquire better learning than I or any of my family.

I appeal to every candid and unprejudiced mind, do not all such men glory in our miseries and degradations; and are there

not millions whose chief glory centres in this horrid wickedness? Now, Mr. President, those are the very humane, philanthropic, and charitable men who proclaim to the world, that
the blacks are such a poor, ignorant and degraded species of
beings, that, were they set at liberty, they would die for the
want of something to subsist upon, and in consequence of
which, they are compelled to keep them in bondage, to do
them good.

O Heaven! what will not avarice and the love of despotic
sway cause men to do with their fellow creatures, when actually
in their power? But, to return whence I digressed; it has been
asked, in what way will the *General Colored Association* (or
the Institution) unite the colored population, so far, in the
United States as may be practicable and expedient? to which
enquiry I answer, by asking the following: Do not two hundred
and eight years very intolerable sufferings teach us the actual
necessity of a general union among us? do we not know indeed,
the horrid dilemma into which we are, and from which, we
must exert ourselves, to be extricated? Shall we keep slumber-
ing on, with our arms completely folded up, exclaiming every
now and then, against our miseries, yet never do the least thing
to ameliorate our condition, or that of posterity? Shall we not,
by such inactivity, leave, or rather entail a hereditary degradation on our children, but a little, if at all, inferior to that which
our fathers, under all their comparative disadvantages and
privations, left on us? In fine, shall we, while almost every other
people under Heaven, are making such mighty efforts to better
their condition, go around from house to house, enquiring what
good associations and societies are going to do us? Ought we
not to form ourselves into a general body, to protect, aid, and
assist each other to the utmost of our power, with the before-
mentioned restrictions?

Yes, Mr. President, it is indispensably our duty to try every
scheme that we think will have a tendency to facilitate our
salvation, and leave the final result to that God, who holds the
destinies of people in the hollow of his hand, and who ever
has, and will, repay every nation according to its works.

Will any be so hardy as to say, or even to imagine, that we are incapable of effecting any object which may have a tendency to hasten our emancipation, in consequence of the prevalence of ignorance and poverty among us? That the major part of us are ignorant and poor, I am at this time unprepared to deny.—But shall this deter us from all lawful attempts to bring about the desired object? nay, sir, it should rouse us to greater exertions; there ought to be a spirit of emulation and inquiry among us, a hungering and thirsting after religion; these are requisitions, which, if we ever be so happy as to acquire, will fit us for all the departments of life; and, in my humble opinion, ultimately result in rescuing us from an oppression, unparalleled, I had almost said, in the annals of the world.

But some may even think that our white brethren and friends are making such mighty efforts, for the amelioration of our condition, that we may stand as neutral spectators of the work. That we have many good friends yea, very good, among that body, perhaps none but a few of those who have ever read at all will deny; and that many of them have gone, and will go, all lengths for our good, is evident, from the very works of the great, the good, and the godlike Granville Sharpe, Wilberforce, Lundy, and the truly patriotic and lamented Mr. Ashmun, late Colonial Agent of Liberia, who, with a zeal which was only equalled by the goodness of his heart, has lost his life in our cause, and a host of others too numerous to mention: a number of private gentlemen too, who, though they say but little, are nevertheless, busily engaged for good. Now, all of those great, and indeed, good friends whom God has given us I do humbly, and very gratefully acknowledge. But, that we should co-operate with them, as far as we are able by uniting and cultivating a spirit of friendship and of love among us, is obvious, from the very exhibition of our miseries, under which we groan.

Two millions and a half of colored people in these United States, more than five hundred thousand of whom are about two thirds of the way free. Now, I ask, if no more than these last were united (which they must be, or always live as enemies) and resolved to aid and assist each other to the utmost

of their power, what mighty deeds could be done by them for
the good of our cause?

But, Mr. President, instead of a general compliance with
these requisitions, which have a natural tendency to raise us in
the estimation of the world, we see, to our sorrow, in the very
midst of us, a gang of villains, who, for the paltry sum of fifty
or a hundred dollars, will kidnap and sell into perpetual slavery,
their fellow creatures! and, too, if one of their fellow sufferers,
whose miseries are a little more enhanced by the scourges of a
tyrant, should abscond from his pretended owner, to take a
little recreation, and unfortunately fall in their way, he is gone!
for they will sell him for a glass of whiskey! Brethren and fellow
sufferers, I ask you, in the name of God, and of Jesus Christ,
shall we suffer such notorious villains to rest peaceably among
us? will they not take our wives and little ones, more particularly our *little ones,* when a convenient opportunity will admit,
and sell them for money to slave holders, who will doom them
to *chains, handcuffs,* and even unto death? May God open our
eyes on those children of the devil and enemies of all good!

But, sir, this wickedness is scarcely more infernal than that
which was attempted a few months since, against the government of our brethren, the Haytiens, by a consummate rogue,
who ought to have, long since, been *haltered,* but who, I
was recently informed, is nevertheless, received into company
among some of our most respectable men, with a kind of
brotherly affection which ought to be shown only to a gentleman of honor.

Now, Mr. President, all such mean, and more than disgrace-
ful actions as these, are powerful auxiliaries, which work for
our destruction, and which are abhorred in the sight of God and
of good men.

But, sir, I cannot but bless God for the glorious anticipation
of a not very distant period, when these things which now help
to degrade us will no more be practised among the sons of
Africa,—for, though this, and perhaps another, generation may
not experience the promised blessings of Heaven, yet, the de-
jected, degraded, and now enslaved children of Africa will

have, in spite of all their enemies, to take their stand among the nations of the earth. And, sir, I verily believe that God has something in reserve for us, which, when he shall have poured it out upon us, will repay us for all our suffering and miseries.

8. DAVID NICKENS: "LET US CHERISH A FRIENDLY UNION WITH OURSELVES"

Fellow Citizens—I arise to address you on the important subject of cultivating a friendly union among ourselves as an oppressed people. We have met on this 5th of July, not under a mock pretence of celebrating the 4th of July, for that would betray in us a want of sound understanding—but to cultivate friendship and good feelings amongst ourselves, with hopes of a reform among our race.

Yesterday our citizens and neighbors, who are of a different cast from us, did with propriety hoist the star-spangled banner and watered the tree planted for them by their fathers fifty-six years ago, when the noise of the drum, the thundering of the cannon, the toasts of the people, all united in forming strong expressions of their joy and tokens of their union;— while we the descendants of Africa, for no alleged crime by us or our forefathers committed, are despised, rejected and excluded from all the privileges calculated to render the life of man comfortable. We are denied the privilege of filling a station in social, political or religious society on terms of equality, amongst a people who differ from us in their complexion! Yes, more— we are deprived measurably of the means of grace, which are calculated to prepare us for the kingdom of glory. The doors of the schools are barred against us by a legislative act, and

David Nickens, "Address to the People of Color in Chillicothe," July 20, 1832, published in LIBERATOR (Boston, Mass.), August 11, 1832.

that too contrary to the legislation of heaven; for we are commanded to train our children in the way they should go. This is a hard task for us or any other people, so long as the means of training are withheld. It needs no argument to confirm this fact. Only let us look to the history of nations, and there we shall see that all people destitute of the revealed will of God, have been enveloped in ignorance, moral gloom and superstition, and possessing a spirit of insubordination. And such, fellow-citizens, has been our unhappy fate: and if ever there have been a people on earth, whose situation and interest called for a combination, it is ours. Then the question is, what can we do to ameliorate our condition? not, what can be done by others?

Let every one of us cherish a friendly union with ourselves: and in order to do this, let the members of our churches be true to their God, and then they will be true to each other—and the non-professing part of our race will, in some degree, follow our example. Let christians throw away the spirit of superiority, and acknowledge every human being their brother and equal, as it respects his creation; for it has been the vain and unfounded notion of superiority, as it respects our creation, which this day, my fellow citizens, excludes us from a friendly and social intercourse on terms of equality with those of our neighbors who differ from us in complexion. This day causes millions of our sable race to groan under the galling yoke of bondage. Let us then, respect each other according to character and merit; and then, and not till then, shall we know what it is to enjoy the comforts of social society.

Permit me, fellow-citizens, in the sequel of my address, to confine myself more particularly to the colored people of our own town and neighborhood.

Twenty years ago, individual attempts were made to benefit the condition of colored individuals in this place; but little general good resulted therefrom. Ten years ago, it entered the hearts of some of our worthy colored citizens, whose names ought to be handed down to our latest posterity, to form a combination to remove the moral gloom, and ameliorate the condition of our rising race, which combination was entered into, and the good effect has been seen by every strict observer in our town, both white and colored. Two churches have since been erected by the people of color—one Baptist—the other Methodist—both of which are attended by colored persons of respectability. Our children have been called from wandering in the streets, and some of our adult profligates called from scenes of debauchery and vice to experience the love of God. Our school has been successfully taught for the last eight years. Many of our children have been educated, enlightened and raised to respectability.

This combination endeared neighbor to neighbor, family to family, and children to children, until the whole mass of the respectable part of the people of color in our town formed one general compact, and became more powerful in doing good than the Philistine giant who defied the armies of the living God.

Away with prejudice and the slanderous assertion that the imbecility of the Africans renders them incapable of improvement. Let those who accuse us of inferiority, as it respects our intellect and structure, look through the dark vista of past ages, and read in the history of Hannibal and others, who were Africans, the strength of intellect, the soundness of judgment, the military skill, which existed in ancient Africa. Africa was the garden and nursery where learning budded and education sprang. From Egypt the arts of civilization were carried into Greece, and from Greece to Europe; therefore all the now civilized world is indebted to sable Africa for the arts of civilization and learning. If our ancestors were instructed and became great on the burning shores of Afric, why may not their descendants, in a milder clime, even on the continent of America? It is not essential that three millions of the sable sons and daughters of Africa must be sent to Liberia before they can be enlightened and become respectable—it can be done at home; and if our neighbors and lawgivers could be induced, by our entreaties, supplications and groans, to remove our heavy burthens, and afford us the means of improvement, the confined

African would leap from his chains, and stand forth with the enlightened men of the earth.

I can say in justice to the honor and credit of my colored citizens of Chillicothe, that this place is the mother and guardian of literature to the colored people west of the Alleghany mountains. With us the spark kindled and burnt till our brethren in neighboring towns caught the flame, and set their hands to the great work of reform; and if we continue our efforts with firm steps and unwearied zeal, guided by an all-wise Ruler, we shall soon be able to stretch our hands across an ocean of three or four thousand miles, and there unite with our sable brethren in cultivating friendship and good feelings, till the whole of our race become enlightened and each one say, 'Let me seek my neighbor's good.'

Suffer me, fellow-citizens, to give a short statement of things at this time among us. For the last two years a spirit of contention and division has entered among us. Division, with his deadly weapon, has smitten, and society, social and religious, has felt the blow. Our churches are shaken—our school is removed from its former basis—families are at variance—our young society divided. Let the good citizens of color arise, male and female, young and old, and give their aid, for the purpose of reconciling and consolidating society again, and set their faces against every person of color who dares to raise his puny arms to interrupt our peace or mar our goodly heritage. Let this maxim be engraven on our memories: UNITED, WE STAND— DIVIDED, WE FALL.

Colonization

The first Negro prominently associated with emigration to or colonization of Africa was Paul Cuffe, a prosperous Quaker shipowner and merchant of Westport, Massachusetts, near New Bedford. In the early part of his career as a race leader he refused to pay taxes during the Revolutionary War because Massachusetts denied Negroes the franchise. Cuffe's fame, however, rests primarily upon his later role as an early colonizationist, and traditionally he has been portrayed as perhaps the first black advocate of expatriation as a solution to the problems of the Negro in America. Shortly before his death in 1817 he was consulted by the founders of the American Colonization Society, which was dedicated to the proposition that the solution to the race problem lay in wholesale Negro emigration to Africa.

Cuffe's papers seem to indicate, however, that although he had a deep sense of affinity and concern for Africa, his interest lay in helping Africa rather than using Africa to solve the problems of the American black man. He sought the emigration of a small group that would Christianize and "civilize" the Africans (for Cuffe shared the stereotypes of his white contemporaries regarding African heathenism and barbarism). "The travail of my soul is that Africa's inhabitants may be favored with reformation,"[1] Cuffe said. He hoped that one result of his work would be elimination of African participation in the slave trade, and thus destruction of the slave trade itself. It was with these purposes in mind that Cuffe

[1] Quoted in Henry N. Sherwood, "Paul Cuffe," *Journal of Negro History*, VIII (April 1923), 167.

visited Sierra Leone in 1811, petitioned Congress in January 1814 for assistance in his project, and finally, in 1815, took 38 free Negroes to Sierra Leone at his own expense. Only after this trip, at the time when Robert Finley and others were laying the groundwork for the American Colonization Society, did Cuffe even begin to consider that substantial emigration might be acceptable for the oppressed blacks of the United States. As he wrote to a London friend in the summer of 1816, Southern planters, fearful of insurrections, would do best to "provide means to effectically abolish the Slave trade and then free their Slaves and Colonyze them either in America or Africa or in both places or free them and give them their plantation to work on . . . until such time as they are capabel of manageing for themselves. . . ."[2]

The first document below, Cuffe's petition to Congress, shows his interest in uplifting and Christianizing the Africans. The second, a letter to Robert Finley, a leading spirit in the founding of the A.C.S., who had written him about likely places for settlements in Africa, reveals that while he was not a true emigrationist, Cuffe was not averse to offering helpful information to those who proposed this solution.

Cuffe corresponded with certain founders of the American Colonization Society, but the majority of articulate Negroes were hostile to the organization. They suspected—and many of the society's white supporters openly said—that its object was to rid the country of the free blacks, whom they regarded as a threat to the system of slavery. One of the chief leaders in the early attacks upon the American Colonization Society was the wealthy sailmaker, abolitionist, and protest leader of Philadelphia, James Forten. Yet Forten was sympathetic with Cuffe's work, and his letter to Cuffe, printed below, suggests that although he was skeptical of the society's purposes at this point in his career he may indeed have been privately inclined

[2] Paul Cuffe to Samuel C. Aiken, August 7, 1816, Paul Cuffe Papers, New Bedford Public Library.

toward emigration as a solution for the race's problems in America. This fact is all the more significant because Forten's place in American history is based on his militant advocacy of antislavery and equal rights.

Like Forten, Richard Allen was a vigorous enemy of the American Colonization Society, but another founder of the A.M.E. Church, Daniel Coker of Baltimore, was not. Maryland was an especially strong center of colonization sentiment among both blacks and whites. In 1820 Coker, who had actually been selected as the first A.M.E. bishop but had, before consecration, declined the honor in favor of Richard Allen, accompanied 86 free Negroes who settled in Sierra Leone under the auspices of the Colonization Society. Coker seems to have been primarily concerned with the Christianization of Africa, but in writing to a Baltimore friend he enthusiastically urged that thousands emigrate.

Though prominent Negroes associated with emigration or colonization projects in this period were essentially interested in uplifting the Africans, there were those whose alienation and disgust with American society led them to view emigration as a permanent escape from America. The short letter from a settler in the Illinois territory, which is the last document in this section, also illustrates the ambivalence of the attitudes of many emigrationists toward the United States.

9. PAUL CUFFE CALLS
FOR THE UPLIFT OF AFRICA

A. PETITION TO THE
PRESIDENT AND CONGRESS

**To the president, senate,
and house of representatives
of the United States of America**

The memorial and petition of Paul Cuffe, of Westport, in the state of Massachusetts, respectfully sheweth, that your memorialist actuated by motives which he conceives are dictated by that philanthropy which is the offspring of Christian benevolence, is induced to ask the patronage of the government of the United States, in affording aid in execution of a plan, which he cherishes a hope may ultimately prove beneficial to his brethren of the African race within their native climate.

In order to give a complete view of the object in contemplation, it may not be considered trespassing too much on your time to premise some of the leading circumstances which have led to the present application. Your memorialist, being a descendant of Africa, and early instructed in habits of sobriety and industry has gratefully to acknowledge the many favors of a bountiful Providence, both in preserving him from many of the evils which the people of his colour too often have fallen into, and also, by blessing his industry with such a portion of the comforts of life as to enable him in some degree not only to commiserate, but to relieve the sufferings of his fellow creatures, and having early found implanted in his heart the prin-

Paul Cuffe, "To the President, Senate, and House of
Representatives of the United States of America," June 1813,
in NILES' WEEKLY REGISTER, January 22, 1814.

ciples of equity and justice, he could but view the practice of his brethren of the African race in selling their fellow creatures into a state of slavery for life as very inconsistent with that Divine principle; and in his mature age, having been greatly interested in the abundant labor of many pious individuals, both in this country and in England to produce a termination of the wrongs of Africa, by prohibiting the slave trade, and also to improve the condition of the degraded inhabitants of the land of his ancestors, he conceived it a duty incumbent upon him, as a faithful steward of the mercies he had received, to give up a portion of his time and his property in visiting that country, and affording such means as might be in his power to promote the improvement and civilization of the Africans.

Under these impressions he left his family, and with a sacrifice of both time and money visited Sierra Leona, and there gained such information of the country and its inhabitants as enabled him to form an opinion of many improvements that appeared to him essential to the well being of that people. These he had an opportunity of communicating to several distinguished members of the royal African institution in London, and he had the satisfaction at that time to find that his recommendations were approved by the celebrated philanthropists the duke of Gloucester, William Wilberforce, Thomas Clarkson, William Allen and others, and has since learned that the institution have so far acceded to his plans, as to make some special provision to carry them into effect. One of these objects was to keep up an intercourse with the free people of color in the United States, in the expectation that some persons of reputation would feel sufficiently interested to visit Africa, and endeavor to promote habits of industry, sobriety and frugality, among the natives of that country.

These views having been communicated by your petitioner to the free people of color in Baltimore, Philadelphia, New York and Boston, they, with a zeal becoming so important a concern have manifested a disposition to promote so laudable an undertaking, and several families whose characters promise usefulness, have come to a conclusion if proper ways could be

opened to go to Africa, in order to give their aid in promoting
the objects already adverted to. Your petitioner, still animated
with a sincere desire of making the knowledge he has acquired,
and the sacrifices he has already made, more permanently
useful in promoting the civilization of Africa, solicits your aid
so far as to grant permission that a vessel may be employed (if
liberty can also be obtained from the British government) between this country and Sierra Leona, to transport such persons
and families as may be inclined to go, as also, some articles of
provision, together with implements of husbandry, and machinery for some mechanic arts and to bring back such of the native
productions of that country as may be wanted.

For although pecuniary profit does not enter into calculation
in the object in contemplation, nor does it afford any very
promising prospects, yet without a little aid from the trifling
commerce of that country, the expense would fall too heavy on
your petitioner, and those of his friends who feel disposed to
patronize the undertaking. Your petitioner therefore craves the
attention of congress to a concern which appears to him very
important to a portion of his fellow creatures who have been
long excluded from the common advantages of civilized life,
and prays that they will afford him and his friends such aid as
they in their wisdom may think best.

With much respect, I am, your assured friend,

Paul Cuffe
Westport, 6th month, 1813

B. LETTER TO
ROBERT FINLEY

Westport
1st mo 8th 1817

Respected friend
   Robert Finley
   Thine of the 5th of December I have duely Receiv'd but not
in time to answer the[e] at Washington. I observe from the
Printed Petition in thy letter, the great and laborous task you
are ingaged in and my desires are that you may be guided by
Wisdom's best means. I stand as it were in a low place and am
not able to see far; but Blessed be God who hath created all
things . . . , he is able to make use of Instruments in such a way
as he Pleases, and may I be Resigned to his Holy Will.— . . . I
Think the colony [of Sierra Leone] from 1811 to 1815 hath
much improved, they are entitled to every Priveledge of free
born citizens, and fill stations in their courts [.] the soil in the
colony of Serrealone for cultivation are not flattering but are
very advantageously situated for a town, and a good ship har-
boar, the course of Africa abound with Rivers, the great River
Gambia hath about 350 miles N.W. of Sierraleone and the
island Buirso that hath at the entrance of the River said to be
very fertile, but are unhealthy for the Northern constatution,
their are another by the name of Shaborow layeth about 50
leagues S.E. of Sierralone, I have had the River of Shaborow
much recommended by John Consell a citizen of Sierrealone.
   These may do for small beginnings, but were there a Willingness for a pretty general removal of the People of colour, and
the south Part of Africa . . . the Cape of Good Hope could be
obtained, I think it looks most favourable, there are the great
River Congo, which lieth near the Equator, it is said she has
very extensive Population, and land fertile—if there were a spot
fixed on the coast of Africa, and another in the United States

From a letter of Paul Cuffe to Robert Finley, January 8, 1817,
Paul Cuffe Papers, New Bedford, Mass. Public Library.

of America, would it not answer the best purpose to Draw off
the coulored Citizens. I think it would be a good Plan, that a
Vessel and suitable Persons, to discover which Place would be
most advantageous to colonize these people. . . .

Ardent labours for the liberation of the African Race, I hope
we may not be unmindful to make use of every wise and Prudent means to more effectively put a stop to the citizens of the
United States being concerned in carrying [on] the slave
trade. . . .

10. JAMES FORTEN EXPRESSES
A DEEP CONCERN ABOUT AFRICA

Philad[a]
January 25th *1817*

Esteemed friend—
. . . The African Institution, met at the Rev. R. Allens, the
very night your letter came to hand. I red that parte to them
that wish them a happy New Year, for which they desired me
to return you many thanks. I must now mention to you that
the whole continent seems to be agetated concerning the Col-
onising [of] the People of Colour. You mention to me in your
letter that a gentleman from Washington, has written you on
the subject, for your opinion. I suppose it must have been The
Rev. Robert Finley, from the state of New Jersey. he convinced
us to gather the other night at the Rev. A[bsolom] Jones on this
interesting subject. he mentioned his intention of writing you.
indeed, the People of Colour, here was very much fritened at
first. they were afrad that all the free people would be compelled to go, particularly in the southern states. we had a large
meeting of Males at the Rev. R. Allens church, the other eve-

From a letter of James Forten to Paul Cuffe, January 25, 1817,
Paul Cuffe Papers, New Bedford, Mass. Public Library.

ning. Three Thousand at least attended, and there was not one soul that was in favor of going to Africa. They think that the slaveholders wants to get rid of them so as to make their property more secure. however it apperes to me that if the Father of all mercies, is in this interesting subject (for it apperes that they all think that something must and aut to be don but do not know were nor how to begin) the way will be made strate and cleare. we however have agreed to remain silent, as the people here bothe white [and] Colour are desided against the measure. my opinion is that they will never become a people until they com out from amongst the white people, but as the majority is disidedly against me I am determend to remain silent, except as to my opinion which I freely give when asked.

I remain very affectionately
yours unalterebly,
James Forten

11. DANIEL COKER:
"MY SOUL CLEAVES TO AFRICA"

Africa, Campalair
April 3, 1820

To Jeremiah Watts, Baltimore

Dear brother,—This comes to inform you of my good health, and safe arrival in Africa. When I wrote to my wife, I did not expect to get time to write to you; and so I gave my love to you in her letter. But having just returned from a visit to one of the kings, with the agent, and finding the ship not gone, I snatch the passing moment to inform you that I have seen and passed through strange things since I last saw you. Oh! my brother, and sister, how great a work is this! The millions in this land, are the thousands in America, and the thousands unborn are

Daniel Coker to Jeremiah Watts, April 3, 1820, JOURNAL OF DANIEL COKER (Baltimore, Md.: Press of Edward J. Coate, 1820), pp. 43–44.

deeply interested in it. Oh! my dears, what darkness has covered the minds of this people. None but those who come and
see, can judge. You would be astonished to see me travelling in
the wilderness, guided by a little foot path, until, coming
suddenly upon a little town of huts in the thickets; and there,
to behold hundreds of men, women and children, naked, sitting
on the ground or on mats, living on the natural productions of
the earth, and as ignorant of God as the brutes that perish. You
would see them coming round me, shaking hands, (but very
different from our way of shaking hands) and gazing on me,
and spreading a mat, and offering me of such food as they live
upon. In a word, they are friendly and kind. Such is their conduct, that any one who loves souls would weep over them, and
be willing to suffer and die with them. I can say, that my soul
cleaves to Africa in such a manner as to reconcile me to the
idea of being separated from my dear friends and the comforts
of a christian land. But I confess, when I think of you all, it is as
much as I can bear. But, my brother and sister, if we don't meet
soon in this life, we may soon meet in heaven. I expect to give
my life to bleeding, groaning, dark, benighted Africa. I expect
to pass through much, if I should live. I should rejoice to see
you in this land; it is a good land; it is a rich land, and I do
believe it will be a great nation, and a powerful and worthy
nation; but those who break the way will suffer much.

If you ask my opinion as to coming oat;—I say, let all that
can, sell out and come; come, and bring ventures, to trade, &c.
and you may do much better than you can possibly do in
America, and not work half so hard. I wish that thousands were
here, and had goods to trade with.—Bring about two hogsheads
of good leaf tobacco, cheap calico, and cheap handkerchiefs,
pins, knives and forks, pocket knives, &c.; with these you may
buy land, hire hands, or buy provisions. I say, come—the land
is good.

I have to refer you to my journal. I have sent it to the secretary, Edward J. Coale; it will, no doubt, be printed. This land
only wants industrious, informed, and christian people, to make
it one of the greatest nations in the world. Dear brother, if you
don't come, I want you to write to me, and let me know how

you come on, and send me something; if it is ever so trifling, from you it will be valuable. I hope, when things get settled, to be able to send you something. But I shall look for you out, till I see or hear from you. Give my love to all dear friends. I am in great haste. Peck is well, and gives his love—all our people are well. The Lord God bless you, and your dear, dear family—

farewell.

D. COKER.

12. A WOULD-BE EMIGRANT: "WE HAD RATHER BE GONE"

Lamott, Illinois Territory
July 13th, 1818

I am a free man of colour, have a family and a large connection of free people of colour residing on the Wabash, who are all willing to leave America whenever the way shall be opened. We love this country and its liberties, if we could share an equal right in them; but our freedom is partial, and we have no hope that it ever will be otherwise here; therefore we had rather be gone, though we should suffer hunger and nakedness for years. Your honour may be assured that nothing shall be lacking on our part in complying with whatever provision shall be made by the United States, whether it be to go to Africa or some other place; we shall hold ourselves in readiness, praying that God (who made man free in the beginning, and who by his kind providence has broken the yoke from every white American) would inspire the heart of every true son of liberty with zeal and pity, to open the door of freedom for us also.[1]

I am, &c.
Abraham Camp

Elias B. Caldwell, Esq.
Secretary of the Colonization Society of the United States.

Abraham Camp to Elias B. Caldwell, July 13, 1818,
American Colonization Society Papers, Library of Congress.

Maturation

PART TWO

The antebellum
colored conventions

The convention movement, which began in 1830 and continued intermittently until 1893, represented an attempt at racial elevation through self-help and racial unity. While the ideologies expressed at the conventions varied greatly, their goal (except for the emigration conventions of 1854, 1856, 1858, and 1893) was to use collective group action to achieve freedom for the slave, recognition of the constitutional rights of the colored freeman, and integration and assimilation of black men in the American social order. As nationalist manifestations, the conventions clearly reflected the ethnic ambivalences in American Negro thought.

The conventions of the 1830s, while an example of racial cooperation and Negro self-help in the face of white oppression, were so directed toward achieving the assimilation of blacks into American society that rarely was the theme of race unity and solidarity overtly articulated at the conclaves. That this theme was present, however, is indicated by the remarks of William Hamilton of New York City, chairman of the 1834 national convention. He said:

Under present circumstances it is highly necessary [that] the free people of colour should combine, and closely attend to their own particular interest. All kinds of jealousy should be swept away from among them, and their whole eye fixed, intently fixed, on their own peculiar welfare. And can they do no better than to meet thus; to take into consideration what are the best means to promote their elevation, and after having decided, to pursue those means with unabating zeal until their end is obtained?[1]

[1] Remarks of William Hamilton, President of the Conventional Board and chairman of the meeting, *Minutes of the Fourth Annual Convention for the Improvement of the Free People of Colour, . . . 1834* (New York: Published by Order of the Convention, 1834).

With the revival of the convention movement in the 1840s the
ideology of racial unity, self-help, and cooperation, the notion
that colored people would have to accomplish their own
advancement rather than depend on the whites, received
more frequent and explicit expression. This spectrum of ideas
was most often enunciated in connection with proposals for the
establishment of an official race journal or newspaper.
It received its most trenchant explication, however, in the 1848
convention's "Address to the Colored People of the
United States" (Document 13).

Frederick Douglass, the greatest of the black abolitionists,
was a consistent agitator for equal rights and the assimilation
of Negroes into American society. For this very reason his pleas
during this period for racial unity and solidarity, for black
self-help and self-uplift, for Negroes taking the lead in the
struggle for their freedom, are particularly significant.
On occasion he expressed an acute sense of alienation. Thus,
addressing an Independence Day celebration in Rochester,
New York, he told a white audience:

I am not included within the pale of this glorious anniversary!
Your high independence only reveals the immeasurable distance
between us. . . . The rich inheritance of justice, liberty, prosperity,
and independence bequeathed by your fathers is shared by you,
not by me. . . . This Fourth of July is *yours,* not *mine.*
You may rejoice, *I* must mourn. . . .[2]

In the pages of his newspaper, *North Star* (later renamed
Frederick Douglass' Paper), Douglass advocated the formation
of a racial union or National League that would implement
his ideology of Negro self-uplift and racial solidarity. Two
documents that follow illustrate this aspect of his antebellum
thought: an editorial from the first issue of *North Star,*
dedicating the newspaper "to the cause of our long oppressed

[2] Frederick Douglass, *Oration Delivered in Corinthian Hall, Rochester,
July 5, 1852,* reprinted in Philip S. Foner (ed.), *The Life and Writings of
Frederick Douglass,* II (New York: International Publishers, 1950), 189.

and plundered fellow countrymen," and an article occasioned
by a letter from Samuel Ringgold Ward, the Congregationalist
clergyman and famous abolitionist orator who was known as
the "black Daniel Webster" (see Document 14). The
concluding document is the proposal—which Douglass largely
shaped—of the 1853 national convention for a National
Council or Union of Colored People. Though this was not
implemented, it expresses a widespread, even characteristic
point of view among black leaders of the 1850s
(see Document 15).

13. COLORED NATIONAL CONVENTION OF 1848 ON "COMPLEXIONAL" AND WHITE INSTITUTIONS

. . . Fellow-countrymen, it is not so much our purpose to cheer
you by the progress we have already made, as it is to stimulate
you to still higher attainments. We have done much, but there
is much more to be done. While we have undoubtedly great
cause to thank God, and take courage for the hopeful changes
which have taken place in our condition, we are not without
cause to mourn over the sad condition which we yet occupy.
We are yet the most oppressed people in the world. In the
Southern States of this Union, we are held as slaves. All over
that wide region our paths are marked with blood. Our backs
are yet scarred by the lash, and our souls are yet dark under the
pall of slavery. Our sisters are sold for purposes of pollution,
and our brethren are sold in the market, with beasts of burden.
Shut up in the prison-house of bondage—denied all rights, and

From "An Address to the Colored People of the United States,"
in REPORT OF THE PROCEEDINGS OF THE COLORED
NATIONAL CONVENTION, . . . 1848 (Rochester, N.Y.: Printed by
John Dick, 1848), pp. 18–20.

deprived of all privileges, we are blotted from the page of human existence, and placed beyond the limits of human regard. DEATH, moral DEATH, has palsied our souls in that quarter, and we are a murdered people.

In the Northern states, we are not slaves to individuals, not personal slaves, yet in many respects we are the slaves of the community. We are, however, far enough removed from the actual condition of the slave, to make us largely responsible for their continued enslavement, or their speedy deliverance from chains. For in the proportion which we shall rise in the scale of human improvement, in that proportion do we augment the probabilities of a speedy emancipation of our enslaved fellow-countrymen. It is more than a mere figure of speech to say, that we are as a people, chained together. We are one people—one in general complexion, one in a common degradation, one in popular estimation.—As one rises, all must rise, and as one falls all must fall. Having now, our feet on the rock of freedom, we must drag our brethren from the slimy depths of slavery, ignorance, and ruin. Every one of us should be ashamed to consider himself free, while his brother is a slave. The wrongs of our brethren, should be our constant theme. There should be no time too precious, no calling too holy, no place too sacred, to make room for this cause. We should not only feel it to be the cause of humanity, but the cause of christianity, and fit work for men and angels. We ask you to devote yourselves to this cause, as one of the first, and most successful means of self improvement. In the careful study of it, you will learn your own rights, and comprehend your own responsibilities, and, scan through the vista of coming time, your high, and God-appointed destiny. Many of the brightest and best of our number, have become such by their devotion to this cause, and the society of white abolitionists. The latter have been willing to make themselves of no reputation for our sake, and in return, let us show ourselves worthy of their zeal and devotion. Attend Antislavery meetings, show that you are interested in the subject, that you hate slavery, and love those who are laboring for its overthrow. Act with white Abolition societies wherever you can, and where you cannot, get up societies among yourselves, but without exclusiveness. It will be a long time before we gain all our rights; and although it may seem to conflict with our views of human brotherhood, we shall undoubtedly for many years be compelled to have institutions of a complexional character, in order to attain this very idea of human brotherhood. We would, however, advise our brethren to occupy memberships and stations among white persons, and in white institutions, just so fast as our rights are secured to us.

Never refuse to act with a white society or institution because it is white, or a black one, because it is black; but act with all men without distinction of color. By so acting, we shall find many opportunities for removing prejudices and establishing the rights of all men.—We say, avail yourselves of *white* institutions, not because they are white, but because they afford a more convenient means of improvement. But we pass from these suggestions, to others which may be deemed more important. In the Convention that now addresses you, there has been much said on the subject of labor, and especially those departments of it, with which we as a class have been long identified. You will see by the resolutions there adopted on that subject, that the Convention regarded those employments, though right in themselves, as being, nevertheless, degrading to us as a class, and therefore, counsel you to abandon them as speedily as possible, and to seek what are called the more respectable employments. While the Convention do not inculcate the doctrine that any kind of needful toil is in itself dishonorable, or that colored persons are to be exempt from what are called menial employments, they do mean to say that such employments have been so long and universally filled by colored men, as to become a badge of degradation, in that it has established the conviction that colored men are only fit for such employments. We therefore advise you, by all means, to cease from such employments, as far as practicable, by pressing into others. Try to get your sons into mechanical trades; press them into the blacksmith's shop, the machine shop, the joiner's shop, the wheelright's shop, the cooper's shop, and the tailor's shop.

Every blow of the sledge-hammer, wielded by a sable arm, is a powerful blow in support of our cause. Every colored mechanic, is by virtue of circumstances, an elevator of his race. Every house built by black men, is a strong tower against the allied hosts of prejudice. It is impossible for us to attach too much importance to this aspect of the subject. Trades are important. Wherever a man may be thrown by misfortune, if he has in his hands a useful trade, he is useful to his fellow-man, and will be esteemed accordingly; and of all men in the world who need trades, we are the most needy.

Understand this, that independence is an essential condition of respectability. To be dependent, is to be degraded. Men may indeed pity us, but they cannot respect us. We do not mean that we can become entirely independent of all men; that would be absurd and impossible, in the social state. But we mean that we must become equally independent with other members of the community. That other members of the community shall be as dependent upon us, as we upon them. That such is not now the case, is too plain to need an argument. The houses we live in are built by white men—the clothes we wear are made by white tailors—the hats on our heads are made by white hatters, and the shoes on our feet are made by white shoe-makers, and the food that we eat, is raised and cultivated by white men. Now it is impossible that we should ever be respected as a people, while we are so universally and completely dependent upon white men for the necessaries of life. We must make white persons as dependent upon us, as we are upon them.—This cannot be done while we are found only in two or three kinds of employments, and those employments have their foundation chiefly, if not entirely, in the pride and indolence of the white people. Sterner necessities, will bring higher respect. . . .

14. FREDERICK DOUGLASS: "OUR ELEVATION AS A RACE, IS ALMOST WHOLLY DEPENDENT UPON OUR OWN EXERTIONS"

A. TO OUR OPPRESSED COUNTRYMEN

We solemnly dedicate the *North Star* to the cause of our long oppressed and plundered fellow countrymen. May God bless the offering to your good! It shall fearlessly assert your rights, faithfully proclaim your wrongs, and earnestly demand for you instant and even-handed justice. Giving no quarter to slavery at the South, it will hold no truce with oppressors at the North. While it shall boldly advocate emancipation for our enslaved brethren, it will omit no opportunity to gain for the nominally free complete enfranchisement. Every effort to injure or de-grade you or your cause—originating wheresoever, or with whomsoever—shall find in it a constant, unswerving and inflex-ible foe.

We shall energetically assail the ramparts of Slavery and Prejudice, be they composed of church or state, and seek the destruction of every refuge of lies, under which tyranny may aim to conceal and protect itself.

Among the multitude of plans proposed and opinions held, with reference to our cause and condition, we shall try to have a mind of our own, harmonizing with all as far as we can, and differing from any and all where we must, but always discrimi-nating between men and measures. We shall cordially approve every measure and effort calculated to advance your sacred cause, and strenuously oppose any which in our opinion may

Frederick Douglass, "To Our Oppressed Countrymen," editorial in THE NORTH STAR, December 3, 1847.

tend to retard its progress. In regard to our position, on questions that have unhappily divided the friends of freedom in this country, we shall stand in our paper where we have ever stood on the platform. Our views written shall accord with our views spoken, earnestly seeking peace with all men, when it can be secured without injuring the integrity of our movement, and never shrinking from conflict or division when summoned to vindicate truth and justice.

While our paper shall be mainly Anti-Slavery, its columns shall be freely opened to the candid and decorous discussion of all measures and topics of a moral and humane character, which may serve to enlighten, improve, and elevate mankind. Temperance, Peace, Capital Punishment, Education,—all subjects claiming the attention of the public mind may be freely and fully discussed here.

While advocating your rights, the *North Star* will strive to throw light on your duties: while it will not fail to make known your virtues, it will not shun to discover your faults. To be faithful to our foes it must be faithful to ourselves, in all things.

Remember that we are one, that our cause is one, and that we must help each other, if we would succeed. We have drunk to the dregs the bitter cup of slavery; we have worn the heavy yoke; we have sighed beneath our bonds, and writhed beneath the bloody lash;—cruel mementoes of our oneness are indelibly marked in our living flesh. We are one with you under the ban of prejudice and proscription—one with you under the slander of inferiority—one with you in social and political disfranchisement. What you suffer, we suffer; what you endure, we endure. We are indissolubly united, and must fall or flourish together.

We feel deeply the solemn responsibility which we have now assumed. We have seriously considered the importance of the enterprise, and have now entered upon it with full purpose of heart. We have nothing to offer in the way of literary ability to induce you to encourage us in our laudable undertaking. You will not expect or require this at our hands. The most that you can reasonably expect, or that we can safely promise, is, a paper of which you need not be ashamed. Twenty-one years of severe bondage at the South, and nine years of active life at the North, while it has afforded us the best possible opportunity for storing our mind with much practical and important information, has left us little time for literary pursuits or attainments. We have yet to receive the advantage of the first day's schooling. In point of education, birth and rank, we are one with yourselves, and of yourselves. What we are, we are not only without help, but against trying opposition. Your knowledge of our history for the last seven years makes it unnecessary for us to say more on this point. What we have been in your cause, we shall continue to be; and not being too old to learn, we may improve in many ways. Patience and Perseverance shall be our motto.

We shall be the advocates of learning, from the very want of it, and shall most readily yield the deference due to men of education among us; but shall always bear in mind to accord most merit to those who have labored hardest, and overcome most, in the praiseworthy pursuit of knowledge, remembering "that the whole need not a physician, but they that are sick," and that "the strong ought to bear the infirmities of the weak."

Brethren, the first number of the paper is before you. It is dedicated to your cause. Through the kindness of our friends in England, we are in possession of an excellent printing press, types, and all other materials necessary for printing a paper. Shall this gift be blest to our good, or shall it result in our injury? It is for you to say. With your aid, co-operation and assistance, our enterprise will be entirely successful. We pledge ourselves that no effort on our part shall be wanting, and that no subscriber shall lose his subscription—"The *North Star* Shall Live."

B. SELF-ELEVATION—REV. S. R. WARD

The letter of our esteemed friend, Ward, published in another column, will well repay an attentive perusal. It will be seen that he is in London, attending to private business. It is said, that "distance lends enchantment to the view"; this declaration may hold good in some cases, but in that of brother Ward, it is completely at variance. For just such men as he, *are needed here on the battle ground*, to work faithfully in the cause of our elevation—our emancipation from every species of servitude.

It is needless to remark, that the views of Mr. Ward, so clearly set forth in this letter, elicit our hearty concurrences. We always admired his characteristic boldness and plainness of utterance. In this letter before us, these features stand out in bold relief. We do not confess to a very extravagant appreciation of the modesty of some of our brethren which precludes them from speaking the truth, at the risk of offending those who arrogate to themselves a position, wholly in conflict with their democratic theory of EQUALITY.

It is well known that we have called down upon our devoted head, the holy (?) horror of a certain class of Abolitionists, because we have dared to maintain our Individuality, and have opened our own eyes, and looked out of them, through another telescope. This has been the head and front of our offending. *This is the way*, we "have thrown our principles to the winds, and substituted policy therefor."

Every day brings with it renewed evidence of the truthfulness of the sentiment, now, in various quarters, gaining the confidence and sympathy of our oppressed People, THAT OUR ELEVATION AS A RACE, IS ALMOST WHOLLY DEPENDENT UPON OUR OWN EXERTIONS. If we are ever elevated, our elevation will have been accomplished through our own instrumentality. The history of other oppressed nations will confirm us in this assertion.

Frederick Douglass, "Self-Elevation—Rev. S. R. Ward," editorial in the FREDERICK DOUGLASS' PAPER, April 15, 1855

No People that has solely depended upon foreign aid, or rather, upon the efforts of those, in any way identified with the oppressor, to undo the heavy burdens, ever stood forth in the attitude of Freedom. Some one, imbued with the spirit of human freedom, from among themselves, has arisen to lead them on to victory. *They* have dashed their fetters to the ground. We do not affirm that no oppressed nation has ever received aid from abroad, which proved conducive to its deliverance. Not at all; but we do say, that the oppressed nation itself, has always taken a prominent part in the conflict, and has not been merely employed by its help-meet or coadjutor, to light camp-fires, bring water to the sick and wounded, and do all the incidental drudgery of the warfare.

We look upon the past as a precedent for the future. Our oppressed people are wholly ignored, in one sense, in the generalship of the movement to effect our Redemption. Nothing is done—no, nothing, as our friend Ward asserts, to inspire us with the Idea of our Equality with the whites. We are a poor, pitiful, dependent and servile class of Negroes, *"unable to keep pace"* with the movement, to which we have adverted—not even capable of *"perceiving what are its demands, or understanding the philosophy of its operations!"* Of course, if we are "unable to keep pace" with our white brethren, in their vivid perception of the demands of our cause, those who assume the leadership of the Anti-Slavery Movement; if it is regarded as having *"transcended our ability,"* we cannot consistently expect to receive from those who indulge in this opinion, a *practical recognition of our Equality.* This is what we are contending for. It is what we have never received. It is what we must receive to inspire us with confidence in the self-appointed generals of the Anti-Slavery host, the Euclids who are *theoretically* working out the almost insoluble problem of our future destiny.

True, our assertions may be misconstrued into a "malicious" misrepresentation of the facts of the case. But we shall present the facts, nevertheless, for none of these things shall ever deter us from the utterance of the truth. Our friend Ward seems to understand, that for the candid expression of his opinion, in this matter, he sets himself up as a target; but *"there I have said it,"* he remarks; and he has said it opportunely, and said it well. He has even dared in his insolence, to peep into the headquarters of the American Garrisonianism, to look at the colored mailwrappers, and waiters in general, who, we fear, will be kept in their "waiting" position, till they satisfy their superiors, that they are able to "keep pace" with them, and that they "understand" the illiberal policy of *their* "operation." This they can never do in their present secondary position, as understrappers. They must *develop their manhood,* and not be too *modest* to attempt such development. Finally, we would remark, that we need, as a people, unity of effort, to impart efficiency to any self elevation movement, we may institute. If we rise, we must rise together; if we fall, we must fall together. We want such men as Ward, and Garnet, and Crummell, *at home.* They *must* come and help us. We know, by experience, that it is very *pleasant* to be where one can inhale a pure atmosphere, and lift up the voice against oppression, wafted as it were to the skies, upon the gratulations of the sympathising multitude, but "any one can perform an agreeable duty." Come home, then, brethren, and help us perform the *"disagreeable duty,"* of telling the truth, and the whole truth, though its promulgation make enemies of "our best friends"; come with an invincible determination to bring your mighty energies to bear upon the redemption of our race, and our whole race, from every species of oppression, irrespective of the form it may assume, or the source whence it may emanate.

Yes! come home, brethren—for, although the Garrisonian host have taken an anti-color position the great mass of Abolitionists call for us now more loudly than ever. There never was a time when your services were more in requisition than now. The field is ripe for the harvest; come, then, for the laborers are few.

15. COLORED NATIONAL CONVENTION
OF 1853: "A NATIONAL COUNCIL
OF THE COLORED PEOPLE"

For the purpose of improving the character, developing the intelligence, maintaining the rights, and organizing a Union of the Colored People of the Free States, the National Convention does hereby ordain and institute the

"NATIONAL COUNCIL OF THE COLORED PEOPLE."

Art. 1. This Council shall consist of two members from each State, represented in this Convention, to be elected by this Convention, and two other members from each State to be elected as follows: On the 15th day of November next, and biennially thereafter, there shall be held in each State, a Poll, at which each colored inhabitant may vote who pay ten cents as a poll-tax; and each State shall elect, at such election, delegates to State Councils, twenty in number from each State, at large. The election to be held in such places and under such conditions as the public meetings in such localities may determine. The members of the National Council in each State, shall receive, canvass and declare the result of such vote. The State Council thus elected, shall meet on the first Monday in January, 1854, and elect additional members to the National Council, in proportion of one to five thousand of colored population of such State; and the members of Council, thus elected, to take office on the 6th day of July next, and all to hold office during two years from that date; at the end of which time another general election by State Council shall take place of members to constitute their successors in office, in the same numbers as

From "National Council of the Colored People," in PROCEEDINGS
OF THE COLORED NATIONAL CONVENTION, . . . 1853
(Rochester, N.Y.: FREDERICK DOUGLASS' PAPER, 1853), pp. 18–19.

above. The State Council of each State shall have full power over the internal concern of said State.

Art. 2. The members of the first Council shall be elected by this Convention, which shall designate out of the number, a President, Vice-President, Secretary, Treasurer, Corresponding Secretary, and Committee of five on Manual Labor School—a Committee of five on Protective Unions—of five on Business Relations—of five on Publications.

Art. 3. The Committee on Manual Labor School, shall procure funds and organize said School in accordance with the plans adopted by this National Convention, with such modifications as experience or necessity may dictate to them. The Committeee shall immediately incorporate itself as an Academy under the general Committee of the State of ——, and shall constitute the Board of Trustees of the Manual Labor School, with full power to select a location in the State designated by the National Council, to erect buildings, appoint or dismiss instructors in the literary or mechanical branches. There shall be a farm attached to the School.

Art. 4. The Committee on Protective Union, shall institute a Protective Union for the purchase and sale of articles of domestic consumption, and shall unite and aid in the formation of branches auxiliary to their own.

Art. 5. The Committee on Business Relations, shall establish an office, in which they shall keep a registry of colored mechanics, artizans and business men throughout the Union. They shall keep a registry of all persons willing to employ colored men in business, to teach colored boys mechanical trades, liberal and scientific professions, and farming; and, also, a registry of colored men and youth seeking employment or instruction. They shall also report upon any avenues of business or trade which they deem inviting to colored capital, skill, or labor. Their reports and advertisements to be in papers of the widest circulation. They shall receive for sale or exhibition, products of the skill and labor of colored people.

Art. 6. The Committee on Publication shall collect all facts, statistics and statements, all laws and historical records and biographies of the Colored People, and all books by colored authors. They shall have for the safe keeping of these documents, a Library, with a Reading Room and Museum. The Committee shall also publish replies to any assaults, worthy of note, made upon the character or condition of the Colored People.

Art. 7. Each Committee shall have absolute control over its special department; shall make its own by-laws, and in case of any vacancy occurring, shall fill up the same forthwith, subject to the confirmation of the Council. Each Committee shall meet at least once a month or as often as possible; shall keep a minute of all its proceedings, executive and financial, and shall submit a full statement of the same, with the accounts audited, at every regular meeting of the National Council.

Art. 8. The National Council shall meet at least once in six months, to receive the reports of the Committees, and to consider any new plan for the general good, for which it shall have power, at its option, to appoint a new Committee, and shall be empowered to receive and appropriate donations for the carrying out of the objects of the same. At all such meetings, eleven members shall constitute a quorum. In case any Committee neglect or refuse to send in its report, according to article 8th, then the Council shall have power to enter the bureau, examine the books and papers of such Committee; and in case the Committee shall persist in its refusal or neglect, then the Council shall declare their offices vacant, and appoint others in their stead.

Art. 9. In all cases of the meetings of the National Council, or the Committees, the travelling expenses (if any) of the members shall be paid out of their respective funds.

Art. 10. The Council shall immediately establish a bureau in the place of its meeting; and the same rooms shall, as far possible, be used by the several Committees for their various purposes. The Council shall have a clerk, at a moderate salary, who shall keep a record of their transactions, and prepare a condensed report of the Committees for publication; and also a registry of the friends of the cause.

Art. 11. The expenses of the Council shall be defrayed by the fees of membership of sub-societies or Councils, to be organized throughout the States. The membership fee shall be one cent per week.

Art. 12. A member of the Council shall be a member of only one of the Committees thereof.

Art. 13. All officers holding funds, shall give security in double the amount likely to be in their hands. This security to be given to the three first officers of the Council.

Art. 14. The Council shall have power to make such By-Laws as are necessary for their proper government.

Revolutionary nationalism

The Reverend Henry Highland Garnet's celebrated address, urging the slaves to revolt against their masters can be considered a nationalist document in two respects. First, it explicitly expresses the sense of identity and solidarity with the slaves felt by the free people of color. Second, it calls for violent overthrow of the Southern economic system, based implicitly upon united and collective action on the part of the slaves themselves. The 1843 national convention, before which the address was made, voted not to publish the document, but only after an intense debate. It did not appear in print until 1848, when Garnet published it himself, bound together with a reprinting of David Walker's *Appeal* of 1829.

16. HENRY HIGHLAND GARNET CALLS FOR SLAVE REBELLIONS

Brethren and Fellow-Citizens:—Your brethren of the North, East, and West have been accustomed to meet together in National Conventions, to sympathize with each other, and to weep over your unhappy condition. In these meetings we have

From Henry Highland Garnet, "An Address to the Slaves of the United States of America" (1843), reprinted in Garnet, A MEMORIAL DISCOURSE BY REV. HENRY HIGHLAND GARNET, DELIVERED IN THE HALL OF THE HOUSE OF REPRESENTATIVES (Philadelphia: Joseph M. Wilson, 1865), pp. 44–51.

addressed all classes of the free, but we have never, until this time, sent a word of consolation and advice to you. We have been contented in sitting still and mourning over your sorrows, earnestly hoping that before this day your sacred liberties would have been restored. But, we have hoped in vain. Years have rolled on, and tens of thousands have been borne on streams of blood and tears, to the shores of eternity. While you have been oppressed, we have also been partakers with you; nor can we be free while you are enslaved. We, therefore, write to you as being bound with you.

Many of you are bound to us, not only by the ties of a common humanity, but we are connected by the more tender relations of parents, wives, husbands, children, brothers, and sisters, and friends. As such we most affectionately address you.

Slavery has fixed a deep gulf between you and us, and while it shuts out from you the relief and consolation which your friends would willingly render, it afflicts and persecutes you with a fierceness which we might not expect to see in the fiends of hell. But still the Almighty Father of mercies has left to us a glimmering ray of hope, which shines out like a lone star in a cloudy sky. Mankind are becoming wiser, and better—the oppressor's power is fading, and you, every day, are becoming better informed, and more numerous. Your grievances, brethren, are many. We shall not attempt, in this short address, to present to the world all the dark catalogue of this nation's sins, which have been committed upon an innocent people. Nor is it indeed necessary, for you feel them from day to day, and all the civilized world look upon them with amazement.

Two hundred and twenty-seven years ago, the first of our injured race were brought to the shores of America. They came not with glad spirits to select their homes in the New World. They came not with their own consent, to find an unmolested enjoyment of the blessings of this fruitful soil. The first dealings they had with men calling themselves Christians, exhibited to them the worst features of corrupt and sordid hearts: and convinced them that no cruelty is too great, no villainy and no robbery too abhorrent for even enlightened men to perform, when influenced by avarice and lust. Neither did they come flying upon the wings of Liberty, to a land of freedom. But they came with broken hearts, from their beloved native land, and were doomed to unrequited toil and deep degradation. Nor did the evil of their bondage end at their emancipation by death. Succeeding generations inherited their chains, and millions have come from eternity into time, and have returned again to the world of spirits, cursed and ruined by American slavery.

The propagators of the system, or their immediate ancestors, very soon discovered its growing evil, and its tremendous wickedness, and secret promises were made to destroy it. The gross inconsistency of a people holding slaves, who had themselves "ferried o'er the wave" for freedom's sake, was too apparent to be entirely overlooked. The voice of Freedom cried, "Emancipate your slaves." Humanity supplicated with tears for the deliverance of the children of Africa. Wisdom urged her solemn plea. The bleeding captive plead his innocence, and pointed to Christianity who stood weeping at the cross. Jehovah frowned upon the nefarious institution, and thunderbolts, red with vengeance, struggled to leap forth to blast the guilty wretches who maintained it. But all was vain. Slavery had stretched its dark wings of death over the land, the Church stood silently by—the priests prophesied falsely, and the people loved to have it so. Its throne is established, and now it reigns triumphant.

Nearly three millions of your fellow-citizens are prohibited by law and public opinion, (which in this country is stronger than law,) from reading the Book of Life. Your intellect has been destroyed as much as possible, and every ray of light they have attempted to shut out from your minds. The oppressors themselves have become involved in the ruin. They have become weak, sensual, and rapacious—they have cursed you— they have cursed themselves—they have cursed the earth which they have trod.

The colonists threw the blame upon England. They said that the mother country entailed the evil upon them, and that they would rid themselves of it if they could. The world thought they were sincere, and the philanthropic pitied them. But time soon tested their sincerity. In a few years the colonists grew strong, and severed themselves from the British Government. Their independence was declared, and they took their station among the sovereign powers of the earth. The declaration was a glorious document. Sages admired it, and the patriotic of every nation reverenced the God-like sentiments which it contained. When the power of Government returned to their hands, did they emancipate the slaves? No; they rather added new links to our chains. Were they ignorant of the principles of Liberty? Certainly they were not. The sentiments of their revolutionary orators fell in burning eloquence upon their hearts, and with one voice they cried, LIBERTY OR DEATH. Oh what a sentence was that! It ran from soul to soul like electric fire, and nerved the arm of thousands to fight in the holy cause of Freedom. Among the diversity of opinions that are entertained in regard to physical resistance, there are but a few found to gainsay that stern declaration. We are among those who do not.

SLAVERY! How much misery is comprehended in that single word. What mind is there that does not shrink from its direful effects? Unless the image of God be obliterated from the soul, all men cherish the love of Liberty. The nice discerning political economist does not regard the sacred right more than the untutored African who roams in the wilds of Congo. Nor has the one more right to the full enjoyment of his freedom than the other. In every man's mind the good seeds of liberty are planted, and he who brings his fellow down so low, as to make him contented with a condition of slavery, commits the highest crime against God and man. Brethren, your oppressors aim to do this. They endeavor to make you as much like brutes as possible. When they have blinded the eyes of your mind— when they have embittered the sweet waters of life—when they have shut out the light which shines from the word of God— then, and not till then, has American slavery done its perfect work.

TO SUCH DEGRADATION IT IS SINFUL IN THE EXTREME FOR YOU

TO MAKE VOLUNTARY SUBMISSION. The divine commandments
you are in duty bound to reverence and obey. If you do not
obey them, you will surely meet with the displeasure of the
Almighty. He requires you to love him supremely, and your
neighbor as yourself—to keep the Sabbath day holy—to search
the Scriptures—and bring up your children with respect for his
laws, and to worship no other God but him. But slavery sets all
these at nought, and hurls defiance in the face of Jehovah. The
forlorn condition in which you are placed, does not destroy your
moral obligation to God. You are not certain of heaven, because
you suffer yourselves to remain in a state of slavery, where you
cannot obey the commandments of the Sovereign of the universe. If the ignorance of slavery is a passport to heaven, then
it is a blessing, and no curse, and you should rather desire its
perpetuity than its abolition. God will not receive slavery, nor
ignorance, nor any other state of mind, for love and obedience
to him. Your condition does not absolve you from your moral
obligation. The diabolical injustice by which your liberties are
cloven down, NEITHER GOD, NOR ANGELS, OR JUST MEN, COMMAND
YOU TO SUFFER FOR A SINGLE MOMENT. THEREFORE IT IS YOUR
SOLEMN AND IMPERATIVE DUTY TO USE EVERY MEANS, BOTH
MORAL, INTELLECTUAL, AND PHYSICAL, THAT PROMISES SUCCESS.
If a band of heathen men should attempt to enslave a race of
Christians, and to place their children under the influence of
some false religion, surely, Heaven would frown upon the men
who would not resist such aggression, even to death. If, on the
other hand, a band of Christians should attempt to enslave a
race of heathen men, and to entail slavery upon them, and to
keep them in heathenism in the midst of Christianity, the God
of heaven would smile upon every effort which the injured
might make to disenthral themselves.

Brethren, it is as wrong for your lordly oppressors to keep
you in slavery, as it was for the man thief to steal our ancestors
from the coast of Africa. You should therefore now use the
same manner of resistance, as would have been just in our ancestors, when the bloody foot-prints of the first remorseless
soul-thief was placed upon the shores of our fatherland. The

humblest peasant is as free in the sight of God as the proudest monarch that ever swayed a sceptre. Liberty is a spirit sent out from God, and like its great Author, is no respecter of persons.

Brethren, the time has come when you must act for yourselves. It is an old and true saying that, "if hereditary bondmen would be free, they must themselves strike the blow." You can plead your own cause, and do the work of emancipation better than any others. The nations of the old world are moving in the great cause of universal freedom, and some of them at least will, ere long, do you justice. The combined powers of Europe have placed their broad seal of disapprobation upon the African slave-trade. But in the slave-holding parts of the United States, the trade is as brisk as ever. They buy and sell you as though you were brute beasts. The North has done much—her opinion of slavery in the abstract is known. But in regard to the South, we adopt the opinion of the *New York Evangelist*—"We have advanced so far, that the cause apparently waits for a more effectual door to be thrown open than has been yet." We are about to point you to that more effectual door. Look around you, and behold the bosoms of your loving wives heaving with untold agonies! Hear the cries of your poor children! Remember the stripes your fathers bore. Think of the torture and disgrace of your noble mothers. Think of your wretched sisters, loving virtue and purity, as they are driven into concubinage and are exposed to the unbridled lusts of incarnate devils. Think of the undying glory that hangs around the ancient name of Africa:—and forget not that you are native-born American citizens, and as such, you are justly entitled to all the rights that are granted to the freest. Think how many tears you have poured out upon the soil which you have cultivated with unrequited toil and enriched with your blood; and then go to your lordly enslavers and tell them plainly, that you *are determined to be free*. Appeal to their sense of justice, and tell them that they have no more right to oppress you, than you have to enslave them. Entreat them to remove the grievous burdens which they have imposed upon you, and to remunerate you for your

labor. Promise them renewed diligence in the cultivation of
the soil, if they will render to you an equivalent for your services. Point them to the increase of happiness and prosperity
in the British West-Indies since the Act of Emancipation. Tell
them in language which they cannot misunderstand, of the
exceeding sinfulness of slavery, and of a future judgment, and
of the righteous retributions of an indignant God. Inform them
that all you desire is FREEDOM, and that nothing else will suffice.
Do this, and for ever after cease to toil for the heartless tyrants,
who give you no other reward but stripes and abuse. If they
then commence the work of death, they, and not you, will be
responsible for the consequences. You had far better all die—
die immediately, than live slaves, and entail your wretchedness
upon your posterity. If you would be free in this generation,
here is your only hope. However much you and all of us may
desire it, there is not much hope of redemption without the
shedding of blood. If you must bleed, let it all come at once—
rather *die freemen, than live to be the slaves.* It is impossible,
like the children of Israel, to make a grand exodus from the
land of bondage. The Pharaohs are on both sides of the blood-
red waters! You cannot move *en masse,* to the dominions of the
British Queen—nor can you pass through Florida and overrun
Texas, and at last find peace in Mexico. The propagators of
American slavery are spending their blood and treasure, that
they may plant the black flag in the heart of Mexico and riot in
the halls of the Montezumas. In the language of the Rev. Robert
Hall, when addressing the volunteers of Bristol, who were rushing forth to repel the invasion of Napoleon, who threatened to
lay waste the fair homes of England, "Religion is too much
interested in your behalf, not to shed over you her most
gracious influences."

You will not be compelled to spend much time in order to
become inured to hardships. From the first moment that you
breathed the air of heaven, you have been accustomed to nothing else but hardships. The heroes of the American Revolution
were never put upon harder fare than a peck of corn and a
few herrings per week. You have not become enervated by the

luxuries of life. Your sternest energies have been beaten out upon the anvil of severe trial. Slavery has done this, to make you subservient to its own purposes; but it has done more than this, it has prepared you for any emergency. If you receive good treatment, it is what you could hardly expect; if you meet with pain, sorrow, and even death, these are the common lot of the slaves.

Fellow-men! patient sufferers! behold your dearest rights crushed to the earth! See your sons murdered, and your wives, mothers and sisters doomed to prostitution. In the name of the merciful God, and by all that life is worth, let it no longer be a debatable question, whether it is better to choose *Liberty* or *death*.

In 1822, Denmark Veazie, of South Carolina, formed a plan for the liberation of his fellow-men. In the whole history of human efforts to overthrow slavery, a more complicated and tremendous plan was never formed. He was betrayed by the treachery of his own people, and died a martyr to freedom. Many a brave hero fell, but history, faithful to her high trust, will transcribe his name on the same monument with Moses, Hampden, Tell, Bruce and Wallace, Toussaint L'Ouverture, Lafayette and Washington. That tremendous movement shook the whole empire of slavery. The guilty soul-thieves were overwhelmed with fear. It is a matter of fact, that at that time, and in consequence of the threatened revolution, the slave States talked strongly of emancipation. But they blew but one blast of the trumpet of freedom, and then laid it aside. As these men became quiet, the slaveholders ceased to talk about emancipation: and now behold your condition to-day! Angels sigh over it, and humanity has long since exhausted her tears in weeping on your account!

The patriotic Nathaniel Turner followed Denmark Veazie. He was goaded to desperation by wrong and injustice. By despotism, his name has been recorded on the list of infamy, and future generations will remember him among the noble and brave.

Next arose the immortal Joseph Cinque, the hero of the

Amistad. He was a native African, and by the help of God he emancipated a whole ship-load of his fellow men on the high seas. And he now sings of liberty on the sunny hills of Africa and beneath his native palm-trees, where he hears the lion roar and feels himself as free as that king of the forest.

Next arose Madison Washington, that bright star of freedom, and took his station in the constellation of true heroism. He was a slave on board the brig Creole, of Richmond, bound to New Orleans, that great slave mart, with a hundred and four others. Nineteeen struck for liberty or death. But one life was taken, and the whole were emancipated, and the vessel was carried into Nassau, New Providence.

Noble men! Those who have fallen in freedom's conflict, their memories will be cherished by the true-hearted and the God-fearing in all future generations; those who are living, their names are surrounded by a halo of glory.

Brethren, arise, arise! Strike for your lives and liberties. Now is the day and the hour. Let every slave throughout the land do this, and the days of slavery are numbered. You cannot be more oppressed than you have been—you cannot suffer greater cruelties than you have already. *Rather die freemen than live to be slaves.* Remember that you are FOUR MILLIONS!

It is in your power so to torment the God-cursed slave-holders, that they will be glad to let you go free. If the scale was turned, and black men were the masters and white men the slaves, every destructive agent and element would be employed to lay the oppressor low. Danger and death would hang over their heads day and night. Yes, the tyrants would meet with plagues more terrible than those of Pharaoh. But you are a patient people. You act as though you were made for the special use of these devils. You act as though your daughters were born to pamper the lusts of your masters and overseers. And worse than all, you tamely submit while your lords tear your wives from your embraces and defile them before your eyes. In the name of God, we ask, are you men? Where is the blood of your fathers? Has it all run out of your veins? Awake, awake; millions of voices are calling you! Your dead fathers speak to you from their graves. Heaven, as with a voice of thunder, calls on you to arise from the dust.

Let your motto be resistance! *resistance!* RESISTANCE! No oppressed people have ever secured their liberty without resistance. What kind of resistance you had better make, you must decide by the circumstances that surround you, and according to the suggestion of expediency. Brethren, adieu! Trust in the living God. Labor for the peace of the human race, and remember that you are FOUR MILLIONS.

Colonization

The purest expression of nationalist ideology during the antebellum generation can be seen in the widespread support for emigration or colonization that developed in the late 1840s and 1850s. Unlike the Garvey movement of the 1920s, this emigration sentiment was a distinctly elite movement, led by some of the most distinguished and successful members of the race. Though their specific proposals varied, as a group they were men who had earlier been in the forefront of the fight for equal rights within the United States. Disillusioned because conditions seemed to be worsening and other tactics had failed, they took refuge in the vision of the glorious opportunities awaiting black people in Africa or Latin America.

Space does not permit a detailed exploration of the many differences of opinion and varieties of thought among the leaders of this mid-century colonizationist movement or of the manner in which specific proposals of individuals changed over the years. Thus Martin R. Delany, antebellum abolitionist, editor, and physician, in the early 1850s was a leading advocate of colonization in Central America, who once had thought that East Africa would be an appropriate place for emigration. By the end of the decade, however, he had settled upon the Niger Delta in West Africa. In 1859 he himself led a Niger Valley exploration expedition and signed a treaty with Yoruba rulers granting him permission to settle American blacks in that African kingdom. Moreover, emigrationists were sharply divided by their attitudes toward the American Colonization Society. Delany, like most Negroes, was severely critical of the society. Others, like Alexander

Crummell, who had originally been a vigorous opponent, turned colonizationist by the middle of the century and became vigorous supporters of the society. Finally most colonizationists, asserting that the future in the United States was hopeless, favored large scale expatriation. As Delany said in a letter to William Lloyd Garrison on May 14, 1852:

I am not in favor of caste, nor a separation of the brotherhood of mankind, and would as willingly live among white men as black, if I had an *equal possession* and enjoyment of privileges . . . If there were any probability of this, I should be willing to remain in the country, fighting and struggling on. . . . But I must admit, that I have no hopes in this country—no confidence in the American people—with a few excellent exceptions—therefore I have written as I have done. Heathenism and Liberty, before Christianity and Slavery.[1]

Yet there were a few who, like Alexander Crummell, while enthusiastic about Liberia, only rarely advocated large-scale emigration. Basically in the tradition of Paul Cuffe, Crummell was chiefly interested in colonization as a means for the uplift of the ancestral continent and the elimination of the slave trade.

This section includes four documents: a group of letters to the American Colonization Society by S. Wesley Jones, a Southern free Negro businessman, who despite his glowing rhetoric in support of the movement never found it possible to emigrate himself; resolutions of a group of Cincinnati colored citizens, representative of the views of Northern colonizationists; the Address of the 1854 national emigration convention, written by Martin R. Delany; and the nationalist vision of James Theodore Holly, Episcopal minister of New Haven and the leading advocate of emigration to Haiti.

[1] Quoted in Carter G. Woodson, ed., *The Mind of the Negro as Reflected in Letters Written During the Crisis, 1800–1860* (Washington, D.C.: Association for the Study of Negro Life and History, 1926), p. 293.

17. AN ALABAMA NEGRO BUSINESSMAN
WANTS TO GO TO LIBERIA

Tuskaloosa, Ala.
June 12, 1848

Rev. and Dear Sir:—After a long silence, I again take up my pen to communicate to you some facts in relation to the subject that lay nearest my heart, save that of the Christian religion, that of African colonization. You no doubt think me a dull and unworthy correspondent, and very justly too, for I ought to have written you months since, and I am quite ashamed of myself for not doing so. Pardon me, kind sir, for the past, and I promise you to do better for the future. Your very kind favor of the 27th February, was duly received; likewise, the different numbers of the Repository you was so pleased to send me, i.e. the January, February, March, and April numbers. . . . I have used some efforts to make the numbers of the Repository that I have received, useful, so far as lay in my power to do so. I have read and caused to be read, to the superstitious and prejudiced of our people, every opportunity, and I am proud to say, with some success. I have not failed in but a single instance, of removing old prejudices; and I still think, with patience in one hand, and perseverance on the other, I may succeed, even in that instance. I have traveled some the past winter, and have met with a great many free persons, and have never failed to bring the subject before them when an opportunity offered; and though I have met with the enemy in his stronghold, I have never failed to completely rout him by and with the aid of your valuable Repository. There are many in the State that are willing to go to Liberia, and all they wait for, is to see certain ones

S. Wesley Jones to William McClain of the American Colonization Society, June 12, 1848, August 4, 1849, undated, 1849, and December 29, 1951; American Colonization Society Papers, Library of Congress.

of their friends make the move. I candidly believe if I were ready at this time to go, I could easily raise a company of an hundred or more; but when I would reason with any upon the subject, they bring this to their relief: That I am willing they should go, but am not willing to go myself. Sir, my intention fully is to go to Liberia if it should please the Lord to spare my life. I have a ten years' business to try to settle up in this country, before I can leave for Africa's shores. If I can succeed only tolerably in collecting what is due me in this country, I shall be able to go to Liberia independent of aid from your benevolent society; but if I can't collect my dues, I shall be poor and dependent. So you percieve, sir, that it only requires a move to be made by some one in whom the people have confidence, to put the whole column in motion. My word for it, whenever there is a start made in Alabama, the whole body of free people will join in a solid phalanx. I intend making a tour through North Alabama, and perhaps I may extend my trip into Tennessee, as I have some business in that part of the country; also some relations, that I desire to confer with concerning Liberia. Should I go, sir, you shall hear from me at Huntsville. . . .

Believe me, sir, with considerations of the highest regard and esteem,

Your obedient servant,
S. Wesley Jones

Tuskaloosa
Aug 4th 1849

Revd & dear Sir

your last favor Came duly to hand & its contents appreciated I have delayed answering untill now for the Purpose of collecting Some information in Regard to the Persons who are likely to Emigrate from the imediate vicinity of this Place that I might inform you of thier intention condition &c.   there is Some 25 in this vicinity of Tuskaloosa with whom I have conversed on the

Subject of Emegrating to Liberea that manifest much anxiety to leave here as Soon as posible & I am Sorry to Say that there is as many more who listen to the well invented Tales of the Enemies of Coln. and Refuse to Emegrate untill Some one have gone to liberia who they Personally know & write or come back and given them information. well Sir when that is done I doubt very much whether it will have the Effect to Remove their foolish Prejudices or not   there is Such an amount of Ignorance among our People i.e.   Some of them that they are Easily gutted [?] by the whites who are disposed to do it the People who want to go from this Region are all free People and nearly all of them free born   they are however Poor there Being a very few of them able to Pay thier Passage or any Part of it   there is Some few that will be able Perhaps to pay there Entire Expences you will See as to that however when I Send the list on I wrote you in my last to Send me a copy of the last anual Report of the A. C. Society   you Sayed nothing of it in your letter and I concluded you had overlooked that Part of my letter or forgoten it   I Renew the Request in this letter   if it is to be abtained please Send it to me as Soon as you can you need not fear to Send me any document that you think would be Serviceable   there is Some information allso I wish to obtain from you Both for myself & for my friends who wish to go to Liberia. do the Society pay the Expenses of those who are unable to pay from the place of their Residence to the Place of Embarkation and are they allowed to carry their Beds and Bed Clothes   these Questions are frequently asked me and I am not able to give satisfactory information   please write me on these Subjects as Soon as Possible   I have information from North Alabama that there are Several in that Section of the State who design going outnext Spring   I Expect a letter from there Soon and I Shall Know all about it and in my next I will give you what additional information I may be able to collect   you need not Entertain any fears as to what you write me doing harm   write freely upon any Subject for your letters comes Safely and no one See them but my Self   I will also write to the Eastern Part of this

State today to Some friends and old acquaintances of mine who told me when I Saw them last that when I Started they would certainly go too of which I will inform you in my next

Yours Respectfully
S. Wesley Jones

P. S. I am certain to go next
Spring if life & health last
I wish you allso to inform me what
is the charge for childrens Passage
of twelve years & under

S. W. J.

Tuskaloosa, Ala.
[1849]

I am proud to be able to inform you that colonization is growing in favor rapidly in this State, among both black and white.

I see in the public journals a proposition laid before Congress by a gentleman from this State by the name of Bryan, for the building of four large steamers of the first class, to ply between Liberia and the ports of the United States, for the purpose of carrying the mails and passengers. I have heard much talk upon this subject. It is one that is received with as much favor in Alabama, as any that has come before the National Legislature for many years. All classes speak of it in the highest terms, and seem to be very anxious that it be carried out. If it is carried out, I candidly believe that in ten years from the date of the first trip, there will not be a free man of color left in the southern or slave-holding States. The most obstinate among us give way, and agree that they will willingly go if this project is carried out. The great length of the voyage, and the time it takes a sailing craft to perform it, deter very many, and the expense of the trip keeps many others away from the Ethiopian Republic; all of which would be obviated, if these steamers were in operation. My since prayer to Almighty God is, that they may be speedily put on the line, and that every free man in these

United States may avail himself of the great advantage of getting to his fatherland.

It is gratifying to me in the highest degree to see colonization taking such strong hold upon the hearts of the people of this great Republic, and upon that class that is able to give the cause that aid which is so much needed—I mean pecuniary assistance: the rich merchant, the wealthy farmer, the large slaveholder, are all joining their hearts and hands to the cause, and raising their voices in its praise and defence, all over the land. And I think it would be well for the friends of colonization to set apart some day for the purpose of returning our sincere, devout and humble thanks to the Disposer of the hearts of men, for his goodness towards us, and offer up our prayers and supplications for the continuation of the same.

Tuskaloosa, Alabama
Dec. 29, 1851

Rev. and Dear Sir: Colonization is rapidly growing in favor in this State. Ere this, doubtless you have heard of the formation of a State Colonization Society in Alabama, having for its object the colonizing her free people of color on the west coast of Africa, or in other words, sending them to Liberia. And I doubt not that the day is not distant when there will be an uprising of the free people of color—not only in Alabama—not only in the much persecuted South, where it is said by the fanatics that we are sorely oppresst, and inhumanly treated, but in the liberal and philanthropic North. We are treated about as well here, at least those who behave themselves, and conduct themselves as they should, as the same class of persons in the North. You ask the question, are you ever going to Liberia? My answer is, yes, without hesitation. I heartily thank you and the society which you represent for your kind and liberal offer of a free passage, and six months support. I regret exceedingly that I shall not be able to avail myself of the offer tendered at so early a day as the 10th January, but trust you will keep the privilege open a few months at least; and I think myself and several others will accept the proffered boon. We would most certainly go now, if we had our little matters closed, but those of us who want to go to Liberia are men who have been striving to do something for ourselves, and consequently have more or less business to close up. I think, however, that we will be able to leave here in a few months. There will be a handsome company from Alabama, I think, about next spring or fall. I have been informed by a correspondent at Huntsville, in the north end of this State, that there is several about there that have in part made up their minds to go, and they only want a little encouragement to settle them fully in favor of Liberia. The day is coming, and I trust is not far distant, when every free person of color in this country will esteem it a privilege to be sent to Liberia.

I am rejoiced to see that the free people in the great North is coming to their right minds at last. I was much pleased with the letter of Mr. Washington, of Hartford, on the subject of the condition of the colored people in this country. I trust there will be found ere long many Washingtons in the field laboring in behalf of Colonization. I was also pleased to see an account of a meeting of the colored people of New York, not long since, to take into consideration the expediency of emigrating to Liberia. I trust that these meetings will be gotten up in every State in the Union. Let the free colored people of every State meet in convention in their respective States, and exchange opinions, and make their views known to each other, and if needs be, hold a grand convention of all the States at such time and place as they may think proper; and let those State conventions send delegates to Liberia, or if they should think proper to have a general convention, let that convention send delegates. There is upwards of two thousand free colored people in Alabama; and if each of these would contribute but twenty-five cents a piece, we could have a fund sufficient to send two delegates to Liberia. Now, it does seem to me, if we, as a people, do feel any interest in our own welfare and that of our children, we will have no objection to inquiring into a matter of so much moment to us, at so small a cost.

I trust my brethren will think of this matter, and arouse themselves, and let national pride be kindled up in their hearts, and
go to and make us a great nation of our own, build our own
cities and towns, make our own laws, collect our own revenues,
command our own vessels, army and navy, elect our own governors and law makers, have our own schools and colleges, our
own lawyers and doctors, in a word, cease to be "hewers of
wood and drawers of water," and be men.

Believe me, yours, and Colonization's devoted friend,

S. W. Jones

18. BLACK CITIZENS OF CINCINNATI "SEEK A HOME WHERE WE MAY BE FREE"

Attention is directed to the following movement:

OHIO IN AFRICA.

At a meeting of colored citizens of Cincinnati, held on the
14th inst., the following preamble and resolutions were offered
and adopted:

Whereas, believing, that with all the exertions on our part,
and the assistance of those friendly to our elevation, we must
despair of ever seeing the prejudice manifested against our
people done away in the United States, for centuries yet to
come, from two ostensible reasons:

First, As no colored persons ever voluntarily emigrated to
this country, but were brought here in chains, consequently, we
that are here, are either slaves or their descendants; and being
thus situated, the vain *pride* of the white race will never admit
the *social equality* of a people who are their bondsmen, or
whose fathers have been their slaves.

"Movement Among the Colored People of Cincinnati," AFRICAN
REPOSITORY (Washington, D.C.), XXVI, (July 1850), 219.

Second, We believe all nations, or men, are respected according to their ability to control, by *numbers*, or *intelligence;* we, possessing neither, can never expect to enjoy a *political equality* where we must fail to command and enforce respect.

Under these considerations, having feelings and aspirations such as other men, we feel it to be a duty which we owe to posterity, to seek a home where we may be free and our children reared under the blessings of liberty. Other nations have colonized and prospered, and why not we? When blessed with the same advantages, we are equal to any and inferior to none. Therefore,

Resolved, That we believe that Liberia offers to the oppressed children of Africa a home where they may be free: and that it is the only place where we can establish a nationality, and be acknowledged as men by the nations of the earth.

Resolved, That the present meeting enter into the organization of an Association for the purpose of emigrating to the territory now being purchased on the coast of Africa, by CHARLES MCMICKEN, Esq., of this city, for the colored people of Ohio.

Resolved, That we believe it expedient, before emigrating to Liberia, to send out efficient agents to examine the country, and bring back some satisfactory report to our people.

Resolved, That this preamble and resolutions be published in several of the papers of this city.

Elias P. Walker,
Chairman

Wm. Byrd, Secretary

19. NATIONAL EMIGRATION CONVENTION OF 1854: "A PEOPLE, TO BE FREE, MUST NECESSARILY BE THEIR OWN RULERS"

To the colored inhabitants of the United States

Fellow-Countrymen!—The duty assigned us is an important one, comprehending all that pertains to our destiny and that of our posterity—present and prospectively. And while it must be admitted, that the subject is one of the greatest magnitude, requiring all that talents, prudence and wisdom might adduce, and while it would be folly to pretend to give you the combined result of these three agencies, we shall satisfy ourselves with doing our duty to the best of our ability, and that in the plainest, most simple and comprehensive manner.

Our object, then, shall be to place before you our true position in this country—the United States,—the improbability of realizing our desires, and the sure, practicable and infallible remedy for the evils we now endure.

We have not addressed you as *citizens*—a term desired and ever cherished by us—because such you have never been. We have not addressed you as *freemen*,—because such privileges have never been enjoyed by any colored man in the United States. Why then should we flatter your credulity, by inducing you to believe that which neither has now, nor never before had an existence. Our oppressors are ever gratified at our manifest satisfaction, especially when that satisfaction is founded upon false premises; an assumption on our part, of the enjoyment of rights and privileges which never have been conceded, and which, according to the present system of the United States policy, we never can enjoy.

From "Political Destiny of the Colored Race, on the American Continent," PROCEEDINGS OF THE NATIONAL EMIGRATION CONVENTION OF COLORED PEOPLE, . . . 1854 (Pittsburgh, Pa.: A. A. Anderson, Printer, 1854), pp. 33–43, 56–63, 69–70.

The *political policy* of this country was solely borrowed from, and shaped and moddled after, that of Rome. This was strikingly the case in the establishment of immunities, and the application of terms in their Civil and Legal regulations.

The term Citizen—politically considered—is derived from the Roman definition—which was never applied in any other sense—*Cives Ingenui;* which meant, one exempt from restraint of any kind. (*Cives*, a citizen; one who might enjoy the highest honors in his own free town—the town in which he lived—and in the country or commonwealth; and *Ingenui. freeborn*—of GOOD EXTRACTION.) All who were deprived of citizenship—that is, the right of enjoying positions of honor and trust—were termed *Hostes* and *Peregrini;* which are public and private *enemies,* and foreigners, or *aliens* to the country. (*Hostis,* a public—and sometimes—private enemy; and *Peregrinus,* an *alien, stranger,* or *foreigner.*)

The Romans, from a national pride, to distinguish their inhabitants from those of other countries, termed them all "citizens," but consequently, were under the necessity of specifying four classes of citizens: none but the *Cives Ingenui* being unrestricted in their privileges. There was one class, called the *Jus Quiritium,* or the wailing or *supplicating* citizen—that is, one who was continually *moaning, complaining, or crying for aid or succor.* This class might also include within themselves, the *jus suffragii,* who had the privilege of *voting,* but no other privilege. They could vote for one of their superiors—the *Cives Ingenui*—but not for themselves.

Such, then, is the condition, precisely, of the black and colored inhabitants of the United States; in some of the States they answering to the latter class, having the privilege of *voting,* to elevate their superiors to positions to which they need never dare aspire, or even hope to attain.

There has, of late years, been a false impression obtained, that the privilege of *voting* constitutes, or necessarily embodies, the *rights of citizenship.* A more radical error never obtained favor among an oppressed people. Suffrage is an ambiguous term, which admits of several definitions. But according to strict political construction, means simply "a vote, voice, appro-bation." Here, then, you have the whole import of the term suffrage. To have the "right of suffrage," as we rather proudly term it, is simply to have the *privilege*—there is no *right* about it—of giving our *approbation* to that which our *rulers may do,* without the privilege, on our part, of doing the same thing. Where such privileges are granted—privileges which are now exercised in but few of the States by colored men—we have but the privilege granted of saying, in common with others, who shall, for the time being, exercise *rights,* which in him, are con-ceded to be *inherent* and *inviolate*: Like the indented appren-tice, who is summoned to give his approbation to an act which would be fully binding without his concurrence. Where there is no *acknowledged sovereignty,* there can be no binding power; hence, the suffrage of the black man, independently of the white, would be in this country unavailable.

Much might be adduced on this point to prove the insignifi-cance of the black man, politically considered in this country, but we deem it wholly unnecessary at present, and conse-quently proceed at once to consider another feature of this important subject.

Let it then be understood, as a great principle of political economy, that no people can be free who themselves do not constitute an essential part of the *ruling element* of the country in which they live. Whether this element be founded upon a true or false, a just or an unjust basis; this position in community is necessary to personal safety. The liberty of no man is secure, who controls not his own political destiny. What is true of an individual, is true of a family; and that which is true of a family, is also true concerning a whole people. To suppose otherwise, is that delusion which at once induces its victim, through a period of long suffering, patiently to submit to every species of wrong; trusting against probability, and hoping against all rea-sonable grounds of expectation, for the granting of privileges and enjoyment of rights, which never will be attained. This delusion reveals the true secret of the power which holds in peaceable subjection, all the oppressed in every part of the world.

A people, to be free, must necessarily be *their own rulers*: that is, *each individual* must, in himself, embody the *essential ingredient*—so to speak—of the *sovereign principle* which composes the *true basis* of his liberty. This principle, when not exercised by himself, may, at his pleasure, be delegated to another—his true representative.

Said a great French writer: "A free agent, in a free government, should be his own governor;" that is, he must possess within himself the *acknowledged right to govern:* this constitutes him a *governor,* though he may delegate to another the power to govern himself.

No one, then, can delegate to another a power he never possessed; that is, he cannot *give an agency* in that which he never had a right. Consequently, the colored man in the United States, being deprived of the right of inherent sovereignty, cannot *confer* a suffrage, because he possesses none to confer. Therefore, where there is no suffrage, there can neither be *freedom* nor *safety* for the disfranchised. And it is a futile hope to suppose that the agent of another's concerns, will take a proper interest in the affairs of those to whom he is under no obligations. Having no favors to ask or expect, he therefore has none to lose.

In other periods and parts of the world—as in Europe and Asia—the people being of one common, direct origin of race, though established on the presumption of difference by birth, or what was termed *blood,* yet the distinction between the superior classes and common people, could only be marked by the difference in the dress and education of the two classes. To effect this, the interposition of government was necessary; consequently, the costume and education of the people became a subject of legal restriction, guarding carefully against the privileges of the common people.

In Rome, the Patrician and Plebeian were orders in the ranks of her people—all of whom were termed citizens *(cives)*—recognized by the laws of the country; their dress and education being determined by law, the better to fix the distinction. In different parts of Europe, at the present day, if not the same, the distinction among the people is similar, only on a modified —and in some kingdoms—probably more tolerant or deceptive policy.

In the United States, our degradation being once—as it has in a hundred instances been done—legally determined, our color is sufficient, independently of costume, education, or other distinguishing marks, to keep up that distinction.

In Europe, when an inferior is elevated to the rank of equality with the superior class, the law first comes to his aid, which, in its decrees, entirely destroys his identity as an inferior, leaving no trace of his former condition visible.

In the United States, among the whites, their color is made, by law and custom, the mark of distinction and superiority; while the color of the blacks is a badge of degradation, acknowledged by statute, organic law, and the common consent of the people.

With this view of the case—which we hold to be correct—to elevate to equality the degraded subject of law and custom, it can only be done, as in Europe, by an entire destruction of the identity of the former condition of the applicant. Even were this desirable—which we by no means admit—with the deep seated prejudices engendered by oppression, with which we have to contend, ages incalculable might reasonably be expected to roll around, before this could honorably be accomplished; otherwise, we should encourage and at once commence an indiscriminate concubinage and immoral commerce, of our mothers, sisters, wives and daughters, revolting to think of, and a physical curse to humanity.

If this state of things be to succeed, then, as in Egypt, under the dread of the inscrutible approach of the destroying angel, to appease the hatred of our oppressors, as a license to the passions of every white, let the lintel of each door of every black man, be stained with the blood of virgin purity and unsullied matron fidelity. Let it be written along the cornice in capitals, "The *will* of the white man is the rule of my household." Remove the protection to our chambers and nurseries, that the places once sacred, may henceforth become the unrestrained resort of the vagrant and rabble, always provided that the licensed commissioner of lust shall wear the indisputable impress of a *white* skin.

But we have fully discovered and comprehended the great political disease with which we are affected, the cause of its origin and continuance; and what is now left for us to do, is to discover and apply a sovereign remedy—a healing balm to a sorely diseased body—a wrecked but not entirely shattered system. We propose for this disease a remedy. That remedy is Emigration. This Emigration should be well advised, and like remedies applied to remove the disease from the physical system of man, skillfully and carefully applied, within the proper time, directed to operate on that part of the system, whose greatest tendency shall be, to benefit the whole.

Several geographical localities have been named, among which rank the Canadas. These we do not object to as places of temporary relief, especially to the fleeing fugitive—which, like a paliative, soothes for the time being the misery—but cannot commend them as permanent places upon which to fix our destiny, and that of our children, who shall come after us. But in this connexion, we would most earnestly recommend to the colored people of the United States generally, to secure by purchase all of the land they possibly can, while selling at low rates, under the British people and government. As that time may come, when, like the lands in the United States territories generally, if not as in Oregon and some other territories and States, they may be prevented entirely from settling or purchasing them; the preference being given to the white applicant.

And here, we would not deceive you by disguising the facts, that according to political tendency, the Canadas—as all British America—at no very distant day, are destined to come into the United States.

And were this not the case, the odds are against us, because the ruling element there, as in the United States, is, and ever must be, white—the population now standing, in all British America, two and a half millions of whites, to but forty thousand of the black race; or sixty-one and a fraction, whites, to one black!—the difference being eleven times greater than in the United States—so that colored people might never hope for anything more than to exist politically by mere suffrance— occupying a secondary position to the whites of the Canadas. The Yankees from this side of the lakes, are fast settling in the Canadas, infusing, with industrious success, all the malignity and negro-hate, inseparable from their very being, as Christian Democrats and American advocates of equality.

Then, to be successful, our attention must be turned in a direction towards those places where the black and colored man comprise, by population, and constitute by necessity of numbers, the *ruling element* of the body politic. And where, when occasion shall require it, the issue can be made and maintained on this basis. Where our political enclosure and national edifice can be reared, established, walled, and proudly defended on this great elementary principle of original identity. Upon this solid foundation rests the fabric of every substantial political structure in the world, which cannot exist without it; and so soon as a people or nation lose their original identity, just so soon must that nation or people become extinct.— Powerful though they may have been, they must fall. Because the nucleus which heretofore held them together, becoming extinct, there being no longer a centre of attraction, or basis for a union of the parts, a dissolution must as naturally ensue, as the result of the nutrality of the basis of adhesion among the particles of matter.

This is the secret of the eventful downfall of Egypt, Carthage, Rome, and the former Grecian States, once so powerful —a loss of original identity; and with it, a loss of interest in maintaining their fundamental principles of nationality.

This, also, is the great secret of the present strength of Great Britain, Russia, the United States, and Turkey; and the endurance of the French nation, whatever its strength and power, is attributable only to their identity as Frenchmen.

And doubtless the downfall of Hungary, brave and noble as may be her people, is mainly to be attributed to the want of identity of origin, and consequently, a union of interests and purpose. This fact it might not have been expected would be admitted by the great Magyar, in his thrilling pleas for the restoration of Hungary, when asking aid, both national and individual, to enable him to throw off the ponderous weight placed upon their shoulders by the House of Hapsburg.

Hungary consisted of three distinct "races"—as they call themselves—of people, all priding in and claiming rights based on their originality—the Magyars, Celts, and Sclaves. On the encroachment of Austria, each one of these races—declaring for nationality—rose up against the House of Hapsburg, claiming the right of self-government, premised on their origin. Between the three a compromise was effected—the Magyars, being the majority, claimed the precedence. They made an effort, but for the want of a unity of interests—and identity of origin, the noble Hungarians failed.—All know the result.

Nor is this the only important consideration. Were we content to remain as we are, sparsely interspersed among our white fellow-countrymen, we never might be expected to equal them in any honorable or respectable competition for a livelihood. For the reason that, acording to the customs and policy of the country, we for ages would be kept in a secondary position, every situation of respectability, honor, profit or trust, either as mechanics, clerks, teachers, jurors, councilmen, or legislators, being filled by white men, consequently, our energies must become paralysed or enervated for the want of proper encouragement.

This example upon our children, and the colored people generally, is pernicious and degrading in the extreme. And how could it otherwise be, when they see every place of respectability filled and occupied by the whites, they pandering to their vanity, and existing among them merely as a thing of conveniency.

Our friends in this and other countries, anxious for our elevation, have for years been erroneously urging us to lose our identity as a distinct race, declaring that we were the same as other people; while at the very same time their own representative was traversing the world and propagating the doctrine in favor of a *universal Anglo-Saxon predominence*. The "Universal Brotherhood," so ably and eloquently advocated by that Polyglot Christian Apostle* of this doctrine, had established as its basis, a universal acknowledgment of the Anglo-Saxon rule.

The truth is, we are not identical with the Anglo-Saxon or any other race of the Caucasian or pure white type of the human family, and the sooner we know and acknowledge this truth, the better for ourselves and posterity.

The English, French, Irish, German, Italian, Turk, Persion, Greek, Jew, and all other races, have their native or inherent peculiarities, and why not our race? We are not willing, therefore, at all times and under all circumstances to be moulded into various shapes of eccentricity, to suit the caprices and conveniences of every kind of people. We are not more suitable to everybody than everybody is suitable to us; therefore, no more like other people than others are like us.

We have then inherent traits, attributes—so to speak—and native characteristics, peculiar to our race—whether pure or mixed blood—and all that is required of us is to cultivate these and develope them in their purity, to make them desirable and emulated by the rest of the world.

That the colored races have the highest traits of civilization, will not be disputed. They are civil, peaceable and religious to a fault. In mathematics, sculpture and architecture, as arts and sciences, commerce and internal improvements as enterprises, the white race may probably excel; but in languages, oratory, poetry, music and painting as arts and sciences, and in ethics, metaphysics, theology and legal jurisprudence; in plain language—in the true principles of morals, correctness of thought, religion, and law or civil government, there is no doubt but the black race will yet instruct the world.

* Elihu Burritt.

It would be duplicity longer to disguise the fact, that the great issue, sooner or later, upon which must be disputed the world's destiny, will be a question of black and white; and every individual will be called upon for his identity with one or the other. The blacks and colored races are four-sixths of all the population of the world; and these people are fast tending to a common cause with each other. The white races are but one-third of the population of the globe—or one of them to two of us—and it cannot much longer continue, that two-thirds will passively submit to the universal domination of this one-third. And it is notorious that the only progress made in territorial domain, in the last three centuries, by the whites, has been a usurpation and encroachment on the rights and native soil of some of the colored races.

The East Indies, Java, Sumatria, the Azores, Madeira, Canary, and Capo Verde Islands; Socotra, Guardifui and the Isle of France; Algiers, Tunis, Tripoli, Barca and Egypt in the North, Sierra Leon in the West, and Cape Colony in the South of Africa; besides many other Islands and possessions not herein named. Australia, the Ladrone Islands, together with many others of Oceania; the seizure and appropriation of a great portion of the Western Continent, with all its Islands, were so many encroachments of the whites upon the rights of the colored races. Nor are they yet content, but, intoxicated with the success of their career, the Sandwich Islands are now marked out as the next booty to be seized, in the ravages of their exterminating crusade.

We regret the necessity of stating the fact—but duty compels us to the task—that for more than two thousand years, the determined aim of the whites has been to crush the colored races wherever found. With a determined will, they have sought and pursued them in every quarter of the globe. The Anglo-Saxon has taken the lead in this work of universal subjugation. But the Anglo-American stands pre-eminent for deeds of injustice and acts of oppression, unparalleled perhaps in the annals of modern history.

We admit the existence of great and good people in America,

England, France, and the rest of Europe, who desire a unity of interests among the whole human family, of whatever origin or race.

But it is neither the moralist, Christian, nor philanthropist whom we now have to meet and combat, but the politician— the civil engineer and skillful economist, who direct and control the machinery which moves forward with mighty impulse, the nations and powers of the earth. We must, therefore, if possible, meet them on vantage ground, or, at least, with adequate means for the conflict.

Should we encounter an enemy with artillery, a prayer will not stay the cannon shot; neither will the kind words nor smiles of philanthropy shield his spear from piercing us through the heart. We must meet mankind, then, as they meet us—prepared for the worst, though we may hope for the best. Our submission does not gain for us an increase of friends nor respectability— as the white race will only respect those who oppose their usurpation, and acknowledge as equals those who will not submit to their rule. This may be no new discovery in political economy, but it certainly is a subject worthy the consideration of the black race.

After a due consideration of these facts, as herein recounted, shall we stand still and continue inactive—the passive observers of the great events of the times and age in which we live; submitting indifferently to the usurpation, by the white race, of every right belonging to the blacks? Shall the last vestage of an opportunity, outside of the continent of Africa, for the national development of our race, be permitted, in consequence of our slothfulness, to elude our grasp and fall into the possession of the whites? This, may Heaven forbid. May the sturdy, intelligent Africo-American sons of the Western Continent forbid.

Longer to remain inactive, it should be borne in mind, may be to give an opportunity to despoil us of every right and possession sacred to our existence, with which God has endowed us as a heritage on the earth. For let it not be forgotten, that the white race—who numbers but *one* of them to *two* of us—

originally located in Europe, besides possessing all of that continent, have now got hold of a large portion of Asia, Africa, all North America, a portion of South America, and all of the great Islands of both Hemispheres, except Paupau, or New Guinea, inhabited by negroes and Malays, in Oceanica; the Japanese Islands, peopled and ruled by the Japanese; Madigascar, peopled by negroes, near the coast of Africa; and the Island of Haiti, in the West Indies, peopled by as brave and noble descendants of Africa, as they who laid the foundation of Thebias, or constructed the everlasting pyramids and catecombs of Egypt.—A people who have freed themselves by the might of their own will, the force of their own power, the unfailing strength of their own right arms, and their unflinching determination to be free.

Let us, then, not survive the disgrace and ordeal of Almighty displeasure, of two to one, witnessing the universal possession and control by the whites, of every habitable portion of the earth. For such must inevitably be the case, and that, too, at no distant day, if black men do not take advantage of the opportunity, by grasping hold of those places where chance is in their favor, and establishing the rights and power of the colored race.

We must make an issue, create an event, and establish for ourselves a position. This is essentially necessary for our effective elevation as a people, in shaping our national development, directing our destiny, and redeeming ourselves as a race.

If we but determine it shall be so, it *will* be so; and there is nothing under the sun can prevent it. We shall then be but in pursuit of our legitimate claims to inherent rights, bequeathed to us by the will of Heaven—the endowment of God, our common parent. A distinguished economist has truly said, "God has implanted in man an infinite progression in the career of improvement. A soul capacitated for improvement ought not to be bounded by a tyrant's landmarks." This sentiment is just and true, the application of which to our case, is adapted with singular fitness.

Having glanced hastily at our present political position in

the world generally, and the United States in particular—the fundamental disadvantages under which we exist, and the improbability of ever attaining citizenship and equality of rights in this country—we call your attention next, to the places of destination to which we shall direct Emigration.

The West Indies, Central and South America, are the countries of our choice, the advantages of which shall be made apparent to your entire satisfaction.

Though we have designated them as countries, they are in fact but one country—relatively considered—a part of this, the Western Continent. . . .

There is but one question presents itself for our serious consideration, upon which we *must* give a decisive reply—Will we transmit, as an inheritance to our children, the blessings of unrestricted civil liberty, or shall we entail upon them, as our only political legacy, the degradation and oppression left us by our fathers?

Shall we be persuaded that we can live and prosper nowhere but under the authority and power of our North American white oppressors; that this (the United States,) is the country most—if not the only one—favorable to our improvement and progress? Are we willing to admit that we are incapable of self-government, establishing for ourselves such political privileges, and making such internal improvements as we delight to enjoy, after American white men have made them for themselves?

No! Neither is it true that the United States is the country best adapted to *our* improvement. But that country is the best in which our manhood—morally, mentally and physically—can be *best developed*—in which we have an untrammeled right to the enjoyment of civil and religious liberty; and the West Indies, Central and South America, present now such advantages, superiorly preferable to all other countries.

That the continent of America was designed by Providence as a reserved asylum for the various oppressed people of the earth, of all races, to us seems very apparent.

From the earliest period after the discovery, various nations

sent a representative here, either as adventurers and specu-
lators, or employed laborers, seamen, or soldiers, hired to work
for their employers. And among the earliest and most numerous
class who found their way to the new world, were those of the
African race. And it has been ascertained to our minds beyond
a doubt, that when the Continent was discovered, there were
found in the West Indies and Central America, tribes of the
black race, fine looking people, having the usual characteristics
of color and hair, identifying them as being originally of the
African race; no doubt, being a remnant of the Africans who,
with the Carthagenian expedition, were adventitiously cast
upon this continent, in their memorable adventure to the "Great
Island," after sailing many miles distant to the West of the
"Pillars of Hercules"—the present Straits of Gibralter.

   We would not be thought to be superstitious, when we say,
that in all this we can "see the finger of God." Is it not worthy
of a notice here, that while the ingress of foreign whites to this
continent has been voluntary and constant, and that of the
blacks involuntary and but occasional, yet the whites in the
southern part have *decreased* in numbers, *degenerated* in
character, and become mentally and physically *enervated* and
imbecile; while the blacks and colored people have studiously
increased in numbers, *regenerated* in character, and have
grown mentally and physically vigorous and active, developing
every function of their manhood, and are now, in their elementary character, decidedly superior to the white race? So
then the white race could never successfully occupy the southern portion of the continent; they must of necessity, every generation, be repeopled from another quarter of the globe. The
fatal error committed by the Spaniards, under Pizarro, was the
attempt to exterminate the Incas and Peruvians, and fill their
places by European whites. The Peruvian Indians, a hale,
hardy, vigorous, intellectual race of people, were succeeded by
those who soon became idle, vicious, degenerated and imbecile.
But Peru, like all the other South American States, is regaining
her former potency, just in proportion as the European race
decreases among them. All the labor of the country is performed
by the aboriginal natives and the blacks; the few Europeans

there, being the merest excrescences on the body politic—consuming drones in the social hive.

Had we no other claims than those set forth in a foregoing part of this Address, they are sufficient to induce every black and colored person to remain on this continent, unshaken and unmoved.

But the West Indians, Central and South Americans, are a noble race of people; generous, sociable and tractible—just the people with whom we desire to unite, who are susceptible of progress, improvement and reform of every kind. They now desire all the improvements of North America, but being justly jealous of their rights, they have no confidence in the whites of the United States, and consequently peremptorily refuse to permit an indiscriminate settlement among them of this class of people; but placing every confidence in the black and colored people of North America.

The example of the unjust invasion and forcible seizure of a large portion of the territory of Mexico, is still fresh in their memory; and the oppressive disfranchisement of a large number of native Mexicans, by the Americans—because of the color and race of the natives—will continue to rankle in the bosom of the people of those countries, and prove a sufficient barrier henceforth against the inroads of North American whites among them.

Upon the American continent, then, we are determined to remain despite every opposition that may be urged against us.

You will doubtless be asked—and that, too, with an air of seriousness—why, if desirable to remain on this continent, not be content to remain *in* the United States. The objections to this—and potent reasons, too, in our estimation—have already been clearly shown.

But notwithstanding all this, were there still any rational, nay, even the most futile grounds for hope, we still might be stupid enough to be content to remain, and yet through another period of unexampled patience and suffering, continue meekly to drag the galling yoke and clank the chain of servility and degradation. But whether or not in this, God is to be thanked and Heaven blessed, we are not permitted, despite our willingness and stupidity, to indulge even the most distant glimmer of a hope of attaining to the level of a well protected slave.

For years, we have been studiously and jealously observing the course of political events and policy, on the part of this country, both in a national and individual State capacity, as pursued toward the colored people. And he who, in the midst of them, can live with observation, is either excusably ignorant, or reprehensibly deceptious and untrustworthy.

We deem it entirely unnecessary to tax you with anything like the history of even one chapter of the unequalled infamies perpetrated on the part of the various States, and national decrees, by legislation, against us. But we shall call your particular attention to the more recent acts of the United States; because whatever privileges we may enjoy in any individual State, will avail nothing, when not recognized as such by the United States.

When the condition of the inhabitants of any country is fixed by legal grades of distinction, this condition can never be changed except by express legislation. And it is the height of folly to expect such express legislation, except by the inevitable force of some irresistible internal political pressure. The force necessary to this imperative demand on our part, we never can obtain, because of our numerical feebleness.

Were the interests of the common people identical with ours, we, in this, might succeed, because we, as a class, would then be numerically the superior. But this is not a question of the rich against the poor, nor the common people against the higher classes; but a question of white against black—every white person, by legal right, being held superior to a black or colored person.

In Russia, the common people might obtain an equality with the aristocracy; because, of the sixty-five millions of her population, forty-five millions are serfs or peasants—leaving but twenty millions of the higher classes, royalty, nobility and all included.

The rights of no oppressed people have ever yet been obtained by a voluntary act of justice on the part of the oppressors.

Christians, philanthropists, and moralists, may preach, argue and philosophise as they may to the contrary; facts are against them. Voluntary acts, it is true, which are in themselves just, may sometimes take place on the part of the oppressor; but these are always actuated by the force of some outward circumstances of self-interest, equal to a compulsion.

The boasted liberties of the American people were established by a Constitution, borrowed from and modeled after the British *magna charta*. And this great charter of British liberty, so much boasted of and vaunted as a model bill of rights, was obtained only by force and extortion.

The Barons, an order of noblemen, under the reign of King John, becoming dissatisfied at the terms submitted to by their sovereign, which necessarily brought degradation upon themselves—terms prescribed by the insolent Pope Innocent III, the haughty sovereign Pontiff of Rome; summoned his majesty to meet them on the plains of the memorable meadow of Runnimede, where presenting to him their own Bill of Rights—a bill dictated by themselves, and drawn up by their own hands—at the unsheathed points of a thousand glittering swords, they commanded him, against his will, to sign the extraordinary document. There was no alternative; he must either do or die. With a puerile timidity, he leaned forward his rather commanding but imbecile person, and with a trembling hand and single dash of the pen, the name KING JOHN stood forth in bold relief, sending more terror throughout the world, than the mystic hand-writing of Heaven throughout the dominions of Nebuchadnezzar, blazing on the walls of Babylon. A consternation, not because of the *name* of the King, but because of the rights of *others*, which that name acknowledged.

The King, however, soon became dissatisfied, and determining on a revokation of the act—an act done entirely contrary to his will—at the head of a formidable army, spread fire and sword throughout the kingdom.

But the Barons, though compelled to leave their castles—their houses and homes—and fly for their lives, could not be induced to undo that which they had so nobly done; the achievement of their rights and privileges. Hence, the act has stood throughout all succeeding time, because never annulled by those who *willed* it.

It will be seen that the first great modern Bill of Rights was obtained only by a force of arms: a resistence of the people against the injustice and intolerance of their rulers. We say the people—because that which the Barons demanded for themselves, was afterwards extended to the common people. Their only hope was based on their *superiority of numbers.*

But can we in this country hope for as much? Certainly not. —Our case is a hopeless one. There was but *one* John, with his few sprigs of adhering royalty; and but *one* heart at which the threatening points of their swords were directed by a thousand Barons; while in our case, there is but a handful of the oppressed, without a sword to point, and *twenty millions* of Johns or Jonathans—as you please—with as many hearts, tenfold more relentless than that of Prince John Lackland, and as deceptious and hypocritical as the Italian heart of Innocent III.

Where, then, is our hope of success in this country? Upon what is it based? Upon what principle of political policy and sagacious discernment, do our political leaders and acknowledged great men—colored men we mean—justify themselves by telling us, and insisting that we shall believe them, and submit to what they say—to be patient, remain where we are; that there is a "bright prospect and glorious future" before us in this country! May Heaven open our eyes from their Bartemian obscurity.

But we call your attention to another point of our political degradation. The acts of State and general governments.

In a few of the States, as in New York, the colored inhabitants have a partial privilege of voting a white man into office. This privilege is based on a property qualification of two hundred and fifty dollars worth of real estate. In others, as in Ohio, in the absence of organic provision, the privilege is granted by judicial decision, based on a ratio of blood, of an admixture of more than one-half white; while in many of the States, there is no privilege allowed, either partial or unrestricted.

The policy of the above named States will be seen and detected at a glance, which while seeming to extend immunities, is intended especially for the object of degradation.

In the State of New York, for instance, there is a constitutional distinction created among colored men—almost necessarily compelling one part to feel superior to the other; while among the whites no such distinctions dare be known. Also, in Ohio, there is a legal distinction set up by an upstart judiciary, creating among the colored people, a privileged class by birth! All this must necessarily sever the cords of union among us, creating almost insurmountable prejudices of the most stupid and fatal kind, paralysing the last bracing nerve which promised to give us strength.

It is upon this same principle, and for the self same object, that the General Government has long been endeavoring, and is at present knowingly designing to effect a recognition of the independence of the Dominican Republic, while disparagingly refusing to recognize the independence of the Haitien nation—a people four-fold greater in numbers, wealth and power. The Haitiens, it is pretended, are refused because they are *Negroes;* while the Dominicans, as is well known to all who are familiar with the geography, history, and political relations of that people, are identical—except in language, they speaking the Spanish tongue—with those of the Haitiens; being composed of negroes and a mixed race. The government may shield itself by the plea that it is not familiar with the origin of those people. To this we have but to reply, that if the government is thus ignorant of the relations of its near neighbors, it is the heighth of presumption, and no small degree of assurance, for it to set up itself as capable of prescribing terms to the one, or conditions to the other.

Should they accomplish their object, they then will have succeeded in forever establishing a barrier of impassable separation, by the creation of a political distinction between those people, of superiority and inferiority of origin or national existence. Here, then, is another strategem of this most determined and untiring enemy of our race—the government of the United States.

We come now to the crowning act of infamy on the part of

the General Government towards the colored inhabitants of the United States—an act so vile in its nature, that rebellion against its demands should be promptly made, in every attempt to enforce its infernal provisions.

In the history of national existence, there is not to be found a parallel to the tantalising and aggravating despotism of the provisions of Millard Fillmore's Fugitive Slave Bill, passed by the thirty-third Congress of the United States, with the approbation of a majority of the American people, in the year of the Gospel of Jesus Christ, eighteen hundred and fifty.

This Bill had but one object in its provisions, which was fully accomplished in its passage; that is, the reduction of every colored person in the United States—save those who carry free papers of emancipation, or bills of sale from former claimants or owners—to a state of relative *slavery;* placing each and every one of us at the *disposal of any and every white* who might choose to *claim* us, and the caprice of any and every upstart knave bearing the title of "Commissioner."

Did any of you, fellow-countrymen, reside in a country the provisions of whose laws were such that any person of a certain class, who whenever he, she or they pleased might come forward, lay a claim to, make oath before (it might be,) some stupid and heartless person, authorized to decide in such cases, and take, at their option, your horse, cow, sheep, house and lot, or any other property, bought and paid for by your own earnings—the result of your personal toil and labor—would you be willing, or could you be induced, by any reasoning, however great the source from which it came, to remain in that country? We pause, fellow-countrymen, for a reply.

If there be not one yea, of how much more importance, then, is your *own personal safety,* than that of property? Of how much more concern is the safety of a wife or husband, than that of a cow or horse; a child, than a sheep; the destiny of your family, to that of a house and lot?

And yet this is precisely our condition. Any one of us, at any moment, is liable to be *claimed, seized* and *taken* into custody by the white as his or her property—to be *enslaved for life*— and there is no remedy, because it is the *law of the land!* And we dare predict, and take this favorable opportunity to fore-warn you, fellow-countrymen, that the time is not far distant, when there will be carried on by the white men of this nation, an extensive commerce in the persons of what now compose the free colored people of the North. We forewarn you, that the general enslavement of the whole of this class of people, is now being contemplated by the whites.

At present, we are liable to enslavement at any moment, provided we are taken *away* from our homes. But we dare venture further to forewarn you, that the scheme is in mature contemplation and has even been mooted in high places, of harmonizing the two discordant political divisions in the country, by again reducing the free to slave States.

The completion of this atrocious scheme, only becomes necessary for each and every one of us to find an owner and master at our own doors. Let the general government but pass such a law, and the States will comply as an act of harmony. Let the South but *demand* it, and the North will comply as a *duty* of compromise.

If Pennsylvania, New York and Massachusetts can be found arming their sons as watch-dogs for southern slave hunters; if the United States may, with impunity, garrison with troops the Court House of the freest city in America; blockade the streets; station armed ruffians of dragoons, and spiked artillery in hostile awe of the people; if free, white, high-born and bred gentlemen of Boston and New York, are smitten down to the earth,* refused an entrance on professional business, into the Court Houses, until inspected by a slave hunter and his counsel;

---

* John Jay, Esq., of New York, son of the late distinguished jurist, Hon. Wm. Jay, was, in 1852, as the counsel of a Fugitive Slave, brutally assaulted and struck in the face by the slave catching agent and counsel, Busteed.

Also, Mr. Dana, an honorable gentleman, counsel for the fugitive Burns, one of the first literary men of Boston, was arrested on his entrance into the Court House, and not permitted to pass the guard of slave catchers, till the slave agent and counsel, Loring, together with the overseer, Suttle, *inspected* him, and ordered that he might be *allowed* to pass in! After which, in passing along the street, Mr. Dana was ruffianly assaulted and murderously fallen to the earth, by the minions of the dastardly southern overseer.

all to put down the liberty of the black man; then, indeed, is there no hope for us in this country! . . .

That, then, which is left for us to do, is to *secure* our liberty; a position which shall fully *warrant* us *against* the *liability* of such monstrous political crusade and riotous invasions of our rights.—Nothing less than a national indemnity, indelibly fixed by virtue of our own sovereign potency, will satisfy us as a redress of grievances for the unparalleled wrongs, undisguised impositions, and unmitigated oppression, which we have suffered at the hands of this American people.

And what wise politician would otherwise conclude and determine? None we dare say. And a people who are incapable of this discernment and precaution, are incapable of self-government, and incompetent to direct their own political destiny. For our own part, we spurn to treat for liberty on any other terms or conditions.

It may not be inapplicable, in this particular place, to quote from high authority, language which has fallen under our notice, since this report has been under consideration. The quotation is worth nothing, except to show that the position assumed by us, is a natural one, which constitutes the essential basis of self-protection.

Said Earl Aberdeen recently in the British House of Lords, when referring to the great question which is now agitating Europe:—"One thing alone is certain, that the only way to obtain a sure and honorable peace, is to *acquire a position* which may *command it;* and to gain such a position *every nerve and sinew* of the empire should be strained. The pickpocket who robs us is not to be let off because he offers to restore our purse;" and his Grace might have justly added, "should never thereafter be entrusted or confided in."

The plea doubtless will be, as it already frequently has been raised, that to remove from the United States, our slave brethren would be left without a hope. They already find their way in large companies to the Canadas, and they have only to be made sensible that there is as much freedom for them South, as there is North; as much protection in Mexico as in Canada;

and the fugitive slave will find it a much pleasanter journey and more easy of access, to wend his way from Louisiana and Arkansas to Mexico, than thousands of miles through the slave-holders of the South and slave-catchers of the North, to Canada. Once into Mexico, and his farther exit to Central and South America and the West Indies, would be certain. There would be no obstructions whatever. No miserable, half-starved, servile Northern slave-catchers by the way, waiting cap in hand, ready and willing to do the bidding of their contemptible southern masters.

No prisons, nor Court Houses, as slave-pens and garrisons, to secure the fugitive and rendezvous the mercenary gangs, who are bought as military on such occasions. No perjured Marshals, bribed Commissioners, nor hireling counsel, who, spaniel-like, crouch at the feet of Southern slave-holders, and cringingly tremble at the crack of their whip. No, not as may be encountered throughout his northern flight, there are none of these to be found or met with in his travels from the Bravo del Norte to the dashing Oronoco— from the borders of Texas to the boundaries of Peru.

Should anything occur to prevent a successful emigration to the South—Central, South America and the West Indies—we have no hesitancy, rather than remain in the United States, the merest subordinates and serviles of the whites, should the Canadas still continue separate in their political relations from this country, to recommend to the great body of our people, to remove to Canada West, where being politically equal to the whites, physically united with each other by a concentration of strength; when worse comes to worse, we may be found, not as a scattered, weak and impotent people, as we now are separated from each other throughout the Union, but a united and powerful body of freemen, mighty in politics, and terrible in any conflict which might ensue, in the event of an attempt at the disturbance of our political relations, domestic repose, and peaceful firesides.

Now, fellow-countrymen, we have done. Into your ears have we recounted your own sorrows; before your own eyes have we exhibited your wrongs; into your own hands have we committed your own cause. If there should prove a failure to remedy this dreadful evil, to assuage this terrible curse which has come upon us; the fault will be yours and not ours; since we have offered you a healing balm for every sorely aggravated wound.

Martin R. Delany, Pa.
William Webb, Pa.
Augustus R. Green, Ohio
Edward Butler, Mo.
H. S. Douglass, La.
A. Dudley, Wis.
Conaway Barbour, Ky.
Wm. J. Fuller, R. I.
Wm. Lambert, Mich.
J. Theodore Holly, N. Y.
T. A. White, Ind.
John A. Warren, Canada

20. JAMES THEODORE HOLLY SPEAKS OF "THE CONTINUED ADVANCEMENT OF THE NEGRO NATIONALITY OF THE NEW WORLD"

Conclusion

But our historical investigations are at an end, and we must hasten to bring our reflections to a conclusion. I have now

From James Theodore Holly, A VINDICATION OF THE CAPACITY OF THE NEGRO RACE FOR SELF-GOVERNMENT AND CIVILIZED PROGRESS, AS DEMONSTRATED BY HISTORICAL EVENTS OF THE HAYTIAN REVOLUTION AND THE SUBSEQUENT ACTS OF THAT PEOPLE SINCE THEIR NATIONAL INDEPENDENCE (New Haven, Conn.: Afric-American Printing Co., 1857), pp. 43–46.

fulfilled my design in vindicating the capacity of the negro race for self-government and civilized progress against the unjust aspersions of our unprincipled oppressors, by boldly examining the facts of Haytian history and deducing legitimate conclusions therefrom. I have summoned the sable heroes and statesmen of that independent isle of the Caribbean Sea, and tried them by the high standard of modern civilization, fearlessly comparing them with the most illustrious men of the most enlightened nations of the earth;—and in this examination and comparison the negro race has not fell one whit behind their contemporaries. And in this investigation I have made no allowance for the negroes just emerging from a barbarous condition and out of the brutish ignorance of West Indian slavery. I have been careful not to make such an allowance, for fear that instead of proving negro equality only, I should prove negro superiority. I shun the point of making this allowance to the negro, as it might reverse the case of the question entirely, that I have been combatting and instead of disproving his alledged inferiority only, would on the other hand, go farther, and establish his superiority. Therefore as it is my design to banish the words "superiority" and "inferiority" from the vocabulary of the world, when applied to the natural capacity of races of men, I claim no allowance for them on the score of their condition and circumstances.

Having now presented the preceding array of facts and arguments to establish, before the world, the negro's equality with the white man in carrying forward the great principles of self-government and civilized progress; I would now have these facts exert their legitimate influence over the minds of my race, in this country, in producing that most desirable object of arousing them to a full consciousness of their own inherent dignity; and thereby increasing among them that self-respect which shall urge them on to the performance of those great deeds which the age and the race now demand at their hands.

Our brethren of Hayti, who stand in the vanguard of the race, have already made a name, and a fame for us, that is as imperishable as the world's history. They exercise sovereign authority over an island, that in natural advantages, is the Eden of America, and the garden spot of the world. Her rich resources invite the capacity of 10,000,000 human beings to adequately use them. It becomes then an important question for the negro race in America to well consider the weighty responsibility that the present exigency devolves upon them, to contribute to the continued advancement of this negro nationality of the New World until its glory and renown shall overspread and cover the whole earth, and redeem and regenerate by its influence in the future, the benighted Fatherland of the race in Africa.

Here in this black nationality of the New World, erected under such glorious auspices, is the stand point that must be occupied, and the lever that must be exerted, to regenerate and disenthrall the oppression and ignorance of the race, throughout the world. We must not overlook this practical vantage ground which Providence has raised up for us out of the depths of the sea, for any man-made and utopian scheme that is prematurely forced upon us, to send us across the ocean, to rummage the graves of our ancestors, in fruitless, and ill-directed efforts at the wrong end of human progress. Civilization and Christianity is passing from the East to the West; and its pristine splendor will only be rekindled in the ancient nations of the Old World, after it has belted the globe in its westward course, and revisited the Orient again. The Serpentine trial of civilization and christianity, like the ancient philosophic symbol of eternity, must coil backward to its fountain head. God, therefore in permitting the accursed slave traffic to transplant so many millions of the race, to the New World, and educing therefrom such a negro nationality as Hayti; indicates thereby, that we have a work now to do here in the Western World, which in his own good time shall shed its orient beams upon the Fatherland of the race. Let us see to it, that we meet the exigency now imposed upon us, as nobly on our part at this time as the Haytians met theirs at the opening of the present century. And in seeking to perform this duty, it may well be a question with us, whether it is not our duty, to go and identify our destiny with our heroic brethren in that independent isle of the Carribean Sea, carrying with us such of the arts, sciences and genius of modern civilization, as we may gain from this hardy and enterprising Anglo-American race, in order to add to Haytian advancement; rather than to indolently remain here, asking for political rights, which, if granted a social proscription stronger than conventional legislation will ever render nugatory and of no avail for the manly elevation and general well-being of the race. If one powerful and civilized negro sovereignty can be developed to the summit of national grandeur in the West Indies, where the keys to the commerce of both hemispheres can be held; this fact will solve all questions respecting the negro, whether they be those of slavery, prejudice or proscription, and wheresoever on the face of the globe such questions shall present themselves for a satisfactory solution.

A concentration and combination of the negro race, of the Western Hemisphere in Hayti, can produce just such a national development. The duty to do so, is therefore incumbent on them. And the responsibility of leading off in this gigantic enterprise. Providence seems to have made our peculiar task by the eligibility of our situation in this country, as a point for gaining an easy access to that island. Then let us boldly enlist in this high pathway of duty, while the watchwords that shall cheer and inspire us in our noble and glorious undertaking, shall be the soul-stirring anthem of GOD and HUMANITY.

Cultural nationalism

Interest in the race's past and in creating a racial literature—
two important themes in what is commonly described as
"cultural nationalism"—developed only in a sketchy way before
the end of the nineteenth century. In fact, historical works,
from J. W. C. Pennington's *Text Book of the Origin and
History of the Colored People* (1841) through William C.
Nell's *Colored Patriots of the American Revolution* (1855) and
William Wells Brown's *The Black Man: His Antecedents,
His Genius, and His Achievements* (1863) to George
Washington Williams' *History of the Negro Race in America*
(1883), were written by integrationists and assimilationists,
and were directed less toward instilling a feeling of race
pride in Negroes than toward convincing whites of the black
man's worth and capacity for citizenship. An exception was
James Theodore Holly, author of *A Vindication of the
Capacity of the Negro Race* (Document 20), who used
historical arguments as part of a larger nationalistic ideology.
Holly's book was mainly devoted to tracing the glorious
history of Haiti, in connection with his vigorous assertion of
the Negro's capacity for self-government and his prediction of
a great national future for the black man in the New World
and in Africa.

Representative of the appeal to the race's past usually made by
black publicists of the antebellum generation is the selection
from Henry Highland Garnet's *The Past and the Present
Condition, and the Destiny, of the Colored Race*. In this
address, delivered to a predominantly white audience in 1848,
Garnet cited the achievements of Africans as proof of the

capability of Negroes. At the time Garnet, a Presbyterian
minister, was the pastor of a white church in Troy, New York.
The author of a call for slave rebellions in 1843 (Document
16), during the 1850s, Garnet was to become a prominent
colonizationist; but at the time of this speech he was a leader
in the fight for emancipation of slaves and equal
rights for free blacks in the United States.

21. HENRY HIGHLAND GARNET
DESCRIBES THE GREATNESS OF AFRICA

In order to pursue my subject I must, for the sake of distinction
use some of the improper terms of our times. I shall, therefore,
speak of *races*, when in fact there is but one race, as there was
but one Adam.

By an almost common consent, the modern world seems
determined to pilfer Africa of her glory. It were not enough that
her children have been scattered over the globe, clothed in
the garments of shame—humiliated and oppressed—but her
merciless foes weary themselves in plundering the tombs of our
renowned sires, and in obliterating their worthy deeds, which
were inscribed by fame upon the pages of ancient history.

The three grand divisions of the earth that were known to the
ancients, were colonized by the three sons of Noah. Shem was
the father of the Asiatics—the Africans descended from Ham,
and Japheth was the progenitor of the Europeans. These men
being the children of one father, they were originally of the
same complexion—for we cannot through the medium of any

From Henry Highland Garnet, THE PAST AND THE PRESENT
CONDITION, AND THE DESTINY OF THE COLORED RACE: A
DISCOURSE DELIVERED AT THE 50TH ANNIVERSARY OF THE FEMALE
BENEVOLENT SOCIETY OF TROY, N. Y., FEBRUARY 14, 1848 (Troy
N. Y.: J. C. Kneeland and Co., 1848), pp. 6–12.

law of nature or reason, come to the conclusion, that one was black, another was copper-colored, and the other was white. Adam was a red man, and by what law of nature his descendants became dissimilar to him, is a problem which is yet to be clearly solved. The fact that the universal Father has varied the complexions of his children, does not detract from his mercy, or give us reason to question his wisdom.

Moses is the patriarch of sacred history. The same eminent station is occupied by Herodotus in profane history. To the chronicles of these two great men we are indebted for all the information we have in relation to the early condition of man. If they are incorrect, to what higher authority shall we appeal —and if they are true, then we may acquaint ourselves with the history of our race from that period,

> When yonder spheres sublime,
> Peal'd their first notes to sound the march of time.

Ham was the first African. Egypt was settled by an immediate descendant of Ham, who, in sacred history, is called Mesraim, and in uninspired history he is known by the name of Menes. Yet in the face of this historical evidence, there are those who affirm that the ancient Egyptians were not of the pure African stock. The gigantic stature of the Phynx has the peculiar features of the children of Ham—one of the most celebrated queens of Egypt was Nitocris, an Ethiopian woman; yet these intellectual resurrectionists dig through a mountain of such evidence, and declare that these people were not negroes.

We learn from Herodotus, that the ancient Egyptians were black, and had woolly hair. These people astonished the world with their arts and sciences, in which they reveled with unbounded prodigality. They became the masters of the East, and the lords of the Hebrews. No arm less powerful than Jehovah's, could pluck the children of Abraham from their hands. The plagues were marshalled against them, and the pillars of cloud and of fire, and at last the resistless sea. "Then the horse and the rider, sank like lead in the mighty waters." But the kingdom of Ptolemys was still great. The most exalted mortal eulogium that could be spoken of Moses, was that he was learned in all the learning of the Egyptians. It was from them that he gathered the materials with which he reared that grand superstructure, partaking of law, poetry, and history, which has filled the world with wonder and praise. Mournful reverses of fortune have passed over that illustrious people. The star that arose in such matchless splendor above the eastern horizon has had its setting. But Egypt, Africa's dark browed queen, still lives. Her pyramid tombs—her sculptured collumns dug from the sands to adorn modern architecture—the remnants of her once impregnable walls—the remains of her hundred gated city, rising over the wide-spread ruins, as if to guard the fame of the race that gave them existence, all proclaim what she once was.

Whatever may be the extent of prejudice against color, as it is falsely called, and is so generally practiced in this country, Solomon, the most renowned of kings, possessed none of it. Among the seven hundred wives, and the three hundred concubines, who filled his houses, the most favored queen was a beautiful sable daughter of one of the Pharoahs of Egypt. In order to take her to his bosom, he trampled upon the laws of his nation, and incurred the divine displeasure—for a Jew might not espouse any heathen or idolater who was not circumcised in heart. When he had secured her, he bowed his great intellect before her, that he might do her that homage which he paid to no other woman. Solomon was a poet, and pure love awakened the sweetest melody in his soul. To her honor and praise he composed that beautiful poem called the *Canticles*, or *Solomon's Song*. For her he wove that gorgeous wreath which is unsurpassed in its kind, and with his own royal hand placed it upon her dark brow. Several persons are represented in the poem, and it is composed of an interesting coloquy. The reader is introduced to "the watchmen that went about the streets," and to "the daughters of Jerusalem," and to the bride and the groom, which are the king and the beauteous Egyptian. It is not at all surprising that she who received such distinguished marks of kingly favors, should encounter the jealousy of the daughters of Jerusalem. They saw that the Egyptian woman had monopolised the heart of the son of David, and the royal poet represents his queen to say to her fairer but supplanted rivals:—

> I am black but comely,
> O ye daughters of Jerusalem,
> As the tents of Kedar,
> As the curtains of Solomon.
> Look not upon me, because I am black,
> Because the sun has looked upon me.

Thus she speaks of the superiority which nature had given her over the women of Jerusalem. She was handsome, and like all handsome women, she knew it.

The bride again speaks, and says to the bride-groom:—

> I have compared thee, O my love,
> To a company of horses in Pharaoh's chariot.

How inappropriate were this allusion if it had been placed in the mouth of any one else but an Egyptian. To give the passage any other interpretation is virtually accusing Solomon of grosser ignorance than my reverence will allow me to attribute to him.

Professor Stowe and President Mahan, and others, agree in giving the following translation to another verse in the first chapter of the song,

> Ere I was aware
> My soul was as the war-chariot
> Of my noble people.

The whole poem, without doubt, is nothing more than a brilliant outburst of Solomon's love for his bride.

Homer, the prince of epic poets, speaks of the Ethiopians, and presents them at the feast of the gods. These men of sun-burnt faces, as their name implies, he calls the excellent Ethiopians.

A distinguished scholar, speaking of this passage in the Grecian's renowned poem, in the presence of an American pedant, the young upstart seriously inquired if the Ethopians were black? "Most assuredly," answered the scholar. "Well," said the young republican, "had I been at that feast, and negroes had been placed at the table, I would have left it." "Had you been living at that time, returned the other, you would have been saved the trouble of leaving the table, for the gods would not have invited you."

Such a man in such a banquet would have been as much out of place as an ass would be in a concert of sacred music.

The interior of Ethiopia has not been explored by modern adventurers. The antiquarian has made his way into almost every dominion where relics of former greatness have promised to reward him for his toil. But this country, as though she had concealed some precious treasure, meets the traveller on the outskirts of her dominions, with pestilence and death. Yet, in the Highlands which have been traversed, many unequivocal traces of former civilization have been discovered. Very lately, British enterprize has made some important researches in that region of Country, all of which go to prove that Homer did not misplace his regards for them, when he associated them with the Gods.

The wife of Moses was an Ethiopian woman, and when Miriam, his sister, murmured against her, the Almighty smote Miriam, and she became white. Whether the murmuring arose on account of the complexion of the great Lawgiver's wife, or from some other cause, I will not attempt to determine. Whatever was the cause, we all see how Jehovah regarded it, how fierce was his indignation, and how terrible his punishment. He came down and stood in a cloudy pillar, and cursed the woman in whose bosom the unholy prejudice was harbored.*

Ethiopia is one of the few nations whose destiny is spoken of in prophecy. This is done in language so plain that we are not driven to dubious inferences.

* Numbers, 12 chap. 10 v.

It is said that "Princes shall come out of Egypt, and Ethiopia shall soon stretch out her hands unto God." It is thought by some that this divine declaration was fulfilled when Philip baptised the converted eunuch of the household of Candes, the Queen of the Ethiopians. In this transaction, a part of the prophecy may have been fulfilled, and only a part.

A vision seen by another prophet has become a matter of history. Hosea, foresaw that God would call his son out of Egypt, and when the infant Redeemer could find no shelter in the land of the Hebrews, he found an asylum in Egypt, where he remained until Herod was dead. He then returned to his native country, and in that event he fulfilled the declaration of the holy seer.

Numerous other instances might be mentioned that would indicate the ancient fame of our ancestors. A fame, which arose from every virtue, and talent, that render mortals pre-eminently great. From the conquests of love and beauty, from the prowess of their arms, and their architecture, poetry, mathematics, generosity, and piety. I will barely allude to the beautiful Cleopatra, who swayed and captivated the heart of Anthony. To Hannibal, the sworn enemy and the scourge of Rome—the mighty General who crossed the Alps to meet his foes—the Alps which had never before been crossed by an army, nor never since, if we except Napoleon, the ambitious corsican. To Terence, Euclid, Cyprian, Origen, and Augustine.

At ths time, when these representatives of our race were filling the world with amazement, the ancestors of the now proud and boasting Anglo Saxons were among the most degraded of the human family. They abode in caves under ground, either naked or covered with the skins of wild beasts. Night was made hideous by their wild shouts, and day was darkened by the smoke which arose from bloody altars, upon which they offered human sacrifice. . . .

Flowering

PART THREE

Race pride, race solidarity

Deterioration of the black man's status in the late nineteenth century produced a broad spectrum of nationalist ideologies, ranging from the advocacy of race unity as a prerequisite to effective protest activity, through a stress upon Negro support of Negro business, to proposals for colonization abroad. One theme underlying all these various nationalistic ideologies was the exhorting of colored men to have pride in themselves. An illustration of this theme of race pride, widely voiced from the 1880s through the 1920s, is Document 22, an editorial from the *A.M.E. Church Review*.

No one was better equipped to articulate the rising tide of nationalist sentiment than the noted nineteenth-century intellectual Alexander Crummell. Crummell, a prominent antebellum colonizationist, had gone to Liberia under the auspices of the American Colonization Society in 1850; 23 years later he returned to the United States and became rector of St. Luke's Episcopal Church in Washington. Crummell's views are of special interest not only because of his prominence but also because the close relationship between the ideology of emigration and that of racial solidarity for advancement within the United States is nowhere shown more clearly than in his sermons and addresses.

In an address, "The Social Principle," printed in 1882, Crummell presented a well-organized brief for the importance of race unity and solidarity. Delivered in 1875 as a Thanksgiving sermon, it was based on a similar talk advocating support for the Liberian national state given at Monrovia in 1859. In the later version (Document 23), Crummell appeals persuasively for race unity as a prerequisite for the development of the race power necessary to advance the black man in the United States.

Crummell believed that the college-educated elite had a special role in elevating the race and bringing it to a position of power. It was the responsibility of the intellectuals to "lift up this people of ours." Here was an elitist conception of racial solidarity and self-help which Crummell, together with W. E. B. Du Bois, was developing in the 1890s and which would in the early twentieth century become famous as Du Bois's theory of the "Talented Tenth." Document 24 is Crummell's inaugural address as the first president of the American Negro Academy. This club of 40 black intellectuals, organized in 1897, aimed to stimulate Negro cultural development as part of a program of racial cooperation and solidarity.

One aspect of the revived emphasis upon race pride and race solidarity was an advocacy of separate institutions. Not only were separate churches carefully justified (see Documents 2 and 3), but there was considerable debate in the black community over the relative advantage of separate or integrated schools. For one thing there was much discussion in the 1880s over whether Negroes should fight for the elimination of public school segregation in the northern states. A large body of opinion held that separate public schools were better for colored children than mixed ones, partly because the elimination of separate schools usually meant a loss of jobs for black teachers, partly because colored youth in Negro schools would not be subject to the ugly prejudice of their white schoolmates and teachers, and partly because black children would find in Negro teachers and principals models who could inspire them to success.

A related matter was the question of control over Negro colleges, the majority of which were in the hands of white missionary boards. One point of contention was whether,

because whites financed these colleges, they had a right
to control the boards of trustees and administrations. A second
was the charge that there was often discrimination against
colored men in the hiring of faculty. Although the number of
black professors and administrators was growing in some
schools, these charges had some substance, especially in the
Congregational and Presbyterian church institutions. Indeed, a
few colleges of these denominations failed to employ black
faculty members until the 1920s or even the 1930s, and others
were slow to place blacks in influential administrative
positions. Third was the argument that black teachers and
administrators would serve as models for the students. Finally,
there was the overriding question of who—whites, blacks,
or both—would really control and make the decisions for
institutions dedicated to the advancement of the race.
In Document 25, the noted Presbyterian minister and protest
leader of Washington, D. C., Francis J. Grimké, persuasively
argues for greater black control of these educational
institutions. Grimké's essay is particularly significant, because
throughout most of his long career he was a passionate
integrationist and assimilationist.

The views discussed above represent what were becoming
widely expressed ideas by the 1880s. Bishop Henry M. Turner
of the African Methodist Episcopal Church was atypical.
Known particularly as a flamboyant colonizationist (see
Document 29), he also used the pages of his newspaper *Voice
of Missions,* to advocate other controversial ideas. Among them
was the assertion that God was black (Document 26).
This theme, like his emigrationist ideology, reflected a belief
that Negroes could achieve racial dignity and pride only by
rejecting American society and culture. Not unnaturally,
therefore, this idea has cropped up several times since among
militant separatist philosophies—most notably those of Marcus
Garvey, the Black Muslims, and, in the late 1960s, of the
Detroit minister, Albert Cleage, pastor of the Shrine of the
Black Madonna.

22. THE A.M.E. CHURCH REVIEW:
"WE MUST LEARN TO LOVE OURSELVES"

There can be no doubt that fish think a deal more of fish, sup-
posing them to be in any way capable of such emotion, than
they do of birds. And the same may be affirmed of birds; these,
beyond question, think more of one another than they do of
beasts; while beasts, in turn, think more of beasts than they do
of man. And man follows the same bent. He thinks more of
man than he does of fish, or of birds, or of beasts. Exactly why
this is so may be more difficult of demonstration than many
might suppose. One of the chief reasons is doubtless found in
the principle of *self-love*. This self-love, or love of self, is everywhere assertive. Indeed, the social structure may be said to rest
upon it. And it is doubtless well that it is so. Without it what
would the individual amount to, and everything depends upon
the individual; for the status of the individual gauges the world.
Let the individual be low, as he most surely would be did not
this self-love exist, and the whole mass would be low; for as is
the part, so is the whole. This principle of self-love is, then, the
preserving and uplifting force of life. And as we have said, it is
well that it is so; nay more, it is necessary that it should be.
Loving self *first*, it is quite natural that we should love next *that
that is nearest to us;* that is, *that looks most like us.* A fish likes
another fish better than it likes a bird, because it is more like
himself. And so of a bird. And so of a beast. And so of a man.
Self *first*. That is nearest like self, *next*. And thus we are brought
to see how natural race love is, or should be. That an Indian
should love an Indian better than he loves a white man, all
things being equal, is of all things to be expected; and for the
reason that the Indian is more nearly like him than the white
man. And so of the Chinaman. And so of the white man. And

"Race Love," an editorial in A.M.E. CHURCH REVIEW, II
(April 1886), 546–548.

so it ought to be of the Negro. That each should be expected to love the one most nearly like himself is as much to be expected as that he should love himself better than he loves another. Nor does this run counter to the teachings of Scripture, which requires universal love of the brotherhood. Scriptures nowhere run counter to or abrogate great principles of being. On the contrary, they simply direct them into right channels. That an Indian who is a Christian should prefer an Indian, but not to the hurt of any other, is to be expected. And he does it in keeping with a great natural law upon which, as we have said, the whole fabric of nature hinges.

And it is just here that the American Negro comes short. He has no self-love. Everybody is better than himself; and, were it possible, he would be somebody else at once. With the average American, he thinks that to be an Indian, Chinaman, Japanese —in short, anybody, is better than to be a Negro. All this is wrong, and it is at the bottom of not a few of our troubles. We must learn to love ourselves. We must learn to respect ourselves. Until this is done, we cannot expect others to love or respect us. Why should they? Are not their tastes as good as ours? Why then expect them to love that that we ourselves despise, or respect that that we condemn. Race pride has need to be cultivated among us; and we rejoice to know that the press is doing its full share in the work of having it done.

And in the shortcoming alluded to above, the Negro-American is the exceptional man of the world. He is the one only who has no respect for self or race. Prof. Whitney . . . feels especially drawn toward those whose similarity was one of speech, though they lived thousands of years ago. Philip Gilbert Hamerton, in his article, "French and English" (*Atlantic,* May), incidentally alludes to the self-love of the three peoples who inhabit the island of Great Britain—the English, the Scotch and the Welsh. Each insists that he shall be known as himself. The Scotchman will have you understand that his is Scotch blood. And so the others.

"Oh, yes," said a Welsh physician to us a few years since in the town of Llanally, "Oh. yes! these English have come down here and subdued us; and while there is nothing for us to do but submit, we yet have to think of the old times, when we had our own government and kings."

And so it must be with the Negro-American before he fully and completely gets upon his feet. *And so it will be.*

23. ALEXANDER CRUMMELL: "WHAT THIS RACE NEEDS IN THIS COUNTRY IS POWER"

The principles of growth and mastery in a race, a nation, or people, are the same all over the globe. The same great agencies which are needed to make a people in one quarter of the globe and in one period of time are needed here, at this time, in this American nationality. We children of Africa in this land are no way different from any other people in these respects. Many of the differences of races are slight and incidental, and ofttimes become obliterated by circumstances, position, and religion. I can take you back to a period in the history of England when its rude inhabitants lived in caves and huts, when they fed on bark and roots, when their dress was the skins of animals. When you next look at some eminent Englishman, the personification, perchance, of everything cultivated, graceful, and refined, you may remember that his distant ancestors were wild and bloody savages, and that it has taken ten centuries to change him from the rudeness of his brutalized forefathers into an enlightened and civilized human being.

The great general laws of growth and superiority are unchangeable. The Almighty neither relaxes nor alters them for

From Alexander Crummell, "The Social Principle Among a People; and Its Bearing on Their Progress and Development" (1875), in Crummell, THE GREATNESS OF CHRIST AND OTHER SERMONS (New York: Thomas Whittaker, 1882), pp. 294–311.

the convenience of any people. Conformity, then, to this demand for combination of forces is a necessity which we, as a
people, cannot resist without loss and ruin. We cannot pay
heed to it too soon; for if there has been anything for which
the colored people of this country have been and now are
noted, it is for disseverance, the segregation of their forces, the
lack of the co-operative spirit. Neither in farming operations,
nor trades, nor business, nor in mechanical employment, nor
marketing, nor in attempts at grocerykeeping, do we find attempts at combination of their forces. No one hears anywhere
of a company of fifty men to start a farm, to manufacture
bricks, to begin a great trading business, to run a mill, or to ply
a set of vessels in the coasting trade. No one sees a spontaneous
movement of thirty or forty families to take possession of a tract
of land for a specific monetary venture. Nowhere do we see a
united movement in any State for general moral and educational improvement, whereby the masses may be delivered from
inferiority and degradation.* The people, as a body, seem delivered over to the same humble, servile occupations of life in
which their fathers trod, because, from a lack of co-operation
they are unable to step into the higher callings of business; and
hence penury, poverty, inferiority, dependence, and even servility is their one general characteristic throughout the country, along with a dreadful state of mortality.

And the cause of this inferiority of purpose and of action is
two-fold, and both the fault, to some extent, of unwise and
unphilosophic leaders. For, since, especially emancipation, *two*
special heresies have influenced and governed the minds of
colored men in this nation: (1.) The one is the dogma which
I have heard frequently from the lips of leaders, personal and
dear, but mistaken, friends, *that the colored people of this
country should forget, as soon as possible, that they* ARE *colored*

---

* I am advised by an intelligent friend, that the above allegations need
modification; that some few such organizations have been made in two
or three of the Southern States and in the City of Baltimore. The
"COLORED EDUCATIONAL CONVENTION" of Virginia deserves distinguished
consideration and great commendation.

people:—a fact, in the first place, which is an impossibility. Forget it, forsooth, when you enter a saloon and are repulsed on account of your color! Forget it when you enter a car, South or West, and are denied a decent seat! Forget it when you enter the Church of God, and are driven to a hole in the gallery! Forget it when every child of yours would be driven ignominiously from four-fifths of the common schools of the country! Forget it, when thousands of mechanics in the large cities would make a "strike" rather than work at the same bench, in the same yard, with a black carpenter or brick-maker! Forget it when the boyhood of our race is almost universally deprived of the opportunity of learning trades, through prejudice! Forget it, when, in one single State, twenty thousand men dare not go to the polls on election-day, through the tyranny of caste! Forget it, when one great commonwealth offers a new constitution for adoption, by which a man like *Dumas* the younger, if he were a North Carolinian, could be indicted for marrying the foulest white woman in that State, and merely because she was white! Forget that you are colored, in these United States! Turn madman, and go into a lunatic asylum, and then, perchance, you may forget it! But, if you have any sense or sensibility, how is it possible for you, or me, or any other colored man, to live oblivious of a fact of so much significance in a land like this! The only place I know of in this land where you can "forget you are colored" is the grave!

But not only is this dogma folly, it is disintegrating and socially destructive. For shut out, for instance, as I am and you are from the cultivated social life of the superior classes of this country, if I forget that I am a black man, if you ignore the fact of race, and we both, ostrich-like, stick our heads in the sand, or stalk along, high-headed, oblivious of the actual distinctions which *do* exist in American society, what are you or I to do for our social nature? What will become of the measure of social life among ourselves which we now possess? Where are we to find our friends? Where find the circles for society and cheerful intercourse?

Why, my friends, the only way you, and I, and thousands of

our people get domestic relations, marry wives and husbands,
secure social relations, form good neighborhood and companionship, is by the very remembrance which we are told to scout
and forswear.

2. The other dogma is the demand *that colored men should
give up all distinctive effort, as colored men, in schools,
churches, associations, and friendly societies.* But this, you will
observe, is equivalent to a demand to the race to give up all
civilization in this land and to submit to barbarism. The cry
is: "Give up your special organization." "Mix in with your
white fellow-citizens."

Now I waive, for the present, all discussion of abstract questions of rights and prerogatives. I direct my attention to the
simple point of practicality; and I beg to say, that this is a
thing which cannot be forced. Grieved, wearied and worried
as humanity has been with the absurd, factitious arrangements
of society in every quarter of the globe, yet men everywhere
have had to wait. You can batter down oppression and tyranny
with forceful implements; not so social disabilities and the exclusiveness of caste. The Saxon could not force it upon the
Norman. Upon this point, if everything is not voluntary, generous, gracious, and spontaneous, the repulsive will is as icy,
and as obstinate too, as Mt. Blanc. I wonder that the men who
talk in the style I have referred to, forget that nine-tenths of
the American people have become so poisoned and stimulated
by the noxious influence of caste, that, in the present day, they
would resist to the utmost before they would allow the affilia-
tions, however remote, that implied the social or domestic
principle.

Nay, more than this: not only would they reject your advances, but, after they had repelled you, they would leave you
to reap the fruits of your own folly in breaking up your own
distinctive and productive organisms, under the flighty stimu-
lants of imaginative conceit.

And the disaster, undoubtedly, would be deserved; not, indeed, morally, for the inflictions of caste are unjust and cruel;
but because of your unwisdom; for it is the office of common

sense to see, as well the exact situation, to comprehend the real condition of things as they exist in this nation; as well as to take cognizance of the pernicious and atrocious virulence of caste!

Few things in policy are more calamitous in result than mere conceit. An unbalanced and blind imagination is one of the most destructive, most disastrous of all guides. Such I believe to be the nature of the suggestions which I reprobate. But remember, I do not condemn the men who hold them. Oppression and caste are responsible for many worse things than unwisdom, or blind speculation. How intolerable are the distinctions which hedge up our ardent, ambitious minds, on every side, I thoroughly apprehend! How the excited mind turns passionately to every fancied and plausible mode of escape, I can easily understand! But remember that the pilotage of a whole people, of an entire race, through the quicksands and the breakers of civil and social degradation, up to the plane of manly freedom and equality, while it is, by its very hazards, calculated to heighten the pulse, and to quicken the activity of the brain, is, nevertheless, just that sort of work which calls for the coolest head, and the hardest, most downright reasonableness. When you are pleading for natural rights, when men are endeavoring to throw off the yoke of oppression, you may indeed

—imitate the action of the tiger,
Stiffen the sinews, summon up the blood.

But a war against a gross public sentiment, a contest with prejudices and repulsions, is a thing of a different kind, and calls for a warfare of an opposite character. You cannot destroy caste with a ten pounder! You cannot sweep away a prejudice with a park of artillery!

I know, to use the words of another, "how difficult it is to silence imagination enough to make the voice of Reason even distinctly heard in this case; as we are accustomed from our youth up to indulge that forward and delusive faculty ever

obtruding beyond its sphere; of some assistance indeed to ap-
prehension, but the author of all error; as we plainly lose ourselves in gross and crude conception of things, taking for
granted that we are acquainted with what indeed we are
wholly ignorant of";* so it seems to me the gravest of all
duties to get rid of all delusions upon this subject; and to learn
to look at it in the light of hard, serious, long-continued, painful, plodding work. It is *work*, you will observe, not abnormal
disturbances, not excitement; but a mighty effort of moral and
mental reconstruction, reaching over to a majestic end. And
then when that is reached and secured, then all the hindrances
of caste will be forever broken down!

Nothing is more idle than to talk of the invincibility of prejudice. The Gospel is sure to work out all the issues and results
of brotherhood, everywhere under the sun, and in this land;
but, until that day arrives, we are a nation, set apart, in this
country. As such, we have got to strive—not to get rid of ourselves; not to agonize over our distinctive peculiarities; but to
accept the situation as Providence allows it, and to quit "ourselves as men," in, if you say so, painful and embarrassing circumstances; determined to shift the groove of circumstance,
and to reverse it.

The special duty before us is to strive for footing and for
superiority in this land, *on the line of race,* as a temporary but
needed expedient, for the ultimate extinction of caste, and all
race distinctions. For if *we* do not look after our own interests,
as a people, and strive for advantage, no other people will. It is
folly for mere idealists to content themselves with the notion
that "we are American citizens"; that, "as American citizens,
ours is the common heritage and destiny of the nation"; that
"special solicitude for the colored people is a superfluity"; that
"there is but one tide in this land; and we shall flow with all
others on it."

On the contrary, I assert, we are just now a "peculiar people"
in this land; looked at, repulsed, kept apart, legislated for, criti-

* Bishop Butler.

cised in journals, magazines, and scientific societies, at an insulting and intolerable distance, *as* a peculiar people; with the doubt against us whether or not we can hold on to vital power on this soil; or whether we have capacity to rise to manhood and superiority.

And hence I maintain that there is the greatest need for us all to hold on to the remembrance that *we* are "colored men," and not to forget it!

While one remnant of disadvantage abides in this land, stand by one another! While proscription in any quarter exists, maintain intact all your phalanxes! While antagonism confronts your foremost men, hold on to all the instincts of race for the support of your leaders, and the elevation of your people! While the imputation of inferiority, justly or unjustly, is cast upon you, combine for all the elements of culture, wealth, and power! While any sensitiveness or repulsion discovers itself at your approach or presence, hold on to your own self-respect, keep up, *and be satisfied with,* your own distinctive circles!

And then the "poor, forsaken ones," in the lanes and alleys and cellars of the great cities; in remote villages and hamlets; on old plantations which their fathers' blood has moistened from generation to generation; ignorant, unkempt, dirty, animal-like, repulsive, and half heathen—brutal and degraded; in some States, tens and hundreds of thousands, not slaves, indeed, according to the letter of the law, but the tools and *serfs* of would-be oppressors: stand by THEM until the school-master and preacher reach them as well as us; and the noble Christian civilization of the land transforms their features and their forms, and changes their rude huts into homes of beauty; and lifts them up into such grand superiority, that no one in the land will associate the word "Negro" with inferiority and degradation; but the whole land, yea, the whole world shall look upon them by-and-by, multitudinous in their brooding, clustered masses, "redeemed, regenerated, disenthralled," and exclaim, "Black, but comely!" But, while they are low, degraded, miserable, almost beastly, don't forget that you are colored men, as well as they; "your brothers' keepers."

Do not blink at the charge of inferiority. It is not a race pecu-
liarity; and whatever its measure or extent in this country, it
has been forced upon you. Do not deny it, but neutralize and
destroy it, not by shrieks, or agonies, or foolish pretence; but
by culture, by probity, and industry.

I know the natural resource of some minds, under these painful circumstances, to cry out, "Agitate! agitate!" But *cui bono?*
What advantage will agitation bring? Everything has a value,
according to its relation to its own natural and specific end. But
what is the bearing of agitation to a purpose which is almost
entirely subjective in its nature. For, as I take it, the object we
must needs have in view, in the face of the disabilities which
confront our race in this land, is the attainment of such general
superiority that prejudice *must* decline. But agitation has no
such force, possesses no such value. Agitation is the expenditure of force: our end and aim is the husbandry of all our vital
resources.

Character, my friends, is the grand, effective instrument
which we are to use for the destruction of caste: Character, in
its broad, wide, deep, and high significance; character, as evi-
denced in high moral and intellectual attainments; as significant of general probity, honor, honesty, and self-restraint; as
inclusive of inward might and power; as comprehending
the attainments of culture, refinement, and enlightenment; as
comprising the substantial results of thrift, economy, and enterprise; and as involving the forces of combined energies and
enlightened coöperation. Make this, *not* the exceptional, but
the common, general reality, amid the diverse, wide-spread
populations of the colored people in this country; and then all
the theories of inferiority, all the assumptions of your native
and invincible degradation will pass, with wonderful rapidity,
into endless forgetfulness; and the people of the very *next,* nay,
multitudes, in the decline of *this* generation, when they look
upon us, will wonder at the degrading facts of a past and
wretched history. Only secure high, commanding, and masterly
Character; and then all the problems of caste, all the enigmas
of prejudice, all unreasonable and all unreasoning repulsion,

will be settled forever, though you were ten times blacker than midnight! Then all false ideas concerning your nature and your qualities, all absurd notions relative to your capacity, shall vanish! Then every contemptuous fling shall be hushed, every insulting epithet be forgotten! Then, also, all the remembrances of a servile heritage, of ancestral degradation, shall be obliterated! Then all repulsive feelings, all evil dislikes shall fly away! Then, too, all timid disconcert shall depart from us, and all cramped and hesitant manhood shall die!

Dear brethren and friends, let there be but the clear demonstration of manly power and grand capacity in our race, in general, in this country; let there only be the wide out-flashings of art and genius, from their brains; and caste will slink, at once, oblivious to the shades. But no mere self-assertion, no strong, vociferous claims and clamor, can ever secure recognition and equality, so long as inferiority and degradation, if even cruelly entailed, abide as a heritage and a cancer. And I maintain we must *organize*, to the end that we may attain such character. The whole of our future on this soil depends upon that single fact of magnitude—character. Race, color, and all the accidents thereof have but little to do with the matter; and men talk idly when they say "we must forget that we are colored men." What is needed is not that *we* should forget this fact, but that we should rise to such elevation that the *people of the land* be forced to forget all the facts and theories of race, when they behold our thorough equality with them, in all the lines of activity and attainment, of culture and moral grandeur. The great necessity in this land is that its *white* population should forget, be made to forget, that we are *colored* men! Hence there is a work ahead for us, for the overthrow of caste, which will consume the best part of a century. He, whoever he may be, commits the greatest blunder, who advises you to disband your forces, until that work is brought to its end. It was only *after* the battle of Waterloo that England and her allies broke up their armies, and scattered their huge battalions. Not until we, as a people, have fully vindicated our race; not until we have achieved to the full their rights and prerogatives; not until,

by character, we challenge universal respect and consideration
in the land, can we sing the song:

> —Come to the sunset tree,
>   The day is past and done,
> The woodman's axe lies free,
>   And the reaper's work is done.

Until that time, far distant from to-day, should the cry be
everywhere among us: "Combine and marshal, for all the highest achievements in industry, social progress, literature, and
religion!"

I hasten to conclude with two brief remarks:

First, then, let me remind and warn you, my friends, that we,
as colored men, have no superfluity of powers or faculties in
the work which is before us, as a race, in this country. First of
all, we all start with maimed and stunted powers. And next, the
work before us is so distinct, definite, and, withal, so immense,
that it tolerates no erratic wanderings to out-of-the-way and
foreign fields.

And yet there are men who tell us that much of our work of
the day is objective, that it lies among another people. But I
beg to say that we have more than we are equal to in the needs
of the six millions of our ignorant and benighted people, yet
crippled and paralyzed by the lingering maladies of slavery.
If we address ourselves strenuously and unitedly to *their* elevation and improvement we shall have our hands full for more
than one generation, without flowing over with zeal and offices
to a masterful people, laden with the enlightenment of centuries.

For one, I say very candidly that I do not feel it *my* special
calling to wage war with and to extirpate caste. I am no way
responsible for its existence. I abominate it as an enormity.
Theirs is the responsibility who uphold it, and theirs is the
obligation to destroy it. My work is special to my own people,
and it is constructive. I beg leave to differ from that class of

colored men who think that ours is a special mission, to leave our camp and to go over, as it were, among the Philistines, and to destroy their idols.

For my part, I am satisfied that my field of labor is with my own race in these times. I feel I have no exuberance of powers or ability to spend in any other field, or to bestow upon any other people. I say, as said the Shunamite woman, "I DWELL AMONG MY OWN PEOPLE" (2 Kings: IV, 13); not, indeed, as mindless of the brotherhood of the entire species, not as forgetful of the sentiment of fellowship with disciples of every name and blood; but as urged by the feeling of kinship, to bind myself as "with hooks of steel" to the most degraded class in the land, my own "kinsmen according to the flesh." I have the most thorough and radical conviction that the very first duty of colored men, in this our day and generation, is in the large field of effort which requires the regeneration and enlightenment of the colored race in these United States.

And second, from this comes the legitimate inference suggested by the text, i. e., of union and co-operation through all our ranks for effective action and for the noblest ends. Everywhere throughout the Union wide and thorough organization of the people should be made, not for idle political logomachy, but for industrial effort, for securing trades for youth, for joint-stock companies, for manufacturing, for the production of the great staples of the land, and likewise for the higher purposes of life, i. e., for mental and moral improvement, and raising the plane of social and domestic life among us.

In every possible way these needs and duties should be pressed upon their attention, by sermons, by lectures, by organized societies, by state and national conventions; the *latter not* for political objects, but for social, industrial ends and attainments. I see nought in the future but that we shall be scattered like chaff before the wind before the organized labor of the land, the great power of capital, and the tremendous tide of emigration, unless, as a people, we fall back upon the might and mastery which come from the combination of forces and the principle of industrial co-operation. Most of your political agitation is but wind and vanity. *What this race needs in this country is* POWER—*the forces that may be felt.* And that comes from character, and character is the product of religion, intelligence, virtue, family order, superiority, wealth, and the show of industrial forces. THESE ARE FORCES WHICH WE DO NOT POSSESS. *We are the only class which, as a class,* IN THIS COUNTRY, IS WANTING IN THESE GRAND ELEMENTS. The very first effort of the colored people should be to lay hold of them; and then they will take such root in this American soil that only the convulsive upheaving of the judgment-day can throw them out! And therefore I close, as I began, with the admonitory tones of the text. God grant they may be heeded at least by YOU who form this congregation, in your sacred work *here,* and in all your other relations: "They helped every one his neighbor, and every one said to his brother, Be of good courage. So the carpenter encouraged the goldsmith, and he that smootheth with the hammer him that smote the anvil, saying, It is ready for the soldering; and he fastened it with nails, that it SHOULD NOT BE MOVED!"

24. ALEXANDER CRUMMELL ON "THE NEED OF . . . SCHOLARLY MEN" TO "LIFT UP THIS PEOPLE OF OURS"

What then, it may be asked, is the special undertaking we have before us, in this Academy? My answer is the civilization of the Negro race in the United States, by the scientific processes of literature, art, and philosophy, through the agency of the

From Alexander Crummell, "Civilization: The Primal Need of the Race," in American Negro Academy, OCCASIONAL PAPERS NO. 3 (Washington, D. C.: The Academy, 1897), pp. 3–7.

cultured men of this same Negro race. And here, let me say, that the special race problem of the Negro in the United States is his civilization.

I doubt if there is a man in this presence who has a higher conception of Negro capacity than your speaker; and this of itself, precludes the idea, on my part, of race disparagement. But, it seems manifest to me that, as a race in this land, we have no art; we have no science; we have no philosophy; we have no scholarship. Individuals we have in each of these lines; but mere individuality cannot be recognized as the aggregation of a family, a nation, or a race; or as the interpretation of any of them. And until we attain the role of civilization, we cannot stand up and hold our place in the world of culture and enlightenment. And the forfeiture of such a place means, despite, inferiority, repulsion, drudgery, poverty, and ultimate death! Now gentlemen, for the creation of a complete and rounded man, you need the impress and the moulding of the highest arts. But how much more so for the realizing of a true and lofty *race* of men. What is true of a man is deeply true of a people. The special need in such a case is the force and application of the highest arts; not mere mechanism; not mere machinery; not mere handicraft; not the mere grasp on material things; not mere temporal ambitions. These are but incidents; important indeed, but pertaining mainly to man's material needs, and to the feeding of the body. And the incidental in life is incapable of feeding the living soul. For "man cannot live by bread alone, but by every word that proceedeth out of the mouth of God." And civilization is the *secondary* word of God, given for the nourishment of humanity.

To make *men* you need civilization; and what I mean by civilization is the action of exalted forces, both of God and man. For manhood is the most majestic thing in God's creation; and hence the demand for the very highest art in the shaping and moulding of human souls.

What is the great difficulty with the black race, in this era, in this land? It is that both within their ranks, and external to themselves, by large schools of thought interested in them, ma-

terial ideas in divers forms are made prominent, as the master-
need of the race, and as the surest way to success. Men are
constantly dogmatizing theories of sense and matter as the
salvable hope of the race. Some of our leaders and teachers
boldly declare, now, that *property* is the source of power; and
then, that *money* is the thing which commands respect. At one
time it is *official position* which is the masterful influence in
the elevation of the race; at another, men are disposed to fall
back upon *blood* and *lineage*, as the root (source) of power and
progress.

Blind men! For they fail to see that neither property, nor
money, nor station, nor office, nor lineage, are fixed factors, in
so large a thing as the destiny of man; that they are not vitaliz-
ing qualities in the changeless hopes of humanity. The greatness of peoples springs from their ability to grasp the grand
conceptions of being. It is the absorption of a people, of a nation, of a race, in large majestic and abiding things which lifts
them up to the skies. These once apprehended, all the minor
details of life follow in their proper places, and spread abroad
in the details and the comfort of practicality. But until these
gifts of a lofty civilization are secured, men are sure to remain
low, debased and grovelling. . . .

Who are to be the agents to lift up this people of ours to the
grand plane of civilization? Who are to bring them up to the
height of noble thought, grand civility, a chaste and elevating
culture, refinement, and the impulses of irrepressible progress?
It is to be done by the scholars and thinkers, who have secured
the vision which penetrates the center of nature, and sweeps
the circles of historic enlightenment; and who have got insight
into the life of things, and learned the art by which men touch
the springs of action.

For to transform and stimulate the souls of a race of a people
is a work of intelligence. It is a work which demands the clear
induction of world-wide facts, and the perception of their application to new circumstances. It is a work which will require
the most skillful resources, and the use of the scientific spirit.

But every man in a race cannot be a philosopher: nay, but

few men in any land, in any age, can grasp ideal truth. Scientific ideas however must be apprehended, else there can be no progress, no elevation.

Just here arises the need of the trained and scholarly men of a race to employ their knowledge and culture and teaching and to guide both the opinions and habits of the crude masses. The masses, nowhere are, or can be, learned or scientific. The scholar is exceptional, just the same as a great admiral like Nelson is, or a grand soldier like Caesar or Napoleon. But the leader, the creative and organizing mind, is the master-need in all the societies of man. But, if they are not inspired with the notion of leadership and duty, then with all their Latin and Greek and science they are but pedants, trimmers, opportunists. For all true and lofty scholarship is weighty with the burdens and responsibilities of life and humanity.

But these reformers must not be mere scholars. They must needs be both scholars and philanthropists. For this, indeed, has it been in all the history of men. In all the great revolutions, and in all great reforms which have transpired, scholars have been conspicuous; in the re-construction of society, in formulating laws, in producing great emancipations, in the revival of letters, in the advancement of science, in the rennaissance of art, in the destruction of gross superstitions and in the restoration of true and enlightened religion.

And what is the spirit with which they are to come to this work? My answer is, that *disinterestedness* must animate their motives and their acts. Whatever rivalries and dissensions may divide man in the social or political world, let generosity govern *us*. Let us emulate one another in the prompt recognition of rare genius, or uncommon talent. Let there be no tardy acknowledgment of worth in *our* world of intellect. If we are fortunate enough, to see, of a sudden, a clever mathematician of our class, a brilliant poet, a youthful, but promising scientist or philosopher, let us rush forward, and hail his coming with no hesitant admiration, with no reluctant praise.

It is only thus, gentlemen, that we can bring forth, stimulate, and uplift all the latent genius, garnered up, in the by-places and sequestered corners of this neglected Race.

It is only thus we can nullify and break down the conspiracy which would fain limit and narrow the range of Negro talent in this caste-tainted country. It is only thus, we can secure that recognition of genius and scholarship in the republic of letters, which is the rightful prerogative of every race of men. It is only thus we can spread abroad and widely disseminate that culture and enlightment which shall permeate and leaven the entire social and domestic life of our people and so give that civilization which is the nearest ally of religion.

25. FRANCIS J. GRIMKÉ URGES BLACK TEACHERS FOR BLACK SCHOOLS

The institutions to which I especially refer under the above head are those founded for the benefit of the colored race, but which have been mainly or exclusively under the control and direction of our white friends. These may be divided into three classes; First, those in which colored men are represented neither in the faculty nor the Trustee Board. Second, those in which they are represented in both. Third, those in which they are represented in one or the other alone. I take it for granted, in entering upon this discussion, that the object in founding these institutions was to secure the largest and best results to the black race. As such they are helpful in two particulars; (1) By affording opportunities of instruction to colored men and women; thus increasing the general intelligence, and swelling the number of those who are to go forth to labor among the masses; (2) by affording opportunities for colored men to exer-

Francis J. Grimké, "Colored Men as Professors in Colored Institutions," A.M.E. CHURCH REVIEW, IV (July 1885), 142–149.

cise their gifts as instructors in the higher departments of learning,—which has an important bearing upon the progress of the race; First, in that it affords time and leisure to members of the race for a broader, deeper culture, and for a larger self-development. In this way these institutions will become not only the soil in which will be grown the men and women who are to labor among the masses, but in which an exceptional scholarship will be fostered, where the men who are to take rank among the great scholars of the land will be grown. Second, in that it accustoms the students to see men of their own race in high and responsible positions, the effect of which is to foster race pride and to engender a feeling of mutual respect. Unfortunately, as a race, we are sadly deficient in this element of respect for each other,—due largely to the influence of slavery. There is no better place in which to educate our people out of this than in these institutions, where are gathered those who are to become its leaders. And there is no better way of effecting this than by the presence of able representatives of their own race as instructors. As many of these schools are at present conducted this feeling is encouraged rather than discouraged. The intellects of our young people are being educated at the expense of their manhood. In the class-room they see only white professors. Vacancies occur, but they are filled only by white men; the effect of which is unconsciously to lead them to associate these places and the idea of fitness for them only with white men. I was especially impressed with this fact, sometime ago, in a conversation which I had with some of the students of one of these institutions, where colored men are represented neither in the faculty nor the Trustee Board. I took the opportunity of suggesting to them that, in my judgment, the time had come for a change, but was surprised, and I confess somewhat annoyed, to find that they were not prepared for such a step,—although this was just what was to be expected in view of their environments. In the third place, the employment of colored professors is helpful in its stimulating effect upon the students in a most laudable direction. Let our colored young men who are being educated in these institutions see colored men filling professor-

ships: let them understand that these positions are open to
them, as soon as they are fitted for them, and the effect is to
stir their ambition, to give a new direction to their thoughts, to
throw open before them the illimitable fields of scholarship and
research. Under such incentives we may expect to find the development of scholarly taste, scholarly aspirations and scholarly attainments. This incentive to high scholarship colored
institutions may afford and should afford to the representatives
of that race for the benefit of which they were founded. Lastly,
the employment of colored professors, would have a beneficial
effect upon an adverse public sentiment. Senator Hoar, in a
letter commending Prof. Wiley Lane in connection with the
application for the professorship of Greek in Howard University, said, among other things: "I think the interest of the colored race will be much promoted as its members take places
of honor requiring capacity in other pursuits than that of
politics." Yes, the interest of the colored race will be much promoted as colored men of ability come to the front, as they are
placed in high and responsible positions where they can have
the opportunity of demonstrating their capacity from an eminence, from which they can be more widely seen and known.
This is a fact which it would be well for our white friends who
have the management and control of colored institutions to
remember. In confining their professorships to white men, in
shutting their doors against colored men, they are losing one of
the grandest opportunities, are failing to use one of the most
effective means in their power, of helping on this race. In
nothing, perhaps, was the greatness of soul of Gen. O. O. Howard, his wisdom, his profound interest in the welfare of the
colored race, his desire to further their interests in every possible way, more strikingly manifested than in this respect. He
did not use his position to advance his own interests or those
of his friends or relatives,—as is so often done in these institutions. No, it was the good of the black race that he had in view
in the founding of Howard University, and he was determined
to make it tell in every possible way in furthering that end.
Hence, recognizing the important fact set forth by Senator

Hoar, among the first things that he did was to associate with himself, in the government and instruction of the University, representative colored men. When he came to organize the Law Department he sought out a representative colored man, in the person of the Hon. John Mercer Langston, and placed him at the head of it. When the Theological Department was to be organized, the able and scholarly Dr. J. B. Reeve, of Philadelphia, was called to its head. The same is true of the Medical Department; the skilful and accomplished surgeon, now at the head of the Freedman's Hospital, Dr. C. B. Purvis, and Dr. Augusta, for many years lecturer on anatomy, early became associated with it. Such was the spirit that pervaded this institution, and continued to preside over it during General Howard's administration. Such is the spirit that should pervade all our colored institutions. Everything should be made subservient to the best interests of the race for which they were founded. The most for the colored man, should be the motto inscribed upon them all, and the principle that should guide in their administration. This unfortunately, has not been the case. These institutions have not been so conducted as to yield the largest and best results to the colored race. They have been helpful mainly in a single direction,—in affording us the opportunity of receiving an education. The help which comes from the opportunity of securing time and leisure for a broader, deeper culture, for a larger self-development; which comes from the opportunity of demonstrating our capacity in a way and manner such as to influence public sentiment in our favor, our white friends have, in nearly all of these institutions, reserved for themselves. They are willing to have us profit by them so far as instruction is concerned, so far as we can be helped in the capacity of students, but in no other way. And if we venture to suggest that this is not the limit of the power of these institutions to help us, and put ourselves in the way of receiving further benefits, we are discouraged or are arrogantly repelled as presumptuous and immodest. It is just here that I take issue with our white friends, and where I think they are doing us a wrong, and allowing themselves to be influenced by other considerations than the good of the race, in depriving us of opportunities which we much need, and which have an important bearing upon our progress and development. The exclusion of colored men at first from these institutions may have been a matter of necessity, owing to a lack of opportunity for preparation. But, however true this may have been in the past, it is not true today. Twenty years of freedom have wrought a great change in our intellectual condition. From scores of colored institutions a steady stream of graduates has flowed into all parts of our country; while on the list of graduates from our leading white institutions,—Harvard, Yale, Dartmouth, Amherst, Brown, Oberlin,—are to be found representatives of our race. The progress has been great, marvelous indeed. Assuming then that we have men who are fitted by training and ability to share the responsibility of instruction in these institutions, the question naturally arises, why are they not admitted, why are they still excluded from many of them, or when applying for a professorship, why are their applications always looked upon with disfavor, and met with decided opposition?

The explanation is to be found in race prejudice on the one side, and selfishness on the other. In the first place, we are shut out, notwithstanding our qualifications, under the operation of the principle of selfishness, which prompts men to look out for themselves and theirs first. We all, more or less, have friends and relatives out of employment, needing something to do, some way of earning a livelihood. It is so natural to think of these, when vacancies occur in these institutions, and desire to see them provided for. In this way the faculties of many of these institutions are built up. One man gets in, and straightway he thinks of an old friend or classmate, and this old friend thinks of some one else, and by and by the uncle thinks of the nephew and the father of the son. As white men usually make up the faculties and trustee boards, only white men are drawn in, under the operation of this principle. I am not finding fault with this exhibition of selfishness on the part of our white friends. I am not saying that it is not perfectly natural, or that colored men, similarly situated, would not do precisely the same thing, but simply directing attention to the fact that, whether natural or unnatural, by it we are effectually excluded from participation in the instruction in many of these institutions.

In the second place, we are excluded because of caste prejudice. I say this in the full knowledge of the fact, that in these institutions there are those who profess to be our friends; who were, many of them, identified with the anti-slavery movement, who bear the name of Christ, and are under ordination vows as ministers of the gospel. All this is true, and yet this accursed prejudice exists. Abolition simply meant freedom for the slave as a man. Christianity, as interpreted by the actions of the great majority of white professors in this country, means recognition of the negro, but in his place,—as an inferior. The election of a colored man as professor in these institutions, means something more than was contemplated in the abolition movement, or is conceded by a spurious, but popular Christianity; it means equality; it means social recognition. This, our white brethren who make up the faculties of colored institutions are not ready for, and are determined not to have, if they can possibly prevent it. In conversation with the financial secretary of one of these institutions,—in which there is not now, and never has been during its history, a colored professor or member of the trustee board,—he frankly confessed that it was not because they did not believe the negro intellectually and mentally qualified to fill such positions. "Then why are they not admitted?" I asked. "Because," said he, "we do not consider it a wise thing to do." He then explained that having been a foreign missionary for many years, and coming almost exclusively in daily contact with people of another race, he did not feel so himself;—thereby showing that the underlying cause, which he skillfully concealed under the term "wise," was no other than caste prejudice. Upon leaving he said, (and I quote his exact language, only omitting the name of the institution, as I do not desire to injure it), This institution "has made no progress in this direction; it does not desire to make any, it has resolved not to." Such, unfortunately, is the spirit which largely prevails in most of these institutions, and will explain, in part, at least, why colored men are excluded from high and responsible positions in them. Upon the character of caste prejudice and selfishness, in themselves considered, I do not desire to enter; but as a colored man, interested in the progress of his race, I have a right to expect our white brethren to so administer the affairs of these institutions as to conserve the best interests of the race, for which they were founded. I have a right to know how they can reconcile their prejudices and their selfishness with their professed interest in us, as a race, and in the objects for which these institutions were founded, when this selfishness and these prejudices operate to exclude us from positions in them which would greatly aid in our development. If our white brethren now holding positions in these institutions are not sufficiently unselfish to forget themselves in their desire for the good of this race, if they are not superior to a petty caste prejudice, which estimates a man by the color of his skin, instead of by his intellectual moral and spiritual worth, then the only manly thing for them to do is to give way to others who will in a truer, nobler spirit carry on the work. Selfishness and caste prejudice are the two greatest obstacles against which the negro has to contend. By them he is excluded from railroad cars and steamboats, from hotels and restaurants, from trades-unions and other associations, and, alas, is discriminated even in his own institutions, where he has a right to expect better things. It is a sad fact, but nevertheless true. It is just as difficult to get a colored man elected to a professorship in some of our colored institutions as it would be in Harvard or Yale, or in the University of Virginia or South Carolina. When vacancies occur he is never thought of, or if he has the hardihood, the presumption, to imagine himself fitted for a professorship, and dares to put in an application, at once everything is done to defeat him. If he chances to have a letter strongly endorsing him, the president, or some one else in whose hands the letter is placed, sits down at once and calls the writer to account for daring to say such complimentary things of a negro; or writes to know if he really meant what he said; or if he fully understood the import of the language used; or if he was quite sure he did not make a mistake; or if he was not laboring under the impression when he wrote, that, because it was a colored institution, anything was good enough for it. I have known this to be done in at least two instances, in relation to the endorsements of colored candidates, while the testimonials in behalf of white applicants were accepted without question. Such examples show the spirit which prevails in many of these institutions, the determination to shut the black man out at all hazards. In one instance I have seen this feeling carried so far that, after the colored candidate was fairly elected at a regular meeting,—though there was barely a quorum present, it is true,—a second meeting was called, and the motion boldly made to rescind the action by which he was appointed. I have heard the president of one of these institutions persist in saying that a black candidate was unfit for a professorship, without having any personal knowledge, whatever, of his unfitness, and in the face of the highest testimonials to his ability and proficiency, from distinguished professors under whom he had studied;—so blinded was he by his prejudices, and so determined was he to defeat his election. It is bad enough to be obliged to contend with this spirit of caste prejudice in white institutions, and on the part of our enemies, but to find it existing, and to such a degree, in our own institutions, and on the part of our professed friends, is almost too much for our patience. The time has come, it seems to me, for black men to speak out, and to direct attention to this evil; to let these pseudo friends,—many of whom have allied themselves with negro institutions only for what they can get out of them, under the pretense of being actuated by philanthropic motives, know, that we understand their true character. The time has come for the purging of these institutions from such hypocrites and pretenders, and filling their places with men who are in hearty sympathy with this oppressed and downtrodden race. The lordly manner in which some of these presidents and professors in colored institutions bear themselves, and the contempt with which they treat the aspirations and attainments of colored men, is as shameful as it is exasperating. The evident pleasure which some of them take in belittling colored men,—the very men for whose good they profess to be laboring, bespeaks their own littleness, and deserves the scorn and contempt of all good men. I have heard the president of one of these institutions labor for nearly an hour to belittle a man in every way his superior in all the elements of a true manhood, and in scholarly attainments in his special line, more than his equal. The attainments, the scholarly tastes and aspirations of the colored applicant, instead of filling him with pride and delight, seemed rather to stir within him the bitterest hatred, which carried him so far in his opposition as to lead him to stoop to a course which can only be characterized as dishonorable. On a recent occasion it was sickening to listen to the character of the remarks made by one of our white brethren respecting the appointment of a colored applicant for a Greek professorship in one of these institutions. One thought it would be too bad to have him leave another institution where he was already laboring,—notwithstanding the reason for his desiring to leave was well understood, and such as would have influenced any man under the circumstances. Another believed in the advancement of colored men to such positions, but was afraid of the bad effect if he should prove a failure; and this in the face of the fact that the applicant had been a successful teacher of Greek for eight years. Another would gladly vote for him if he were the equal of the white man, a fact, however, which he was unwilling to concede. Every line of argument was only to prepare the way for voting against the black man. This is always the case; the effort is to discover reasons, not why he should be supported, but why he should not. On a similar occasion, I remember but one white man, and he an ex-officer in the confederate army, and an ex-slaveholder, who boldly espoused the cause of the colored applicant, and showed by his earnest words that his heart was in it. In view of such facts it is not surprising that we are sometimes inclined to become discouraged, and yet we should not be. There are some signs of progress. Two years ago, when the case of Professor Wiley Lane came up before the trustees of Howard University the principle was laid down that in colored institutions the preference should be given to competent colored men; which was strongly controverted by the president, who maintained that no consideration whatever was to be accorded to colored men, on account of their color, even in their own institutions. At the last meeting of the board the same principle was again laid down, and met with hearty applause. This is one step of progress. The principle was also advanced that colored institutions were to be conducted in the interest of the colored race; that when vacancies occurred the colored man was first to be thought of, and the white man only when it was impossible to secure competent colored men. "We must decrease in these institutions, but they (i.e., the colored people,) must increase," said a white trustee in addressing his white brethren. What he meant was, that as white men, they were to make way for colored men, as fast as they were fitted to assume the duties and responsibilities of these institutions themselves; that these positions were to be held by white men only provisionally, to be vacated as soon as competent colored men could be found to fill them. At some future time I hope to see this principle also recognized and applauded. It is not at present orthodox, I am sorry to say. The spirit which it embodies is not the spirit which today rules in these institutions. The disposition is not to open the door to the colored man and bid him welcome, but to shut him out; not to hold these places provisionally, but absolutely; not with a view of benefiting the colored man, but of benefiting themselves through him. The fact that professorships in all the white institutions in the land, from which we are absolutely excluded, are open to our white brethren, ought to dictate to them the propriety of not putting themselves forward, and of allowing us a chance, at least in our own institutions. But instead of this, the disposition is to challenge our right to hold such positions, even in these; to take advantage of their superior numbers on the trustee boards, to monopolize every important position. If this is philanthropy, then I, for one, think we have had quite enough of it. If this is the treatment we are to continue to receive from our friends, then it is time for us to begin to pray to be deliv... d from our friends.

To all that has been said, it may be objected that as colored men we have no right to complain, since the money for carrying on these institutions is furnished by white men. In answer to this I would say, First, the poverty of the colored man is no fault of his. For two hundred and fifty years the white man has been enriched by his toil. Though he may not furnish the money directly, therefore, it does not follow that he is not entitled to it. Second, whether we furnish the money or not, we have a right to insist that these institutions, which are founded for our good, be so administered as to secure to us the largest possible results; to see that we are deprived of no benefits to be derived from them. If we are thus deprived, which is un-doubtedly the case in many of these institutions, we have not only the right, but it is our sacred duty to direct attention to the evil with a view to its removal. This I trust we will continue to do until the last vestige of this accursed caste prejudice, and narrow selfishness which so largely prevail in many of these institutions shall be swept away, and the black man be accorded that recognition which he deserves, and which he has a right to expect.

26. BISHOP HENRY M. TURNER:
"GOD IS A NEGRO"

Bishop Turner of the African Methodist Church says, "that God is a Negro." The good Bishop has been represented as one of the ablest men of his race and we thought justly so, for he is not only an intelligent thinker, but upon all subjects connected with his people his reasoning is profound, and in most instances unanswerable, but he is evidently becoming demented if he used the language attributed to him.   OBSERVER.

The Observer has our thanks for the compliment tendered in respect to our thinking faculties, notwithstanding our demented condition when we understand God to be a Negro. We have as much right biblically and otherwise to believe that God is a Negro, as you buckra or white people have to believe that God is a fine looking, symmetrical and ornamented white man. For the bulk of you and all the fool Negroes of the country believe that God is white-skinned, blue-eyed, straight-haired, projecting nosed, compressed lipped and finely robed *white* gentleman, sitting upon a throne somewhere in the heavens. Every race of people since time began who have attempted to describe their God by words, or by paintings, or by carvings, or by any other form or figure, have conveyed the idea that the God who made them and shaped their destinies was symbolized in themselves, and why should not the Negro believe that he resembles God as much so as other people? We do not believe that there is any hope for a race of people who do not believe they look like God.

Demented though we be, whenever we reach the conclusion that God, or even that Jesus Christ, while in the flesh, was a

Henry M. Turner, "God is a Negro," VOICE OF MISSIONS, February 1, 1898.

white man, we shall hang our gospel trumpet upon the willow and cease to preach.

We had rather be an atheist and believe in no God, or a pantheist and believe that all nature is God, than to believe in the personality of a God, and not to believe that He is a Negro. Blackness is much older than whiteness, for black was here before white, if the Hebrew word, coshach, or chashach, has *any* meaning. We do not believe in the eternity of matter, but we do believe that chaos floated in infinite darkness or blackness millions, billions, quintillions and eons of years before God said, "Let there be light," and that during that time God had no material light Himself and was shrouded in darkness, so far as *human* comprehension is able to grasp the situation.

Yet we are no stickler as to God's color, anyway, but if He has any we would prefer to believe that it is nearer symbolized in the blue sky above us and the blue water of the seas and oceans; but we certainly protest against God being a white man or against God being white *at all;* abstract as this theme must forever remain while we are in the flesh. This is one of the reasons we favor African emigration, or Negro naturalization, wherever we can find a domain, for, as long as we remain among the whites, the Negro will believe that the devil is black and that he (the Negro) favors the devil, and that God is white and that he (the Negro) bears no resemblance to Him, and the effects of such a sentiment is contemptuous and degrading, and one-half of the Negro race will be trying to get white and the other half will spend their days in trying to be white men's scullions in order to please the whites; and the time they should be giving to the study of such things as will dignify and make our race great will be devoted to studying about how unfortunate they are in not being white.

We conclude these remarks by repeating for the information of the Observer what it adjudged us, demented, for "*God is a Negro.*"

Territorial separatism and emigration

During the half century that followed the end of Reconstruction, territorial separatism and emigration were recurrent and interrelated themes. Their base was among the masses; and except for some of the all-Negro towns like Mound Bayou, Mississippi, and an occasional advocate of African colonization like Bishop Henry M. Turner, few of the elite spokesmen for the race endorsed proposals along these lines.

During the late 1870s, the growing racism that accompanied the close of Reconstruction combined with economic depression to produce considerable interest among working-class Negroes in the possibilities of migrating to a more favorable location. Both the American Midwest, especially Kansas, and Africa were regarded as likely places of refuge (see Documents 27 and 28). Sentiment for moving to either area, though undoubtedly basically precipitated by stark economic conditions, involved disillusionment with the South and revealed distinct nationalist overtones. Later in the century, both the attempt, on the one hand, to create an all-black state in Oklahoma and all-Negro towns like Mound Bayou, Mississippi, and the brilliant rhetoric of Bishop Henry M. Turner on the other, were to offer more dramatic evidence of nationalist feelings. These in turn would be overshadowed in the twentieth century by the Garveyites and the Black Muslims. The desire for a "territory of our own" (as Henry Adams puts it in Document 27), whether within the United States or Africa, is an old and recurring theme, as the selections here illustrate.

One of the few members of the black elite to espouse

colonization with any degree of consistency was the noted A.M.E. cleric, Bishop Turner. A leading Negro politician during Reconstruction, Turner had become an advocate of emigration by the middle 1870s. Thereafter he was known for his colorful denunciations of the United States and his ringing calls for expatriation. As Document 29 indicates, he foreshadowed the views of the more celebrated twentieth-century nationalist movements, like the Garvey Movement and the Black Muslims, in his damning of the American white society, in his advocacy of the necessity of a separate nation, and in his cultural nationalism, including the belief that God is black.

Actually, during the late nineteenth and early twentieth centuries, emigration was a less prominent form of territorial-separatist ideology than were proposals to create all-black communities within the United States. A number of all-Negro towns were created, the most noted of which was Mound Bayou, Mississippi, founded in 1887, a community in which prominent spokesmen like Booker T. Washington were deeply interested. More ambitious was the attempt to turn the Oklahoma Territory into an all-Negro state during the 1890s; the result was 25 black towns, like Boley and Langston. These communities, despite enormous difficulties and often failure, proudly considered themselves examples of what Negroes themselves could accomplish through mobilization on the basis of race pride and solidarity.

On the fringes of the movement for separation was the plan of an obscure man named Arthur Anderson for the creation of a black nation within the geographical confines of the U.S. Like Garvey later, he had been associated with African nationalists abroad, most notably with Duse Mohamed Ali, the Sudanese-Egyptian nationalist and editor of the London *African Times and Orient Review,* whose writings were largely responsible for the striking similarities in the doctrines of Anderson and the more recent Black Muslims. Like the Black Muslims, Anderson asserted that the blacks were the original race of mankind from

which the whites, an inferior and diseased race, evolved; and
he envisioned a glorious future for the American black man
in a separate territory provided by the United States
government as an indemnity for past oppression
(see Document 30).

The most important of the movements for territorial separatism
and colonization was the Universal Negro Improvement
Association, which was founded in Jamaica in 1914 under the
leadership of Marcus Garvey. His propaganda found fertile
ground in the slum-shocked migrants who had been moving to
the cities—especially to the cities of the North during and
after the war. Garvey, a Jamaican citizen, was the one man who
really reached the frustrated and disillusioned masses in the
ghettos. During its heyday after the war his U.N.I.A. had
branches in many cities in the United States and in several
foreign countries. Garvey aimed to liberate both Africans and
American Negroes from their oppressors. His utopian means
of accomplishing both goals was the wholesale migration of
American Negroes to Africa. Garvey contended that whites
would always be racist and insisted that the black man must
develop "a distinct racial type of civilization of his own and . . .
work out his salvation in his motherland, all to be
accomplished under the stimulus and influence of the slogan,
'Africa for the Africans, at home and abroad.'" On a more
practical level he urged Negroes to support Negro businesses,
and the U.N.I.A. itself organized a chain of groceries,
restaurants, laundries, a hotel, a doll factory, and a printing
plant. Thousands bought stock in the U.N.I.A.'s Black Star
Steamship Line, which proposed to establish a commercial link
between the United States, the West Indies, and Africa. Tens of
thousands of Negroes swelled with pride at the parades of
massed units of the African Legion in blue and red uniforms
and the white-attired contingents of the Black Cross Nurses.
Garvey's followers proudly waved the association's flag (black
for Negro skin, green for Negro hopes, and red for Negro
blood), and sang the U.N.I.A. anthem, "Ethiopia, Thou Land of

Our Fathers." Stressing race pride, Garvey gloried in the
African past and taught that God and Christ were black.

He denounced the light-skinned, integrationist, middle- and
upper-class Negroes active in the NAACP for being ashamed of
their black ancestry and wanting to amalgamate with the
white race. Garvey insisted that the U.N.I.A. was the only
agency able to protect the black masses against the Du Bois-led
"caste aristocracy" of college graduates. The established
Negro leaders resented and feared the "provisional President
of the African Republic," and several of them called the
attention of the United States government to irregularities in
the management of the Black Star Line. Garvey was jailed
and then deported on charges of using the mails to defraud,
and his movement collapsed. But he dramatized as no one
before had done the bitterness and alienation of the black
masses. Thus the Garvey movement provided a compensatory
escape for black people for whom the urban promised
land had turned out to be a hopeless ghetto.
The selections below include a description by Roi Ottley,
a black journalist who was a close observer of the Harlem
scene (Document 31), and three selections from *Philosophy
and Opinions of Marcus Garvey*, illustrating his advocacy
of racial unity, his denunciation of the light-skinned
assimilationist Negro elite, and his belief that the solution for
the black man's problems lay in emigration and
national independence (Document 32).

The documents in this section are of interest in part because
they indicate the close relationship between colonization in a
separate territory within the United States and actual
expatriation to Africa. Both ideologies have a common source
in the disillusionment of the black masses. The testimony
of Henry Adams, for example, shows explicitly that emigration
to Liberia was viewed as an alternative to colonization in
Kansas. Again, a generation later in 1915, many of the
Oklahoma colonizationists, thoroughly disillusioned when their
vision of an all-black state faded, and faced with

disfranchisement and economic misery, became enthusiastic followers of an alleged Ashanti ruler, "Chief Alfred C. Sam," and his abortive effort to establish a settlement in West Africa. Most of the documents presented here reflect the fact that late nineteenth and twentieth-century territorial separatism and colonization were rooted mainly in the black masses, rather than in the black elite, as they were before the Civil War.

Henry Adams, like other witnesses before the Senate committee investigating the Kansas Exodus of 1879, was a farm laborer who was born a slave in Georgia and had moved to Louisiana at the close of the Civil War. Arthur Anderson was semiliterate. Henry M. Turner and the leaders of the South Carolina emigration movement, including Martin R. Delany and Congressman and later A.M.E. Bishop R. H. Cain, were, it is true, outstanding clerics and political leaders. But as an English traveler reported, "The upper class do not go themselves, but preach to their countrymen the advantage of going."[1] And those who did go on the ill-fated expedition of the bark *Azor* were of humble origins. Finally, Garvey's organization was a striking example of a movement based upon the lower classes, with only a handful of middle-class participants, chiefly in the leadership ranks.

[1] Sir George Campbell, *White and Black* (London, 1879), p. 347.

27. A LEADER OF THE KANSAS EXODUS:
"WE WANTED TO GO
TO A TERRITORY BY OURSELVES"

Q. What is your business, Mr. Adams?—*A.* I am a laborer. I was raised on a farm and have been at hard work all my life.

Q. Now tell us, Mr. Adams, what, if anything you know about the exodus of the colored people from the Southern to the Northern and Western States; and be good enough to tell us in the first place what you know about the organization of any committeee or society among the colored people themselves for the purpose of bettering their condition, and why it was organized. Just give us a history of that as you understand it.—*A.* Well, in 1870, I believe it was, or about that year, after I had left the Army—I went into the Army in 1866 and came out the last of 1869—and went right back home again where I went from, Shreveport; I enlisted there, and went back there. I enlisted in the Regular Army, and then I went back after I came out of the Army. After we had come out a parcel of we men that was in the Army and other men thought that the way our people had been treated during the time we was in service—we heard so much talk of how they had been treated and opposed so much and there was no help for it—that caused me to go into the Army at first, the way our people was opposed. There was so much going on that I went off and left it; when I came back it was still going on, part of it, not quite so bad as at first. So a parcel of us got together and said that we would organize ourselves into a committeee and look into affairs and see the true condition of our race, to see whether it was possible we could

From testimony of Henry Adams in REPORT AND TESTIMONY OF THE SELECT COMMITTEE OF THE UNITED STATES SENATE TO INVESTIGATE THE CAUSES OF THE REMOVAL OF THE NEGROES FROM THE SOUTHERN STATES TO THE NORTHERN STATES, Senate Report No. 693, Part 2, 46th Cong., 2nd sess. (Washington, D. C. U.S. Government Printing Office, 1880), pp. 101–105, 108–11.

stay under a people who had held us under bondage or not. Then we did so and organized a committee.

Q. What did you call your committee?—A. We just called it a committee, that is all we called it, and it remained so; it increased to a large extent, and remained so. Some of the members of the committee was ordered by the committee to go into every State in the South where we had been slaves there, and post one another from time to time about the true condition of our race, and nothing but the truth.

Q. You mean some members of your committee?—A. That committee; yes, sir.

Q. They traveled over the other States?—A. Yes, sir; and we worked some of us, worked our way from place to place and went from State to State and worked—some of them did— amongst our people in the fields, everywhere, to see what sort of living our people lived; whether we could remain in the South amongst the people who had held us as slaves or not. We continued that on till 1874. . . .

Q. Was the object of that committee at that time to remove your people from the South, or what was it?—A. O, no, sir; not then; we just wanted to see whether there was any State in the South where we could get a living and enjoy our rights.

Q. The object, then, was to find out the best places in the South where you could live?—A. Yes, sir; where we could live and get along well there and to investigate our affairs—not to go nowhere till we saw whether we could stand it.

Q. How were the expenses of these men paid?—A. Every one paid his own expenses, except the one we sent to Louisiana and Mississippi. We took money out of our pockets and sent him, and said to him you must now go to work. You can't find out anything till you get amongst them. You can talk as much as you please, but you have got to go right into the field and work with them and sleep with them to know all about them.

Q. Have you any idea how many of your people went out in that way?—A. At one time there was five hundred of us.

Q. Do you mean five hundred belonging to your committee? —A. Yes, sir.

Q. I want to know how many traveled in that way to get at the condition of your people in the Southern States?—*A.* I think about one hundred or one hundred and fifty went from one place or another.

Q. And they went from one place to another, working their way and paying their expenses and reporting to the common center at Shreveport, do you mean?—*A.* Yes, sir.

Q. What was the character of the information that they gave you?—*A.* Well, the character of the information they brought to us was very bad, sir.

Q. In what respect?—*A.* They said that in other parts of the country where they traveled through, and what they saw they were comparing with what we saw and what we had seen in the part where we lived; we knowed what that was; and they cited several things that they saw in their travels; it was very bad.

Q. Do you remember any of these reports that you got from members of your committee?—*A.* Yes, sir; they said in several parts where they was that the land rent was still higher there in that part of the country than it was where we first organized it, and the people was still being whipped, some of them, by the old owners, the men that had owned them as slaves, and some of them was being cheated out of their crops just the same as they was there.

Q. Was anything said about their personal and political rights in these reports, as to how they were treated about these? —*A.* Yes; some of them stated that in some parts of the country where they voted they would be shot. Some of them stated that if they voted the Democratic ticket they would not be injured. . . .

Q. The result of this investigation during these fours years by your committee was the organization of this colonization council. Is that the way you wish me to understand it?—*A.* It caused it to be organized.

Q. It caused it to be organized. Now, what was the purpose of this colonization council?—*A.* Well, it was to better our condition.

Q. In what way did you propose to do it?—*A.* We first organized and adopted a plan to appeal to the President of the United States and to Congress to help us out of our distress, or protect us in our rights and privileges.

Q. Your council appealed first to the President and to Congress for protection and relief from this distressed condition in which you found yourselves, and to protect you in the enjoyment of your rights and privileges?—A. Yes, sir.

Q. Well, what other plan had you?—A. And if that failed our idea was then to ask them to set apart a territory in the United States for us, somewhere where we could go and live with our families.

Q. You preferred to go off somewhere by yourselves?—A. Yes.

Q. Well, what then?—A. If that failed, our other object was to ask for an appropriation of money to ship us all to Liberia, in Africa; somewhere where we could live in peace and quiet.

Q. Well, and what after that?—A. When that failed then our idea was to appeal to other governments outside of the United States to help us to get away from the United States and go there and live under their flag.

Q. Have you given us all the objects of this colonization council?—A. That is just what we was organized for, to better our condition one way or another. . . .

Q. Now, let us understand more distinctly, before we go any further, the kind of people who composed that association. The committee, as I understand you, was composed entirely of laboring people?—A. Yes, sir.

Q. Did it include any politicians of either color, white or black?—A. No politicianers didn't belong to it, because we didn't allow them to know nothing about it, because we was afraid that if we allowed the colored politicianer to belong to it he would tell it to the Republican politicianers, and from that the men that was doing all this to us would get hold of it, too, and then get after us.

Q. So you did not trust any politicians, white or black?—A. No; we didn't trust any of them.

Q. That was the condition of things during the time the committee were at work in 1870 to 1874?—*A*. Yes, that was the condition.

Q. Now, when you organized the council what kind of people were taken into it?—*A*. Nobody but laboring men. . . .

Q. At the time you were doing that, was there anything political in your organization?—*A*. Nothing in the world.

Q. You were simply looking out for a better place in which you could get work and enjoy your freedom?—*A*. Yes, sir; that was all.

Q. When did the idea first enter your council to emigrate to the northern and northwestern States; if you remember, what were the first movements in that direction?—*A*. Well, in that petition we appealed there, if nothing could be done to stop the turmoil and strife, and give us our rights in the South, we appealed then, at that time, for a territory to be set apart for us to which we could go and take our families and live in peace and quiet.

Q. The design of your organization, then, as you understood it, was not so much to go north to live among the white people in the Northern and Western States as it was to have a territory somewhere that you could occupy in peace and quiet for yourselves?—*A*. That is what we wanted, provided we could not get our rights in the South, where we was. We had much rather staid there if we could have had our rights.

Q. You would have preferred to remain in the South?—*A*. Yes, sir.

Q. And your organization was not in favor of your moving, providing you could get your rights and be protected in the enjoyment of them as any other men?—*A*. No, sir; we had rather staid there than go anywhere else, though the organization was very careful about that, and we said so from the first; and then, if that could not be done under any circumstances, then we wanted to go to a territory by ourselves.

Q. Well, about what time did this idea of a territory first occur to you; did it occur at all during the organization of your committee, or after the council was organized?—*A*. After the committee had made their investigations.

Q. Well, what did you do after that?—*A.* We organized the council after that.

Q. About what time did you lose all hope and confidence that your condition could be tolerated in the Southern States?—*A.* Well, we never lost all hopes in the world till 1877.

Q. Not until 1877?—*A.* No, sir. In 1877 we lost all hopes.

Q. Why did you lose all hope in that year?—*A.* Well, we found ourselves in such condition that we looked around and we seed that there was no way on earth, it seemed, that we could better our condition there, and we discussed that thoroughly in our organization along in May. We said that the whole South—every State in the South—had got into the hands of the very men that held us slaves—from one thing to another —and we thought that the men that held us slaves was holding the reins of government over our heads in every respect almost, even the constable up to the governor. We felt we had almost as well be slaves under these men. In regard to the whole matter that was discussed, it came up in every council. Then we said there was no hope for us and we had better go.

Q. You say, then, that in 1877 you lost all hope of being able to remain in the South, and you began to think of moving somewhere else?—*A.* Yes; we said we was going if we had to run away and go into the woods.

Q. Well, what was the complaint after you failed to get the territory?—*A.* Then, in 1877 we appealed to President Hayes and to Congress, to both Houses. I am certain we sent papers there; if they didn't get them that is not our fault; we sent them.

Q. What did that petition ask for?—*A.* We asked for protection, to have our rights guaranteed to us, and at least if that could not be done, we asked that money should be provided to send us to Liberia.

Q. That was 1877, was it?—*A.* Yes, sir; that was in 1877.

Q. Still, up to that time you did not think at all of going into the Northern States; at least you had taken no steps toward going into those States, had you?—*A.* No, sir.

Q. When did that idea first occur to your people?—*A.* In 1877, too, we declared that if we could not get a territory we would go anywhere on God's earth; we didn't care where.

Q. Even to the Northern States?—*A.* Yes; anywhere to leave them Southern States. We declared that in our council in 1877. We said we would go anywhere to get away.

Q. Well, when did the exodus to the Northern States from your locality, or from your country you are acquainted with best, begin?—*A.* Well, it didn't begin to any extent until just about a year ago.

Q. It didn't begin to any extent until 1879, you mean?—*A.* No, sir; not till the spring of 1879.

Q. But you had prior to that time been organized and ready to go somewhere, as I understand you?—*A.* Yes, sir; we had several organizations; there were many organizations; I can't tell you how many immigration associations, and so forth, all springing out of our colonization council. We had a large meeting, some five thousand people present, and made public speeches in 1877 on immigration.

Q. What was the character of those speeches as to what you intended to do?—*A.* We intended to go away, to leave the South, if Congress would not give us any relief; we were going away, for we knowed we could not get our rights.

Q. Where were these meetings held?—*A.* Some were held at Shreveport, in Caddo Parish, some were held in Madison, and some were held in Bossier Parish.

Q. Was there any opposition to these meetings in which you talked about going away?—*A.* No, sir. There didn't nobody say anything to us against our having our meetings, but I will tell you we had a terrible struggle with our own selves, our own people there; these ministers of these churches would not allow us to have any meeting of that kind, no way.

Q. They didn't want you to go?—*A.* No; they didn't want us to go.

Q. Why?—*A.* They wanted us to stay there to support them; I don't know what else. Mighty few ministers would allow us to have their churches; some few would in some of the parishes. There was one church, Zion, in Shreveport, that allowed us to talk there.

Q. Were the ministers opposed to it?—*A.* Yes, sir; they was opposed to it. . . .

Q. Your meetings were composed, then, of men in favor of going away?—*A*. Yes, and of the laboring class.

Q. Others didn't participate with you?—*A*. No, sir.

Q. Why didn't the politicians want you to go?—*A*. They were against it from the beginning.

Q. Why?—*A*. They thought if we went somewhere else they would not get our votes. That is what we thought.

Q. Why were the ministers opposed to it?—*A*. Well, because they would not get our support; that is what we thought of them.

Q. They thought it might break up their churches?—*A*. Yes; that is what they thought; at least we supposed the ministers thought that.

Q. About how many did this committee consist of before you organized your council? Give us the number as near as you can tell.—*A*. As many as five hundred in all.

Q. The committee, do you mean?—*A*. Yes; the committee has been that large.

Q. What was the largest number reached by your colonization council, in your best judgment?—*A*. Well, it is not exactly five hundred men belonging to the council, that we have in our council, but they all agreed to go with us and enroll their names with us from time to time, so that they have now got at this time 98,000 names enrolled

Q. Women and men?—*A*. Yes, sir; women and men, and none under twelve years old. . . .

Q. How many of your people have gone from that part of the country to the North, if you know?—*A*. I don't know exactly how many have gone.

Q. Of course you cannot tell us exactly, but as near as you know; give some idea of the number, if you can.—*A*. My reports from several members of the committee, in parts I have not been in and seen for myself—I take their words and put their words down as mine, because they are not allowed to lie on the subject. And so from what I have learned from them from time to time I think it is about five thousand and something.

Q. Do you mean from that section of country down there?—
A. Yes, sir.

Q. From Louisiana?—*A.* Yes, sir. . . .

Q. Now, Mr. Adams, you know, probably, more about the causes of the exodus from that country than any other man, from your connection with it; tell us in a few words what you believe to be the causes of these people going away.—*A.* Well, the cause is, in my judgment, and from what information I have received, and what I have seen with my own eyes—it is because the largest majority of the people, of the white people, that held us as slaves treats our people so bad in many respects that it is impossible for them to stand it. Now, in a great many parts of that country there our people most as well be slaves as to be free; because, in the first place, I will state this: that in some times, in times of politics, if they have any idea that the Republicans will carry a parish or ward, or something of that kind, why, they would do anything on God's earth. There ain't nothing too mean for them to do to prevent it; nothing I can make mention of is too mean for them to do. If I am working on his place, and he has been laughing and talking with me, and I do everything he tells me to, yet in times of election he will crush me down, and even kill me, or do anything to me to carry his point. If he can't carry his point without killing me, he will kill me; but if he can carry his point without killing me, he will do that. . . .

28. THE SOUTH CAROLINA EXODUS TO AFRICA: "AFRICA IS THE ONLY LAND THAT A COLORED MAN CAN SAY IS HIS"

Rooms of The Liberia
Joint Stock Steamship Company
Charleston, S. C.
Nov. 6th, 1877

To the President of the Republic of Liberia:

Dear Sir,—This will inform you that the colored people of America and especially of the Southern States desire to return to their fatherland.

We wish to come bringing our wives and little ones with what wealth and education, arts, and refinement we have been able to acquire in the land of our exile and in the house of bondage. We come pleading in the name of our common Father that our beloved brethren and sisters of the Republic, which you have the high and distinguished honor of presiding over, will grant unto us a home with you and yours in the land of our Fathers. We would have addressed you before on this subject, but we have waited to see what would come of the sudden up-heaval of this movement. We are now in position to say, if you will grant us a home in your Republic where we can live and aid in building up a nationality of Africans, we will come, and in coming we will be prepared to take care of ourselves and not be burdensome to the Government. By our present plan of operations, we will be able to furnish food, medicine and clothing to last us for from six months to a year.

We desire to ask you the question, can we come? Will you be able to furnish us with a receptacle, where we could spend the first few weeks of our arrival, or will it be necessary for us to build our own? Would it be convenient for us to settle on the St. Paul's river? We hope to hear your decision at your earliest convenience.

Yours, for and in behalf of 150,000 exiles enrolled for Liberia,
Benj. F. Porter,
Pres. Liberia J. S. S. S. Co.

The following letter is from an emigrant from Littleton, N. C., where he was a school teacher of high repute and deservedly popular. He was accompanied to Liberia by his family, his parents and a number of other relations and acquaintances:—

"*Brewerville*
January 28, 1880
Dear Sir: Thank God and the American Colonization Society for aiding me to remove to Liberia. After a pleasant run of thirty-one days from New York, I landed at Monrovia, the capital city of this republic. I remained in Monrovia one day, and then came to the town of Brewerville, on the St. Paul river, some ten miles distant. I never was so well pleased as when I set my feet on Africa's shore, for here I am at home. All that is wanted in this country is intelligent, enterprising and mon-eyed men from the United States. By this class a large and powerful republic can be built on the coast of Africa. Ministers are also wanted to preach to our brethren that are in heathen-ism. I find this to be a good country—the only country for the Negro. Africa, dear Africa, is the only land that a colored man can say is his. I expect to start a school soon at Brewerville for the natives—to teach them the truths of the gospel, the bless-ings of civilization, and the elevating beauties of the English language. I say to my brethren in America, come to your own country. Here you can feel that your soul is your own; here you will not be despised as of another race; here you can rule in-stead of being ruled; here are no white men to say whether you shall vote or not, and here you will not be kicked about from pillar to post as a football by white people or politicians. The Western coast of Africa was wisely selected by Ameri-

can benevolence and philanthropy for the settlement of the exiled people of color. I find here all kinds of fruit, vegetables and grain, as in the United States. It is not so hot here—and January is the warmest month—as to burn the fish in the rivers or the fine coffee growing on trees. It is pleasant; the air is sweet and soft, and it is quite cool in the morning and evening. At noonday it is not hotter than in North Carolina in summer time.

If I were again in the United States I would not remain, but would return to Liberia, even if I had to grieve my bones with labor until I should raise money enough to bury my body here. The emigrants that left with me are all well. They have selected their lands and are at work upon them.

Please have this statement published and send it to Rev. Lewis Browne, my minister, and to Mr. Alexander Browne, my brother, both at Littleton, N. C. I write them to come; and please aid them all you can in removing to this republic of true liberty, equality and happiness.

Very respectfully yours,
Norfleet Browne

29. BISHOP HENRY M. TURNER DEMANDS AN INDEMNITY "TO GO HOME TO AFRICA"

A. "THE NEGRO HAS NOT SENSE ENOUGH"

We remained in slavery two hundred and fifty years, and have been free the best end of fifty more years. In other words we have been dominated over by the buckra, or white race, for about three hundred years. We have worked, enriched the

Henry M. Turner, "The Negro Has Not Sense Enough,"
VOICE OF MISSIONS, July 1, 1900.

country and helped give it a standing among the powers of
the earth, and when we are denied our civil and political
rights, the fool Negro who has no more sense than a jackass,
yet he wants to be a leader, ridicules the idea of asking for a
hundred million of dollars to go home, for Africa is our home,
and is the one place that offers us manhood and freedom,
though we are the subjects of nations that have claimed a
part of Africa by conquest. A hundred million of dollars can
be obtained if we, as a race, would ask for it. The way we
figure it out, this country owes us forty billions of dollars, and
we are afraid to ask for a hundred million. Congress, by its
legislation, throws away over a hundred million annually, and
we are so little, such contemptible pigmies, so insignificant that
we shudder at the very idea of a hundred million. It shows
what little minds we have, what little money we are used to,
and what little souls we possess. Every man that has the sense
of an animal must see there is no future in this country for the
Negro. In the north we have some kind of civil rights, we grant,
and the same in the east and west, but in the south, where the
great bulk of our people are, we haven't the rights of a dog.
We are tried in the courts, but the judge and jury are all white,
and justice is unknown, if the suit is against a white man or
woman. Jails are broke open, and we are taken out and burned,
shot, hanged, unjointed and murdered in every way. Our civil
rights are taken from us by force; our political rights are a
farce. Can't the fool Negro see that there is no future in this
country for him? If he cannot, then he should return to slavery.
We would be better off as slaves than as freemen. The Negro
that can't understand the folly of attempted existence here is
an inferior man or an inferior woman, and the white people are
right when they call us inferiors. If we could believe that men
were in earnest, such as lawyers, Bishops, ministers of the gospel, doctors, professors in colleges, teachers of public schools,
politicians and scholars, we would pronounce the Negro race
as an inferior, to the day of our death, and hereafter we shall
join with the white people in declaring the Negro race as inferiors, unless they wake up soon to the dreadful condition

before them. Big names do not impart sense. Fine clothes and finely furnished houses do not give sense. Before God I believe we are inferiors, and were born to be slaves. We are certainly a set of fools.

B. "WAR WITH SPAIN"

Being out of the country when the present war with Spain broke out, we could not define our position relative to the part that the colored man should play upon the bloody programme.

Since our arrival home we have been asked a thousand times for our opinion, and we have simply replied that the war is now in progress and the black man is in it and it would be useless to say anything; but just as we expected, we see that he is made the butt of ridicule, his faults are magnified and he is still the bone of contention. He is being snubbed while even defending the stars and stripes. This is no news to us, however, for we knew it would be the case before we returned to the country, or before we had even heard a word uttered. We do not see what the Negro is so anxious to fight for anyway, he has no country here and *never will* have.

Much is being said about fighting poor little Spain, the eighth power of the world for the purpose of humanity, that the Spanish are so cruel and brutal in their treatment toward the Cubans. "Physician, heal thyself," very appropriately comes in here. Enough men have been lynched to death to reach a mile high if laid one upon the other, and enough women and children to form the head and foot slab if they could be arranged to stand upon the head of each other. The United States puts more people to death without law than all the other nations of earth combined. So our humanitarianism is too ridiculous to be made a count in the argument of justification.

Henry M. Turner, "War with Spain," VOICE OF MISSIONS, July 1, 1898.

The Negro will be exterminated soon enough at best, without being overanxious to die in the defense of a country that is decimating his numbers daily.

The colored men would far better be employed in remaining at home, marrying wives and giving the race sons and daughters, and perpetuating our existence, than rushing into a death struggle for a country that cares nothing for their rights or manhood, and wait till they are wanted, and then the nation will feel and know his worth and concede to him the respect due the defenders of a nation.

It is very likely that the Negro will be wanted before this little fuss is over, anyway, for we have but little doubt that the greater part of Europe will have a hand in this affair before it is ended, and should it so turn out the black man will be wanted, and inducements will be offered for his blood and bravery in common with other men. One thing can be said to the everlasting credit of Spain—a man is a man in her domain. We have been from one end of Spain to the other, and we have seen black men and black women enjoying every privilege that was being enjoyed by people of any other color. We have stopped at some of her finest hotels and have enjoyed such respect and honors that some Americans who were there exhibited their disapproval because we were seated at the table in the midst of them. We pretended not to notice it, however, although we *did* notice it. Governor Atkinson of Georgia, who said that he would not enlist Negroes in this war, according to what we saw in the English papers before our arrival home, shows himself a greater friend to the Negro than those governors who are enlisting his aid and service. Governor Atkinson knows that the Negro has nothing for which he should fight, and he has too much respect for the Negro to encourage him to die for nothing.

We endorse Governor Atkinson in toto and tender him our gratitude for the interest he exhibits in behalf of our race.

C. "EMIGRATION"

A big emigration has set in from Georgia to the west. People are leaving by thousands and are sacrificing their property and giving away their places or are getting a mere song for them. Some are not getting one-tenth or one-ninth of their true value. They had far better be emigrating to Africa; for instance, Liberia, where they will have a permanent home and their children after them will have a permanent home. The white people are all alike and the same condition of things that drive them from Georgia will prevail in Mississippi, Arkansas and the western states. We are told that nearly one thousand assembled at the depot at Athens last night, that hundreds and thousands have left for the western states during the last month or three weeks. The cars have been crowded to density and in some instances they have been refused the conveniences of the car and had to wait and take freight trains and cattle boxes. The fools appear to have nothing to say or nothing to do with this emigration, but the moment Africa is mentioned they swarm like bees and pour the vituperation and scandal upon the only spot that offers manhood and freedom. If the whole crowd of these anti-emigrationists were hung dead by the neck it would be better for the race, and in a majority of instances, they are preachers and the money they spend is wrung from poor women and poor men at the sacrifice of their lives. We will not say any more upon the subject lest we say too much. We have no patience with them. We mean these so-called leaders who are not fit to lead a flea.

Henry M. Turner, "Emigration," VOICE OF MISSIONS, April 1, 1900.

30. ARTHUR A. ANDERSON:
"PROPHETIC LIBERATOR OF
THE COLOURED RACE," DEMANDS
AN INDEMNITY FOR A SEPARATE TERRITORY
IN THE UNITED STATES

This, whether now, or 50 years hence, by the acceptance or rejection of this command, will ultimately be, the only way, by which the said people may be, or, rather will be liberated and, placed on equality with other men who inhabit this continent. Not a slow process of evolution—but now to-day—the climax in the lives of the colored and white of the U.S. America, is reached—something must be done now to prevent a bloody war of extermination—mark you! for both, if this command is ignored, it is startling near sure and inevitable. But this advice acted upon at once, can settle the question without the single fire of a rifle, or, a single slash of a sword, of which the pen is indeed the mightier, and in less than 5 years the difference of the two races will be adjusted in a contented compromise.

The plan

First a Few Plain Facts.—It is astonishing upon what facts and fancies the ignorance of a so-called civilization, has allowed prejudice, to the dark races, and particularly the Negro, to find a basis. Africa, the mother of civilization, the black and dark people—the origin of mankind, the father of nations, of whom the white man is but a diseased brother, and, yet assumes a superiority.

We will settle once and for all the question of the Negro's skin. His is the original color, while the white man, is but a

From Arthur A. Anderson, PROPHETIC LIBERATOR OF THE COLOURED RACE OF THE UNITED STATES OF AMERICA: COMMAND TO HIS PEOPLE (New York: New York Age Print, 1913).

tribe of the dark man, who having wandered far from the original family, into new climatic environments antagonistic to his former tropical surroundings, found themselves overcome with privations and disease which blanched his blood, and, skin into the so-called white man of to-day.

Through centuries of time he has survived it all, until he has developed into a formidable adversary and tyrant over his black brother. We have medical and historical science as proof when necessary.

So it is rather a question how the white man acquired his color that solves the problem of the Negro's colored or dark skin.

The dark skin which has produced the very head and front of the "polite savages" the white man's religion.

The strength upon which his Empire is based and thrives, Christianity, descending from Christ, who was of the Jews direct descendants of Abraham of Negro blood,—so if the Negro can give to the white man a Christ, a God, surely his dark skin should command more respect.

If geneology counts for anything we have King Menelik of Abyssinia, who to-day traces his ancestry back to King Solomon, a King like Solomon in his day a King amongst Kings, of what more noble ancestors can one wish to boast. . . .

. . . The American Negro has reached the heights of oratory; in literature he has equalled, in art we have Tanner, in music, the only music by which the American people, "white" is recognized abroad, is embodied in Swanee River and "Rag-Time that stirs that ancient blood of the Negro in white man, that cries out for recognition and that will never be suppressed." So that it is not education the white man longer pleads for as an excuse for recognition of the Negro. Not industry, for we had in slavery days superior Negro mechanics and agriculturists, so to what excuse can he longer look for the delay? Until the Negro has turned white? In that the slave holders nearly succeeded, by the abominable advantage they took in the rape of the slave women, that has produced the colored race of America to-day, he still persecutes, as in those days he sold his own flesh and blood, and to-day appropriates in many localities the prettiest mulattos and octoroons for his own lascivious tastes. White slavery indeed! What about black slavery. Jack Johnson will yet be crowned hero and martyr. This oppression and tyrannizing over the American colored people by his white brother, is but another,—a modern form of slavery. How slow men of my race you are to perceive it.

But it must end and now—I command it! Since all the requirements, as education, morality, industry, arts all have failed to satisfy the white people, what more can we do? What more would they have us do? I must be plain there is no time for artistic or aesthetic flights of fancy, but to the truth plain, simple, inevitable, secret of solution, and if not the white man's desire, it must be ours. Inevitable destiny that must be to the satisfaction of both races. As I predicted 20 years ago on a return visit from Europe and 30 years of travel in as many different countries comparing "ever" social conditions and the modern trend of events, convinces me and others who view us from the outside world as the "only plan."

Segregation. How?

The American colored people must unite more firm, there will always be dissenters, even, amongst race lovers—many differences of opinion on this plan and other matters will arise. I can almost picture in my mind, the amount of discussion pro and con the furor of this movement is going to create—more black eyes, epithets, lauding and damning will be hurled one at the other, in fact more opposition and energy will be expended in its discussion than that would be required to put the plan in operation. So did Christianity and other great world movements have for its beginning such struggles. Some men of the race will fear to jeopardize their positions, politically, religiously, educationally, industrially or socially, this all along has been the trouble—the drawback, until as yet the race has never had an ideal leader of the race itself. What are those positions to the first principle of manhood, savage or civilized—"Liberty"—I wouldn't accept the best position the Government of the United States could offer me, the best that has ever been offered a Negro, were it the presidency itself, unless it was to better my people, no slow process, but at once, the Negro question settled before, I begin. That would act as an inducement to accept, but until then, I had rather walk the roads in rags, living on the charity of a single sympathizer than even vote in a country where a vote, does not entitle one to the rights of a man. If I had 300 million dollars I'd spend it in the same cause. I am ashamed to walk the streets as the lowest type of manhood. I am ashamed that my beautiful daughters and son must now feel on their return home this oppressing indignity to my race.

So what is the first step necessary in this great plan. If the race in a majority cannot unite on this plan as organization is their weak point, then 100 men staunch and true can carry out the work others will follow.

You must know by now, that all questions of races or nations, in their dealings with one or the other, in commerce, aggrandisement, war or peace comes under international law, as accepted by the great powers, in which the great European powers have greatest control. Now when we are firmly united as a people—a nation apart, we are in a position to present our cause, before the great tribunal, The Hague, even if it be left to the 100 men, we must be presented as a nation modern in every respect, equipped with the highest knowledge of their own modern civilization, yet without protection, without a flag, without a country.

And in case of failure of this appeal (following) to the American people to accept or demand the protection of some other power outside the U.S.A.

Now then that we have arranged the first step in Union, comes the first actual movement. We, the colored race of the U.S.A. and our representatives, your wards, your half brothers and sisters by blood demand of the Government of this United States $600,000,000 indemnity for slavery, for the trail of blood sacrificed in human lives, the loss of country. The years of tyranny and oppression that followed and continues until to-

day on the ex-slaves and their offsprings, created by the institution of a cruel slavery by the American people of the U.S.A.

In addition to the $600,000,000 indemnity, we the colored
people of the U.S.A. and our representatives, demand of the
U.S.A. Government a suitable territory, a part of the United
States of America, not some distant land over the sea, but the
U.S.A. The land, every inch of which is hallowed by the blood
of the Negro, shed in the upbuilding of this Empire. A suitable
territory of ample spacious dimensions—in which to propagate,
to develop their resourcefulness, necessary to its maintenance
as a modern nation, a race apart, the people to be free from
further oppression, but the U.S.A. Government to help the
colored people to form and make laws themselves for themselves conducive to the welfare of the colored race.

The whole to be under the protectorate of the U.S.A. but
only in case of invasion from another foreign country, or the
invasion by the white race of the U.S.A. unauthorized, or the
invasion unauthorized by the U.S.A. of the colored people into
the U.S.A. But the protectorate to in no way interfere with the
civil affairs of the colored peoples territory. And I would like
to state here to my people that a Monarchy would be preferable to a Republic; the reasons are many and the question may
be discussed at the proper time.

I am simply outlining in a general way this great plan, the
details of which will be many and intricate and can be left in
better hands of Negro diplomats, of which the race can produce
many competent. In fact I am conceited enough to know, not
believe, that there are men of our race capable of occupying
the chair at the White House itself. . . .

You would be astonished in traveling abroad to see how little
is known by the man in the street, or the average European
about the Negroes of the U.S.A. We will call ourselves Negroes
or colored people or Africans. There is some controversy as to
the correct term, but we will say colored people of the U.S.A.
to distinguish us from the real African who is pushing the
American colored people close in the race for the re-establishment of the race.

As I said it is astonishing how little the European and Orientals know of the colored people of America's early struggles, his advancement, his ambitions, his cry for recognition, his claim for reward. Many know there are Negroes in America and particularly in the south, but they could scarcely tell you whether that meant the southern states or South America, which is thought by them, to be the same. The race needs a few men to do what Ida B. Wells, a woman did. So you see how necessary it is to let the world know what we are doing, and what we want.

Now then, historians and writers, we want a book wrote of the history of the American Negro from the slave down to the aeroplane. Slavery with all its horrors, the slaying of men, the debauchery of Negro women, with nothing too revolting or terrible to tell which truth, will not equal by half the actual brutal deeds. The white people (these polite savages) has left no stone unturned to depreciate and humiliate us in the eyes of the world, before whose Royalty and nobility they cringe and crawl for social favors, read any society doings abroad— in London, Paris, Berlin, Rome, or Cairo, Egypt, it is current news, they must be held up to the same ridicule as have we.

We have the writers, and means of publishing of our own selves this book to benefit by, socially and financially, and show to the world how America has treated its wards within its own dominions, yet assuming the Protectorate of Honolulu, San Domingo, Liberia, Philippines and others—loudest to decry the Congo atrocities. Ye God! what hypocrisy and look at us! A reflection of themselves, we are what they have made us.

Now then we are beginning to get things into shape, now that we have the Land and Indemnity Bill before Congress, the history of the American colored people on the press.

We have work for other writers, and students of genealogy to prove their ancestry of some of the colored people of the U.S.A.; men capable of research in Africa and the Orient along those lines. We've a few smart men of other dark races in London that can help and white men too. Much has already been published in the *African Times and Orient Review* of London to prove that among Negro American slaves, are de-

scendants of African Kings, Egyptian Potentates, Nubian nobility exiles and slaves of Turkish aristocracy. I have myself,
while in Algiers, North Africa, been by the Algerians proudly
pointed out, as the American Negro descendants of their African, Arabic blood. Now then we want this all looked into mi-
nutely and accurately from slavery to the present. . . .

So you see there is work for the writers, and mind you, these
books are later to be translated into many languages. Now,
then we have the book agoing and the genealogical tree set up
to be presented to the world—a moment I forgot and believe
important enough to mention. The *African Times and Orient
Review* I frequently mention and with whom I have the honor
to be associated, gives a few statistics of the American Negroes
advancement. I tell you the eyes of the world are upon us, and
it behooves us to hustle and from words pass into deeds.

The aforesaid statistics when, at the close of the Civil War
the American Negroes, started on their career as farmers, they
had no land as farm-owners or tenants. When the great difference in the conditions of white and black farmers fifty years
ago is taken into account, the fact that, the relative number of
owners, among the Negro farmers in the south, is now more
than one-half as great as the relative number of owners among
the white farmers makes a very commendable showing. The
Negroes now in the U.S.A. own 20,000,000 acres of land or
31,000 square miles. If all the land they own, were placed in
one body, it would equal the area of the states of New Hamp-
shire, Vermont, Massachusetts and Rhode Island (by the way
that's about the size and a little more we want for our colony,
in the U.S.A. with a sea front for marine instructions). There
are now over 50,000 Negroes in the professions—teachers,
preachers, lawyers, doctors, dentists, editors, etc.; 30,000 engaged in businesses of various sorts, photography, druggists,
pharmacists, mine owners, cottonmills, dry-goods, stores, insurance companies, theatres, wholesale merchants, newspapers,
undertakers, real estate dealers. 20,000 grocers, blacksmiths,
skilled mechanics, engineers, iron, gold and silver workers,
3,950 in the postal service. They have accumulated $700,000,000

enough! So you see are we not ripe for taking a recognized
place in the world of nations? And capable of ruling ourselves
as a distinct nation in a country of our own? Yes! and yet we
are deprived of political, social and industrial rights, lynched,
burned, submitted to brutal atrocities and ostracism.

That's what we want the world outside to know what we
have accomplished under adverse circumstances. So writers get
busy with the books with appropriate beautiful illustrations, of
race characters, industries, etc. Pardon me for the digression
from my original subject at times, but you can imagine how my
blood is fired with the hope of this great scheme. . . .

Now then we've a year or so to plan out and get this work
in shape, while we are awaiting the decision of the great Indemnity and Land Bill, which time will be thus utilized.

First to appoint these 100 men select race men, capable
travelers by land and sea, good orators, singers, musicians, imposing characters, some linguists if possible. We could easily
scrape up their expenses out of the rich race men, the societies
and other organizations of those 7 hundred millions, with what
might be made, from sociables, concerts and meetings previous
to the departure of the representatives, saying nothing of what
will be made from the sale of these books, concerts, lectures,
contributions while en route. This organization to be known as

THE COLORED LIBERTY LEAGUE

. . . Now we are ready with select body of men, for a tour of
the world, to lecture on the race, its achievements, its desire
for protection of some nation in case of the failure of America's
passing of the indemnity bill,—but, rather the object of laying
stress on the demand of America which owes us that right, and
rather to seek the co-operation of foreign countries in influenc-
ing America's favorable decision.

Off for a six months' tour, while awaiting the decision strain-
ing every effort to bring about the required results.

If through sickness or disease or accident to our ambassadors, men there will be already assigned to take their place, as
in these days of rapid transit, little time would be lost. There

will be other commissions aside from the general plan. You will agree with me men of my race, the importance of this mode of operation.

If America fails us, we know that blood is thicker than water, we know too that American people may oppose this plan, and had rather spend 600,000,000 to thwart it in its consummation, even if they have to pay some of our own race to betray us as traitors are easily found with greased hands, but the idea alone of the plan generally known will have sown the seed of determination. As for me, I believe the white people at least some will think a thousand deaths would not appease their wrath for even proposing such a scheme. But once the scheme is made known by every colored newspaper, to reach every Negro home, in words only, leaving the deed to be accomplished when I live no more, I will gladly welcome those thousand deaths. As I know this is the inevitable means of averting a race war in the U.S.A. as predicted last year by a famous French traveler and writer. . . .

No time should be lost in organizing this plan, so that clubs and leagues may be formed all over the U.S.A. to accelerate the movements for good of the U.S.A. colored people.

In presenting the Indemnity and Land Bill to Congress we want 10,000,000 signatures of colored and white, to give impetus to this propaganda!

Picture if you can, men of our race, those of you who have any romance in your souls, or temporary flights of fancy, or dreams of blissful contentment, a country all our own. Say we will call it Moderna and ourselves Modernites or Modernitians, ruled by a king, and a monarchy can be an ideal government. Look at England to-day, whose king is the most powerful of earthly monarchs, and from modern ideas the most approaching the ideal of perfect peace-makers and to whom all of you, all races bow in submission. It speaks not badly for power in monarchy.

Picture if you can as I said our own country ruled by a king how grand! "From slave to king." The king with his ministers and courtiers, robed in beautiful flowing garments, dispensing justice righteous justice and encouragement to a people, who but yesterday could not go into the meanest restaurant, to ask and pay for food. Compelled to travel in cars set apart, as if for the beasts of the field, that he might not contaminate a still lower beast, but boasted a white skin.

Picture our king ruling over us by our united sanction. A king but, too, our servant our guide. Our kingdom sending out men of our race as ambassadors, proud to represent our little country, at the grand courts of the world, with our wives, and we have some ladies too that would grace any court of the world—I have seen many worse, but none better.

Picture our fêtes in magnificent halls and gardens over the door of which is no sign of "No colored people allowed here." Palaces, schools, industries, turning out our young ready and fitted for positions long denied them while those positions are ready and eagerly awaiting their sortie.

In which every accomplishment will find responsive demands, and no question raised as to "color." Yet those who still have a hankering for their white friends will still remember they are under their protection, but free from their ridicule and ostracism. I have heard it said on several occasions by our own people, Oh we are not capable of ruling ourselves. What monstrous rot and infidelity.

Look at Abyssinia with King Menlik, and they have not the advantages like we of a so-called high speed civilization. Still they have their picturesque court of Oriental splendor, of high potentates, and lesser nobles, gentry and citizens of noble and industrious characters. They defied and triumphed over a European modern nation, and to-day is allied with one of Europe's greatest empires.

We have Hayti with its black president ruling his own people. True civil differences arise at times amounting to war, but that is between themselves and invariably satisfactorily adjusted by themselves. Such things occur with the great nations, did you not fight in the Civil War? America, England, France, all all, have their internal troubles but it does not always stand for dismemberment, if still loyally cemented to the country.

Yes! we are fully capable and ready to rule ourselves.

Imagine the employment, the opening up of such a colony would entail.

In which every accomplishment, bought and borrowed from the highest of modern civilizations, would be brought into play, and everyone needed.

The raising up as if in a day, or a dream, by hands of fairies, a permanent kingdom in which Dinah, Hannah, and Uncle Ben would be transformed into Lady Hannia, Duchess Diana or Lord Ben Micaelas, with lesser nobles and gentry in their train, in a permanent and lasting country, in which a long tired submissive and oppressed people, might proudly end their days in peace, leaving everlasting monuments of triumph over tyranny and injustice to future posterity in black.

Arthur A. Anderson join the Colored Liberty League. Now we shall see who are the men willing to sacrifice all for the first principal of manhood not a "vote" but, "liberty."

31. THE GARVEY MOVEMENT DESCRIBED: "UP, YOU MIGHTY RACE!"

I asked, where is the black man's government? Where is his president, his country, and his ambassadors, his army, his navy, and his men of big affairs? I could not find them and then I declared, I will help make them.
. . . MARCUS GARVEY

Marcus Manasseh Garvey, tempestuous and flamboyant, was unique among Negro leaders. To begin with, he was *black*, an *immigrant,* and without much formal education—decidedly not

From Roi Ottley, 'NEW WORLD A-COMING' (Boston: Houghton Mifflin Co., 1943), chap. 7, pp. 68–81. Copyright 1943 by Roi Ottley. Reprinted by permission of Farrar, Straus & Giroux, Inc.

Du Bois' idea of Talented Tenth material. He was born in Jamaica, British West Indies, in 1887, the grandson of an African slave—a fact that was his proudest boast. Neighbors called him 'Ugly Mug.' He grew up under a color caste system— white, mulatto, and black—which even as a boy aroused his resentment, not only against whites but against mulattoes as well, and it was this resentment that was to be translated into one of the cardinal doctrines of the movement he was to lead. Indeed, it began his odyssey, at the age of twenty-one, in search of a place to escape color prejudice.

His wanderings took him to London, where he lived for several years working at his trade as a printer. Here he soon became acquainted with native Africans to whom he listened attentively while they described the exploitation and squalor of Africa amidst immense riches. It was probably here that Garvey first had dreams of an empire ruled by black men. At any rate he returned to Jamaica and led a printers' strike, but when the men compromised, he was thrown out of work permanently. He then shifted his emphasis to the establishment of a school, and in search of a plan read Booker T. Washington's inspiring autobiography, *Up from Slavery.* He wrote to the American educator and received an encouraging offer to come to the United States, but before he arrived in 1916 the Southern leader died.

A squat, ugly black man with intelligent eyes and big head, Marcus Garvey began to harangue loiterers along Lenox Avenue in the spring of 1917. Harlem ignored him. Worse, he was dismissed as an immigrant carpetbagger. Two years later an insane man dashed into his rooms in a beaten brownstone house on 135th Street near Lenox Avenue and shot him. The bullet grazed his forehead, but with a keen sense of publicity that was to characterize his entire extraordinary career, he rushed into the streets with the blood of the martyr coursing down his cheeks. The next day his assailant, captured and jailed by the police, leaped to his death from a prison window. The affair, involving a woman (later to become his wife), who attempted to shield him from his attacker, was given heroic proportions in the local press. And the name of Harlem's first messiah was on the lips of everyone. . . .

Garvey leaped into the ocean of black unhappiness at a most timely moment for a savior. He had witnessed the Negro's disillusionment mount with the progress of the World War. Negro soldiers had suffered all forms of Jim Crow, humiliation, discrimination, slander, and even violence at the hands of the white civilian population. After the war, there was a resurgence of Ku Klux Klan influence; another decade of racial hatred and open lawlessness had set in, and Negroes again were prominent among the victims. Meantime, administration leaders were quite pointed in trying to persuade Negroes that in spite of their full participation in the war effort they could expect no change in their traditional status in America. Newton D. Baker was particularly vocal on this issue. The liberal white citizens were disturbed by events, but took little action beyond viewing with alarm.

Negroes were more than ready for a Moses—one done in black preferably. Intellectuals of the race tried to rationalize the situation, but not so the broad masses; their acknowledged leader, Du Bois, had gone overboard with the war effort and now found himself estranged from his people. Negroes were faced with a choice between *racialism* and *radicalism*. Marcus Garvey settled the question for thousands by forming the Universal Negro Improvement Association, called U.N.I.A. for brevity, and preaching with great zeal for a pilgrimage of black men 'Back to Africa.' He rallied men to the slogan, 'Africa for Africans!'—for talk was then current about self-determination for subject peoples.

His voice was heard in every corner and crevice of the Black Belts of the country. Leaders like Du Bois who sought to *integrate* Negroes into American life were shocked and dismayed by such heresy, but helpless. Ignoring them, Garvey set up headquarters in Harlem and made his first appeal directly to the foreign-born elements in the community; not only the British West Indians but also the Spanish and French. They flocked to his banner, eventually to form the basic element of his movement. Next, he went on a tour that swept through thirty-eight states. He was acclaimed everywhere, Negroes seeing in him the inspired leader. When the little messiah returned to Harlem, with thousands following in his wake, he built Liberty Hall, a great zinc-roofed shed. Then, he started a weekly newspaper, the *Negro World,* which proved to be his most potent instrument for wielding opinion.

The character of this project deserves a brief word. It had a Spanish and French section and sold for five cents a copy in New York and ten cents elsewhere. Within a few months it had an international circulation. Usually the pages of the *Negro World,* some ten to sixteen, were crowded with 'the philosophy and opinions' of its editor. Edged between his long polemic articles were essays, reports of African and European affairs, patent medicine and beauty preparation advertisements (though skin-whitening ads were excluded), and occasionally a display of Lucky Strike cigarettes. His bombastic editorials referred to the 'glorious' history of the Negro, with particular emphasis on Africa's past regal splendor; recalled the slave struggles for freedom, and recounted stirring tales of the heroism of such Southern leaders of slave revolts as Denmark Vesey, Gabriel (Prosser), and Nat Turner. The exploits of long dead Zulu and Hottentot warriors who had fought against British rule were not forgotten, nor the histories of the Moorish and Ethiopian empires. Toussaint L'Ouverture's leadership of the Haitian Rebellion was stock copy. It was for this reason, perhaps, that the *Negro World* was cited in the report on radicalism made in 1919 by Attorney General A. Mitchell Palmer.

Marcus Garvey sought an economic solution of the Negro's problem through the establishment of Negro business. The Negro, he held, must become independent of white capital and white employers if he wants salvation. This was a page from the philosophy of Booker T. Washington, who had preached individual thrift and enterprise. His disciple, Garvey, envisioned an independent 'Black Economy' within the white capitalistic world, completely ignoring the fact that he himself was dependent on the large finance corporations and banks owned by whites for setting his projects in motion.

Tangible expression was given to his idea when he formed a Negro merchant marine, known as the Black Star Line, to develop trade relations among the darker peoples of the world. Ten million dollars was the announced need to capitalize the Black Star Line. Shares were sold to followers for five dollars each. While the pundits, according to Claude McKay, were proving the scheme a mathematical impossibility, Garvey proudly announced the acquisition of the first boat, the *Yarmouth*. It was purchased from the North American Steamship Company for one hundred and sixty-five thousand dollars and with proper fuss and feathers rechristened the *Frederick Douglass*. Negroes were thrilled. From every black belt in America they swarmed into Harlem to see (and indeed feel) the wonderful miracle. Thousands journeyed down to the Hudson River, where the boat was moored, and happily paid a half-dollar to go aboard and shake hands with the all-Negro crew.

'Up, you mighty race,' Marcus Garvey thundered in response to hosannas. 'You can accomplish what you will!'

The ship's launching was spectacular. Thousands were on hand, cheering and waving flags and dangerously jamming the pier. There were anxious moments until the ship slid out of port on its maiden voyage under the colors of the Black Star Line. Loaded down with a cargo of liquor to be delivered in Cuba, the boat foundered a few miles outside of Newport News. Five hundred cases of expensive whiskies and champagnes had to be thrown overboard to keep the ship afloat. When the news reached Garvey, he hotly denounced the crew for becoming drunk on the cargo and navigating dice instead of the ship. He charged the Negro captain with being in the pay of enemy white folks, and gained tremendous sympathy which he carefully exploited. Imperceptibly the emphasis of the movement shifted to the nationalistic scheme for the redemption of Africa.

'It is only a question of a few more years,' he solemnly assured his followers, 'when Africa will be completely colonized by Negroes, as Europe is by the white race. No one knows when the hour of Africa's redemption cometh. It is in the wind. It is coming. One day, like a storm, it will be here.'

Anticipating that great day, he formed a social order modeled on a somewhat feudal pattern, and called it the 'Court of Ethiopia.' Trusted aides and large financial contributors were elevated to the ranks of duke, duchess, and lady-in-waiting. He himself modestly assumed the title of 'Provisional President-General of Africa.' But his boldest stroke was the creation of a Black Religion with a Black God!

He had been a convert to the Roman Catholic faith, and for a time was a devout follower—it was in fact the Saint Mark's Roman Catholic Church which provided him with his first platform in the United States. But he felt that the logic of an all-black world demanded a *Black God*. So his official historians and theologians delved into Biblical writings, reconstructed the nativity of Jesus, properly documented their interpretation, and the African Orthodox Church emerged as the true church of the black man. The Reverend George Alexander McGuire, an imposing man who had kicked over the Episcopalian traces of dogma, was called from his Boston pulpit, and after being consecrated by a white archbishop of the Greek Orthodox Church, he was installed as Primate. The fundamental outlines of the Roman Catholic Church were borrowed, even to much of its ritual and liturgy, and the Holy Trinity acknowledged—in black, of course. An impressive ceremony was held at Liberty Hall, and a 'Special Form of Divine Service' was performed by His Grace, Archbishop McGuire, for the purpose of 'canonization' of the Lord Jesus Christ as 'the Black Man of Sorrow' and the Blessed Virgin Mary as a Black Madonna.

'You must forget the white gods,' Archbishop McGuire was heard to say. 'Erase the white gods from your hearts. We must go back to the native church, to our own true God.'

Since a chosen people must be undefiled, Marcus Garvey naturally pontificated that only those who were 'one hundred per cent Negroid' could hold office in the organization, and thus carried his all-black world to its logical conclusion—*racial purity*. Accordingly, he admonished both whites and blacks that the purity of the races was being endangered. 'It is the duty of the virtuous and morally pure of both the white and black races,' he declared, 'to thoughtfully and actively protect the future of the two peoples, by vigorously opposing the destructive propaganda and vile efforts of the miscegenationists of the white race, and their associates, the hybrids of the Negro race.'

A racial doctrine of this sort brought him the open support of the notorious E. S. Cox, of the Ku Klux Klan, and that of John Powell, of the Anglo-Saxon clubs. Both men spoke several times from the platform of Liberty Hall and extolled the Back-to-Africa Movement, its leader, and its racial-purity program. Negro leaders rained criticism on Garvey, some even saying he had entered into a secret deal with the Klan. A. Philip Randolph, then editor of the radical *Messenger* magazine and today president of the Brotherhood of Sleeping Car Porters, denounced him as an ally of anti-Negro forces, and cited the fact that he was the only Negro who could hold rallies—some mighty boisterous ones too—in Southern cities and not be beaten, driven out, or even lynched. Garvey replied with devastating frankness.

'I regard the Klan,' he countered, 'as a better friend of the race than all the groups of hypocritical whites put together. You may call me a Klansman if you will, but, potentially, every white man is a Klansman, as far as the Negro in competition with whites socially, economically, and politically is concerned, and there is no use lying about it.'

Not alone did he advocate that sharp racial lines be drawn between whites and blacks, but he also insisted upon divisions within the Negro race—between blacks and mulattoes. He formulated this policy under the false assumption that there were three distinct races in the United States—white, black, and mulatto—divisions which existed concretely in his native Jamaica. He began his anti-mulatto campaign with scorching attacks on the 'near-white' leaders of the N.A.A.C.P. In so doing he hoped to create a buffer class which would bear the brunt of race prejudice between whites and blacks. For a time this type of propaganda inflated the darker Negroes, and succeeded in driving a wedge between the blacks and light-complexioned Negroes. But the success of this policy was limited because

White Americans, unlike Englishmen, make no distinctions between mulattoes and blacks, nor do American Negroes.

Fanaticism soon took its obvious toll—there were casualties among the wayward. In the year of Garvey's greatest poularity —1923, to be exact—James W. H. Eason was tried and found guilty of 'acts unbecoming a high officer of the High Executive Council,' and he was promptly removed from his job. Smarting under his disgrace, he attempted to form a rival organization in New Orleans, where he and a disgruntled few set up headquarters. The challenge was met swiftly, inexorably. One evening as Eason made his way to a meeting, he was ambushed and assassinated. His assailants were never apprehended, though it was frankly said at the time that Garvey was in possession of the facts. The incident served to stifle further open revolt and sent his opponents underground for a while.

Garvey's movement had gathered terrific momentum, even to a detail like the manufacture of black baby dolls for children. Negroes swept into Harlem, carried on a tidal wave of race consciousness. The cotton-picker of the South, bending over his basket, the poor ignorant worker of the Delta, crushed beneath a load of prejudice, the domestic of the city, trudging wearily to white folks' kitchens, and even the peasant of the Caribbean islands, dispossessed from the land, lifted his head and cried, 'Let's go to Harlem and follow this Black Moses!' The organization's phenomenal growth was reflected by its reported worldwide membership of more than six million followers. A former official of the organization told me that actually the movement had *two* million 'active dues-paying members' and four million sympathizers scattered throughout the world.

As a youngster I witnessed the movement's first 'Universal Negro Convention' held in Harlem. It was a monster affair, almost approaching medieval splendor in regalia of lush colors. During the whole month of August, 1920, delegates from all the states, the West Indies, South America, and Africa assembled in Liberty Hall, in a demonstration that proved to be a series of rousing 'bravos' and 'hallelujahs' to the black leader. People were fascinated by all the bustle, color, and animation in the

streets. There were loud speeches, stock-selling from the curb-
stones, and indeed fisticuffs as men clashed.

'Is Garvey greater than Jesus Christ?' people asked.

'Give he a chance,' shot back his devout West Indian followers in their quaint English dialect. 'He's a young mon yet!'

Noisy meetings at Liberty Hall were climaxed by a magnificent parade in which more than fifty thousand 'Garveyites'
marched through Harlem. His Excellency, Marcus Garvey, Provisional President of Africa, led the demonstration bedecked in
a dazzling uniform of purple, green, and black, with gold braid,
and a thrilling hat with white plumes 'as long as the leaves of
Guinea grass.' He rode in a big, high-mounted black Packard
automobile and graciously, but with restraint becoming a sovereign, acknowledged the ovations of the crowds that lined
the sidewalks. Behind him rode His Grace, Archbishop Mc-
Guire, in silk robes of state, blessing the populace. Then, the
Black Nobility and Knight Commanders of the Distinguished
Order of the Nile followed, the hierarchy of the state, properly
attired in regalia drawn from a bold palette. Arrayed in gorgeous uniforms of black and green, trimmed with much gold
braid, came the smartly strutting African Legion; and in white,
the stretcher-bearing Black Cross nurses. Then came troops of
kilt-clad Boy and Girl Scouts, trailed by a multitude of bump-
tious black subjects.

Harlem was spellbound. For the first time white New York
became aware of the proportions of the movement, its implications, and indeed its divertissements. Marcus Garvey had become a world figure, and his movements and utterances were
noted by every European Power with possessions in Africa. He
sent a good-will greeting to Abd el Krim, the rebel leader of
Spanish Morocco; and advocated unity with all darker peoples
—in the Caribbeans, Africa, India, China, and Japan.

On his return from abroad, Claude McKay reported two interesting incidents in connection with the movement. When the
African Prince Kogo, darling of smart Parisian circles, embraced
the Back-to-Africa Movement, he was driven out of France;
and when Garvey elevated Gabriel Johnson, Negro mayor of

Monrovia, capital of Liberia, to the rank of 'High Potentate of Monrovia,' the title nearly got the poor man lynched by the black aristocracy.

Incidents like these were only minor swirls on the smooth stream of Garvey's nationalistic course. But he was hardly prepared for the first real surging wave which was eventually to engulf and finally wash away his organization. Early in 1923, after repeated complaints by Negroes, the federal government investigated the Black Star Line. Garvey was indicted soon afterward and put on trial for using the mails to defraud. Yet, with his amazing energy and daring, as James Weldon Johnson observed, he might have carried on longer. He had stirred the imagination of Negroes. But in hypnotizing many credulous people, he had also attracted numerous crafty men who sought to enrich themselves. It was upon the latter group that he laid the blame for his failure. The inescapable fact is that he himself made the fundamental blunder by advancing an amazingly meager design (indeed impossible idea)—not to mention the poor economics of the program—for colonizing the possessions of imperialist nations.

'The whole scheme of a black empire, in the raging sea of imperialism,' Randolph declared, 'would make it impossible to maintain power; nor would it bring liberation to Africa, for Negro exploiters and tyrants are as bad as white ones.'

In reality, the Back-to-Africa Movement was a restatement of colonization schemes advanced on three other occasions in the history of the United States. A plan to colonize Negroes in Africa was vigorously put forth by the American Colonization Society, early in the last century, having such sponsors as Henry Clay, Andrew Johnson, and Thomas Jefferson. Liberia was chosen as the Site. Negro opposition was immediate, militant, and widespread. Numerous protest meetings were held. One in Philadelphia in 1817 assumed the proportions of a national demonstration, when three thousand delegates attended and passed resolutions declaring it their right and intention to remain in the United States.

The next plan, ironically enough, was advanced by Lincoln. Before he signed the Emancipation Proclamation, he urged Congress to colonize black men in the West Indies, at an initial cost of twenty million dollars. Six hundred thousand dollars was appropriated and the government signed a contract with Bernard Kock, a promoter who had procured a lease on the island of Vache, off the coast of Haiti. He turned out to be 'an irresponsible and untruthful adventurer,' according to Lincoln, and his contract was canceled. The first boat sailed with a contingent of some five hundred men, women, and children. Kock, despite his reputation, was sent along to govern the colony. The venture proved to be a miserable failure. Two hundred colonists died, and Kock was driven from the island. Lincoln brought back the survivors under a beating shower of abolitionist criticism. The bill for Negro colonization was repealed, not to be heard of again until President Grant's administration; and finally in 1939 when the Mississippi Senator Bilbo, with typical obtuseness, introduced a bill to colonize Negroes in Africa.

Garvey went on trial before Judge Julian Mack in 1923, while Arthur Brisbane, the Hearst columnist, protested that to hold him was equivalent to 'jailing a rainbow.' The trial lasted about a month, during which time Garvey dismissed his Negro attorney and hired a white one. Meanwhile the government's witnesses placed the total deficit of the Black Star Line at seven hundred thousand dollars—though Garvey's wife and secretary, Amy Jacques, estimated that between 1919 and 1921, he took in ten million dollars. The government revealed that there were more than forty thousand stockholders in this project—and there were several such projects.

Besides the ill-fated *Frederick Douglass,* two ships had been purchased—the *Kanawha,* a former H. H. Rogers yacht which was bought for sixty thousand dollars; and the *Shadyside,* a discarded Hudson River steamer, for which thirty-five thousand dollars was paid. Driven by his critics Garvey had acquired them when ships were at a premium, many being needed at the time to bring home the A.E.F. But soon afterward the demand fell off, and they became a drug on the market. The Black Star Line, such as it was, was worth only the scrap iron in its construction.

Plenty of cash had been splashed about, but the government was unable to find any tangible assets. There were none! Garvey testified that all the money he had in the world was some forty dollars and two hundred and eighty-nine shares of his own worthless stock. In his summation to the jury, the psychological factors that underscored this wild spending were touched upon by Henry Lincoln Johnson, a Negro attorney who represented one of Garvey's co-defendants. 'If every Negro,' he said, 'could have put every dime, every penny into the sea, and if he might get in exchange the knowledge that he was somebody, that he meant something in the world, he would gladly do it. . . . The Black Star Line was a loss in money but it was a gain in soul.'

The case against Garvey was admittedly weak, but he succumbed to the temptation to strut before a crowded courtroom and to see his name on the front pages of the New York newspapers. He brushed aside his lawyer, and handled the case himself. He cross-examined himself and the witnesses, and corrected their English; he harangued the judge and jury, and was finally convicted.

But this was hardly the end of this magnificent dreamer of empire. Released on bail, pending appeal, he rallied his followers in a terrific demonstration at the old Madison Square Garden and they quickly subscribed more than a hundred thousand dollars. The next day the Black Cross Navigation Company was formed and a ship, the *General Goethals,* was purchased from the Panama-American Railroad Company. The vessel was in good condition, and the price paid for it was said to be one hundred and seventy thousand dollars. Renamed the *Booker T. Washington,* the ship sailed from New York with passengers and United States mail, but upon arrival at a Caribbean port it was impounded for debt and never seen again.

The Black Moses had a sudden change of heart—but too late. Up to this point, the central idea of his program had meant

absolute abdication of the Negro's rights and place in American
life. He reversed his stand completely and urged his followers
to take immediate interest in American politics and urged his
foreign-born members to become naturalized. He formed the
Universal Negro Political Union and in 1924 issued a nation-
wide list of candidates for whom his followers were to vote.
But new lawsuits brought the final financial collapse. Meantime Garvey lost his appeal, was fined a thousand dollars and
sentenced to serve five years in prison. He entered Atlanta Penitentiary in 1925. Two years later President Coolidge—whose
election he had supported—pardoned him and he was deported
as an undesirable alien.

Without its dynamic little leader, the U.N.I.A. fell into quar-
reling segments. From his island exile in Jamaica, Marcus Garvey made futile efforts to re-form his movement. But without
the vast stage of the Black Metropolis and the loud acoustics
of Black America—to say nothing of the New York press—his
voice failed to carry. He finally gave up and went to London to
begin again. He died there in obscurity in 1940, deserted by
his followers, but holding tenaciously to his Pan-African dream
—though he was never to see the land of his ancestors. Nor
were his followers to set eyes on the Promised Land. The truth
is, a few may have consented to making an excursion to Africa,
but the vast majority had no idea of leaving the United States.
The dream of an all-black nation had simply given a sorely
driven people a new and abundant dignity, enough to squander.

Concretely, the movement set in motion what was to become
the most compelling force in Negro life—race and color consciousness, which is today that ephemeral thing that inspires
'race loyalty'; the banner to which Negroes rally; the chain that
binds them together. It has propelled many a political and
social movement and stimulated racial internationalism. It is
indeed a philosophy, an ethical standard by which most things
are measured and interpreted. It accounts for much constructive
belligerency today.

'Marcus Garvey opened windows in the minds of Negroes!'
one of his followers said.

32. MARCUS GARVEY:
"ETHIOPIA SHALL ONCE MORE
SEE THE DAY OF HER GLORY"

A. LACK OF CO-OPERATION IN THE NEGRO RACE

It is so hard, so difficult to find men who will stick to a purpose, who will maintain a principle for the worth of that principle, for the good of that purpose, and if there is a race that needs such men in the world today, God Almighty knows it is the race of which I am a member.

The race needs men of vision and ability. Men of character and above all men of honesty, and that is so hard to find.

The greatest stumbling block in the way of progress in the race has invariably come from within the race itself. The monkey wrench of destruction as thrown into the cog of Negro Progress, is not thrown so much by the outsider as by the very fellow who is in our fold, and who should be the first to grease the wheel of progress rather than seeking to impede it.

But notwithstanding the lack of sympathetic co-operation, I have one consolation—That I cannot get away from the race, and so long as I am in the race and since I have sense and judgment enough to know what affects the race affects me, it is my duty to help the race to clear itself of those things that affect us in common.

From Amy Jacques-Garvey, ed., PHILOSOPHY AND OPINIONS OF MARCUS GARVEY, 2 vols. (New York: Universal Publishing House, 1923, 1925), I, 37; II, 55–61; I, 38–39.

B. AN EXPOSÉ OF THE
CASTE SYSTEM AMONG NEGROES

(Written from the Tombs Prison August 31st, 1923)
The policy of the Universal Negro Improvement Association is so clean-cut, and my personal views are so well known, that no one, for even one moment, could reasonably accuse us of having any other desire than that of working for a united Negro race.

The Program of the Universal Negro Improvement Association is that of drawing together, into one universal whole, all the Negro peoples of the world, with prejudice toward none. We desire to have every shade of color, even those with one drop of African blood, in our fold; because we believe that none of us, as we are, is responsible for our birth; in a word, we have no prejudice against ourselves in race. We believe that every Negro racially is just alike, and, therefore, we have no distinction to make, hence wherever you see the Universal Negro Improvement Association you will find us giving every member of the race an equal chance and opportunity to make good.

Unfortunately, there is a disposition on the part of a certain element of our people in America, the West Indies and Africa, to hold themselves up as the "better class" or "privileged" group on the caste of color.

This subject is such a delicate one that no one is honest enough to broach it, yet the evil of it is working great harm to our racial solidarity, and I personally feel it my duty to right now bring it to the attention of all concerned. The Universal Negro Improvement Association is founded on truth, and, therefore, anything that would menace or retard the race must be gotten out of the way, hence our stand in this direction. During the early days of slavery our people were wrested from the bosom of our native land—Africa—and brought into these climes. For centuries, against their will, our mothers were subjected to the most cruel and unfair treatment, the result of which has created among us a diversity of colors and types, to the end that we have become the most mixed race in the world.

The abuse of our race

The abuse of our race was, up to eighty-five years ago in the West Indies and fifty-seven years ago in America, beyond our control, because we were then but chattel slaves of our masters; but since emancipation we have had full control of our own moral-social life and cannot, therefore, complain against anyone other than ourselves, for any social or moral wrongs inflicted upon us.

The Universal Negro Improvement Association realizes that it is now our duty to socially and morally steady ourselves, hence our desire to bring about a united race with one moral code and principle. The types in our race should not be blameable to our generation, but to the abuse and advantage taken of us in the past; but that should not be reason for us to further open ourselves to a continuation of this abuse and thereby wreck our racial pride and self-respect. The Universal Negro Improvement Association believes that the time has come for us to call a halt, and thus steady ourselves on the basis of race and not be allowed to drift along in the world as the outcasts or lepers of society, to be laughed at by every other race beneath their social breath.

Near whites

Some of us in America, the West Indies and Africa believe that the nearer we approach the white man in color the greater our social standing and privilege and that we should build up an "aristocracy" based upon caste of color and not achievement in race. It is well known, although no one is honest enough to admit it, that we have been, for the past thirty years at least, but more so now than ever, grading ourselves for social honor and distinction on the basis of color. That the average success in the race has been regulated by color and not by ability and merit; that we have been trying to get away from the pride of race into the atmosphere of color worship, to the damaging extent that the whole world has made us its laughing stock.

There is no doubt that a race that doesn't respect itself forfeits the respect of others, and we are in the moral-social position now of losing the respect of the whole world.

There is a subtle and underhand propaganda fostered by a few men of color in America, the West Indies and Africa to destroy the self-respect and pride of the Negro race by building up what is commonly known to us as a "blue vein" aristocracy and to foster same as the social and moral standard of the race. The success of this effort is very much marked in the West Indies, and coming into immediate recognition in South Africa, and is now gaining much headway in America under the skillful leadership of the National Association for the Advancement of "Colored" People and their silent but scattered agents.

The observant members of our race must have noticed within recent years a great hostility between the National Association for the Advancement of "Colored" People and the Universal "Negro" Improvement Association, and must have wondered why Du Bois writes so bitterly against Garvey and vice versa. Well, the reason is plainly to be seen after the following explanation:

Group that hates Negro

Du Bois represents a group that hates the Negro blood in its veins, and has been working subtly to build up a caste aristocracy that would socially divide the race into two groups: One the superior because of color caste, and the other the inferior, hence the pretentious work of the National Association for the Advancement of "Colored" People. The program of deception was well arranged and under way for success when Marcus Garvey arrived in America, and he, after understudying the artful doctor and the group he represented, fired a "bomb" into the camp by organizing the Universal "Negro" Improvement Association to cut off the wicked attempt of race deception and distinction, and, in truth, to build up a race united in spirit and ideal, with the honest desire of adjusting itself to its own moral-social pride and national self-respect. When Garvey arrived in America and visited the office of the National Association for the Advancement of "Colored" People to interview Du Bois, who was regarded as a leader of the Negro people, and who had recently visited the West Indies, he was dumfounded on approach to the office to find that but for Mr. Dill, Du Bois, himself and the office boy, he could not tell whether he was in a white office or that of the National Association for the Advancement of "Colored" People. The whole staff was either white or very near white, and thus Garvey got his first shock of the advancement hypocrisy. There was no representation of the race there that anyone could recognize. The advancement meant that you had to be as near white as possible, otherwise there was no place for you as stenographer, clerk or attendant in the office of the National Association for the Advancement of "Colored" People. After a short talk with Du Bois, Garvey became so disgusted with the man and his principles that the thought he never contemplated entered his mind—that of remaining in America to teach Du Bois and his group what real race pride meant.

Garvey at N.A.A.C.P.'s office

When Garvey left the office of the National Association for the Advancement of "Colored" People, to travel through and study the social life of Negro America, he found that the policy of the Association was well observed in business and professional life, as well as in the drawing room, etc., all over the country. In restaurants, drug stores and offices all over the nation where our people were engaged in business it was discoverable that those employed were the very "lightest" members of the race—as waitresses, clerks and stenographers. Garvey asked, "What's the matter? Why were not black, brown-skin and mulatto girls employed?" And he was told it was "for the good of the trade." That to have trade it was necessary and incumbent to have "light" faces, as near white as possible. But the shock did not stop there. In New York, Boston, Washington and Detroit, Garvey further discovered the activities of the "Blue Vein Society" and the "Colonial Club." The West Indian "lights" formed the "Colonial Club" and the American "lights" the "Blue Vein" Society. The "Colonial Club" would give annual balls besides regular or monthly *soirees* and no one less than a quadroon would be admitted, and gentlemen below that complexion were only admitted if they were lawyers, doctors or very successful business men with plenty of "cash," who were known to uphold the caste aristocracy. At St. Philip's Church, New York, where the Very Rev. Dr. Daniels held sway and dominion, the "society" had things so arranged that even though this man was a brown-skin clergyman, and his rector a very near white gentleman, he had to draw the line and give the best seats in the church and the places of honor to the "Blue Veins" and the others would have a "look in" when they, by fawning before and "humbling" themselves and by giving lavishly to the church, admitted the superiority of caste. (By the way, Dr. Daniels was also an executive officer or director of the National Association for the Advancement of "Colored" People.) In Washington one or two of the churches did the same thing, but in Detroit the Very Rev. "Bob" Bagnall, now director of branches of the National Association for the Advancement of "Colored" people held sway. In his church no dark person could have a seat in the front, and, to test the truthfulness of it after being told, Garvey, incog, one Sunday night attempted to occupy one of the empty seats, not so very near the front, and the effort nearly spoiled the whole service, as Brother Bob, who was then ascending the pulpit, nearly lost his "balance" to see such a face so near the "holy of holies." Brother Bob was also an officer of the National Association for the Advancement of "Colored" People. On Garvey's return to New York he made (incog) a similar test at St. Philip's Church one Sunday, and the Rev. Daniels was nearly ready to fight.

Now, what does all this mean? It is to relate the hidden program and motive of the National Association for the Advancement of "Colored" People and to warn Negro America of not being deceived by a group of men who have as much love for the Negro blood in their veins as the devil has for holy water.

Scheme to destroy race

The National Association for the Advancement of "Colored" People is a scheme to destroy the Negro Race, and the leaders of it hate Marcus Garvey, because he has discovered them at their game and because the Universal Negro Improvement Association, without any prejudice to color or caste, is making headway in bringing all the people together for their common good. They hate Garvey because the Universal Negro Improvement Association and the Black Star Line employed every shade of color in the race, according to ability and merit, and put the N.A.A.C.P. to shame for employing only the "lightest" of the race. They hate Garvey because he forced them to fill Shiladay's place with a Negro. They hate Garvey because they had to employ "black" Pickens to cover up their scheme after Garvey had discovered it; they hate Garvey because they have had to employ brown-skin "Bob" Bagnall to make a showing to the people that they were doing the "right" thing by them; they hate Garvey because he has broken up the "Pink Tea Set"; they hate Garvey because they had been forced to recognize mulatto, brown and black talent in the association equally with the lighter element; they hate Garvey because he is teaching the unity of race, without color superiority or prejudice. The gang thought that they would have been able to build up in America a buffer class between whites and Negroes, and thus in another fifty years join with the powerful race and crush the blood of their mothers, as is being done in South Africa and the West Indies.

The imprisonment of Garvey is more than appears on the surface, and the National Association for the Advancement of Colored People knows it. Du Bois and those who lead the Association are skillful enough to be using the old method of getting the "other fellow" to destroy himself, hence the activities of "brown-skin" Bagnall and "black" Pickens. Walter White, whom we can hardly tell from a Southern gentleman who lives with a white family in Brooklyn, is kept in the background, but dark Bagnall, Pickens and Du Bois are pushed to the front to make the attack, so that there would be no suspicion of the motive. They are to drive hard and hot, and then the silent influence would bring up the rear, hence the slogan, "Garvey must go!" and the vicious attacks in the different magazines by Pickens, Du Bois and Bagnall.

Garvey caught the tune

Gentlemen, you are very smart, but Garvey has caught your tune. The conspiracy to destroy the Negro race, is so well organized that the moment anything interferes with their program there springs up a simultaneous action on the part of the leaders. It will be observed that in the September issue of the "Crisis" is published on the very last page of its news section what purports to be the opinion of a Jamaica paper about Marcus Garvey and his case. The skillful editor of the "Crisis," Dr. Du Bois, reproduces that part of the article that would tend to show the opinion about Garvey in his own country taken from a paper called the "Gleaner," (edited by one Herbert George de Lisser) and not the property of Negroes.

The article in the original was clipped from the "Gleaner" when it appeared, and was sent by a friend to Garvey, so that he knew all that appeared in it. In it the editor extolled the leadership and virtues of Dr. Du Bois, and said it was the right kind of leadership for the American Negro people, and bitterly denounced Garvey. Du Bois published that part that denounced Garvey, but suppressed the part that gave him the right of leadership; and he failed to enlighten his readers that the editor of the "Gleaner" is a very light man, who hates the Negro blood of his mother and who is part of the international scheme to foster the Blue Vein Society scheme. Dr. Du Bois failed to further enlighten his readers that he visited Jamaica and was part of the "Colonial Society" scheme; he also failed to state that in the plan De Lisser is to "hold down" the West Indian end of the "caste scheme" and he and others to "hold down" the American end, while their agents "hold down" the South African section.

Entire race must get together

But now we have reached the point where the entire race must get together and stop these schemers at their game. Whether we are light, yellow, black or what not, there is but one thing for us to do, and that is to get together and build up a race. God made us in His own image and He had some purpose when He thus created us. Then why should we seek to destroy ourselves? If a few Du Boises and De Lissers do not want their progeny to remain of our race, why not be satisfied to abide their time and take their peaceful exit? But why try in this subtle manner to humiliate and destroy our race?

We as a people, have a great future before us. Ethiopia shall once more see the day of her glory, then why destroy the chance and opportunity simply to be someone else?

Let us work and wait patiently, for our day of racial triumph will come. Let us not divide ourselves into castes, but let us all work together for the common good. Let us remember the sorrow of our mothers. Let us not forget that it is our duty to remedy any wrong that has already been done, and not ourselves perpetuate the evil of race destruction. To change our race is no credit. The Anglo-Saxon doesn't want to be a Japanese; the Japanese doesn't want to be a Negro. Then, in the name of God and all that is holy, why should we want to be somebody else?

Let the National Association for the Advancement of Colored People stop its hypocrisy and settle down to real race uplift.

If Dr. Du Bois, Johnson, Pickens and Bagnall do not know, let me tell them that they are only being used to weaken the race, so that in another fifty or a hundred years the race can easily be wiped out as a social, economic and political force or "menace."

The people who are directing the affairs of the National Association for the Advancement of "Colored" People are keen observers, it takes more than ordinary intelligence to penetrate their motive, hence you are now warned.

All the "gas" about anti-lynching and "social equality" will not amount to a row of pins, in fact, it is only a ruse to raise money to capitalize the scheme and hide the real motive. Negroes, "watch your step" and save yourselves from deception and subsequent extermination.

C. THE TRUE SOLUTION
OF THE NEGRO PROBLEM—1922

As far as Negroes are concerned, in America we have the problem of lynching, peonage and dis-franchisement.

In the West Indies, South and Central America we have the problem of peonage, serfdom, industrial and political governmental inequality.

In Africa we have, not only peonage and serfdom, but outright slavery, racial exploitation and alien political monopoly.

We cannot allow a continuation of these crimes against our race. As four hundred million men, women and children, worthy of the existence given us by the Divine Creator, we are determined to solve our own problem, by redeeming our Motherland Africa from the hands of Alien exploiters and found there a government, a nation of our own, strong enough to lend protection to the members of our race scattered all over the world, and to compel the respect of the nations and races of the earth.

Do they lynch Englishmen, Frenchmen, Germans or Japanese? No. And Why? Because these people are represented by great governments, mighty nations and empires, strongly organized. Yes, and ever ready to shed the last drop of blood and spend the last penny in the national treasury to protect the honor and integrity of a citizen outraged anywhere.

Until the Negro reaches this point of national independence, all he does as a race will count for naught, because the prejudice that will stand out against him even with his ballot in his hand, with his industrial progress to show, will be of such an overwhelming nature as to perpetuate mob violence and mob rule, from which he will suffer, and which he will not be able to stop with his industrial wealth and with his ballot.

You may argue that he can use his industrial wealth and his ballot to force the government to recognize him, but he must understand that the government is the people. That the majority of the people dictate the policy of governments, and if the majority are against a measure, a thing, or a race, then the government is impotent to protect that measure, thing or race.

If the Negro were to live in this Western Hemisphere for another five hundred years he would still be outnumbered by other races who are prejudiced against him. He cannot resort to the government for protection for government will be in the hands of the majority of the people who are prejudiced against him, hence for the Negro to depend on the ballot and his industrial progress alone, will be hopeless as it does not help him when he is lynched, burned, jim-crowed and segregated. The future of the Negro therefore, outside of Africa, spells ruin and disaster.

The rhetoric of protest
and revolution

Although the era from the 1880s on was dominated increasingly by an ideology of accommodation, the protest tradition always maintained some vitality. And in an era marked by a pervasive belief in the value of self-help and racial solidarity, programs for the achievement of citizenship rights were often couched in these terms. This was particularly true of the Afro-American League, founded in 1890 by the militant editor of the New York *Age*, T. Thomas Fortune.

The organization was to have a curious history. It became defunct before the middle of the decade, and was revived in 1898 as the Afro-American Council. In many respects it was a continuation of the earlier convention movement, serving as a platform for most of the race's best-known leaders and spokesmen. Early in the twentieth century it was captured by Booker T. Washington, and for several years its annual resolutions were far less militant than before, although they continued to ask explicitly for the black man's full Constitutional rights. Finally, the Council became a battleground in which the conservative supporters of Booker T. Washington were challenged by the small but rising protest movement among the Negro intellectuals. The latter were victorious in 1908, but this victory only paved the way for the death of the Council a year or so later.

Actually, the Council accomplished little as an organization, though it was the vehicle through which Washington secretly attacked the disfranchisement constitutions of the southern states in 1903–1904. As well as being a forum for the most distinguished persons of the race for nearly two decades, it was

significant in that it exemplified—and explicitly articulated
—the view that only through united collective efforts,
through race unity and self-help, could black men
achieve their citizenship rights.

The speech given by T. Thomas Fortune at the founding
convention of the Afro-American League in 1890 sets forth
this philosophy (Document 33). Beyond that it was a clarion
call to action, a trenchant advocacy of agitation, even
revolution. Fortune, the most brilliant black editor of the
period, during the 1880s had been probably the most radical.
In fact he was the outstanding Negro representative of the
native American radicalism exemplified by men like Henry
George. In the following years Fortune was to become
entangled in a complex web of relationships with Booker T.
Washington, but his speech at the founding meeting of
the League, delivered when he stood at the far left wing of
Negro thought, is an able fusion of the doctrine of agitation
with the ideology of self-help and racial solidarity.

33. T. THOMAS FORTUNE:
"WE KNOW OUR RIGHTS . . . AND
HAVE THE COURAGE TO DEFEND THEM"

Ladies and Gentlemen of the Afro-American Leagues—We are
here to-day, as representatives of 8,000,000 freemen, who know
our rights and have the courage to defend them. We have met
here to-day to emphasize the fact that the past condition of
dependence and helplessness upon men who have used us for

From an address of T. Thomas Fortune in OFFICIAL COMPILATION
OF PROCEEDINGS OF THE AFRO-AMERICAN LEAGUE
NATIONAL CONVENTION, . . . 1890 (Chicago: J. C. Battles and
R. B. Cabbell, 1890), pp. 8–18.

selfish and unholy purposes, who have murdered and robbed and outraged us, must be reversed. . . .

Fellow-members of the League, I congratulate you upon your presence here. I congratulate you upon the high resolve, the manly inspiration, which impelled you to this spot. I congratulate you that you have aroused from the lethargy of the past, and that you now stand face to face, brave men and true, with the awful fact that "Who would be free must themselves strike the first blow." I congratulate you that you now recognize the fact that a great work remains for you to do, and that you are determined, with the countenance of Jehovah, to do it. And, finally, I congratulate myself that I have been chosen as the humble spokesman to voice at this time and in this manner the high resolves which move you as one man to perfect an organization which shall secure to ourselves and to our children the blessings of citizenship so generally denied us.

The spirit of agitation which has brought us together here comprehends in its vast sweep the entire range of human history. The world has been rocked in the cradle of agitation from Moses to Gladstone. . . .

Apathy leads to stagnation. The arsenal, the fort, the warrior are as necessary as the school, the church, the newspapers and the public forum of debate. It is a narrow and perverted philosophy which condemns as a nuisance agitators. It is this sort of people who consider nothing to be sacred which stands in the pathway of the progress of the world. Like John crying in the wilderness, they are the forerunners of change in rooted abuses which revolutionize society.

Demosthenes, thundering against the designs of Philip of Macedon upon the liberties of Greece; Cicero, holding up to scorn and ridicule the schemes of Cataline against the freedom of Rome; Oliver Cromwell, baring his sturdy breast to the arrows of royalty and nobility to preserve to Englishmen the rights contained in Magna Charta; Patrick Henry, fulminating against the arrogant and insolent encroachments of Great Britain upon the rights of the American colonies; Nat Turner, rising from the dust of slavery and defying the slave oligarchy of Virginia, and John Brown, resisting the power of the United States in a heroic effort to break the chains of the bondsman—these are some of the agitators who have voiced the discontent of their times at the peril of life and limb and property. Who shall cast the stone of reproach at these noblest children of the race? Who shall say they were not heroes born to live forever in the annals of song and story?

Revolutions are of many sorts. They are either silent and unobservable, noiseless as the movement of the earth on its axes, or loud and destructive, shaking the earth from center to circumference, making huge gaps in the map of earth, changing the face of empires, subverting dynasties and breaking fetters asunder or riveting them anew.

Jesus Christ may be regarded as the chief spirit of agitation and innovation. He himself declared, "I come not to bring peace, but a sword."

St. Paul, standing upon Mars Hill, read the death sentence of Greek and Roman mythology in the simple sentence, "Whom ye ignorantly worship him I declare unto you."

A portion of mankind remains always conservative, while the other portion is moved by the spirit of radicalism; and no man can predict where the conflict may lead when once the old idea and the new one conflict, and must needs appeal to the logic of revolution to arbitrate between them. Few Romes are large enough to hold a Caesar and a Brutus. The old idea and the new idea, the spirit of freedom and the spirit of tyranny and oppression cannot live together without friction. The agitator must never be in advance of his times. The people must be prepared to receive the message he brings them. The harvest must be ripe for the sickle when the reaper enters the field.

As it was in ancient Greece and Rome, so it is in modern Europe and America. The just cause does not always prevail. The John Browns and the Nat Turners do not always find the people ready to receive the tidings of great joy they bring them. . . .

Fellow-members of the League, it is matter of history that the 'abolition of slavery' was the fruit of the fiercest and most pro-

tracted agitation in the history of social reforms. Begun practically in 1816 by Benjamin Lundy, having been the chief bone
of contention at the very birth of the republic, the agitation for
the emancipation of the slave did not cease until Abraham
Lincoln issued the Emancipation Proclamation in 1863. When
emancipation was an established fact, when the slave had been
made a freeman and the freeman had been made a citizen, the
nation reached the conclusion that its duty was fully discharged.
A reaction set in after the second election of Gen. Grant to the
presidency in 1872, and terminated after the election of Mr.
Hayes in 1876, when the Afro-American citizen was turned over
to the tender mercies of his late masters—deserted by the
nation, deserted by the party he had served in peace and in
war, left poor and defenceless to fight a foe who had baffled
the entire nation through four years of bloody and destructive
war. . . .

Ladies and gentlemen, we have been robbed of the honest
wages of our toil; we have been robbed of the substance of our
citizenship by murder and intimidation; we have been outraged
by enemies and deserted by friends; and because in a society
governed by law, we have been true to the law, true to treacherous friends, and as true in distrust of our enemies, it has been
charged upon us that we are not made of the stern stuff which
makes the Anglo-Saxon race the most consummate masters
of hypocrisy, of roguery, of insolence, of arrogance, and of cowardice, in the history of races.

Was ever race more unjustly maligned than ours? Was ever
race more shamelessly robbed than ours? Was ever race used
to advance the political and pecuniary fortunes of others as
ours? Was ever race so patient, so law abiding, so uncomplain-
ing as ours?

Ladies and gentlemen, it is time to call a halt. It is time to begin a fight fire with fire. It is time to stand shoulder to shoulder
as men. It is time to rebuke the treachery of friends in the only
way that treachery should be rebuked. It is time to face the
enemy and fight him inch by inch for every right he denies us.

We have been patient so long that many believe that we are

incapable of resenting insult, outrage and wrong; we have so long accepted uncomplainingly all that injustice and cowardice and insolence heaped upon us, that many imagine that we are compelled to submit and have not the manhood necessary to resent such conduct. When matters assume this complexion, when oppressors presume too far upon the forebearance and the helplessness of the oppressed, the condition of the people affected is critical indeed. Such is our condition to-day. Because it is true; because we feel that something must be done to change the condition; because we are tired of being kicked and cuffed by individuals, made the scapegoats of the law, used by one party as an issue and by another as a stepping stone to place and power, and elbowed at pleasure by insolent corporations and their minions, corporations which derive their valuable franchises in part by consent of these very people they insult and outrage—it is because of the existence of these things that we are assembled here to-day—determined to perfect an organization whose one mission shall be to labor by every reasonable and legal means to right the wrongs complained of, until not one right justly ours under the constitution is denied us.

Ladies and gentlemen, I stand here to-day and assert in all soberness that we shall no longer accept in silence a condition which degrades our manhood and makes a mockery of our citizenship. I believe I voice the sentiments of each member of the League here assembled when I assert that from now and hence we shall labor as one man, inspired with one holy purpose, to wage relentless opposition to all men who would degrade our manhood and who would defraud us of the benefits of citizenship; guaranteed alike to all born upon this soil or naturalization, by the constitution which has been cemented and made indestructible by our blood in every war, foreign or domestic, waged by this grand Republic. . . .

There come periods in the history of every people when the necessity of their affairs makes it imperative that they take such steps as shall show to the world that they are worthy to be free, and therefore entitled to the sympathy of all mankind and to the co-operation of all lovers of justice and fair play. To do this they must unequivocally show that while they may solicit the sympathy and co-operation of mankind, they have the intelligence and courage to know what are their rights and to manfully contend for them, even though that sympathy and co-operation be ungenerously denied them.

I am in no sense unmindful of the vastness of the undertaking; but this, instead of being a drawback, is rather an incentive to prosecute the matter with more earnestness and persistence.

I now give in consecutive order the reasons which, in my opinion, justify the organization of the National Afro-American League, to-wit:

1. The almost universal suppression of our ballot in the South, and consequent "taxation without representation," since in the cities, counties and states where we have undisputed preponderating majorities of the voting population we have, in the main, no representation, and therefore no voice in the making and enforcing the laws under which we live.

2. The universal and lamentable reign of lynch and mob law, of which we are made the victims, especially in the South, all the more aggravating because all the machinery of the law making and enforcing power is in the hands of those who resort to such outrageous, heinous and murderous violations of the law.

3. The unequal distribution of school funds, collected from all taxpayers alike, and to the equal and undivided benefits of which all are alike entitled.

4. The odious and demoralizing penitentiary system of the South, with its chain gangs, convict leases and indiscriminate mixing of males and females.

5. The almost universal tyranny of common carrier corporations in the South—railroad, steamboat and other—in which the common rights of men and women are outraged and denied by the minions of these corporations, acting under implicit orders in most cases, as well as by common passengers, who take the matter in their own hands as often as they please, and are in no instances pursued and punished by the lawful authorities.

6. The discrimination practiced of those who conduct places

of public accommodation, and are granted a license for this purpose, such as keepers of inns, hotels and conductors of theaters and kindred places of amusement, where one man's money, all things being equal, should usually be as good as another's.

7. The serious question of wages, caused in the main by the vicious industrial system in the South, by the general contempt employers feel for employes, and by the overcrowded nature of the labor market.

These matters reach down into the very life of our people; they are fundamentally the things which in all times have moved men to associate themselves together in civil society for mutual benefit and protection, to restrain the rapacious and unscrupulous and to protect the weak, the timid and the virtuous; and whenever and wherever a condition of affairs obtains when these principles are disregarded and outraged, it becomes the imperative duty of the aggrieved to take such steps for their correction as the condition of affairs seems to warrant.

I know, ladies and gentlemen of the league, that those who are looking to this organization, loyal people in every section of the country, for some sensible action which shall assist in solving the great problems which confront us, as well as the croaking, skeptical few, who do not expect that we shall be able to advance or to accomplish anything which shall survive the hour of our adjournment, have their eyes upon us. I have confidence in the great race of which I am proud to be a member. I have confidence in its wisdom and its patriotism, and in its self-sacrifice for the common good. I have faith in the God who rules in the affairs of men, and who will not leave us alone to our own devices if we shall make an honest effort to assist ourselves. Thus fortitude in my faith, what have I to propose as remedies for some if not all of the evils against which we have to contend? It shall not be said that I have called you here to a barren feast; it shall not be said by friend or foe that I am an impracticable visionary, a man chasing shadows—a man who denounces the fearful structure in which we abide and would tear it down without offering at least a substitute to replace it.

I have pondered long and seriously on the evils which beset us, and I have sought, as light was given me, for an antidote to them, if such there be. I lay them before you, and you are here to adopt or reject them. I propose, then,

1. The adoption by this league of an Afro-American Bank, with central offices in some one of the great commercial centres of the republic and branches all over the country. We need to concentrate our earnings, and a bank is the proper place to concentrate them. And I shall submit a bank scheme which I have devised in the hope to meet the requirements of the situation.

I propose (2) the establishment of a Bureau of Emigration. We need to scatter ourselves more generally throughout the republic.

I propose (3) the establishment of a committee on legislation. We need to have a sharp eye upon the measures annually proposed in the federal and state legislatures affecting us and our interests, and there are laws everywhere in the republic the repeal of which must engage our best thought and effort.

I propose (4) the establishment of a bureau of technical industrial education. We need trained artisans, educated farmers and laborers more than we need educated lawyers, doctors, and loafers on the street corners. The learned professions are overcrowded. There is not near so much room at the top as there was in the days of Daniel Webster.

And I propose (5) lastly the establishment of a bureau of cooperative industry. We need to buy the necessaries of life cheaper than we can command them in many states. We need to stimulate the business instinct, the commercial predisposition of the race. We not only want a market for the products of our industry, but we want and must have a fair, and a living return for them.

To my mind the solution of the problems which make this league a necessity is to be found in the five propositions here stated. Their successful execution will require the very highest

order of executive ability and the collection and disbursement
of a vast sum of money. Have we brains and the necessary capital to put these vast enterprises into successful motion? I think
we have. There are 8,000,000 of us in this country. Some of us
are rich and some of us are poor. Some of us are wise and some
of us are foolish. Let us all—the rich and the poor, the wise
and the foolish—resolve to unite and pull together, and the results will speak for themselves. Let us destroy the dead weight
of poverty and ignorance which pulls us down and smothers
us with the charity, the pity, and the contempt of mankind, and
all other things will be added unto us. . . .

The people suffer in silence. This should not be. They should
have a voice.

The grievances they are forced to suffer should be known of
all the world and they must be. An organization national in its
ramification, such as we propose, would be such a voice, so loud
that it would compel men to hear it; for if it were silenced in
the South, it would be all the louder in the North and the West.

Whenever colored men talk of forming anything in which
they are to be the prime movers and their grievances are to be
the subjects to be agitated, a vast array of men, mostly politicians, and newspaper editors, more or less partisan, and therefore interested in keeping colored voters in a helpless state as
far as disorganization and absence of responsible leadership
can affect this, cry aloud that "colored men should be the last
persons to draw the color line." So they should be; so they have
been; and they would never have drawn any such line, or proposed that any such should be drawn, if white men had not
first drawn it, and continue to draw it now in religion, in politics, in educational matters, in all moral movements, like that
of temperance for instance. We have not drawn the color line.
The A. M. E. Church did its founders establish it because they
did not care to worship with their white co-religionists? Not a
bit of it. They established that magnificent religious organization as a rebuke and a protest to the peanut gallery accommodations offered by white Christians, so-called, to colored Christians. The same spirit actuated the founders of the Zion A. M. E.
Church and the colored M. E. Church.

It was not the colored Christians, but the white Christians, who, to their eternal shame and damnation, drew the color line, and continue to draw it, even unto this hour. Turn to the Masonic, the Odd Fellows and the Knights of Pythias orders—did colored men draw the line in these? Did they set up colored lodges all over the country because they did not care to fraternize with the white orders? The answer can be inferred when it is stated that white Masons, white Odd Fellows and white Knights of Pythias even at this hour refuse to fraternize with or to recognize the legality or regularity of the orders their actions caused Afro-Americans to establish. . . .

Ladies and gentlemen, let us stand up like men in our own organization where color will not be a brand of odium. The eternal compromises of our manhood and self-respect, true of the past, must cease. Right is right, and we should at no time or under any circumstances compromise upon anything but absolute right. If the white man cannot rescue our drunkards and evangelize our sinners except by insulting us, let him keep away from us. His contamination under such conditions does us more harm than good. It is not we who have drawn the color line. That is pure nonsense.

Take our public schools—take the schools and colleges throughout the land; who draw the color line in these? Is there an Afro-American school of any sort in the South where a white applicant would be refused admission on account of his color? Not one! Is there a white school in the South where a colored applicant would not be refused admission on account of his color? Not one! The thing is plain. The white man draws the color line in everything he has anything to do with. He is saturated with the black mud of prejudice and intolerance.

Leadership must have a following, otherwise it will run to seed and wither up, be of no benefit to the race or to the persons possessing the superior capacity. An army without a general is a mob, at the mercy of any disciplined force that is hurled against it; and a disorganized, leaderless race is nothing more than a helpless, restless mob.

All those men who have profited by our disorganization and fattened on our labor by class and corporate legislation, will oppose this Afro-American League movement. In the intensity of their opposition they may resort to the coward argument of violence; but are we to remain forever inactive, the victims of extortion and duplicity on this account? No, sir. We propose to accomplish our purposes by the peaceful methods of agitation, through the ballot and the courts, but if others use the weapons of violence to combat our peaceful arguments, it is not for us to run away from violence. A man's a man, and what is worth having is worth fighting for. It is proudly claimed that "the blood of the martyrs is the seed of the church." Certainly the blood of anti-slavery champions was the seed of Garrison's doctrine of "the genius of universal emancipation." Certainly the blood of Irish patriots has been the seed of Irish persistence and success; certainly the blood of Negro patriots was the seed of the independence of Hayti and San Domingo; and in the great revolution of our own country the cornerstones of American freedom were cemented with the blood of black patriots who were not afraid to die; and the refrain which celebrates the heroism and martyrdom of the first men who died that the American colonies might be free will reverberate down the ages.

> Long as in freedom's cause the wise contend
> Dear to your country shall your fame extend;
> While to the world the lettered stone shall tell
> Where Caldwell, Attucks, Gray and Maverick fell.

Attucks, the black patriot—he was no coward! Toussaint L'Ouverture—he was no coward! Nat Turner—he was no coward! And the two hundred thousand black soldiers of the last war—they were no cowards! If we have a work to do, let us do it. And if there come violence, let those who oppose our just cause "throw the first stone." We have wealth, we have intelligence, we have courage; and we have a great work to do. We should therefore take hold of it like men, not counting our time and means and lives of any consequence further than they contribute to the grand purposes which call us to the work. . . .

The ideology
of accommodation

Roughly from 1890 to 1910 nationalist expression was
associated mainly with an ideology of accommodation rather
than protest. Separatism, self-help, and racial solidarity were
all part of a constellation of ideas that accepted white
supremacy as an irrefutable fact of life—for the immediate
future at least—soft-pedaled demands for the franchise and
civil rights, and placed the blame for the Negroes' condition on
Negroes themselves. Instead of agitating for acceptance into
white society, this school of thought maintained that Negroes
should withdraw from contact with whites, develop their own
institutions and businesses, and uplift themselves along
economic and moral lines. When they had thus acquired
middle-class virtues and style of life, education and economic
competence, the prejudice against them would wither away
and the whites would accord them citizenship rights. Holders
of this view even pointed to the "advantages of the
disadvantages" in discrimination, which, it was believed,
compelled Negroes to work hard, help themselves, and acquire
education and property.

Booker T. Washington, dominant figure in Negro life at the
turn of the century, is the man most prominently identified
with the philosophy of accommodation. An even more extreme
accommodator than Washington was William Hooper Councill,
president of the State Normal School at Huntsville, Alabama
(Document 34). A statement by Washington (Document 35)
displays the breadth of his application of the ideas of race
pride and race solidarity. Like many writers of the period, the
Tuskegeean suggested that Negroes use the Jews as a model in

these particulars. Booker T. Washington's nationalism
concentrated particularly on economic self-help by Negroes.
His views in this regard are best expressed by the National
Negro Business League (Documents 37 and 38).

34. WILLIAM HOOPER COUNCILL: "THE NEGRO CAN GROW ONLY . . . IN HIS OWN SPHERE, AS GOD INTENDED"

American prejudice plays an important part in Negro opportunity. Never before in the history of any people has prejudice
had such high valuation. Instead of seeking admission into
places of amusement, pleasure and instruction run by white
people for white people, let colored men open such places for
their own accommodation and grow rich. Instead of knocking
for admission into white circles, adorn, beautify, elevate, enlarge Negro circles and find scope for our broadest and most
lofty ambition.

Every hotel which refuses the Negro a meal, every soda
fountain which declines to serve him are voices telling him to
go and open these places and make himself rich. That Negro
is unwise who goes around asking for such accommodations
among whites when the denial is only a friendly advice to open
up this business for himself, place his own boys and girls in
position and build up his own race by his own patronage. I
want my race to find admission wherever honest service is
wanted, and we will take care of the fun and pleasure places.

The Negro can grow only by being true to his own nature
in his own sphere, as God intended. When he seeks to unrace
himself—to run from his black skin, his flat nose, his thick lips
and flat feet—then he will make himself despicable in the eyes
of other races, and deserves the curse of God. We cannot make

a white man a Negro, nor a Negro a white man. God has made the distinction, and set the bounds of each. Each will grow strong and great only as he is true to his own nature. I honor the white man because he honors himself. I honor him because he places his mother, sister, wife and daughter on a platform up among the stars, gets a thousand gatling guns, and decrees death to him who seeks to drag them down. I honor him because he throws his powerful arms around every little red-headed, freckled-face, poor white girl and boy in the land and makes the way possible for them to rise in this world. I honor him because he does not go around whining and begging to be helped up, but by faith in his own muscle he cuts and carves out his own destiny. Let the Negro do likewise, according to his own nature, and in his own sphere, without prejudice to any, with love for all mankind, and he will succeed. Seize these opportunities; cultivate the most friendly relations with all men, feel a deep interest in our southland, and our deeds will count for something with man and God. . . .

Political reverses

I shall not be surprised to see the Negro stripped of every privilege and right which were thrust upon him. People do not retain things for which they do not struggle. The Negro fought for his freedom. He won it. He is worthy of it. No man seeks to take it away. No earthly power can take it away. He did not struggle for the reins of southern state governments in 1866, when backed by southern bayonets; he stood upon the bosom of the white south prostrate in the dust of defeat. The white south rose up, threw him off, and chased him from the legislatures and the national congress. The ballot was thrust upon him without his knowledge of consent. He has lost it. He is being stripped of all unpurchased rights. He stands naked and bare, from which point all men must start, procure and secure the things which are precious and sacred to them. Your race does not enjoy a right for which it did not pour out its life blood or toil and struggle. If the Negro is not willing to labor and strive for rights, he is not worthy of them. When he wins

them by toil no man, in a free country, will dare seek to rob
him of them. He must stand upon a solid foundation, and then
he will recover through intelligence and merit what he now
seems to be losing through ignorance. Injustice will strengthen
him. No power outside of himself can harm him. When thus
equipped he will rise to the zenith in his own sphere as a
Negro, and sink to rest amid the golden splendors of usefulness, having cut out his own way, and having carved his own
history in the imperishable marble of time.

Salvation through Negro women

We complain too much of a lack of honor among our youth
when we do not exert ourselves to give them proper encouragement. We complain of the hardships of our women when we
never do one thing to relieve them. Our female element, under
mother influence, attends school and church, eschews the broth-
els, stays at home, works, and to our shame is the backbone of
the Negro race today. Were it not for the Negro woman the
outlook would be dark. I am aware of the breadth of my speech
when I say that the world has never furnished a higher womanhood under like conditions than the Negro woman of the south
today. With strong appetites and passions, penniless, house-
less, working on "starvation wages," practically left to shift
alone, amid stumbling, falling, rising, fleeing—she goes on
washing, cooking, plowing, sowing, reaping—educating her
daughter, building the cottage, erecting churches and schools,
often supporting husband and son—this black woman deserves
the admiration of the gods. Every business man will say that a
Negro woman's word is worth just what she values it at. Herein
we see the nobility of white southern womanhood of long ago
running through the black slave womanhood and lifting up her
offspring of today—still lifting her up regardless of great draw-
backs and weights.

Social separation—but justice

Can the strong Anglo-Saxon afford to be otherwise than just

with the weak Negro in his midst? Treat the Negro fairly in the courts, in the common business transactions of life, in the labor markets of the south. I stand here, having affiliated for twenty-five years with the best white south in all that it considered its best welfare in politics and otherwise, and now with all the earnestness of my soul appeal for better treatment of the nurses, cooks and black mammies on the common carriers of the south. Separate the races in everything that looks like social intermingling, but in God's name treat us fairly. Do not subject us to treatment and to accommodation unworthy the gallantry and chivalry of the south. If the Negro girl is to be the servant girl of the south, then the white south is interested in making her refined and filling her with the tenderness, dignity, and virtue necessary for domestics in the best southern homes. Gentlemen, is there anything in the treatment of Negro women on the common carriers, and at the railroad stations to find them for service in good homes? You do not only run from social contact with the Negro, but you flee from the rough and riotous element in your own race. Help us to separate, as far as you can, from the unworthy of our race. The best blood of the south does not know that that nurse so well-beloved by their sunny haired children, that cook praised by the whole family, that "black mammy" the glory of many a southern heart are piled in a "jim crow" car, with dogs, convicts, train tools, roughs, their eyes, ears and noses insulted in a most ungodly manner, and forced with low men in the same dirty closets of waiting stations. As the white south honors its noble womanhood and precious childhood, it must throw around its servant class, everywhere, environments of integrity and refinement.

Organic forces in the south

The few disturbances and outbreaks in the south show the wonderful organic forces in the south. We have here more than ten millions of Negroes and fifteen million whites, and yet we have probably in the whole south only one Negro and white man in ten thousand who clash. The other nine thousand nine hundred and ninety-nine rub against one another every hour

of the day, in every walk of life, transact their business and go
their way in perfect friendship. These peaceful relations of the
9,999 give a bolder prominence to the one exception which is
held up by the enemies of the south as the general rule. The
love and attachment between the races of the south are more
than wonderful when we consider the untiring efforts of busy
and meddlesome enemies—the politician, the newspaper, the
magazine, and even the pulpit seeking to scatter seeds of dis-
cord and break up our peace. We 9,999 will stand firmly for
good will and happiness of both races in the south. No enemy
shall take that one sinner in ten thousand and disrupt and tear
us asunder.

Lessons of the monuments

The world's monuments tell the story of human struggle.
Where man has shed most tears and moistened the earth with
his blood there the monuments have their foundations deepest.
I have found that where man has toiled and struggled for man
there the foundation of the monuments are broadest. I have
found that where man has fought fiercest in the realm of mind
there he has conquered most and there the monuments rear
their heads highest. My race has built a monument in America
which the hand of Time can not efface. As long as a man loves
true liberty, as long as the spirit of justice finds lodgement in
the human breast, as long as the virtues of fidelity and patience
live among men, so long will the memory of the Negro race in
America live. All efforts to discount or wipe out our glorious
record of the past will only brighten it, and cause it to reflect
its refulgent glories far away across the ages to come.

Lesson from the Jews

Nothing is immortal but mind. Nothing survives but spirit.
Nothing triumphs but soul. The Jewish people are the fittest
people in the annals of man. They alone live. All others die.
All nations, whether ancient or modern, have been broken and

shattered in proportion to the intensity with which they have thrown themselves against this spiritual people. Oppress them, they increase. Persecute them, they flourish. Discriminate against them, they grow rich. They go right on growing stronger by the cruelty of their enemies. Babylon carried them into captivity. The Jew is here. Where is Babylon? Egypt has beat him with many stripes while he built her pyramids, her sphinx and her gigantic lake. The Jew is here, the pyramids and sphinx which he built are here. Where is Egypt? Rome whipped the Colosseum out of his muscles. The Colosseum is here. The Jew is here. Where is bloody Rome? Such will be the history of spiritual races unto the end. The Negro is a spiritual race.

A coward; a brave man

Any coward can oppress a people—can be unfair—but it takes a brave man to treat all men of whatever race and condition fairly and justly. Any other ideals, any other treatment of men transmits to posterity a race of moral weaklings and cowards. Teach every Negro boy and girl that the salvation of life, the salvation of everything in the world is the glorious end of education and duty. Then there could be no race conflict. I would rather see every Negro, of the ten million in this country, driven into the Gulf of Mexico and sink beneath its waters with spotless souls, than continue to live with the blood of human beings, with the blood of another race dropping from victorious daggers in Negro hands.

Put up thy sword

Violence is the argument of cowards and unwise people. Shot guns correct nothing. Swords conquer nothing. Those who use the sword must perish by it. The Negro has the most powerful weapon known among men. It is the only convincing argument. It is the only weapon which brings lasting conquest. It is the sword of the spirit. It is faith in God. The Negro cannot hope to succeed with carnal armament. But with spirit forces there is no ocean which he cannot cross, no Alps which he cannot scale. Persecutions in time turn on the persecutor with a thousand fold more destructive malignity than were visited upon the persecuted. Wrongs are like the boomerang and return to the one who hurls them with more deadly results than they inflicted upon the intended victim. No people were ever persecuted down. They were always persecuted up. If we have been persecuted in this country, such persecution has more than doubled our population in thirty-five years and has increased our material wealth by a billion dollars in the same time.

His vivid imagination

It is not extravagant to say that a people so spiritual, so vivid in imagination, will yet put an interpretation upon the religion of Christ which will startle and refine more favored races. Such imagination, or spiritual insight, has never been more highly shown in any other people than in the Negro. He sees lights, dreams dreams, has visions, hears voices where other people can see or hear nothing, because until recently the Negro could exercise only his religious imagination which was cultivated to the highest degree. The Negro fills all the air with heavenly music, or heavenly hosts to soothe, lead or protect the faithful servants of God. It is not extravagant to say that such vivid imagination when turned into the channels of art, will rival Phydias or Raphael, when turned toward science will discover and develop new worlds around about us and bring forth inventions for human salvation beyond the reach of materialistic races.

"No history"

It is said that we have no history. Blot out Egypt. Forget Hannibal. Do not remember noble Attucks. Wipe from history's page great Toussaint L'Ouverture or grand Douglass and still the Negro has done enough in the last forty years to give him creditable standing in the society of races, and to place his name in letters of gold across the azure blue above. Light up his wonderful imagination and emotion by the lamp of culture. Turn his imagination into mechanical and philosophical invention. Turn his deep emotion into music and poetry. Turn his constant stream of feeling into painting and sculptuary. Then the Negro, standing upon the shoulders of his Anglo-Saxon brother, will send wonder and amazement through the scientific and literary world. There are more inventions to be thought out, higher classes of forces yet undiscovered to be harnessed to appliances; more worlds to be discovered and dissected—more of God to be brought down to man. If the Negro is true to himself he will be God's instrument to bring it all about. God does not pay large prices for small things. Two millions of men did not meet forty years ago upon the battle field and redden the earth with their blood for nothing, God is helping the Negro to rise in the world.

Not solution—but evolution

We must train the hand to strike for man. Teach the heart to bear an injury, but never inflict one. All solutions of all human problems are simply evolutions. As man evolves out of selfishness into deep and broad sympathy, out of ignorance into light, out of sect, out of party into boundless humanity, then will racial conflict be diminished. There can be no racial solution, but amelioration of condition. Each individual must do his best at the black board of life, write plus, then go and "take his place in the silent halls of death." No three hundred years of human history have presented such wonderful evolutions as the three hundred years of Negro American history. Four millions of industrious Christians were evolved in the south from four million savages.

From four millions of penniless Negroes have evolved in thirty-five years ten millions of citizens worth a billion dollars, right here in the land of their bondage. From eight million

white slave-holders have evolved fifteen million white tax pay-
ers who support churches and schools for their former slaves.
Thus while all the outside world discusses solution, the glorious
old south goes from one triumph to another in the process of
evolution in thought and industry. This is our work in the
south. By it the law of love shall reign supreme in all the land,
and gentle peace shall come to abide forever in the Negro
cabin, in the white man's mansion.

35. BOOKER T. WASHINGTON URGES "CULTIVATING . . . FAITH IN THE RACE"

Now, if we wish to bring the race to a point where it should be,
where it will be strong, and grow and prosper, we have got to,
in every way possible, encourage it. We can do this in no
better way than by cultivating that amount of faith in the race
which will make us patronise its own enterprises wherever
those enterprises are worth patronising. I do not believe much
in the advice that is often given that we should patronise the
enterprises of our race without regard to the worth of those
enterprises. I believe that the best way to bring the race to the
point where it will compare with other races is to let it understand that, whenever it enters into any line of business, it will
be patronised just in proportion as it makes that business as
successful, as useful, as is true of any business enterprise conducted by any other race. The race that would grow strong
and powerful must have the element of hero-worship in it that
will, in the largest degree, make it honour its great men, the
men who have succeeded in that race. I think we should be
ashamed of the coloured man or woman who would not vener-
ate the name of Frederick Douglass. No race that would not

From Booker T. Washington, FUTURE OF THE AMERICAN NEGRO
(Boston: Small, Maynard & Co., 1899), pp. 178–183.

look upon such a man with honour and respect and pride could ever hope to enjoy the respect of any other race. I speak of this, not that I want my people to regard themselves in a narrow, bigoted sense, because there is nothing so hurtful to an individual or to a race as to get into the habit of feeling that there is no good except in its own race, but because I wish that it may have reasonable pride in all that is honourable in its history. Whenever you hear a coloured man say that he hates the people of the other race, there, in most instances, you will find a weak, narrow-minded coloured man. And, whenever you find a white man who expresses the same sentiment toward the people of other races, there, too, in almost every case, you will find a narrow-minded, prejudiced white man.

That person is the broadest, strongest, and most useful who sees something to love and admire in all races, no matter what their color.

If the Negro race wishes to grow strong, it must learn to respect itself, not to be ashamed. It must learn that it will only grow in proportion as its members have confidence in it, in proportion as they believe that it is a coming race.

We have reached a period when educated Negroes should give more attention to the history of their race; should devote more time to finding out the true history of the race, and in collecting in some museum the relics that mark its progress. It is true of all races of culture and refinement and civilisation that they have gathered in some place the relics which mark the progress of their civilisation, which show how they lived from period to period. We should have so much pride that we would spend more time in looking into the history of the race, more effort and money in perpetuating in some durable form its achievements, so that from year to year, instead of looking back with regret, we can point to our children the rough path through which we grew strong and great.

We have a very bright and striking example in the history of the Jews in this and other countries. There is, perhaps, no race that has suffered so much, not so much in America as in some of the countries in Europe. But these people have clung together. They have had a certain amount of unity, pride, and love of race; and, as the years go on, they will be more and more influential in this country,—a country where they were once despised, and looked upon with scorn and derision. It is largely because the Jewish race has had faith in itself. Unless the Negro learns more and more to imitate the Jew in these matters, to have faith in himself, he cannot expect to have any high degree of success.

Bourgeois economic nationalism

An important component of the nationalism of accommodation was economic chauvinism—the view that Negroes should support the development of Negro business. This belief was not inherently part of an accommodating philosophy, however, and it was often expressed by protest leaders. In fact, next to the general themes of race solidarity and self-help, the propaganda for Negro support of Negro business was the leading doctrine expressed by articulate blacks in the half-century under consideration in this part of the book, and was very marked in the militant decade of the 1920s.

Four selections illustrate this view. The first is from a convention held in Kansas City, Missouri, in 1879; it expresses succinctly the major components of this doctrine (Document 36). It is followed by three documents illustrating the philosophy of the National Negro Business League, founded by Booker T. Washington in 1900, following a suggestion made by W. E. B. Du Bois at the Atlanta University Conference in 1899 (Document 41).

The 1879 convention, evidently influenced by the Grange and labor union ideologies of the 1870s, called for the creation of cooperative stores as well as joint stock companies. In any case, all these documents exemplify what may be termed a bourgeois economic nationalism, advocating the creation of capitalistic enterprise. This is in contrast to the later economic nationalism of W. E. B. Du Bois, with its stress on a cooperative, quasi-socialistic economy (see Document 42).

36. A COLORED CONVENTION
RECOMMENDS NEGRO SUPPORT
FOR NEGRO BUSINESS

The committee on Farming made the following report which
was adopted:

Report of Committee on Farming

Mr. President:—Your committee to whom was referred the
topic, "How can we best encourage our young men to engage
in farming?" have had the same under consideration, and beg
leave to submit the following:

Resolved, That in order to encourage our young men to engage in farming as a vocation, it is necessary to impress them
with the fact that farming is an independent, honorable, and
lucrative business, affording ample opportunity for all the pleasure and enjoyment of any other calling and is the sure road to
individual independence.

Signed:

Rev. R. Ricketts, A. Williams, Jas. Groze, Committee

T. Newton offered the following preamble and resolutions
which were adopted:

Whereas, There are colored farmers, mechanics, and artizans
in the states of Colorado, Iowa, Nebraska, Missouri and Kansas, and

Whereas, It is important that we should use every means in
our power to stimulate and encourage them to renewed efforts
in their respective callings. Therefore

Resolved, That we recommend the above named states to
hold a Mechanical and Industrial fair in Leavenworth, Kansas,
commencing Aug. 1st, 1879.

From PROCEEDINGS OF THE COLORED LABORER'S AND
BUSINESS MEN'S INDUSTRIAL CONVENTION, . . . 1879 (Kansas
City, Mo.: H. R. Graham, 1879), pp. 12–13.

The committee on Mercantile industry made the following report, which was adopted:

Report of Committee on Mercantile Industries

We your committee to whom was referred the question of securing a better representation for colored men in the mercantile industries of the country beg leave to report.

1. That we recommend to our young men not only, but men of all classes to engage in individual enterprises of a mercantile nature; to open a store, office or place of business on their own account, that their example and success may create a confidence and establish a precedent that shall induce others to join labor and capital in larger and better enterprises or business operations.

2. We recommend the establishment of co-operative stores and joint stock companies for engaging in the pursuits of lumbering, milling, wood and coal yards, mining, fishing, and in short any other occupations that promise a competence or a livelihood.

3. We urge upon our people everywhere to patronize in every way possible all movements and enterprises, whether individual or co-operation of a mercantile character. If one of our race learns a trade, let us support him; if a shoemaker, let us buy our shoes of him; if he keeps a store, let us encourage him by our influence and our cash. All other nationalities give more liberal support to themselves than do we. Where then must we look for support and encouragement, if not to one another? Can we expect more assistance from the whites than from ourselves?

4. Again, if one of our business men desires success, let him first prepare himself for his vocation. Let him have faith in himself, and some experience to sustain him, and when he comes to engage in business, let him possess sufficient capital to furnish such a business as shall enable him to come into competition with other men. Our business enterprises generally have failed for lack of sufficient capital. Now, to succeed in business, the merchant must keep what the people want in his

line, and sell his wares as cheap as they can be had elsewhere. Our people are like other races; they go where they can do the best for themselves, where they can buy the cheapest and goods of the best quality.

5. We suggest that plans for joint stock companies and co-operative stores be published from time to time in our colored newspapers, and in such other papers as are accessible, to the end that our people desiring to engage in such enterprises may have the benefit of the wisdom and experience of our most successful business men. All of which is respectfully submitted.

37. FRED R. MOORE: "NEGROES SHOULD NOW BEGIN TO SUPPORT NEGROES"

The way to organize is to ORGANIZE. Where there is a will there is always a way. If an individual or individuals are anxious to see results and believe in the advancement of the race and of individuals in their communities, they will use every effort to get the people together in an organization. Some say that those engaged in business should get together; this is quite true. My contention is, however that business men and those who believe in giving them support should get together. Your local leagues will be stronger when you bring into them all the citizens of character who believe in race effort. I would require every person who joins a local league to pledge himself to support all worthy enterprises managed by men and women of the race, and when I found him doing otherwise, unless for good reason, I would fire him out of the local organization. When a prescription is to be filled or medicine purchased, the drug

From Fred R. Moore, "Organizing Local Business Leagues," REPORT OF THE FIFTH ANNUAL CONVENTION OF THE NATIONAL NEGRO BUSINESS LEAGUE, . . . 1904 (Pensacola, Fla.: M. M. Lewey, n.d.), pp. 42–48.

store kept by a member of the race should have the filling of
the same. The doctor of your race when in need of medical
attention, the lawyer of your race when in need of legal advice
or having legal papers drawn. When in need of literature subscribe to those periodicals published by members of the race.
All business enterprises should be supported, how else can we
expect to be respected by the world at large and be representative of something if we do not begin to practice what a great
many of us preach? How can we otherwise succeed? Some
would say that this was drawing the color line. I do not believe
it. Jews support Jews; Germans support Germans; Italians support Italians, until they get strong enough to compete with
their brothers in the professions and trades; and Negroes should
now begin to support Negroes. Don't delay this, but begin today. The preacher says: "To-day is the day of salvation; harden
not your hearts, for to-morrow ye may die."

I say to-day is the time to organize, and this should be your
slogan. Organize, organize and don't delay.

When the white race sees us organized in support of one another they will have greater respect for us. I lose respect for
the individual who doubts the capacity of his people to do;
that we cannot do as well as the whites. How can we ever prove
that we have the ability to compete unless supported by our
people. I believe that we can do anything the white man does,
if only given the chance. We are constantly appealing to the
whites to hold open the door of opportunity, but we are not
doing it for ourselves as we should. We must begin to recognize the true principle and we should educate the race up to it;
and that principle is—believe in your race and practice it by
giving them proper support in all proper undertakings. What a
mighty power we shall be when we begin to do this, and we
shall never be a mighty people until we do begin.

What a local league should stand for
to make it effective

It should have direct oversight over the interests of the people; in fact, it should be the Chamber of Commerce; guarding, and, as far as possible, protecting the people against unwise investments, and exposing fake companies organized to take advantage of the ignorant by promising large profits. The local league should seek constantly to better the business engaged in by individuals, by suggesting improvements; insist on business methods, fair prices and cleanliness in appearance; guard against failures by advocating loyal support, and a good supply of common sense. A local business league should control the employment of labor and bestow it where it will do the most good.

A local business league to be effective, must hold regular monthly meetings, and where our people are in large numbers and are not thoroughly organized, the meetings should be held weekly. A general interchange of ideas as to the conduct of business, with experienced persons to discuss the question, or read a paper on business effort, would be most helpful. There should be charged a fee for joining of not more than twenty-five cents, and monthly dues of ten cents to cover cost of necessary stationery and meeting place. With a good corps of officers and a very active secretary, the wisdom and the helpfulness of such an organization would soon be apparent, and would be appreciated by the people.

As to the individual who is always advocating the support of enterprises with his mouth. Watch the man who believes in supporting all of the enterprises instituted by members of the race with his mouth, but has never been known to go down in his pocket and give tangible evidence of his sympathy and support; he is a "fakir." The one way to demonstrate is to produce the goods.

The dreamers who believe that everything comes to him who waits and are constant critics of the doers, are usually lost in the shuffle. You must get together in support of the individual or individuals, learn to concentrate your monies and make a success of one thing at a time. Learn to value money and study thoroughly the plan of investment. Don't always be governed by sentiment; let it be business all the way through, all other things being equal.

The power of organization is in what is accomplished. It is

not necessary to wait for large numbers, but get together four or five active men in your community and have your plans well thought out and put them into immediate operation. Hold weekly meetings, constantly adding to your membership. Do not be discouraged if you should be unsuccessful at the start, but persevere. It is the determined individual who succeeds, and to succeed you must be willing to make sacrifices.

The National Organization had its being by and through this very idea. Its object is to give encouragement to the people to stand together, to build up individuals in various communities, and show to the world the capabilities and possibilities of the race along all lines if given a chance; and to demonstrate to the race that largely our success is with ourselves. Let me, therefore urge upon you the great importance of keeping together. Do not argue for organization here and when you return to your homes lose sight of putting it in actual operation. Have the same interest in the race at home that some of you have when away from home. Be as big a man at home as you seek to be away from home. Advocate the value of a local league in your community as strongly as you do when absent. Urge the people to stand together; assist them in bettering their condition by showing them how to be helpful to one another. All of this can be done, if you will but make the effort.

38. A KANSAS CITY BUSINESSMAN URGES NEGROES TO "PATRONIZE THE COLORED MAN"

Mr. F. J. Weaver, of Kansas City, Missouri: We have a very active body of business men in our State Business League, and we have a Local League in Kansas City, Mo., comprising 15

From Report of the FOURTEENTH ANNUAL CONVENTION OF THE NATIONAL NEGRO BUSINESS LEAGUE, . . . 1913 (Nashville, Tenn.: A.M.E. Sunday School Union, 1913), pp. 184–185.

members. There, about four years ago, our people were seemingly asleep, doing practically nothing by way of organized effort to advance the material interest of our people. So we organized some of the business men, got the cooperation of various ministers of the city to help carry on this campaign, and we inaugurated a campaign that has done a great deal of good. We started the campaign by having public meetings in the various churches of different denominations, and created a sentiment there, until now, it is almost considered a crime for a representative Negro to be caught going into a white place, unless to get something which cannot be obtained from members of our own race. When we first started to mould public sentiment on the part of our people in favor of their own racial enterprises, we were told that it was utterly impossible to get the big Negroes, the educated ones of our race to patronize the colored man in business. We found that even some of the colored school teachers rarely spent their money with the struggling business establishments conducted by our people in Kansas City; but now, since we have crystallized sentiment in that direction, every man and woman who is a teacher in our public schools thoroughly understands the fact, if they don't support the Negro in business and do their full duty in helping to build up our race in that city, their general influence won't be worth very much. (Prolonged applause and hearty laughter.) The same is true of our professional men; they have been given the same kind of cue. We have given them to understand that if they expect help, they must help others. (Hearty applause.) They understand well enough that unless they send their prescriptions and spend their money at Dr. Greiger's drugstore and support our other colored business enterprises, that the result will be disastrous to them, and they needn't look to us for any assistance. Judging from the rapid improvement made in this direction, I think within the next year we will have a strong business organization in the State of Missouri.

Our Local League in Kansas City meets once a month, and we derive a great deal of good through mutual counsel. Kansas City, Mo., has the distinction of being the "town of homebuyers among Negroes;" almost every Negro you see in that town who amounts to anything owns his home, and nearly every month we hear of a new colored business being opened up. (Hearty applause.) This of course, is very encouraging to us, and the splendid results which have followed from creating public sentiment in the way I have indicated, leads me to prescribe the same remedy for other communities throughout this country. (Laughter and applause.) Tell your schoolteachers, your professional men and other public servants that if they can't support the Negro in business and help our race to get on its feet in your community, their jobs and professions will not be worth anything to them. (Prolonged applause.)

39. A CALIFORNIA NEWSPAPER LOOKS AT THE NATIONAL NEGRO BUSINESS LEAGUE

At the recent meeting just closed in Boston, Mass., many telling experiences were recited of the rise of individual Negroes from lowly walks of life to merchants and bankers of affluence and standing. A Business League is a very much needed organization in every city where there is any percentage of the population of the Negro race. Such an organization is needed to teach Negroes to unite, to teach Negroes the value of cooperation, to teach Negro housewives to buy their groceries and sundries from the colored grocery store on the corner. Although the flour may be 5 per cent higher, you are more than repaid to have a Negro driver deliver it and probably making a job for a Negro girl as clerk or stenographer. Negroes must be taught that the insurance on their property can be placed through colored agents as cheaply and as safe as a white agent.

Editorial, "Value of Negro Business Leagues,"
SUNSHINE (Oakland, Calif.), September 4, 1915.

Negroes must be taught that they can stay out of a white restaurant, except in a very few cities and out of the way places,
just as easy as they can and do shun a white barber shop. Negroes must be taught to admire shops kept and run by Negroes.
Negroes must be taught to think before they buy and ask if
there are any Negro places of business that they might look
them over and see if it is possible to leave a few dimes or
dollars with the race. Negroes must be taught to know that
when they build up a Negro enterprise they are creating positions for their sons and daughters.

The Negro Business League should teach Negro preachers
the value of reciprocity; that is, that as a rule colored preachers
will use a Negro or race journal to prop up their case and give
publicity to their notices, but very few of them ever take time
during their services to advise their flock to sustain race journals and build up their own. They should be taught that it is
no more out of place to tell their flock to patronize a Negro
store, shop or place of business run by a colored man than it is
to desecrate their pulpits with vulgar songs and telling funny
stories and the like. As a rule, our people listen to what the
preacher and the church says, but we know of a few Negro
ministers that have not learned what reciprocity is and what
their duty is with regard to colored business men and women.
Still, the blame lies largely with the individual Negro, who in
some cases is so deceitful and hypocritical when it comes to
placing any business in the hands of a Negro business man.
Every Negro church in the bay cities should be insured by a
Negro agent and this could be done. Every Negro church
should buy its furniture from a Negro merchant. We know of
a Negro church not a hundred miles away from the city of
Oakland that promised to buy a lot of new carpet through a
Negro firm, but some mule head darky on the board thought
that the white man must have a chance in that carpet purchase
and must have sidetracked their plans, as the carpet was bought
and nothing said to the Negro dealer. Now, if our churches, our
pastors and our church officers do this kind of thing, when they
call for money, which they sometimes do, will they expect the

Negro merchant that did not get the carpet contract, to donate, or will they find that white man in their midst every Sunday putting coin in the collection box? The answer is plain. Now these Negro leaders must be taught consistency and common sense. There was no good reason why this particular church could not have purchased the carpet from the Negro store or through him and they know it.

We need a Negro Business League to help secure employment for our girls that are qualifying themselves to do office work. Why should they not have a chance? Why should we not begin to make positions for them? A few weeks ago in one of our big cities a Negro contractor was turned down and the job given to his white competitor to build a Negro church because the colored contractor was a few dollars higher. Just think what folly. Great guns of wonder, is not that inconsistency? Yes, we need the Business League.

The nationalism of W. E. B. Du Bois

Of all the black leaders and spokesmen in the history of the United States, W. E. B. Du Bois most explicitly revealed—and most cogently expressed—the impact of oppression and of American equalitarian values in creating ambivalent loyalties toward race and nation in the minds of Afro-Americans. Du Bois has described himself as integrally a part of western Civilization, and "yet, more significant, one of its rejected parts, one who expressed in life and action and made vocal to many, a single whirlpool of social entanglement and inner psychological paradox."[1]

The strain of nationalism in Du Bois's thinking is nowhere more persuasively argued than in an early paper (1897) entitled *The Conservation of Races* (Document 40). This has become one of the most important of Du Bois's essays because it contains many of the themes to which he later returned and developed: (1) American Negroes were the vanguard of blacks the world over whose destiny was "Pan-Negroism"—the doctrine that Negroes, regardless of what nation they lived in, should feel an emotional commitment to one another. (2) Negroes everywhere have a special attachment to Africa as the race's "greater fatherland." (3) Salvation would come only from an educated black elite who would chart the way to cultural and economic elevation. (4) Black People "MUST DO FOR THEMSELVES" by developing their own organizations, such as businesses, newspapers, and schools. (5) Negroes have "a distinct mission as a race"—"to soften the whiteness" of an

[1] W. E. B. Du Bois, *Dusk of Dawn: An Essay Toward an Autobiography of a Race Concept* (New York: Harcourt, Brace & Co., 1940), p. 2.

uninspiring, materialistic Anglo-Saxon culture. He argued that "the Negro people as a race have a contribution to make in civilization and humanity, which no other race can make."

Du Bois, when he rose to prominence as a protest leader early in the twentieth century, was identified with an elitist doctrine of racial advancement through collective endeavor known as the theory of the "Talented Tenth." At the time, the ideologists of accommodation (who emphasized the primacy of economic accomplishment in the solution of the race's problems) downgraded the usefulness of college-educated and professional men and advocated agricultural and industrial education to the subordination, if not the exclusion, of higher education. In this view Negroes, having proven their worth to society by first establishing themselves as farmers and landowners, artisans and businessmen, would be in a position to cultivate scholarship and the arts, or what Booker T. Washington called the "nonessentials." In contrast, a tiny group of intellectuals stressed the importance of a college-educated elite that would lead and uplift the masses of Negroes. Such a class, it was maintained, was necessary to the advancement and civilization of any race. Members of this elite, like the philosophers in Plato's Republic, had a duty to subordinate their private interests to the welfare and advancement of the race. This ideology had been foreshadowed in Du Bois's thinking since he was a student at Fisk University in the late 1880s, and it had been cogently developed by Alexander Crummell in his address of 1897, "Civilization, The Primal Need of the Race." (Du Bois's essay on the "Talented Tenth" is not included here because Crummell's essay articulated all the essential ideas that Du Bois a few years later made pivotal in his ideological battle with the accommodator and industrial educator, Booker T. Washington; see Document 24.)

Du Bois's economic nationalism took two forms. At first he advocated bourgeois nationalism, urging the development of black capitalist enterprise based on the Negro market. Later, after coming under the influence of socialist doctrines beginning in 1904, he became an earnest advocate of consumer and producer cooperatives. Du Bois, as a professor at Atlanta University from 1897 to 1910, attempted to popularize his ideas through annual conferences sponsored by the university. Each conclave devoted itself to a different theme of black community life. In 1899, the Negro in Business was explored, with Du Bois largely writing the resolutions which the conference ratified. He told Negroes to patronize black stores even if they charged higher prices. Black businessmen were asked to unite into Leagues—an idea which Booker T. Washington borrowed a year later when he established the National Negro Business League (Document 41).

Du Bois, a founder of the NAACP, was editor of its monthly magazine, *The Crisis*, from 1910 to 1934. In its pages he repeatedly propagandized on behalf of economic cooperation among black consumers and producers (see Document 42).

A central theme in Du Bois's writings throughout his career was his interest in Africa and its cultures. At a time when most American Negroes were embarrassed by the alleged "primitiveness" of their ancestral societies in Africa, Du Bois appears to have been the first American author—black or white—to describe the great medieval kingdoms of West Africa; and he was among the first to regard the nonliterate peoples of sub-Saharan Africa as possessing complex and sophisticated cultures. Finally, he also maintained that the way of life of New World Negroes had been significantly influenced by the cultures of Africa.

Believing that blacks throughout the world should work together for each other's freedom and development, Du Bois, between 1919 and 1927, convened four Pan-African Congresses in Europe and the United States. Calling for recognition of the "absolute equality of races" and the end of imperialist exploitation of blacks everywhere, all these conclaves stressed the condition of the race in Africa. The "Manifesto of the Second Pan-African Congress" of 1921 (Document 43) is typical in articulating such demands as popular education and self-government for blacks. This document is also representative of Du Bois's thinking concerning the role of intellectuals, the "Talented Tenth." The Pan-African Congresses were in fact a concrete application of the theory that black intellectuals should lead the way in the elevation of the race, in Africa and the New World.

Repeatedly Du Bois used *The Crisis* magazine to teach lessons of cultural nationalism and show Afro-Americans that there is "beauty in black." In the 1920s he proclaimed that Negro writers, artists, and sculptors, representatives of "Negro Youth . . . a different kind of Youth," could create beauty and truth for the black race and for all mankind. He insisted that while blacks should demand "all the rights of other American citizens," they should be satisfied with nothing less than the elevation and purification of America's "present goals and ideals," which he found ugly both spiritually and materially. Addressing the NAACP convention of 1926, he expressed his thoughts about Negro art. His speech, reflecting an increasing sense of racial solidarity within the black community, was delivered at the height of the "Harlem Renaissance," the literary and artistic movement summed up by the term "New Negro." Along with many other black intellectuals of the period, he believed that intellectually and artistically Negroes should have pride in their past and their traditions and use the themes from Negro life and Negro history as an inspiration for literary creation. Above all, blacks could enrich themselves and America only if they defined their own standards of beauty and truth, rather than permitting whites to define them (Document 44).

Massive Negro unemployment and the general deterioration of social conditions during the depression of the 1930s led Du Bois to resign as editor of *The Crisis* because he was convinced that the NAACP's emphasis on attacking disfranchisement and segregation had been a failure. In a series of *Crisis* editorials in 1934 he advocated a separate Negro cooperative economy as a solution to the problems posed by the Depression. This action led to a clash with those who supported the NAACP's traditional opposition to any form of segregation and resulted in withdrawal not only from his position with the NAACP but also from a position of effective leadership in the black community. In his last editorials he attempted to explain his belief in the value of collective racial economic endeavor—a view he had long espoused but which now became his new central thrust instead of racial integration (Document 45).

40. ON THE CONSERVATION OF RACES: "THE NEGRO PEOPLE AS A RACE HAVE A CONTRIBUTION TO MAKE TO CIVILIZATION . . . WHICH NO OTHER RACE CAN MAKE"

The American Negro has always felt an intense personal interest in discussions as to the origins and destinies of races: primarily because back of most discussions of race with which he is familiar, have lurked certain assumptions as to his natural abilities, as to his political, intellectual and moral status, which he felt were wrong. He has, consequently, been led to deprecate and minimize race distinctions, to believe intensely that out of one blood God created all nations, and to speak of human brotherhood as though it were the possibility of an already dawning to-morrow.

Nevertheless, in our calmer moments we must acknowledge that human beings are divided into races; that in this country the two most extreme types of the world's races have met, and the resulting problem as to the future relations of these types is

W. E. B. Du Bois, THE CONSERVATION OF RACES (Washington, D. C.: American Negro Academy, OCCASIONAL PAPERS No. 2, 1897).

not only of intense and living interest to us, but forms an epoch
in the history of mankind.

It is necessary, therefore, in planning our movements, in
guiding our future development, that at times we rise above
the pressing, but smaller questions of separate schools and cars,
wage-discrimination and lynch law, to survey the whole question of race in human philosophy and to lay, on a basis of
broad knowledge and careful insight, those large lines of policy and higher ideals which may form our guiding lines and
boundaries in the practical difficulties of every day. For it is
certain that all human striving must recognize the hard limits
of natural law, and that any striving, no matter how intense
and earnest, which is against the constitution of the world, is
vain. The question, then, which we must seriously consider is
this: What is the real meaning of Race; what has, in the past,
been the law of race development, and what lessons has the
past history of race development to teach the rising Negro
people?

When we thus come to inquire into the essential difference
of races we find it hard to come at once to any definite conclusion. Many criteria of race differences have in the past been
proposed, as color, hair, cranial measurements and language.
And manifestly, in each of these respects, human beings differ
widely. They vary in color, for instance, from the marble-like
pallor of the Scandinavian to the rich, dark brown of the Zulu,
passing by the creamy Slav, the yellow Chinese, the light
brown Sicilian and the brown Egyptian. Men vary, too, in the
texture of hair from the obstinately straight hair of the Chinese
to the obstinately tufted and frizzled hair of the Bushman.
In measurement of heads, again, men vary; from the broad-
headed Tartar to the medium-headed European and the nar-
row-headed Hottentot; or, again in language, from the highly-
inflected Roman tongue to the monosyllabic Chinese. All these
physical characteristics are patent enough, and if they agreed
with each other it would be very easy to classify mankind. Unfortunately for scientists, however, these criteria of race are

most exasperatingly intermingled. Color does not agree with texture of hair, for many of the dark races have straight hair; nor does color agree with the breadth of the head, for the yellow Tartar has a broader head than the German; nor, again, has the science of language as yet succeeded in clearing up the relative authority of these various and contradictory criteria. The final word of science, so far, is that we have at least two, perhaps three, great families of human beings—the whites and Negroes, possibly the yellow race. That other races have arisen from the intermingling of the blood of these two. This broad division of the world's races which men like Huxley and Raetzel have introduced as more nearly true than the old five-race scheme of Blumenbach, is nothing more than an acknowledgment that, so far as purely physical characteristics are concerned, the differences between men do not explain all the differences of their history. It declares, as Darwin himself said, that great as is the physical unlikeness of the various races of men their likenesses are greater, and upon this rests the whole scientific doctrine of Human Brotherhood.

Although the wonderful developments of human history teach that the grosser physical differences of color, hair and bone go but a short way toward explaining the different roles which groups of men have played in Human Progress, yet there are differences—subtle, delicate and elusive, though they may be—which have silently but definitely separated men into groups. While these subtle forces have generally followed the natural cleavage of common blood, descent and physical peculiarities, they have at other times swept across and ignored these. At all times, however, they have divided human beings into races, which, while they perhaps transcend scientific definition, nevertheless, are clearly defined to the eye of the Historian and Sociologist.

If this be true, then the history of the world is the history, not of individuals, but of groups, not of nations, but of races, and he who ignores or seeks to override the race idea in human history ignores and overrides the central thought of all history. What, then, is a race? It is a vast family of human beings, generally of common blood and language, always of common history, traditions and impulses, who are both voluntarily and involuntarily striving together for the accomplishment of certain more or less vividly conceived ideals of life.

Turning to real history, there can be no doubt, first, as to the widespread, nay, universal, prevalence of the race idea, the race spirit, the race ideal, and as to its efficiency as the vastest and most ingenious invention for human progress. We, who have been reared and trained under the individualistic philosophy of the Declaration of Independence and the laissez-faire philosophy of Adam Smith, are loath to see and loath to acknowledge this patent fact of human history. We see the Pharaohs, Caesars, Toussaints and Napoleons of history and forget the vast races of which they were but epitomized expressions. We are apt to think in our American impatience, that while it may have been true in the past that closed race groups made history, that here in conglomerate America *nous avons changer tout cela*—we have changed all that, and have no need of this ancient instrument of progress. This assumption of which the Negro people are especially fond, can not be established by a careful consideration of history.

We find upon the world's stage today eight distinctly differentiated races, in the sense in which History tells us the word must be used. They are, the Slavs of eastern Europe, the Teutons of middle Europe, the English of Great Britain and America, the Romance nations of Southern and Western Europe, the Negroes of Africa and America, the Semitic people of Western Asia and Northern Africa, the Hindoos of Central Asia and the Mongolians of Eastern Asia. There are, of course, other minor race groups, as the American Indians, the Esquimaux and the South Sea Islanders; these larger races, too, are far from homogeneous; the Slav includes the Czech, the Magyar, the Pole and the Russian; the Teuton includes the German, the Scandinavian and the Dutch; the English include the Scotch, the Irish and the conglomerate American. Under Romance nations the widely-differing Frenchman, Italian, Sicilian and Spaniard are comprehended. The term Negro is, perhaps, the most indefinite of all, combining the Mulattoes and Zamboes of America and the Egyptians, Bantus and Bushmen of Africa. Among the Hindoos are traces of widely differing nations, while the great Chinese, Tartar, Corean and Japanese families fall under the one designation—Mongolian.

The question now is: What is the real distinction between these nations? Is it the physical differences of blood, color and cranial measurements? Certainly we must all acknowledge that physical differences play a great part, and that, with wide exceptions and qualifications, these eight great races of to-day follow the cleavage of physical race distinctions; the English and Teuton represent the white variety of mankind; the Mongolian, the yellow; the Negroes, the black. Between these are many crosses and mixtures, where Mongolian and Teuton have blended into the Slav, and other mixtures have produced the Romance nations and the Semites. But while race differences have followed mainly physical race lines, yet no mere physical distinctions would really define or explain the deeper differences—the cohesiveness and continuity of these groups. The deeper differences are spiritual, psychical, differences—undoubtedly based on the physical, but infinitely transcending them. The forces that bind together the Teuton nations are, then, first, their race identity and common blood; secondly, and more important, a common history, common laws and religion, similar habits of thought and a conscious striving together for certain ideals of life. The whole process which has brought about these race differentiations has been a growth, and the great characteristic of this growth has been the differentiation of spiritual and mental differences between great races of mankind and the integration of physical differences.

The age of nomadic tribes of closely related individuals represents the maximum of physical differences. They were practically vast families, and there were as many groups as families. As the families came together to form cities the physical differences lessened, purity of blood was replaced by the requirement of domicile, and all who lived within the city bounds became gradually to be regarded as members of the group; *i.e.,* there was a slight and slow breaking down of physical barriers. This, however, was accompanied by an increase of the spiritual and social differences between cities. This city became husbandmen, this, merchants, another warriors, and so on. The *ideals of life* for which the different cities struggled were different. When at last cities began to coalesce into nations there was another breaking down of barriers which separated groups of men. The larger and broader differences of color, hair and physical proportions were not by any means ignored, but myriads of minor differences disappeared, and the sociological and historical races of men began to approximate the present division of races as indicated by physical researches. At the same time the spiritual and physical differences of race groups which constituted the nations became deep and decisive. The English nation stood for constitutional liberty and commercial freedom; the German nation for science and philosophy; the Romance nations stood for literature and art, and the other race groups are striving, each in its own way, to develope for civilization its particular message, its particular ideal, which shall help to guide the world nearer and nearer that perfection of human life for which we all long, that

one far off Divine event.

This has been the function of race differences up to the present time. What shall be its function in the future? Manifestly some of the great races of today—particularly the Negro race— have not as yet given to civilization the full spiritual message which they are capable of giving. I will not say that the Negro race has as yet given no message to the world, for it is still a mooted question among scientists as to just how far Egyptian civilization was Negro in its origin; if it was not wholly Negro, it was certainly very closely allied. Be that as it may, however, the fact still remains that the full, complete Negro message of the whole Negro race has not as yet been given to the world: that the messages and ideal of the yellow race have not been completed, and that the striving of the mighty Slavs has but begun. The question is, then: How shall this message be delivered; how shall these various ideals be realized? The answer is plain: By the development of these race groups, not as individuals, but as races. For the development of Japanese genius, Japanese literature and art, Japanese spirit, only Japanese, bound and welded together, Japanese inspired by one vast ideal, can work out in its fullness the wonderful message which Japan has for the nations of the earth. For the development of Negro genius, of Negro literature and art, of Negro spirit, only Negroes bound and welded together, Negroes inspired by one vast ideal, can work out in its fullness the great message we have for humanity. We cannot reverse history; we are subject to the same natural laws as other races, and if the Negro is ever to be a factor in the world's history—if among the gaily-colored banners that deck the broad ramparts of civilization is to hang one uncompromising black, then it must be placed there by black hands, fashioned by black heads and hallowed by the travail of 200,000,000 black hearts beating in one glad song of jubilee.

For this reason, the advance guard of the Negro people— the 8,000,000 people of Negro blood in the United States of America—must soon come to realize that if they are to take their just place in the van of Pan-Negroism, then their destiny is *not* absorption by the white Americans. That if in America it is to be proven for the first time in the modern world that not only Negroes are capable of evolving individual men like Toussaint, the Saviour, but are a nation stored with wonderful possibilities of culture, then their destiny is not a servile imitation of Anglo-Saxon culture, but a stalwart originality which shall unswervingly follow Negro ideals.

It may, however, be objected here that the situation of our race in America renders this attitude impossible; that our sole hope of salvation lies in our being able to lose our race identity in the commingled blood of the nation; and that any other course would merely increase the friction of races which we call race prejudice, and against which we have so long and so earnestly fought.

Here, then, is the dilemma, and it is a puzzling one, I admit.

No Negro who has given earnest thought to the situation of his people in America has failed, at some time in life, to find himself at these cross-roads; has failed to ask himself at some time: What, after all, am I? Am I an American or am I a Negro? Can I be both? Or is it my duty to cease to be a Negro as soon as possible and be an American? If I strive as a Negro, am I not perpetuating the very cleft that threatens and separates Black and White America? Is not my only possible practical aim the subduction of all that is Negro in me to the American? Does my black blood place upon me any more obligation to assert my nationality than German, or Irish or Italian blood would?

It is such incessant self-questioning and the hesitation that arises from it, that is making the present period a time of vacillation and contradiction for the American Negro; combined race action is stifled, race responsibility is shirked, race enterprises languish, and the best blood, the best talent, the best energy of the Negro people cannot be marshalled to do the bidding of the race. They stand back to make room for every rascal and demagogue who chooses to cloak his selfish deviltry under the veil of race pride.

Is this right? Is it rational? Is it good policy? Have we in America a distinct mission as a race—a distinct sphere of action and an opportunity for race development, or is self-obliteration the highest end to which Negro blood dare aspire?

If we carefully consider what race prejudice really is, we find it, historically, to be nothing but the friction between different groups of people; it is the difference in aim, in feeling, in ideals of two different races; if, now, this difference exists touching territory, laws, language, or even religion, it is manifest that these people cannot live in the same territory without fatal collision; but if, on the other hand, there is substantial agreement in laws, language and religion; if there is a satisfactory adjustment of economic life, then there is no reason why, in the same country and on the same street, two or three great national ideals might not thrive and develop, that men of different races might not strive together for their race ideals as well, perhaps even better, than in isolation. Here, it seems to me, is the reading of the riddle that puzzles so many of us. We are Americans, not only by birth and by citizenship, but by our political ideals, our language, our religion. Farther than that, our Americanism does not go. At that point, we are Negroes, members of a vast historic race that from the very dawn of creation has slept, but half awakening in the dark forests of its African fatherland. We are the first fruits of this new nation, the harbinger of that black to-morrow which is yet destined to soften the whiteness of the Teutonic to-day. We are that people whose subtle sense of song has given America its only American music, its only American fairy tales, its only touch of pathos and humor amid its mad money-getting plutocracy. As such, it is our duty to conserve our physical powers, our intellectual endowments, our spiritual ideals; as a race we must strive by race organization, by race solidarity, by race unity to the realization of that broader humanity which freely recognizes differences in men, but sternly deprecates inequality in their opportunities of development.

For the accomplishment of these ends we need race organizations: Negro colleges, Negro newspapers, Negro business organizations, a Negro school of literature and art, and an intellectual clearing house, for all these products of the Negro mind, which we may call a Negro Academy. Not only is all this necessary for positive advance, it is absolutely imperative for negative defense. Let us not deceive ourselves at our situation in this country. Weighted with a heritage of moral iniquity from our past history, hard pressed in the economic world by foreign immigrants and native prejudice, hated here, despised there and pitied everywhere; our one haven of refuge is ourselves, and but one means of advance, our own belief in our great destiny, our own implicit trust in our ability and worth. There is no power under God's high heaven that can stop the advance of eight thousand thousand honest, earnest, inspired and united people. But—and here is the rub—they *must* be honest, fearlessly criticising their own faults, zealously correcting them; they must be *earnest*. No people that laughs at itself, and ridicules itself, and wishes to God it was anything but itself ever wrote its name in history; it *must* be inspired with the

Divine faith of our black mothers, that out of the blood and dust of battle will march a victorious host, a mighty nation, a peculiar people, to speak to the nations of earth a Divine truth that shall make them free. And such a people must be united; not merely united for the organized theft of political spoils, not united to disgrace religion with whoremongers and ward-heelers; not united merely to protest and pass resolutions, but united to stop the ravages of consumption among the Negro people, united to keep black boys from loafing, gambling and crime; united to guard the purity of black women and to reduce that vast army of black prostitutes that is today marching to hell; and united in serious organizations, to determine by careful conference and thoughtful interchange of opinion the broad lines of policy and action for the American Negro.

This, is the reason for being which the American Negro Academy has. It aims at once to be the epitome and expression of the intellect of the black-blooded people of America, the exponent of the race ideals of one of the world's great races. As such, the Academy must, if successful, be

(a). Representative in character.
(b). Impartial in conduct.
(c). Firm in leadership.

It must be representative in character; not in that it represents all interests or all factions, but in that it seeks to comprise something of the *best* thought, the most unselfish striving and the highest ideals. There are scattered in forgotten nooks and corners throughout the land, Negroes of some considerable training, of high minds, and high motives, who are unknown to their fellows, who exert far too little influence. These the Negro Academy should strive to bring into touch with each other and to give them a common mouthpiece.

The Academy should be impartial in conduct; while it aims to exalt the people it should aim to do so by truth—not by lies, by honesty—not by flattery. It should continually impress the fact upon the Negro people that they must not expect to have things done for them—they MUST DO FOR THEMSELVES; that they have on their hands a vast work of self-reformation to do, and that a little less complaint and whining, and a little more dogged work and manly striving would do us more credit and benefit than a thousand Force or Civil Rights bills.

Finally, the American Negro Academy must point out a practical path of advance to the Negro people; there lie before every Negro today hundreds of questions of policy and right which must be settled and which each one settles now, not in accordance with any rule, but by impulse or individual preference; for instance: What should be the attitude of Negroes toward the educational qualification for voters? What should be our attitude toward separate schools? How should we meet discriminations on railways and in hotels? Such questions need not so much specific answers for each part as a general expression of policy, and nobody should be better fitted to announce such a policy than a representative honest Negro Academy.

All this, however, must come in time after careful organization and long conference. The immediate work before us should be practical and have direct bearing upon the situation of the Negro. The historical work of collecting the laws of the United States and of the various States of the Union with regard to the Negro is a work of such magnitude and importance that no body but one like this could think of undertaking it. If we could accomplish that one task we would justify our existence.

In the field of Sociology an apalling work lies before us. First, we must unflinchingly and bravely face the truth, not with apologies, but with solemn earnestness. The Negro Academy ought to sound a note of warning that would echo in every black cabin in the land: *Unless we conquer our present vices they will conquer us;* we are diseased, we are developing criminal tendencies, and an alarmingly large percentage of our men and women are sexually impure. The Negro Academy should stand and proclaim this over the housetops, crying with Garrison: *I will not equivocate, I will not retreat a single inch, and I will be heard.* The Academy should seek to gather about it the talented, unselfish men, the pure and noble-minded women, to fight an army of devils that disgraces our manhood and our womanhood. There does not stand today upon God's earth a race more capable in muscle, in intellect, in morals, than the American Negro, if he will bend his energies in the right direction; if he will

> Burst his birth's invidious bar
> And grasp the skirts of happy chance,
> And breast the blows of circumstance,
>   And grapple with his evil star.

In science and morals, I have indicated two fields of work for the Academy. Finally, in practical policy, I wish to suggest the following *Academy Creed:*

1. We believe that the Negro people, as a race, have a contribution to make to civilization and humanity, which no other race can make.

2. We believe it the duty of the Americans of Negro descent, as a body, to maintain their race identity until this mission of the Negro people is accomplished, and the ideal of human brotherhood has become a practical possibility.

3. We believe that, unless modern civilization is a failure, it is entirely feasible and practicable for two races in such essential political, economic and religious harmony as the white and colored people of America, to develop side by side in peace and mutual happiness, the peculiar contribution which each has to make to the culture of their common country.

4. As a means to this end we advocate, not such social equality between these races as would disregard human likes and dislikes, but such a social equilibrium as would, throughout all the complicated relations of life, give due and just consideration to culture, ability, and moral worth, whether they be found under white or black skins.

5. We believe that the first and greatest step toward the settlement of the present friction between the races—commonly called the Negro Problem—lies in the correction of the immorality, crime and laziness among the Negroes themselves, which still remains as a heritage from slavery. We believe that only earnest and long continued efforts on our own part can cure these social ills.

6. We believe that the second great step toward a better ad-

justment of the relations between the races, should be a more impartial selection of ability in the economic and intellectual world, and a greater respect for personal liberty and worth, regardless of race. We believe that only earnest efforts on the part of the white people of this country will bring much needed reform in these matters.

7. On the basis of the foregoing declaration, and firmly believing in our high destiny, we, as American Negroes, are resolved to strive in every honorable way for the realization of the best and highest aims, for the development of strong manhood and pure womanhood, and for the rearing of a race ideal in America and Africa, to the glory of God and the uplifting of the Negro people.

41. ON SUPPORT FOR
BLACK BUSINESS ENTERPRISE

The resolutions passed at the last session of the conference were as follows:

1. Negroes ought to enter into business life in increasing numbers. The present disproportion in the distribution of Negroes in the various occupations is unfortunate. It gives the race a one-sided development, unnecessarily increases competition in certain lines of industry, and puts the mass of the Negro people out of sympathy and touch with the industrial and mercantile spirit of the age. Moreover the growth of a class of merchants among us would be a far-sighted measure of self-defense, and would make for wealth and mutual cooperation.

2. We need as merchants the best trained young men we can find. A college training ought to be one of the best preparations

"Resolutions of the Atlanta University Conference on the Negro in Business," in W. E. B. Du Bois (ed.), THE NEGRO IN BUSINESS (Atlanta, Ga.: ATLANTA UNIVERSITY PUBLICATIONS, No. 4, 1899), p. 50.

for a broad business life; and thorough English and high school training is indispensable.

3. Negroes going into business should remember that their customers demand courtesy, honesty, and careful methods, and they should not expect patronage when their manner of conducting business does not justify it.

4. The mass of the Negroes must learn to patronize business enterprises conducted by their own race, even at some slight disadvantage. We *must* cooperate or we are lost. Ten million people who join in intelligent self-help can never be long ignored or mistreated.

5. The 1,900 business men reported to the conference are to be congratulated. They are pioneers in a great movement, and some of them have made a creditable record. We earnestly ask Negroes—and especially the better class of thinking Negroes—to patronize these establishments and encourage them in every way.

6. The most advisable work for the immediate future would seem to be: (a) Continued agitation in churches, schools, and newspapers, and by all other avenues, of the necessity of business careers for young people.

(b) Increased effort to encourage saving and habits of thrift among the young that we may have more capital at our disposal.

(c) The organization in every town and hamlet where colored people dwell, of Negro Business Men's Leagues, and the gradual federation from these of state and national organizations.

42. ON COOPERATION
AMONG BLACK CONSUMERS

A. COOPERATION, 1917

But how shall we enter? Shall we try the old paths of individual exploitation, develop a class of rich and grasping brigands of Industry, use them to exploit the mass of the black laboring people and reproduce in our own group all the industrial Hell of old Europe and America? No! This method has been advocated but it has been advocated by people who did not realize the new spirit that has come to the industrial world. Slowly and with great difficulty this new spirit is going to work itself out in the white world; but if we American Negroes are keen and intelligent we can evolve a new and efficient industrial co-operation quicker than any other group of people, for the simple reason that our inequalities of wealth are small, our group loyalty is growing stronger and stronger, and the necessity for a change in our industrial life is becoming imperative. Think of the teeming thousands, not to say millions, of colored working-men who are literally mad to get simply the ordinary decencies of employment, who are anxious and eager for proper industrial leadership on the part of their own people.

Brethren, the door of opportunity is open before us, leading to such kingdoms as neither Alexander nor Napoleon ever dreamed of.

In the next number of *The Crisis* we shall pursue further this line of argument.

Editorial in THE CRISIS, XIV (August 1917), 166.

B. A REPORT

In August, 1918, the Editor of THE CRISIS held a meeting in New York, of those persons interested in the idea of co-operation and its spread and adoption among colored people. Among those present was B. M. Roddy of Memphis, Tenn., who returned home and who entered upon an active campaign for the introduction of co-operation throughout the South—beginning, naturally enough, with Memphis. It is to Mr. Roddy that we are indebted for the main facts of this article.

Several people in Memphis becoming, through Mr. Roddy, interested in co-operation, got together small groups of people who studied the subject. By February, 1919, a charter of incorporation for the State of Tennessee was secured and a co-operative organization founded. It was made plain to the members that the purpose of such an organization was to secure and protect the interest of the members. They themselves were to control the distribution of necessities and all profits were to be divided among them. The basis of division of profits rested on the amount of shares owned by each member, however, and not on the amount of goods purchased, which is the better plan.

In the case of this particular co-operative organization, incorporated, by the way, under the name of The Citizens' Co-operative Stores, the capital stock was originally $5,000, to which the members were invited to subscribe at $12.50 per share. This amount might be paid cash down or in weekly installments of no less than fifty cents. No member might purchase more than ten shares and each member was to receive dividends on his holdings whenever the net assets of the corporation so permitted.

Within ninety days after receiving the charter the organization had sold the entire $5,000 worth of stock and was obliged to amend the charter and capitalize anew at $15,000. By August

Untitled article in THE CRISIS, XIX (December 1919), 48, 50.

30, 1919, $10,000 worth of this stock had been sold and now five stores with meat markets are operating.

In the vicinity of each store is a Negro co-operative guild composed of the stockholders of the Company,—those who have already paid for their shares,—and of the prospective stockholders—those who are buying shares on the installment plan. The members of these guilds meet at least once a month, keep abreast of co-operative literature, open discussions and offer suggestions.

We regret that the stores thus auspiciously established have not adopted the full co-operative principle, namely, one vote to each shareholder, regardless of the number of shares he holds; and distribution of profits according to purchase made and not according to shares bought. This is a wise and fundamental principle and we hope to see it followed in the future.

Despite this, one sees that what is actually happening is the phenomenon of a group of people buying and selling to themselves,—buying necessities at cost and selling them back to themselves at retail prices. But just because the group that buys is also the group that sells, it is possible for the difference between the wholesale and the retail price to be returned to the members of the group as profits. In other words, the group is its own *middle-man* and reaps the benefit of such a procedure.

The good results of co-operation among colored people do not lie alone in the return of savings. They show, also, new opportunities for the earning of a livelihood, and in the chance offered our colored youth to become acquainted with business methods. For naturally in enterprises of this sort colored property is used whenever possible, colored management and colored clerks, typists, book-keepers, and the like, are employed. Thus, in a larger and different sense, we have another form of co-operation. Colored people are furnishing their own with work and money for services received and the recipients are handing the money back for re-distribution to the original colored sources. The possibilities of such an organization are almost boundless. Thus, as the co-operative society in Memphis grows, it proposes to own its own buildings. From this the ownership of co-operative warehouses would be a natural and easy step, and so the circle widens.

Business is not all there is to life. Co-operation aims at something else besides the establishment of food and clothing stores. Its main object is organization among a people who are in sad lack of that particular thing. It hopes to introduce insurance against unemployment, sickness, old age; to establish a system whereby loans can be made to deserving members without the onus of high interest rates. It aspires to help out in time of strikes and lock-outs, to provide club-houses, hospitals, recreation-centres.

Finally, co-operation establishes the spirit of brotherhood. We have Mr. Roddy's word for it in Memphis. These five stores are serving 75,000 people who are rallying to a concern which shows that the interest of one is the interest of all, that no man in this organization can lose without the reflection of his loss in the returns of all those connected with him. An attitude enforced may easily become a habit. Interest for self-protection in other people finally develops into an interest in those people for their own sake. This is the lesson of co-operation.

Co-operation is an organized non-political effort of the people to control the production and distribution of the things needed to satisfy their wants. Its first requisite is loyalty and friendship toward one's fellowmen. Usually shares cost $10. No society should start with less than 20 members and $200 subscribed. With this amount, at first, they buy at wholesale a few of the most used commodities—sugar, flour, coffee, tea, eggs, etc. These they sell at the current *retail* price—not at cost—to their members. They save the amount which represents the difference between the cost and the selling price (the profit that had previously gone to the private merchant) and return it to the members in *proportion to their purchases.*

Persons interested may write to the editor.

C. COOPERATION, 1920

Several cooperative efforts are starting among colored people. Probably today, there are fifty or more local efforts. Most of them are sporadic, and will fail. Some few are the efforts of individuals who use the magic word cooperation for stores in which there is not a trace of the cooperation principle.

There are a dozen or more which are largely cooperative, but not entirely—for instance, they have shares, and the number which one man may own is limited. The shareholders are obliged to buy a certain minimum amount of goods before they can share in the profits.

This is only partially cooperative. Full cooperation requires: cheap shares, of which anyone can own any number; BUT there is no temptation to own large numbers of shares, because PROFITS ARE DIVIDED ACCORDING TO THE AMOUNT THE PERSON BUYS.

Why, now, do beginners hesitate to make this last provision? Because having stirred up the people by the argument of race loyalty and opened the store, they say: "Why should I surrender the coming profits to a mass of people whom the driblets will not greatly benefit? Why not keep them and GROW RICH!"

Hesitate, brother, hesitate, RIGHT THERE! Remember that with the present chain grocery store and trust system, your individual grocery has a small chance to succeed, because the Trust can and will undersell you.

But with the true cooperative principle, your clientele is nailed down. Your shareholders are pledged by their own interests to trade with you, and to trade often and much. The more they spend the more they make. Your business is no guesswork. You know just how much to buy. If the chain store cuts prices below cost, your people will buy of you at the higher price, because they know that the low price is a temporary trick for which they themselves will eventually pay. Whatever happens, you CANNOT fail as long as your shareholders are true, and they will be true as long as they share in the profits according to their purchases.

Don't be afraid. Try the whole cooperative program. Write us.

43. ON PAN-AFRICANISM: "THE DIVINE RIGHT OF SUPPRESSED . . . PEOPLES TO . . . BE FREE"

To the world

The absolute equality of races,—physical, political and social —is the founding stone of world peace and human advancement. No one denies great differences of gift, capacity and attainment among individuals of all races, but the voice of science, religion and practical politics is one in denying the God-appointed existence of super-races, or of races naturally and inevitably and eternally inferior.

That in the vast range of time, one group should in its industrial technique, or social organization, or spiritual vision, lag a few hundred years behind another, or forge fitfully ahead, or come to differ decidedly in thought, deed and ideal, is proof of the essential richness and variety of human nature, rather than proof of the co-existence of demi-gods and apes in human form. The doctrine of racial equality does not interfere with individual liberty, rather, it fulfils it. And of all the various criteria by which masses of men have in the past been prejudged and classified, that of the color of the skin and texture of the hair, is surely the most adventitious and idiotic.

It is the duty of the world to assist in every way the advance

W. E. B. Du Bois, "Manifesto of the Second Pan-African Congress" (1921), THE CRISIS, XXIII (November 1921), 5–10.

of the backward and suppressed groups of mankind. The rise of all men is a menace to no one and is the highest human ideal; it is not an altruistic benevolence, but the one road to world salvation.

For the purpose of raising such peoples to intelligence, self-knowledge and self-control, their intelligentsia of right ought to be recognized as the natural leaders of their groups.

The insidious and dishonorable propaganda, which, for selfish ends, so distorts and denies facts as to represent the advancement and development of certain races of men as impossible and undesirable, should be met with widespread dissemination of the truth. The experiment of making the Negro slave a free citizen in the United States is not a failure; the attempts at autonomous government in Haiti and Liberia are not proofs of the impossibility of self-government among black men; the experience of Spanish America does not prove that mulatto democracy will not eventually succeed there; the aspirations of Egypt and India are not successfully to be met by sneers at the capacity of darker races.

We who resent the attempt to treat civilized men as uncivilized, and who bring in our hearts grievance upon grievance against those who lynch the untried, disfranchise the intelligent, deny self-government to educated men, and insult the helpless, we complain; but not simply or primarily for ourselves—more especially for the millions of our fellows, blood of our blood, and flesh of our flesh, who have not even what we have—the power to complain against monstrous wrong, the power to see and to know the source of our oppression.

How far the future advance of mankind will depend upon the social contact and physical intermixture of the various strains of human blood is unknown, but the demand for the interpenetration of countries and intermingling of blood has come, in modern days, from the white race alone, and has been imposed upon brown and black folks mainly by brute force and fraud. On top of this, the resulting people of mixed race have had to endure innuendo, persecution, and insult, and the penetrated countries have been forced into semi-slavery.

If it be proven that absolute world segregation by group, color or historic affinity is best for the future, let the white race leave the dark world and the darker races will gladly leave the white. But the proposition is absurd. This is a world of men, of men whose likenesses far outweigh their differences; who mutually need each other in labor and thought and dream, but who can successfully have each other only on terms of equality, justice and mutual respect. They are the real and only peacemakers who work sincerely and peacefully to this end.

The beginning of wisdom in interracial contact is the establishment of political institutions among suppressed peoples. The habit of democracy must be made to encircle the earth. Despite the attempt to prove that its practice is the secret and divine gift of the few, no habit is more natural or more widely spread among primitive people, or more easily capable of development among masses. Local self-government with a minimum of help and oversight can be established tomorrow in Asia, in Africa, in America and in the Isles of the Sea. It will in many instances need general control and guidance, but it will fail only when that guidance seeks ignorantly and consciously its own selfish ends and not the people's liberty and good.

Surely in the 20th century of the Prince of Peace, in the millenium of Buddha and Mahmoud, and in the mightiest Age of Human Reason, there can be found in the civilized world enough of altruism, learning and benevolence to develop native institutions for the native's good, rather than continue to allow the majority of mankind to be brutalized and enslaved by ignorant and selfish agents of commercial institutions, whose one aim is profit and power for the few.

And this brings us to the crux of the matter: It is the shame of the world that today the relation between the main groups of mankind and their mutual estimate and respect is determined chiefly by the degree in which one can subject the other to its service, enslaving labor, making ignorance compulsory, uprooting ruthlessly religion and customs, and destroying government, so that the favored Few may luxuriate in the toil of the tortured Many. Science, Religion and Philanthropy have thus been made the slaves of world commerce and industry, and bodies, minds, souls of Fiji and Congo, are judged almost solely by the quotations on the Bourse.

The day of such world organization is past and whatever excuse be made for it in other ages, the 20th century must come to judge men as men and not as material and labor.

The great industrial problem which has hitherto been regarded as the domestic problem of culture lands, must be viewed far more broadly, if it is ever to reach just settlement. Labor and capital in England, France and America can never solve their problem as long as a similar and vastly greater problem of poverty and injustice marks the relations of the whiter and darker peoples. It is shameful, unreligious, unscientific and undemocratic that the estimate, which half the peoples of earth put on the other half, depends mainly on their ability to squeeze profit out of them.

If we are coming to recognize that the great modern problem is to correct maladjustment in the distribution of wealth, it must be remembered that the basic maladjustment is in the outrageously unjust distribution of world income between the dominant and supressed peoples; in the rape of land and raw material, and monopoly of technique and culture. And in this crime white labor is *particeps criminis* with white capital. Unconsciously and consciously, carelessly and deliberately, the vast power of the white labor vote in modern democracies has been cajoled and flattered into imperialistic schemes to enslave and debauch black, brown and yellow labor, until with fatal retribution, they are themselves today bound and gagged and rendered impotent by the resulting monopoly of the world's raw material in the hands of a dominant, cruel and irresponsible few.

And, too, just as curiously, the educated and cultured of the world, the well-born and well-bred, and even the deeply pious and philanthropic, receive their training and comfort and luxury, the ministrations of delicate beauty and sensibility, on condition that they neither inquire into the real source of their income and the methods of distribution or interfere with the

legal props which rest on a pitiful human foundation of writh-
ing white and yellow and brown and black bodies.

We claim no perfectness of our own nor do we seek to
escape the blame which of right falls on the backward for failure to advance, but *noblesse oblige,* and we arraign civilization
and more especially the colonial powers for deliberate trans-
gressions of our just demands and their own better conscience.

England, with her Pax Britannica, her courts of justice, established commerce and a certain apparent recognition of native
law and customs, has nevertheless systematically fostered
ignorance among the natives, has enslaved them and is still
enslaving some of them, has usually declined even to try to train
black and brown men in real self-government, to recognize
civilized black folks as civilized, or to grant to colored colonies
those rights of self-government which it freely gives to white
men.

Belgium is a nation which has but recently assumed responsibility for her colonies, and has taken some steps to lift them
from the worst abuses of the autocratic regime; but she has not
confirmed to the people the possession of their land and labor,
and she shows no disposition to allow the natives any voice in
their own government, or to provide for their political future.
Her colonial policy is still mainly dominated by the banks and
great corporations. But we are glad to learn that the present
government is considering a liberal program of reform for the
future.

Portugal and Spain have never drawn a legal caste line
against persons of culture who happen to be of Negro descent.
Portugal has a humane code for the natives and has begun their
education in some regions. But, unfortunately, the industrial
concessions of Portuguese Africa are almost wholly in the hands
of foreigners whom Portugal cannot or will not control, and
who are exploiting land and re-establishing the African slave
trade.

The United States of America after brutally enslaving millions of black folks suddenly emancipated them and began their
education; but it acted without system or forethought, throwing

the freed men upon the world penniless and landless, educating them without thoroughness and system, and subjecting them the while to lynching, lawlessness, discrimination, insult and slander, such as human beings have seldom endured and survived. To save their own government, they enfranchized the Negro and then when danger passed, allowed hundreds of thousands of educated and civilized black folk to be lawlessly disfranchised and subjected to a caste system; and, at the same time, in 1776, 1812, 1861, 1898, and 1917, they asked and allowed thousands of black men to offer up their lives as a sacrifice to the country which despised and dispises them.

France alone of the great colonial powers has sought to place her cultured black citizens on a plane of absolute legal and social equality with her white and given them representation in her highest legislature. In her colonies she has a widespread but still imperfect system of state education. This splendid beginning must be completed by widening the political basis of her native government, by restoring to the indigenes the ownership of the soil, by protecting native labor against the aggression of established capital, and by asking no man, black or white, to be a soldier unless the country gives him a voice in his own government.

The independence of Abyssinia, Liberia, Haiti and San Domingo, is absolutely necessary to any sustained belief of the black folk in the sincerity and honesty of the white. These nations have earned the right to be free, they deserve the recognition of the world; notwithstanding all their faults and mistakes, and the fact that they are behind the most advanced civilization of the day, nevertheless they compare favorably with the past, and even more recent, history of most European nations, and it shames civilization that the treaty of London practically invited Italy to aggression in Abyssinia, and that free America has unjustly and cruelly seized Haiti, murdered and for a time enslaved her workmen, overthrown her free institutions by force, and has so far failed in return to give her a single bit of help, aid or sympathy.

What do those wish who see these evils of the color line and racial discrimination and who believe in the divine right of supressed and backward peoples to learn and aspire and be free?

The Negro race through its thinking intelligentsia is demanding:

I—The recognition of civilized men as civilized despite their race or color

II—Local self government for backward groups, deliberately rising as experience and knowledge grow to complete self government under the limitations of a self governed world

III—Education in self knowledge, in scientific truth and in industrial technique, undivorced from the art of beauty

IV—Freedom in their own religion and social customs, and with the right to be different and non-conformist

V—Co-operation with the rest of the world in government, industry and art on the basis of Justice, Freedom and Peace

VI—The ancient common ownership of the land and its natural fruits and defence against the unrestrained greed of invested capital

VII—The establishment under the League of Nations of an international institution for the study of Negro problems

VIII—The establishment of an international section in the Labor Bureau of the League of Nations, charged with the protection of native labor.

The world must face two eventualities: either the complete assimilation of Africa with two or three of the great world states, with political, civil and social power and privileges absolutely equal for its black and white citizens, or the rise of a great black African state founded in Peace and Good Will, based on popular education, natural art and industry and freedom of trade; autonomous and sovereign in its internal policy, but from its beginning a part of a great society of peoples in which it takes its place with others as co-rulers of the world.

In some such words and thoughts as these we seek to express our will and ideal, and the end of our untiring effort. To our aid we call all men of the Earth who love Justice and Mercy.

Out of the depths we have cried unto the deaf and dumb masters of the world. Out of the depths we cry to our own sleeping souls.

The answer is written in the stars.

44. ON CULTURAL NATIONALISM: "LET US TRAIN OURSELVES TO SEE BEAUTY IN BLACK"

A. IN BLACK

It was in Chicago. John Haynes Holmes was talking.

He said: "I met two children—one as fair as the dawn—the other as beautiful as the night." Then he paused. He had to pause for the audience guffawed in wild merriment. Why?

It was a colored audience. Many of them were black. Some black faces there were as beautiful as the night.

Why did they laugh?

Because the world had taught them to be ashamed of their color.

Because for 500 years men had hated and despised and abused black folk.

And now in strange, inexplicable transposition the rising blacks laugh at themselves in nervous, blatant, furtive merriment.

They laugh because they think they are expected to laugh—because all their poor hunted lives they have heard "black" things laughed at.

Editorial in THE CRISIS, XX (October 1920), 263, 266.

Of all the pitiful things of this pitiful race problem, this is the pitifullest. So curious a mental state tends to further subtleties. Colored folk, like all folk, love to see themselves in pictures; but they are afraid to see the types which the white world has caricatured. The whites obviously seldom picture brown and yellow folk, but for five centuries they have exhausted every ingenuity of trick, of ridicule and caricature on black folk: "grinning" Negroes, "happy" Negroes, "gold dust twins," "Aunt Jemimas," "solid" headed tacks—everything and anything to make Negroes ridiculous. As a result if THE CRISIS puts a black face on its cover our 500,000 colored readers do not see the actual picture—they see the caricature that white folk intend when *they* make a black face. In the last few years a thoughtful, clear eyed artist, Frank Walts, has done a number of striking portraits for THE CRISIS. Mainly he has treated black faces; and regularly protests have come to us from various colored sources. His lovely portrait of the bright-eyed boy, Harry Elam, done in thoughtful sympathy, was approved by few Negroes. Our photograph of a woman of Santa Lucia, with its strength and humor and fine swing of head, was laughed at by many.

Why?

"O—er—it was not because they were black," stammer some of my office companions, "but they are *too* black. No people were ever so—"

Nonsense! Do white people complain because their pictures are too white? They ought to, but they do not. Neither do we complain if we are photographed a shade "light."

No. It is not that we are ashamed of our color and blood. We are instinctively and almost unconsciously ashamed of the caricatures done of our darker shades. Black *is* caricature in our half conscious thought and we shun in print and paint that which we love in life. How good a dark face looks to us in a strange white city! How the black soldiers, despite their white French sweethearts, yearned for their far-off "brown-skins." A mighty and swelling human consciousness is leading us joyously to embrace the darker world, but we remain afraid of black pictures because they are the cruel reminders of the crimes of Sunday "comics" and "Nigger" minstrels.

Off with these thought-chains and inchoate soul-shrinkings, and let us train ourselves to see beauty in black.

B. CRITERIA OF NEGRO ART

I do not doubt, but there are some in this audience who are a little disturbed at the subject of this meeting, and particularly at the subject I have chosen. Such people are thinking something like this: "How is it that an organization like this, a group of radicals trying to bring new things into the world, a fighting organization which has come up out of the blood and dust of battle, struggling for the right of black men to be ordinary human beings—how is it that an organization of this kind can turn aside to talk about Art? After all, what have we who are slaves and black to do with Art?"

Or perhaps there are others who feel a certain relief and are saying, "After all it is rather satisfactory after all this talk about rights and fighting to sit and dream of something which leaves a nice taste in the mouth."

Let me tell you that neither of these groups is right. The thing we are talking about tonight is part of the great fight we are carrying on and it represents a forward and an upward look —a pushing onward. You and I have been breasting hills; we have been climbing upward; there has been progress and we can see it day by day looking back along blood-filled paths. But as you go through the valleys and over the foothills, so long as you are climbing, the direction,—north, south, east or west,— is of less importance. But when gradually the vista widens and you begin to see the world at your feet and the far horizon, then

W. E. B. Du Bois, "Criteria of Negro Art," THE CRISIS, XXXII (October 1926), 290, 292, 294, 296–297.

it is time to know more precisely whither you are going and what you really want.

What do we want? What is the thing we are after? As it was phrased last night it had a certain truth: We want to be Americans, full-fledged Americans, with all the rights of other American citizens. But is that all? Do we want simply to be Americans? Once in a while through all of us there flashes some clairvoyance, some clear idea, of what America really is. We who are dark can see America in a way that white Americans cannot. And seeing our country thus, are we satisfied with its present goals and ideals?

In the high school where I studied we learned most of Scott's "Lady of the Lake" by heart. In after life once it was my privilege to see the lake. It was Sunday. It was quiet. You could glimpse the deer wandering in unbroken forests; you could hear the soft ripple of romance on the waters. Around me fell the cadence of that poetry of my youth. I fell asleep full of the enchantment of the Scottish border. A new day broke and with it came a sudden rush of excursionists. They were mostly Americans and they were loud and strident. They poured upon the little pleasure boat,—men with their hats a little on one side and drooping cigars in the wet corners of their mouths; women who shared their conversation with the world. They all tried to get everywhere first. They pushed other people out of the way. They made all sorts of incoherent noises and gestures so that the quiet home folk and the visitors from other lands silently and half-wonderingly gave way before them. They struck a note not evil but wrong. They carried, perhaps, a sense of strength and accomplishment, but their hearts had no conception of the beauty which pervaded this holy place.

If you tonight suddenly should become full-fledged Americans; if your color faded, or the color line here in Chicago was miraculously forgotten; suppose, too, you became at the same time rich and powerful;—what is it that you would want? What would you immediately seek? Would you buy the most powerful of motor cars and outrace Cook County? Would you buy the most elaborate estate on the North Shore? Would you be a

Rotarian or a Lion or a What-not of the very last degree? Would you wear the most striking clothes, give the richest dinners and buy the longest press notices?

Even as you visualize such ideals you know in your hearts that these are not the things you really want. You realize this sooner than the average white American because, pushed aside as we have been in America, there has come to us not only a certain distaste for the tawdry and flamboyant but a vision of what the world could be if it were really a beautiful world; if we had the true spirit; if we had the Seeing Eye, the Cunning Hand, the Feeling Heart; if we had, to be sure, not perfect happiness, but plenty of good hard work, the inevitable suffering that always comes with life; sacrifice and waiting, all that—but, nevertheless, lived in a world where men know, where men create, where they realize themselves and where they enjoy life. It is that sort of a world we want to create for ourselves and for all America.

After all, who shall describe Beauty? What is it? I remember tonight four beautiful things: The Cathedral at Cologne, a forest in stone, set in light and changing shadow, echoing with sunlight and solemn song; a village of the Veys in West Africa, a little thing of mauve and purple, quiet, lying content and shining in the sun; a black and velvet room where on a throne rests, in old and yellowing marble, the broken curves of the Venus of Milo; a single phrase of music in the Southern South —utter melody, haunting and appealing, suddenly arising out of night and eternity, beneath the moon.

Such is Beauty. Its variety is infinite. Its possibility is endless. In normal life all may have it and have it yet again. The world is full of it; and yet today the mass of human beings are choked away from it, and their lives distorted and made ugly. This is not only wrong, it is silly. Who shall right this well-nigh universal failing? Who shall let this world be beautiful? Who shall restore to men the glory of sunsets and the peace of quiet sleep?

We black folk may help for we have within us as a race new stirrings; stirrings of the beginning of a new appreciation of joy; of a new desire to create, of a new will to be; as though in this morning of group life we had awakened from some sleep that at once dimly mourns the past and dreams a splendid future; and there has come the conviction that the Youth that is here today, the Negro Youth, is a different kind of Youth, because in some new way it bears this mighty prophecy on its breast, with a new realization of itself, with new determination for all mankind.

What has this Beauty to do with the world? What has Beauty to do with Truth and Goodness—with the facts of the world and the right actions of men? "Nothing," the artists rush to answer. They may be right. I am but an humble disciple of art and cannot presume to say. I am one who tells the truth and exposes evil and, seeks with Beauty and for Beauty to set the world right. That somehow, somewhere eternal and perfect Beauty sits above Truth and Right I can conceive, but here and now in the world in which I work they are for me unseparated and inseparable.

This is brought to us peculiarly when as artists we face our own past as a people. There has come to us—and it has come especially through the man we are going to honor tonight*—a realization of that past, of which for long years we have been ashamed, for which we have apologized. We thought nothing could come out of that past which we wanted to remember; which we wanted to hand down to our children. Suddenly, this same past is taking on form, color and reality, and in a half shamefaced way we are beginning to be proud of it. We are remembering that the romance of the world did not die and lie forgotten in the Middle Age; that if you want romance to deal with you must have it here and now and in your own hands.

I once knew a man and woman. They had two children, a daughter who was white and a daughter who was brown; the daughter who was white married a white man; and when her wedding was preparing the daughter who was brown prepared to go and celebrate. But the mother said, "No!" and the brown daughter went into her room and turned on the gas and died. Do you want Greek tragedy swifter than that?

Or again, here is a little Southern town and you are in the

---

* Carter Godwin Woodson, 12th Spingarn Medallist.

public square. On one side of the square is the office of a colored lawyer and on all the other sides are men who do not like colored lawyers. A white woman goes into the black man's office and points to the white-filled square and says, "I want five hundred dollars now and if I do not get it I am going to scream."

Have you heard the story of the conquest of German East Africa? Listen to the untold tale: There were 40,000 black men and 4,000 white men who talked German. There were 20,000 black men and 12,000 white men who talked English. There were 10,000 black men and 400 white men who talked French. In Africa then where the Mountains of the Moon raised their white and snow-capped heads into the mouth of the tropic sun, where Nile and Congo rise and the Great Lakes swim, these men fought; they struggled on mountain, hill and valley, in river, lake and swamp, until in masses they sickened, crawled and died; until the 4,000 white Germans had become mostly bleached bones; until nearly all the 12,000 white Englishmen had returned to South Africa, and the 400 Frenchmen to Belgium and Heaven—all except a mere handful of the white men died; but thousands of black men from East, West and South Africa, from Nigeria and the Valley of the Nile, and from the West Indies still struggled, fought and died. For four years they fought and won and lost German East Africa; and all you hear about it is that England and Belgium conquered German Africa for the allies!

Such is the true and stirring stuff of which Romance is born and from this stuff come the stirrings of men who are beginning to remember that this kind of material is theirs; and this vital life of their own kind is beckoning them on.

The question comes next as to the interpretation of these new stirrings, of the new spirit: Of what is the colored artist capable? We have had on the part of both colored and white people singular unanimity of judgment in the past. Colored people have said: "This work must be inferior because it comes from colored people." White people have said: "It is inferior because it is done by colored people." But today there is coming to both the realization that the work of the black man is not always inferior. Interesting stories come to us. A professor in the University of Chicago read to a class that had studied literature a passage of poetry and asked them to guess the author. They guessed a goodly company from Shelley and Robert Browning down to Tennyson and Masefield. The author was Countee Cullen. Or again the English critic John Drinkwater went down to a Southern seminary, one of the sort which "finishes" young white women of the South. The students sat with their wooden faces while he tried to get some response out of them. Finally he said, "Name me some of your Southern poets." They hesitated. He said finally, "I'll start out with your best: Paul Laurence Dunbar!"

With the growing recognition of Negro artists in spite of the severe handicaps, one comforting thing is occurring to both white and black. They are whispering, "Here is a way out. Here is the real solution of the color problem. The recognition accorded Cullen, Hughes, Fauset, White and others shows there is no real color line. Keep quiet! Don't complain! Work! All will be well!"

I will not say that already this chorus amounts to a conspiracy. Perhaps I am naturally too suspicious. But I will say that there are today a surprising number of white people who are getting great satisfaction out of these younger Negro writers because they think it is going to stop agitation of the Negro question. They say, "What is the use of your fighting and complaining; do the great thing and the reward is there." And many colored people are all too eager to follow this advice; especially those who are weary of the eternal struggle along the color line, who are afraid to fight and to whom the money of philanthropists and the alluring publicity are subtle and deadly bribes. They say, "What is the use of fighting? Why not show simply what we deserve and let the reward come to us?"

And it is right here that the National Association for the Advancement of Colored People comes upon the field, comes with its great call to a new battle, a new fight and new things to fight before the old things are wholly won; and to say that the Beauty of Truth and Freedom which shall some day be our heritage and the heritage of all civilized men is not in our hands yet and that we ourselves must not fail to realize.

There is in New York tonight a black woman molding clay by herself in a little bare room, because there is not a single school of sculpture in New York where she is welcome. Surely there are doors she might burst through, but when God makes a sculptor He does not always make the pushing sort of person who beats his way through doors thrust in his face. This girl is working her hands off to get out of this country so that she can get some sort of training.

There was Richard Brown. If he had been white he would have been alive today instead of dead of neglect. Many helped him when he asked but he was not the kind of boy that always asks. He was simply one who made colors sing.

There is a colored woman in Chicago who is a great musician. She thought she would like to study at Fountainebleau this summer where Walter Damrosch and a score of leaders of Art have an American school of music. But the application blank of this school says: "I am a white American and I apply for admission to the school."

We can go on the stage; we can be just as funny as white Americans wish us to be; we can play all the sordid parts that America likes to assign to Negroes; but for anything else there is still small place for us.

And so I might go on. But let me sum up with this: Suppose the only Negro who survived some centuries hence was the Negro painted by white Americans in the novels and essays they have written. What would people in a hundred years say of black Americans? Now turn it around. Suppose you were to write a story and put in it the kind of people you know and like and imagine. You might get it published and you might not. And the "might not" is still far bigger than the "might." The white publishers catering to white folk would say, "It is not interesting"—to white folk, naturally not. They want Uncle Toms, Topsies, good "darkies" and clowns. I have in my office a story with all the earmarks of truth. A young man says that he started out to write and had his stories accepted. Then he began to write about the things he knew best about, that is, about his own people. He submitted a story to a magazine which said, "We are sorry, but we cannot take it." "I sat down and revised my story, changing the color of the characters and the locale and sent it under an assumed name with a change of address and it was accepted by the same magazine that had refused it, the editor promising to take anything else I might send in providing it was good enough."

We have, to be sure, a few recognized and successful Negro artists; but they are not all those fit to survive or even a good minority. They are but the remnants of that ability and genius among us whom the accidents of education and opportunity have raised on the tidal waves of chance. We black folk are not altogether peculiar in this. After all, in the world at large, it is only the accident, the remnant, that gets the chance to make the most of itself; but if this is true of the white world it is infinitely more true of the colored world. It is not simply the great clear tenor of Roland Hayes that opened the ears of America. We have had many voices of all kinds as fine as his and America was and is as deaf as she was for years to him. Then a foreign land heard Hayes and put its imprint on him and immediately America with all its imitative snobbery woke up. We approved Hayes because London, Paris and Berlin approved him and not simply because he was a great singer.

Thus it is the bounden duty of black America to begin this great work of the creation of Beauty, of the preservation of Beauty, of the realization of Beauty, and we must use in this work all the methods that men have used before. And what have been the tools of the artist in times gone by? First of all, he has used the Truth—not for the sake of truth, not as a scientist seeking truth, but as one upon whom Truth eternally thrusts itself as the highest handmaid of imagination, as the one great vehicle of universal understanding. Again artists have used Goodness—goodness in all its aspects of justice, honor and right—not for sake of an ethical sanction but as the one true method of gaining sympathy and human interest.

The apostle of Beauty thus becomes the apostle of Truth and

Right not by choice but by inner and outer compulsion. Free he is but his freedom is ever bounded by Truth and Justice; and slavery only dogs him when he is denied the right to tell the Truth or recognize an ideal of Justice.

Thus all Art is propaganda and ever must be, despite the wailing of the purists. I stand in utter shamelessness and say that whatever art I have for writing has been used always for propaganda for gaining the right of black folk to love and enjoy. I do not care a damn for any art that is not used for propaganda. But I do care when propaganda is confined to one side while the other is stripped and silent.

In New York we have two plays: "White Cargo" and "Congo." In "White Cargo" there is a fallen woman. She is black. In "Congo" the fallen woman is white. In "White Cargo" the black woman goes down further and further and in "Congo" the white woman begins with degradation but in the end is one of the angels of the Lord.

You know the current magazine story: A young white man goes down to Central America and the most beautiful colored woman there falls in love with him. She crawls across the whole isthmus to get to him. The white man says nobly, "No." He goes back to his white sweetheart in New York.

In such cases, it is not the positive propaganda of people who believe white blood divine, infallible and holy to which I object. It is the denial of a similar right of propaganda to those who believe black blood human, lovable and inspired with new ideals for the world. White artists themselves suffer from the narrowing of their field. They cry for freedom in dealing with Negroes because they have so little freedom in dealing with whites. DuBose Heyward writes "Porgy" and writes beautifully of the black Charleston underworld. But why does he do this? Because he cannot do a similar thing for the white people of Charleston, or they would drum him out of town. The only chance he had to tell the truth of pitiful human degradation was to tell it of colored people. I should not be surprised if Octavius Roy Cohen had approached the *Saturday Evening Post* and asked permission to write about a different kind of colored folk than the monstrosities he has created; but if he has, the *Post* has replied, "No. You are getting paid to write about the kind of colored people you are writing about."

In other words, the white public today demands from its artists, literary and pictorial, racial pre-judgment which deliberately distorts Truth and Justice, as far as colored races are concerned, and it will pay for no other.

On the other hand, the young and slowly growing black public still wants its prophets almost equally unfree. We are bound by all sorts of customs that have come down as second-hand soul clothes of white patrons. We are ashamed of sex and we lower our eyes when people will talk of it. Our religion holds us in superstition. Our worst side has been so shamelessly emphasized that we are denying we have or ever had a worst side. In all sorts of ways we are hemmed in and our new young artists have got to fight their way to freedom.

The ultimate judge has got to be you and you have got to build yourselves up into that wide judgment, that catholicity of temper which is going to enable the artist to have his widest chance for freedom. We can afford the Truth. White folk today cannot. As it is now we are handing everything over to a white jury. If a colored man wants to publish a book, he has got to get a white publisher and a white newspaper to say it is great; and then you and I say so. We must come to the place where the work of art when it appears is reviewed and acclaimed by our own free and unfettered judgment. And we are going to have a real and valuable and eternal judgment only as we make ourselves free of mind, proud of body, and just of soul to all men.

And then do you know what will be said? It is already saying. Just as soon as true Art emerges; just as soon as the black artist appears, someone touches the race on the shoulder and says, "He did that because he was an American, not because he was a Negro; he was born here; he was trained here; he is not a Negro—what is a Negro anyhow? He is just human; it is the kind of thing you ought to expect."

I do not doubt that the ultimate art coming from black folk

is going to be just as beautiful, and beautiful largely in the same ways, as the art that comes from white folk, or yellow, or red; but the point today is that until the art of the black folk compels recognition they will not be rated as human. And when through art they compel recognition then let the world discover if it will that their art is as new as it is old and as old as new.

I had a classmate once who did three beautiful things and died. One of them was a story of a folk who found fire and then went wandering in the gloom of night seeking again the stars they had once known and lost; suddenly out of blackness they looked up and there loomed the heavens; and what was-it that they said? They raised a mighty cry: "It is the stars, it is the ancient stars, it is the young and everlasting stars!"

45. ON BLACK SEPARATISM: "ORGANIZE OUR ECONOMIC AND SOCIAL POWER, NO MATTER HOW MUCH SEGREGATION IT INVOLVES"

I have read with interest the various criticisms on my recent discussions of segregation. Those like that of Mr. Pierce of Cleveland, do not impress me. I am not worried about being inconsistent. What worries me is the Truth. I am talking about conditions in 1934 and not in 1910. I do not care what I said in 1910 or 1810 or in B.C. 700.

The arguments of Walter White, George Schuyler and Kelly Miller have logic, but they seem to me quite beside the point. In the first place, Walter White is white. He has more white companions and friends than colored. He goes where he will in New York City and naturally meets no Color Line, for the

W. E. B. Du Bois, "Segregation in the North,"
THE CRISIS, XLI (April 1934), 115–117.

simple and sufficient reason that he isn't "colored"; he feels his new freedom in bitter contrast to what he was born to in Georgia. This is perfectly natural and he does what anyone else of his complexion would do.

But it is fantastic to assume that this has anything to do with the color problem in the United States. It naturally makes Mr. White an extreme opponent of any segregation based on a myth of race. But this argument does not apply to Schuyler or Miller or me. Moreover, Mr. White knows this. He moved once into a white apartment house and it went black on him. He now lives in a colored apartment house with attendant limitations. He once took a friend to dine with him at the celebrated café of the Lafayette Hotel, where he had often been welcomed. The management humiliated him by refusing to serve Roland Hayes.

The attitudes of Schuyler and Kelly Miller are historically based on the amiable assumption that there is little or no segregation in the North, and that agitation and a firm stand is making this disappear; that obvious desert and accomplishment by Negroes can break down prejudice. This is a fable. I once believed it passionately. It may become true in 250 or 1,000 years. Now it is not true. No black man whatever his culture or ability is today in America regarded as a man by any considerable number of white Americans. The difference between North and South in the matter of segregation is largely a difference of degree; of wide degree certainly, but still of degree.

In the North, neither Schuyler nor Kelly Miller nor anyone with a visible admixture of Negro blood can frequent hotels or restaurants. They have difficulty in finding dwelling places in better class neighborhoods. They occupy "Lower 1" on Pullmans, and if they are wise, they do not go into dining cars when any large number of white people is there. Their children either go to colored schools or to schools nominally for both races, but actually attended almost exclusively by colored children. In other words, they are confined by unyielding public opinion to a Negro world. They earn a living on colored newspapers or in colored colleges, or other racial institutions.

They treat colored patients and preach to colored pews. Not one of the 12 colored Ph.D's of last year, trained by highest American and European standards, is going to get a job in any white university. Even when Negroes in the North work side by side with whites, they are segregated, like the postal clerks, or refused by white unions or denied merited promotion.

No matter how much we may fulminate about, "No segregation," there stand the flat facts. Moreover, this situation has in the last quarter century been steadily growing worse. Mr. Spingarn may ask judicially as to whether or not the N.A.A.C.P. should change its attitude toward segregation. The point that he does not realize is that segregation has changed its attitude toward the N.A.A.C.P. The higher the Negro climbs or tries to climb, the more pitiless and unyielding the color ban. Segregation may be just as evil today as it was in 1910, but it is more insistent, more prevalent and more unassailable by appeal or argument. The pressing problem is: What are we going to do about it?

In 1910, colored men could be entertained in the best hotels in Cleveland, Detroit and Chicago. Today, there is not a single Northern city, except New York, where a Negro can be a guest at a first-class hotel. Not even in Boston is he welcome; and in New York, the number of hotels where he can go is very small. Roland Hayes was unable to get regular hotel accommodations, and Dr. Moton only succeeds by powerful white influence and by refraining from use of the public dining room or the public lobbies.

If as Spingarn asserts, the N.A.A.C.P. has conducted a quarter-century campaign against segregation, the net result has been a little less than nothing. We have by legal action steadied the foundation so that in the future, segregation must be by wish and will and not law, but beyond that we have not made the slightest impress on the determination of the overwhelming mass of white Americans not to treat Negroes as men.

These are unpleasant facts. We do not like to voice them. The theory is that by maintaining certain fictions of law and administration, by whistling and keeping our courage up, we can stand on the "principle" of no segregation and wait until public opinion meets our position. But can we do this? When we were living in times of prosperity; when we were making post-war incomes; when our labor was in demand, we perhaps could afford to wait. But today, faced by starvation and economic upheaval, and by the question of being able to survive at all in this land in the reconstruction that is upon us, it is ridiculous not to see, and criminal not to tell, the colored people that they can not base their salvation upon the empty reiteration of a slogan.

What then can we do? The only thing that we not only can, but must do, is voluntarily and insistently to organize our economic and social power, no matter how much segregation it involves. Learn to associate with ourselves and to train ourselves for effective association. Organize our strength as consumers; learn to co-operate and use machines and power as producers; train ourselves in methods of democratic control within our own group. Run and support our own institutions.

We are doing this partially now, only we are doing it under a peculiar attitude of protest, and with only transient and distracted interest. A number of excellent young gentlemen in Washington, having formed a Negro Alliance, proceed to read me out of the congregation of the righteous because I dare even discuss segregation. But who are these young men? The products of a segregated school system; the talent selected by Negro teachers; the persons who can today, in nine cases out of ten, earn only a living through segregated Negro social institutions. These are the men who are yelling against segregation. If most of them had been educated in the mixed schools in New York instead of the segregated schools of Washington, they never would have seen college, because Washington picks out and sends ten times as many Negroes to college as New York does.

It would, of course, be full easy to deny that this voluntary association for great social and economic ends is segregation; and if I had done this in the beginning of this debate, many people would have been easily deceived, and would have yelled

"No segregation" with one side of their mouths and "Race pride and Race initiative" with the other side. No such distinction can possibly be drawn. Segregation may be compulsory by law or it may be compulsory by economic or social condition, or it may be a matter of free choice. At any rate, it is the separation of human beings and separation despite the will to humanity. Such separation is evil; it leads to jealousy, greed, nationalism and war; and yet it is today and in this world inevitable; inevitable to Jews because of Hitler; inevitable to Japanese because of white Europe; inevitable to Russia because of organized greed over all the white world; inevitable to Ethiopia because of white armies and navies; inevitable, because without it, the American Negro will suffer evils greater than any possible evil of separation: we would suffer the loss of self-respect, the lack of faith in ourselves, the lack of knowledge about ourselves, the lack of ability to make a decent living by our own efforts and not by philanthropy.

This situation has been plunged into crisis and precipitated to an open demand for thought and action by the Depression and the New Deal. The government, national and state, is helping and guiding the individual. It has entered and entered for good into the social and economic organization of life. We could wish, we could pray, that this entrance could absolutely ignore lines of race and color, but we know perfectly well it does not and will not, and with the present American opinion, it cannot. The question is then, are we going to stand out and refuse the inevitable and inescapable government aid because we first wish to abolish the Color Line? This is not simply tilting at windmills; it is, if we are not careful, committing race suicide.

"No segregation"

Back of all slogans lies the difficulty that the meanings may change without changing the words. For instance, "no segregation" may mean two very different things:

1. A chance for the Negro to advance without the hindrances which arise when he is segregated from the main group, and the main social institutions upon which society depends. He becomes, thus, an outsider, a hanger on, with no chance to function properly as a man.

2. It may mean utter lack of faith of Negroes in Negroes, and the desire to escape into another group, shirking, on the other hand, all responsibility for ignorance, degradation and lack of experience among Negroes, while asking admission into the other group on terms of full equality and with full chance for individual development.

It is in the first sense that I have always believed and used the slogan: "No Segregation." On the other hand, in the second sense, I have no desire or right to hinder or estop those persons who do not want to be Negroes. But I am compelled to ask the very plain and pertinent question: Assuming for the moment that the group into which you demand admission does not want you, what are you going to do about it? Can you demand that they want you? Can you make them by law or public opinion admit you when they are supreme over this same public opinion and make these laws? Manifestly, you cannot. Manifestly your admission to the other group on the basis of your individual desert and wish, can only be accomplished if they, too, join in the wish to have you. If they do so join, all problems based mostly on race and color disappear, and there remains only the human problems of social uplift and intelligence and group action. But there is in the United States today no sign that this objection to the social and even civic recognition of persons of Negro blood is going to occur during the life of persons now living. In which case there can be only one meaning to the slogan "No Segregation;" and that is, no hindrance to my effort to be a man. If you do not wish to associate with me, I am more than willing to associate with myself. Indeed, I deem it a privilege to work with and for Negroes, only asking that my hands be not tied nor my feet hobbled.

Objects of segregation

What is the object of those persons who insist by law, custom and propaganda to keep the American Negro separate in rights and privileges from other citizens of the United States? The real object, confessed or semiconscious, is to so isolate the Negro that he will be spiritually bankrupt, physically degenerate, and economically dependent.

Against this it is the bounden duty of every Negro and every enlightened American to protest; to oppose the policy so far as it is manifest by laws; to agitate against customs by revealing facts; and to apeal to the sense of decency and justice in all American citizens.

I have never known an American Negro who did not agree that this was a proper program. Some have disagreed as to the emphasis to be put on this and that method of protest; on the efficacy of any appeal against American prejudice; but all Negroes have agreed that segregation is bad and should be opposed.

Suppose, however, that this appeal is ineffective or nearly so? What is the Negro going to do? There is one thing that he can or must do, and that is to see to it that segregation does *not* undermine his health; does *not* leave him spiritually bankrupt; and does *not* make him an economic slave; and he must do this at any cost.

If he cannot live in sanitary and decent sections of a city, he must build his own residential quarters, and raise and keep them on a plane fit for living. If he cannot educate his children in decent schools with other children, he must, nevertheless, educate his children in decent Negro schools and arrange and conduct and oversee such schools. If he cannot enter American industry at a living wage, or find work suited to his education and talent, or receive promotion and advancement according to his desserts, he must organize his own economic life so that just as far as possible these discriminations will not reduce him to abject exploitation.

Everyone of these movements on the part of colored people

are not only necessary, but inevitable. And at the same time, they involve more or less active segregation and acquiescence in segregation.

Here again, if there be any number of American Negroes who have not in practical life made this fight of self-segregation and self-association against the compulsory segregation forced upon them, I am unacquainted with such persons. They may, of course, explain their compulsory retreat from a great ideal, by calling segregation by some other name. They may affirm with fierce insistency that they will never, no never, under any circumstances acquiesce in segregation. But if they live in the United States in the year of our Lord 1934, or in any previous year since the foundation of the government, they are segregated; they accept segregation, and they segregate themselves, because they must. From this dilemma I see no issue.

Boycott

Whither does all this sudden talk of segregation lead? May I illustrate by an appositive example. Several times THE CRISIS has commended what seemed to us the epoch-making work of The *Chicago Whip* when it instituted boycotts against stores in the black belt which refused to employ Negro clerks. Recently, in Washington, a group of young intellectuals sought to do the same thing but fell afoul of the ordinances against picketing. These efforts illustrate the use of mass action by Negroes who take advantage of segregation in order to strengthen their economic foundation. The Chicago success was applauded by every Negro in the land and the Washington failure deserved success. Today the same sort of move is being made in Richmond.

Yet, mind you, both these efforts were efforts toward segregation. The movement meant, in essence, Negro clerks for Negro customers. Of course, this was not directly said but this is what it amounted to. The proponents knew that Negro clerks would only be hired if Negro customers demanded it, and if the Negro customers, as happened in some cases, did not want to be waited on by Negro clerks, or even felt insulted if the Negro clerk came to them, then the proprietors had a perfect right to refuse to employ Negro clerks. Indeed, this happened in several cases in Harlem, New York.

And yet given the practically compulsory segregation of residence, and the Negro race is not only justified but compelled to invoke the additional gesture which involves segregation by asking Negro clerks for Negro customers. Of course, the logical demand of those who refuse to contemplate any measure of segregation, would be to demand the employment of Negro clerks everywhere in the city, and in all stores, at least in the same proportion that the Negro population bears to the total population. This was not demanded because such a demand would be futile and have no implement for its enforcement. But you can enforce the employment of Negroes by commercial houses in a Negro community and this ought to be done and must be done, and this use of the boycott by American Negroes must be widened and systematized, with care, of course, to avoid the ridiculous laws which make boycotts in so many cases illegal.

The funny postscript to all this, is that the same group of young Negroes who sought in Washington to fight segregation with segregation, or better to build a decent living on compulsory segregation, immediately set up a yell of "No Segregation," when they read THE CRISIS.

Integration

Extreme opponents of segregation act as though there was but one solution of the race problem, and that, complete integration of the black race with the white race in America, with no distinction of color in political, civil or social life. There is no doubt but what this is the great end toward which humanity is tending, and that so long as there are artificially emphasized differences of nationality, race and color, not to mention the fundamental discriminations of economic class, there will be no real Humanity.

On the other hand, it is just as clear, that not for a century and more probably not for ten centuries, will any such consummation be reached. No person born will ever live to see national and racial distinctions altogether abolished, and economic distinctions will last many a day.

Since this is true, the practical problem that faces us is not a choice between segregation and no segregation, between compulsory interferences with human intercourse and complete liberty of contact; the thing that faces us is given varying degrees of segregation. How shall we conduct ourselves so that in the end human differences will not be emphasized at the expense of human advance.

It is perfectly certain that, not only shall we be compelled to submit to much segregation, but that sometimes it will be necessary to our survival and a step toward the ultimate breaking down of barriers, to increase by voluntary action our separation from our fellowmen.

When my room-mate gets too noisy and dirty, I leave him; when my neighbors get too annoying and insulting I seek another home; when white Americans refuse to treat me as a man, I will cut my intercourse with white Americans to the minimum demanded by decent living.

It may be and often has been true that oppression and insult have become so intense and so unremitting that there is no alternative left to self-respecting men but to herd by themselves in self-defense, until the attitude of the world changes. It happens that today is peculiarly a day when such voluntary union for self-expression and self-defense is forced upon large numbers of people. We may rail against this. We may say that it is not our fault, and it certainly is not. Nevertheless, to do nothing in the face of it: to accept opposition without united counter opposition is the program of fools.

Moreover if association and contact with Negroes is distasteful to you, what is it to white people? Remember that the white people of America will certainly never want us until we want ourselves. We excuse ourselves in this case and say we do not hate Negroes but we do hate their condition, and immediately the answer is thrown back on us in the very words. Whose job is it to change that condition? The job of the white people or the job of the black people themselves, and especially of their uplifted classes?

Ethics in education

A puzzling problem of ethics has arisen in one of the largest Negro universities. A graduate student of unblemished character and excellent scholarship sent a letter to the public press condemning certain occurrences in the University. The University immediately asked this student to withdraw.

There comes now the nice question as to why he was asked to withdraw? Was it because what he said in the letter was untrue, or was it because it was true? If it was untrue, would not a sufficient answer have been a publication of the exact truth, and then perhaps an investigation as to how far the student had deliberately lied or had been mistaken. It seems, however, fortunately or unfortunately, that the student charge was true, certainly in its essential particulars, and that he was compelled to withdraw because this expenditure was "bad publicity" for the institution. This raises a very grave question of ethics in an institution of learning for Negro youth. If the truth about a situation in a university is bad publicity, the way to attack it is to change that truth and reform or not repeat the facts upon which it is based. But it is certainly an extraordinary thing to try to defend an institution by punishing a good student for telling what the university knows is true. Under such circumstances, the student who has been made to suffer ought to receive welcome and sufficient scholarship funds to pursue his work in every Negro university worth a name, not to mention white schools.

Cultural nationalism

The half-century from about 1880 to 1930 witnessed the flowering of a clear-cut cultural nationalism. It was evident particularly in a rising self-conscious interest in the race's past and in efforts to stimulate a distinctively black literature. Generally speaking, as the selections presented here indicate, this cultural nationalism was pervaded by the ethnic dualism that characterized Negro thinking. The advocates of a distinctive racial literature were quite explicit in insisting that the black artistic contribution would be part of the American cultural heritage (Documents 50 and 52). Only in the case of an emigrationist like Marcus Garvey did the strong interest in the race heritage involve a complete rejection of identification with American society.

The propagandists for black history stressed the importance of building race pride as a basis for racial advancement. E.A. Johnson, a North Carolina school principal who subsequently became the first black member of the New York legislature, wrote a popular text to help disseminate knowledge of the race's past among colored school children (see Document 46). The noted bibliophile Arthur A. Schomburg, whose library later formed the basis of the Schomburg Collection of the New York Public Library, was an active figure in the Negro Society for Historical Research, founded in 1911, and a leader in the movement to introduce courses in black history and literature into the curriculum of the Negro colleges (see Document 47). In fact, around the time of World War I, courses in these subjects began to appear in the Negro college

catalogs—a development stimulated by such figures as
Benjamin Brawley, a professor at Morehouse College.

Meanwhile, Negro history achieved a scholarly and professional
status, even though it was ignored by all but a few white
historians. George Washington Williams' two-volume *History
of the Negro Race in America* (1883) was the first serious
attempt to write a scholarly history of the black man in the
United States. Williams himself lacked professional training as
a historian. Rather, living just before the professionalization
of history that accompanied the emergence of American
graduate departments, he belonged to that school of gifted
amateur historians who dominated the writing of American
history until late in the nineteenth century. Two men who
received the Ph.D. degree from Harvard University were
responsible for putting the study of black history on
professional, scholarly foundations: W. E. B. Du Bois, whose
doctoral dissertation, *The Suppression of the African Slave
Trade,* appeared in 1896, and Carter G. Woodson, who received
his doctorate in 1912. In 1915 Woodson established the
Association for the Study of Negro Life and History. He often
declared that his objective was to prevent the race from
becoming "a negligible factor in the thought of the world."
Through the Association Woodson performed a dual function:
he carried out his mission of propagandizing the study of
Negro history as a basis for race pride, and he made
incalculable contributions to scholarship, especially through
the *Journal of Negro History.* The selection by Woodson,
summarizing the work of the Association from 1915 to 1947,
illustrates both phases of his work (Document 48).

Negro history enthusiasts like Schomburg, Du Bois, and
Woodson displayed a passionate interest in the race's African
past. Representative of this concern is the essay by Monroe
Work, which discusses the evidence for complex civilizations in
ancient and medieval Africa, and their significance for black
men in America (Document 49). Work was later well known as
editor of the *Negro Year Book: An Annual Encyclopedia of*

the Negro, and as compiler of *A Bibliography of the Negro in Africa and America* (1928).

The post-World War I years witnessed a literary and artistic ferment, known as the Harlem Renaissance, comparable to the frenetic cultural activity of the middle and late 1960s. These movements were one aspect of an increased militance among Negroes; both emphasized the uniqueness and value of black culture and the way of life of the Negro masses. On the other hand, where the artists of the Harlem Renaissance were forced to depend primarily upon a white audience, the artists of today often deliberately address themselves entirely to blacks, and frequently display a hostility toward whites absent from the works of the 1920s.

The Harlem Renaissance was crystallized for the general book-buying white public with the appearance of *Survey Graphic's* Harlem number in 1925, edited by Alain Locke and later published in book form as *The New Negro.* Locke, the first Negro Rhodes Scholar and for many years professor of philosophy at Howard University, was a leading interpreter of the Renaissance and subsequent Negro culture. As he himself noted, the roots of this movement, which he viewed as similar to the cultural and artistic movements among awakening nationalities the world over, was found in intellectual developments evident in the black community as far back as the turn of the century. The article by Benjamin Brawley, an English professor, historian, and college administrator, is representative of the writings of those intellectuals who were calling for the creation of a distinctive Negro literature that would reflect the soul and aspirations of the race (Document 50). Similarly, many leading writers and artists of the postwar period believed that the black subculture was the fruit of a unique racial experience and a distinctive racial soul. Representative of this thinking is the selection by the noted actor and singer, Paul Robeson. This essay, although published in 1934, is a product of the Renaissance period (Document 51).

The Renaissance, although rooted in prewar currents among black intellectuals, was encouraged by white philanthropists and more particularly by the editors of *The Crisis*, organ of the NAACP, and of *Opportunity*, organ of the National Urban League. In fact, Du Bois himself, as editor of *The Crisis*, was a leading propagandist for the cultural pluralism of the Renaissance (see Document 44). The essay by Locke which closes this section appeared in 1925, at the height of the Renaissance, as the introduction to *The New Negro*. It sums up with grace and perception the ideological thrust of this high point of black cultural nationalism (Document 52).

46. E. A. JOHNSON URGES THE STUDY OF AFRO-AMERICAN HISTORY "FOR A NEW SELF-RESPECT AND CONFIDENCE"

To the many thousand colored teachers in our country this book is dedicated. During my experience of eleven years as a teacher, I have often felt that the children of the race ought to study some work that would give them a little information on the many brave deeds and noble characters of their own race. I have often observed the sin of omission and commission on the part of white authors, most of whom seem to have written exclusively for white children, and studiously left out the many creditable deeds of the Negro. The general tone of most of the histories taught in our schools has been that of the inferiority of the Negro, whether actually said in so many words, or left to be implied from the highest laudation of the deeds of one race to the complete exclusion of those of the other. It must, indeed be a stimulus to any people to be able to refer to their

E. A. Johnson, A SCHOOL HISTORY OF THE NEGRO RACE
IN AMERICA FROM 1619 TO 1891 (New York: Isaac Goldmann Co., 1891),
Preface, pp. iii–v.

ancestors as distinguished in deeds of valor, and peculiarly so
to the colored people. But how must the little colored child feel
when he has completed the assigned course of U. S. History
and in it found not one word of credit, not one word of favorable comment for even one among the millions of his fore-
parents, who have lived through nearly three centuries of his
country's history! The Negro is hardly given a passing notice
in many of the histories taught in the schools; he is credited
with no heritage of valor; he is mentioned only as a slave, while
true historical records prove him to have been among the most
patriotic of patriots, among the bravest of soldiers, and constantly a God-fearing, faithful producer of the nation's wealth.
Though a slave to this government, his was the first blood shed
in its defence in those days when a foreign foe threatened its
destruction. In each of the American wars the Negro was faithful—yes, faithful to a land not his own in point of rights and
freedom, but, indeed, a land that, after he had shouldered his
musket to defend, rewarded him with a renewed term of slavery. Patriotism and valor under such circumstances possess a
peculiar merit and beauty. But such is the truth of history; and
may I not hope that the study of this little work by the boys
and girls of the race will inspire in them a new self-respect and
confidence? Much, of course, will depend on you, dear teachers,
into whose hands I hope to place this book. By your efforts, and
those of the children, you are to teach from the truth of history
that complexions do not govern patriotism, valor, and sterling
integrity.

My endeavor has been to shorten this work as much as I
thought consistent with clearness. Personal opinions and comments have been kept out. A fair impartial statement has been
my aim. Facts are what I have tried to give without bias or
prejudice; and may not something herein said hasten on that
day when the race for which these facts are written, following
the example of the noble men and women who have gone before, level themselves up to the highest pinnacle of all that is
noble in human nature?

I respectfully request that my fellow-teachers will see to it that the word *Negro* is written with a capital *N*. It deserves to be so enlarged, and will help, perhaps, to magnify the race it stands for in the minds of those who see it.

47. ARTHUR A. SCHOMBURG ADVOCATES THE CREATION OF CHAIRS OF NEGRO HISTORY

. . . I am here with a sincere desire to awaken the sensibilities, to kindle the dormant fibres in the soul, and to fire the racial patriotism by the study of the Negro books. We often feel that so many things around us are warped and alienated. Let us see, if we cannot agree to arrange a formula or create a basic construction, for the establishment of a substantial method of instruction for our young women and men in the material and the useful. The object of this paper is not to revolutionize existing standards, but simply to improve them by amending them, so that they will include the practical history of the Negro Race, from the dawn of civilization to the present time. We are reminded that the earliest instruction was imparted orally, and the system is still found extant in Africa and among other Oriental nations. It is useful, because it trains the mind to listen, and retain. The modern school with its many books, but without systematic lectures, turns out many graduates who are lacking in retentiveness and no sooner than the sound of the words has left their teachers' lips, the subject has been forgotten; and if they are called upon to explain the theme, it is reduced to an incomprehensible mass of meaningless words. The university graduate is wont to overestimate his ability, fresh from the ma-

From Arthur A. Schomburg, RACIAL INTEGRITY: A PLEA FOR THE ESTABLISHMENT OF A CHAIR OF NEGRO HISTORY IN OUR SCHOOLS AND COLLEGES (Yonkers, N. Y.: Negro Society for Historical Research, OCCASIONAL PAPERS NO. 3, 1913), 5–8, 10–13, 17–19.

chinery that endows him with a parchment and crowns him with knowledge, he steps out into the world to meet the practical men with years of experience and mother wit. It is a contrast, the professional man with the veneer of high art, and the acquaintance with the best authors, and up to date histories demanding recognition. All these books take their proper places when applied to the white people, but when applied or measured up to the black people, they lack the substantial and the inspiring. They are like meat without salt, they bear no analogy to our own; and for this reason it would be a wise plan for us to lay down a course of study in Negro History and achievements, before or after men and women have left certain schools. By this I mean, the reading and acquaintance with those writers whose "good books are the precious life blood of master spirits embalmed and treasured up on purpose to a life beyond life." (Milton)

The fables of Aesop, the cherished and enjoyable book of our youth, was originally related as folk-lore by a Negro from Aethiopia to the Greeks, who in turn published them. The early editions of this book speaking of the author says: "All agree that his person was uncommonly deformed, his head was long, nose flat, lips thick and pendant, a hump-back and complexion dark, from which he contracted his name Aesopus being the same as Aethiops, large belly and bow-legs; but his greatest infirmity was, that his speech was slow, inarticulate, and very obscure. Such was the person of Aesop." It does not require any length or breadth of the imagination for us to locate Aesop socially. Were we to see such a slave amongst us would we believe him to be a Negro? Yet we have lived so many years to read his book and think that it was the workmanship of Grecian lettered men.

It is the season for us to devote our time in kindling the torches that will inspire us to racial integrity. Milton was inspired by the shepherd to his great song. We need it more than the Jews who though not a practical nation, live in theory a nation of most powerful intellects. They live on the very groups of nations who destroyed them; and this concentration of force,

energy, power and vitality has made them a combination of
forces to be relied on whenever the sinews of war are a prerequisite to defence or offence. The Negro must strive to follow
in the good examples of the Jews—they cling to their customs
and traditions, no matter whether they live in Timbuctoo or in
the highest peaks of the Andean mountains; they cling together and uphold the maxim that "in unity there is strength."
We need a collection or list of books written by our men and
women. If they lack style, let the children of tomorrow correct
the omission of their sires. Let them build upon the crude
work. Let them, because of the opportunities that colleges and
universities grant, crystalize the crude work and bring it out
flawless. . . .

Juan Latino, who sang the praises of Don Juan de Austria at
the battle of Lepanto, and whose book was printed at Granada
in 1573 (one of the most remarkable and rarest of books), can
be seen and read at the Boston Public Library in the Ticknor
collection of Spanish literature. Latino's life is full of romantic
episodes for a slave. He applied for the degree of Doctor of Arts
at the University of Granada, and the preceptors who opposed
him, were the first after his successful examination to publicly
acclaim him the most learned in the Latin language. When the
chair of Poetry became vacant, he came out ahead of his com-
petitors and won the cathedra. Antonio in his "Bibliotheca
Nova" pays an excellent tribute to his learning and wisdom.
It should be remembered that Juan took the name Latino when
he applied for his degree and it was not given him as a nick-
name as some writers claim.

Anthony William Amo was born on the coast of Guinea and
studied at Halle, Saxony, and at the University of Wittenberg.
He was learned in Latin, Greek, and spoke Hebrew, Dutch,
French and German. He is well remembered by Blumenbach
and Gregoire. He wrote two books, one a philosophical dissertation on the "want of feeling" which obtained the approbation
of the University and won the doctor's degree for him. The
other was a philosophical treatise containing a succinct discussion of those sensations which pertain both to the mind and to

the living organic body. These volumes were published in the
year 17[3]4. . . .

Phillis Wheatley was our peerless poetess. Her first book of
poems was printed in London 1773, it was followed by a second London edition the same year. Another edition was printed
in Walpole, N. H., 1802, thence followed a Philadelphia, an
Albany and several other issues, with a short biography during
the years 1834–5–6–7–8 at Boston. Still another edition was
published in Denver, Colorado in 1887. The first edition published by a Negro was by R. R. Wright Jr., at Philadelphia, Pa.
Mr. Deane published an edition of 100 copies of her letters in
1804, which was read before the Mass. Historical Society. Individual broadside poems preceded her book. After her marriage
many of her poems were published under the name of Phillis
Peters.

"The Poems by a Slave" by George M. Horton of North Carolina, the author of Praises of Creation and in whose behalf
Joshua Coffin took great interest to purchase his freedom, is
a booklet of unusual merit, and deserves the consideration of
disinterested racial men who will reprint it for the better appreciation of this generation.

The poets Whitefield of Buffalo, Islay Walden, the blind poet
of North Carolina and Whitman of Florida are additional evidence of the mental ability of our men to scale the heights of
Mount Olympus.

The late Frances E. Watkins Harper, a novelist as well as a
poetess and lecturer whose lyre was always tuned in defence
of righteousness and who ever pleaded for as clean a ministry
as for our rights, should be remembered. Mr. J. J. Thomas, the
author of the "Creole Grammar" says, "But it is as a poet that
posterity will hail her in the coming ages of our race; for pathos,
depth of spiritual insight, and magical exercise of a rare power
of self utterance, it will hardly be questioned that she has sur-
passed every competitor among females—white or black—save
and except Elizabeth Barrett Browning, with whom the gifted
African stands on much the same plane of poetic excellence"
(p. 259, "Froudacity"). . . .

"Walker's Appeal" was a remarkable brochure. Very few persons of this generation know of it, and those of the past have expressed a cold desire to inspect its pages. It was written by a Negro named David Walker, formerly of Wilmington, N. C., but at that time of Boston, Mass. His pamphlet was circulated carefully wherever that stain of slavery was apparent, it ran through three editions. And the Rev. Henry Highland Garnet republished it and had it added to a lecture he gave in 1844. It created the wildest feeling in the Southern States and every effort was made by the Southern executives to quench the spirit that animated Walker's Appeal. Samuel J. May in his "Recollections of Our Anti-Slavery Conflict" (p. 163) says: "In September 1829, he published his "Appeal" to the colored citizens of the world, in particular and very expressly to those of the United States." "It was a pamphlet of more than 80 octavo pages, ably written very impassioned and well adapted to its purposes. The 2nd and 3rd editions of it were published in less than twelve months, and to them Mr. Walker devoted himself until his death, which happened soon after the distribution of his appeal to colored men." Walker's Appeal is one of the rarest anti-slavery tracts. I have only seen two copies and a reprint of the Appeal, in the possession of Mr. W. C. Bolivar. Here is an illustration of a Negro, sending seditious literature to disseminate the ghastly truth of the debasing influence of slavery, or as Crummell has said, the "bold outcry." So is the Rev. Coker's "A Dialogue between a Virginian and an African Minister," printed in Baltimore, Md.

The slave narratives offer a vast field to select from; they represent a collection of facts mingled with pain. The anguish and the vissicitudes are related, with candor and pathos. And yet there is much of invaluable use, pertaining to different states, telling of conditions to be found elsewhere. John Brown's narrative deals with slavery in Georgia, William Wells Brown with Kentucky and Missouri, whereas Frederick Douglass and Samuel Ringgold Ward deal with conditions in Maryland. Each one gives the different shading to the subject and portrays with remarkable fidelity the naked truth. These men lived for the attainment of greater usefulness.

Frederick Douglass of imperishable memory was the "cataract that roared." His imagery was fine, vivid. Douglass was the lecturer, powerful in invective. He told the story of his wrongs, so that they stood out in all their naked ugliness. And Samuel Ringgold Ward was the debater, the wit, always self-possessed and never disconcerted, always clear and forcible. He had the power not only to examine but to enable you to see the fairness of that examination and the justness of its conclusions. Such was the opinion of William J. Wilson, after having heard these two champions debate. The work carried on and done independently by Samuel R. Ward in England in behalf of our cause, has not received the proper appreciation of our people. The "Narrative," "My Bondage and My Freedom" and others of Douglass' pamphlets together with Samuel R. Ward's "Autobiography of a Runaway Slave," are useful and inspiring models for our children to have before them.

Alexandre Poushkin, a Negro descendant, has crowned himself with glory in Russia. Few of his works have been translated into English, except "Prose Tales" (Keane, ed.) "Marie," "The Captain's Daughter" and his narrative of his grandfather, an unfinished work. He was a prolific writer. Suffice it to say that he was a luminary in Russian literature and as a poet was called the "Black Byron."

The works of Alexandre Dumas are too well known for me to bring to your notice. He was the king of romance and historical novels.

"Clothel or the President's Daughter" by William Wells Brown was one of the first anti-slavery novels written by our men. It was originally printed in London 1853 and in America at the close of the same year. The London publication says, that Thomas Jefferson was the father of two slave girls Clothel and Althesa. But in the later the American edition, no mention is made of the circumstance. Frank J. Webb published in London "The Garies and Their Friends" with an introduction by Mrs. Harriet B. Stowe and a prefatory letter from Lord Brougham. Dunbar's novels, his "Uncalled," "Fanatics," "The Heart of Happy Hollow" and others are sure indication of the usefulness of this kind of reading matter. No one, I am sure,

decries the classics. They stand as models of excellence. The
description of the battle of Waterloo by Victor Hugo is claimed
to be a perfect literary composition. But we like to read of the
exploits of our men, we love to read of them doing a manly act.
There is courage beneath the black skin as well as the white
skin. So let us have our deeds and our meeds of praise set up
for the inspiration and edification of our people. . . .

We have reached the crucial period of our educational existence. I have shown by a few examples of the past available
and useful material upon which we can base our future structure. We have chairs of almost everything, and believe we lack
nothing, but we sadly need a chair of Negro history. The white
institutions have their chair of history; it is the history of their
people and whenever the Negro is mentioned in the text books
it dwindles down to a foot note. The white scholar's mind and
heart is fired, because in the temple of learning he is told how
on the 5th of March, 1770, the Americans were able to beat the
English; but to find Crispus Attucks it is necessary to go deep
into special books. In the orations delivered at Bunker Hill,
Daniel Webster never mentioned the Negroes having done anything, and is silent about Peter Salem. In the account of the
battle of Long Island City and around New York under Major-
General Nathaniel Greene, no mention is made of the 800
Negro soldiers who periled their lives in the Revolutionary war.
Cases can be shown right and left of the palpable omissions.
Weiss in his Life of Theodore Parker publishes a letter from
Parker to historian Bancroft telling him "here is what I get
about Africans at the battle of Bunker Hill; fighting in it, I
mean; my friend Wm. C. Nell, a colored man of this city,
helped me to the facts. He has written quite a valuable book
on 'The Colored Patriots of the Revolution.' Boston, 1855.
* * * When you publish your volume I wish you would send
Nell a copy. Negroes get few honors, Yours faithfully, Theodore Parker."

Where is our historian to give us, our side view and our chair
of Negro History to teach our people our own history. We are
at the mercy of the "flotsam and jetsam" of the white writers.
The very learned Rev. Alexander Crummell before the Ameri-

can Negro Academy, stated that he heard J. C. Calhoun say that the inferiority of the Negro was so self evident that he would not believe him human unless he could conjugate Greek verbs; and yet it must have been self evident to Calhoun that in North Carolina there were many Negroes held as slaves who could read and write Arabic (see Hodgson, W. B. "The Gospels in the Negro patois," etc., N. Y. 1857) that in those days men like Juan Latino, Amo, Capitein, Francis Williams, Rev. J. C. Pennington and others could not only conjugate the Greek and Hebrew verbs, but had shown unmistakably evidences of learning, for they had received degrees from Universities of world famed reputation. Yet in those days there were many whites unrestrained, enjoying the opportunities of education, who could not conjugate Greek roots nor verbs of the spoken language of the land. Yet this barrier was set up to persons restrained by force from the enjoyment of the most ordinary rights.

We need in the coming dawn the man, who will give us the background for our future, it matters not whether he comes from the cloisters of the university or from the rank and file of the fields. We await his coming, a

> Slave to no sect, who takes no private road,
> But looks through nature up to nature's God.—POPE

The Anglo-Saxon is effusive in his praises to the Saxon Shepherds who lived on the banks of the river Elbe, to whom he pays blind allegiance. We need the historian and philosopher to give us, with trenchant pen, the story of our forefathers and let our soul and body, with phosphorescent light, brighten the chasm that separates us. And we should cling to them just as "blood is thicker than water." When the fact has been put down in the scroll of time, that the Negroes of Africa smelted iron and tempered bronzes, at the time Europe was wielding stone implements; that "the use of letters was introduced among the savages of Europe about 1500 B.C. and the European carried them to America about the XV century after the Christian era" that "Phoenicia and Palestine will forever live in the memory of mankind, since America as well as Europe has received letters from the one and religion from the other" (Decline and

Fall of the Roman Empire.—Gibbons), we will feel prouder of the achievements of our sires. We must research diligently the annals of time and bring back from obscurity the dormant examples of agriculture, industry and commerce, upon these the arts and sciences and make common the battle ground of our heritage.

48. CARTER G. WOODSON DESCRIBES THE WORK OF THE ASSOCIATION FOR THE STUDY OF NEGRO LIFE AND HISTORY

Beginnings

1. Organized by Carter G. Woodson in Chicago, September 9, 1915, with George Cleveland Hall, W. B. Hartgrove, J. E. Stamps, and Alexander L. Jackson, the four out of the many invited by the founder to participate in this organization.

2. Incorporated under the laws of the District of Columbia, October 2, 1915, with Carter G. Woodson, J. E. Moorland, and J. A. Bigham as trustees.

3. Brought out the first number of THE JOURNAL OF NEGRO HISTORY, January 1, 1916, and since that date has published this scientific magazine regularly every quarter. Complete files are available in bound or unbound form.

Purposes

1. To promote historical research.
2. To publish books on Negro life and history.
3. To promote the study of the Negro through clubs and schools.

From [Carter G. Woodson], THE A.S.N.L.H. (leaflet, n.p., n.d. [1947]).

4. To bring about harmony between the races by interpreting the one to the other.

Promoters

1. Well-known gentlemen like Harold H. Swift, C. B. Powell, Arthur W. Mitchell, Oswald Garrison Villard, Elmer A. Henderson, and F. D. Patterson.

2. Distinguished scholars like Roland G. Usher, Frederick L. Hoffman, Evarts B. Greene, Charles M. Andrews, H. N. Sherwood, Ambrose Caliver, Benjamin E. Mays, Charles H. Wesley, Henry J. Cadbury, F. J. Klingberg, and J. R. Angell.

Achievements

1. It has directed the attention of investigators to this neglected field.

2. It has extended the circulation of THE JOURNAL OF NEGRO HISTORY into South America, Europe, Asia, and Africa.

3. It has published twenty-five volumes of articles and documents giving facts which are generally unknown.

4. It has produced twenty-seven monographs on Negro life and history.

5. It has organized and stimulated the studies of local clubs and classes, which have done much to change the attitude of communities toward the Negro.

6. It has collected thousands of valuable manuscripts on the Negro which have been made accessible to the public in the Library of Congress.

7. It has had thirteen young men and women trained for research in social science and for instruction in colleges and universities.

The development of the idea

Directing attention to the study of the Negro as a neglected field, the Association could soon report important results. It led men to see the unreasonableness of the claim made for superiority of race and encouraged them to arrive at their conclusions by scientific investigation. Giving such a stimulus to the reconstruction of thought, then, the Association has changed the attitude of many persons toward the Negro and other races. The Negro himself, too, has been stimulated to higher endeavor by learning from his significant record that he is not the most despised of men.

In 1922 the Association was enabled by a grant to undertake systematic research. Prior to that time its investigation had been purely voluntary. That year the Department of Research was established and a number of investigators were employed to undertake definite tasks. These researches have resulted in the publication of twenty-seven monographs embracing almost every aspect of Negro life and history. The Department of Research has recently undertaken the special task of investigating the social and economic conditions of the Negro since the Civil War, and it has given some attention to Negro Folklore and African Anthropology.

In 1926 the Association began the celebration of Negro History Week. This was made an occasion for public exercises inviting special attention to the achievements of the Negro. The thought emerged from the mind of the founder. With the cooperation of ministers, teachers and professional and business men throughout the country, the celebration proved to be an unusual success. Negro History Week has helped to arouse the people to a keener appreciation of the contribution of the Negro to civilization. Negro History Week has become "Negro History Year" in that schools are now taking up the study of the Negro as a required course. Men are now learning to think of civilization as the heritage of the centuries to which all races have made some contribution.

Owing to the demand for more service in the dissemination of information than its facilities then afforded, the Association established in 1927 an Extension Division to embrace the imparting of information by public lectures and the study of Negro Life and History by mail. This department, therefore, offers instruction given by the Association staff under the administrative supervision and control of the Association. Such an opportunity for self-improvement is widely sought by literary societies, study clubs, and other institutions for persons who have no other chance for this kind of instruction.

Why the Negro in history?

If a race has no history, if it has no worthwhile tradition, it becomes a negligible factor in the thought of the world, and it stands in danger of being exterminated. The American Indian left no continuous record. He did not know the value of history; and where is he today? The Hebrew keenly appreciated the worth of tradition, as is attested by the Bible itself. In spite of world-wide persecution, therefore, he is still a great factor in the universe.

The case of the Negro may be stated concretely. For example, a man writes a book on the *New Freedom*. Some one inquires as to how he can harmonize his anti-Negro policy with his progressive doctrine. He replies that he was not thinking of the Negro when he wrote that book. An order is given for the training of all young men for military service. A Negro applies to equip himself for this duty, but he is told that the principles involved in the war concern only white men, and that Negroes will be encouraged to serve only in subordinate positions. A Negro supports the successful party in a campaign and then asks for the accustomed recognition in the personnel of the new administration, but he is told that public opinion is such that the Negro cannot be safely exalted to positions of trust in the government. A bond issue is voted to improve the facilities of education, but the Negro school is denied its share or it is permitted to receive what the white system abandons as antiquated and inadequate. A Negro is passed on the street and is shoved off into the mud; he complains or strikes back and is lynched as a desperado who attacked a gentleman.

And what if the Negro is handicapped, segregated, or lynched? According to our education and practice, if you kill one of the group, the world goes on just as well or better; for the Negro is nothing, has never been anything and never will be anything but a menace to civilization. The Negro therefore has no respect for himself, and others have the utmost contempt for him.

We call this race prejudice, and it may be thus properly named; but it is not something inherent in human nature. It is merely the logical result of tradition, the inevitable outcome of thorough instruction to the effect that the Negro has never contributed anything to the progress of mankind. The doctrine has been thoroughly drilled into the whites, and the Negroes have learned well the lesson themselves; for many of them look upon other races as superior and accept the status of recognized inferiority.

All races make contributions

The fact is, however, that one race has not accomplished any more good than any other race, for it would be contrary to the laws of nature to have one race inferior to the other. But if you leave it to the one to set forth his special virtues while disparaging those of others, it will not require many generations before all credit for human achievements will be ascribed to one particular stock. Such is the history taught the youth today.

On the other hand, just as thorough education in the belief in the inequality of races has brought the world to the cat-and-dog stage of religious, racial and political strife, so may thorough instruction in the equality of races bring about a reign of brotherhood through an appreciation of the virtues of all races, creeds and colors. In such a millennium the achievements of the Negro properly set forth will crown him as a factor in early human progress and a maker of modern civilization. He has supplied the demand for labor of a large area of our own country, he has been a conservative force in its recent economic development, he has given the nation a poetic stimulus, he has developed the most popular music of the modern era, and he has preserved in its purity the brotherhood taught by Jesus of

Nazareth. In his native country, moreover, the Negro produced in ancient times a civilization contemporaneous with that of the nations of the early Mediterranean, he influenced the cultures then cast in the crucible of time, and he taught the modern world trial by jury, music by stringed instruments, the domestication of the sheep, goat and cow, and the use of iron by which science and initiative have remade the universe. Must we let this generation continue ignorant of these eloquent facts?

The publications of the Association

1. THE JOURNAL OF NEGRO HISTORY, a scientific quarterly, regularly published since January, 1916. Thirty-one volumes now available in bound or unbound form.

2. Twenty-seven monographs and reports treating almost every phase of Negro life and history, such as, *The Negro in the Reconstruction of Virginia, The Negro in South Carolina during the Reconstruction, Free Negro Heads of Families, Negro Owners of Slaves, The Relations between Negroes and Indians, The Controversy over the Distribution of Abolition Literature,* and *The Mind of the Negro Reflected in Letters.*

3. Special studies of the economic and social aspects of the record of the Negro in the modern world, like *The Rural Negro, The Negro Wage Earner, The Black Man in White America, Negro Education in Alabama* and *The Negro Professional Man.*

4. Translations of the works of reputable foreign scholars who have made scientific studies of Negroes, such as Delafosse's *Negroes of Africa, History and Culture,* and Ramos's *The Negro in Brazil.*

5. Textbooks of Negro History, with the assistance of the Associated Publishers, such as *The Child's Story of the Negro, Negro Makers of History, The Story of the Negro Retold,* and *The Negro in Our History.*

6. Works of biography like Charles H. Wesley's *Richard Allen,* Sadie I. Daniel's *Women Builders,* and C. G. Woodson's *African Heroes and Heroines.*

7. Works treating in detail special contributions of the Negro

like *Negro Poets and Their Poems, Negro Orators and Their Orations, Negro Musicians and Their Music,* and *The African Background Outlined, or Handbook for the Study of the Negro.*

8. Special service in seeking abroad rare books on the Negro in order to facilitate the study of the race at important centers in the United States.

Branches of the Association

For the expansion of the work the Association for the Study of Negro Life and History has organized a number of branches. Others may be established only where the national office believes that the interest is sufficient to keep them alive.

The purposes of a branch are:

1. To save the records of the Negro and send them to the central office in Washington, D. C., where they are being assorted and classified and kept under fireproof protection to be used by investigators from all parts of the world.

2. To write the life histories of the "near great" but useful Negroes of whom editors and authors take no account, and to publish the records of local institutions which the "near great" established.

3. To promote the actual study of the Negro in a club or class proceeding according to a definite outline and under the supervision of the Director of the Association.

4. To secure the cooperation of a number of persons who will learn to tell intelligently to children in schools and churches interesting stories of distinguished Negroes who have achieved things worth while as promoters of business, professional men, teachers, and ministers. . . .

Junior societies

To root more deeply the work of the Association in the mind of the youth, junior societies are now being organized in connection with the local branches. For such societies the following plan has been agreed upon:

1. The junior societies shall be organized in churches, in junior and senior high schools, and among such other groups as may become interested.

2. In cities or communities where chapters for the study of Negro life and history already exist the organization of the junior branch shall be under the supervision of the president of the local branch or someone designated by him.

3. In places where no branch exists the junior society or societies shall be organized and supervised by someone interested in Negro history. This person shall be designated by the home office. . . .

49. MONROE N. WORK: "NEGROES SHOULD NOT DESPISE THE ROCK FROM WHICH THEY WERE HEWN"

A close examination shows that what we know about the Negro both of the present and the past vitally affects our opinions concerning him. Men's beliefs concerning things are to a large extent determined by where they live and what has been handed down to them. We believe in a hell of roaring flames wherein the fiercest of heat the souls of the wicked are subject to eternal burnings. This idea of hell was evolved in the deserts of the Arabian Peninsula where heat is one of the greatest forces of nature with which man has to contend. Among the native tribes of Northern Siberia dwelling in the regions of perpetual ice and snow, hell is a place filled with great chunks of ice upon which the souls of the wicked are placed and there subjected to eternal freezings. This idea of hell was evolved in the regions where man is in a continual battle with the cold.

Monroe N. Work, "The Passing Tradition and the African Civilization," JOURNAL OF NEGRO HISTORY, I (January 1916), 34–41.
Copyright © 1916 by the Association for the Study of Negro Life and History, Inc. Reprinted by permission.

The beliefs of Negroes concerning themselves have to a large extent been made for them. The reader no doubt will be interested to know that the prevailing notions concerning the inferiority of the Negro grew up to a large extent as the concomitant to Negro slavery in this country. The bringing of the first Negroes from Africa as slaves was justified on the grounds that they were heathen. It was not right, it was argued, for Christians to enslave Christians, but they could enslave heathen, who as a result would have an opportunity to become Christians. These Negro slaves did actually become Christians and as a result the colonists were forced to find other grounds to justify their continuation of the system. The next argument was that they were different from white people. Here we have a large part of the beginnings of the doctrine of the inferiority of the Negro.

When, about 1830, anti-slavery agitation arose in this country, a new set of arguments were brought forward to justify slavery. First in importance were those taken from the Bible. Science also was called upon and brought forward a large number of facts to demonstrate that by nature the Negro was especially fitted to be a slave. It happened that about this time anthropology was being developed. Racial differences were some of the things which especially interested scientists in this field. The races were defined according to certain physical characteristics. These, it was asserted, determined the superiority or inferiority of races. The true Negro race, said the early anthropologists, had characteristics which especially indicated its inferiority. Through our geographies, histories and encyclopedias we have become familiar with representations of this so-called true Negro, whose chief characteristics were a black skin, woolly hair, protuberant lips and a receding forehead. Caricaturists seized upon these characteristics and popularized them in cartoons, in songs and other ways. Thus it happened that the Negro, through the descriptions that he got of himself, has come largely to believe in his inherent inferiority and that to attain superiority he must become like the white man in color, in achievements and, in fact, along all lines.

In recent years it has been asked, "Why cannot the Negro attain superiority along lines of his own," that is, instead of simply patterning after what the white man has done, why cannot the Negro through music, art, history, and science, make his own special contributions to the progress of the world? This question has arisen because in the fields of science and history there have been brought forward a number of facts which prove this possibility. First of all, the leading scientists in the field of anthropology are telling us that while there are differences of races, there are no characteristics which per se indicate that one race is inferior or superior to another. The existing differences are differences in kind not in value. On the other hand, whatever superiority one race has attained over another has been largely due to environment.

A German writer in a discussion of the origin of African civilizations said some time ago "What bold investigators, great pioneers, still find to tell us in civilizations nearer home, proves more and more clearly that we are ignorant of hoary Africa. Somewhat of its present, perhaps, we know, but of its past little. Open an illustrated geography and compare the 'Type of the African Negro,' the bluish-black fellow of the protuberant lips, the flattened nose, the stupid expression and the short curly hair, with the tall bronze figures from Dark Africa with which we have of late become familiar, their almost fine-cut features, slightly arched nose, long hair, etc., and you have an example of the problems pressing for solution. In other respects, too, the genuine African of the interior bears no resemblance to the accepted Negro type as it figures on drug and cigar store signs, wearing a shabby stovepipe hat, plaid trousers, and a vari-colored coat. A stroll through the corridors of the Berlin Museum of Ethnology teaches that the real African need by no means resort to the rags and tatters of bygone European splendor. He has precious ornaments of his own, of ivory and plumes, fine plaited willow ware, weapons of superior workmanship. Justly can it be demanded 'What sort of civilization is this? Whence does it come?' "

It is also pointed out that one of the most important contributions to the civilization of mankind was very probably made by the Negro race. This was the invention of the smelting of iron. The facts brought forward to support this view are: that no iron was smelted in Europe before 900 B. C.; that about 3000 B. C., there began to appear on the Egyptian monuments pictures of Africans bringing iron from the South to Egypt; that at a time considerably later than this iron implements began to appear in Asia; that there is no iron ore in Egypt; and that in Negro Africa iron ore is abundant. In many places it is found on top of the ground and in some parts it can be melted by simply placing a piece of ore in the fire very much as you would a potato to be roasted.

Studies in the fields of ancient and medieval history are also showing that in the past there were in Negro Africa civilizations of probable indigenous origin which attained importance enough to be mentioned in the writings of the historians and poets of those periods. The seat of one of the highest of these civilizations was Ethiopia. Here the Negro nation attained the greatest fame. As early as 2,500 years before the birth of Christ the Ethiopians appeared to have had a considerable civilization. It was well known to the writers of the Bible and is referred to therein some forty-nine times. In Genesis we read of Cush, the eldest son of Ham. Cush is the Hebrew word for black and means the same as Ethiopia. One of the most famous sons of Cush was Nimrod, whom the Bible mentions as being "a mighty hunter before the Lord; whereof it is said, like Nimrod, a mighty hunter before the Lord." The Bible refers to Ethiopia as being far distant from Palestine. In the book of Isaiah we read "the land of the rustling of wings which is beyond the rivers of Ethiopia that sendeth ambassadors by the sea." The rivers of Ethiopia mentioned in Isaiah are the upper tributaries of the Nile, the Atbara, the Blue Nile and the Sobat.

The later capital of Ethiopia was Meroe. Recent excavations have shown Meroe to have been a city larger than Memphis. The Temple of Ammon, where kings were crowned, was one of the largest in the valley of the Nile. The great walls of cut stones were 15 feet thick and 30 feet high. Heaps of iron-slag and furnaces for smelting iron were discovered, and there were magnificent quays and landing places on the river side, for the export of iron. Excavations have also shown that for 150 years Egypt was a dependency of Ethiopia. The kings of the twenty-third and twenty-fourth Egyptian dynasties were really governors appointed by Ethiopian overlords, while the twenty-fifth dynasty was founded by the Ethiopian king, Sabako, in order to check Assyrian aggression. Palestine was enabled to hold out against Assyria by Ethiopian help. Sennacherib's attempt to capture Jerusalem and carry the Jews into captivity, was frustrated by the army of the Ethiopian king, Taharka. The nation and religion of Judah were thus preserved from being absorbed in heathen lands like the lost Ten Tribes. The Negro soldiers of the Sudan saved the Jewish religion.

The old Greek writers were well acquainted with Ethiopia. According to them in the most ancient times there existed to the South of Egypt a nation and a land designated as Ethiopia. This was the land where the people with the sunburnt faces dwelt. The Greek poet, Homer, mentions the Ethiopians as dwelling at the uttermost limits of the earth, where they enjoyed personal intercourse with the gods. In one place Homer said that Neptune, the god of the sea, "had gone to feast with the Ethiopians who dwell afar off, the Ethiopians who are divided into two parts, the most distant of men, some at the setting of the sun, others at the rising." Herodotus, the Greek historian, described the Ethiopians as long lived and their country as extending to the Southern Sea.

The great fame of the Ethiopians is thus sketched by the eminent historian, Heeren, who in his historical researches says: "In the earliest traditions of nearly all the more civilized nations of antiquity, the name of this distant people is found. The annals of the Egyptian priests were full of them; the nations of inner Asia, on the Euphrates and Tigris, have interwoven the fictions of the Ethiopians with their own traditions of the conquests and wars of their heroes; and, at a period equally remote, they glimmer in Greek mythology. When the Greeks scarcely knew Italy and Sicily by name, the Ethiopians were celebrated in the verses of their poets; they spoke of them as the 'remotest nation,' the 'most just of men,' the 'favorites of the gods.' The lofty inhabitants of Olympus journey to them and take part in their feasts; their sacrifices are the most agreeable of all that mortals can offer them. And when the faint gleam of tradition and fable gives way to the clear light of history, the luster of the Ethiopians is not diminished. They still continue the object of curiosity and admiration; and the pens of cautious, clear-sighted historians often place them in the highest rank of knowledge and civilization."

Of these facts most modern historians know but little and Negroes in general almost nothing. For example, how many have ever heard of Al-Bekri, the Arab writer, who in the eleventh century wrote a description of the Western Sudan of such importance that it gained him the title of "The Historian of Negro Land"? How much, by means of research, might be learned of the town of Ghana situate on the banks of the Niger, which the historian Al-Bekri described as a meeting place for commercial caravans from all parts of the world? This town, he said, contained schools and centers of learning. It was the resort of the learned, the rich, and the pious of all nations. Likewise, most of us have never heard perhaps of another Arab writer, Iben Khaldun, who in writing about the middle of the fourteenth century of Melle, another of the kingdoms of the Sudan, reported that caravans from Egypt consisting of twelve thousand laden camels passed every year through one town on the eastern border of the empire on their way to the capital of the nation. The load of a camel was three hundred pounds. 12,000 camel loads amounted, therefore, to something like 1,600 tons of merchandise. At this time we are told that there was probably not a ship in any of the merchant navies of the world which could carry one hundred tons. 250 years later the average tonnage of the vessels of Spain was 300 tons and that of the English much less. The largest ship which Queen Elizabeth had in her navy, the *Great Mary*, had a capacity of a thousand tons; but it was considered an exception and the marvel of the age.

Another thing that is not generally known is the importance to which some of these Negro kingdoms of the Western Sudan attained during the middle ages and the first centuries of the modern era. In size and permanency they compared favorably with the most advanced nations of Europe. The kingdom of Melle of which the historian, Iben Khaldun, wrote, had an area of over 1,000 miles in extent and existed for 250 years. It was the first of the kingdoms of the Western Sudan to be received on equal terms with the contemporary white nations. The greatest of all the Sudan states was the kingdom of Songhay which, in its golden age, had an area almost equal to that of the United States and existed from about 750 A. D. to 1591. There is a record of the kings of Songhay in regular succession for almost 900 years. The length of the life of the Songhay empire coincides almost exactly with the life of Rome from its foundation as a republic to its downfall as an empire.

The greatest evidences of the high state of civilization which the Sudan had in the fourteenth and fifteenth centuries were the attention that was paid to education and the unusual amount of learning that existed there. The university of Sankore at Timbuctu was a very active center of learning. It was in correspondence with the universities of North Africa and Egypt. It was in touch with the universities of Spain. In the sixteenth century Timbuctu had a large learned class living at ease and busily occupied with the elucidation of intellectual and religious problems. The town swarmed with students. Law, literature, grammar, theology and the natural sciences were studied. The city of Melle had a regular school of science. One distinguished geographer is mentioned, and allusions to surgical science show that the old maxim of the Arabian schools, "He who studies anatomy pleases God," was not forgotten. One of these writers mentions that his brother came from Jenne to Timbuctu to undergo an operation for cataract of the eyes at the hands of a celebrated surgeon there. It is said that the operation was wholly successful. The appearance of comets, so amazing to Europe of the Middle Ages and at the present time to the ignorant, was by these learned blacks noted calmly as a matter of scientific interest. Earthquakes and eclipses excited no great surprise.

The renowned writer of the Sudan was Abdurrahman Essadi. He was born in Timbuctu in 1596. He came of learned and distinguished ancestors. He is chief author of the history of Sudan. The book is said to be a wonderful document. The narrative deals mainly with the modern history of the Songhay Empire, and relates the rise of this black civilization through the fifteenth and sixteenth centuries and its decadence up to the middle of the seventeenth century. The noted traveller, Barth, was of the opinion that the book forms one of the most important additions that the present age has made to the history of mankind. The work is especially valuable for the unconscious light which it throws upon the life, manners, politics, and literature of the country. It presents a vivid picture of the character of the men with whom it deals. It is sometimes called the Epic of the Sudan.

From this brief sketch which I have given of the African in ancient and medieval times it is clear that Negroes should not despise the rock from which they were hewn. As a race they have a past which is full of interest. It is worthy of serious study. From it we can draw inspiration; for it appears that not all black men everywhere throughout the ages have been "hewers of wood and drawers of water." On the contrary, through long periods of time there were powerful black nations which have left the records of their achievements and of which we are just now beginning to learn a little. This little, however, which we have learned teaches us that the Negroes of today should work and strive. Along their own special line and in their own peculiar way they should endeavor to make contributions to civilization. Their achievements can be such that once more black will be dignified and the fame of Ethiopia again spread throughout the world.

50. BENJAMIN BRAWLEY:
"EVERY RACE HAS A PECULIAR GENIUS"

In his lecture on "The Poetic Principle," in leading down to his
definition of poetry, Edgar Allan Poe has called attention to
the three faculties, intellect, feeling, and will, and shown that
poetry, that the whole realm of esthetics in fact, is concerned
primarily and solely with the second of these. Does it appeal
to a sense of beauty? This is his sole test of a poem or of any
work of art, the aim being neither to appeal to the intellect by
satisfying the reason or inculcating truth, nor to appeal to the
will by satisfying the moral sense or inculcating duty.

This standard has often been criticized as narrow; yet it embodies a large and fundamental element of truth. If, now, we
study the races that go to make up our cosmopolitan American
life we shall find that the three which most distinctively represent the faculties, intellect, feeling, and will, are respectively the
Anglo-Saxon, the Negro, and the Jewish. Whatever achievement has been made by the Anglo-Saxon has been primarily in
the domain of pure intellect. In religion, in business, in invention, in pure scholarship, the same principle holds; and examples are found in Jonathan Edwards, J. Pierpont Morgan,
Thomas A. Edison, and in such scholars as Royce and Kittredge
of the Harvard of today. Similarly the outstanding race in the
history of the world for emphasis on the moral or religious
element of life has been the Jewish. Throughout the Old Testa-
ment the heart of Israel cries out to Jehovah, and through the
law given on Sinai, the songs of the Psalmist, and the prophesies
of Isaiah, the tradition of Israel has thrilled and inspired the
entire human race.

With reference now to the Negro two things are observable.
One is that any distinction so far won by a member of the race

Benjamin Brawley, "The Negro Genius,"
SOUTHERN WORKMAN, XLIV (May 1915), 305–308.

in America has been almost always in some one of the arts; and the other is that any influence so far exerted by the Negro on American civilization has been primarily in the field of esthetics. A man of science like Benjamin Banneker is the exception. To prove the point we may refer to a long line of beautiful singers, to the fervid oratory of Douglass, to the sensuous poetry of Dunbar, to the picturesque style of Du Bois, to the impressionism of the paintings of Tanner, and to the elemental sculpture of Meta Warrick Fuller. Even Booker Washington, most practical of Americans, proves the point, the distinguishing qualities of his speeches being anecdote and brilliant concrete illustration.

Everyone must have observed the radical difference in the appearance of the homes of white people and Negroes of the peasant class in the South. If the white man is not himself cultivated, and if he has not been able to give to his children the advantages of culture, his home is most likely to be a bare, blank abode with no pictures and no flowers. Such is not the case with the Negro. He is determined to have a picture, and if nothing better is obtainable he will paste a circus poster or a flaring advertisement on the walls. The instinct for beauty insists upon an outlet; and there are few homes of Negroes of the humbler class that will not have a geranium on the windowsill or a rosebush in the garden. If, too, we look at the matter conversely, we shall find that those things which are most picturesque make to the Negro the readiest appeal. Red is his favorite color, simply because it is the most pronounced of all colors. Goethe's "Faust" can hardly be said to be a play designed primarily for the galleries. In general it might be supposed to rank with "Macbeth" or "She Stoops to Conquer" or "Richelieu." One never sees it fail, however, that in any Southern city "Faust" will fill the gallery with the so-called lower class of Negro people, who would never dream of going to see one of the other plays just mentioned; and the applause never leaves one in doubt as to the reasons for Goethe's popularity. It is the suggestiveness of the love scenes, the red costume of Mephistopheles, the electrical effects, and the rain of fire, that give the thrill desired—all pure melodrama of course. "Faust" is a good show as well as a good play.

In some of our communities Negroes are frequently known to "get happy" in church. Now a sermon on the rule of faith or the plan of salvation is never known to awaken such ecstacy. This rather accompanies a vivid portrayal of the beauties of heaven, with its walls of jasper, the angels with palms in their hands, and (*summum bonum!*) the feast of milk and honey. And just here is the dilemma faced by the occupants of a great many pulpits in Negro churches. Do the Negroes want scholarly training? Very frequently the cultured preacher will be inclined to answer in the negative. Do they want rant and shouting? Such a standard fails at once to satisfy the ever-increasing intelligence of the audience itself. The trouble is that the educated Negro minister too often leaves out of account the basic psychology of his audience. That preacher who will ultimately be the most successful with the Negro congregation will be the one who to scholarship and culture can join brilliant imagination and fervid rhetorical expression. When all of these qualities are brought together in their finest proportion the effect is irresistible. Some distinguished white preachers, who to their deep spirituality have joined lively rhetorical expression, have never failed to succeed with a Negro audience as well as with an Anglo-Saxon one. Noteworthy examples within recent years have been Dr. P. S. Henson and Dr. R. S. MacArthur.

Gathering up the threads of our discussion so far, we find that there is constant striving on the part of the Negro for beautiful or striking effect, that those things which are most picturesque make the readiest appeal to his nature, and that in the sphere of religion he receives with most appreciation those discourses which are most imaginative in quality. In short, so far as the last point is concerned, it is not too much to assert that the Negro is thrilled, not so much by the moral as by the artistic and pictorial elements in religion.

But there is something deeper than the sensuousness of beauty that makes for the possibilities of the Negro in the realm of the arts, and that is the soul of the race. The wail of the old melodies and the plaintive quality that is ever present in the Negro voice are but the reflection of a background of tragedy. No race can rise to the greatest heights of art until it has yearned and suffered. The Russians are a case in point. Such has been their background in oppression and striving that their literature and art today are marked by an unmistakable note of power. The same future beckons to the American Negro. There is something very elemental about the heart of the race, something that finds its origin in the African forest, in the sighing of the night-wind, and in the falling of the stars. There is something grim and stern about it all too, something that speaks of the lash, of the child torn from its mother's bosom, of the dead body riddled with bullets and swinging all night from a limb by the roadside.

What does all this mean but that the Negro is a thorough-going romanticist? The philosophy, the satires, the conventionalities of the age of reason mean little to him; but the freedom, the picturesqueness, the moodiness of Wordsworth's day mean much. In his wild, weird melodies we follow once more the wanderings of the Ancient Mariner. In the fervid picture of the New Jerusalem we see the same emphasis on the concrete as in "To a Skylark" or the "Ode to the West Wind;" and under the spell of the Negro voice at its best we once more revel in the sensuousness of "The Eve of St. Agnes."

All of this of course does not mean that the Negro cannot rise to distinction in any sphere other than the arts, any more than it means that the Anglo-Saxon has not produced great painting and music. It does mean, however, that every race has its peculiar genius, and that, so far as we are at present able to judge, the Negro, with all of his manual labor, is destined to reach his greatest heights in the field of the artistic. But the impulse needs to be watched. Romanticism very soon becomes unhealthy. The Negro has great gifts of voice and ear and soul; but so far much of his talent has not soared above the vaudeville stage. This is due most largely of course to economic instability. It is the call of patriotism, however, that America should realize that the Negro has peculiar gifts which need all possible cultivation, and which will one day add to the glory of the country. Already his music is recognized as the most distinctive that the United States has yet produced. The possibilities of the race in literature and oratory, in sculpture and painting, are illimitable.

51. PAUL ROBESON: NEGRO SPIRITUALS ARE "THE SOUL OF THE RACE MADE MANIFEST"

Critics have often reproached me for not becoming an opera star and never attempting to give recitals of German and Italian songs as every accomplished singer is supposed to do. I am not an artist in the sense in which they want me to be an artist and of which they could approve. I have no desire to interpret the vocal genius of half a dozen cultures which are really alien to me. I have a far more important task to perform.

When I first suggested singing negro spirituals for English audiences, a few years ago, I was laughed at. How could these utterly simple, indeed, almost savage songs interest the most sophisticated audience in the world? I was asked. And yet I have found response amongst this very audience to the simple, direct emotional appeal of negro spirituals. These songs are to negro culture what the works of the great poets are to English culture: they are the soul of the race made manifest. No matter in what part of the world you may find him the negro has retained his direct emotional response to outside stimuli; he is constantly aware of an external power which guides his destiny. The white man has made a fetish of intellect and worships the God of thought; the negro feels rather than thinks, experiences emotions directly rather than interprets them by roundabout and devious abstractions, and apprehends the outside world

Paul Robeson, "The Culture of the Negro,"
THE SPECTATOR (London), June 15, 1934, pp. 916–917.

by means of intuitive perception instead of through a carefully built up system of logical analysis. No wonder that the negro is an intensely religious creature and that his artistic and cultural capacities find expression in the glorification of some deity in song. It does not matter who the deity is. The American and West Indian negro worships the Christian God in his own particular way and makes him the object of his supreme artistic manifestation which is embodied in the negro spiritual. But, what of the African negro? What is the object of his strong religious sense, and how does his artistic spirit manifest itself? These are the questions I have set myself to answer.

As a first step I went to the London School of Oriental Languages and, quite haphazardly, began by studying the East Coast languages, Swahili and the Bantu group which forms a sort of Lingua Franca of the East Coast of Africa. I found in these languages a pure negro foundation, dating from an ancient culture, but intermingled with many Arabic and Hamitic impurities. From them I passed on to the West Coast Negro languages and immediately found a kinship of rhythm and intonation with the negro-English dialect which I had heard spoken around me as a child. It was to me like a home-coming, and I felt that I had penetrated to the core of African culture when I began to study the legendary traditions, folksong and folklore of the West African negro. I hope to be able to interpret this original and unpolluted negro folksong to the Western world and I am convinced that there lies a wealth of uncharted musical material in that source which I hope, one day, will evoke the response in English and American audiences which my negro spirituals have done; but for me this is only one aspect of my discovery.

Culturally speaking, the African negro, as well as his American and West Indian brothers, stands at the parting of the ways. The day is past when they were regarded as something less than human and little more than mere savages by the white man. Racial tolerance and political equality of status have taken the place of oppression and slavery for the greater part of the negro race. But the sufferings he has undergone have left an indelible mark on the negro's soul, and at the present stage he suffers from an inferiority complex which finds its compensation in a desire to imitate the white man and his ways; but I am convinced that in this direction there is neither fulfilment nor peace for the negro. He is too radically different from the white man in his mental and emotional structure ever to be more than a spurious and uneasy imitation of him, if he persists in following this direction. His soul contains riches which can come to fruition only if he retains intact the full spate of his emotional awareness, and uses unswervingly the artistic endowments which nature has given him.

It is astonishing and, to me, fascinating to find a flexibility and subtlety in a language like Swahili, sufficient to convey the teachings of Confucius, for example, and it is my ambition to make an effort to guide the negro race by means of its own peculiar qualities to a higher degree of perfection along the line of its natural development. Though it is a commonplace to anthropologists these qualities and attainments of negro languages are entirely unknown to the general public of the Western world and, astonishingly enough, even to the negroes themselves. I have met negroes in the United States who believed that the African negro communicated his thoughts solely by means of gestures, that, in fact, he was practically incapable of speech and merely used sign language!

It is my first concern to dispel this regrettable and abysmal ignorance of the value of its own heritage in the negro race itself. As a first step in this direction I intend to make a comparative study of the main language groups: Indo-European, Asiatic and African, choosing two or three principal languages out of each group, and indicate their comparative richness at a comparable stage of development. It may take me five years to complete this work but I am convinced that the results will be adequate to form a concrete foundation for a movement to inspire confidence in the negro in the value of his own past and future.

52. ALAIN LOCKE ON THE NEW NEGRO: A "FORCED ATTEMPT TO BUILD . . . AMERICANISM ON RACE VALUES"

In the last decade something beyond the watch and guard of statistics has happened in the life of the American Negro and the three norns who have traditionally presided over the Negro problem have a changeling in their laps. The Sociologist, the Philanthropist, the Race-leader are not unaware of the New Negro, but they are at a loss to account for him. He simply cannot be swathed in their formulae. For the younger generation is vibrant with a new psychology; the new spirit is awake in the masses, and under the very eyes of the professional observers is transforming what has been a perennial problem into the progressive phases of contemporary Negro life.

Could such a metamorphosis have taken place as suddenly as it has appeared to? The answer is no; not because the New Negro is not here, but because the Old Negro had long become more of a myth than a man. The Old Negro, we must remember, was a creature of moral debate and historical controversy. His has been a stock figure perpetuated as an historical fiction partly in innocent sentimentalism, partly in deliberate reactionism. The Negro himself has contributed his share to this through a sort of protective social mimicry forced upon him by the adverse circumstances of dependence. So for generations in the mind of America, the Negro has been more of a formula than a human being—a something to be argued about, condemned or defended, to be "kept down," or "in his place," or "helped up," to be worried with or worried over, harassed or patronized, a social bogey or a social burden. The thinking Negro even has been induced to share this same general attitude, to focus his attention on controversial issues, to see him-

Alain Locke, "The New Negro," in Locke (ed.), THE NEW NEGRO (New York: Albert and Charles Boni, 1925), pp. 3–16.

self in the distorted perspective of a social problem. His shadow, so to speak, has been more real to him than his personality. Through having had to appeal from the unjust stereotypes of his oppressors and traducers to those of his liberators, friends and benefactors he has had to subscribe to the traditional positions from which his case has been viewed. Little true social or self-understanding has or could come from such a situation.

But while the minds of most of us, black and white, have thus burrowed in the trenches of the Civil War and Reconstruction, the actual march of development has simply flanked these positions, necessitating a sudden reorientation of view. We have not been watching in the right direction; set North and South on a sectional axis, we have not noticed the East till the sun has us blinking.

Recall how suddenly the Negro spirituals revealed themselves; suppressed for generations under the stereotypes of Wesleyan hymn harmony, secretive, half-ashamed, until the courage of being natural brought them out—and behold, there was folk-music. Similarly the mind of the Negro seems suddenly to have slipped from under the tyranny of social intimidation and to be shaking off the psychology of imitation and implied inferiority. By shedding the old chrysalis of the Negro problem we are achieving something like a spiritual emancipation. Until recently, lacking self-understanding, we have been almost as much of a problem to ourselves as we still are to others. But the decade that found us with a problem has left us with only a task. The multitude perhaps feels as yet only a strange relief and a new vague urge, but the thinking few know that in the reaction the vital inner grip of prejudice has been broken.

With this renewed self-respect and self-dependence, the life of the Negro community is bound to enter a new dynamic phase, the buoyancy from within compensating for whatever pressure there may be of conditions from without. The migrant masses, shifting from countryside to city, hurdle several generations of experience at a leap, but more important, the same thing happens spiritually in the life-attitudes and self-expression of the Young Negro, in his poetry, his art, his education and his new outlook, with the additional advantage, of course, of the poise and greater certainty of knowing what it is all about. From this comes the promise and warrant of a new leadership. As one of them has discerningly put it:

> We have tomorrow
> Bright before us
> Like a flame.
>
> Yesterday, a night-gone thing
> A sun-down-name.
>
> And dawn today
> Broad arch above the road we came.
> We march!

This is what, even more than any "most creditable record of fifty years of freedom," requires that the Negro of to-day be seen through other than the dusty spectacles of past controversy. The day of "aunties," "uncles" and "mammies" is equally gone. Uncle Tom and Sambo have passed on, and even the "Colonel" and "George" play barnstorm rôles from which they escape with relief when the public spotlight is off. The popular melodrama has about played itself out, and it is time to scrap the fictions, garret the bogeys and settle down to a realistic facing of facts.

First we must observe some of the changes which since the traditional lines of opinion were drawn have rendered these quite obsolete. A main change has been, of course, that shifting of the Negro population which has made the Negro problem no longer exclusively or even predominantly Southern. Why should our minds remain sectionalized, when the problem itself no longer is? Then the trend of migration has not only been toward the North and the Central Midwest, but city-ward and to the great centers of industry—the problems of adjustment are new, practical, local and not peculiarly racial. Rather they are an integral part of the large industrial and social problems of our

present-day democracy. And finally, with the Negro rapidly in
process of class differentiation, if it ever was warrantable to
regard and treat the Negro *en masse* it is becoming with every
day less possible, more unjust and more ridiculous.

In the very process of being transplanted, the Negro is
becoming transformed.

The tide of Negro migration, northward and city-ward, is not
to be fully explained as a blind flood started by the demands
of war industry coupled with the shutting off of foreign migration, or by the pressure of poor crops coupled with increased
social terrorism in certain sections of the South and Southwest.
Neither labor demand, the boll weevil nor the Ku Klux Klan is
a basic factor, however contributory any or all of them may
have been. The wash and rush of this human tide on the beach
line of the northern city centers is to be explained primarily in
terms of a new vision of opportunity, of social and economic
freedom, of a spirit to seize, even in the face of an extortionate
and heavy toll, a chance for the improvement of conditions.
With each successive wave of it, the movement of the Negro
becomes more and more a mass movement toward the larger
and the more democratic chance—in the Negro's case a deliberate flight not only from countryside to city, but from medieval
America to modern.

Take Harlem as an instance of this. Here in Manhattan is not
merely the largest Negro community in the world, but the first
concentration in history of so many diverse elements of Negro
life. It has attracted the African, the West Indian, the Negro
American; has brought together the Negro of the North and
the Negro of the South; the man from the city and the man
from the town and village; the peasant, the student, the business man, the professional man, artist, poet, musician, adventurer and worker, preacher and criminal, exploiter and social
outcast. Each group has come with its own separate motives
and for its own special ends, but their greatest experience has
been the finding of one another. Proscription and prejudice
have thrown these dissimilar elements into a common area of
contact and interaction. Within this area, race sympathy and

unity have determined a further fusing of sentiment and experience. So what began in terms of segregation becomes more and more, as its elements mix and react, the laboratory of a great race-welding. Hitherto, it must be admitted that American Negroes have been a race more in name than in fact, or to be exact, more in sentiment than in experience. The chief bond between them has been that of a common condition rather than a common consciousness; a problem in common rather than a life in common. In Harlem, Negro life is seizing upon its first chances for group expression and self-determination. It is—or promises at least to be—a race capital. That is why our comparison is taken with those nascent centers of folk-expression and self-determination which are playing a creative part in the world to-day. Without pretense to their political significance, Harlem has the same rôle to play for the New Negro as Dublin has had for the New Ireland or Prague for the New Czechoslovakia.

Harlem, I grant you, isn't typical—but it is significant, it is prophetic. No sane observer, however sympathetic to the new trend, would contend that the great masses are articulate as yet, but they stir, they move, they are more than physically restless. The challenge of the new intellectuals among them is clear enough—the "race radicals" and realists who have broken with the old epoch of philanthropic guidance, sentimental appeal and protest. But are we after all only reading into the stirrings of a sleeping giant the dreams of an agitator? The answer is in the migrating peasant. It is the "man farthest down" who is most active in getting up. One of the most characteristic symptoms of this is the professional man, himself migrating to recapture his constituency after a vain effort to maintain in some Southern corner what for years back seemed an established living and clientele. The clergyman following his errant flock, the physician or lawyer trailing his clients, supply the true clues. In a real sense it is the rank and file who are leading, and the leaders who are following. A transformed and transforming psychology permeates the masses.

When the racial leaders of twenty years ago spoke of developing race-pride and stimulating race-consciousness, and of the desirability of race solidarity, they could not in any accurate degree have anticipated the abrupt feeling that has surged up and now pervades the awakened centers. Some of the recognized Negro leaders and a powerful section of white opinion identified with "race work" of the older order have indeed attempted to discount this feeling as a "passing phase," an attack of "race nerves" so to speak, an "aftermath of the war," and the like. It has not abated, however, if we are to gauge by the present tone and temper of the Negro press, or by the shift in popular support from the officially recognized and orthodox spokesmen to those of the independent, popular, and often radical type who are unmistakable symptoms of a new order. It is a social disservice to blunt the fact that the Negro of the Northern centers has reached a stage where tutelage, even of the most interested and well-intentioned sort, must give place to new relationships, where positive self-direction must be reckoned with in ever increasing measure. The American mind must reckon with a fundamentally changed Negro.

The Negro too, for his part, has idols of the tribe to smash. If on the one hand the white man has erred in making the Negro appear to be that which would excuse or extenuate his treatment of him, the Negro, in turn, has too often unnecessarily excused himself because of the way he has been treated. The intelligent Negro of to-day is resolved not to make discrimination an extenuation for his shortcomings in performance, individual or collective; he is trying to hold himself at par, neither inflated by sentimental allowances nor depreciated by current social discounts. For this he must know himself and be known for precisely what he is, and for that reason he welcomes the new scientific rather than the old sentimental interest. Sentimental interest in the Negro has ebbed. We used to lament this as the falling off of our friends; now we rejoice and pray to be delivered both from self-pity and condescension. The mind of each racial group has had a bitter weaning, apathy or hatred on one side matching disillusionment or resentment on the other; but they face each other to-day with the possibility at least of entirely new mutual attitudes.

It does not follow that if the Negro were better known, he would be better liked or better treated. But mutual understanding is basic for any subsequent coöperation and adjustment. The effort toward this will at least have the effect of remedying in large part what has been the most unsatisfactory feature of our present stage of race relationships in America, namely the fact that the more intelligent and representative elements of the two race groups have at so many points got quite out of vital touch with one another.

The fiction is that the life of the races is separate, and increasingly so. The fact is that they have touched too closely at the unfavorable and too lightly at the favorable levels.

While inter-racial councils have sprung up in the South, drawing on forward elements of both races, in the Northern cities manual laborers may brush elbows in their everyday work, but the community and business leaders have experienced no such interplay or far too little of it. These segments must achieve contact or the race situation in America becomes desperate. Fortunately this is happening. There is a growing realization that in social effort the co-operative basis must supplant long-distance philanthropy, and that the only safeguard for mass relations in the future must be provided in the carefully maintained contacts of the enlightened minorities of both race groups. In the intellectual realm a renewed and keen curiosity is replacing the recent apathy; the Negro is being carefully studied, not just talked about and discussed. In art and letters, instead of being wholly caricatured, he is being seriously portrayed and painted.

To all of this the New Negro is keenly responsive as an augury of a new democracy in American culture. He is contributing his share to the new social understanding. But the desire to be understood would never in itself have been sufficient to have opened so completely the protectively closed portals of the thinking Negro's mind. There is still too much possibility of being snubbed or patronized for that. It was rather the necessity for fuller, truer self-expression, the realization of the unwisdom of allowing social discrimination to segregate him mentally, and a counter-attitude to cramp and fetter his own living—and so the "spite-wall" that the intellectuals built over the "color-line" has happily been taken down. Much of this reopening of intellectual contacts has centered in New York and has been richly fruitful not merely in the enlarging of personal experience, but in the definite enrichment of American art and letters and in the clarifying of our common vision of the social tasks ahead.

The particular significance in the re-establishment of contact between the more advanced and representative classes is that it promises to offset some of the unfavorable reactions of the past, or at least to re-surface race contacts somewhat for the future. Subtly the conditions that are molding a New Negro are molding a new American attitude.

However, this new phase of things is delicate; it will call for less charity but more justice; less help, but infinitely closer understanding. This is indeed a critical stage of race relationships because of the likelihood, if the new temper is not understood, of engendering sharp group antagonism and a second crop of more calculated prejudice. In some quarters, it has already done so. Having weaned the Negro, public opinion cannot continue to paternalize. The Negro to-day is inevitably moving forward under the control largely of his own objectives. What are these objectives? Those of his outer life are happily already well and finally formulated, for they are none other than the ideals of American institutions and democracy. Those of his inner life are yet in process of formation, for the new psychology at present is more of a consensus of feeling than of opinion, of attitude rather than of program. Still some points seem to have crystallized.

Up to the present one may adequately describe the Negro's "inner objectives" as an attempt to repair a damaged group psychology and reshape a warped social perspective. Their realization has required a new mentality for the American Negro. And

as it matures we begin to see its effects; at first, negative, iconoclastic, and then positive and constructive. In this new group
psychology we note the lapse of sentimental appeal, then the
development of a more positive self-respect and self-reliance;
the repudiation of social dependence, and then the gradual re-
covery from hyper-sensitiveness and "touchy" nerves, the repudiation of the double standard of judgment with its special
philanthropic allowances and then the sturdier desire for
objective and scientific appraisal; and finally the rise from
social disillusionment to race pride, from the sense of social
debt to the responsibilities of social contribution, and offsetting
the necessary working and commonsense acceptance of restricted conditions, the belief in ultimate esteem and recognition. Therefore the Negro to-day wishes to be known for what
he is, even in his faults and shortcomings, and scorns a craven
and precarious survival at the price of seeming to be what he is
not. He resents being spoken of as a social ward or minor, even
by his own, and to being regarded a chronic patient for the
sociological clinic, the sick man of American Democracy. For
the same reasons, he himself is through with those social nos-
trums and panaceas, the so-called "solutions" of his "problem,"
with which he and the country have been so liberally dosed in
the past. Religion, freedom, education, money—in turn, he has
ardently hoped for and peculiarly trusted these things; he still
believes in them, but not in blind trust that they alone will
solve his life-problem.

Each generation, however, will have its creed, and that of
the present is the belief in the efficacy of collective effort, in
race co-operation. This deep feeling of race is at present the
mainspring of Negro life. It seems to be the outcome of the
reaction to proscription and prejudice; an attempt, fairly successful on the whole, to convert a defensive into an offensive
position, a handicap into an incentive. It is radical in tone, but
not in purpose and only the most stupid forms of opposition,
misunderstanding or persecution could make it otherwise. Of
course, the thinking Negro has shifted a little toward the left
with the world-trend, and there is an increasing group who

affiliate with radical and liberal movements. But fundamentally
for the present the Negro is radical on race matters, conservative on others, in other words, a "forced radical," a social protestant rather than a genuine radical. Yet under further pressure
and injustice iconoclastic thought and motives will inevitably
increase. Harlem's quixotic radicalisms call for their ounce of
democracy to-day lest to-morrow they be beyond cure.

The Negro mind reaches out as yet to nothing but American
wants, American ideas. But this forced attempt to build his
Americanism on race values is a unique social experiment, and
its ultimate success is impossible except through the fullest sharing of American culture and institutions. There should be no
delusion about this. American nerves in sections unstrung with
race hysteria are often fed the opiate that the trend of Negro
advance is wholly separatist, and that the effect of its operation
will be to encyst the Negro as a benign foreign body in the
body politic. This cannot be—even if it were desirable. The
racialism of the Negro is no limitation or reservation with respect to American life; it is only a constructive effort to build
the obstructions in the stream of his progress into an efficient
dam of social energy and power. Democracy itself is obstructed
and stagnated to the extent that any of its channels are closed.
Indeed they cannot be selectively closed. So the choice is not
between one way for the Negro and another way for the rest,
but between American institutions frustrated on the one hand
and American ideals progressively fulfilled and realized on
the other.

There is, of course, a warrantably comfortable feeling in
being on the right side of the country's professed ideals. We
realize that we cannot be undone without America's undoing.
It is within the gamut of this attitude that the thinking Negro
faces America, but with variations of mood that are if anything
more significant than the attitude itself. Sometimes we have it
taken with the defiant ironic challenge of McKay:

> Mine is the future grinding down to-day
> Like a great landslip moving to the sea,

> Bearing its freight of débris far away
> Where the green hungry waters restlessly
> Heave mammoth pyramids, and break and roar
> Their eerie challenge to the crumbling shore.

Sometimes, perhaps more frequently as yet, it is taken in the fervent and almost filial appeal and counsel of Weldon Johnson's:

> O Southland, dear Southland!
> Then why do you still cling
> To an idle age and a musty page,
> To a dead and useless thing?

But between defiance and appeal, midway almost between cynicism and hope, the prevailing mind stands in the mood of the same author's *To America,* an attitude of sober query and stoical challenge:

> How would you have us, as we are?
> Or sinking 'neath the load we bear,
> Our eyes fixed forward on a star,
> Or gazing empty at despair?

> Rising or falling?   Men or things?
> With dragging pace or footsteps fleet?
> Strong, willing sinews in your wings,
> Or tightening chains about your feet?

More and more, however, an intelligent realization of the great discrepancy between the American social creed and the American social practice forces upon the Negro the taking of the moral advantage that is his. Only the steadying and sobering effect of a truly characteristic gentleness of spirit prevents the rapid rise of a definite cynicism and counter-hate and a defiant superiority feeling. Human as this reaction would be, the majority still deprecate its advent, and would gladly see it forestalled by the speedy amelioration of its causes. We wish our race pride to be a healthier, more positive achievement than a feeling based upon a realization of the shortcomings of others. But all paths toward the attainment of a sound social attitude have been difficult; only a relatively few enlightened minds have been able as the phrase puts it "to rise above" prejudice. The ordinary man has had until recently only a hard choice between the alternatives of supine and humiliating submission and stimulating but hurtful counter-prejudice. Fortunately from some inner, desperate resourcefulness has recently sprung up the simple expedient of fighting prejudice by mental passive resistance, in other words by trying to ignore it. For the few, this manna may perhaps be effective, but the masses cannot thrive upon it.

Fortunately there are constructive channels opening out into which the balked social feelings of the American Negro can flow freely.

Without them there would be much more pressure and danger than there is. These compensating interests are racial but in a new and enlarged way. One is the consciousness of acting as the advance-guard of the African peoples in their contact with Twentieth Century civilization; the other, the sense of a mission of rehabilitating the race in world esteem from that loss of prestige for which the fate and conditions of slavery have so largely been responsible. Harlem, as we shall see, is the center of both these movements; she is the home of the Negro's "Zionism." The pulse of the Negro world has begun to beat in Harlem. A Negro newspaper carrying news material in English, French and Spanish, gathered from all quarters of America, the West Indies and Africa has maintained itself in Harlem for over five years. Two important magazines, both edited from New York, maintain their news and circulation consistently on a cosmopolitan scale. Under American auspices and backing, three pan-African congresses have been held abroad for the discussion of common interests, colonial questions and the future co-operative development of Africa. In terms of the race question as a world problem, the Negro mind has leapt, so to speak, upon the parapets of prejudice and extended its cramped horizons. In so doing it has linked up with the growing group consciousness of the dark-peoples and is gradually learning their common interests. As one of our writers has recently put it: "It is imperative that we understand the white world in its relations to the non-white world." As with the Jew, persecution is making the Negro international.

As a world phenomenon this wider race consciousness is a different thing from the much asserted rising tide of color. Its inevitable causes are not of our making. The consequences are not necessarily damaging to the best interests of civilization. Whether it actually brings into being new Armadas of conflict or argosies of cultural exchange and enlightenment can only be decided by the attitude of the dominant races in an era of critical change. With the American Negro, his new internationalism is primarily an effort to recapture contact with the scattered peoples of African derivation. Garveyism may be a transient, if spectacular, phenomenon, but the possible rôle of the American Negro in the future development of Africa is one of the most constructive and universally helpful missions that any modern people can lay claim to.

Constructive participation in such causes cannot help giving the Negro valuable group incentives, as well as increased prestige at home and abroad. Our greatest rehabilitation may possibly come through such channels, but for the present, more immediate hope rests in the revaluation by white and black alike of the Negro in terms of his artistic endowments and cultural contributions, past and prospective. It must be increasingly recognized that the Negro has already made very substantial contributions, not only in his folk-art, music especially, which has always found appreciation, but in larger, though humbler and less acknowledged ways. For generations the Negro has been the peasant matrix of that section of America which has most undervalued him, and here he has contributed not only materially in labor and in social patience, but spiritually as well. The South has unconsciously absorbed the gift of his folk-temperament. In less than half a generation it will be easier to recognize this, but the fact remains that a leaven of humor, sentiment, imagination and tropic nonchalance has gone into the making of the South from a humble, unacknowledged source. A second crop of the Negro's gifts promises still more largely. He now becomes a conscious contributor and lays aside the status of a beneficiary and ward for that of a collaborator and participant in American civilization. The great social gain in this is the releasing of our talented group from the arid fields of controversy and debate to the productive fields of creative expression. The especially cultural recognition they win should in turn prove the key to that revaluation of the Negro which must precede or accompany any considerable further betterment of race relationships. But whatever the general effect, the present generation will have added the motives of self-expression and spiritual development to the old and still unfinished task of making material headway and progress. No one who understandingly faces the situation with its substantial accomplishment or views the new scene with its still more abundant promise can be entirely without hope. And certainly, if in our lifetime the Negro should not be able to celebrate his full initiation into American democracy, he can at least, on the warrant of these things, celebrate the attainment of a significant and satisfying new phase of group development, and with it a spiritual Coming of Age.

A plea for unity

The spirit of race pride and cultural pluralism that was widespread among black intellectuals and artists, the bourgeois economic nationalism that called for Negro support of Negro business, and the lower-class, emigrationist Garvey movement had their counterparts in political and civic life. Many even saw advantages in the development of the vast black ghettos of the northern cities that followed the large northward migration of the World War I and postwar years; they shared the vision of a black community that would support black business and professional men and send Negroes to public office. Ministers and other leaders denounced race disunity and called upon the blacks to imitate the cohesiveness of the Jewish community.

The most specific proposal—and the most widely published call—for effecting racial unity was Kelly Miller's plan for a national organization of all race organizations to be known as the "Negro Sanhedrin." Miller, prolific essayist and popular sociologist, and dean of the College of Liberal Arts at Howard University, had long been known as a man who occupied the middle of the road among the conflicting Negro schools of thought.

Though a functioning "Sanhedrin" did not grow out of the 1924 conference called by Miller, his proposal received careful consideration. It caused considerable comment and discussion in the black community. More important, in its call for unity and manhood and independence, in its analysis of psychological and other factors standing in the way of racial unity, in its discussion of the need for all-black institutions and organizations, it sums up the thinking of the majority of articulate spokesmen in the period of the New Negro.

53. KELLY MILLER:
"BEFORE THE NEGRO BECOMES ONE
WITH THE REST OF THE AMERICAN PEOPLE,
HE MUST BECOME ONE WITH HIMSELF"

Sanhedrin

The Sanhedrin was a Jewish assembly or council. The Great Sanhedrin was composed of seventy-one members, and sat at Jerusalem with supreme jurisdiction. The Lesser Sanhedrin, composed of twenty-three members, sat in each province with local and limited jurisdiction.

The use of the term in its present application grew out of the circumstances surrounding the Jews in Europe under the domination of Napoleon Bonaparte. The Emperor found that the relation between the Jew and the Gentile world was a fruitful source of antagonism, persecution and race friction. In order to compose this troublesome situation he called a Sanhedrin of all of the Jews under his jurisdiction, which assembled upon his invitation and perfected a scheme of working relationship between the two groups that has operated with more or less success and satisfaction down to the present time. Similarity of situation suggests a like conference of the Negro peoples of the United States to-day under the ancient designation. The Greater Sanhedrin with nation-wide function, and the Lesser Sanhedrin limited to city and local jurisdiction, also suggest a happy comparison.

The Negro Sanhedrin

The All-Race Conference, commonly known as the Negro Sanhedrin, has been called to convene in the city of Chicago, during the week of February 11, 1924. The civil rights bodies

From Kelly Miller, THE NEGRO SANHEDRIN:
A CALL TO CONFERENCE (n.p., 1924).

which joined in the issuance of the call are: The National Association for the Advancement of Colored People, The Equal Rights League, The Race Congress, The Blood Brotherhood, the International Uplift League and the Friends of Negro Freedom. The special competence of this type of organization to issue such a call grows out of the fact that these civil rights bodies profess to function for the race as a whole, as against religious denominations, benevolent and fraternal orders, and business, economic and industrial agencies, which operate in limited and special spheres. The preliminary arrangements are in the hands of a central committee with plenary powers. The conference is not to be a mass meeting, but a delegated body, composed of representatives from national organizations functioning in general or special fields. In addition, there will be a minority of individual delegates composed of leading citizens in the various walks of life.

The object of the conference

There are already innumerable organizations in the racial field operating separately and severally. Each is efficient in its sphere, but no one of them, nor yet all of them combined, can claim to be sufficient as concerns the general welfare of the race. They are all aiming at the same objective, without correlation, unity of plan or harmony of procedure. Nor does any existing organization deal fundamentally with the whole problem of racial life and relationship. Each is concerned with some special feature rather than with the problem as a whole. The religious, political, educational, industrial, economic, and social features are but emanations and special emergences from a common racial background. The Negro Sanhedrin hopes to reduce all of these social fractions to a common denominator. The whole is greater than any of its parts, and equal to the sum of all of its parts. The Negro Sanhedrin does not propose to interfere with any existing organization or to usurp its function. In a nutshell, its object is to make for understanding and unity. It hopes to reach an understanding of the problem as a whole and to promote harmonization of effort of existing agencies to secure the desired end. The All-Race Conference must consider the state of the race, I am almost persuaded to say, the united state of the race.

The psychology of the problem

The Negro question is a problem of psychology. The white race in America has a certain more or less fixed and definite attitude concerning the place and sphere of the Negro in the general scheme. A race consciousness will necessarily arise under compulsion of external circumstances. Purposive intelligence must be brought to bear to give it orderliness and direction. To inquire into the origin of race prejudice or to seek the limits within which it is modifiable would indeed furnish a theme of interesting and curious speculation. But we do know that it is a present, pressing, persistent fact which conditions the entire scheme of the Negro's life and relationship. Race statesmanship requires that we study to understand the operation of this controlling influence, to withstand as far as we may its hurtful effect, and to stand the residue that may not be withstood. It cannot be conceded for a moment that the race has not sufficient wisdom to formulate its own philosophy and to state its own case. This must be done in terms that are so comprehensive, clear and precise that the race will be compelled to accept and the world to take notice. So far, the Negro has not undertaken, in any serious way, to formulate a declaration of principles for his own guidance. The white man has spoken for him and told him what he thinks he ought to do. We have followed the leading strings of material charity and intellectual philanthropy. But the time has now come when the Negro must think for himself and speak for himself in terms of his own understanding of his own condition. If he is not now prepared to use his own brain and his own tongue to think out and express the policy for his own intimate guidance, his helplessness is indeed pitiable. The white man has been generous and kind. He has spoken for us when our tongues were tied;

but now our tongues have been loosed and our intellectual energies released. The white man at his best can no longer speak for us within the circumscribed area to which his prejudice confines us. Any group that is devoid of enlightened self-expression is doomed.

The temper of the conference

The spirit of the Conference must be sane, temperate and determined. It must avoid the fatuous extremes of idle boasting and cowardly surrender. Such conferences usually open the cave of the winds. The time is wasted with vacuous verbosity, loud-voiced loquacity and sonorous silliness. It is in vain that we denounce the white race as being unpatriotic, unchristian and inhuman; and to no useful purpose do we excoriate the South for its sins of commission and the North for its sins of omission, beyond the natural expression of righteous indignation. Wild demands which the demandant has no means of enforcing, are but vain vociferations whose echo returns to torment his own ears. It is to be hoped that no such impotent waste of while will invade the conference. We are a group of ten millions in the midst of ten times our own numbers. The welfare of one must not be sought at the expense of ten. All of our policies must be patriotic and considerate of the whole equation of which we constitute but a minor factor. We can surrender no rights, inalienable nor conferred. But we must measure our powers against the task imposed. We must know where the task exceeds our strength. It is as suicidal to excite impotency to try conclusions with might, as it is to yield supinely without the fullest trial of strength. We must avoid the folly of defying the facts of the universe and of shaking the fist of defiance at forces we cannot combat. . . .

Is an all-Negro conference possible?

Will an all-race conference lead to an all-race wrangle? The critical white world anticipates the spectacle of internal, interminable dissension whenever the Negro assembles to consider his own affairs. There is abundant precedent to justify this expectation. Minorities are ever prone to work at cross purposes. The helplessness of the weak is accentuated by their inability to agree among themselves. The policy of the powerful has always been to divide and conquer. The laboring man represents four-fifths of our electorate. The control of the government would fall quickly into his hands if he could only agree upon a plan of political action. But the crafty capitalist keeps him under by keeping him asunder. The labor party of England now represents the major minority party in parliament. It is only their fatal lack of harmony that keeps this party from manning and controlling the British government. The Democratic minorities in the North and the Republican minorities in the South always furnish the greater number of contests at our national conventions. . . .

The Negro has never been admitted to responsible participation in government. He naturally enough shows the evil consequences of this deprivation. Internal dissension is his besetting sin. His chief dynamic is derived from dissent. He would a hundred times rather fight his fellow Negro than an enemy of the white race. Animosity is always intensified by nearness of relationship. Would to God the Negro might spend half the energy in combating the common enemy that he wastes in bootless internal strife. How long, O Lord, how long, must these things be? Slavery sowed the seed of dissension whose tree hangs big with bitter fruit. We still partake thereof and contend needlessly one with another. But we must throw off this infirmity, if need be, by sheer calculation and prudence. Hamlet said to his mother: "Assume chastity, if you have it not." The Negro leaders must assume the semblance of unity of aim and effort, even though they have it not. We may, by assuming a virtue and by persistent practice, make the assumption true. If we proceed on the basis that this present disposition to disunion and strife is inherent and cannot be overcome, then our case is hopeless and our cause is lost. The longer we delay, the stronger will the disposition grow.

We are now divided into a hundred separate camps. Each is aiming, in its own way, at the same objective. There is untold waste in friction, rivalry and jealous antagonism. Everyone is prone to think that his way is *the* way. Where none is certain each is infallible. A philosopher once said that men never fall out about what they know, but about what they don't know. If any one of us had the sure infallible key to the solution of the problem, it would only be necessary for him to proceed to solve the problem by his method, and satisfy us all. After we have said all we have to say, and done all that we know how to do, in separate alignments, the problem persists in all of its perplexing forms and phases. The only thing left untried is united wisdom and judgment.

There is no need of despair. As long as the objective is possible, the trial is worth while. We shall probably not all think as one on any particular detail but we will all agree on essential principles. Programs will vary with local and individual circumstances and conditions; principles are universal and unvarying. If, as an outcome of the proposed conference, the various agencies and organizations reach a common understanding, and agree upon plans of procedure, so that the contributions of each will reinforce, and not neutralize, those of the other, we shall be well on the way toward the accomplishment of the end we all have in view. Nothing can keep ten million of our group from their just share in the civilization in which they are involved and which they help to maintain, except their own folly. If in this year of our Lord, after two generations of education and opportunity, we are not able to unify our forces and solidify the power resident within us, then our faith is vain and our hope is vain.

We have an educated class sufficient in numbers and understanding to cope with the most complex human condition. Great will be the condemnation of our *intelligentsia* if it continues to hide its light under a bushel. Let the best minds the best hearts and the best consciences of the race compose their petty diversities, and come together in conference for the common good. "Come, let us reason together," says the voice of wisdom.

The necessity for the Negro Sanhedrin

. . . The ten million American Negroes occupy a unique position among the racial groups of the world. Transplanted from a distant continent, thrust servilely into the midst of a disdaining civilization, given the full status of citizenship by the exigencies of economic and political exactions, the Negro is a part of the American people, and yet apart from them. They cannot completely isolate him; they will not wholly assimilate him. His interests and activities are so intricately intermixed with those of the general population that the welfare of one becomes the welfare of all. And yet he is assigned to separate areas within whose boundaries he must work out his own destiny, mainly through his own endeavor. A semi-subject people in the midst of democracy is an anomaly. If the law breaks down at the color line, democracy becomes a self-confessed failure. If the law applies alike to all, the color line will wipe out itself. And so we must adjust ourselves between alternate perplexities of the white man's mood.

Within the next half generation there will be a tremendous change in the scheme of race adjustment in the United States. The quickened conscience of the nation will not consent to go on living forever on the basis of a lie. The relation of the Negro will become more firmly established on a basis of equality, or will settle into a status of frankly declared inferiority. Which it shall be, will depend upon the Negro himself. The time is ripe for treatment. Instant action is demanded, hesitancy is dangerous. Delay may prove fatal.

Why a Negro conference?

The Negro group has special and peculiar interests and relations, infinitely more serious and vital than any other subordinate group into which our population is divided. There are fourteen million foreigners in this country. Their peculiar problems are limited to one generation, and will pass away within a half century. Three million Jews are segregated only in reli-

gious alignment and domestic relations. The separation is of
the Jew's own preference. He labors under no political, civil or
social disabilities by virtue of race or color. Twenty million
Catholics differ from the Protestant majority only in forms of
belief and modes of worship. The Negro alone is separated
from the rest of the nation by the whole diameter of the social
intimacies of life. This *regime* is imposed upon him. He did not
make it; he cannot unmake it. Special group interests call
for special treatment. If the Jews find it necessary to meet in
nation-wide conferences to consider matters that concern Jewry
alone; if the Catholics form national organizations to promote
interests peculiar to their religion, surely the Negro group
needs to give attention to its own intimate affairs.

The Negro is the only section of the American people which
is assigned to separate cars, is segregated in residential areas,
confined to separate schools, disfranchised by tricky contrivances, and is denied accommodations in theaters, hotels and
places of public resort. He alone is lynched on account of his
race and color rather than his crime. The terms "white" and
"colored" carry all but the separative connotations "Jew and
Gentile," "Greek and Barbarian," "Christian and Heathen," as
historical lines of cleavage of mankind. The Negro constitutes
a nation within a nation with a body of intra-racial needs and
demands which make the all-race conference imperative.

The origin of race churches

About the beginning of the nineteenth century, Negro communicants found themselves frozen out of the Christian
Church. They were confined to the rear pews and upper galleries where mayhap the droppings of the showers of the Gospel might fall even on them. The function of the church is to
unite men in one solid phalanx of Christian brotherhood. And
yet the Christian Church in America has been the one separative agency between the races. There always has been a closer
racial unity in politics, business and education than in religion.
Even to-day the Negro finds it more comfortable to deal with
the white man in his office where he manipulates politics or

conducts business than at his church were he professes to be concerned with the affairs of the soul.

In these early years the sense of manly self-respect prompted the Negro religionists to organize independent denominations where they might worship God face to face without being hidden behind the screen of servility. Thus the African Methodist Episcopal Church, the African Methodist Episcopal Zion Church and the great Negro Baptist Church had their origins. A century and more of ecclesiastic independence justifies the faith and manly courage of the founders. We may indeed speculate what would have been the religious state of the race to-day had the Negro accepted the inferior position in the church to which the "master and servant" interpretation of Christianity relegated him. He would still be in the rear pews and upper galleries.

Early Negro conventions

In the middle thirties of the last century when large numbers of manumitted and fugitive slaves found their way into the free states, they began to think collectively upon the proscriptive lot that was forced upon them and to devise means to promote and safeguard their own welfare. Negro conventions were organized to take into consideration the civil rights of the race throughout the free states. Such organizations met annually or at intervals until the downfall of slavery and the Reconstruction of the South. In reading the deliberations and addresses of these early Negro conventions, one is forced to wonder if the intelligence, race patriotism and power of leadership of that day suffers or shines by comparison with this day. One thing is clear—their statemanship was better calculated to meet the requirements of their day than ours is of ours. . . .

African movements

The Universal Negro Improvement Association is the contrivance of Marcus Gravey whose chief aim is to set up an independent civilization on the continent of Africa largely through the instrumentality of Afro-Americans. The Pan-African Congress originated by Dr. DuBois purports to be a consultive body composed of representative people of African blood now sojourning in the different countries of the world. It is the analogue of the League of Nations for the African race.

The Negro Sanhedrin, on the other hand, is concerned with the immediate problems of the Negro in the United States. While it cannot be incurious as to the destiny of the Negro peoples as a whole, yet it must limit its deliberations to our domestic situation. Whatever is to be the destiny of the black race, and whatever part the Afro-American is to play in that destiny, it is perfectly plain that he must first demonstrate his capacity to cope with his own problems before he can claim competence to assume the leadership and direction of his blood brothers now scattered over the face of the earth.

Lack of leadership

It will be readily conceded that there is no group of ten million people in the world that have the absolute and relative opportunity of the American Negroes which is making such little use of them. The Negro possesses every political right that the most favored citizen possesses, and yet he is a practical nullity in the state. He holds the industrial destiny of large and fertile areas stored up in the energy of his arm, and yet he is mainly a hewer of wood and drawer of water. In him is the start of great enterprises and great achievements, and yet we still pray to the white man: "Give us this day our daily bread." He indulges in vainglorious boasting over his accomplishments, when they are but the earnest of the greater things which he should do.

It is conceded that the race possesses emotional and religious possibilities surpassing the material coldness and indifference of the white world by which he is environed, and yet the Negro still looks to the white man to interpret the meaning and mission of Christianity. He has been, and still is, overpowered and intimidated. He does not dare to stretch himself out at full length. His powers must be loosened; his energies released. He is too dependent on the white man and too deferential to him. He is too prone to interpret all of the practical and higher values of life in terms of the experience and forms of expression manifested by other race varieties than his own. He has yet to feel that all fundamental virtues and values grow out of the basic needs and necessities of humanity. The Negro Sanhedrin will serve to create in us a new heart and to renew a right spirit of manly independence within the race.

Race aim and ideal

I have been in an exceptional position to observe the ultimate aims and ideals by which ambitious Negro youth are actuated. I have had the intimate handling of more Negro collegians than has fallen to the fortune of any other American citizen white or black, during the past twenty-five years. The vitally weak spot in our racial armor is the lack of some consuming motive which actuates the educated Negro youth of this day and generation. Technical intelligence is rapidly increasing, but the quickening power of the spirit grows not apace. The chief task of Negro leadership to-day is to impart to our youth an inspiring motive. The statesman is one who can formulate a workable policy and impress it upon the minds of his constituency in such persuasive form that they will be constrained to adopt it as a guiding rule of action. This is the supreme task of race statesmanship. We must delve below the surface into the deep philosophy of things.

There are but three great social motives which actuate the conduct of men. These are based respectively upon patriotism, religion and race. The appeal of country is easily made and quickly responded to. The Negro possesses unsurpassed patriotic capacity. If this country would only permit him to love it to the fullest extent of his affection, the patriotic motive would be all-compelling. But, except in times of war, when emotionalism is aroused, patriotism does not make a compelling appeal to him. I have seen Negro audiences refuse to sing

"My country, 'tis of thee." Patriotism does not mean the same thing to the Negro boy in Mississippi that it does to the white boy, and cannot elicit the same response. The Negro is altruistically loyal by nature; he is faithful to his country even when it is not faithful to him; and let us hope that he may be permitted to be patriotic in the same sense as other citizens can be. But at the present time reasoned patriotism does not quicken and inspire the Negro youth to develop, exert and assert his highest powers and possibilities.

In the second place, religion is the great source of inspiration and aspiration which calls out the best endeavor of its adherents. But sad to say, religion to-day is appealing but feebly to the youthful ambition of America, and perhaps feeblest of all to the Negro youth. On a great missionary occasion attended by thousands of white and hundreds of Negro college students, appeal was made for student volunteers for the African field. Scores of white students, male and female, stepped forward in answer to the call; but not a single brother or sister in black. The Negro is allowing the white man's religious false face to obscure the Christ he hides behind it. It seems to me that a simpler interpretation of the secret and method of Jesus, divested of much of its ceremonial accretions and racial arrogance, should appeal to Negro youth as to no other, and as nothing else can hope to do. Meekness, forgiveness, long suffering and non-resentfulness of spirit—the essential Christian virtues—are imbedded in the soul-stuff of the Negro race. The Negro has to try hard, not to be religious. The Christian religion vibrates in harmony with his spiritual wave-length. It beats in sympathetic resonance with the impulse of his soul. It is not thinkable to formulate a controlling motive for the Negro without including the religious element which is the dominant note of his nature. The Negro's religion must not be derived from the white man but from its original source. Religion is always refracted by the medium through which it passes. One sees the Christ but dimly who views him through Teutonic glasses. The heavenly light will yet shine directly on the Negro's face; this he will reflect for the spiritual enlightenment of the world, without deviation in its direction or dimming of its brightness.

The third factor in the formation of a social ideal is the racial or group appeal. Here the Negro motive is at low ebb. We have a race without territorial or ethnic unity. The infusion of diverse bloods helps to frustrate orderly formation of race consciousness. The cunning policy of the white overlordship, which insists that all models of excellence shall be made in its own image, tends to the same end. The flesh and blood basis of brotherhood is the gospel of the Ku Klux Klan. Kinship of blood though not essential to, easily awakes, kinship of the spirit. The white and the non-white races form the separate American groups for the practical purposes with which we need now to concern ourselves. The race pride of our group must be based partly on blood and partly on social classification. The definition of a Negro that will meet all of the requirements of the Negro Sanhedrin, is anyone who would be jim-crowed in Virginia. Blood and color are but a badge of identification. This racial group, shut into itself by the pressure of prejudice, will perforce form a group consciousness, and the opportunities, possibilities, outlook and upreachings of this circumscribed circle must be presented to its youth in a manner to inspire them with hope and zeal.

Weaving these three threads of motive into one strand of duty, and service, and inspiration, the Negro youth can be made to feel that his function in the vineyard of humanity is not merely equal to, but superior to, that of any other group in this day and generation. The Sanhedrin will fail of its essential aim unless it holds up an ideal to Negro youth which is worth living for, worth striving for, and, if need be, worth dying for.

Inter- and intra-race conferences

President Coolidge has recommended a joint commission composed of white and colored men to make a careful study of the entire fabric of race relationship and to recommend suitable legislation to put its findings into effect. I was a member of the delegation that brought this question to the President's attention. The commission on race relationship appointed by Governor Lowden of Illinois, has issued a report which contains many interesting facts and wise suggestions. Great good may be expected to flow from such commissions, both local and national. The Negro is almost wholly dependent upon the white man for employment, and is conditioned by him in many of the essential relations of life. In all such inter-related matters the races can no more be divorced than capital from labor. We may also expect a wholesome measure of good understanding to flow from these inter-racial conferences. Mutual exclusion begets mutual distrust and suspicion. The Negro still needs much help from the benevolent whites whose human impulse is to help those less fortunate than themselves. But the best help is that which leads most quickly to self-help. Dependence tends to perpetuate itself. We should look to philanthropy only so far and so long as it may be necessary, and no farther and no longer.

"To the feasts of lesser men, the Gods unbidden go." The white man is disposed to feel that his superior position confers upon him the right to know all the Negro's secrets and to participate in all of his plans. There are many well-meaning colored people who decry the formation of any purely Negro movement which does not let the white man in on the ground floor. They argue that such projects but tend to widen the gap between the races and confuse rather than clarify the situation. Some have asked me if it is the plan of the Negro Sanhedrin to have white men participate in its proceedings. On receiving a negative response, they have shaken their heads in sad dissent, and gone away sorrowful. Too many Negro gatherings waste the time listening to well-meaning white men tell how their grandfathers were kind to their slaves, and how they themselves used to play with Negro playmates. They flatter their audiences by repeating the familiar recital of the race's wonderful progress and accomplishments but add nothing to the constructive purpose of the proceedings. The Negro is more

likely to gain self-respect and the respect of his fellows by
sailing under his own steam, when the craft is to carry only
Negro passengers. We gain the esteem of our fellow men by
having what they want rather than by wanting what they have.
Before the Negro becomes one with the rest of the American
people, he must become one with himself.

Inter-racial conferences are made necessary by the segregated life which the race is forced to live. The laboring man
would be kept forever in a weak and dependent position if he
held only joint meetings with the capitalists. The Jews have innumerable relations with the gentiles which they consider on
common grounds and in common council. But when they deal
with matters peculiar to their race and religion, they meet behind closed doors. The Catholics form a solid part of our common citizenship. Most of their relations are considered along
with the rest of the population. There is no hint or squint of religion in their ordinary dealings with their Protestant fellow
citizens. But when it comes to the intimate internal affairs of
their religion, no Protestant would dare suggest a share in
shaping their plans and policies. The Congregational, Presbyterian, and Episcopalian denominations operate as general organizations for all of their membership; and yet the colored
contingents of these several religious bodies find it necessary to
meet in separate councils to consider plans and formulate policies to meet the peculiar needs of their semi-segregated relationship. The Young Men's Christian Association has its Negro
department, which, though a part of, is yet apart from, the
Christian organization to which it belongs. The colored membership seeks its own management, and meets in separate conclaves to discuss the peculiar problems of its racial circumstances and situation.

If the white race should consent never to hold a meeting
without the presence of the Negro, then the Negro might agree
to hold no separate sessions. The Negro Sanhedrin has no sin-
ister secrets. It does not seek the wizardry of darkness to conceal its evil deeds. All of its aims are in harmony with the Ten
Commandments, the Golden Rule, the Sermon on the Mount,

the Declaration of Independence, and the Constitution of the United States.

Politics

Senator Ingalls, of Kansas, once defined politics as the metaphysics of force. It is the dynamic factor in social control. The Government is assuming a larger and larger share in shaping the general welfare, as the affairs of the country become more and more complex. It used to be a maxim that the Negro does well enough so long as he lets politics alone. It is no longer possible for any class of citizens to be indifferent to the affairs of government or to be ignored by them. We must all look to the government for the cure of existing ills and for the protective measures of the future. The government is but the social agency through which society carries out its collective will. The Negro's place in the national scheme is peculiarly related to and conditioned by political considerations. In a democracy conducted by partizan government, politics is a game. To the victors belong the power of office, if not the spoils thereof. Any group may expect greater consideration from that party which it places in power. The politicians who make the game of politics a profession find easy favor with the administration which owes its success to their prowess. Our Negro politicians do well to corral the Negro vote for their favorite party, and to hold that party to its just obligations to the race. As practical men, we must use practical methods. The much-abused politicians constitute a factor and a force which can neither be denied or ignored. But it is dangerous to let politicians get the underhold on any movement which aims to function broadly for the welfare of the people. Political ethics never rises above barter in the commodity of votes. The dynamic power of the ballot is the most effective agency through which to promote many of the aims of the race. But no race organization should sell its soul to any political party. Negro organizations too often fall victims to this evil. The Negro Sanhedrin must avoid any such entangling alliance. After all, our fundamental problems are deeply sociological rather than narrowly political.

The agenda

Negro organizations usually indulge in a recital of wrongs, recount exciting incidents, make denunciatory speeches, pass high-sounding resolutions, and adjourn *sine die,* with little abiding result. Such pronounced evils as lynchings, jim-crowism, disfranchisement, segregation and race proscription will inevitably form a large part of the program of any race meeting. Irritating symptoms cannot be ignored. A man with the toothache has little patience with abstract philosophy. The sufferer from any painful malady seeks immediate relief. Protest against wrong is but a natural reaction.

The Negro can hardly be expected to forget his grievances or cease to complain about them until they have been removed. But symptoms are merely surface indications of deep-seated underlying causes. We must remove the seeds of disease from the system by determining, if we may, its nature and cause and finding an effective cure.

The outcome of the Sanhedrin

"Let me write 'union' at the top of the page, and I care not what you write underneath," was Lincoln's famous reply to the representatives of the seceding states seeking to effect a settlement of differences. If the Negro Sanhedrin can but effect union of aim and harmony of purpose its chief aim will have been accomplished. It is more essential that the Race should act in unison than that it should act in any given direction. The Negro Sanhedrin is an influence rather than an organization. Principles must be laid down and programs outlined. The plans must be constructive, remedial, ameliorative and inspirational. The resulting type of agency which is to put into effective operation the things agreed on must be the outcome of the conference itself. Its sessions will probably be triennial. It is not without significance that the Sanhedrin is to be held during the week covering the birthdays of Frederick Douglass and Abraham Lincoln.

A Negro national anthem

The ethnic dualism and the quality of optimism exhibited in Alain Locke's essay on the New Negro were also reflected in a song, "Lift Ev'ry Voice and Sing." It was written in 1900 by a Jacksonville, Florida, high school principal, James Weldon Johnson, later famous as an author and as executive secretary of the NAACP. His brother, the composer J. Rosamond Johnson, set the poem to music. First performed at a local Lincoln's birthday celebration in 1900, it gradually spread among school and church groups, and by the 1920s it was widely sung and generally known as the "Negro National Hymn" or the "Negro National Anthem."

This anthem expresses both black consciousness and the ethnic ambivalences of American Negroes. Thus, not once mentioning the black man by name, Johnson's lyrics exhibit a sense of identity based upon suffering in the past, hopefulness for the future, belief in liberty, and faith in God and America. Johnson believed that in the last verse—which ends, "May we forever stand,/True to our God, True to our native land"—"the American Negro was, historically and spiritually, immanent."[1]

[1] James Weldon Johnson, *Along This Way* (New York: The Viking Press, 1933), p. 155.

54. JAMES WELDON JOHNSON:
"SING A SONG FULL OF THE FAITH
THAT THE DARK PAST HAS TAUGHT US"

Lift Ev'ry Voice and Sing

Lift ev'ry voice and sing,
Till earth and heaven ring,
Ring with the harmonies of liberty;
Let our rejoicing rise,
High as the list'ning skies,
Let it resound loud as the rolling sea.
Sing a song full of the faith that the dark past has taught us,
Sing a song full of hope that the present has brought us,
Facing the rising sun,
Of our new day begun,
Let us march on till victory is won.

Stony the road we trod,
Bitter the chast'ning rod,
Felt in the days when hope unborn had died;
Yet with a steady beat,
Have not our weary feet
Come to the place for which our fathers sighed?
We have come over a way that with tears has been watered,
We have come, treading our path thro' the blood of the
    slaughtered,
Out from the gloomy past,
Till now we stand at last
Where the white gleam of our bright star is cast.

God of our weary years,
God of our silent tears,

James Weldon Johnson and J. Rosamond Johnson, LIFT EV'RY VOICE
AND SING (New York: Edward B. Marks Music Corporation, 1900).

Thou who has brought us thus far on our way,
Thou who has by Thy might
Let us into the light,
Keep us forever in the path, we pray;
Lest our feet stray from the places, our God, where we met
    Thee,
Lest, our hearts drunk with the wine of the world, we forget
    Thee;
Shadowed beneath Thy hand,
May we forever stand,
True to our God, True to our native land.

Eclipse

PART FOUR

55. CHICAGO IN THE 1930s:
"MAKING JOBS FOR THE RACE"

During the 1920s, the blacks of Chicago, probably more than those of any other city, had been known for their militant economic nationalism. This ideology, expressed principally through the doctrine of Negro support of Negro business, took the form of "Don't-Buy-Where-You-Can't-Work" campaigns with the onset of economic depression at the end of the decade. Like the direct-action demonstrations for employment in white-owned enterprises, the ideology of patronizing black businesses, though it served the interests of Negro entrepreneurs and professional men, was justified as a method for increasing the number of jobs for blacks.

The two selections from St. Clair Drake's and Horace Cayton's classic sociological treatise, *Black Metropolis*, illustrate both themes. As participant-observers in Chicago's black community, Drake and Cayton have written not only a sociological masterpiece but also a primary source document. The selection about the "double-duty dollar" illustrates the continuing importance of the ideology of Negro support for Negro business through the depression, while the chart of employment campaigns indicates the scope and variety of collective efforts to obtain jobs in white-owned corporations.

From St. Clair Drake and Horace R. Cayton, BLACK METROPOLIS: A STUDY OF NEGRO LIFE IN A NORTHERN CITY (New York: Harcourt, Brace & World, Inc., 1945), pp. 430–434, 743. Copyright 1945 by St. Clair Drake and Horace R. Cayton. Reprinted by permission of Harcourt, Brace & World, Inc.

The doctrine of the double-duty dollar[1]

It is Sunday morning in the "black belt." The pastor of one of the largest churches has just finished his morning prayer. There is an air of quiet expectancy, and then—a most unusual discourse begins. The minister, in the homely, humorous style so often affected by Bronzeville's "educated" leaders when dealing with a mass audience, is describing a *business exposition:*

The Business Exposition at the Armory was one of the finest achievements of our people in the history of Chicago. Are there any members of the Exposition Committee here? If so, please stand. [A man stands.] Come right down here where you belong; we've got a seat right here in front for you. This man is manager of the Apex Shoe Store—the shoes that I wear. . . . We can get anything we want to wear or eat from Negroes today. If you would do that it would not only purchase the necessities of life for you, but would open positions for your young folks. You can strut as much as you want to, and look like Miss Lizzie [an upper-class white person], but you don't know race respect if you don't buy from Negroes. As soon as these white folks get rich on the South Side, they go and live on the Gold Coast, and the only way you can get in is by washing their cuspidors. Why not go to Jackson's store, even if you don't want to buy nothin' but a gingersnap? Do that and encourage those girls workin' in there. Go in there and come out eating. Why don't you do that?

This is the doctrine of the "Double-Duty Dollar," preached from many Bronzeville pulpits as a part of the weekly ritual. Church newspapers, too, carry advertisements of all types of business from "chicken shacks"[2] to corset shops. Specific businessmen are often pointed out to the congregations as being worthy of emulation and support, and occasional mass meetings stress the virtues of buying from Negroes—of making the dollar

[1] The term "Double-Duty Dollar" seems to have been first popularized by a Negro minister, Dr. Gordon B. Hancock, who runs a column called *Between the Lines* in several weekly Negro newspapers. In Chicago, the term is frequently used by public speakers and writers.

[2] Restaurants which specialize in fried chicken.

do "double-duty": by both purchasing a commodity and "advancing The Race." The pastor quoted above had been even more explicit in an address before the Business Exposition crowd itself:

Tomorrow I want all of you people to go to these stores. Have your shoes repaired at a Negro shop, buy your groceries from a Negro grocer . . . and for God's sake, buy your meats, pork chops, and yes, even your chitterlings,[3] from a Negro butcher. On behalf of the Negro ministers of Chicago, I wish to commend these Negro businessmen for promoting such an affair, and urge upon you again to patronize your own, for that is the only way we as a race will ever get anywhere.

Residents of the Negro community rather generally approve of those churches and ministers who lend their support to Negro enterprises, and church members sometimes cite such actions as evidence that their pastors are "progressive." As one woman phrased it: "Reverend Moss is one of the progressive ministers. . . . He tells us that we are too dependent on other races for employment and that we must establish good sound business enterprises and at least give employment to the many youths that finish their education each year. His one principal subject is co-operation and racial solidarity, for in union there is strength."

Preachers who do not preach the gospel of the "Double-Duty Dollar" are liable to such caustic criticisms as this:

God have mercy on our preachers! They are the supposed-to-be leaders of The Race. But all they are interested in is money for themselves. . . . We pay hundreds of thousands of dollars for churches, but when it comes to building Negro businesses, it seems that our people are not interested.

Some of the Holiness sects protest vigorously against this mixture of religion, business, and race pride, but they are definitely a minority voice in Bronzeville.

[3] A southern delicacy prepared from the intestines of the hog.

This endorsement of business by the church simply dramatizes, and brings the force of sacred sanctions to bear upon, slogans that the press, the civic organizations, and even the social clubs repeat incessantly, emphasizing the duty of Negroes to trade with Negroes and promising ultimate racial "salvation" if they will support racial business enterprises.

The efficacy of these appeals is difficult to measure. There is no way of knowing, for instance, how many of the hearers react like the person referred to in this (probably apocryphal) story told by a colored merchant:

A Negro came in here with five dollars worth of Jew stuff[4] in his arms and bought ten cents' worth of salt pork from me. He said: "Every Sunday morning the Reverend wants all who bought groceries from a colored grocer to raise their hands. Now I can hold *mine* up with a clear conscience."

To the Negro community, a business is more than a mere enterprise to make profit for the owner. From the standpoints of both the customer and the owner it becomes a symbol of racial progress, for better or for worse. And the preacher is expected to encourage his flock to trade with Negroes.

That these ministerial appeals do have some effect is suggested by the rather general comments of white businessmen in

[4] In 1938, about three-fourths of the merchants in Bronzeville were Jewish. During that year an organized anti-Semitic drive arose in Bronzeville. A small newspaper, *Dynamite,* scurrilously attacked all Jews. Jewish philanthropists were accused of trying to dominate Negro institutions; Jewish merchants were dubbed exploiters. Suggestions were made that all Jews should be expelled from Bronzeville. Finally, after conferences between Negro and Jewish leaders as well as representatives of various labor unions, the editor of the paper was dissuaded from publishing further attacks. Because many of the interviews we quote were made when the campaign was at its height, the repeated references to Jews may represent an abnormal situation; in other years such references might be less frequent. Yet, as the most highly visible and most immediately available white persons in the community, Jewish merchants tend to become the symbol of the Negroes' verbal attack on all white businessmen, and anti-Semitic waves sometimes sweep through Bronzeville. In New Orleans, where Italian merchants predominate in Negro areas, "Dagoes" are the target of attack. In Bronzeville it is the Jew who is the scapegoat.

the Black Belt, such as that of one man who told an interviewer:

"There has been a great deal of propaganda created against the white merchants in this neighborhood, some of it coming from the ministers in the pulpits of their churches, advising the people to patronize Negro merchants whenever possible. And they are doing it!"

The elevation of the Double-Duty Dollar slogan into the realm of almost sacred dogma results primarily from the fact that Negroes participate in two worlds—the larger community of city, state, and nation, and the smaller, socially isolated, and spatially separate Negro world. As participants in the general American culture, they are exposed to a system that places a high premium upon business success and white-collar occupations. Financial power and economic control bring those political and social rewards which have traditionally been supposed to serve as incentives to thrift, enterprise, and hard work. Negroes, using the same school textbooks as whites, reading the same papers, attending the same movies, and in constant contact with the white world, tend to incorporate the general ideals of American life. Inevitably, they measure progress since slavery partly in terms of the positions of power and prestige which Negroes attain in the business world.

Objective reality, however, is at variance with the ideal. No Negro sits on a board of directors in La Salle Street; none trades in the grain pit or has a seat on the Stock Exchange; none owns a skyscraper. Negro girls are seldom seen in the offices and stores of the Loop except as maids. Colored traveling salesmen, buyers, and jobbers are a rarity. The largest retail stores and half of the smaller business enterprises in Bronzeville are owned and operated by white persons, and until recently many of these did not voluntarily employ Negroes.

Making jobs for the race

Campaigns	Date	Groups Involved	Technique	Outcome
"Spend Your Money Where You Can Work" Campaign (directed at white stores in the Black Belt)	1929	Sponsored by *Negro Professionals and Business men.* (Led by Race Radicals, with broad community support)	Boycott; picketing	Successful: 2,000 jobs in Black Belt stores
51st Street Riot (directed at white laborers)	1930	Spontaneous outburst by laborers	Violence	Successful
Fight for Skilled Jobs on Construction in Black Belt (directed at AFL building trades unions)	1929–1938	*Consolidated Trades Council* — group of Negro artisans	Picketing; political pressure; some violence	Partial success with advent of New Deal
Fight for Branch Managers with *Daily Times*	1937		Threat of boycott	Six managers appointed after one week campaign
Fight for Branch Managers, *Evening American*	1937	*Negro Labor Relations League*— group of young men and women; some co-operation from Urban League and politicians	Conference; implied threat of boycott	Eight managers appointed
Campaign for Motion Picture Operators in Black Belt (directed against AFL Unions)	1938		Picketing; threat of boycott	Ten operators appointed after short campaign
Campaign for Telephone Operators (directed against phone company)	1937–1939		Threat that all Negroes would remove telephones	Unsuccessful; threat not carried out fully
Drive for Negro Milkmen (directed against major dairies and the AFL unions)	1929–1939	Fight begun by *Whip;* revived in 1937 by *Council of Negro Organizations and Negro Labor Relations League*	Threat of boycott; attempt to organize "Milkless Sundays"	Unsuccessful due to lack of community support
Campaign for bus drivers and motormen on transit lines	1930–1944	*"United front"* with strong left-wing influence; campaign aided by FEPC.	Demonstrations; threat of boycott; strong political pressure	Successful in securing a few positions

56. THE NEW NEGRO ALLIANCE:
"WE MUST ORGANIZE
OUR PURCHASING POWER"

The New Negro Alliance in Washington was one of many local
organizations formed during the depression, in order to combat
employment discrimination by obtaining jobs for black
workers in white-owned businesses serving the ghetto people.
Ralph Bunche's description of this movement indicates very
clearly the ethnic ambivalence which characterized its ideology.
The New Negro Alliance, as Bunche points out, was a
middle-class organization; in some cities, as in the case of
The Future Outlook League of Cleveland, the
movement was a lower-class one.

The New Negro Alliance, Incorporated, of Washington, D. C.,
is an excellent example of the Negro boycott organizations.
Its motto is "Buy Where You Work—Buy Where You Clerk."
The factors giving rise to this organization are significant.
Early in 1933 the management of a Hamburger Grill on "U"
Street, N.W., in Washington, discharged its Negro employees
and replaced them with white workers. This establishment was
in the heart of the Negro belt of Northwest Washington and
its entire trade was Negro. Several young Negroes happened to
witness the discharge of the Negro employees and the injustice
of the situation struck them with full force. They decided to
organize a picket line in front of the grill and in a surprisingly
short time the discharged Negro workers were back on their
jobs. In setting up the picket line in front of the Grill, these
young Negroes had perfected an organization. Inspired by

From Ralph J. Bunche, "The Programs, Ideologies, Tactics, and
Achievements, of Negro Betterment and Interracial Organizations"
(unpublished memorandum prepared for the Carnegie-Myrdal Study of
the Negro in America, 1940), pp. 380–92.
Printed by permission of Ralph J. Bunche.

their victory at the Grill, they decided to expand their organization and to make it a permanent force in the Negro community. It was named the New Negro Alliance, Incorporated. It was proposed as "an organization with a new vision, a new thought, and spirit, fearless in its undertakings, and willing to sacrifice and fight for its principles even if it meant being thrown in jail."[1]

From this beginning the organization went on to develop its policy of picketing stores in Negro districts which refused to employ Negro clerks. The Alliance tackled the Kaufman Department Store on upper Seventh Street, N. W. and caused it to lose the greater part of its Christmas trade. The Sanitary, the A. & P., and the High Ice Cream Company Stores were next tackled. The Kaufman, High and Sanitary Stores succeeded in getting injunctions against the Alliance. The injunction obtained by the Sanitary Stores went so far as to stipulate that in addition to no picketing, Alliance officials were enjoined from door to door campaigns—another weapon that had been employed effectively by the Alliance. While this litigation was pending and while the organization was thus deprived of its most effective weapon, the organization prepared a Civil Rights Bill for the District of Columbia, modeled after those in Pennsylvania and New York. This bill was introduced by Congressman Koppleman in the House of Representatives as HB No. 5333. In 1938 after four years of bitter court action, the Supreme Court of the United States dismissed the injunction. The opinion was handed down by Mr. Justice Roberts on March 28, 1938. The court ruled that the relationship of employer-employee is not essential in order to bring an organization such as the Alliance within the purview of the Norris-LaGuardia Act which permits peaceful picketing. Thus, the Alliance—striving to obtain employment for persons from employers who discriminated against them on account of race and color—was interpreted as a "person interested" in a labor dispute and so within the protection of the law prohibiting "interference."[2]

1 *New Negro Alliance Yearbook* (1939), p. 15
2 "The Supreme Court Speaks," by Leon A. Ransom, *New Negro Alliance Yearbook* (1939), p. 17.

The New Negro Alliance is directed by regularly elected officers and maintains a number of committees and subcommittees. The officers and committee members work without remuneration. The Alliance claims to be non-political and non-sectarian.[3]

The program of the New Negro Alliance is set forth as follows: (1) the securing of positions which will increase the earning capacity of Negroes: (2) the securing of opportunities for advancement and promotion in positions secured; (3) the uniting of the purchasing power of the colored people to be used as a lever in securing economic advantages; (4) the creation of bigger and better Negro business through increased earning power of Negroes, through a better business outlook resulting from contact and experience with successful businesses of the other group, and through the stimulation of businesses now run by Negroes to higher levels of efficiency and service; (5) the concentrated support of all businesses which employ Negroes or in which Negro capital is invested[4]; (6) research and investigation which will discover and thoroughly analyze the possibility for Negro business and Negro labor in new fields.[5]

The tactics of the Alliance are those of a pressure group dependent largely upon the weight of the Negro consuming public. The proposal is to organize Negro consumers and to get them to support or withhold their support from designated stores and other business enterprises, and to persuade or force them to employ Negroes in proportion to Negro purchasing power. The Alliance essays a thorough survey of the trading area from which the store draws its patronage and definite efforts are made to determine the exact percentage of Negro

[3] Cf. Article by John A. Davis, in *Opportunity* (August 1938), pp. 230–37.
[4] Though this is an official statement of the organization's program, this item is misleading. The Alliance does not give its support to "all businesses which employ Negroes," since this would embrace businesses such as the Peoples' Drug Stores, which it has vigorously picketed. The Alliance supports those businesses which employ Negro clerks and other white collar workers.
[5] *New Negro Alliance Yearbook* (1939), p. 11.

business enjoyed by the store in question. Such statistics are presented by a committee representing the Alliance to officials of the store, and on the basis of such facts definite demands are made in proportion to the percentage of income from Negro trade. If no action has been taken upon these demands after a reasonable time has elapsed, a picket line is placed in front of the establishment. Negroes in this trading area are acquainted with the program of the organization and the reasons for the boycott through the distribution of circular letters from door to door.[6]

The support of the Alliance is through membership fees and voluntary contributions. Membership fees range from one to twelve dollars per year. For some time the Alliance published the "New Negro Opinion" as the official organ of the organization. This was a weekly set up in newspaper style.

The "New Negro Opinion" in its issue of February 3, 1934, presented a comparative study of the records of the New Negro Alliance under the heading "Figures Don't Lie" in order to demonstrate the profitable returns gotten for the Negro community on a very small investment through the efforts of the Alliance. These figures read as follows: Expenditures for office, stenographer, postage, etc.—$225; for printing, advertising signs, pickets, etc.—$175; total expenditures—$400. Returns—A. & P.—18 clerks per year, $13,104; Hamburger Grill—four clerks per year, $3,744; Sanitary—four clerks per year, $2,912; others—nine clerks per year, $5,594; total returns—$25,354.[7]

The organization boasts a number of successes with local employers and in two instances with large chain stores. However, in its attempt to compel the Peoples Drug Stores to employ Negro clerks, it met with failure. The People's Drug Stores is a chain of some 56 stores in Washington and nearby states. The Alliance began its campaign against these stores with a letter to the management requesting a conference on the matter of the employment of Negro clerks and professional workers in those stores in which the preponderance of trade

[6] *New Negro Alliance Yearbook* (1939), p. 48.
[7] Reprinted in the *New Negro Alliance Yearbook* (1939), p. 15.

was Negro. After a second letter, a conference with the district manager was obtained, and on June 21, 1938, a committee from the Alliance met with the district manager. The Alliance Committee was told on behalf of the executive committee of the Peoples Drug Stores Corporation that the definite policy of the company was that Negroes be barred from clerical and professional positions and that they be refused service at soda fountains. The committee was told that since the management of the stores did not believe that colored people would stay out of the stores because of such policy, no change was contemplated. On June 25, 1938, the New Negro Alliance placed a picket in front of the Peoples Drug Store at Fourteenth and U Streets, N.W., where a check had shown that approximately 75% of the trade was Negro. The signs carried by the pickets urged all fair-minded people to stay out of the store and circulars were distributed explaining the nature of the controversy. On July 15, 1938 a second picket line was begun in front of the Peoples Drug Store at Seventh and M. Streets, N.W., where a check had shown that approximately 70% of the trade was Negro. These picket lines were maintained for well over a year and a half, yet, despite the claims of the Alliance that the number of Negro patrons entering the Fourteenth and U Streets store immediately dropped from approximately 1,000 per day to a little more than 100 a day, the management of the store remained adamant and ultimately the Alliance was compelled to abandon its struggle without any concession from the management.[8]

The membership of the Alliance is "ninety-nine and forty-four one hundred per cent pure Negro" with a "few unsolicited whites as members."[9] The organization has no affiliation with any other group—political or civic—and claims to be free from all restraining influence in its work.[10]

[8] "We picket the Peoples Drug Stores," *New Negro Alliance Yearbook* (1939), p. 21.
[9] Interview with Eugene Davidson, Administrator of the New Negro Alliance, December, 1939. William Bryant's memo.
[10] *Ibid.*

The main problem of the organization is that of financial support. Since membership fees are its sole source of revenue and since the number of members who pay dues within the course of the year does not exceed 1,500, the Alliance is hard pressed for funds to meet its normal expenditures. In its picketing campaigns it has found that it cannot recruit enough volunteer pickets and has been compelled to resort to paid pickets to carry on the work. During the picketing of the Peoples Drug Stores the monthly payroll was in the neighborhood of $150.[11]

The administrator of the organization states that the maintenance of the picket line before the two Peoples Drug Stores was chiefly a "symbol." He claims that the particular stores picketed became dead-weights and the firm was able to carry them only because of the chain character of the organization. Proof of the effectiveness of the picketing was claimed to be found in the fact that following its inception the clerical staff of the Fourteenth Street store was reduced by seven. Moreover it is contended that the maintenance of these lines proved invaluable because of its effect upon individual white enterprises in the same neighborhood. The owners of such businesses were said to realize that they cannot keep their stores open on the strength of other holdings and have usually capitulated to the demands of the Alliance without struggle. It is claimed that Seventh Street from New York Avenue to Florida Avenue is an excellent example of the influence of the Alliance since there is now scarcely a store on upper Seventh Street which does not have at least one colored clerk.[12]

The organization is now proposing to train its sights on the public utilities in Washington, but appreciates the fact that considerable mass education of Negroes is a necessary prerequisite to such a move. The Alliance contemplates the employment of tactics similar to those used by Negroes in New York under the direction of the New York Coordinating Committee. This involves a closely knit organization of the Negro masses so that when the organization decides to have all of the Negroes

11 *Ibid.*
12 *Ibid.*

in Washington turn off their electric lights on any particular night of the week, it would get impressive cooperation. The Alliance is also putting its active support behind the new proposed Civil Rights Bill of the District of Columbia.

It is stated that frequently the Alliance has run across the problem of union labor. In some cases employers have expressed a willingness to put on Negro employees, but are faced with the fact that the white employees are union men and that the unions will not accept Negro members. In the case of Heurich Brewers, for example, the company got around the difficulty with the union by employing Negroes as truck drivers and paying them union wages for their work. It was explained that, though the unions would not accept Negroes into their ranks, they did issue permits to the Negroes to drive the trucks for union wages. This was made necessary because of the fact that some fourteen Negro establishments had withdrawn their trade from the Heurich Company.[13]

In the statements of its aims, the New Negro Alliance points out that

In our cities we find two types of businesses. First there is the 'neighborhood' store which caters to and relies upon the trade of the people living within a few blocks of the store. The other type of business whether a street railway company or a large department store, is one which serves the entire city. The neighborhood store owes to the community which supports it a fair return in the form of such employment as the store can give. The business which serves the entire city and makes a profit out of city-wide trade should give all persons in the community an opportunity to work as need arise and fitness can be shown. Where a neighborhood store is located in a colored neighborhood, its obligation to the neighborhood is an obligation to colored people. Where the neighborhood is one of white persons those are the persons who can rightly insist on a chance to work in neighborhood stores. . . . In each case the right is based not on race, but on the obligation of the neighborhood store to the neighborhood. . . .

[13] *Ibid.*

The New Negro Alliance does not sponsor jim-crow economy, but we must organize our purchasing power behind the demands for equal opportunity to work and also in support of those businesses in which Negroes can do work without discrimination. The support of businesses owned and operated by Negroes is, of course, an essential part of such a program.[14]

As to the effect of its policy upon the relations between Negro and white workers the Alliance explains that it has

never fought to drive white workers into the streets. In every case the Alliance has sought to place Negroes it has taken the position that in any business of any size the normal course of replacements, displacements, and additions to personnel causes vacancies to arise from time to time. Moreover where Negroes represent the large part of the patronage of a store, the additional cost of adding a few Negroes to the payroll is more than compensated for by the increase of business the establishment will receive.[15]

Despite its protestations to the contrary, it is clear that the New Negro Alliance pursues a narrowly racial policy—one that has no orientation in terms of labor unity or organization, and one that definitely opposes Negro against white workers.[16] Its membership is middle class and so is its ideology. Its efforts are devoted almost entirely to obtaining white collar jobs for Negroes and this is amply demonstrated by the claims made as to its successes.[17] Practically all of the jobs it has gotten for Negroes have been white collar jobs and these mainly clerks. It emphasizes the support of Negro business and says very little about the importance of organized labor to the Negro worker. Though employing the tactics and weapons of labor it is in no sense a labor organization. In terms of economic status it is quite clear that the ultimate results of the efforts of this organi-

[14] *The New Negro Alliance Yearbook* (1939), p. 47.
[15] *Ibid.*
[16] "The Why of the Alliance," by William H. Hastie, *The New Negro Alliance Yearbook* (1939), p. 14.
[17] See "Notes from Alliance Case Book," *New Negro Alliance Yearbook* (1939), pp. 24ff.

zation will be of slight consequence to the Negro community.

Although both have been connected with the New Negro Alliance in an official capacity since its very beginning, Mr. Hastie and Mr. Fitzhugh have widely different conceptions of the organization's sympathizers. Mr. Fitzhugh places the membership at 1500 and the number of sympathizers at 5,000. Mr. Hastie, on the other hand places the membership at 1,000, but estimates 50,000 sympathizers.

Critique of the "don't buy where you can't work" organizations

The "Don't Buy Where You Can't Work" or "Buy Where You Can Work" movements are a logical corrolary of the Negro business philosophy. This credo has been expressed through organizations such as the New Negro Alliance, the League for Fair Play and the Afro-American Federation of Labor. The movement began in Chicago about 1931 and rapidly spread to the East and more recently to the South and West.

The organizations participating in this recent movement occasionally have employed the labor weapons of boycott and picketing against white stores in Negro districts which refuse to employ Negro white collar workers. This has undoubtedly been of educational value to the Negro in that it has given him some inkling of his latent economic power and an acquaintance with the recognized weapons of organized labor. The most violent manifestation of this movement was in the Harlem Riot of 1935 when thousands of Harlem Negroes vented their fury, born of poverty, against the small white—mostly Jewish—shopowners on Lennox and Seventh Avenues.

The philosophy of this movement is narrowly racial. If successful, it could only result in a vicious cycle of job displacement since it creates no new jobs but only struggles to displace white workers, and, since Negro communities do not offer sufficient economic activity to absorb even a small number of the Negroes now employed in white industry. Its appeal has been primarily in the interest of the Negro white collar worker and its support has come chiefly from Negro middle class professional and intellectual groups. It appears unable to realize that there is an economic system as well as a race problem in America and that when a Negro is unemployed, it is not just because he is a Negro but more seriously because of the defective operation of the economy under which we live—an economy that finds it impossible to provide an adequate number of jobs and economic security for the population. More seriously, still, this movement tends to widen the menacing gap between white and black workers by insisting that jobs be distributed on a racial basis. It is a philosophy which, like that of Negro business, offers only racialism with no significant hope for the mass Negro population.

57. BENJAMIN J. DAVIS, JR., ARGUES THE COMMUNIST POSITION: "THE NEGRO PEOPLE A NATION"

The Communist International, at its Sixth World Congress held in Moscow in 1928, affirmed the Negroes' right to self-determination in the black belt of the American South. This proposal for a black Soviet Socialist Republic was a mechanical adaptation of Joseph Stalin's early ideas for dealing with the ethnic minorities in Russia, and it clearly failed to attract Negroes to the American Communist party. In 1946, the national committee of the American Communist party reaffirmed this right of black self-government in the heart of the South. Benjamin J. Davis, a black city councilman of New York and a member of the national committee of the party and chairman of its Harlem division, elaborates on this proposal in a pamphlet, *The Path of Negro Liberation,* an excerpt from

From Benjamin J. Davis, Jr., THE PATH OF NEGRO LIBERATION (New York: New Century Publishers, 1947), pp. 8–10, 20–22.

which appears here. A distinctly peripheral brand of nationalist
ideology without any visible relation to the thinking of the
black community, it does represent the official viewpoint of
the Communist party and its black spokesmen.

Since the prime roots of the oppression of the Negro people,
on a nation-wide scale, are in the Black Belt areas of the South,
we must look here to ascertain their true status. In order to
wage a successful fight on the day-to-day issues of Negro rights
and to defeat the objectives of capitalist tories, the ultimate,
long-range perspective of democratic solution of the Negro
question must be clarified and fully settled. Otherwise, one
cannot distinguish which trends and developments are growing
and permanent, however weak at the moment, and those which
are temporary and disappearing, however strong at the moment.
The conscious seizure and development of that which is new
and rising, sound and permanent—even though not fully developed—is the key to the complete liberation of the Negro people,
as it is to the emancipation of the working class of our country.

The Negro people in the Black Belt are a nation and possess
the basic characteristics of a nation. According to the only
scientific definition of nationhood, given by Stalin:

A nation is an historically evolved, stable community of language,
territory, economic life, and psychological make-up manifested in a
community of culture.

Fears may be expressed that this definition comes from Stalin
as if from the brow of Jove. However, it will be found that
every country or people in the world today which is popularly
as well as accurately described as a nation, possesses the basic
characteristics of nationhood analyzed by Stalin. The Black
Belt area in the South is the core and main center of the Negro
nation in America.

When, over 300 years ago, the Negroes were first brought to
this country against their will, they were enchained in chattel
slavery and did not ripen into nationhood over night. Even

before the Civil War they had certain common characteristics, namely, a common land, language and psychological make-up growing out of their common oppression. But it was not until after the Civil War and the abolition of slavery that they developed the higher qualities of nationhood even though in elementary form.

They have developed a strong proletariat, a petty-bourgeoisie, professionals and middle class, and a distinct, although weak capitalist class, landowners and industrialists. The Negro bourgeoisie is almost 100 per cent confined to the Negro market for its profits. All sections of the Negro people are subject to national Jim Crow oppression. The great majority of the Negroes in the Black Belt area are sharecroppers and poor farmers —almost physically attached to the soil through peonage and debt slavery. They tend the land which has been their common territory for over 300 years, but which they have never owned due to semifeudalism and poverty. This land is owned by the big Northern trusts, insurance companies and banks in an alliance with the semifeudal landlords of the South.

Under the conditions of capitalism and the abolition of slavery since 1865, the Negro has become a composite whole— that is, a nation—and are no longer just a transplanted agrarian people living under conditions of slavery or semifeudal plantation system. Obviously, the Negro people would have reached a higher level of maturity as a nation, had their growth not been partially stunted by the extreme rigors and double oppression of the Jim Crow system which served to blunt and smother their consciousness of nationhood. No one can speak of the full freedom of the Negro people in the Black Belt of the South unless willing to remove all obstacles to their full, conscious growth as a nation, leading to their own self-government. . . .

Toward a bi-national state

The orientation of the Negro people is such, however, that statehood would take place within the confines of the United

States. The growing development of the Negro people has practically disintegrated any remaining nationally organized centers of separatism among them; and the Negroes look, and justly so, with extreme skepticism upon any concepts which would isolate them from their American citizenship rights.

Indications are that the Negro people are not seeking a separate Negro Republic in the South, but are more definitely veering toward relationships obtaining in a bi-national state, toward the relationships analagous in some respects to those of the French-Canadians toward the rest of the Canadian people.

However, while supporting the right of the Negro people to self-determination, the Communist Party does not seek to impose any specific solution in advance, nor does it prematurely raise self-determination as an immediate slogan of action. The solution must arise from the living movement itself, out of the struggles for democracy and equal rights. Its form of expression or coming into being will also be determined by the level of class relationships in the country as a whole and by the relation of the Negro people to the progressive coalition. The lessons of the bi-national and multi-national states in other parts of the world will be extremely helpful in helping to arrive at a final solution appropriate to the specific and peculiar conditions of our own country.

We must not underestimate the stake of the white workers and poor farmers in the Black Belt area, in achieving the right of self-determination. For the first time, they would have the guarantee of freedom from the exploitation and poverty imposed upon them by the common enemy, the big trusts and semifeudal landlords. Equal citizenship among Negro and white in such a state would be the highest expression of Negro-white unity. The increasing unity between Southern Negroes and whites shows this is possible. During the Reconstruction period only, where the Negro people approached self-government, did the white masses, impoverished by slavery, enjoy the benefits of full suffrage and progressive government.

In summary, while boldly supporting the right of self-determination of the Negro people, as the logical, necessary and only solution to the growing national aspirations of the Negro people:

1. We should avoid presenting the slogan in any manner whatsoever that creates the impression that self-determination would necessarily lead to the creation of a separate Negro Republic. Separation is only one form it could take, and life itself shows that the Negroes have a contrary orientation. Nor would self-determination entail the forced migration of Negroes elsewhere to the area of self-government.

2. The question of race should not be brushed aside as in the past. The role of racial prejudice in intensifying the oppression of the Negro people must be recognized, and its relation to the larger, more basic political question of national oppression of the Negroes shown. This question must be further studied.

3. Our advocacy of the slogan must correspond more closely to the general stage of the national development which the young Negro nation has attained. We must adopt as a major task the awakening of the Negro people's consciousness of nationhood, purposefully seizing upon those sound and permanent trends developing among them and fighting beside them to develop them to higher levels. The slogan of self-determination should not be presented in schematic, or mechanical manner or in any other fashion as would assume that the Negro people are a nation fully matured politically.

4. We must more concretely connect the question of Socialism with the fight of the Negro people against oppression. We must point out that while their present fight for economic, social, and political equality, and their eventual struggle for national self-determination are indispensable for their welfare and freedom, it will only be under the Socialist transformation of society, that they, together with the white working masses, finally and irrevocably achieve full liberty, equality and prosperity.

5. We must not make this a slogan of immediate action but must point out its long-range character flowing out of existing

conditions and class relationships involving many factors. We must be sensitive to the past that the bourgeoisie and all its henchmen will seek to distort and discredit it even as they do Socialism and every other major step toward progress proposed in the country.

6. The adoption of this slogan in no way interferes with, but strengthens, the effectiveness of the fight for the basic policy of our Party on the current issues, all over the country—namely for full, unconditional, social, economic and political equality of the Negro people in all aspects of American life.

58. A. PHILIP RANDOLPH AND THE MARCH ON WASHINGTON MOVEMENT: "OPPRESSED PEOPLE MUST ASSUME THE RESPONSIBILITY . . . TO FREE THEMSELVES"

A. Philip Randolph came to prominence during and after World War I as editor of the radical socialist magazine, *The Messenger*. He established himself as a race leader by his successful effort to organize and secure recognition of the Brotherhood of Sleeping Car Porters during the 1920s and 1930s. In 1936 he became the first president of the National Negro Congress, an "organization of organizations," created on the initiative of a group of black intellectuals and evidently inspired partly by Kelly Miller's proposals for a Negro Sanhedrin (see Document 53). The Congress, however, never seems to have expressed an overtly nationalist ideology. Rather, it adopted a platform of broad racial advancement, with special emphasis upon the problems of black workers.

From A. Philip Randolph, "Keynote Address to the Policy Conference of the March on Washington Movement," in MARCH ON WASHINGTON MOVEMENT: PROCEEDINGS OF THE CONFERENCE HELD IN DETROIT, SEPTEMBER 26–27, 1942 (n.p., n.d.), pp. 6–7, 37.

Randolph, the old socialist and trade unionist, resigned as president of the Congress in 1940, when it became evident that Communists had infiltrated and turned it into a popular-front organization. A year later he started what was the most significant black nationalist movement between the 1920s and the 1960s—the avowedly all-Negro March on Washington Movement. Randolph, concerned about discrimination in the expanding defense industries, proposed a mass march of ten thousand Negroes to the nation's capital in 1941 to petition for equal opportunities in employment. In June 1941, as a result of the ensuing pressure, President Franklin D. Roosevelt promulgated his executive order establishing a Fair Employment Practices Committee. Randolph called off the March but tried to keep the movement intact, and the selection included here is an excerpt from his address to the September 1942 conference of the March on Washington Movement.

This aggressively all-black movement excluded white participation. Criticized by a number of his contemporaries, Randolph and his followers defended the color barrier on the ground that white participation inevitably led to Communist infiltration and that the National Negro Congress had proved the divisive and destructive nature of such infiltration. However, the policy was certainly also rooted in a genuine belief in the necessity for Negroes to direct their own fight for freedom—as Frederick Douglass had declared nearly a century before. Yet the movement's ideology not unexpectedly revealed the common ethnic paradox, and Randolph made it clear that it was in no way antiwhite, nor did he close the doors on cooperation with white and interracial groups.

As to the composition of our movement. Our policy is that it be all-Negro, and pro-Negro but not anti-white, or anti-semitic or anti-labor, or anti-Catholic. The reason for this policy is that all oppressed people must assume the responsibility and take the initiative to free themselves. Jews must wage their battle to abolish anti-semitism. Catholics must wage their battle to abolish anti-catholicism. The workers must wage their battle to advance and protect their interests and rights.

But this does not mean that because Jews must take the responsibility and initiative to solve their own problems that they should not seek the cooperation and support of Gentiles, or that Catholics should not seek the support of Negroes, or that the workers should not attempt to enlist the backing of Jews, Catholics, and Negroes in their fight to win a strike; but the main reliance must be upon the workers themselves. By the same token because Negroes build an all-Negro movement such as the March, it does not follow that our movement should not call for the collaboration of Jews, Catholics, Trade unions and white liberals to help restore the President's Fair Employment Practice Committee to its original status of independence, with responsibility to the President. That was done. William Green, President of the A. F. of L. and Philip Murray, President of C. I. O. were called upon to send telegrams to the President to restore the Committee to its independence. Both responded. Their cooperation had its effects. Workers have formed citizens committees to back them while on strike, but this does not mean that they take those citizens into their unions as members. No, not at all.

And while the March on Washington Movement may find it advisable to form a citizens committee of friendly white citizens to give moral support to a fight against the Poll tax or white primaries, it does not imply that these white citizens or citizens of any racial group should be taken into the March on Washington Movement as members. The essential value of an all-Negro movement such as the March on Washington is that it helps to create faith by Negroes in Negroes. It develops a sense of self-reliance with Negroes depending on Negroes in vital matters. It helps to break down the slave psychology and inferiority-complex in Negroes which comes and is nourished with Negroes relying on white people for direction and support. This inevitably happens in mixed organizations that are supposed to be in the interest of the Negro.

Now, in every community there are many and varied problems. Some are specialized and others are generalized. For instance the problem of anti-semitism is a specialized one and must be attacked by the Jews through a Jewish organization which considers this question its major interest. The organization of the unorganized workers and the winning of wage increases, shorter hours, and better working conditions, is a specialized problem of workers which must be handled through a trade union composed of workers, not lawyers, doctors, preachers, or business men or by an organization of Catholics or Negroes.

The problem of lynching is a specialized one and Negroes must take the responsibility and initiative to solve it, because Negroes are the chief victims of it just as the workers are the victims of low wages and must act to change and raise them.

But the problems of taxation, sanitation, health, a proper school system, an efficient fire department, and crime are generalized problems. They don't only concern the workers or Jews or Negroes or Catholics, but everybody and hence it is sound and proper social strategy and policy for all of these groups in the community to form a generalized or composite movement, financed by all, to handle these problems that are definitely general in nature. Neither group can depend upon the other in dealing with a general social problem. No one group can handle it properly. But this same general organization could not be depended upon to fight for the abolition of segregation of Negroes in the government, or to abolish company unionism in the interest of the workers, or to fight anti-semitism. It's structure is too general to qualify it to attempt to solve a special problem. And, by the same logic, the Zionist Movement, or the Knights of Columbus, or the Longshoremen Union is too special in structure and purpose to be qualified to deal with such a general problem as crime, or health, or education in a community.

Therefore, while the March on Washington Movement is interested in the general problems of every community and will lend its aid to help solve them, it has as its major interest and task the liberation of the Negro people, and this is sound social economy. It is in conformity with the principle of the division of labor. No organization can do everything. Every organization can do something, and each organization is charged with the social responsibility to do that which it can do, it is built to do.

I have given quite some time to the discussion of this question of organizational structure and function and composition, because the March on Washington Movement is a mass movement of Negroes which is being built to achieve a definite objective, and is a departure from the usual pattern of Negro efforts and thinking. As a rule, Negroes do not choose to be to themselves in anything, they are only to themselves as a result of compulsive segregation. Negroes are together voluntarily for the same reason workers join voluntarily into a trade union. But because workers only join trade unions, does not mean that the very same workers may not join organizations composed of some non-workers, such as art museums or churches or fraternal lodges that have varying purposes. This same thing is true of Negroes. Because Negroes only can join the March on Washington Movement, does not indicate that Negroes in the M.O.W.M. may not join an inter-racial golf club or church or Elks Lodge or debating society or trade union.

No one would claim that a society of Filipinos is undemocratic because it does not take in Japanese members, or that Catholics are anti-Jewish because the Jesuits won't accept Jews as members or that trade unions are illiberal because they deny membership to employers. Neither is the March on Washington Movement undemocratic because it confines its members to Negroes. Now this reasoning would not apply to a public school or a Pullman Car because these agencies are public in nature and provide a service which is necessary to all of the people of a community. . . .

The very nature of an all-Negro led and supported group lays the way open to the charge of "Black Nationalism." The strategy of the March On Washington Movement, should be to consistently avoid always and everywhere public statements, decorum, or activities that will corroborate such a charge. The Movement should seek to use tested American techniques of pressure and militant action, never losing sight of the fact that its final goal is to secure full integration of Negro citizens into all phases of American life on a par with other citizens. Recognizing the dual nature of its task, it should make clear to membership and to the public that its basic reason for existence is to develop a continuous technique of mass pressure and militant action until its objectives have been secured. The March On Washington Movement, should make clear that it is not nor is it akin to so-called "Back To Africa Movements," and should emphasize its program of stimulating Negroes to assume initial responsibility for the solution of their problems within the framework for the larger social and economic problems of the American scene.

59. W. E. B. DU BOIS EMIGRATES TO AFRICA: "AFRICA HAD COME NOT UP FROM HELL, BUT FROM THE SUM OF HEAVEN'S GLORY"

During the 1940s W. E. B. Du Bois gradually soft-pedalled his separate economy plan and embraced a "world conception of proletarian liberation." He became increasingly sympathetic toward the Communist nations Russia and China. In 1961, shortly before his ninety-fourth birthday, he officially joined the Communist party and moved to Ghana, where he died in 1963, an expatriate from America. His return to Africa, where he had visited once nearly forty years earlier, filled him with exultation. His mood is reflected in the poem, "Ghana Calls," which he dedicated to President Kwame Nkrumah, with whom he had been associated in the Fifth Pan-African Congress in 1945. The poem illustrates the consistency of his lifelong nationalistic views about the "dream" of Pan-Africa and of his belief in Africa's greatness and special mission to illumine the world.

W. E. B. Du Bois, "Ghana Calls," FREEDOMWAYS, II (Winter 1962), 71–74. Reprinted by permission of FREEDOMWAYS.

To Kwame Nkrumah

I was a little boy, at home with strangers.
  I liked my playmates, and knew well,
  Whence all their parents came;
  From England, Scotland, royal France
  From Germany and oft by chance
  The humble Emerald Isle.

But my brown skin and close-curled hair
  Was alien, and how it grew, none knew:
  Few tried to say, some dropped a wondering word or stray;
  Some laughed and stared.

And then it came: I dreamed.
  I placed together all I knew
  All hints and slurs together grew.
  I dreamed.

I made one picture of what nothing seemed
  I shuddered in dumb terror
  In silence screamed,
  For now it seemed this I had dreamed:

How up from Hell, a land had leaped
  A wretched land, all scorched and seamed
  Covered with ashes, chained with pain
  Streaming with blood, in horror lain
  Its very air a shriek of death
    and agony of hurt.

Anon I woke, but in one corner of my soul
  I stayed asleep.
  Forget I could not,
  But never would I remember
  That hell-hoist ghost
  Of slavery and woe.

I lived and grew, I worked and hoped
  I planned and wandered, gripped and coped

With every doubt but one that slept
Yet clamored to awaken.

I became old; old, worn and gray;
   Along my hard and weary way
   Rolled war and pestilence, war again;
   I looked on Poverty and foul Disease
   I walked with Death and yet I knew
   There stirred a doubt: Were all dreams true?
      And what in truth was Africa?

One cloud-swept day a Seer appeared,
   All cloaked and veiled as me he hailed
   And bid me make three journeys to the world
   Seeking all through their lengthened links
   The endless Riddle of the Sphinx.

I went to Moscow; Ignorance grown wise taught me Wisdom;
   I went to Peking; Poverty grown rich
   Showed me the wealth of Work.
   I came to Accra.

Here at last, I looked back on my Dream;
   I heard the Voice that loosed
   The long-locked dungeons of my soul
   I sensed that Africa had come
   Not up from Hell, but from the sum of Heaven's glory.

I lifted up mine eyes to Ghana
   And swept the Hills with high Hosanna;
   Above the sun my sight took flight
   Till from that pinnacle of light
   I saw dropped down this earth of crimson, green and gold
   Roaring with color, drums and song,

Happy with dreams and deeds worth more than doing
   Around me velvet faces loomed
   Burnt by the kiss of everlasting suns
   Under great stars of midnight glory
   Trees danced, and foliage sang;

The lilies hallelujah rang
   Where robed with rule on Golden Stool
   The gold-crowned Priests with duty done
   Pour high libations to the sun
   And danced to gods.

Red blood flowed rare 'neath close-clung hair
   While subtle perfume filled the air
   And whirls and whirls of tiny curls
   Crowned heads.

Yet Ghana shows its might and power
   Not in its color nor its flower
   But in its wondrous breadth of soul
   Its Joy of Life
   Its selfless role
   Of giving.

School and clinic, home and hall
   Road and garden bloom and call
   Socialism blossoms bold
   On Communism centuries old.

I lifted my last voice and cried
   I cried to heaven as I died:
   O turn me to the Golden Horde
   Summon all western nations
   Toward the Rising Sun.

From reeking West whose day is done,
   Who stink and stagger in their dung
   Toward Africa, China, India's strand
   Where Kenya and Himalaya stand
   And Nile and Yang-tze roll:
   Turn every yearning face of man.

Come with us, dark America:
   The scum of Europe battened here
   And drowned a dream
   Made fetid swamp a refuge seem:

Enslaved the Black and killed the Red
   And armed the Rich to loot the Dead;
   Worshipped the whores of Hollywood
   Where once the Virgin Mary stood
   And lynched the Christ.

Awake, awake, O sleeping world
   Honor the sun;
   Worship the stars, those vaster suns
   Who rule the night
   Where black is bright
   And all unselfish work is right
   And Greed is sin.

And Africa, leads on;
   Pan Africa!

Revival

PART FIVE

The Nation of Islam

Throughout the 1940s and early 1950s, the Nation of Islam, founded in 1930 by W. Fard Muhammad as a breakaway faction of the Moorish Science Temple and led by Elijah Muhammad after 1933, slowly built up its strength among the lower classes and prison inmates. By the end of the fifties, with the ferment of black protest and the rebirth of Africa, the number and influence of the Muslims was increasing rapidly. The Muslim program (Document 60), while espousing equal opportunity and equal justice, contrasts radically with the integrationist ideology that dominated this period. Elijah Muhammad states clearly his desire for "complete separation in a state or territory of our own," and for prohibition of "intermarriage or race mixing." He moved to set up Muslim schools and establish Muslim businesses such as dry cleaning shops, grocery stores, and restaurants, as a first step toward developing black self-sufficiency. These actions in the economic sector carry on Garvey's ideas and foreshadow the black capitalist ideology of the late 1960s. *Muhammad Speaks*, the Muslim weekly newspaper, published accounts of the activities and struggles of black people throughout the world in addition to those of the Muslims themselves.

In 1965 Elijah Muhammad published a book about his views, *Message to the Blackman*. The brief selection from it includes a plea for racial separatism and illustrates the emphasis on self-definition that was a factor in the revival of the black pride and black-is-beautiful concepts in the mid-sixties (Document 61).

60. ELIJAH MUHAMMAD:
"WHAT DO THE MUSLIMS WANT?"

What do the Muslims want?

This is the question asked most frequently by both the whites and the blacks. The answers to this question I shall state as simply as possible.

Since we cannot get along with them in peace and equality, after giving them 400 years of our sweat and blood and receiving in return some of the worst treatment human beings have ever experienced, we believe our contributions to this land and the suffering forced upon us by white America, justifies our demand for complete separation in a state or territory of our own.

1. We want freedom. We want a full and complete freedom.

2. We want justice. Equal justice under the law. We want justice applied equally to all, regardless of creed or class or color.

3. We want equality of opportunity. We want equal membership in society with the best in civilized society.

4. We want our people in America whose parents or grandparents were descendants from slaves, to be allowed to establish a separate state or territory of their own—either on this continent or elsewhere. We believe that our former slave masters are obligated to provide such land and that the area must be fertile and minerally rich. We believe that our former slave masters are obligated to maintain and supply our needs in this separate territory for the next 20 to 25 years—until we are able to produce and supply our own needs.

5. We want freedom for all Believers of Islam now held in federal prisons. We want freedom for all black men and women now under death sentence in innumerable prisons in the North as well as the South.

Elijah Muhammad, "The Muslim Program," MUHAMMAD SPEAKS, July 31, 1962. Reprinted by permission of MUHAMMAD SPEAKS.

We want every black man and woman to have the freedom to accept or reject being separated from the slave master's children and establish a land of their own.

We know that the above plan for the solution of the black and white conflict is the best and only answer to the problem between two people.

6. We want an immediate end to the police brutality and mob attacks against the so-called Negro throughout the United States.

We believe that the Federal government should intercede to see that black men and women tried in white courts receive justice in accordance with the laws of the land—or allow us to build a new nation for ourselves, dedicated to justice, freedom and liberty.

7. As long as we are not allowed to establish a state or territory of our own, we demand not only equal justice under the laws of the United States, but equal employment opportunities —NOW!

We do not believe that after 400 years of free or nearly free labor, sweat and blood, which has helped America become rich and powerful, that so many thousands of black people should have to subsist on relief, charity or live in poor houses.

8. We want the government of the United States to exempt our people from ALL taxation as long as we are deprived of equal justice under the laws of the land.

9. We want equal education—but separate schools up to 16 for boys and 18 for girls on the condition that the girls be sent to women's colleges and universities. We want all black children educated, taught and trained by their own teachers.

Under such schooling system we believe we will make a better nation of people. The United States government should provide, free, all necessary text books and equipment, schools and college buildings. The Muslim teachers shall be left free to teach and train their people in the way of righteousness, decency and self respect.

10. We believe that intermarriage or race mixing should be prohibited. We want the religion of Islam taught without hinderance, or suppression.

These are some of the things that we, the Muslims, want for our people in North America.

What the Muslims believe

1. WE BELIEVE in the One God Whose proper Name is Allah.

2. WE BELIEVE in the Holy Qura-an and in the Scriptures of all the Prophets of God.

3. WE BELIEVE in the truth of the Bible, but we believe that it has been tampered with and must be reinterpreted so that mankind will not be snared by the falsehoods that have been added to it.

4. WE BELIEVE in Allah's Prophets and the Scriptures they brought to the people.

5. WE BELIEVE in the resurrection of the dead—not in physical resurrection—but in mental resurrection. We believe that the so-called Negroes are most in need of mental resurrection; therefore, they will be resurrected first.

Furthermore, we believe we are the people of God's choice, as it has been written, that God would choose the rejected and the despised. We can find no other persons fitting this description in these last days more than the so-called Negroes in America. We believe in the resurrection of the righteous.

6. WE BELIEVE in the judgement; we believe this first judgement will take place, as God revealed, in America. . . .

7. WE BELIEVE this is the time in history for the separation of the so-called Negroes and the so-called white Americans. We believe the black man should be freed in name as well as in fact. By this we mean that he should be freed from the names imposed upon him by his former slave masters. Names which identified him as being the slave master's slave. We believe that if we are free indeed, we should go in our own people's names —the black peoples of the earth.

8. WE BELIEVE in justice for all, whether in God or not; we believe as others, that we are due equal justice as human beings. We believe in equality—as a nation—of equals. We do not believe that we are equal with our slave masters in the status of "freed slaves."

We recognize and respect American citizens as independent peoples and we respect their laws which govern this nation.

9. WE BELIEVE that the offer of integration is hypocritical and is made by those who are trying to deceive the black peoples into believing that their 400-year-old open enemies of freedom, justice and equality are, all of a sudden, their "friends." Furthermore, we believe that such deception is intended to prevent black people from realizing that the time in history has arrived for the separation from the whites of this nation.

If the white people are truthful about their professed friendship toward the so-called Negro, they can prove it by dividing up America with their slaves.

We do not believe that America will ever be able to furnish enough jobs for her own millions of unemployed, in addition to jobs for the 20,000,000 black people as well.

10. WE BELIEVE that we who declared ourselves to be righteous Muslims, should not participate in wars which take the lives of humans. We do not believe this nation should force us to take part in such wars, for we have nothing to gain from it unless America agrees to give us the necessary territory wherein we may have something to fight for.

11. WE BELIEVE our women should be respected and protected as the women of other nationalities are respected and protected.

12. WE BELIEVE that Allah (God) appeared in the Person of Master W. Fard Muhammad, July, 1930; the long-awaited "Messiah" of the Christians and the "Mahdi" of the Muslims.

We believe further and lastly that Allah is God and besides HIM there is no God and He will bring about a universal government of peace wherein we all can live in peace together.

61. ELIJAH MUHAMMAD: "SEPARATION OF THE SO-CALLED NEGROES FROM THEIR SLAVEMASTERS' CHILDREN IS A MUST"

Understand self

There are some efforts to celebrate a so-called "Negro History Week," and some of my people will participate. The planning of that week to teach the slave a knowledge of his past is not complete, sufficient or comprehensive enough to enable my people to learn the true knowledge of themselves. It is important that my people learn the true knowledge of self, as it means their salvation.

We are not Negroes, because God, whose proper name is Allah, has taught me who we are. We are not "colored" people because God has taught me who the colored people are. The American Negro is without a knowledge of self. You are a so-called Negro because you are "not" a Negro. Allah has given to me our proper names, the people from whom we were taken and brought here to the shores of North America and the history of our forefathers. Allah has taught me and today I do not fear to tell you, that you can discard that name "Negro." We are not "Negroes." We are not colored! Those are some of the main things which we should remember.

We must become aware of the knowledge of self and the time in which we are living. You must know these things whether you agree that Elijah Muhammad is on time or out of time. If what I say is out of season, it goes for nothing. If I am on time or in season, then all I say will bear fruit.

There is much misunderstanding among us because of our

From Elijah Muhammad, MESSAGE TO THE BLACKMAN (Chicago: Muhammad Mosque of Islam No. 2, 1965), pp. 34–37. Reprinted by permission of MUHAMMAD SPEAKS.

inferior knowledge of self. We have been to schools where they do not teach us the knowledge of self. We have been to the schools of our slave-master children. We have been to their schools and gone as far as they allowed us to go. That was not far enough for us to learn a knowledge of self. The lack of knowledge of self is one of our main handicaps. It blocks us throughout the world. If you were the world and you were a part of the world, you would also turn a man down if he did not know who he actually was. If we, the so-called Negroes, do not know our own selves, how can we be accepted by a people who have a knowledge of self?

Are we representing ourselves as Negroes and "colored" people in the ancient history of black men? Our search of the ancient history of the black man of the earth will prove that not once in time were Negroes or "colored" people living in Asia or Africa. How did we come by those names? The names are from the slave-masters. They have called us by their names and the nicknames used among themselves.

It even seems that we like being called by the slave-masters' name. After nearly a hundred years of freedom, we are still representing ourselves by the names our slave-masters called us! We must learn that the slave-master's names are not accepted by God or by the righteous people of God.

It is time for us to learn who we really are, and it is time for us to understand ourselves. That true knowledge is here for you today whether you accept it or reject it. God has said that we are members of the original people or black nation of the earth. Original means first. Historian J. A. Rogers points out in his book that beyond the cotton fields of the South and long before the white man himself was a part of our planet, we were the original people ruling the earth, and according to the Holy Qur-an, we had governments superior to any we are experiencing today. Trace over the earth. Check back 5,000, 10,000 or 20,000 years ago. Look at history. Who were those people? They were our people. Today, we are confronted with proof of who the original people are and who shall live on this earth and call it their own.

Help self before helping others

Many of my people, the so-called Negroes, say we should help the nations of Africa which are awakening. This has been said as if we owned America. We are so foolish! What part of America do you have that you can offer toward helping Africa? Who is independent, the nations of Africa or we? The best act would be to request the independent governments of Africa and Asia to help us. We are the ones who need help. We have little or nothing to offer as help to others. We should begin to help at home first.

We are 20 million strong. Many of the nations today that have their independence, and those who are getting their independence, are much smaller in number than my people in America. We are dependent on the slave-master. We do not have 2 feet of earth for our nation of people. You and I, here in America, are licking the boots of the slave-master, begging him for the right of independent people. Yes, we are licking his boots. "Sir, let me shine your shoes?" You have been doing that for approximately 400 years. Today, if one rises up in your midst and says, "We should not lick the slave-master's boots, we should lick our own boots," you would say, "He should be killed! He should be killed because he is teaching us to hate." My people, you are in a dangerous position. Get that fear out of you and stand up for your people! Who are you not to die for your people? Who am I not to die for my people! If I am shot down or cut down today, who is little Elijah Muhammad to 20 million of you! If a million of us throw ourselves in the fire for the benefit of the 20 million, the loss will be small compared to the great gain our people will make as a result of that sacrifice. Hundreds of thousands of Muslims gave their lives in Pakistan to get their nation's independence. They were successful. The black men in Africa are fighting and dying today in unity for their independence.

We sit here like pampered babies. We cannot even stand up on the floor, not to mention taking a chance of crawling out of the door. We are too careful of shedding blood for ourselves.

We are willing to shed all of it for the benefit of others. I am not trying to get you to fight. That is not even necessary; our unity will win the battle! Not one of us will have to raise a sword. Not one gun would we need to fire. The great cannon that will be fired is our unity. Our unity is the best. Why are you afraid to unite? Why are you afraid to accept Allah and Islam?

It is only because the slave-master did not teach you of this! We must unite to ourselves as a nation of people.

Separation of the so-called Negroes from their slave-masters' children is a MUST. It is the only solution to our problem.

You must know that this is the time of our separation and the judgment of this world (the Caucasian), which you and I have known. Therefore, Allah has said to me that the time is ripe for you and me to accept our own, the whole planet earth. Are you waiting for the Divine Destruction? Come! Let us reason together. First, in order for us to reason, you must have a thorough knowledge of self. Who is going to teach you that knowledge of self? Who are you waiting for to teach you the knowledge of self? Surely, not your slave-master, who blinded you to that knowledge of self. The slave-master will not teach you the knowledge of self, as there would not be a master-slave relationship any longer.

Malcolm X

More than any single person, Malcolm X symbolized the nationalist revival of the 1960s, first as the brilliant, articulate, and charismatic spokesman for the Nation of Islam, and then as a revolutionary nationalist. Leading the short-lived Organization of Afro-American Unity, Malcolm kept the doctrines of nationalism—self-determination, self-defense, separatism—before the American public as alternatives to racial integration and nonviolence. A school dropout and underworld figure in his late teens, Malcolm was convicted of burglary and sentenced to prison at the age of twenty-one. He was converted to the Nation of Islam while in prison, and after his release in 1952 he became an active follower of Elijah Muhammad.

While he served as a minister in New York and Washington, Malcolm's intelligence and ability to command the immediate respect of those he met were factors in his rise to national prominence as the Nation of Islam's leading spokesman. The speech at the Harlem Unity Rally in 1960 is typical of this period in Malcolm's career (Document 62). The scathing denunciations of Western society and of those who advocate integration into it, the disapproval of interracial marriage, the plea for black self-discipline and unity, and the emphasis on land as an essential prerequisite to black nationhood are all included. This is the Malcolm who became a symbol of black manhood.

Because of differences with Elijah Muhammad, Malcolm left the Nation of Islam, issuing a "Declaration of Independence" in March 1964. Shortly afterward he formed the Organization of

Afro-American Unity, a movement largely inspired by the Organization of African Unity. The views expressed in his public statement issued June 28, 1964, outlining the aims and objectives of the organization (Document 63) contrast with those in the earlier document in secular tone, concern with specific problems, and international orientation. Since his assassination in February 1965, Malcolm's status has grown, and his *Autobiography of Malcolm X* (1965) has a commanding place in the nationalist literature of the sixties.

62. MINISTER MALCOLM X ENUNCIATES THE MUSLIM PROGRAM

AS-SALAAM-ALAIKUM, Beloved Brothers and Sisters
WELCOME TO OUR HARLEM FREEDOM RALLY
When we say "our" we do not mean Muslim nor Christian, Catholic nor Protestant, Baptist nor Methodist, Democrat nor Republican, Mason nor Elk. By "our" Harlem Freedom, we mean the Black people of Harlem, the Black people of America, and the Black people all over this earth.

The largest concentration of Black people on earth is right here in Harlem, so we are gathered here today in Harlem Square to a Freedom Rally, of Black people, by Black people, and for the benefit of Black people.

We are not here at this Rally because we have already gained freedom. No!!! We are gathered here rallying for the freedom which we have long been promised, but have as yet not received. This Rally is for that perfect freedom which up until now this government has not granted us. There would be no need to protest to the government if we were already free.

From MUHAMMAD SPEAKS, September 1960, pp. 2, 20–22.
Reprinted by permission of MUHAMMAD SPEAKS.

Freedom is essential to life itself. Freedom is essential to the development of the human being. If we don't have freedom we can never expect justice and equality. Only after we have freedom do justice and equality become a reality.

Today we are gathered at this Rally to hear from our leaders who have been acting as our spokesmen, and representing us to the white man downtown. We want to know how our leaders really think, how they talk, how they feel . . . and most important of all, we want them to know how we feel.

Many of these leaders have suddenly become "experts on Harlem" and as such are often regarded by the white man as the "voice of Harlem." If this must be the case, then we want the voice of these leaders to ring sometimes in Harlem too.

Leaders have differences, and these differences offtimes cause serious division among the masses. But the HOUR is too short today for Black people to afford the luxury of "differences."

Again I repeat, we are not gathered here today because we are Muslims or Christians, Protestants or Catholics, Baptists or Methodists, Democrats or Republicans, Masons or Elks . . . but, because as a collective mass of Black people we have been colonized, enslaved, lynched, exploited, deceived, abused, etc.

As a collective mass of Black people we have been deprived, not only of civil rights, but even our human rights, the right to human dignity . . . the right to be a human being!

This Freedom Rally is to be a united effort by all our leaders. We have set aside all petty differences, and in the Spirit of Bandung we have come together on this same platform, wherein each one can voice his personal feelings and his personal solution to this grave crisis we face.

The Western World today faces a great catastrophe. It stands on the brink of disaster. Mr. Muhammad says the only way our people can avoid the fiery destruction that God Himself will soon unleash upon this wicked world, is for our people to come together among themselves in unity and practice true brotherhood. Mr. Muhammad says God is with us to unite our people into one brotherhood, and to aid those that are oppressed, and to uplift those who are downtrodden.

The Western World, filled with evil and wickedness, is groping and stumbling blindly through spiritual darkness toward its inevitable doom. Mr. Muhammad says we must qualify ourselves so that God's Spiritual Light will guide us past the pitfalls of destruction.

The Western World is filled with drunkedness, dope addiction, lying, stealing, gambling, adultery, fornication, prostitution and hosts of other evils. These evils must be removed if the world is to have peace. These evils are the primary cause of troubles all over the earth. These evils promote greed and lust, increase wickedness and unrest, and destroy all hopes for peace.

You want peace. I want peace. Everyone craves for a world of peace. Mr. Muhammad says anyone who will submit to the God Of Peace will have peace. Even the white man himself can prolong his time today if he will submit to the God of Peace, and give Freedom, Justice and Equality to the "people of God" . . . the so-called Negroes here in America.

The city of Nineveh in the bible to whom Jonah was sent to warn is a good prophetic example of today. They were actually spared because they repented when the warning came to them from God. God will spare our slavemaster today too if he will repent.

The whole Dark World wants peace. When I was in Africa last year I was deeply impressed by the desire of our African Brothers for peace, but even they agree that there can be no peace without freedom from colonialism, foreign domination, oppression and exploitation.

The God of Peace and Righteousness is about to set up His Kingdom of Peace and Righteousness here on this earth. Knowing that God is about to establish His Righteous Government, Mr. Muhammad is trying to clean up our morals and qualify us to enter into this new Righteous Nation of God.

The American so-called Negroes must recognize each other as Brothers and Sisters . . . stop carrying guns and knives to harm each other, stop drinking whiskey, taking dope, reefers, and even cigarettes. No more gambling! Save your money. Stop fornication, adultery and prostitution. Elevate the Black woman; respect her and protect her. Let us rid ourselves of immoral habits and God will be with us to protect and guide us.

Then, we must form a platform that will be good for all of our own people, as well as for others. As Black people we must unite. We must recognize and give intelligent active support to our political leaders who fight for us unselfishly, sincerely, and fearlessly.

But, to prove their sincerity and their right for the support of the Black Masses, these leaders must first display fearlessness, intelligence, and unity among themselves. They must stop their public bickering with each other. They must stop attacking each other in front of the white man, and for the benefit of the white man.

If the Black leaders must have differences of opinion, learn to go into the closet with each other, but when you come from behind closed doors, show a united front in the face of the one who is a common enemy to all of us.

Mr. Muhammad has invited all of the leaders here today for that purpose. He wants our people united, but unity will never exist among the Black masses as long as our leaders are not united.

We want to get behind leaders who will fight for us . . . leaders who are not afraid to demand freedom, justice, and equality. We do not want leaders who are handpicked for us by the white man. We don't want any more Uncle Toms. We don't want any more leaders who are puppets or parrots for the white man.

We want brave leaders as our spokesmen, who are not afraid to state our case, who can intelligently demand what we need, what we want, and what is rightfully ours. We don't want leaders who are beggars, who feel they must compromise with the enemy. And we don't want leaders who are selfish or greedy . . . who will sell us out for a few pieces of silver.

A big election is coming up this year. What kind of leaders do we want in office? Which ones will the Black masses get behind? Mr. Muhammad has thousands of followers, and millions of sympathisers. He will place his weight behind any fearless Black leaders who will stand up and help the so-called American Negroes get complete and immediate freedom.

If these Black leaders are afraid that to be identified with us they will irk the white man, or lose the white man's favor or his support, then they can no longer expect the support of the Black masses.

They call us racial extremists. They call Jomo Kenyatta also a racial extremist and Tom Mboya a moderate. It is only the white man's fear of men like Kenyatta that make him listen to men like Mboya. If it were not for the extremists, the white man would ignore the moderates. To be called a "moderate" in this awakening Dark World today, that is crying for freedom, is to receive the "kiss of death" as spokesman or leader of the masses . . . for the masses are ready to burst the shackles of slavery whether the "moderates" will stand up or not.

We have many Black leaders who are unafraid, especially when they know the Black masses stand behind them. Many of them are qualified to represent us not only in this United States government, but could also represent us in this government if we are given 100% citizenship and the opportunity for FIRST CLASS participation . . . or else we can get behind these same leaders in setting up an independent government of our own.

We, the Black masses, don't want these leaders who seek our support coming to us representing a certain political party. They must come to us today as Black Leaders representing the welfare of Black people.

We won't follow any leader today who comes on the basis of political party. Both parties (Democrat and Republican) are controlled by the same people who have abused our rights, and who have deceived us with false promises every time an election rolls around.

Mr. Muhammad grieves over the disunity that exists even among the intellectual and professional so-called Negroes. It is these "educated" so-called Negroes who should be leading us out of this maze of misery and want. They possess the academic knowhow, great amounts of technical skills . . . but they can't use it for the benefit of their own kind simply because they themselves are also disunited. If these intellectuals and professional so-called Negroes would unite, not only Harlem would benefit, but it will benefit our people all over the world.

Mr. Muhammad says disunity is our number one stumbling block, and this disunity exists only because we lack knowledge of SELF (our own kind). So-called Negro "intellectuals" seem to think integration is the answer. But, is it? "Integrate" means to become as one unit. How can these "intellectuals" expect the white man to accept us into his social unit, political unit, or economic unit when we are not yet in unity (as a unit) among our own kind?

We, the Muslims, are for "Brotherhood," but not for integration! What is the difference? Brotherhood is based on love, which automatically produces voluntary acts of "sincere benevolence." But integration produces hypocrisy. It forces the white man to pose as a "liberal," to be pretensive and false. Thus, "benevolent" acts which are "forced by integration laws" are producing white hypocrites, and reducing chances of creating a "mutual-working-agreement" between the two races.

Your thirst for integration makes the white man think you want only to marry his daughter. We (Muslims) who follow Mr. Muhammad don't think God ever intended for Black men to marry white women. Mr. Muhammad and his followers are violently opposed to intermarriage.

This is conveniently and purposely misinterpreted by our enemies to mean that we are anti-white, anti-christian, and anti-American (simply because we refuse to chase after the white man's women!). Let the white man keep his women, and let us keep ours.

Some Negroes who love race-mixing, and want white women, are angry at Mr. Muhammad because he teaches against race-mixing . . . so they slip around and make the white man think we are anti-white. (I'm surprised that the white man is dumb enough to believe these Uncle Toms, who stoop so low, like JUDAS, to be stool pigeons against their own kind.)

We have oceans of Dark People on this earth: in Africa, Asia, and even here in America. Our women are the most beautiful, like a bouquet of flowers. Why should we chase white women?

In this "changing" world today, what would we do married to a white woman? Her people don't want you in their neighborhood around them, and our fast awakening people don't want you to bring her back into our neighborhood any more to live around us. Thus, you both become a "misfit" . . . unwelcomed and unwanted in either society . . . where can you go?

Because we Muslims look at this as it is and face reality does not mean we are anti-white. We don't want his white mother, his white sister, nor his white daughter. We want only an equal chance on this earth, but to have an equal chance we must have the same thing the white man himself needed before he could get this nation started . . . WE MUST HAVE SOME LAND OF OUR OWN!

Why do we want some land of our own? Because land is essential to freedom. How else can 20 million Black people who now constitute a nation in our own right, a NATION WITHIN A NATION, expect to survive forever in a land where we are the last ones hired and the first ones fired . . . simply because we have no land of our own?

For over 400 years we have been very faithful to our American slave masters. Now God is warning them through Mr. Muhammad that they should be nice enough to give us some land so we can separate ourselves from them and get started for ourselves.

This is no more than what the white man should do. It is in complete accord with the Christian religion. Their bible says that when a slave is set free, his slave master should give him something to help him get started on his own . . . never send him away empty-handed.

If the Hebrews in the bible numbered only 600,000 in the land of their bondage, and God was concerned with giving them freedom in a land of their own, a land "flowing with milk and honey," . . . then what about 20 million so-called Negroes here in America, who have the "freedom" only to look for a job?

Can you not see that our former "leaders" have been fighting for the wrong thing . . . the wrong kind of freedom? Mr. Muhammad says we must have some land where we can work hard for ourselves, make ourselves equal, and live in dignity. Then and only then we won't have to beg the white man for the crumbs that fall occasionally from his table. No one respects or appreciates a beggar.

Since we say Lincoln freed us, let us avail ourselves of that freedom by uniting together and doing something for our own kind. But, we must have some of this earth. We have been in America over 400 years. We have been so-called "free" a 100 years, and yet he still calls us "the white man's burden."

We Muslims don't want to be a burden on America any longer. God has given Mr. Muhammad a Divine Message, Program, and Solution. WE MUST HAVE SOME LAND! The white man should be glad to give his loyal "slaves" some land so we can get out of his way and go for ourselves.

We will then set up our own farms, factories, business, and schools . . . and show him how much we appreciate the education he has given us, by using it to become self-sustaining . . . economically and otherwise.

We want some land where we can create unity, harmony and brotherhood . . . and live together in peace. Since America now sees that this false show of integration and intermarriage will not work, she should make immediate steps to set aside a few of these states for us, and put us there to ourselves.

If America will repent and do this, God will overlook some of her wicked deeds (as in the days of Nineveh) . . . but if America refuses to give Mr. Muhammad what God instructed him to ask for, . . . then, like the biblical houses of Egypt and Babylon (slave empires of the bible), God will erase the American government and the entire race that it favors and represents, from this planet . . . and God will then give the whole earth back to the Original Owners, The Black Man!

63. THE ORGANIZATION
OF AFRO-AMERICAN UNITY:
"FOR HUMAN RIGHTS AND DIGNITY"

The Organization of Afro-American Unity, organized and structured by a cross-section of the Afro-American people living in the U. S. A., has been patterned after the letter and spirit of the Organization of African Unity established at Addis Ababa, Ethiopia, May, 1963.

We, the members of the Organization of Afro-American Unity gathered together in Harlem, New York:

Convinced that it is the inalienable right of all people to control their own destiny;

Conscious of the fact that freedom, equality, justice and dignity are essential objectives for the achievement of the legitimate aspirations of the people of African descent here in the Western Hemisphere, we will endeavor to build a bridge of understanding and create the basis for Afro-American unity;

Conscious of our responsibility to harness the natural and human resources of our people for their total advancement in all spheres of human endeavor;

Inspired by a common determination to promote understanding among our people and co-operation in all matters pertaining to their survival and advancement, we will support the aspirations of our people for brotherhood and solidarity in a larger unity transcending all organizational differences;

Convinced that, in order to translate this determination into a dynamic force in the cause of human progress, conditions of peace and security must be established and maintained;

Determined to unify the Americans of African descent in

"Statement of Basic Aims and Objectives of the Organization of Afro-American Unity" (June 28, 1964), in George Breitman, THE LAST YEAR OF MALCOLM X: THE EVOLUTION OF A REVOLUTIONARY (New York: Merit Publishers, 1967), pp. 105–111.

their fight for human rights and dignity, and being fully aware that this is not possible in the present atmosphere and condition of oppression, we dedicate ourselves to the building of a political, economic, and social system of justice and peace;

Dedicated to the unification of all people of African descent in this hemisphere and to the utilization of that unity to bring into being the organizational structure that will project the black people's contributions to the world;

Persuaded that the Charter of the United Nations, the Universal Declaration of Human Rights, the Constitution of the U. S. A. and the Bill of Rights are the principles in which we believe and these documents if put into practice represent the essence of mankind's hopes and good intentions;

Desirous that all Afro-American people and organizations should henceforth unite so that the welfare and well-being of our people will be assured;

Resolved to reinforce the common bond of purpose between our people by submerging all of our differences and establishing a non-religious and non-sectarian constructive program for human rights;

Do hereby present this charter.

I—Establishment

The Organization of Afro-American Unity shall include all people of African descent in the Western Hemisphere, as well as our brothers and sisters on the African Continent.

II—Self-Defense

Since self-preservation is the first law of nature, we assert the Afro-American's right of self-defense.

The Constitution of the U. S. A. clearly affirms the right of every American citizen to bear arms. And as Americans, we will not give up a single right guaranteed under the Constitution. The history of the unpunished violence against our people clearly indicates that we must be prepared to defend ourselves or we will continue to be a defenseless people at the mercy of a ruthless and violent racist mob.

We assert that in those areas where the government is either unable or unwilling to protect the lives and property of our people, that our people are within their rights to protect themselves by whatever means necessary. A man with a rifle or club can only be stopped by a person who defends himself with a rifle or club.

Tactics based solely on morality can only succeed when you are dealing with basically moral people or a moral system. A man or system which oppresses a man because of his color is not moral. It is the duty of every Afro-American and every Afro-American community throughout this country to protect its people against mass murderers, bombers, lynchers, floggers, brutalizers and exploiters.

III—Education

Education is an important element in the struggle for human rights. It is the means to help our children and people rediscover their identity and thereby increase self-respect. Education is our passport to the future, for tomorrow belongs to the people who prepare for it today.

Our children are being criminally shortchanged in the public school system of America. The Afro-American schools are the poorest run schools in New York City. Principals and teachers fail to understand the nature of the problems with which they work and as a result they cannot do the job of teaching our children. The textbooks tell our children nothing about the great contributions of Afro-Americans to the growth and development of this country. The Board of Education's integration program is expensive and unworkable; and the organization of principals and supervisors in the New York City school system has refused to support the Board's plan to integrate the schools, thus dooming it to failure.

The Board of Education has said that even with its plan there are ten per cent of the schools in the Harlem-Bedford-Stuyvesant community they cannot improve. This means that the Organization of Afro-American Unity must make the Afro-American community a more potent force for educational self-improvement.

A first step in the program to end the existing system of racist education is to demand that the ten per cent of the schools the Board of Education will not include in its plan be turned over to and run by the Afro-American community. We want Afro-American principals to head these schools. We want Afro-American teachers in these schools. We want textbooks written by Afro-Americans that are acceptable to us to be used in these schools.

The Organization of Afro-American Unity will select and recommend people to serve on local school boards where school policy is made and passed on to the Board of Education.

Through these steps we will make the ten per cent of schools we take over educational showplaces that will attract the attention of people all over the nation.

If these proposals are not met, we will ask Afro-American parents to keep their children out of the present inferior schools they attend. When these schools in our neighborhood are controlled by Afro-Americans, we will return to them.

The Organization of Afro-American Unity recognizes the tremendous importance of the complete involvement of Afro-American parents in every phase of school life. Afro-American parents must be willing and able to go into the schools and see that the job of educating our children is done properly.

We call on all Afro-Americans around the nation to be aware that the conditions that exist in the New York City public school system are as deplorable in their cities as they are here. We must unite our effort and spread our program of self-improvement through education to every Afro-American community in America.

We must establish all over the country schools of our own to train our children to become scientists and mathematicians. We must realize the need for adult education and for job retraining programs that will emphasize a changing society in which automation plays the key role. We intend to use the tools of education to help raise our people to an unprecedented level of excellence and self-respect through their own efforts.

IV—Politics—Economics

Basically, there are two kinds of power that count in America: economic and political, with social power deriving from the two. In order for the Afro-Americans to control their destiny, they must be able to control and affect the decisions which control their destiny: economic, political and social. This can only be done through organization.

The Organization of Afro-American Unity will organize the Afro-American community block by block to make the community aware of its power and potential; we will start immediately a voter-registration drive to make every unregistered voter in the Afro-American community an independent voter; we propose to support and/or organize political clubs to run independent candidates for office, and to support any Afro-American already in office who answers to and is responsible to the Afro-American community.

Economic exploitation in the Afro-American community is the most vicious form practiced on any people in America; twice as much rent for rat-infested, roach-crawling, rotting tenements; the Afro-American pays more for food, clothing, insurance rates and so forth. The Organization of Afro-American Unity will wage an unrelenting struggle against these evils in our community. There shall be organizers to work with the people to solve these problems, and start a housing self-improvement program. We propose to support rent strikes and other activities designed to better the community.

V—Social

This organization is responsible only to the Afro-American people and community and will function only with their support, both financially and numerically. We believe that our communities must be the sources of their own strength politically, economically, intellectually and culturally in the struggle for human rights and dignity.

The community must reinforce its moral responsibility to rid itself of the effects of years of exploitation, neglect and apathy, and wage an unrelenting struggle against police brutality

The Afro-American community must accept the responsibility for regaining our people who have lost their place in society. We must declare an all-out war on organized crime in our community; a vice that is controlled by policemen who accept bribes and graft, and who must be exposed. We must establish a clinic, whereby one can get aid and cure for drug addiction; and create meaningful, creative, useful activities for those who were led astray down the avenues of vice.

The people of the Afro-American community must be prepared to help each other in all ways possible; we must establish a place where unwed mothers can get help and advice; a home for the aged in Harlem and an orphanage in Harlem.

We must set up a guardian system that will help our youth who get into trouble and also provide constructive activities for our children. We must set a good example for our children and must teach them to always be ready to accept the responsibilities that are necessary for building good communities and nations. We must teach them that their greatest responsibilities are to themselves, to their families and to their communities.

The Organization of Afro-American Unity believes that the Afro-American community must endeavor to do the major part of all charity work from within the community. Charity, however, does not mean that to which we are legally entitled in the form of government benefits. The Afro-American veteran must be made aware of all the benefits due him and the procedure for obtaining them. These veterans must be encouraged to go into business together, using G. I. loans, etc.

Afro-Americans must unite and work together. We must take pride in the Afro-American community, for it is home and it is power.

What we do here in regaining our self-respect, manhood, dignity and freedom helps all people everywhere who are fighting against oppression.

VI—Culture

"A race of people is like an individual man; until it uses its own talent, takes pride in its own history, expresses its own culture, affirms its own selfhood, it can never fulfill itself."

Our history and our culture were completely destroyed when we were forcibly brought to America in chains. And now it is important for us to know that our history did not begin with slavery's scars. We come from Africa, a great continent and a proud and varied people, a land which is the new world and was the cradle of civilization. Our culture and our history are as old as man himself and yet we know almost nothing of it. We must recapture our heritage and our identity if we are ever to liberate ourselves from the bonds of white supremacy. We must launch a cultural revolution to unbrainwash an entire people.

Our cultural revolution must be the means of bringing us closer to our African brothers and sisters. It must begin in the community and be based on community participation. Afro-Americans will be free to create only when they can depend on the Afro-American community for support and Afro-American artists must realize that they depend on the Afro-American for inspiration. We must work toward the establishment of a cultural center in Harlem, which will include people of all ages, and will conduct workshops in all the arts, such as film, creative writing, painting, theater, music, Afro-American history, etc.

This cultural revolution will be the journey to our rediscovery of ourselves. History is a people's memory, and without a memory man is demoted to the lower animals.

Armed with the knowledge of the past, we can with confidence charter a course for our future. Culture is an indispensable weapon in the freedom struggle. We must take hold of it and forge the future with the past.

Toward a black cultural revolution

One aspect of the nationalism of the 1960s is concern with breaking away from the cultural and psychological oppression that has fostered black self-hatred and belief in black inferiority. The selections in this section relate the struggle for cultural liberation to the struggle for political and economic liberation.

L. Eldridge Cleaver's 1962 essay was written while he was still in San Quentin. With perception and sensitivity Cleaver explores the implications of the Negro's acceptance of white standards of physical beauty. He discusses the connotation of the words "black" and "white" in Western society, declaring it absurd for one "ethnic group to judge itself by the standard of some other group." Of particular interest are Cleaver's insistence on use of the word "black" in a positive sense, an idea not often expressed during the heyday of the integration struggle, his awareness that emerging African nations evoke pride in Afro-Americans, and his use of the term "black power." After his release from prison, Cleaver, who is now in exile, served as Minister of Information of the Black Panther Party in Oakland, California, and as an editor of *Ramparts* magazine. He has published two books of essays, *Soul on Ice* (1967) and *Eldridge Cleaver* (1969).

The two articles by Askia Muhammad Touré—the first under his original name, Rolland Snellings—a leading poet and cultural critic, are significant for the skill with which the folk culture of the urban ghetto is linked to the struggles going on around it. The first essay, which is itself a work of art, uses the sounds and rhythms of black music to effectively evoke the mood of the period. Touré does not attempt to assert the existence of a separate black culture; he assumes it exists, and goes on to relate the uses that should be made of it. The second selection discusses the problems facing cultural nationalism and its relationship to revolutionary nationalism. The including of "concrete tasks" for black intellectuals and artists expresses Touré's concern for the translation of theory into practice.

64. L. ELDRIDGE CLEAVER: "BLACK IS COMING BACK!"

In every society, in every historical period, it is demonstrable that human beings have always made some type of judgment as to what is beautiful and what is not beautiful. The things, or aspects of things, esteemed as beautiful have changed; but always men have looked upon some things as beautiful and others as unbeautiful or, condemnatorily, as ugly. Indeed, an entire branch of philosophy—Esthetics—has this phenomenon as its subject-matter.

As time goes by, these judgments seep into, and become deeply entrenched in, the culture of a people, and are looked upon as standards by which value judgments are made. To each cultural group, the acceptance of these traditional standards is as natural and unquestioned as is the acceptance by the group of any other aspect of its culture.

It seems that, from time immemorial, mankind has passed judgment on the human body, pronouncing these characteristics and traits beautiful and these un-beautiful—or ugly. As the judgments are reiterated over the years, they become objectified into standards by which the merits and demerits of individual human beings are determined. This practice can be observed

L. Eldridge Cleaver, "As Crinkly as Yours," NEGRO HISTORY BULLETIN, XXV (March 1962), 127–132. Copyright © 1962 by Association for the Study of Negro Life and History, Washington, D. C. Reprinted by permission.

amongst all people, be they so-called civilized or so-called primitive. They all ornament themselves in various ways—in conformity to an accepted standard of beauty; and failure to do so marks one as an oddity, an eccentric, or one type of freak or another.

This phenomenon would not be the subject of remark outside the bounds of the discipline which embraces it, were it not for the fact that the traditional judgments which Western Man has made, and still tenaciously clings to, are now (and, indeed, have been) the cause of very serious maladjustments in our society and, much more seriously, in the world at large. In this essay, the attempt will be made to show that the continued application of these judgments is the cause of an untold amount of mental illness and frustration.

In our culture, the recognized standard of beauty—one could just as well say, "the official standard of beauty"—is that of the Caucasian peoples; and since the Caucasian has possessed hegemony over the world for the duration of the epoch which is now drawing to a close, along with other values of Western culture, he has also exported *his* standard of beauty. In a profound sense, the Caucasian standard of beauty has been—and is now—one of the corner-stones of the doctrine of "White Supremacy." We have only to observe in order to see the destructive psychological impact of this standard of beauty on the people around the world who have unknowingly fallen under its subtle influence. In this essay, the discussion will be confined chiefly to the situation as it relates to the American Negro; but by extension, most of what is said here can be applied in a general way.

It is generally held that the first incidence of Africans being seized and abducted from their native soil and brought to America and enslaved, occurred in the year 1619; if that is so, then that is the date on which the traditional standard of beauty of the transplanted African was first undermined and the corroding process of subversion began. Certainly, up until that time, the Africans had their own standards of beauty, and they accepted them just as naturally, proudly, and unquestioningly as all other people accepted their own.

But after being crushed down into a position of slavery, degradation, poverty and general wretchedness—but most important, after the arbitrary and more or less total disruption of his
cultural continuity, due largely to the indiscriminate and un-
ceremonious mixing of different tribes and cultural groups by
the Slavers, who cared not a tack for the cultures of their prey—
the black slave began to identify everything that fell to his lot
with the conditions under which he suffered. The lodging that
was forced upon him; the food that was parceled out to him;
the crude work-a-day clothing that he was obliged to wear—all
of these items became in his eyes, badges of bondage; and therefore he passionately hated them.

Under the harsh physical brutality, the taunts, castigations
and deprecatory harassments of his slavemasters, who looked
upon the black man as a sub-human beast of burden, after generation on top of generation of slaves, born into slavery and
knowing nothing but the miseries of their state and the constant
brain-washing of their every-day life, totally stripped of their
own culture—under that pressure the slaves began to identify
everything that is good and desirable with the Caucasians for
whom they toiled. It was the Caucasians whom they saw
dressed in the finest garments and attire that the fabulous profits
of slavery could command; it was the Caucasians whom they
saw inhabiting the palatial mansions of the plantations in the
"great white world beyond . . ."—consequently the slaves came
to regard the surroundings of the "whites" as a veritable heaven
on earth; something to dream of, yet never attain. The pomp
and show of the ostentatious Southern Aristocracy served to
hammer the black man down, dwarfing his pride and extirpat-
ing his self-esteem by shackling to his neck the huge, iron
collar of the inferiority complex. This went on for some 240
years, and after this blanket annihilation of his traditional way
of life, the black man was set free in a "white" oriented society.
With the advent of freedom, the adverse effects of the Caucasian standard of beauty on the black men upon whom it had
been imposed became more apparent.

Following the Civil War, the great mass of "Freedmen," now
designated as "Negro," were able, in a quasi-free way, to deter-

mine their own destiny. For the first time in the history of the race, black men found themselves 'free' en masse in the midst of Western culture and civilization. And if Negroes, while in slavery, identified the fabled 'Good Life' with the standards of the Caucasians, after freedom was achieved the desires and dreams of attaining this 'Good Life' mushroomed and took on new tantalizing proportions in their minds by virtue of the fact that the actual conditions to which they aspired were ever-present and all around them, as it were "so near and yet so far."

Negroes migrated to the big cities, to the fashion capitals of the nation, there to be fascinated and dazzled by, what must have seemed to them, splendor and finery fit for kings—treasures unparalleled in their most inspired dreams. And who possessed the objects of these dreams? The Caucasians. (It is important to remember that the ideals and values which were born in slavery were carried over and persisted into the new era.)

There were deeply imbedded in the thinking and folklore of the race such adages and beliefs as: "If you're white you're all right; if you're brown stick around; but if you're black—GET BACK!" And some of these same old sayings are still current in the Negro community.

Think on it: this was the era of the camera. Negroes saw photographs, paintings and portraits in which the beauty of the Caucasian was extolled saturatingly throughout the land. Negroes witnessed beauty contests in which Caucasian men and women were held up and proclaimed the most beautiful creatures that God had fashioned and placed upon the face of the earth (it never dawning on the Negroes that it was the Caucasians themselves who were pinning roses on their own lapels). Great numbers of Negroes were learning to read and write; and in the books which they read, the process took on a sweeping new dimension. When a Negro retired in solitude to relax and enjoy a *great* book, it was the Caucasian standard of beauty which was flaunted before him and held up for him to praise—and praise it he did, unable to resist or dispute, having no criterion by which to refute. In the novels, he met heroines with *creamy white skin, sparkling blue eyes, and long flowing blonde tresses;* and heroes with *rugged Roman noses, wavy black hair* and perhaps a *gentle* sun-tan. And then the motion-picture industry sprang into being, and with it, a constant deluge reiterating and indisputably establishing the Caucasian standard of beauty.

At this point let it be recalled that *physical appearance,* i.e., skin color and texture of hair, is what primarily distinguishes the great majority of Negroes from other Americans. It is this salient factor—physical appearance—which points out the Negro and makes him readily available as a target of abuse and a more vulnerable mark for exploitation. Significantly, the historical fact is that the other despised minority groups which America has known were able, after a comparatively brief time, to disappear into the main-stream of our national life and take active parts in the social, political and economic affairs of the country. Unlike the Negro, the other minority groups could not be identified as such merely on the basis of physical appearance. For those minorities, assimilation was an accomplished fact simply by learning to speak English and smoothing out the family name from Schmidt to Smith.

To an excruciatingly painful degree, Negroes were very much aware of their "burden of color and bad hair."

How can the effects of the Caucasian standard of beauty be identified in the thinking and actions of Negroes? Why, observe the great vogue of hair-straighteners, wigs, and skin-bleaches that sprang into being! Great geniuses were at work! One such savant, after much pondering and tedious toil, emerged and created a revolution amongst Negro women when he introduced that Magic Wand—the Straightening Comb:

"After one preparation, Madam, you too can have *silky-straight* flowing tresses, just as *beautiful* and *lovely* as your pale sister. Or perhaps you *require* a hank of this *flattering* Store Bought Hair? Just come as you are and when we are finished with you—well just come in to see us—then you be the judge!"

Another great benefactor was at work, but due to the fact that the Negro male would run the risk of burning out his brains if he took to the Hot Comb, this Einstein had a more difficult, arduous and exacting quest. But not to be daunted, he experimented, researched and concocted: and then one fateful day he returned victorious and announced to the world that, at long last, the Negro male, too, could have *silky-straight* locks, wavy and curly which, if you master the technique, you can even toss around a bit; it will even fall down in front of your eyes, just like the movie stars—that is, if you are prudent and do not overdo it.

"All you have to do, Sammy, my boy, is go see your barber, or go to the Beauty Parlor (oh, it's all right); just tell them to 'tighten' your mop for you, man, and when they get through applying their Lye Solutions, their Caustic Soda Preparations, their Miracle Acids and Combinations of Acids—after that, you will be just like Boss Charlie! You will have such Beautiful Straight Hair!"

Ah! Love that scientific spirit.

"After Madam and Monsieur have finished their coiffure, why go right around the corner to the Drug Store and buy a big fat bottle of Skin Bleach! Get the six-month economy size! Oh, don't worry about which brand, all of them are medically tested, proven, and guaranteed to bleach your dull skin Pretty-Pink and White!"

According to Ebony's Hall of Fame, Madame C. J. Walker, the "founder of the world's oldest and biggest Negro cosmetics company," became "the first Negro woman millionaire, after starting business with $2 and an original formula for "refining the scalp and straightening hair," (as if the Negro's head was an unfinished product!). Madame Walker is acclaimed as a "pioneer in the field of Negro beauty culture," and was elected to the Hall of Fame for her "contributions to the progress of the Negro and the American way of life." Incidentally, Madame Walker mixed her first batch of hair straightener in a washtub; and her last prayer went thus:

"Not for me, O Lord, but for my race."

Apparently she felt that her "formula" had delivered the Negro from all evil.

Now it is not surprising that the Negro reacted so. That is the logical outcome of his historical experience. But it is time that he checked himself. That he should continue to react in this way is not only surprising—it is beginning to be something of a scandal. Do not think that the reasons for such behavior have disappeared: on the contrary, they have gathered force and broadened. All of the mass media are constantly busy publicizing the Caucasian standard of beauty: the motion pictures, magazines, newspapers, television, literature, illustrated wall posters and bill boards—an unthinking (or money-hungry) Negro press—and most obvious and telling of all, the beauty contests.

What reaction do you think a young Negro girl has when a blonde haired, blue eyed 'white' girl is held up and proclaimed as Miss America, or Miss Universe? When this is done, implicitly they are saying:

"This type of female is the ideal, the most beautiful female on earth, and the more closely you approximate her characteristics the more beautiful you will be, otherwise, my dear little black girl, you are just plain ugly!"

What unspoken and unspeakable wretchedness must scorch and flame in the heart of the young black girl when she witnesses this type of thing! especially when the values of her friends, the Negro press—and in many cases—her own values, seem to acquiesce in applauding the Caucasian standard of beauty.

What Negro is there who has not felt an inarticulate questioning—deep down inside—upon being confronted with the Caucasian standard of beauty, especially if he has to make a decision, in his own mind, as to whether or not this is really beauty upon which he is looking? What rationalizations he is forced to make! And, oh! what frustration and feelings of inferiority result! How much pathological, insane, peculiar behavior, do you think, is a direct result of this frustration caused by the standard of beauty which Negroes have accepted? Undoubtedly the proportion would prove alarming. With all the mass media disseminating this doctrine, it would be difficult, if not impossible, to find a Negro who has not been influenced by it.

Implicit in the very acceptance of the Caucasian standard of beauty is the negation of typical Negroid traits. If it is believed that blue eyes, long straight blonde hair, and non-colored skin are the component parts of beauty—then it logically follows that since Negroes generally do not share this particular variety of attributes, Negroes generally are not beautiful. To be sure, Negroes have eyes, and hair, and skins; but if you will just think about the words which Negroes employ to describe themselves, you will see that the words reflect degrees and gradations *away* from the Caucasian ideal of beauty.

Eye color does not present much of a problem, but notice that a Negro who possesses blue eyes, grey eyes, hazel eyes, light-brown eyes—a Negro with eyes of either of these colors is generally looked upon as being fortunate, whereas the majority of Negroes have eyes of a dark hue. It is axiomatic of the eye that when we look at it in search of beauty, we look for such things as the clearness—the sparkle, as it were—of the eyeball; the length and density of the eye-lashes and eye-brows, and the general contour of the eye. And it does not matter too much what the type of face is in which a beautiful eye is set. But still, when we consider the eye, we take our cue from the Caucasian standard of beauty.

But what happens when we consider skin color and hair texture? The very words that we use indicate that we have set a premium on the Caucasian ideal of beauty. When discussing inter-racial relations, we speak of "white people" and "non-white people." We will refer to people all over the world as "white" and "non-white." Notice that that particular choice of words gives precedence to "white people" by making them a center—a standard—to which "non-white" bears a negative relation. Notice the different connotations when we turn it around and say "colored" and "non-colored," or "black" and "non-black." Our thinking is so foggy on this issue that we describe our complexions as if they are qualities strewn along a yard-stick, the opposite ends of which are painted black and white respectively—black being the negative end. In this type of thinking, to be black is extremely unfortunate, and the higher up towards the white end of the yard-stick your complexion is located, the better off you are. We have a host of terms to fit the ascending graduations of the yard-stick: passing for white, high-yellow, real-light, light, high-brown, dark-brown, dark, black, blue-black, jet-black. In a sense these descriptive terms are accurate, because the complexions of those designated as 'Negro' run the gamut of the spectrum from 'jet-black' to 'passing for white.' However, it is our thinking—the relative value which we set on these various hues: and the fact that we do set *values* on them—that is what we are concerned with herein.

Now, when we consider the hair, we reach a topic on which we are extremely sensitive. This is because of the obvious variation between the texture of the typical Negro's hair and that of the typical Caucasian. But if Negroes are going to adhere to the Caucasian standard of beauty, must they not also pass judgment on the hair? Of course we must, and we have: we look upon our texture of hair as an affliction, a fiendish mockery of us by Mother Nature. Consequently we have another yard-stick for *evaluating* the relative *quality* of our hair. This one progresses from "bad hair" to "good hair." The straighter the hair— that is to say, the more one's hair resembles that of the Caucasian—the "better" it is. Good hair, bad hair, nappy hair, kinky hair and so on. And *short-haired women?* Good Gravy! (God bless the soul to whom we must forever be humble for inventing the "Boyish Bob") Short hair is looked upon as an especial abomination. We do not have even any flattering words with which to describe our hair: but this is not surprising since we do not look upon our hair as being particularly flattering.

In her brilliant play, *A Raisin in the Sun,* Lorraine Hansberry focuses the spot light squarely on this problem. But as it turned out, the lady Hansberry filed charges against the American Negro woman, and then refused to prosecute. In Act One, Scene Two, she has Asagai, the young Nigerian student who symbolizes the rebirth of Africa, tell Beneatha, an American Negro girl who is looking for her *identity,* that she has "mutilated" her hair; and this is what follows:

Beneatha A (Turning suddenly)—My hair—what's wrong with my hair?

Asagai (Shrugging)—Were you born with it like that?

Beneatha (Reaching up to touch it)—No . . . of course not.

(She looks back to the mirror, disturbed)

Asagai (Smiling)—How then?

Beneatha—You know perfectly well how . . . as crinkly as yours . . . that's how.

Asagai—And it is ugly to you that way?

Beneatha (Quickly)—Oh, no—not ugly . . . (More slowly, apologetically) But it's so hard to manage when it's well—raw.

Asagai—And so to accommodate that—you mutilate it every week?

Beneatha—It's not mutilation!

Asagai (Laughing aloud at her seriousness)—Oh . . . please! I am only teasing you because you are so very serious about these things. (He stands back from her and folds his arms across his chest as he watches her pulling at her hair and frowning in the mirror)

How much worry, frustration—and wasted money—is a direct result of our attempts to run away from ourselves! We can pick up any issue of probably any Negro newspaper, and we will see a report of some opportunistic itinerant witch doctor, or perhaps an entire troup of witch doctors, touring the country, hitting the big "progressive" cities, teaching the eager populace the latest methods of becoming carbon copies of the Caucasian via the "last word" in beauty culture.

That the Negro press is a primary sower of these seeds of inferiority complexes, feelings of rejection and self-rejection, can be seen at a glance. Open almost any one of the Negro publications which carry advertisements of skin bleaches and skin lighteners, hair straighteners, false hair and wigs, etc., all with an emotion-charged indictment such as "Why should you *suffer* with hard to manage kinky ugly hair? Use Dr. Flop's Hair Straightener and become a big hit!" "Do you suffer from dull ugly skin? Get Hosana Bleaching Cream and have a fair, beautiful complexion!" This type of advertising is usually accompanied by one of those convincing "Before and After" illustrations of some wretched, despondent young Negro girl or boy who, immediately after applying the product advertised, is suddenly transformed into a sparkling young center of attraction.

Ebony Magazine, which is probably the most widely read Negro magazine, periodically runs a feature which it presumptuously entitles "The World's Most Beautiful Negro Women" or something to that effect.

And what are the contents of this feature? Why the Caucasian standard of beauty, of course! Invariably, they will crown Lena Horne, Dorothy Dandridge, or someone else whose appearance would nominate them to compete rather for the title of Miss Scandinavia, Miss Greater Europe, or Miss Anything—other than that which is indicated by the title of the feature. And what emotions do you think the typical Negro girl experiences when she reads this feature? Why obviously, exactly the ones that are evoked when she sees the results of the Miss America or Miss Universe contests!

Thus, it is obvious that while on one hand, through no fault of his own, the Negro is a victim of a set of cultural values—on the other hand it is equally true that the Negro's response to this vicious situation has been to adjust to the environment through the dubious process of "mutilating" his natural ethnic characteristics in order to conform as best he could, to the Caucasian standard of beauty.

Of course, it would be facetious of us to campaign for a law to ban the Caucasian standard of beauty; but it is of paramount importance that we realize that there is absolutely no such thing as a universal standard of beauty for all people—black, brown, red, yellow, white—measuring up to which they stand or fall. The standards of beauty which exist in the world today are nothing but manifestations of ethnocentrism. Our concepts of beauty enter our minds through social indoctrination. We think a person with a certain complexion, a certain type of hair, a certain shape of nose, a certain color of eyes—we think that person possessed of beauty, not because he is beautiful per se, but rather because we have been culturally conditioned to look upon the particular traits of which he is possessed as being the most desirable, the most becoming: the beautiful.

Let it be remembered that, historically, each ethnic group has looked upon it's own characteristic traits as being beautiful.

If Negroes continue to respond blindly and unthinkingly to this indoctrination, then they as surely will continue to be plagued by the divisive self-hatreds, feelings of inferiority, etc., which are vestiges of the bygone days of the unchallenged sway of the odious doctrine of "White Supremacy." When we judge ourselves by the Caucasian standard of beauty and find that it does not fit us, if we have accepted that standard as absolute, then our reaction is not merely that we think our own individual selves ugly, it extends much farther than that: it touches every facet of our existence, it influences the very value which we set on ourselves as individuals, it colors our thinking and our opinion of the race as a whole—in short—it has a disastrous effect. This confusion pursues many of us all through life, "like the Furies in a Greek play," driving us deeper into a private hell.

To be sure, it is a hyper-ethnocentric act—but one consonant with the doctrine of "White Supremacy"—for the Caucasian to hold up one of his members and crown him or her Mister or Miss Universe; but it is *something* else when the Negro accepts this standard, and then proceeds with a host of contrivances to warp his natural characteristics in a vain effort to measure up to that alien standard. Until the social values of human beings evolve to the point where we no longer feel the need to aggrandize ourselves above our fellow men on the quicksand ground of ethnic superiority, until that time, we will have with us the spectacle of the Eskimos in Alaska saying that they are the most beautiful people in creation; the Chinese in China saying that they alone are beautiful; the Japanese, the Arabs, the Australian Aborigines, all in their own lands saying the same thing, while the Caucasian proclaims it to the entire world. But let us hope that the Negro will not still be running along behind in the "white shadows" with his Hot Combs and Bleaching Creams in an orgy of self-destroying mimicry.

It is superficially absurd for a given ethnic group to judge itself by the standard of some other group. If we were to take a

Caucasian man and woman and judge their beauty by a people's standard other than their own, that Caucasian man and woman would be judged as ugly. The same will be the result when we judge others by the Caucasian standard of beauty, or when we judge a member of one ethnic group by the prevailing standard of another ethnic group.

Would it not be superfluous for the Pygmys to take for their standard of beauty that of the Watusi? The average height of the Watusi is about 7 feet, while that of the Pygmy is about 4½ feet! In addition, the Watusi are rather large of body while the Pygmys are rather small. Would it not be a fallacy for the Pygmy to set about inventing contrivances with which to eradicate their natural physical endowments in order to measure up to the Watusi ideal of beauty? They could invent stretching machines to elongate their diminutive bodies; and they could inflate their torsos with helium and become Watusi-like! And wouldn't the Watusi seem ridiculous to try to approximate the ideal of the Pygmy? They would have quite a shrinking job on their hands! But should either of them consider himself inferior because of their differences? This is analogous to the Negro's present position.

Let it be remembered that the purpose of this essay is to call attention to certain unhealthy concepts and ideals which currently are held by all to many Negroes. Essentially, the problem is a psychological one. It concerns unexamined ideals and practices which are an integral part of our social heritage, and which are fostered and inculcated by the white oriented culture of which we are members. By becoming aware of the nature and origin of our beliefs and ideals, we are better able to understand and manipulate them if it becomes apparent that they need readjustment. When a group of ideals and beliefs become the authors of as much evil as the ones under discussion, then it is obvious that they require examination and readjustment. If there is a general stigma attached to the Negro because of his previous condition of servitude, and if the Negro does have something of an inferiority complex, it is composed of elements such as the ones isolated in this essay. We try to escape this stigma and complex by becoming 'passively Negro,' i.e., we accept our status as Negroes only because we can not escape it. The danger lies in the fact that there are only three main positions from which one must choose on the issue of belonging to a particular ethnic group: there is a positive, a neutral, and a negative position. The ethnocentric bigot will take the positive; he who realizes that all men are brothers and that they are all of the same moral value must, in order to be consistent, take the neutral position; the negative is owned by those who despise what they are, consciously or subconsciously, their vociferations to the contrary not withstanding.

Psychologically, a Negro of the negative position, i.e., a Negative Negro, attempts to purge himself of any and all traits which identify him as Negro. This brings us to a very important point, one which goes hand in hand with the Caucasian standard of beauty, and yet runs deeper and cuts deeper than any other facet of the entire affair.

The polarized western mind

What we term as *The Polarized Western Mind* derives from the symbolism attached to the two colors, black and white, in the mind of Western man. These two colors are highly charged and the symbolization is deeply ingrained in the thinking and culture of the West. Everything that is good, desirable, beautiful, morally elevated, pure—in short, the highest abstractions of the Western mind are denoted by the celestial hue of white. And at the opposite end of the pole lies the degrading shade of black. Everything that is debased, corrupt, feared, evil, and ugly, is identified with the color black.

Even in those activities which touch us deepest, such as religion, we find manifestations of this polarization. For an instance, when persons are united in the *sacred* rites of matrimony the traditional garments worn by the bride to symbolize her virtue and chastity are of the color white. While at the other end of the pole, at the time of death, or rather the funeral following death, the traditional attire of those in mourning is of the *dreary* hue of black. Instances of this polarization could be cited from now until dooms-day: there is an old Negro Spiritual which calls upon Jesus to "wash my sins away and make me white as snow." We speak of black cats causing bad luck, and black magic, and individuals with malignant black hearts.

This polarization affects the mind in very subtle ways. We are not conscious of it, as such, when it is in motion, but it colors our thinking just the same. An obvious and striking example of polarized thinking came to our attention recently. It concerned an illustrated cartoon satirizing the fallacious stupidity of the non-policy of segregation. The artist presents Jesus Christ hanging sufferingly from his cross; there ran a barbed wire fence through the center of Jesus and the cross, bisecting them; on one side of the fence kneeled a black man, and on the other side kneeled a white man; everything on the black man's side was painted black to symbolize the separation, and everything on the other side was painted white to further emphasize the separation; the cross, too, was painted black and white on the respective sides—but Jesus himself was pure white! If the artist had been logically consistent, he would have painted Jesus one-half black and one-half white. But the artist's polarized mind would not allow him to represent the Savior in the infamous hue of despised black.

And just as the Negro lives in the shadows cast by the connotations of the terms Negro and black, the Caucasian is living in the reflected glory of the term white. By describing himself as white, the Caucasian associates himself with the highest ideals and values in our culture.

Have you ever see such a thing as a *white* man? Wow, what a sight that would be! Actually, if the Caucasian were forced to describe his hue realistically, he would be hard pressed to discover a hue in the spectrum that would plausibly coincide with his own. But, having labeled himself *white,* whenever he hears that name called, a flattering process of association goes on in his mind. And whenever a non-Caucasian with a polarized mind utilizes the term white in referring to the Caucasian, the same associations are made.

When the term *black* is applied to the Negro (Negro being the Latin for *black*), the process is reversed. Along with all of the unsavory connotations of the word *black*, in the polarized mind, the Negro is subconsciously condemned and degraded. Not that the term *black* is, in itself, derogatory, but rather that it is incumbent upon the polarized mind to make the associations that the connotations of the term carry, and through those associations, the imperative condemnation follows.

A Negro with a polarized mind is daily committing a type of mental suicide on the installment plan. The component parts of his polarization are constantly gnawing away at his sanity. He has to make myriad rationalizations; but there are times when the mind is unable to come up with the appropriate rationalization; these are the times when the conscious mental aberrations occur, the crushing of the personality under the leaden weight of the inferiority complex, the slow burn of suppressed rage; and these are the times when the black hand will reach for the bottle of whiskey, narcotics, or what have you, to blot out the insupportable reality which hovers above one in a stultifying cloud of condemnation, and one is further crushed when this occurs because one will describe the burdensome reality as: "Ah, the *black* clouds!"

It is manifest, then, that for the sake of the people who are the victims of this polarization, they must shatter these antiquated clichés of thought and, as it were, de-polarize their minds. It is not to be supposed that values so deeply rooted in our culture can be refashioned overnight; but, by realizing .that the problem exists the job is half-done.

What we must do is to stop associating the Caucasian with these exalted connotations of the word *white* when we think or speak of him. At the same time, we must cease associating ourselves with the unsavory connotations of the word *black*. "A house divided against itself cannot stand," how much truer this must be for the mind! We can talk, preach, and write about race pride and self-respect interminably, but in the last analysis, if we are indeed to have any pride, we must root-out from our thinking and folklore those elements which have robbed us of our pride.

When a black President Kwame Nkrumah of Ghana, arrayed majestically in colorful tribal robes, can stride in towering dignity and pride onto the highest rostrum of the United Nations General Assembly, and deliver a rousing, epoch-making speech —without first pausing to either 'straighten' his hair or 'bleach' his skin, the unspoken message to his brethren is unmistakable: Black is Coming Back! The rebirth of Africa, black dignity and black power, is destined to raise the black end of the yard-stick from the depths to which it was crushed by the oppressive weight of the doctrine of "White Supremacy"—raise it back into proper equilibrium. And then when Africa asks the American Negro with what type of hair was he born, he will answer loud and clear, with dignity and pride: "As crinkly as yours."

65. ROLLAND SNELLINGS: "WE ARE ON THE MOVE AND OUR MUSIC IS _MOVING_ WITH US"

In the Lash Years when we wore the chains of our dishonor, we were a defiant, spirited people. So much so, that there occurred a slave revolt on the average of once every three weeks. The slave revolts were the outward PHYSICAL manifestations of the inner SPIRIT of the captive people. The inner SPIRIT was also manifested in what were to become the rudiments or foundations of African-american culture: the spirituals, hollers, field-chants, etc.

The African-american spiritual was an ingenius instrument

Rolland Snellings, "Keep on Pushin': Rhythm & Blues as a Weapon,"
LIBERATOR, V (October 1965), 6–8.

molded in the fires of oppression—disguised as mere "sacred songs," the spiritual was a vessel which carried the message of resistance, escape, or revolt. Resistance, escape, or revolt, the message of the spiritual, has been handed down through the years, in the collective memory of our people, in the "double-talk" of the parables, folk-tales, folksongs, etc. of the Black Man.

Given the primary powerlessness of our people to Whitey's brute force, we had to create a subtle instrument which would increase our "value" to the Beast while "taking care of business" for ourselves. "Boy, those niggers sure can sing; gather 'em up at the big house tonight from all over the plantation, so they can serenade us." So, the "get togethers" were very instrumental in providing many coded messages, details, etc. to the Underground Railroad and networks developing throughout the South.

From the period of "Reconstruction," where the neo-colonialism of White America was exposed for what it was, down to the outright betrayal and institution of color segregation, our people shifted their emphasis to the painful irony of the Blues (or Country Blues) to describe or "run down" our philosophy, attitudes, and outlooks. It is recorded that when Gertrude "Ma" Rainey gave a show in the Southern "back country," the Black farmers and sharecroppers (landless peasants) came from miles around, from neighboring districts and counties, to view the scene.

Such songs as "Backwater Blues" (describing the tragedy of the floods), "Yellow Dog Blues," and others were the crystallized philosophies, hopes, and aspirations voice FOR our people by their PRIEST-PHILOSOPHERS: the Black singers and musicians. (This attitude of the Black musician and poet as priest-philosoper goes back to the indigenous African civilizations, where the artist-priest had a functional role as the keeper or guardian of the spirit of the nation—as well as the ancestors.) This attitude, curiously enough, has remained among us despite the dehumanization of chattel slavery and the "white-washing" of the Western Missionary Educational System. It has, of course been either ignored or by-passed by bourgeois "negro" sociologists, either through ignorance of heritage or fear of being classified "alien" to American cultural standards.

ONCE MORE: We are a defiant, spirited people who have a history of over three hundred years of constant slave revolts, in which our music played a vital role. Our main philosophical and cultural attitudes are displayed through our MUSIC, which serves as the ROOT of our culture; from which springs our art, poetry, literature, etc. Our creative artists—especially singers and musicians—function as PRIESTS, as PHILOSOPHERS of our captive nation; a holdover from our ancient past.

"I got to keep on pushin', can't stop now. Move up a little higher, some way, some how.
'Cause I got my strength, don't make sense: Keep on pushin'!"

In the smoldering epoch of our times, eruptions of the Captive Nation are once again reflected in the songs of Black Folks. In the period of the early Fifties, JAZZ, which had been a vital part of Black people's music, was taken over by the racketeers and moved downtown into the clubs and bars of the middle-class pleasure-seekers, away from the roots, away from the Heart, the Womb, away from the home of the people: uptown-ghetto!

With JAZZ—Bird, Diz, Miles, Max, Lady Day, Lester Young —JAZZ all gone away: Rhythm and Blues was the only music left to sing out the aspirations and soul stirrings of Blacks folks uptown N.Y. and "uptown-ghetto" across the face of the land. This was, at first, a blow to the Soul Folks: What would they possibly DO without BIRD, DIZ, MILES or LADY DAY or LESTER YOUNG to make them "feel alright" deep down in the nitty-gritty of their hearts? But, being a people raised on change, raised with the insecurities of change throbbing in the nerve-ends of their lives, they ADAPTED themselves to expression with their only cultural weapon or potential weapon: Rhythm and Blues.

Yes, JAZZ, fine JAZZ, great JAZZ was gone away, gone away, away into the Ofay night, away from the warm earth smell of their rhythms and soul vibrations, to make the cash registers clang and sing, ring and pile up green capital for the "negroes' 'FRIEND' " and sponsor "downtown" in the air-conditioned nightmares of the West.

The Fifties, the early Fifties, the later Fifties of suicidal Johnny Ace, Big Mabel, Chuck Willis, Chuck Jackson: all legendary Blues People, scorched with the pain reflected in bleary red-eyed heartbreak sweat-stained songs and tears flooding into the "Ebb-tide" of Roy Hamiltons or the Moonglows; Clyde McPhatter and the Drifters blown to the "White Cliffs of Dover" on the "Wind" of the Diablos; "Crying in the Chapels" of the Orioles; or shot down, cut and beaten up in "Smokey Joe's Cafe."

These were OUR songs, OUR lives reflected in a thousand blue notes, notes of hopelessness marked with thicker callouses on black hands, more muscle cramps in mama's knees, more heartache and unemployment for our fathers and brothers, as Korea loomed distantly and we went away to slaughter up the Yellow race for Whitey's cause.

My people, YES, a million lonely eyes burning to touch Happiness, to touch Human Sympathy, Brotherhood, Justice: all those BIG words that BIG white learned men invented to taunt us into dissatisfaction with eight kids to a room, bedside roach-crawl and rats gnawing at the eight kids to a room on gloom street, on your street, my street: Ghetto-uptown U.S.A.!

My people, YES, my love, my Fifties of Martin Luther King, minister of youth: Large liquid eyes then searching for the Gandhi-secret Freedom-message looming huge and idealistic from Southern horizons bleeding in the sun of a thousand lynch-fires; echoing whitely in the poison-voice of Eastland, Talmadge, Russell, Earl Long and other Favorite Sons of the "Land of the Tree." (In those years of Martin Luther King, bus boycotts and other evidence of our growing struggle, we grew up, developed, expanded our souls, our minds churning to the beat of our people's only music, Rhythm and Blues. We lived it; sang it in vocal groups, in cabarets, on street corners: junkies nodding in the rain. We didn't call it "culture," didn't call it "negro art," it was just OUR music, OUR soul, like OUR girl-

friends, OUR comrades, OUR families who didn't understand.
It, again, was OUR voice, OUR ritual, OUR understanding of
those deep things far too complicated to put into words—except
those of Fats Domino, Little Richard, Ray Charles, Dinah
Washington, Faye Addams, Ruth Brown, Lloyd Price and many
more.)

> "Look, a 'look a 'yonder: what's that I see?
> Great big stone wall standing straight ahead of me.
> But I've got my pride, move the wall aside:
> Keep on pushin'!"

The Sixties, roaring in like a rocket, roaring through the
Southland with freedom riders, more boycotts, sit-ins, wade-
ins, stand-ins, kneel-ins; Black Muslims rising in the Northland
new angry voice, young copper-skinned Malcolm X shaking up
the psyche of the nations—Black and White. Lumumba, the
U.N. Congo demonstrations, Robert Williams defends a Southern town against the Klan. WE are on the move, WE are moving to a New Tempo, to a New Dynamism—like Coltrane blow-
ing SCREAMING in the downtown nightclubs: "Afro-Blue,"
"Blue Trane," "Africa," "Out of This World;" and we hear in his
screams the bloody Whiplash moans and screams of our great-
grandfathers and grandmothers bending low; eyes ablaze with
terror at castration, rape, mutilation, SCREAMING into the
Raven Universe, SCREAMING into the coming generations,
SCREAMING into the Womb of Mother Africa violated
and crushed by the Roman Prophylactic: AAAAAAAIIIIII-
EEEEEEE! AAAAAAAIIIIIIIEEEEEEEE!

We sing in our young hearts, we sing in our angry Black
Souls: WE ARE COMING UP! WE ARE COMING UP! And
it's reflected in the Riot-song that symbolized Harlem, Philly,
Brooklyn, Rochester, Patterson, Elizabeth; this song, of course,
"Dancing in the Streets"—making Martha and the Vandellas
legendary. Then FLASH! it surges up again: "We Gonna' Make
It" (to the tune of Medgar Evers gunned down in Mississippi:
POW! POW! POW! POW!) "Keep On Trying" (to the tune of
James Powell gunned down in Harlem: POW! POW! POW!

POW!) "Nowhere to Run, Nowhere to Hide," "Change Is Gonna' Come" (to the tune of Brother Malcolm shot down in the Audobon: POW! POW! POW! POW! POW! POW! POW! POW!)

THIS is, once again, a people's music, THIS is the reflection of their rising aspirations, THESE are the Truths sung by their modern PRIESTS and PHILOSOPHERS: We are on the move and our music is MOVING with us. WE are expressing our heartfelt anger, conjuring up strong Black Armies marching to the tune of "The Same Old Song" while gas bombs and myths explode in Watts, Los Angeles, explode into the putrid white heart of the racist hell that has us STILL IN CHAINS! YES, IN CHAINS! Look at our Rhythm and Blues singers! Look at the musicians! WHO own their contracts? WHO are their agents, managers; WHO speaks for them? CHAINS! CHAINS! MORE CHAINS! WHITE CHAINS CLANKING IN OUR SOULS! But we are coming out, we are coming up (WHITE AMER-ICA: DO YOU HEAR?), we are coming out from the chains that bind us: whether culture, economics, politics, military chains: WE ARE COMING OUT! FORGET about his com-puters, jetplanes, rocketships, blue-eyed troops; FORGET about atomic bombs, police-dogs, cattle-prods and dynamite. OUR songs are turning from "love," turning from being "songs," turning into WAYS, into WAYS, into "THINGS." We are making BLACK magic, BLACK NIGGER magic with our SONGS, with our LIVES: this is our BOMB, our BLACK BOMB, our TIME BOMB, our TIME BOMB which will bring on the "DESTRUCTION OF AMERICA," A PLAY BY LE-ROI JONES. This Social Voice of Rhythm and Blues is only the beginning of the end. Somewhere along the line, the "Keep On Pushin' " in song, in Rhythm and Blues is merging with the Revolutionary Dynamism of COLTRANE of ERIC DOLPHY of BROTHER MALCOLM of YOUNG BLACK GUERRIL-LAS STRIKING DEEP INTO THE HEARTLAND OF THE WESTERN EMPIRE. The Fire is spreading, the Fire is spread-ing, the Fire made from the merging of dynamic Black Music (Rhythm and Blues, Jazz), with politics (GUERRILLA WAR-

FARE) is spreading like black oil flaming in Atlantic ship-
wrecks spreading like Black Fire: the Black Plague spreads
across Europe in the Middle Ages—raining death. WORK your
magic, BLACK magic, NIGGER magic across the Empire to
the beat, to the dynamism of Social-conscious RHYTHM AND
BLUES, NEW JAZZ, BLACK POETRY: WORK your NIG-
GER MAGIC in the sweaty smile of the Boston Monkey,
"SUGAR PIE, HONEY-BUNCH:" twist and shimmy frug
monkey down the Empire with thick ruby lips grinning like
MAD like BLAZING RED EYES LURKING IN THE MOON.

EACH TIME a Black song is born, EACH TIME a Black
Sister has another child, EACH TIME Black Youth says NO!
to the racist draft boards, EACH TIME someone remembers
Brother Malcolm's smile, EACH TIME we write a poem an
essay as a Way into "Things," EACH TIME we love each
other a little more: THIS THING QUAKES! WE are moving
forward, WE are on the move, WE record it all in Rhythm and
Blues, New Jazz, Black Poetry, WE—the Captive Nation listening to its priests and wisemen; growing stronger; donning
Black Armor to get the job done so Rhythm and Blues can once
again sing about "Love," "mellow" black women, and happy
children: after it sings this Empire to the grave, after it sings
the Sun of the Spirit back into the lonely heart of man. (For
Dinah Washington, Sam Cooke, Nat Cole, Eric Dolphy, James
Chaney, James Powell, Medgar Evers, Brother Malcolm, Leon
Ameer, Walter Bowe, Khaleel Sayyed, Robert Collier: Many
Thousand Gone!)

> Maybe someday, I'll reach that higher goal.
> I know I can make it with just a little bit of soul.
> 'Cause I've got my strength, don't make sense:
> Keep on Pushin'!
> Ha-al-lelujah! Ha-al-lelujah!:
> Keep on Pushin'!
> Keep on Pushin'!

66. ASKIA MUHAMMAD TOURÉ (ROLLAND SNELLINGS): "WE MUST CREATE A NATIONAL BLACK INTELLIGENTSIA IN ORDER TO SURVIVE"

Introduction

The title of this essay was derived from a number of observations and conversations that I've had with conscious Black people across the country for the last two years; and last but not least, from a very recent conversation with Bro. Joe Goncalves.

If one would speak with the seemingly endless number of young nationalist intellectuals anywhere in the country about Black culture, one would be reassured that we're "T.C.B." (takin' care of business) in that area, and that things are getting better and better, " 'cause we're really showing whitey that we don't need his western thing." But frankly, are things *really* getting better? Or are we so focused upon "anti-whitism" (the first stages of nationalism) that we're neglecting the hard, serious business of building Black cultural/spiritual awareness—the very core of a National Psyche or Consciousness?

And let's be *realistic:* when Black people talk about "Black Consciousness or Power," they are speaking indirectly of Nationalism—whether cultural, political, or economic. (America, according to Bro. Harold Cruse and others, is a nation of nations: white Protestant Anglo-Saxon, Jewish, Catholic, what remains of the Indian, and on the bottom, the African-American. The problem with the Afro-American is, unlike other groups, his intellectuals and professionals have never recognized their innate nationalism and proceeded to create the proper cultural philosophy, organizations, and attitudes to gear their people

Askia Muhammad Touré, "The Crises in Black Culture," JOURNAL OF BLACK POETRY, I, 8 (Spring 1968), 2–10. Reprinted by permission of Askia Muhammad Touré.

for concrete survival in the West.) Anyone who denies this is either ignorant, blind, or dishonest. Because ultimate Black Power means *self-determination, not "equality"* (with mass murderers?), but self-determination. The main example of this is the Third World. The African, Asian, South and Central American Bros. are not asking for "equality" with racist colonialists and neo-colonialists, but are *demanding* self-determination: the right of nations and peoples to determine their own destinies; which means self-government or the setting up of a National State as an ultimate goal.

I am clarifying my position from the beginning in order to get to the basis of my perspective. We have among us a number of naive young Bros. today who are screaming "Black Power! Black Revolution!" etc., and when one naturally follows up the logical trend of their thought with Nationalism, they back off and reply: "No we're not Black Nationalists! No not Nationalists—Revolutionaries!" and who, may I ask, ever heard of a "revolutionary" who wasn't a Revolutionary *Nationalist?* Lenin, Mao, Ho, Fidel, Nkrumah were Revolutionary Nationalists, *first,* then Revolutionary Internationalists. Those "revolutionaries" who want Black Power, but are not Black Nationalists, you'll find, are really *integrationists (assimilationists) in green field jackets;* for *ultimate* Black Power means Black Nationhood. They realize that the masses, being basically nationalistic, are not going to hear any of that old, March on Washington nonsense about "Black and white together" or "Love your enemies" or "nonviolence," so they are opportunistically out-revolutionizing and out-"Blacking" the *true* revolutionaries—Revolutionary Nationalists—in order to maintain their waning influence over the awakening masses.

Now these polemics might seem rather far-fetched or off the subject, but my position is that when we view Black Culture in White America, we *must* view it from a straight-up, no monkey-business Nationalist perspective if we wish to resurrect the lives of our people. We must see ourselves as a separate entity, an alien Nation/Race—"alien" from white America—and that this is *really* how the whites view us and treat us (Southern colo-

nialism, Northern ghetto-colonialism) whether they *tell* us this
or not. Now, from this perspective, everything that we as a
separate entity produce is a product of our own special consciousness or world-view. So that our culture should be viewed
as separate or belonging to Black People (our most important
wealth, since we produce no raw resources) since it is the product of our spirit/awareness, consciousness, and reflects our Collective Psyche. Now if this culture is a product of Black Minds
in motion in the world, Black consciousness, and is controlled
politically and economically by whites (Jews, Italians, WASPS,
etc.) *then Black Culture is indeed in crisis.*

I

Black people are world renown[ed]—and have been since the
Fisk Jubilee Singers of the nineteenth century—for Black
music, which in this day seems to capture the dynamism, alienation, flux and change that is the "modern era." Black music,
especially Modern Afro-American Music ("jazz"), is the main
music that has been played in most countries world-wide and
serves as the root or core of African-American culture. This is
true because Afro-Americans, during chattel slavery, became
more musically inclined due to the fact that we were not allowed
to read or write, and were only permitted to keep our music because it helped to get the work done and *seemed* to keep us
quiet. When they stripped us of our obvious African culture
(robes, drums, language, religion, etc.) the "abstract" non-arti-
fact producing aspect of culture—our music—was the only
thing, in altered form, permitted to remain. So, given this situation, Black people were forced to become more musically oriented than anything else; and the Black Man began to express
his thoughts and feelings about Life, God, and the Universe
musically. As time passed, the Black Musician became *and remains* the major philosopher, priest, myth-maker and cultural-
hero of the Black Nation. What, again, we must be aware of is
that Black Music is the *core* of our National Culture. Being the
core or root, as *it* goes, so goes our spiritual/cultural life as a

nation of people. (Permit me to savor this term, "nation." Anywhere upon this planet twenty to sixty million souls, with a common history, language, and culture, constitute a good-sized nation.) We must remember that, with the exception of a few people of genius, Black People have only been producing literature in any large amount since the 'twenties of this current century. (Oh I know, Chestnutt, DuBois, Dunbar, Weldon Johnson, but I mean on a *massive* scale.) And yet, taking all of these facts into consideration, we see Black People today, possessing only a *few* literary journals. As far as Black Literature is concerned, the New Black Writing has produced a number of brilliant poets—Larry Neal, Jewel Latimore, Ronald Stone, LeRoi Jones, William Kgotsitsile, Don Lee, Le Graham, Sonia Sanchez, S. E. Anderson, to mention a few. Some of these writers also deal in essays, Ed Bullins and Jones in playwriting, but we still have much to accomplish in terms of serious fiction. In Bro. C. H. "Charlie" Fuller of Philly, we have perhaps the best short story writer that New Black Writing has produced so far; but the major Black literary journals—with the exception of *Black Dialogue*—have refused to publish his work. Bro. S. E. Anderson shows much promise as a short story writer also.

What New Black Writers must remember is that if we represent a New Black world-view, then this must be reflected in our creative literature which must be well-rounded: plays, short stories, novels, essays *as well as* poetry. We must remember that there have been Black literary movements of the past that can offer comparison with us. The so-called "Talented Tenth" generation of the early 1900's—Du Bois, Paul Lawrence Dunbar, James Weldon Johnson, etc.—were poets also, but where is the fiction work of the new writing that can compare with Du Bois' "Dark Princess," or Weldon Johnson's "Autobiography of an Ex-Colored Man"?* What new fiction can compare to Claude McKay's "Home to Harlem"? The "Talented Tenth" generation of writers offers an accurate comparison with us, because they were political activists and leaders—Du Bois,

---

* What new book of essays can compare with the classic, "Souls of Black Folk"?

Weldon Johnson, journalist Monroe Trotter, historian Carter G. Woodson—as well as creative writers. If one seriously studies the writings of this "Talented Tenth" group—whether one shares their politico-cultural views or not—one can see that they had a *philosophy*, a clear-cut vision of themselves and of the world, and always projected this in their creative writing. Some of us write fairly good plays and essays; what we must remember is that many times a good short story will get across a new viewpoint or philosophy quicker and more effectively than a "hard-line," no monkey-business political essay—which might tend to alienate new readers.

Also, we Black writers *must* produce more literary journals. It's a shame that our main journals—*Soulbook, Black Dialogue, Journal of Black Poetry*—are all located on the West Coast! There should be some kind of regular literary publication representing each area—East Coast, Mid-west, South, and West Coast—as well as publications geared for national and international circulation. The writers in each region should make it their responsibility to organize *workshops* to train young thinkers and writers in Black Consciousness and New Black writing. Presently we are organizing this for *Black Dialogue*. (More than likely, we'll become more organized and develop these things as our movement matures and as we gain more confidence in deciding just what we're really proposing to accomplish.) All magazines having to do with serious "jazz" criticism, or having to do with Rhythm and Blues, Country Blues, etc., *are in white hands*. With the notable exceptions of LeRoi Jones and A. B. Spellman, all serious critics of Afro-American music *are white men*. WHY??? It will be agreed by both Blacks and whites, that "jazz" is the main musical contribution of people in this country to the modern world. It will be agreed that Black music—Blues, Rhythm and Blues, Gospel, "jazz"—is surely the most dynamic musical culture in this land. *Then why don't Black intellectuals and Black people control Black Music and Black musical/cultural criticism???*

We are cultural slaves! Dig it! Victims of what Bro. Harold Cruse calls "Cultural Imperialism." This means that since we

didn't have any raw resources for whites to exploit, they were able to exploit our cheap labor and the products of our National Black Culture (mainly music). Broken down further, this means that the recording companies are white-owned.†
Broken down *even further,* this means, baby, that James Brown and the late Otis Redding, not to mention Aretha, are sending a lot of Jewish and Italian boys and girls to college and making their parents *rich* with the products of their Black souls. And further, *none, or very little, of this bread is going into the Black communities that inspire the music.* Yes, Brothers and Sisters, "intellectuals," whether we dig it or not, we are supporting Zionist Israel and the Mafia (Italian nationalism) with our Soul Music—and further helping to impoverish the Black Nation.

What is to be done:
the role of an authentic black intelligensia

First, we will say that the role of an authentic intelligensia is to organize Black people politically, culturally, spiritually, and economically. In other words, a true intelligensia of a people would seek to create the *forms,* the organizations, through which that particular people can, first survive, then prosper, and finally, rise to eminence or world power. The "negro" intellectuals (or "civil writers"), due to the ignorance of their roles, again as Bro. Harold Cruse points out, have failed to do this and thus the Black Nation/Race at the present time is defenseless.

The aware Black people who realize these dangerous weaknesses in our Nation must proceed to correct them: *we must create a National Black Intelligensia in order to survive.* What is this "intelligensia"? Again, it comes down to this, it is the *living mind* of the Black Nation/Race. Today we in Black America are like a tremendous giant with amnesia: we cannot remember who and what we are. However, our Memory is

† The booking agencies are white owned; the radio stations, the theatres, and the night clubs where the music is heard, are white (usually immigrant) owned.

gradually returning—piecemeal. We must set about to organize methods through which we can speed-up the process of "re-membering who we are," or Self-Realization. First and fore-most, we must create a Black Cultural Philosophy and Ideol-ogy: the projection of the Black Spirit/Awareness, or the Dy-namic Black Psyche, into the realm of intellectual ideas. This Philosophy/Ideology is the most important thing at this time because it will provide the Basis for any future moves that we collectively make in the world. In other words, when we define and articulate our collective World-view, we will *know* how to move and act in the future. This philosophy/ideology should create a system of ethics which would show our people how to live life. Much of Afro-American thought is based upon a defense-reaction to White American racism. In other words, we are caught up in reacting to Ofays, in being "anti-white" rather than "pro-Black"; we have loosely defined what we're *against,* but not what we're *for,* what we really want.

Where will this Black Intelligensia come from? The New Black Intelligensia is emerging today from independent radi-cals, the campuses—especially the new Black Student Unions that are in formation—and from those youth from the streets who've been awakened and influenced by Elijah Muhammad, Malcolm X, and the young Black Power advocates. Black Youth is reading and studying like never before in our history. Black Youth is the most dynamic element of the Black Nation—as goes Black Youth, so goes Black America—as well as being the majority of the population: according to reliable sources, the major portion of our people is under thirty-five (35) years of age and growing.

Concrete Tasks: Even at this time, with the Philosophy/Ideology still in formation, there are some things that Black intellectuals can be/should be doing. First, there should be concrete moves made to bring about a working unity among the Black creative artists. There is no reason in the world why James Brown and Aretha Franklin should not know LeRoi Jones, Larry Neal, or Abdul Karim. Some of the newer Black writers are familiar with the New Musicians—and are even influenced by them—but this does not, however, extend to Rhythm and Blues or Gospel. Of all of the Black creative artists, the Black writers are the most "conscious" in terms of Black political/cultural awareness, and should, therefore, take the lead in unifying the creative artists. Moves should be made to "collectize" Black culture: in other words, bring it all under one standard or banner. This can be initiated by many methods. Some older thinkers have suggested the formation of such organizations as Black writers, artists, and musicians' leagues and unions leading, finally, to a National Congress of Black Culture. Also, the institution of a National Journal of Black Music. Locally, in our communities, such institutions as Black Musical/Cultural Institutes, and Black Repertory Theaters (in formation in Harlem), as well as community liberation schools should be initiated. These are relatively simple undertakings: look at the progress of the Chicago artists—the Wall of Respect plus the community workshops in the arts that they formed. (As far as I am concerned, every large Black community should have a Wall of Respect. *We must learn from each other.*) Yes, these moves are relatively simple, if the creative artists are consciously dedicated to preserving Black culture.

Again I would like to stress the important link-up of the New Black intelligensia with the Black popular artists. The Rhythm and Blues singers are the cultural heroes of the Black Masses (Black Youth), along with the popular disc jockeys. The Impressions are *obviously* Nationalistic Black Artists; who ever disagrees with this should listen to their latest release, "We're a Winner." (In 1965, I wrote, for *Liberator* Magazine, the first creative essay to center around Black Music, mainly Rhythm and Blues and New Music, for the New Black writing. At that time, my theme was the Impressions' "Keep on Pushin," which I had borrowed from David Henderson's epic poem based upon the famous Harlem uprising of '64. More of these things must be attempted by Black writers.) Also, Black Student Unions should strive to create on campus/off campus Black Studies and cultural programs which would involve the Black communities closest to their schools. Black students should see themselves as the political/cultural/intellectual extension of the Black community upon the local college campus. They should also participate in Black community forums and engage in tutorial programs in the community, thus solidifying mass intellectual unity.

The crisis

Probably quite a few Black people who read this essay will judge me an impractical, utopian schemer, because they do not realize the seriousness of the current crisis in Black culture. Let me illustrate my point. White musicians and intellectuals have hung around Black musicians and entertainers since the 'twenties. Always they have attempted to imitate these musicians and produce a diluted "hip" white style of their own. In the twenties we had white "Dixieland," in the 'thirties and 'forties we had white "Swing" music and "jazz" with Harry James, Benny Goodman, Paul Whiteman and other white "Fathers of (ha!) 'jazz.'" In the 'fifties we had whites pushing harder—inventing the cold, sterile "Third Stream" music (a mixture of "jazz" with western "serious" music), and in the popular field, the Elvis Presley—Bobby Darin raucous, rowdy "Rock and Roll" that sought to challenge the smooth, lyrical Black Rhythm and Blues. Now, in the 'sixties, we have the final "successful" white imitation: so-called hippy or "Rock" music. This music was, at first, a carry-over from the Everly Brothers— Elvis Presley "Rock and Roll" school; but with the emergence of the British Beatles (who rode to glory by imitating the great Chuck Berry, Muddy Waters and others) and the Hippies, this white cultural-hybrid, "Rock," stands to replace *both* Rhythm & Blues and New Music or "jazz" as the popular music of this country. Now, due to their dependence upon the merchants of the white music industry for economic subsistence, the Black musicians, both "jazz" and R & B, are in trouble. In many Eastern cities—and, indeed, on the West Coast—the white musical establishment is beginning to *replace* Black musicians—on the radio and in the clubs—with hippie groups.

Opportunistic white music "critics" such as Frank Kofsky, who writes for *Jazz* Magazine which has lately been changed to *Jazz & Pop* (Rock?), have recently pointed out that certain Black Music is too "ivy-league," too establishment, not "Revolutionary" enough, etc. That "Rock" is now *the* new music, *the* thing; and "jazz" should become more "soulful" by linking up with hippie rock music. Dig it!! Due to this latest example of opportunist, white cultural nationalism, many young "jazz" musicians are being thrown out of work and are, in some cases, starving—than going and setting up their music in the Black community, for the interests of their own people. Now this does not mean that the merchants of the white music industry have finished draining Black music; no, on the contrary, the white music merchants continue to feed upon the *top* Black artists, James Brown, Aretha and others, while gradually beginning to cut the young "up-an-coming" musicians, who follow them, loose. As they see the growing popularity of hippie "Rock" music with white youth, they will begin to substitute it for Rhythm & Blues and "jazz." The young "jazz" musicians and vocal groups will find themselves unable to survive unless they return to the roots of "Home," the Black community. Efforts are now in progress to begin to link Black Music totally with the Black community. Jihad Productions (LeRoi Jones), Milford Graves and other musicians are beginning to cut their own sides. The controversial Don Warden pointed out on his San Francisco "talk" show that Bro. Otis Redding and his group were assassinated by the Mafia for *daring* to attempt to organize an independent, all-Black music corporation with some of the major Black recording artists. If this is true, we can see that the Italian nationalists (the Mafia) have robbed the Black Nation of a cultural giant. I don't know the truth of the matter, but Warden and others have stated that the white authorities *refused* to raise Bro. Otis' plane from the Minnesota lake in order to investigate the reasons behind the tragic crash. (And poor *Jet* magazine talking about the "eery" similarities of Otis' death with Bro. Sam Cooke's death; but only "eery" in terms of similar dates, etc. *God help us!*)

If what Warden implied is even *remotely* true, we are indeed pitiful; and we must speed up the proposed contacts between the Black Intelligensia and the popular artists. If Bro. Otis Redding did, indeed, proceed upon this basically *nationalistic* music venture, he should have been aware of its consequences, and should have had *protection* until he completed the deal. This is another role that strong organized nationalists can play: protection of Black artists, writers, and political figures. Had Bro. Otis been conscious enough to have contacted a group like Bro. Karenga's "US" organization for protection, he might still be thrilling us today. (Also, Dammit, there was no, *absolutely no*, reason for 'Roi Jones and the brothers to be riding around Newark *alone*, without protection, or Huey Newton to be gunned down, again unprotected, in Oakland. If we don't protect our leading people, how do we expect to survive?)

So we must see that many risks will be involved in organizing Black people on even cultural levels; but we have no choice if we expect to continue to exist as a national/cultural entity. Only in this way—the creation of a National Black Intelligensia; the development of a Black Cultural Philosophy/Ideology; the creation of a working unity of all Black artists; the development of National Black Cultural Institutions and Bodies—can we overcome the current Crisis in Black Culture and move to fulfill our National and Racial Destiny. "MOVIN ON UP!"

Black Power

The slogan "Black Power" covered a wide variety of ideologies and specific strategies. Where SNCC stressed revolutionary rhetoric, CORE emphasized a reformist program. In the first months after the "Black Power" slogan became popular, CORE enunciated a program of broad scope. Its leaders hoped to attack a wide range of issues by organizing and mobilizing the potential power of the people in the black ghettos. CORE's outlook at this stage is illustrated by an address of Mrs. Ruth Turner Perot (Document 67), who was special assistant to the national director of CORE. Subsequently CORE, funded in part by foundation grants, engaged in specific action projects in selected urban centers. Particular efforts were directed at political organization, as in Cleveland, and, more recently, at the development of black capitalism (see Document 71).

SNCC, reflecting a growing disillusionment with the inadequate progress of the civil rights movement in the South and the mounting rebelliousness of the ghettos, shifted its focus from civil rights protest and voter registration in the South to radicalizing youth in the ghettos and on the college campuses. Beginning in the summer of 1966, when the "Black Power" slogan first gained national prominence, SNCC spokesman Stokely Carmichael (chairman 1966–67), and H. Rap Brown (chairman 1967–68) espoused their brand of racial solidarity and black revolution. The speech by Carmichael presented here (Document 68), which he delivered in the summer of 1966 to an audience of black Chicago youth, typifies his utterances to black audiences during that period. The themes of black unity, self-awareness and Black Power are discussed.

Typical of the new militancy of black students to which Carmichael addressed himself was the confrontation that took place at Northwestern University in Evanston, Illinois, in the spring of 1968. On May 3 the black students, who were organized in two groups—F.M.O. (For Members Only) and the Afro-American Student Union—seized and occupied the university business office. They held it until a list of demands was negotiated the following day. Such demonstrations have since become commonplace on the nation's campuses and the sequence of events leading up to the confrontation is familiar: the entrance into predominantly white schools of large numbers of ghetto blacks fortified by assertive pride in their blackness and intent to maintain their cultural identity; a refusal of university officials and faculty to comprehend or accede to the distinctive outlook of the black students; a period of tension and conflict between black and white students, faculty and administration; unsuccessful negotiation for changes black students feel to be necessary and conducive to their pursuit of education; a realization by black students that existing university arrangements do not easily accommodate these special needs; confrontation or some move to force the university to act on their demands. The resolution of the Northwestern confrontation, with the University administration agreeing in substance to meet the demands, created a model for black students throughout the country. These demands ranged from those relating specifically to the needs of black college students to those that spoke to the larger needs of the black community. The unifying theme of the demands is self-determination for black people (Document 69).

67. RUTH TURNER PEROT: "ORGANIZING THE BLACK COMMUNITY FOR THE PURPOSE OF PROMOTING THE INTERESTS AND CONCERNS OF THE BLACK PEOPLE"

What would America have done in recent months without "black power"? What subject could have drawn so many headlines, editorials and TV news comments? What theme would have been so timely for discussion groups or seminars? How else would politicians have explained their loss of grip and unions the growing conservatism of their ranks? How else would liberals have rationalized their disenchantment with a civil rights movement they could no longer lead nor understand? What would many Americans have used as a scapegoat —Americans insecure and frightened, anxious about a War in Vietnam and convinced that Negroes had gone far enough in their pursuit of total equality? What could they all have blamed for their performance at the polls in California or Florida, Georgia or New York, if it had not been for "black power"?

Interestingly enough, black power was never intended to render such service. In fact, it was never intended for the ears of white America at all. Black power was a rallying cry aimed directly at the black community and, in particular, the many millions who had not yet been touched by the efforts and gains of the old civil rights movement. It was timely and necessary and called for, if we will but analyze where the civil rights movement had arrived in the summer of 1966 and where it had to go.

Where had we come by 1966? We had seen a massive march on Washington—the granddaddy of all efforts to prick America's conscience. You will recall that a month or two later, four

Ruth Turner Perot, "Black Power: A Voice Within," OBERLIN ALUMNI MAGAZINE, LXIII, May 1967), 17–19. Reprinted by permission of Mrs. Ruth Turner Perot and OBERLIN ALUMNI MAGAZINE little girls were bombed to death in Birmingham. A year later, three civil rights workers were found dead in Mississippi. We had also seen two civil rights bills, 1964 and 1965. Although many young militants maintained that they were unnecessary since they reiterated the Constitution, they represented *some* kind of progress. Yet they had to be enforced.

Today, there are still not enough federal registrars in Southern counties. The Office of Education moved reluctantly and when it finally began to enforce the law, was criticized by no other than liberal Majority Leader Mike Mansfield, one of the chief architects of the empowering legislation. We had seen further, the shooting of James Meredith—proof that a Negro could still be assaulted in 1966 while exercising his rights under the Constitution.

CORE listened. From deep in the hearts of Northern ghettoes and the backwoods of the South we heart little people speak:

"Marches are fine and bills are fine, *but* I can't afford a hamburger or a room in that fancy integrated hotel."

"I have nobody worth voting for."

"I can't get a good education."

"I've gotten an education but I still cannot find a decent job that pays decent money."

"I don't want to live in an integrated neighborhood, but I do want a decent place to live and raise my family."

We took a closer look. Dazzled by the successes of the Thurgood Marshalls, Constance Baker Motleys, the Edward Brookes, Robert Weavers, etc., we had overlooked the plight of the millions. That plight was actually getting worse.

Schools were more and more segregated. In Cleveland over 90% of the children were attending public schools that were Negro or nearly all Negro. Schools were also getting worse. In Central Harlem 87% of the pupils are reading below level, 50% were in that position in 1954.

Negroes were closing the educational gap very rapidly (less than one year's difference between Negroes and whites 24 and under), but Negro income remained only 56% of white income in 1965. (It was 57% in 1952.) It is also estimated that in 1966,

Negro college graduates could expect to earn as much in a lifetime as whites finishing three years of high school.

Unemployment rates among Negroes remained consistently at 2.1 times those of whites (and are now almost triple), although black soldiers were overrepresented in Vietnam and this was a period of relative prosperity. Neighborhood deterioration often is the result of federal programs supposedly designed to help. There is no better example than the ravages of urban renewal on Cleveland's Hough area.

After this analysis, the logical question became: where were decisions made affecting schools, housing, jobs and neighborhoods? The answer was obvious: city halls, state houses, Capital Hill and Wall St. No moral appeals could succeed in these places. Rather the pertinent questions were "Can you buy, can you sell, how much and how many votes can you deliver?" That, in anybody's language added up to power. And if black men wanted to influence those decisions, they had to have black power.

There was more feedback from the ghettoes and the backwoods—psychological feedback from stress on integration as a goal in and of itself. The civil rights movement had been saying "Good schools are integrated schools and only integrated schools are good schools. Good neighborhoods are integrated neighborhoods and only integrated neighborhoods are good neighborhoods."

Integration simply could not be gained at the expense of black self-worth. No other ethnic group had been forced to lose its identity to succeed in integrated society. Why was it necessary for black people to do so?

Thus "black power" was born, the organizing of the black community for the purpose of promoting the interests and concerns of black people. An old American tradition, by the way, as David Danzig wrote in *Commentary*: "The effort to encourage Negroes to see themselves as a power bloc and to act as one is entirely in keeping with American minority politics." It was, in fact, the procedure by which the Irish captured Boston and Tammany Hall, the Italians Newark and Cleveland.

Black power is further an audacious prideful affirmation of self, without which Negroes cannot assume a *respected* position in an integrated American society.

So why the hue and cry? Clearly there was and is a good deal of deliberate distortion of "black power"—to sell newspapers, to divide and weaken the civil rights movement, to create a convenient scapegoat, for an anticipated swing to the right. There is also the inability to adjust to change. White men have been startled by the phenomenon of Negroes "no longer plodding and asking for eventual freedom" but insisting and demanding it now, as men and women not as their younger counterparts.

Others feel threatened. Of course, none need feel threatened unless they have misused power or have too much of it. Least of all should the poor white feel threatened since he has no power except that which his white skin may represent and black power does not want that.

Then of course, there is a panicky reaction to black power because of fear. If it is fear of power that drives us, then we had better come to terms with that. This is the most powerful nation on earth and we ought to understand who has it, why, and what we are doing with that power.

More operative, probably, is the fear of blackness. Whatever the fear and its cause, white men had better discover why they fear lest they fall prey to those who will exploit fear for selfish and evil purposes, as in Nazi Germany or more recently, in the New York City elections.

Does black power exist? Is it myth or reality? The answer to that question appears obvious. The political emasculation of Adam Clayton Powell who represents not only his district, but *all* black people, gives the key. That and the President's decision to substitute a constituency of South Vietnamese for a constituency of Negroes indicate that Negroes have no political power the Democratic or Republican parties are bound to respect.

However, that is not the whole story. Black power to CORE means the organization of the black community into a tight and disciplined group, for six purposes:

1. Growth of political power.
2. Building economic power.
3. Improvement of self-image.
4. Development of Negro leadership.
5. Demanding federal law enforcement.
6. Mobilization of Negro consumer power.

Let me give some examples of how CORE programs the concept:

—In Baltimore, MFU, an independent union organized by CORE, raised wages of nearly 100 members, workers regular labor unions did not want to organize, from 35¢ to $1.50.

—Baltimore, CORE's 1966 Target City, also demonstrates black power in the November elections. As a result an intensive mobilizing and organizing by CORE and other groups, Negroes switched 35 to 1 to vote for Republican Agnew over "Home is your castle" Mahoney. Mahoney was defeated. We were so effective, in fact, that the Ku Klux Klan has chosen Baltimore as Target City.

—CORE ran eight Negro candidates for school board elections in Democratic primaries in Louisiana. All won, first time since Reconstruction.

—Also—Louisiana (Opelousas)—Sweet potato cooperative. 375 farmers, 15 white, growing and marketing their sweet potato crops. This is economic black power.

—Watts, Operation Bootstraps, "Learn, Baby, Learn." 12 teenagers, graduates of computer course, have set up their own business, offering up-to-date skills for pay.

—Freedom School in Baltimore and plans for Black Arts and Afro-American Institute. A place where black people learn of history and contributions to world culture and civilization. Power of self-knowledge. Also in Baltimore, a leadership training for neighborhood people.

—As result of CORE insistence, federal examiners sent to South Carolina and Mississippi counties. Result: registration climbed.

We believe that these building blocks will become a bulwark that will protect the next Adam Clayton Powell, multiplied many times over. There is no other choice. If power for the powerless is not achieved so that changes within its structure can be made, this nation will not survive.

What can black power mean for America?

It can mean the reaffirmation of the concept of a pluralistic American society, respect of an individual's heritage and contribution, and a respect of difference in a nation that tends too readily to become amorphous, dull and conformist.

It can and has meant increased dialogue and conversation about methods and goals within the civil rights movement.

It can offset the growing strength of reactionary forces which would reverse progress and stifle growth. Black power can build cities, communities, institutions and men worthy of American ideals.

Black power can force the honest appraisal of who, what, and where we are.

68. STOKELY CARMICHAEL: "WE ARE GOING TO USE THE TERM 'BLACK POWER' AND WE ARE GOING TO DEFINE IT BECAUSE BLACK POWER SPEAKS TO US"

This is 1966 and it seems to me that it's 'time out' for nice words. It's time black people got together. We have to say things nobody else in this country is willing to say and find the strength internally and from each other to say the things that need to be said. We have to understand the lies this country has spoken about black people and we have to set the record straight. No one else can do that but black people.

From a speech by Stokely Carmichael, July 28, 1966, in NOTES AND COMMENT (Chicago: Student Nonviolent Coordinating Committee, 1966), mimeographed.

I remember when I was in school they used to say, "If you work real hard, if you sweat, if you are ambitious, then you will be successful." I'm here to tell you that if that was true, black people would own this country, because we sweat more than anybody else in this country. We have to say to this country that you have lied to us. We picked your cotton for $2.00 a day, we washed your dishes, we're the porters in your bank and in your building, we are the janitors and the elevator men. We worked hard and all we get is a little pay and a hard way to go from you. We have to talk not only about what's going on here but what this country is doing across the world. When we start getting the internal strength to tell them what should be told and to speak the truth as it should be spoken, let them pick the sides and let the chips fall where they may.

Now, about what black people have to do and what has been done to us by white people. If you are born in Lowndes County, Alabama, Swillingchit, Mississippi or Harlem, New York and the color of your skin happens to be black you are going to catch it. The only reason we have to get together is the color of our skins. They oppress us because we are black and we are going to use that blackness to get out of the trick bag they put us in. Don't be ashamed of your color.

A few years ago, white people used to say, "Well, the reason they live in the ghetto is they are stupid, dumb, lazy, unambitious, apathetic, don't care, happy, contented," and the trouble was a whole lot of us believed that junk about ourselves. We were so busy trying to prove to white folks that we were everything they said we weren't that we got so busy being white we forgot what it was to be black. We are going to call our black brothers hand.

Now, after 1960, when we got moving, they couldn't say we were lazy and dumb and apathetic and all that anymore so they got sophisticated and started to play the dozens with us. They called conferences about our mamas and told us that's why we were where we were at. Some people were sitting up there talking with Johnson while he was talking about their mamas. I don't play the dozens with white folks. To set the record straight, the reason we are in the bag we are in isn't because of my mama, it's because of what they did to my mama. That's why I'm where I'm at. We have to put the blame where it belongs. The blame does not belong on the oppressed but on the oppressor, and that's where it is going to stay.

Don't let them scare you when you start opening your mouth —speak the truth. Tell them, "Don't blame us because we haven't ever had the chance to do wrong." They made sure that we have been so blocked-in we couldn't move until they said, "Move." Now there are a number of things we have to do. The only thing we own in this country is the color of our skins and we are ashamed of that because they made us ashamed. We have to stop being ashamed of being black. A broad nose, a thick lip and nappy hair is us and we are going to call that beautiful whether they like it or not. We are not going to fry our hair anymore but they can start wearing their hair natural to look like us.

We have to define how we are going to move, not how they say we can move. We have never been able to do that before. Everybody in this country jumps up and says, "I'm a friend of the civil rights movement. I'm a friend of the Negro." We haven't had the chance to say whether or not that man is stabbing us in the back or not. All those people who are calling us friends are nothing but treacherous enemies and we can take care of our enemies but God deliver us from our 'friends.' The only protection we are going to have is from each other. We have to build a strong base to let them know if they touch one black man driving his wife to the hospital in Los Angeles, or one black man walking down a highway in Mississippi or if they take one black man who has a rebellion and put him in jail and start talking treason, we are going to disrupt this whole country.

We have to say, "Don't play jive and start writing poems after Malcolm is shot." We have to move from the point where the man left off and stop writing poems. We have to start supporting our own movement. If we can spend all that money to send a preacher to a Baptist convention in a Cadillac then we can spend money to support our own movement.

Now, let's get to what the white press has been calling riots. In the first place don't get confused with the words they use like "anti-white," "hate," "militant" and all that nonsense like "radical" and "riots." What's happening is rebellions not riots and the extremist element is not RAM. As a matter of fact RAM is a very reactionary group, reacting against the pressures white people are putting on them. The extremists in this country are the white people who force us to live the way we live. We have to define our own ethic. We don't have to (and don't make any apologies about it) obey any law that we didn't have a part to make, especially if that law was made to keep us where we are. We have the right to break it.

We have to stop apologizing for each other. We must tell our black brothers and sisters who go to college, "Don't take any job for IBM or Wall Street because you aren't doing anything for us. You are helping this country perpetuate its lies about how democracy rises in this country." They have to come back to the community, where they belong and use their skills to help develop us. We have to tell the Doctors, "You can't go to college and come back and charge us $5.00 and $10.00 a visit. You have to charge us 50¢ and be thankful you get that." We have to tell our lawyers not to charge us what they charge but to be happy to take a case and plead it free of charge. We have to define success and tell them the food Ralph Bunche eats doesn't feed our hungry stomachs. We have to tell Ralph Bunche the only reason he is up there is so when we yell they can pull him out. We have to do that, nobody else can do that for us.

We have to talk about wars and soldiers and just what that means. A mercenary is a hired killer and any black man serving in this man's army is a black mercenary, nothing else. A mercenary fights for a country for a price but does not enjoy the rights of the country for which he is fighting. A mercenary will go to Viet Nam to fight for free elections for the Vietnamese but doesn't have free elections in Alabama, Mississippi, Georgia, Texas, Louisiana, South Carolina and Washington, D.C. A mercenary goes to Viet Nam and gets shot fighting for his country and they won't even bury him in his own home town. He's a mercenary, that's all. We must find the strength so that when they start grabbing us to fight their war we say, "Hell no."

We have to talk about nonviolence among us, so that we don't cut each other on Friday nights and don't destroy each other but move to a point where we appreciate and love each other. That's the nonviolence that has to be talked about. The psychology the man has used on us has turned us against each other. He says nothing about the cutting that goes on Friday night but talk about raising one finger-tip towards him and that's when he jumps up. We have to talk about nonviolence among us first.

We have to study black history but don't get fooled. You should know who John Hullett is, and Fanny Lou Hamer is, who Lerone Bennett is, who Max Stanford is, who Lawrence Landry is, who May Mallory is and who Robert Williams is. You have to know these people yourselves because you can't read about them in a book or in the press. You have to know what Mr. X said from his own lips not the Chicago Sun-Times. That responsibility is ours. The Muslims call themselves Muslims but the press calls them black Muslims. We have to call them Muslims and go to their mosque to find out what they are talking about firsthand and then we can talk about getting together. Don't let that man get up there and tell you, "Oh, you know those Muslims preach nothing but hate. You shouldn't be messing with them." "Yah, I don't mess with them, yah, I know they bad." The man's name is the Honorable Elijah Muhammad and he represents a great section of the black community. Honor him.

We have to go out and find our young blacks who are cutting and shooting each other and tell them they are doing the cutting and shooting to the wrong people. We have to bring them together and spend the time if we are not just shucking and jiving. This is 1966 and my grandmother used to tell me, "The time is far spent." We have to move this year.

There is a psychological war going on in this country and it's whether or not black people are going to be able to use the terms they want about their movement without white peoples blessing. We have to tell them we are going to use the term 'Black Power' and we are going to define it because Black Power speaks to us. We can't let them project Black Power because they can only project it from white power and we know what white power has done to us. We have to organize ourselves to speak from a position of strength and stop begging people to look kindly upon us. We are going to build a movement in this country based on the color of our skins that is going to free us from our oppressors and we have to do that ourselves.

We have got to understand what is going on in Lowndes County, Alabama, what it means, who is in it and what they are doing so if white people steal that election like they do all over this country then the eyes of black people all over this country will be focused there to let them know we are going to take care of business if they mess with us in Lowndes County. That responsibility lies on all of us, not just the civil rights workers and do-gooders.

If we talk about education we have to educate ourselves, not with Hegel or Plato or the missionaries who came to Africa with the bible and we had the land and when they left we had the bible and they had the land. We have to tell them the only way anybody eliminates poverty in this country is to give poor people money. You don't have to headstart, uplift and upward-bound them into your culture. Just give us the money you stole from us, that's all. We have to say to people in this country, "We don't really care about you. For us to get better, we don't have to go to white things. We can do it in our own community, ourselves if you didn't steal the resources that belong there." We have to understand the Horatio Alger lie and that the individualist, profit-concept nonsense will never work for us. We have to form cooperatives and use the profits to benefit our community. We can't tolerate their system.

When we form coalitions we must say on what grounds we are going to form them, not white people telling us how to form them. We must build strength and pride amongst ourselves. We must think politically and get power because we are the only people in this country that are powerless. We are the only people who have to protect ourselves from our protectors. We are the only people who want a man called Willis removed who is a racist, that have to lie down in the street and beg a racist named Daley to remove the racist named Willis. We have to build a movement so we can see Daley and say, "Tell Willis to get hat," and by the time we turn around he is gone. That's Black Power.

Everybody in this country is for "Freedom Now" but not everybody is for Black Power because we have got to get rid of some of the people who have white power. We have got to get us some Black Power. We don't control anything but what white people say we can control. We have to be able to smash any political machine in the country that's oppressing us and bring it to its knees. We have to be aware that if we keep growing and multiplying the way we do in ten years all the major cities are going to be ours. We have to know that in Newark, New Jersey, where we are 60% of the population, we went along with their stories about integrating and we got absorbed. All we have to show for it is three councilmen who are speaking for them and not for us. We have to organize ourselves to speak for each other. That's Black Power. We have to move to control the economics and politics of our community. . . .

69. NORTHWESTERN UNIVERSITY BLACK STUDENTS: "IF OUR DEMANDS ARE IMPOSSIBLE, THEN PEACE BETWEEN US IS IMPOSSIBLE TOO"

Having rejected the basic principles on which our demands were based, the administration has forced us to speak for the last time on those matters discussed at the meeting of Wednes-

"Revised Demands of the Black Students,"
in "Black and White at Northwestern University: Documents,"
INTEGRATED EDUCATION, VI (May–June 1968), 36–41.

day, April 24, 1968. We demand that such action be taken to meet this, our final list of demands. The University must show itself flexible enough to take in the "peculiarities" of our culture and background. The only way, we feel, the University can display its understanding and flexibility is by the immediate approval and implementation of those demands submitted by the Black student body on April 22, 1968.

I. Policy statement

Northwestern cannot begin to deal effectively with racism on this campus until it first realizes and openly acknowledges the extent of racism in American society. For this reason we reject the statement given to us in response and demand that a "new" policy statement be issued and made public from President J. Roscoe Miller asserting that the racism of American society which has penetrated all American institutions has also penetrated Northwestern University, and has thus affected the social and academic life here.

This statement is to include a declaration that the University is attempting to provide a multi-racial and cultural society within the university walls and that any racist attack and/or abuses shall be considered in direct opposition to the University's goals and a danger to the peaceful existence of such a society. The extent of this danger is such that the perpetrator shall be immediately excluded from this institution.

In order to alter the racist structure of this University, a change has to take place in the judiciary structures, attitudes, and practices. As of now, the University Disciplinary Committee is ineffective in dealing with racism on campus (examples include the Fiji incidents and the many encounters with Sigma Chi). We demand that this judiciary be changed and implemented to bring about swifter and fairer decisions, or that a special judiciary be created to deal with these special cases.

On acknowledging the racist structure of this country and this institution, Northwestern is committed to understand the negative effects of racism on Black people and other oppressed

people. The entire concept of justice has to be re-evaluated for
this reason. Justice for Black people at this time does not mean
equal treatment before a law or rule which is insensitive to
our oppressive position in this country. We contend that justice
for Black people means that extra consideration and efforts are
to be made in order to balance the effects of racism. This means
in effect that the U.D.C. decision to place 3 white students and
2 Black students on disciplinary warning is not justice and is
thus unacceptable in our eyes.

Our experience in America has not been characterized by
justice in any way. No white institution can right our hundreds
of years of history and experience by suddenly treating us the
same as white people (only at those times when it is strategic to
do so) and call it justice and equality. No matter how one looks
at it, idealistically or realistically, Black people know that we
are still getting the short end of the deal. A new basis for
administering justice must be developed and put into effect and
it is with this that U.D.C., or any new judiciary which intends
to deal with racism, has to concern itself.

The only concrete response from the administration was the
establishment of a special University Committee on Human
Relations. However, we are not satisfied with that response and
demand the right of the Black student community to approve
all appointments to this committee and to determine at least
50% of these appointments.

II. Admissions

We understand that Northwestern has suddenly made a
"substantial effort to change the composition of the undergrad-
uate student body." However, this statement or any of the
others which followed says nothing about a guaranteed increase
of the number of Black students at Northwestern. We demand
that each forthcoming freshman class be 10-12% Black and that
it will be financially feasible for all those Black students accepted to come.

We demanded that 50% of each year's incoming Black students be from the inner city school systems. The administration emphasized that in the past the Black enrollment contained at least 50% from the inner city and ended with the statement "There is no reason to believe that this percentage should change." In lieu of this statement there is no reason why we should not be given a guarantee that this percentage will remain the same.

We agreed that a committee will be appointed by the Black student community to assist the Admissions Office, especially in the area of recruitment. We demand that there be no restrictions placed on our selections, that this committee be in a salaried position, and that it have shared power with the Office of Admissions and Financial Aid in making all decisions relevant to Black students, including decision on which Black students are to be admitted.

The University has agreed to provide us with the names of all Black students who are known to the Administration as well as a list of all entering Black students. We demand a list of all Black students accepted as well as those entering with information relevant to our purposes such as residence (city and state). We further demand that such lists be compiled and turned over to F.M.O. for each subsequent freshman class.

In addition, the University agreed to arrange a meeting between us and the incoming Black freshman.

III. Scholarships

As all Black people in America categorically suffer from the oppressiveness of this white society, we conclude that all Black students at Northwestern in turn categorically suffer from economic and social oppression and on that basis should categorically be given special consideration for increased financial aid which is not covered in the data of the financial aid form. The process of evaluating financial need and administering financial aid must be restructured to meet our vital needs. This re-organization can be done in conjunction with our established Admissions and Financial Aid Committee.

The acceptance of job and loan offers may be optional for white students attending Northwestern, but due to our plight in this country, they are not optional for us. Black students are forced to take jobs and loans to lessen the financial burden of our families who suffer categorically under the American political, economic, and social structure. Therefore the problems and pressures encountered by a Black student receiving financial aid are not the same one encountered by a white financial aid student.

The University has already acknowledged the deficiency in our high school preparation. By virtue of this fact, we contend that this deficiency can best be removed by allowing all Black students to attend the summer session as they so desire. Also, we strongly feel that Black students should have the same opportunity to continue their education through the summer as any other Northwestern student. Whether or not we work or attend classes should be *our option* and therefore the University should not restrict us by requiring that we work in order to substantiate our scholarships for the other three quarters.

As it stands now, Northwestern has neither a fair admissions policy nor a fair financial aid arrangement. Equal opportunity and rights for us imply much more than whites care to admit. Our demands still stand that our scholarships be increased to cover what is now included in our "required jobs" and to include funds for those who want or need to attend Summer session.

IV. Housing

As taken from the University's reply to our demands of April 22nd: "While we [the administration] can understand and appreciate the frustrations that lead to the demands . . ." We, the Black students of Northwestern, cannot *appreciate* the *frustrations* that led to making these demands. How the University can claim to understand our problems and/or frustrations and not concede to our demands is beyond our comprehension!

The University might be living with a severe shortage of on-campus housing. However, this does not affect us in that a

Black living unit would not necessarily call for additional space, only the relocation of students.

Furthermore, the Administration contends that the most important reason for denying this demand lies in the function the residence hall serves in the educational program of the University. "[The residence hall] is a place where students learn from each other and thereby further the education in which this institution is engaged. This function of University housing depends on a mixture of student types which cannot be achieved if certain groups are segregated from the rest of the living environment." Why, we ask, are the fraternities and sororities exempt from this educational program?

The University evidently helps to support living units (fraternities and sororities) on this campus which are in direct opposition to the above-quoted University policy. Therefore, the University should have no objection to supporting another living unit (Black) without this educational program.

Furthermore, according to the minutes of the March 5, 1968 CUL Subcommittee meeting, "Mr. Ihlanfeldt stated that as Director of Admissions, he feels his charge from the faculty is to recruit quality and dissimilarity within the student body. He sees the Greek groups as selecting others like themselves and opposes the extension of the system on that basis. He stated that he would accept the fraternity idea but not in the same way that it has been in the past where there is discrimination based on the same type of criterion. He would only accept an extension of the idea, such as converting Hobart and Rogers to models of the future that may tend to represent the philosophical idea of a master house plan. This could be all or predominantly Negro, but it would not be copying the fraternity system as it is." Evidently the idea of a Black living unit was at one time feasible. Why is it that this is no longer the case?

If the University genuinely believes that a Black living unit would be in direct conflict with their program and/or basic university policy, then we demand that the University should make a policy statement condemning the existing living units of this sort (i. e., fraternities and sororities) with a commitment to get rid of them immediately. Otherwise, on the basis of this argument, we restate our demand that the University provide us with a Black living unit.

V. Curriculum

Dean Strotz received a copy of our demands on April 21, 1968 as did the rest of the administration. It is our understanding that Dean Strotz heads the Committee for Curriculum Revisions. We have received no reply either from him or through the administration on the creation of a Black Studies Course. Therefore, we assume that he has either denied our request or he is thoroughly disinterested in the condition of the Black student at Northwestern.

Through University funds, the Administration has the influence to promote the hiring of Black faculty members. We demand that this influence be immediately put into effect and used to its fullest extent.

One concrete step in meeting our demand would be the creation of a visiting chair in Black Studies. However, we demand that the Black community have the ultimate decision as to which professor would occupy this chair from year to year.

VI. Counseling

We want it understood that any hiring of personnel in the position of counseling to the Black community of Northwestern University must be approved by the Black community. Without such approval, we will totally absolve ourselves from recognizing or interacting with such persons. Further understand our position on the hiring of Mr. Calvin Smith. We will review his "qualifications"; however, if he does not meet our approval, steps must be taken to find an acceptable Black counselor.

VII. Facilities

We acknowledge the Administration's reply to our demand for facilities.

VIII. Open occupancy

We acknowledge the University's efforts toward the passage of the Evanston Open Occupancy Law. However, we demand access to the committee which has been studying open occupancy and discrimination, as well as review rights to the matters which they are discussing so that we may determine both their relevance and effectiveness.

The legitimacy of these demands cannot be debated. What is important to Black people is not necessarily important to the Administration or this University as a whole. The Administration has demonstrated that they are less concerned about our reasons and motivations for presenting these demands than about their own intentions to maintain ultimate control over our lives. Likewise, we are not interested in the reasons why these demands cannot be met.

In lieu of this, tension between us is inevitable and it is this tension which has to be reconciled. We realize that the factors leading to our presently being students at Northwestern were basically politically motivated and had little or nothing to do with a social interest in the plight of Black people in America. Being brought here essentially for purposes of exploitation, Northwestern has subsequently shown little interest in our needs except for those which were compatible with theirs. Therefore, the main responsibility for reconciling the tension between us lies with the Administration and not with us. All we can say is that if our demands are impossible, then peace between us is impossible, too.

In summary, we demand positive responses from the Administration to the following:

Policy statement

1. That the Administration will accept and issue a policy statement as outlined in this paper.

2. That the Administration restructure the UDC or create a new judiciary to adequately and justly cope with racial problems and incidents.

3. That the Administration effect a new judiciary standard (as outlined) and apply this standard retroactively to the UDC decision of April 15.

4. That the Administration allow the Black community to (a) approve all appointments to the Human Relations Committee and (b) determine at least 50% of those appointments.

Admission

5. That each forthcoming freshman class consist of 10%-12% Black students, half of which are from the inner city school systems.

6. That the Administration will institute a committee selected by the Black community to aid the Admissions Office, especially in recruitment, and which will have shared power with the Office of Admissions and Financial Aid in making decisions relevant to us.

7. That the members constituting this committee be in a salaried position.

8. That F.M.O. will be supplied with (a) a list of all Black students presently enrolled at Northwestern (b) a list including names, addresses, etc. of all accepted and incoming Black freshmen, (c) a similar list of each forthcoming freshman class.

Financial aid

9. That the process of evaluating financial need and administering financial aid be restructured in conjunction with our Admissions and Financial Aid Committee.

10. That our scholarships be increased to cover what is now included in our "required jobs and that funds be allocated for those who want or need to attend summer session.

Housing

11. That the University provide us with a Black living unit or commit themselves to immediately getting rid of the present fraternity and sorority housing arrangements.

Counseling

12. That any hiring of personnel in the position of counseling the Black community of NU be approved by that Black community.

Facilities

13. That a committee of Black students selected by us work with the Administration in meeting our needs for a Black Student Union.

Open occupancy

14. That we have access to the committee studying open occupancy and discrimination with review rights to the matters which they are discussing.

Black capitalism

Economic nationalism survived the ebbing of black nationalist thought during the 1930s and 1940s. A number of splinter groups from Garvey's UNIA continued to advocate "buying black" and to urge development of black capitalism. One such organization was the Harlem-based African Nationalist Pioneer Movement. Led by Carlos Cooks in the late 1950s, this group opposed the religious nationalism of the Nation of Islam and reiterated Garvey's secular goals of a separate black economy.

With the emergence of the Black Power slogan in 1966, one of the many definitions given it was black economic power. Floyd McKissick, a former national director of CORE, in a brochure promoting McKissick Enterprises, Inc., offers a rationale for the new thrust of black capitalism, and a description of the purpose, scope, and structure of the company and its specific projects. The ideas of a strong black business class coupled with the appeal to wealthy whites for assistance echoes turn-of-the-century economic nationalism.

70. AFRICAN NATIONALIST PIONEER MOVEMENT: "WE ADVOCATE COMPLETE ECONOMIC CONTROL BY THE BLACKS OF ALL AFRICAN COMMUNITIES IN AMERICA"

A. A MANIFESTO

Buy Black!   **Buy Black!**

WHAT WE KNOW!!

THE AFRICAN NATIONALIST PIONEER MOVEMENT advocates the uniting of all people of the African ethnic group into one, healthy, vigorous Black Race.

We are against miscegenation or race suicide.

We are against rich Blacks marrying poor whites.

We believe in the purity of the Black Race, and the purity of all other races.

We are against the white race or any race taking advantage of Black Women.

We know that the Black Race is as good as any other; therefore, should be as proud of itself as other races are.

We know that the social, political and physical separation of all races to the extent that they may promote their own Ideals and Civilization, and with the privilege of trading and doing Business with each other, is positively necessary.

We know that Nature has drawn indelible lines forever restricting the Black and White Races,—upon being integrated—from living equally free.

We know that the communist whiteman, as well as the capi-

"What We Know! !" THE BLACK CHALLENGE (1959), p. 15.

talist whiteman, stands on one platform, where it concerns the Blackman, that is White Supremacy.

We know that the Mongolians are interested in their own security, the Arabs have shown by their record as slave traders that they would gladly exploit the Blacks and Africa and are currently doing so through Mohammedanism.

We know that the Idea of God was conceived by man; hence man made God and that brotherhood among men is possible only between members of any one given race.

We know the rights of black men must be achieved and maintained by Blacks.

We adhere to: One Cause, One Goal, One Destiny.

We know that the Black Race's salvation cannot be attained within the realm of any religion, or apologetic Uncle Tom leadership; it must be BLACK NATIONALISM of eternal vassalage.

We are against all caste names whether; Negro, Colored, Sepia, Tan or "what have you." We prefer to be called what we are: Black Men and Black Women.

We strongly advocate the promotion of a powerful Black Nation in Africa (AFRICA FOR THE AFRICANS).

We believe in the Political and Physical Independence of all men.

We advocate complete economic control by the Blacks of all African Communities in America, creating thereby *Self-Determination* and Race Pride.

WE say. BUY BLACK! So that your children will revere your memory. Patronize your own people's Business Enterprises, build a solvent economic future,

We know that we are not obligated to or bound by the opinions of others, therefore, are entitled to our own opinions, and the right to guide our own destiny.

B. "BUY BLACK"

Blacks were brought from Africa by whites. They were brought here as slaves. In the year 1619, the first slave ship landed at James Town, Virginia. The master determined the status of the slaves then, and he determines their status now!

In 1619 the slaves could not go to school with him, sit in buses beside him, nor go to church with him.

In 1959 the slaves still can't go to school with him, sit in buses beside him, nor go to church with him.

The master knows what the slaves are, and regardless of what they say or do, it does not change their status.

The Negro, as he has been called since slavery, has made all kinds of sacrifices for the master, including 245 years of free labor.

If he is no more today in the eyes of his master, than he was then, doesn't it seem foolhardy to waste his time trying to prove otherwise?

The master says he is a Negro, and a Negro he is!

Pere John criticizes Mr. Carlos A. Cook's ideas of retaining the wealth we lavish so freely in white establishments. In this Country there are millionaires—known as Industrialists. These fellows invest billions of dollars all over the world: Yet, they have protective tariff to safeguard their markets, so that no foreign enterprise can compete with them, for their money, in their own Country.

This simple minded Negro amuses me. Then if this is true, the Negro should keep every red cent he earns, out of the hands of those who do not look like him. More so, since he has to work like a horse to earn it.

If protective tariff is good for the millionaires, then "BUY BLACK" is more than good for Negroes, who earn $25.00 to $45.00 a week.

From Oscar Brown, " 'Buy Black' Is the Only Logical Solution," THE BLACK CHALLENGE (1959), p. 28.

I say that if the Negro is only 10% of the population, he should not have a 75% ratio on relief. Nor should he have a 70% or more in penal and other institutions.

Harlem is not the only place where prostitution exist. Nor where drunks and dope fiends hang out. But if the Negroes wants to share the white man's vices, he should also share his virtues.

Are there any Negro Hospitals? Railroads? Textile Mills? Or any Negro Industrialists? You cannot tell a Negro business man who has nothing to sell because of lack of support, to give service. You first have to tell the Negroes to buy what he has, then he in turn will learn to give service if he wants their patronage.

Some of these white establishments are not only filthy, but they actually insult Negroes. Yet you see these Negroes crowding into these stores, not for bargains as Pere John would have us believe, but paying unheard of prices, for worthless merchandise.

Business is based on profit. Nobody gives anything away. Of course these are white establishments, and that is how they are supposed to treat Negroes. These are the same people who refuse to serve Negroes in the South. If Pere John is writing for a white newspaper, he is a hireling! If he is writing for a Negro newspaper, all he has to do is turn to page one. There he will see it in big bold letters, "Negro is last hired, and first fired."

Then let the Negro create employment for his own kind. This he can do only through business. And in order to have business, he must first learn to support Negroes in business. That is simple enough for even the Negro to understand.

Incidentally: I read a book on Gun Smithing. There the Author wrote, "Think Nigger—Think."

If Pere John had written this in 1800, I could see it. But not in 1959, when every group wants the right to control themselves Politically and economically. Note: Chinese, Mexicans, etc. etc.

But the Negro! He wants to remain a hireling. The master expects only so much patriotism. More than that, he know that you are either an ass, or expect special favors.

You claim that you wrote in 1931. How come you neglected to tell us of the then, existing slave market in the Bronx, where Negro women use to go to look for work? These women took garbage cans, put paper and wood in them, to light a fire to keep themselves warm. These women use to stand around these cans in colonies, and waited to be employed. Not only that, but they had to have their own clocks, because after 6 p.m. in winter, every hour look alike. Their employers use to turn their clocks back in order to get a day and a half work for one day's pay. Of course as a Negro writer, you are not suppose to know these things.

When we say Black, we don't mean Black in color, as some of you are prone to believe. We would prefer it that way. But in as much as Negroes are so mixed up, we are using a standard. We are Members of the Black Race. Since some Negroes are any-thing but Black in color, and many of them feel that to say Black, would mean a loss of Status. They fight like hell when you say Black, and strangely enough, they enlist the aid of persons who are Black in color to assist them.

People have rights to a certain extent. We support Whites, Chinese, etc, etc. They don't live among us. Then if a Negro Business man sees fit to move to the suburbs, although I can't see how any Negro Business man can move anywhere if no one supports him, grant it—he has his rights, and that should not offend us. True, Negroes do not look after each other's interest but after all, isn't that the way they were trained?

If however, we had a daily or weekly Newspaper that was really voicing our sentiments, we could change this.

71. FLOYD B. McKISSICK:
"BLACK BUSINESS DEVELOPMENT
WITH SOCIAL COMMITMENT
TO BLACK COMMUNITIES"

An introductory message

The many promises by the white society to achieve equality and economic freedom have not materialized. The tokens we have received have had the effects of drops of water in the sea.

Many of the promises of the past have raised the hopes of the Black Man, but by and large he is still in the economic bread line. What he has received is intended to placate him and lull him into false security. The result, however, has been turmoil in our great cities. Turmoil bred of frustration and growing fury. What has been done has been too little, too slow and much too late.

Many of the efforts may have been sincere, but have not been meaningful. Additional millions poured into unplanned poverty programs and welfare will not solve the dilemma posed by our ghettos. Billions of dollars are required, but the nature and control of the programs are more important than press releases about the amount.

I feel that my best service to the movement and to my people can be rendered by my full-time commitment to Black Economic Independence. The Black Man and Woman will no longer be content to eat leftovers in the kitchen. We want to sit at our own table and carve the financial turkey with all its trimmings.

The Black Man's sweat and tears have fertilized this economy. His blood has been shed in many wars to protect it. Even

A brochure describing Floyd B. McKissick Enterprises, Inc., 1968. Reprinted by permission of Floyd B. McKissick Enterprises, Inc.

now, it is being expended in a greater proportionate ratio than any other group in the world in Vietnam. Most of the Black folk, as well as white, still do not know what they are fighting for. While our Black Brothers are fighting to save the white capitalist society in Vietnam, we are going to fight here at home to create a strong Black Society for those fortunate enough to return home. We are going to create the economic tools and we will finish the job. The Black Man's only salvation is through his own efforts.

All over the world the struggle is for Economic Power and Self-determination. These bring respect to those who gain them. Black People are fighting for respect and dignity, not a handout.

Throughout American History, Black People have lived in circumstances and conditions dictated by whites and we have been urged to sit by while white people fulfilled their promises to us. From slavery, we were promised freedom. That freedom became separate and unequal apartheid. From segregation, we were promised integration into the life of affluent America. That integration became growing slum squalor and violence.

The very co-existence of Black and Whites in this society is being threatened. It is my belief that the development of Black Economic Power offers White America its last chance to save the Republic. If we are to exist together, it will be as equals. Equality depends on Black control of its own institutions.

This can be accomplished only through the rapid growth of *Black Corporate Structures.*

To coordinate and catalyze the formation of Black Business Enterprises, I have formed the organization, known as Floyd B. McKissick Enterprises, Incorporated. It is a corporation formed to create and distribute profits to millions of Black Americans. McKissick Enterprises will be a national resource center for Black individuals and communities who need assistance in developing new businesses.

McKissick Enterprises is located in the heart of Harlem. We are utilizing Black experts from all levels of business and industry.

We are currently organizing the following departments within the Company:

—Capital Resources   —Technical Resources
—Training Resources   —Planning Resources
—Management Resources   —Real Estate Development

Each of the Departments will be manned by knowledgeable and expert staff and will be supported by a panel of consultants who will represent the highest achievements in their respective areas.

In addition to providing assistance to other companies, McKissick Enterprises will invest directly in the formation of new companies, some of which will be so constructed that ownership will be eventually transferred to local persons.

Much of the capital for our undertakings will be forthcoming from white financial institutions and business corporations. The success of our endeavors is dependent, however, on the efforts and toil of Black People—the same Blacks who have loyally contributed to the strength of this nation, and who spend over 40 billion dollars each year, but who realize little economic return. The Black man will no longer be a consumer, but a producer.

If a Black Man has no bread in his pocket—the solution to his problem is not integration; it's to get some bread. Real simple—that's what McKissick Enterprises, Inc. is all about.

The corporate goals of McKissick Enterprises

McKissick Enterprises is planning to become a major American Corporation. Unlike most companies, however, its major objectives are *Black Business Development with Social Commitment to Black Communities*. Nevertheless, it recognizes that its social goals will be obtained only to the extent that it prospers and is able to reinvest and distribute profits.

The social goal may be stated very simply: to provide a means for Black People to become a part of the American capitalist system and thereby achieve social and economic parity with the white community.

Translating these social goals into corporate objectives is a major challenge to McKissick Enterprises. Some of the dimensions of the challenge are discussed below.

The unique nature of the company

There have been many attempts to institute Black Economic Independence on this continent. Most of these attempts have been hampered, however, by unrealistic, even romantic, notions or by a lack of sound business practices, or both.

McKissick Enterprises, on the other hand, recognizes the requirement to work within the capitalistic system. *It neither supports nor condemns capitalism.* It simply recognizes it as a power fact of life and realizes that if Black Men and Women are to share in the productive wealth of the nation, they have no alternative at this time other than full participation as entrepreneurs.

No other business corporation is attempting to build Black Capitalism on a national scale. McKissick Enterprises is doing so and has the ability to channel the resources which will make success possible.

The scope of the company

McKissick Enterprises is concerned with the fate of Black People throughout this country—and the world. It is not limited to big city problems, rural areas or a particular social class. It is concerned with large and small businesses, with sales, services and production.

McKissick Enterprises will actively seek to stimulate business activities among Black people and it will encourage the formation of numerous new independent undertakings. It will foster broad ownership and community control through stock corporations and "community corporations." It will also help to establish family stores and shops.

In the course of expanding its activities, McKissick Enterprises will carefully develop priorities for areas in which it will concentrate.

The structure of the company

McKissick Enterprises is formed to make profit and to return profits to those Black Persons who participate in its activities.

In certain regards, the company will function as a holding company. That is, it will organize new corporations with limited goals. Some of these corporations may be subsidiaries, while McKissick Enterprises may own only a minority interest in others. For most major activities a new corporation will be formed.

McKissick Enterprises will also enter into contracts with local organizations, corporations, communities and individuals to provide services and to bring together the talents and resources required to mount individual business endeavors and projects for total community development.

In all cases, McKissick Enterprises will be concerned only with viable business ventures which appear to offer real opportunity for growth and stability and which promise to yield a high return relative on investment.

The resources of the company

McKissick Enterprises has a unique wealth of resources. The political climate of the nation demands Black participation and control. Presently, there are forward looking businessmen and politicians who stand ready to cooperate with sound, well planned Black Business ventures.

The major asset of the Company is, however, its President, F. B. McKissick. Mr. McKissick, a highly successful lawyer and businessman, has earned an international reputation for boldness and integrity of leadership. As Director of CORE, he was the first man in recent times to clearly articulate the meaning of "Black Power." More important, he was the only one to draft a realistic program and design a structure for achieving Black Power and self-determination.

His drive and farsightedness led him to the founding of McKissick Enterprises, since he clearly perceived that the key to power in the United States was economic power.

McKissick Enterprises will be able to attract substantial capital backing for its projects. Lack of such capital has been a major problem facing Black Businesses. McKissick Enterprises will also develop the managerial skills which are required in order to mount new businesses. It is currently putting together a staff and body of consultants who will provide a management talent pool which is unsurpassed.

McKissick Enterprises is Black owned and controlled, but it recognizes the need to acquire talent and skill from a broad range of experienced businessmen and planners. It will utilize persons from every background as consultants, and in other capacities, as long as these individuals are willing to work to realize the long-term goals of the company.

The primary goal of McKissick Enterprises is economic independence for the Black Community. Economic Independence demands that comprehensive Black Industry be developed. Black People cannot hope to achieve a strong Black Economy without controlling their own industry from beginning to end. They cannot merely process and sell products designed and developed by the white community. In order to be effective, new Black corporations must be involved in production of goods as well as the import and export of products. Black American corporations can significantly affect positive trade relations with African countries, and stimulate a vast new market for the products of Black America. Such healthy economic relations should serve to further unite Black Americans with their brothers in Africa—resulting in a new awareness and harmony between the developing African nations and their western neighbors.

Existing Black Communities are, in many ways, like colonies. These communities are plagued by an imbalance of trade. Black People presently depend upon the larger community for their employment as well as the goods and services necessary to urban life. Therefore, they must leave their communities to earn their money as well as to spend it. The few existing economic institutions in Black Communities are almost exclusively white owned and operated. Therefore, there is no funnel for capital into the Black Community. There is no chance for Black People to seriously affect the conditions in which they must live.

McKissick Enterprises future plans is to develop a Non-profit Small Business Development Cooperative which will function as a consultant for Black Businesses, and will serve to bring Black Businessmen together to exchange information and ideas pertinent to Black Economic Growth. Representatives of white corporations will also be encouraged to contribute by aiding in the development of a skills bank which would provide trained and skilled planners and workers for Black Industry.

In addition, McKissick Enterprises will aid young Black Businessmen by providing technical assistance and funds to people with sound business ideas. At times, new companies will be owned by McKissick Enterprises until they are sufficiently viable to become independent. At that point, these companies would become the property of those who provided the original inspiration.

McKissick Enterprises will be instrumental in the development of Profit-making economic institutions across America. McKissick Enterprises can provide the expert legal and technical assistance to prevent unnecessary failures in Black Economic ventures. It can provide information and arrange for mortgages and financing for new undertakings which will be ultimately beneficial to Black Communities. In this capacity, it is likely that McKissick Enterprises will be involved in the establishment of such diversified institutions as hosiery factories, construction companies and supermarkets.

McKissick Enterprises will be able to present Management Development Packaged Programs for operational Black Businesses and Communities. It will be able to provide training systems, secure private or public funds, in order to launch new Black Business Enterprises.

While consulting will be an important function of McKissick Enterprises, the primary function will be to develop Black Economic structures in as many Black Communities as possible. In order to accomplish such a complex task, the structure of McKissick Enterprises must remain flexible—adaptable to the requirements of each individual community.

McKissick Enterprises will distribute and operate franchises as well as build businesses, maintain businesses and bring together entire industries. McKissick Enterprises will acquire profits by the creation and operation of innovative training programs—ongoing programs throughout the nation which will be owned and operated by McKissick Enterprises—Automobile, Secretarial Training Centers, schools of Business Administration. The Black Community needs training programs to provide skilled personnel to work on every level of the economy. McKissick Enterprises will play a primary role in providing these programs.

McKissick Enterprises will participate in land development; acquiring land to be used for projects of benefit to the Black community. Such projects will be undertaken only after careful and thorough consultation with the community. *No project will be undertaken without the support of the local Black Community.*

Profits made in one community by McKissick Enterprises will be used to establish other profit-making projects in other Black Communities across America. In this way, great numbers of Black People will be positively affected by the activities of McKissick Enterprises. Most profits will be reinvested rather than distributed.

We will seek capital from two major sources. The Black community will provide much of the capital. Further capital will be provided by insurance companies, banks and private industry. Sources of substantial capital will have a number of incentives to make loans to McKissick Enterprises instead of investing funds in other companies in Black Areas. Black People will no longer accept white domination. The Black Community has made it clear that it will not be exploited by white individuals or corporations. Therefore, if White Businessmen are to continue to reap any economic benefit from the Black Community, they will have to invest through Black Organizations and Corporations. At all times, these Black Organizations must retain control. The final decisions must be made by Black men when those decisions vitally affect the Black Community.

Banking institutions will also find it profitable to initiate loans to McKissick Enterprises. Frequently, rigid standards prevent banks from investing in businesses which do not meet stringent and often arbitrary standards. Therefore, if McKissick Enterprises can guarantee the bank's investment, the bank will be far more likely to invest.

Black Businessmen have historically received little help from banking institutions. There is hence a great reluctance on the part of many businessmen to deal with these banks. In many cases, these men would rather deal through a broker such as McKissick Enterprises, knowing that McKissick Enterprises was operating in their best interests and was aware of their special difficulties. In this way, McKissick Enterprises will serve to bring together businessmen and bankers who might not otherwise cooperate. The result will be the creation of new and viable businesses which might not otherwise be possible.

Already, plans are being outlined for the acquisition of a block of property in central Harlem. This is an area which is currently plagued with the worst problems of ghetto life,— drug addiction, poor housing, unemployment, crime. It is an area which can be successfully redeveloped, while retaining the existing dwellers and small businesses in the area. An arcade could be built, which could include training centers, a motel or hotel, as well as shops and stores. Other companies such as Corn Products Company have expressed interest in this project. This project would provide a model for Black Economic Development, and demonstrate the potential for growth in the Black Community.

Small businessmen or private tenants will not be dispossessed to make way for McKissick Enterprises. There is no doubt that hotels can be built to include new and attractive apartments for those people already living in the area. Businessmen temporarily moved out can return to new and vastly improved quarters. But the culture of the community will be preserved. In many cases, renovation rather than rebuilding will be preferable.

Feasibility studies will, of course, be necessary. McKissick Enterprises cannot hope to be successful if it undertakes projects with a high potential for failure. Nevertheless, every effort will be made to meet the demands of the community. It is the belief of McKissick Enterprises that the demands of the Black Community are just and reasonable. In the few cases where McKissick Enterprises will be unable to meet these demands, full and detailed explanations will be given to the community.

The following projects are under development:

A. *Black Top Restaurants, Incorporated*
Consideration is being given to establishing a chain of restaurants. A corporation has been formed. Currently a plan of action is being formulated, and a site for an initial Harlem restaurant is being sought.

B. *Shopping Center Development*
An initial proposal for the development of a shopping center in Harlem and/or Mount Vernon, New York has been prepared. Following several discussions, the International Council of Shopping Centers has agreed to participate. Plans are currently being drawn up to specify the nature of the corporate structure which would maximize community ownership and control.

C. *Harlem Human Development Consortium*
We have organized a Consortium and submitted a proposal to the United States Department of Labor for training the hardcore unemployed under the MA-4 Program. The Consortium will include large employers of cooks, bakers and meat cutters as well as Harlem civic and civil rights organizations.

D. *Publishing Company*

We are negotiating with several publishing companies for purchase of rights to a number of titles related to the history, struggle and future of Black America. Active consideration is being given to forming a new publishing company, alone or in conjunction with an already existing publisher.

E. *Black Drama Productions Incorporated*

A number of prominent Black Playwrights and Authors have secured the assistance of McKissick Enterprises in organizing and launching this company. Pioneer Productions will initially produce lecture series for colleges. It also plans to present Black Art, Music and Drama Programs as well as produce several plays. The nature of the agreement between our company and pioneer is being negotiated.

The feasibility of these additional projects is being investigated:

A. *Black Top Clubs, Inc.*

A chain of clubs presenting entertainment and African style dining is being considered. A corporation has been formed, but has not begun activities.

B. *New City Development*

Under consideration is the building of a new city in rural North Carolina. Initial talks have been held with Rouse and Company.

At present, resources do not allow McKissick Enterprises to develop its own market projections. Outside consultations will be required. Eventually, marketing and consulting firms will be added to McKissick Enterprises.

Numerous other business ideas are scheduled for consideration. Currently, McKissick Enterprises is investigating the possibility of further dealing in African artifacts, jewelry, sculpture, etc. Such a project could be not only economically rewarding, but would help arouse Black consciousness and cultural understanding.

McKissick Enterprises might also establish a bonding company, primarily for the purpose of bonding businessmen starting in the construction business. This is necessary since construction companies depend on such performance bonds and white companies have been unwilling to bond most Black People. Another worthwhile project might be an insurance company which would provide adequate and fair insurance coverage for Black Businessmen throughout the nation.

McKissick Enterprises believes that the development of Black Capitalism is so long overdue and of such importance that it takes precedence over job training programs and general education. Until now, Black People have been relegated to the bottom of the economic ladder. The only way to reverse this trend is to firmly establish Black People on every level of the capitalist structure—thereby guaranteeing organizations receptive to the Black Community and willing to aid in the training and education of the masses of Black People.

The success of McKissick Enterprises will have a tremendously revitalizing effect upon the Black American population. The development of products by Black People to be sold primarily, but not exclusively, to Black People, will have a beneficial effect upon young Blacks. Young people will be encouraged to participate in the economy and to study and train to assume responsible roles within that economy. They will be faced with strong evidence that they have a chance to make it. Presently, the number of Black Capitalists is so small and frequently so far removed from their community that their achievements mean little to most Black Youngsters. *The establishment of Black Economic institutions which are responsive to the needs and desires of the Black Community can be a force for positive change and optimism. It can be a force for the elimination of apathy and despair, the most volatile social components in this society.*

Revolutionary nationalism

Revolutionary nationalism developed rapidly in the middle 1960s. The following documents illustrate the complexity and variety of its ideologies and organizational forms. A letter from General G. Baker, Jr., a young nationalist from Detroit, to his draft board (Document 72) responds to its request that he report for a physical examination. The spirit of this letter, written in 1964, echoes that of Bishop Turner in the war with Spain in 1898 (Document 29B) and anticipates the later chant, "Hell, no! We won't go!" The identification of the struggles of black Americans with those of oppressed peoples throughout the world epitomizes the outlook of *Soulbook*, the journal in which the letter appeared, begun late in 1964 by college-age blacks from New York and California.

One aspect of recent revolutionary nationalism is the belief that a violent confrontation will, and indeed must, take place before black people can really be free. All these documents reflect this view. The first article by Max Stanford, a young Philadelphia nationalist who was formerly field chairman of the Revolutionary Action Movement (RAM), is a secular alternative to the revolutionary, but essentially religious, nationalism preached by Malcolm X. It illustrates the transition from civil rights protest to the later nationalism. The second article was issued as a news release from the Queens County House of Detention in New York City where Stanford was held for alleged conspiracy to commit criminal anarchy and related charges. It calls for the establishment of an independent black nation within the present boundaries of the United States (Document 73). Brother Gaidi (Milton Henry), first vice-president of the Republic of New Africa, explains in Document 74 how his separatist group intends to establish just such a nation consisting of Louisiana, Mississippi, Alabama, Georgia, and South Carolina.

Whereas RAM and the Republic of New Africa see the black revolution culminating in the formation of a separate black nation, James Boggs (Document 75) views the cities as the major focus of the impending struggle, foreseeing a series of black-controlled cities within a drastically restructured American society. Boggs, long an automobile worker in Detroit, has written widely on the theory and strategies of black liberation. His major works are *The American Revolution: Pages from a Negro Worker's Notebook* (1963) and *Manifesto for a Black Revolutionary Party* (1969).

The revolutionary nationalism espoused by Robert Williams and Malcolm X, propagated in the pages of *Soulbook* and *Liberator,* and given wider currency by the militant speeches of Stokely Carmichael and H. Rap Brown, manifested itself dramatically in the Black Panther Party, formed in Oakland, California, in 1966. Led by Huey P. Newton, Bobby Seale, and Eldridge Cleaver, the Panthers attracted wide publicity by their distinctive dress—black berets and black leather coats— and by their brandishing of weapons. The party platform and an interview with Huey Newton (Document 76) indicate their underlying belief that the needs of black people cannot be met within the capitalist system and their advocacy of self-determination. Such views were becoming increasingly common among local groups. Even at the time, as the interview with Huey Newton indicates, the Black Panthers were not averse to working with revolutionary white radicals. This tendency has recently become so marked that Stokely Carmichael has denounced the Panthers for deserting the nationalist cause.

One local organization, Dodge Revolutionary Union Movement (DRUM), was founded in 1968 by automobile workers in Detroit who believed that both the union and the employers oppressed them. Successfully organizing on the basis of the specific problems of young black laborers, DRUM inspired similar groups in other automobile plants who early in 1969 formed a League of Revolutionary Black Workers. The DRUM constitution (Document 77) presents an analysis of the present condition of black people, a solution, and an organizational structure. This spreading of revolutionary nationalist ideologies to the factories is perhaps one of the most significant developments of this period.

72. GENERAL G. BAKER, JR.: "MY FIGHT IS FOR FREEDOM: UHURU, LIBERTAD, HALAUGA, AND HARAMBEE!"

Gentlemen:

This letter is in regards to a notice sent to me, General Gordon Baker, Jr., requesting my appearance before an examining station to determine my fitness for military service.

How could you have the NERVE knowing that I am a black man living under the scope and influence of America's racist, decadent society??? You did not ask me if I had any morals, principles, or basic human values by which to live. Yet, you ask if I am qualified. QUALIFIED FOR WHAT, might I ask? What does being "Qualified" mean: qualified to serve in the U.S. Army? . . . To be further brainwashed into the insidious notion of "defending freedom"?

You stand before me with the dried blood of Patrice Lumumba on your hands, the blood of defenseless Panamanian

General G. Baker, Jr., "Letter to Draft Board 100, Wayne County, Detroit, Michigan," SOULBOOK, II (Spring 1965), 133–134. Reprinted by permission of the author.

students, shot down by U.S. marines; the blood of my black brothers in Angola and South Africa who are being tortured by the Portuguese and South African whites (whom you resolutely support) respectively; the dead people of Japan, Korea, and now Vietnam, in Asia; the blood of Medgar Evers, six Birmingham babies, the blood of one million Algerians slaughtered by the French (whom you supported); the *fresh* blood of ten thousand Congolese patriots dead from your ruthless rape and plunder of the Congo—the blood of defenseless women and children burned in villages from Napalm jelly bombs . . . With all of this blood of my non-white brothers dripping from your fangs, you have the damned AUDACITY to ask me if I am "qualified." White man; listen to me for I am talking to you!

I AM A MAN OF PRINCIPLES AND VALUES: principles of justice and national liberation, self-determination, and respect for national sovereignty. Yet, you ask if I am "physically fit" to go to Asia, Africa, and Latin America to fight my oppressed brothers (who are completely and resolutely within their just rights to free their fatherland from foreign domination). You ask me if I am qualified to join an army of FOOLS, ASSASSINS and MORAL DELINQUENTS who are not worthy of being called men! You want me to defend the riches reaped from the super-exploitation of the darker races of mankind by a few white, rich, super-monopolists who control the most vast empire that has ever existed in man's one million years of History—all in the name of "Freedom"!

Why, here in the heart of America, 22 million black people are suffering unsurmounted toil: exploited economically by every form of business—from monopolists to petty hustlers; completely suppressed politically; deprived of their social and cultural heritage.

But, all men of principle are fighting-men! My fight is for Freedom: UHURU, LIBERTAD, HALAUGA, and HARAMBEE! Therefore, when the call is made to free South Africa; when the call is made to liberate Latin America from the United Fruit Co., Kaiser and Alcoa Aluminum Co., and from Standard Oil; when the call is made to jail the exploiting Brahmins in

India in order to destroy the Caste System; when the call is made to free the black delta areas of Mississippi, Alabama, South Carolina; when the call is made to FREE 12TH STREET HERE IN DETROIT!: when these calls are made, send for me, for these shall be Historical Struggles in which it shall be an honor to serve!

Venceremos!
General G. Baker, Jr.

73. MAX STANFORD:
"REVOLUTIONARY NATIONALISM,
BLACK NATIONALISM,
OR JUST PLAIN BLACKISM"

A. TOWARDS REVOLUTIONARY ACTION
MOVEMENT MANIFESTO

RAM was officially organized in the winter of 1963 by Afro-Americans who favored Robert F. Williams and the concept of organized violence. Through a series of workshop discussions, the group decided there was a need for a "Third Force" or movement that would be somewhere between the Nation of Islam (Black Muslims) and SNCC (Student Non-Violent Co-ordinating Committee.)

Objectives

1. To give black people a sense of racial pride, dignity, unity and solidarity in struggle.

Max Stanford, "Towards Revolutionary Action Movement Manifesto," CORRESPONDENCE (March 1964), pp. 3, 5.

2. To give black people a new image of manhood and womanhood.

3. To free black people from colonial and imperialist bondage everywhere and to take whatever steps necessary to achieve that goal.

4. To give black people a sense of purpose.

The motto was "One Purpose, One Aim, One Destiny," meaning:

ONE PURPOSE—To free black people from the universal slave-master (slang for capitalist oppression).

ONE AIM—To develop black people through struggle to the highest attainment possible.

ONE DESTINY—To follow in the spirit of black revolutionaries such as Gabriel Prosser, Toussaint L'Overture, Denmark Vesey, Nat Turner, Sojourner Truth, Harriet Tubman, Frederick Douglass, Marcus Garvey, Dr. DuBois, Robert F. Williams, and to create a new world free of colonialism, racism, imperialism, exploitation, and national oppression.

Thus RAM was officially organized as a movement. With rotating chairmen to develop leadership, RAM immediately plunged into action. It helped organize one of Philadelphia's largest black mass rallies for the NAACP over the issue of a "research project" designed by white liberals for the black community.

We felt a need for "fresh, young and new ideas" to be discussed in the black community, so we began publishing a bi-monthly *Black America*. RAM then organized several street meetings in the heart of the black ghetto to bring its program to our people, obtained an office, and began to hold free weekly African and Afro-American history classes. Through a free weekly publication, *Ram Speaks*, RAM attempted to raise the consciousness of the black community by the discussion of political issues.

RAM found, through its active involvement and living with the black masses, that one of the main reasons that we (black people) are unorganized is because we (black people) are politically unaware. RAM then reorganized its program to education in political revolution. We soon saw that the key to the black man's plight is his lack of revolutionary organization. We felt that this could best be brought about by the organization of a black political party. But we also felt that this black political party must have revolutionary objectives and not that of peaceful co-existence with the oppressor. In other words, we felt the need for a black revolution that could and would seize power.

In spreading revolutionary concepts throughout the community and especially among youth, RAM became a target for the power structure. When RAM demonstrated, along with many other groups over the racist-fascist police tactics used against unarmed women, children and men in Birmingham, the NAACP tried to oust RAM from a "united" picket line because of its sign stating, "We do not advocate non-violence in a police state." The more RAM pushed, the more the reformist leadership had to sound aggressive. When the NAACP decided to organize demonstrations over union discrimination on a school construction site, RAM played a major role. The racist-fascist police seized the opportunity to attack some RAM organizers and frame them on trumped-up charges of assault and battery, cutting, disorderly conduct, disturbing the peace, and conspiracy.

It soon became apparent that the NAACP and CORE were fighting to get headlines, so RAM ceased its public program and began to develop its members and those around them. RAM felt this was necessary since, in order to make our black revolt into a successful black revolution, we would have to train people in what real revolution means and what it is going to take.

To answer some questions raised by "orthodox black nationalists" and charges that RAM is an integrationist group, I will explain why we participated in the school construction site struggle.

As revolutionary black nationalists, we do not believe that standing on the street corners alone will liberate our people. Revolutionary black nationalists must act as a vanguard to show our people how to seize power so that they may gain some control over their lives. The main reason they are treated the way they are is that they are powerless. In the school construction site demonstration, our people saw the system denying them opportunity. As our struggle developed, they saw that the police who represent the state or state power were not on our side but on the side of those who uphold racism. This brought in the concept of government, protection of the community by a black people's police force, and the concept that we are at war with white America. Thus by our action, our people gained a vital lesson in the need for a revolutionary organization that has power by physical example and involvement.

RAM soon found that just being out in the streets was not enough and that national revolutionary organization was the key to victory of our revolution. RAM also shifted its program to an accent on youth. After careful analysis through action and study, RAM feels that black youth are the key to our revolution. We see youth all over the world leading the revolutions of our people. In the Angolan liberation army the soldiers' age range is 17-20; in the Congo's guerilla force called "Youth" the age range is 14-20; in the Viet Cong the age range is 14-19; in Kenya the Mau Mau was started by roving bands of youth. In Cuba Castro's forces were very young.

During the summer of 1963 RAM reorganized and sent field organizers throughout the North to help local groups organize demonstrations. Through our experience we have developed an organization on three levels of involvement: 1) *Field Organizers*, who are full-time organizers with a period of orientation and training in the movement; 2) *Active Members*, who cannot be full-time but actively support RAM by physical, financial and other help, and have also been through a period of orientation; 3) *Associate Members*, who have been through a period of orientation but, for reasons approved by the movement, cannot give physical support but do pledge financial support. During the fall of 1963, RAM field organizers helped groups throughout the South develop a perspective beyond the limits of the integrationist movement. Also in Philadelphia, RAM's home base, RAM in 1962 and 1963 fought several cases of police brutality and in one case achieved unity among the young black militant groups for a brief period. RAM has recently been active in organizing demonstrations around the frame-up of Mae Mallory and the other Monroe defendants.

RAM philosophy

RAM philosophy may be described as revolutionary nationalism, black nationalism or just plain blackism. It is that black people of the world (darker races, black, yellow, brown, red, oppressed peoples) are all enslaved by the same forces. RAM's philosophy is one of the world black revolution or world revolution of oppressed peoples rising up against their former slave-masters. Our movement is a movement of black people who are coordinating their efforts to create a "new world" free from exploitation and oppression of man to man.

In the world today there is a struggle for world power between two camps, the haves (Western or white capitalist nations) and the have-nots (Eastern or newly independent nations struggling for independence, socialist nations). There are two types of nationalism. One type suppresses or oppresses, that is, a nation or particular group reaps profits or advances materially at the expense, exploitation, slavery or torture of another group or nation. In this nation and in the world today, this nationalism is considered "white nationalism" or the cooperation of the white Western nations to keep the new emerging oppressed world in bondage. This is capitalist or reactionary nationalism. The other type of nationalism is to liberate or free from exploitation. That is the binding force of a nation or particular group to free itself from a group or nation that is suppressing or oppressing it. In this country and in the world, this is considered black nationalism or revolutionary nationalism.

We can see that black nationalism is the opposite of white nationalism; black nationalism being revolutionary and white being reactionary. We see also that nationalism is really inter-nationalism today.

While defining nationalism as a force towards black libera-tion, we define nationalism as black patriotism.

Nationalism is an identification and consciousness of our own kind and self. Knowledge of self is an integral part of national-ism. Knowledge of our own history of struggle is an essential part of nationalism. Love for our own people and not for the enemy is nationalism.

RAM feels that with the rise of fascism, the black man must not only think of armed self-defense but must also think aggressively.

Our black nation is still in captivity. RAM feels that the road to freedom is self-government, national liberation and black power. Our slogan is "Unite or perish." Our definition of revo-lution is one group's determination to take power away from another.

In ending this manifesto, we (RAM) say, "Think what you wish, but we shall accomplish what we will."

B. A MESSAGE FROM JAIL

The following proposals were released by Brother Stanford on March 5, 1968:

1. The African-American in the U.S. should demand inde-pendent Black Nationhood and take the U.S. government to the world court, the United Nations, and bring international indictment against the U.S. for its violation of Human Rights and racial war crimes of Genocide.

2. Black people in the U.S. must demand independent Black

"Max Stanford Calls for Independent Black Nation," press release, Afro-American News Service, April 17, 1968, mimeographed.

Nationhood (Land) and Reparations (repayment for racial crimes committed by the U.S. government).

The following message from Max Stanford thoroughly explains and supports his call for Independent Black Nationhood:

The Blackman in America must realize that integration of the Black and white races in the U.S. will never work. He must realize that he is not a citizen denied his rights but a colonized captive held in colonial bondage inside the U.S. Black people in America are a nation within a nation; a colonialized captive African nation. Instead of America establishing a colony in Africa as other European nations did, it brought its colony within its national boundaries.

A second class citizen is a 20th century slave. Our struggle is not a struggle for civil rights; it's a struggle for human rights and self determination. Our struggle is not a domestic problem, it is not a national problem, it is an international problem.

America is an enemy to all freedom loving peoples of the world. America spreads racism all over the world. It is an international racist criminal. It is the Fourth Reich worse than Nazi Germany. America doesn't want us to realize our struggle is one of human rights and nationhood because it knows it could be brought before the U.N. and tried by the world court for its racial crimes of Genocide and branded as a racist colonial power. Our friends worldwide could then help us and our real enemies would be exposed.

But this can never happen as long as we are begging for civil rights. The U.S. government can slaughter us in the streets as it's preparing to do and say it's a domestic problem. As long as we demand integration, we will be shot down in the streets. We must realize there is no mercy in this racist beast. He has proved this by bombing our children in churches, kidnapping young girls, raping our women, assassinating our leaders, lynching and shooting our young men.

We must fight for independence and nationhood like all other freedom loving peoples have done. By demanding an independent Black nation from the land that is rightfully ours: Mississippi, Louisiana, Alabama, Georgia, Florida, Texas, Virginia, South Carolina and North Carolina. The land we tilled, shed blood for 300 years for nothing (slave labor) and a 100 years for dry bones (sharecropping); we can get support from others.

We demand Reparations: repayment for racial crimes and injustices done to us for over 400 years. If we make no demand, how can anyone help us?

We must see through the oppressor's tricknology and take our question of human rights and self determination before the world court. Wake up before you find out too late *America is the Blackman's Battleground.*

THE YEAR 1968,
THE YEAR THE BLACK NATION WILL REALIZE
THAT AMERICA IS THE BLACKMAN'S
BATTLEGROUND

The year 1968 will go down in history as the worst year yet of racial war between blacks and whites since the end of the civil war. It will also be recorded as the year the African-American challenged the question of his so-called second class U.S. citizenship and raised the question of separate nationhood. IT will be remembered as the year the Blackman realized *America is the Blackman's Battleground.*

It's too late to save America. America has a bad case of cancer called racism. For 300 years this cancer has been bred and spread all throughout American society without being checked. At first America benefited from this disease getting free profits, having her economy built from slave labor. America eventually built herself an empire from the economic and political exploitation of the Blackman. Its empire became so huge it could send its armies and navy around the world and dominate any nation at will. But like the invincible Greek warrior, Achilles, America had only one weakness, its cancer—racism. Now in the year 1968, America is about to be destroyed by its own creation—the so-called American Negro.

America is about to reap what it has sown. The reason why it's too late for her is because white Americans no longer need

Black slaves or servants; they have machines to replace us. With the rise of automation America doesn't have enough jobs for white people, let alone Black people. The average white man sees the Blackman as a threat. Racist groups are busy inflaming the average white middle-class American into believing the only way to save their way of life is by exterminating 22 million Black Americans. Instead of America admitting the truth of injustices done to the African-American and attempting to repay him, it has chosen instead to eliminate him. These racist groups led by the John Birch Society, Minutemen and KKK have infiltrated the army, government, police force, national guard and are preparing to unleash mass slaughter, a blood bath on the Blackman. The Fourth Reich is here. As time goes on these groups are gaining more control over the white masses. The more the Reich gains control of the white masses, the less tolerant they are to Black demands. Armageddon is here, race war is at hand.

Instead of racial tension getting better, it's getting worse. America is at the point of a race war. As America's economy drains in gold in order to maintain its world empire, it cannot afford racial turmoil within, it has decided to have complete control of the African-American or exterminate him. America is the 20th century Rome. America is the new Nazi Germany— the Fourth Reich.

The year 1968 will be recorded as the year when integration efforts proved a total failure. As the U.S. Army is training special "Black extermination" units, the Black Nation must realize it cannot depend on the federal government to help it or be on its side.

The U.S. government is a government of the majority, by the majority, for the majority—the white majority. When Black peoples fight for freedom no longer helps or benefits the white majority, the white U.S. government will not be on our side. Neither will the white National Guard, white state troopers, white city cops and white state and city governments be on our side. The whole Fourth Reich will be against us and will try to wipe us out when Black Americans rebel against racism.

The Fourth Reich will use the latest techniques of electronic, biological and chemical warfare against us. They know if they lose this war their whole empire will crumble. The Fourth Reich is designing chemicals such as Mace that can paralyze thousands of people at one time and make them helpless; they are working on sirens that make one's bowels break and nerves shatter. They have devices that can be sprayed on crowds that sting, blinds, shines in the dark and can't be washed off. The Fourth Reich will unleash a more brutal war on us than they're waging against the Vietnamese. It wants to kill two birds with one stone this summer—us and the Vietcong. Yes, they will eventually drop Napalm bombs on us. They will throw everything at us they can. This is what the U.S. government is preparing to do to us. Will this stop us? No.

Being outnumbered 9 to 1, each Black American must be physically, mentally and spiritually superior to the enemy. *All forms of self-defense must be well known in the Black community.* Karate, Aikdo, Kung Fu and other forms of martial arts should become the new national past time for Black youth. You must unite and prepare to survive the most vicious racist attack the world has ever seen. Time will teach the Blackman to be as swift as the wind and never fight on the enemy's terms. Time will teach the Blackman never to be where the enemy expect him, *never to fight when the enemy wants him to fight,* to rise in the west, strike in the east; *retreat when the enemy advances.*

The summer of 1968 will be a summer of a fight for survival for Black militants. Black militants will have to be very *wise* if they are to be around in 1969. As H. Rap Brown said when attacked, it's time to stop lootin' and to start shootin'. There are some who say Black Power will come from the barrel of a gun. Only time will tell. Anyway, one thing for sure, 1968 is the year the Blackman had better Arise, Awake, before he realizes too late: America is the Blackman's Battleground.

74. THE REPUBLIC OF NEW AFRICA: "WE ARE THE GOVERNMENT FOR THE NON-SELF-GOVERNING BLACKS HELD CAPTIVE WITHIN THE UNITED STATES"

How would it be possible to effect the transfer of power, money and land from the United States to the Republic of New Africa? In the following interview, Henry attempts to explain it:

Q: Do you consider your government already in existence?

A: Certainly. We are the government for the non-self-governing blacks held captive within the United States. We meet once a week in every consulate, and we have consulates in most of the larger cities right now. New York, Baltimore, Pittsburgh, Philadelphia, Washington, Chicago, Cleveland—you name it. We're thin in the West, but we have strong consulates in Los Angeles and San Francisco. Soon we will be organizing a Congress.

Q: Are these just paper consulates?

A: They are real consulates with a consul and a vice-consul and at least two secretaries. We *should* be issuing passports but if we did the U.S. government would probably use that as an excuse to crack down on us.

Q: How do you propose shifting your government-in-exile into the Deep South and setting up a government-in-fact?

A: We have already begun the shift. We have bought a hundred acres in Mississippi. That isn't much land but it is sufficient for a base headquarters. Like the Jews moving into Israel we will start to organize along the lines of cooperative and collective farms. You have to be able to feed your people. But the collective farm does more than just provide food. It's a center where people can get together, can politic themselves and can protect themselves.

From Robert Sherill, interview with Milton Henry, ESQUIRE (January 1969), pp. 73, 75. Reprinted by permission of ESQUIRE magazine. © 1968 by Esquire, Inc.

Q: How many blacks will you ship into Mississippi to take control?

A: It won't have to be many. With a small movement of people we can do it. There are less than three million people in Mississippi and the blacks are already more than forty percent; in some counties they are fifty to seventy-five percent. Having a majority isn't meaningful until the day comes when we have enough people standing at the polls with guns to protect our vote.

Q: Does that mean you intend to seize the ballot machinery by democratic methods or by force?

A: Nothing is really peaceful. We may have to use arms. We will take over Mississippi county by county. To do that, we must have the power to get our votes counted. This embraces two needs: the power to ward off economic pressure and the power to ward off physical pressure. The reason we are setting up a Black Legion is so we will get our votes counted. If you bring in enough voters to take over a county, that gives you a sheriff. If you are wise in selecting your county—particularly in the Mississippi delta—you will have a large number of blacks to build with. Then we will have a legitimate military force, legitimate under U.S. law, made up of people who can be deputized and armed. The influence we will then exercise over the whole area of Mississippi will immediately be disproportionate to the numbers under our command. If we had only four sheriffs down there, with all that can be done with deputizing, we could change the state of Mississippi. Why did the Jews go into the Palestinian area and buy land? Because it gave them a base from which they could legitimately say, "We have land and we want to change the sovereignty." That's the way we are operating already.

Q: Where are you getting your money to buy the land? And where will you get your money to ship in blacks from the North?

A: Each black citizen is asked to buy one-hundred-dollar Malcolm X land certificates. It's something he can cherish and show to his children to prove he helped set up the black nation. The average black man can afford a hundred dollars. He can afford money for everything else under the sun—he doesn't have any objection to buying the most expensive automobiles and everything else, and they wear out in three years. He sure can afford a hundred dollars to put down on his land.

Q: Will you feel you can take over the five states when you have five black governors?

A: We may not have to wait until we control these governors' offices before we make our demands as a new nation. The real question is not whether we control the governors but whether we control the land, and we can do that by controlling the sheriffs. That's the important thing: having physical control of the land. In terms of real control of the land and real confrontation—there will be other things going on in this country. It could be burned to the ground while U.S. officials are playing games with us. They could be engaged in very costly guerrilla activities. The problems in the North aren't going to be settled. We say the U.S. government will talk to us, and they will talk seriously to us about separation prior to the time we control the governors.

Q: If the government sees what you are up to and moves in to stop you, do you think you could whip the U.S. Army?

A: With the aid of nuclear weapons from our allies, such as China, sure we could. China could never help us until we could show that we were capable of a separate, independent existence. But we could show that by controlling a land mass. We could show it by the actual fact that we were there and had a majority of the people and were not subject to U.S. jurisdiction. Then China would back us with missiles. But we don't want to fight. It's better to have nice relations. We would only have to neutralize the U.S. Army, not fight it. We don't want another Vietnam, flames and napalm. Neutralizing the U.S. is the only way Castro could survive, and that's the way we would do it, too.

Q: At this point China is only a tentative hope for you to rely on. What do you have in the way of retaliatory firepower to fall back on until you can be sure of China's help?

A: We've got second-strike power right now in our guerrillas within the metropolitan areas—black men, armed. Say we started taking over Mississippi—which we are capable of doing right now—and the United States started to interfere. Well, our guerrillas all over the country would strike. Our second-strike capability would be to prevent the United States Armed Forces from working us over, not the local forces. The local forces couldn't compete with our forces. We can handle them. The second-strike capability already exists, and all the United States has to do to find out is to make the wrong move. The guerrillas will be operative until we take possession of the physical land. Ultimately, when we have the land, we will get the missiles from around the world.

Q: What makes you think the U.S. will let you have the land when they wouldn't let the Confederacy secede?

A: It's a different situation. The South could be defeated separately, but if the whites defeat our objectives, the country will be ruined in the process. There are a sizable number of people who want self-determination, separation, land. They want that more than life itself. They can't shoot all of us. They can't shoot enough to discourage others. You see, the Revolutionary War would not have worked if that could have happened. And the war in Vietnam *isn't* doing so good. They aren't going to win in Vietnam and they can't win in the United States. We can fight from within. How are they going to get us out of here? Where would they make the guns to shoot us—in the United States? Do you think we are just going to let them keep on making guns? How will they transport their guns and soldiers —on railroad trains? The United States can be destroyed.

Q: Do you mean you would do all this by sabotage and guerrilla warfare?

A: Obviously. We're within the country. This country will either talk to the separatists today or will talk to them later. At which time perhaps this country will have lost a great deal, in terms of lives and property.

Q: As for the blacks who stay behind in the United States after you separate, how do you foresee defending them from revenge?

A: I don't think that is possible, and this is one reason why most of them will come with us. It would be like Germany. Some would want to stay behind, but you get rid of ambivalence by oppression. There were some Zionists who even kind of welcomed the oppression because it helped unify the people toward the ideal of creating a nation. We've always said the white man is making more converts than we ever could. Every day the police walk through the black ghettos they make more converts than we can.

Q: When you have cut away the South as your own nation, what would happen to the industries that are already there, such as the steel companies around Birmingham?

A: We keep them. We take them and we keep them. The United States would pay reparations to those companies as part of our conditions for separation. The U.S. could give the companies tax credits for their losses. In those terms it wouldn't be very costly to the U.S. And of course our government would operate the plants. We don't have any hang-ups on socialism, which we call "ujaama," which is broader than socialism. It's an African conception of the organization of society. It means we have total responsibility for one another.

Q: Where will you get your technicians during the transition period?

A: If we need outside technicians, they'll be given resident visas. White people who feel they can live in the kind of society we're talking about can stay. But they'll have to be cognizant of the fact that we'll have a new kind of law. The white industrialists and technicians have too much power in Africa. I'm impressed every time I go back there—they have too damn much power in Africa. One of the things Castro did that helped his survival was to cut off the head of the industrial monster in the midst of his government. This is one of the problems in Algeria—they can't get out from under this economic thing. Those industrial guys are *powerful*.

Q: Since many of the whites who stayed on would hate your guts, wouldn't you be afraid of sabotage and guerrilla reprisals from them?

A (laughing): That kind of white would want to move. They'd

say, "Those goddamned niggers." I know there'd be a lot of people calling the President a bastard. Some of us who are helping getting the thing underway may never live to see the actual fruition of the government. But the government will go on.

Q: You say that your black followers are arming themselves for the day of separation. But where is this evident? If the blacks were really arming in large numbers, seriously, wouldn't the destruction and bloodshed in the riots of recent years have been far greater than it was?

A: The blacks have been arming along defense lines so far. We are now going through the period of holding action. But most astute people see that a different pattern is developing. Everywhere you can see a frustration, the willingness on the part of black people to say the hell with it. Some black people right now are so keyed up they just want to shoot it out. They want it all right now—right now. They don't want to wait. So far there has been sparing use of the gun and the Molotov cocktail. But we are urging that every black home have a gun for self-defense against the possibility of a Treblinka.

75. JAMES BOGGS: "THE FINAL CONFRONTATION"

Back in the early 1960's, at the time of the burning of the buses in Anniston, Alabama, which is not far from Birmingham, I proposed to the UAW that it immediately dispatch a busload of workers, Black and white, to Alabama to test what the Klan in 'Bama would do. I was, of course, not only interested in testing the Alabama Klan. I was also testing the readiness of the

James Boggs, "The Final Confrontation," LIBERATOR, VIII (March 1968), pp. 4–8. Copyright © 1968 by LIBERATOR. Reprinted by permission of LIBERATOR.

organized labor movement and of Northern white workers to clash with other whites on the issue of integration, which they allegedly supported.

The UAW took the easy way out. Instead of confronting the rank and file with this proposal, the leadership made a financial contribution to the NAACP—an organization which had already discredited itself by ousting Robert Williams (now in exile in China) from the presidency of the Monroe, North Carolina, branch of the NAACP because he had advocated Black people defending themselves from nightriding terrorist Klansmen (in his famous "Meet violence with violence" proposal). Today, nearly seven years later, the same Northern white workers who thought it was so noble for Black men and women not to defend themselves and their children from howling, club-swinging mobs in the South have themselves formed part of cursing, howling, bottle-throwing mobs and are openly arming and calling upon official and unofficial bodies to equip themselves with the most modern weaponry to try to push Blacks back into their place.

It was this same bus-burning incident which caused me to write an article entitled "The Second Civil War Has Begun in the U.S.A." I was at that time chairman of a small radical newspaper called *Correspondence,* and there was much heated debate in the organization (which was primarily white) over the article. People argued that a civil war situation did not exist in the United States on the race issue because there were not enough people on each side clashing over fundamental issues. After all, they said, Blacks were only asking to be like whites and to be a part of the system. They were not clashing with whites, and they were not clashing with the system.

In one sense their argument was a sound one. At that time, Black people were still appealing to the moral conscience of America. They were only asking for civil rights, which are, after all, only the normal rights which a nation grants to its citizens. Black people had not yet learned that rights are what you make and take, and that it takes power to beget rights and even more power to secure and insure those rights after they have been begotten. Black people had also not realized that any claims which the American people—Christian, atheist or agnostic— had to moral behavior had been refuted by their own history. This nation was built on the extermination of one race and the systematic degradation of another. It saw nothing wrong in fighting a war to free itself from colonial oppression and then continuing to keep Blacks in colonial oppression. Nearly a hundred years later it saw nothing wrong in allegedly fighting a civil war to free Blacks from slavery and then making a compromise to establish a new form of servitude for those Blacks, so that the nation could go on its merry way industrializing itself with the labor of immigrants.

But this is history we all know. What is new is that we are now in the early stages of another civil war and the system which was created by the last civil war is collapsing all around us. *The key to the future lies in being able to resist the temptation to reform the system so that it can work*. It is not difficult to recognize that a system is in trouble. What is difficult is to recognize this and at the same time recognize that *all* attempts to reform the system will in the end only create more bitterness and conflict with those forces already in motion, forces which can only survive by transforming the system from top to bottom. The example of Vietnam should always be kept in mind. In Vietnam, anything short of total revolutionary control of the entire country by the National Liberation Front—in other words, any attempt to set up other institutions to reform the system as the United States is attempting to do with one South Vietnamese government after another—means a bloody and extended civil war. *The only way to make the civil war briefer and less bloody is to hasten the destruction of the system by the revolutionary social forces*.

In Detroit today the Establishment is now trying to save the system by placing its own negro leader, William Patrick, at the head of a task force to build a "New Detroit" in the closest relation to multi-county government. It is the same thing that the United States is attempting in Vietnam, and it is sowing the seeds for the same kind of result.

There is a great difference between the issues that were posed in the first civil war and those that are being posed in today's civil war. The first was fought because one force in American society—the industrialists and the working people in the North—wanted to be the one to decide how the West should be developed, while another force, in the South, had its own plans. The issue was whether the West should be developed as a wheat-growing country by homesteading Northerners to act as a breadbasket for the rapidly industrializing North, or as cotton country developed by slave-owning Southerners. In other words, the fight was over who should control the West, *not* over any general principle of slave labor vs. free labor and certainly not over that of slave labor vs. free labor in the South.

Once this is understood, it is easy to see why the North was so willing to make the infamous Compromise of 1877 which allowed the South to reintroduce a new form of servitude for Black people in the South. But the American people always prefer to think that they are fighting for great moral principles rather than admit that the real issue is one of power and control. This genius that Americans have for disguising real issues of power as moral issues of principle is one of the chief reasons why we are today faced with a second civil war, one potentially much more complex and dangerous than the first.

The fight today is between two sets of people of two different races, one race having been systematically damned into underdevelopment in every facet of daily life—political, economic and social—by the other, a race which has pretended that both races were equal while at the same time discriminating against Blacks on the basis of race. The first group, the oppressed race, can therefore only free itself from the second, the oppressing race, by liberating itself as a race. Thus, for Blacks it is a war of national liberation, a war to free themselves as Black people from white America, past, present, and future—from its culture, its way of thinking, its history, its economic system and its politics.

The conflict is not only national but international, because the same white people who have colonized Black people at home have done and are continuing to do the same thing to people of color all over the world.

How have we arrived at this point? For years radicals and liberals have been calling for unity between white and Black workers on the theory that white and Black were only divided by some external force, the ruling class, which is supposed to have created the division so that it could rule. But what this theoretical construct of "Divide and Rule" has failed to recognize is that the so-called lack of unity between white and Black is and has been in reality an antagonism between white workers and Black people, the kind of antagonism which is inevitable between oppressor and oppressed.

When Blacks were unable to get their rights through moral appeal, then they began to realize that they had to get them through power. And getting something through power means that one set of people who are powerless replace another set of people who are in power. Power is always concrete. It involves control of very concrete resources and institutions: (a) *economic resources and institutions,* such as banks and industries and stores; (b) *political resources and institutions,* such as local, state and national governments, courts and police forces; (c) *social resources and institutions,* such as schools and universities, churches, public places, foundations, etc.

Step by step, as Black people have rid themselves of the old rag-thoughts of moral misconceptions which cluttered up their minds, and as white people have revealed their determination to hold on to the resources and institutions of power, the clash has become inevitable. As usual, the more those in power are determined to hold on to their power, the more phrases they use to disguise the real issue. So today, everywhere, the hue and cry is that we must save democracy, enforce law and order, protect majority rule, defend property rights, save the free world, restore liberty and equality, etc., etc. All of these are the empty phrases of those who know that their power is being challenged and who are determined not to yield any real power.

To have some vision of what is necessary we must start not at the bottom but at the very top of this collapsing society. It is a cold fact that neither the present President of the United States nor any of his aides nor any of the present aspirers to the Presidency of the United States could possibly resolve either the chief international issue or the chief domestic issue which faces this nation. The reason is that not one of them, from the moment that he began to exercise any power, could gain or maintain the confidence of the Third World either inside or outside this nation. There is no reason for any of the non-white nations of the world—which contain the majority of the world's people—to believe that the United States, as long as it is ruled by whites, could make a binding treaty that would respect their national sovereignty. The American people say that they believe in majority rule. Yet these two hundred million Americans are led to believe and do believe that they, a minority in the world, are entitled to use all necessary force and all the force at their disposal, to decide the course of the world. Only a Black people in power in this country could sign a treaty safeguarding the national sovereignty of other nations and setting up fair trade and technical exchange relations with other nations which could be acknowledged and respected by other nations.

The first civil war was fought over who would control the West. This civil war is to be fought over who will control the cities. In every major city inside this country, Black people are fast becoming the biggest ethnic majority, having been driven to the cities by the agricultural revolution in the South where they were at one time the only working class, but where their labor is no longer needed. They are also being driven to the cities for political reasons, the Southern whites having realized that if Afro-Americans remained in the counties of the South, they would soon constitute the ruling power in county government by virtue of majority rule. But whether in the North or South, when it comes to Black people the beautiful principle of majority rule is no longer a principle, just as in ancient Greece the beautiful principle of democracy was no longer a principle when it came to the slaves. Throughout the North, as is now obvious, the whites have run away to the suburbs, abandoning the inner city to the Blacks. But they still want to run the city from the suburbs, maintaining their control of the reservation by their blue occupation army of the police at night until they return the next morning to civilize it by their presence. That is how Washington, D.C., is controlled, and the rest of the country follows the pattern of the nation's capital.

It is obvious that Blacks must rule the city from top to bottom. But it is not simply a question of the cities, because the cities are part of a nation. So the city must change its relation to the federal and the state governments. In place of the city-state relations, which have never worked adequately to supply the social and economic needs of the city, new city-federal relations must now be developed. These in turn require a new federal constitution. Therefore, Black political power in the cities is not only a challenge to the suburban whites who want to continue to rule the city and who are devising all kinds of multi-county regional schemes to do so; it is also a direct challenge to the federal government. But the federal government, which is constantly being called upon to intervene in local, city and state matters, is ruling on the basis of a set of constitutional rules and procedures in whose establishment Black people had no voice.

Thus the question of *whose* constitution, *whose* law and order, *whose* equality, *whose* justice, *whose* welfare, becomes a question of what kind of constitution, what kind of law and order, what kind of equality, what kind of justice, what kind of welfare, and the need arises to create a new political, economic and social system.

Let me say right here that no whites can participate directly in the resolution of any of these issues until they have recognized that other whites—not only those in power but those who support the ones in power (i.e., the majority)—are their enemies.

What does this recognition of other whites as enemies mean? Firstly, that these seriously concerned whites have acknowledged that the *others can't be changed by moral persuasion or reason.* Only when this old rag-thought is thrown out will they be able to understand that a struggle for power between them-selves and other whites is inevitable. And only then will they be able to prepare for such a clash. Secondly, it means the recognition that those in power and those who support the whites in power are a direct danger and threat not only to the Black man but to themselves; and that taking control away from those in power is, in fact, a matter of survival.

Only when some whites begin to act upon these fundamental recognitions and achieve power by virtue of their actions on these foundations, can there be a meeting of whites with power with Blacks with power to work out new constitutional pro-cedures under which we can coexist. I am not saying that this will be easy, or even that it is likely to happen, because it is very difficult for the landlord to listen to the tenant, and it is even harder for those who are identified with those in power in every way except in intentions to recognize that the party is over and that it is not whether or not they like it but the cold realities which force the re-evaluation.

(I have not up to now mentioned the church. Whatever it could have done or should have done, it, too, is now caught up in the whirlwind of the revolution. Castro delivered the best message to the church in the early 60's when America thought it could use the church against the revolution. In his May Day speech in 1961, Castro made two important points about the Christian church. Christianity, he pointed out, originated as the religion of the humble, the slaves and the oppressed of Rome. He then reminded the church that it had been able to coexist with the Roman Empire, feudalism, absolute monarchies, and with the democratic republican bourgeoisie, always adapting itself. Why then, he asked, should it not be able to "coexist with a regime which in its social laws and social perspectives, in its defense of human interests and its defense of all men in society, its struggle against exploitation, is so much more like Christi-anity than are the exploitation and cruelty of feudalism, the absolute monarchs, the Roman Empire, the republican bour-geoisie or Yankee imperialism?"

Today most churchgoers are part and parcel of "the man"—no better, no worse. Only history can absolve them, and history may not be so kind.)

White Americans must realize that this country is already in the early stages of a great civil conflict between the revolution and the counterrevolution, both inside the country and outside, a conflict which can end only in the victory of the revolution or in the common ruin of the contending forces.

This conflict already has its own momentum, and as the President's Commission on Riots has pointed out, it is a momentum the majority of Americans will be virtually powerless to alter, whether they want to or not.

76. THE BLACK PANTHER PARTY: "POLITICAL POWER COMES THROUGH THE BARREL OF A GUN"

A. THE BLACK PANTHER PARTY PROGRAM

WHAT WE WANT NOW! WHAT WE BELIEVE

What we want

1. We want freedom. We want power to determine the destiny of our black community.

2. We want full employment for our people.

3. We want an end to the robbery by the white man of our black community.

4. We want decent housing, fit for shelter of human beings.

5. We want education for our people that exposes the true

The Black Panther program, "What we Want Now! What we Believe," THE BLACK PANTHER, March 16, 1968, p. 4.

nature of this decadent American society. We want education that teaches us our true history and our role in the present day society.

6. We want all black men to be exempt from military service.

7. We want an immediate end to *police brutality* and *murder* of black people.

8. We want freedom for all black men held in federal, state, county, and city prisons and jails.

9. We want all black people when brought to trial to be tried in court by a jury of their peer group or people from their black communities, as defined by the Constitution of the United States.

10. We want land, bread, housing, education, clothing, justice and peace.

What we believe

1. We believe that black people will not be free until we are able to determine our destiny.

2. We believe that the federal government is responsible and obligated to give every man employment or a guaranteed income. We believe that if the white American business men will not give full employment, then the means of production should be taken from the business men and placed in the community so that the people of the community can organize and employ all of its people and give a high standard of living.

3. We believe that this racist government has robbed us and now we are demanding the overdue debt of forty acres and two mules. Forty acres and two mules was promised 100 years ago as retribution for slave labor and mass murder of black people. We will accept the payment in currency which will be distributed to our many communities. The Germans are now aiding the Jews in Israel for the genocide of the Jewish people. The Germans murdered 6,000,000 Jews. The American racist has taken part in the slaughter of over 50,000,000 black people; therefore, we feel that this is a modest demand that we make.

4. We believe that if the white landlords will not give decent housing to our black community, then the housing and the

land should be made into cooperatives so that our community, with government aid, can build and make decent housing for its people.

5. We believe in an educational system that will give to our people a knowledge of self. If a man does not have knowledge of himself and his position in society and the world, then he has little chance to relate to anything else.

6. We believe that black people should not be forced to fight in the military service to defend a racist government that does not protect us. We will not fight and kill other people of color in the world who, like black people, are being victimized by the white racist government of America. We will protect ourselves from the force and violence of the racist police and the racist military, by whatever means necessary.

7. We believe we can end police brutality in our black community by organizing black *self defense* groups that are dedicated to defending our black community from racist police oppression and brutality. The Second Amendment of the Constitution of the United States gives us a right to bear arms. We therefore believe that all black people should arm themselves for *self defense*.

8. We believe that all black people should be released from the many jails and prisons because they have not received a fair and impartial trial.

9. We believe that the courts should follow the United States Constitution so that black people will receive fair trials. The 14th Amendment of the U.S. Constitution gives a man a right to be tried by his peer group. A peer is a person from a similar economic, social, religious, geographical, environmental, historical and racial background. To do this the court will be forced to select a jury from the black community from which the black defendant came. We have been and are being tried by all white juries that have no understanding of the "average reasoning man" of the black community.

10. When in the course of human events, it becomes necessary for one people to dissolve the political bonds which have connected them with another, and to assume among the powers of the earth, the separate and equal station to which the laws of

nature and nature's God entitle them, a decent respect to the opinions of mankind requires that they should declare the causes which impel them to separation. We hold these truths to be self-evident, that all men are created equal, that they are endowed by their Creator with certain inalienable rights, that among these are life, liberty and the pursuit of happiness. That to secure these rights, governments are instituted among men, deriving their just powers from the consent of the governed,— that *whenever any form of government becomes destructive of these ends, it is the right of people to alter or to abolish it, and to institute new government, laying its foundation on such principles and organizing its powers in such form as to them shall seem most likely to effect their safety and happiness.*

Prudence, indeed, will dictate that governments long established should not be changed for light and transient causes; and accordingly all experience hath shewn, that mankind are more disposed to suffer, while evils are sufferable, than to right themselves by abolishing the forms to which they are accustomed. *But when a long train of abuses and usurpations, pursuing invariably the same object, evinces a design to reduce them under absolute despotism, it is their right, it is their duty, to throw off such government, and to provide new guards for their future security.*

GUNS BABY GUNS

B. AN INTERVIEW WITH HUEY P. NEWTON

An Exclusive Interview with Minister of Defense, Huey P. Newton in the Attornies' Room, Alameda County Jail, March 8, 1968. Present were: Charles R. Garry, [Newton's] Attorney;

"In Defense of Self Defense: An Exclusive Interview
with Minister of Defense, Huey P. Newton,"
THE BLACK PANTHER, March 16, 1968, pp. 4, 16–18.

Ray Rodgers, Los Angeles Times; *Joan Didia,* Saturday Evening Post; *Colin Edwards, KPFA; and Eldridge Cleaver,* Ramparts Magazine *and* The Black Panther *Newspaper.*

Q: Why did you drop the words for self defense from the official name of your organization?

A:. We ran into the problem of people misinterpreting us as a political party. They use the words for self defense to define us as a group that is paramilitary, or body guards, or something of this nature. But we found that it was very difficult, even though in our program we described or defined ourselves as a political party, people seemed to misinterpret the definition of what self defense was all about. We realize that when we are assaulted in the community by the gestapo tactics of the police that this is also a political thing. We are assaulted because we are black people, because the power structure finds it to their advantage to keep us imprisoned in our black community as colonized people are kept by a foreign power. So, the police is only an arm of the white power structure used very similarly to their military force—which it is—the local police is a military force, then there's the National Guard as the national police, and then there's the regular military as the international police. These police are used to occupy our community just as foreign troops occupy territory. The police don't live in our community, they have no respect for black people who do live in the community, yet they occupy the community. And they are not there occupying the community for the welfare and benefit of the people who live there, they are occupying it to make sure that the white businessmen who are systematically robbing our community are safe. So, this was part of our political stand—to make the Party basically clear for the intellectuals, because the grass roots of the community, the people we're most concerned with, the lower class black who represents about ninety-five per cent of the black population throughout this nation understood very well what we stood for. But, to make it clear to every one we changed the name to the Black Panther Party, to make it clear what our political stand was about.

Q: Mr. Newton, some newspapers, radio stations and television sort of brands the Black Panther leadership, you and

Mr. Seale and others, as anti-white, racists, or counterracists. Would you like to clear up this matter?

A: Yes, the Black Panther Party is against racism, we're not racists. But we stand to protect the black community, to rid America of racism. We're subject to the tactics of racists by the white establishment, but it's a very common thing for the people who are in control of the mass media to define the victim as a criminal, or to define the victim of racism as a racist. This is just a propaganda device that's used by the power structure so that they will gain support throughout the white community, a small portion of which happens not to be racist. But to consolidate *their* troops, they will claim that *we* want racism, and therefore turn all white people against us.

Q: Have you felt good about some of the young white people coming out in support of your case, and taking a political position on it?

A: Yes, the white revolutionaries or the enlightened part of the white community has responded and come to the defense of the vanguard group of the black community, which is the Black Panther Party. We think that we'll see more of this in the future.

Q: Would you tell us some more about yourself, your life, before the Black Panther Party?

A: I think that before the Black Panther Party that my life was very similar to that of most black people in the country. I'm from a lower class, working class family and I've suffered abuses of the power structure and I've responded as black people are responding now, so I see very little difference in my personality than any other black person living here in racist America.

Q: What shapes your attitude towards the racist institutions you're indicting?

A: Living here in America. It reminds me of a quote from James Baldwin. He says that, "To be black and conscious in America is to be in a constant state of rage," and I think that this is very true of black people in general in this country. Many black people, most black people, as I said, are uneducated and they're not used to handling academic things and administrating. So their response might have been somewhat different than mine, but they will rally behind a political party that's representing their grievances. So, all the Black Panther Party has done is to articulate and bring out the grievances of the black community.

Q: Can you recall some incident that sort of brought home to you the attitude of the majority of white people toward Negroes and the attitude of the white establishment?

A: You would like a specific incident?

Q: To bring home to people how this can scar one's soul.

A: I can understand that, it's very difficult for me to cite one specific incident because it's a very long process. I started to say that, "for a white person to understand, let him come to the black community," but this wouldn't be a good example, because he couldn't experience the alienation and the antagonistic attitudes of blacks that we receive in the white community. We live in a world, in white America here and any time a white person goes to the black community or a black country I doubt very seriously whether he experiences this alienation, because black people seem to have some priority on being humanist for some reason. Perhaps its a historical reason, I can't pinpoint why, but we seem to be more fair, as a people, to other people, than anyone else in the world.

Q: Have you had a chance to see this President's Commission on Civil Disorders Report?

A: I read a couple of accounts of it, yes.

Q: Did it seem pretty close to the mark?

A: I think that some of the statements in the report hit the mark, but as far as the conclusions or the solutions to the problem, I think they were wanting in that direction.

Q: Do you think the white establishment and white people as a whole will take it to heart and do something really effective to solve this problem of racism that it portrays?

A: I doubt seriously whether white America is mature enough and mentally well enough to solve this problem without a great catastrophe.

Q: Are you optimistic about your trial? Do you think it will be a fair trial?

A: Well, I think that black people will make sure that I receive a fair trial. I have no faith at all in the court system, because I've already suffered an injustice by being indicted by an all-white middle class Grand Jury, and so from my prior experiences I would expect no change. I also expect black people to come to my aid and to put pressure and see by any means necessary that all black men receive a fair trial, that's including those who are held in the various prisons and county jails at the present time. We're demanding immediate release for them because we realize they've suffered the same kind of injustice that I'm suffering now.

Q: You know the Peace and Freedom Party has sought to have you run as their candidate in the Seventh Congressional District, and we understand that you stated that if the Peace and Freedom Party would endorse the Ten Point Program of the Black Panther Party, then you would feel free to run. Would you like to comment on that?

A: That's very true. The Black Panther Party feels that the essentials that we cited in our platform, the Ten Point Program, is necessary for any group to accept if we're going to work in coalition with them. It's the basic things that the black community desires and needs; it's the basic demands of the black community. And without accepting the basic demands we would feel that the person who is seeking coalition is insincere if he cannot accept these ten basic philosophies.

Q: One of the points in the Ten Point Program [is to release] all black people from the draft, right?

A: Yes, that's part of it, we have a Ten Point Program of what we want and what we believe. We state that black people should not be made to fight in a war, to serve a military, to serve a government that is not working in our benefit, that's not working for our general welfare. That if the government is working against black people, and for the destruction of black people, we don't see any need at all for black people to serve in that military that's oppressing other colored peoples throughout the world. So we are demanding that all black men be released from the military service until this government rights the wrongs that have been perpetrated against us.

Q: Is this in objection to a specific war or an objection to our government?

A: It's an objection to the specific war in particular and the governmental in general. We don't see where we would fight anyone for this racist government. It's only oppressing people for economic and racial reasons, as they're oppressing us in our black colony throughout America.

Q: How do you stand in relation to some black nationalist group, like Ron Karenga's in Watts, let's say?

A: In the first place, the Black Panther Party is a political party. I don't believe that Ron Karenga claims to be a political organ. And secondly, Ron Karenga and some other nationalistic groups seem to be somewhat hung up on surviving Africanisms, or what we call cultural nationalism. Cultural Nationalism deals with a return to the old culture of Africa and that we are somehow freed by identifying and returning to this culture, to the African cultural stage of the 1100's or before then. Somehow they believe that they will be free through identifying in this manner. As far as we are concerned, we believe that it's important for us to recognize our origins and to identify with the revolutionary black people of Africa and people of color throughout the world. But as far as returning, per se to the ancient customs, we don't see any necessity in this. And also, we say that the only culture that is worth holding on to is revolutionary culture, for change, for the better. We say the only way we're going to be free is by seizing political power which comes through the barrel of a gun. We say that we will identify so that we will have this consolidation of people: so we will have strength and we will respect ourselves and have the dignity of our past, but there are many things connected to the culture that we don't feel is necessary to return to.

Q: The Black Panther Party title and symbol was produced. I believe, by SNCC in Mississippi and Alabama when they started the Black Panther Party or movement down there. Was this what gave inspiration to the creation of the Black Panther Party?

A: Yes, I was very impressed by the political party in Lowndes County. It called itself a freedom organization and they used the black panther as their symbol. They used the black panther because of the nature of a panther—a panther will not attack anyone but will back up first. But if the assailant is persistent, then the black panther will strike out and wipe out his aggressor, thoroughly, wholly, absolutely, and completely. So we thought that the symbol would be very appropriate for us. Also, I was very proud of the move that black people in Lowndes County made.

Q: Do you get any support from overseas?

A: At this time, black people all over the world are supporting each other. We realize that we're being treated by racist America within the country as other colonized people are treated abroad. We are abused for economic and race reasons.

Q: The communications are kind of bad up here between Huey and the outside world. They have imposed restrictions on newspapers and magazines, books, and so forth, which would keep him informed on what's going on around the world, very essential information. Were he able to get news from the outside, he would know that while Stokely Carmichael was in Africa, a Free Huey rally was held in Tanzania and President Kwame Nkrumah and Sékou Touré issued public statements to the effect that Huey Newton should be set free. So there is an awareness. News, clippings, and so forth are sent around the world and people around the world are aware of the pivotal nature of the case. If you are acquitted and set free, I presume you'll continue into a political career. Have you thought of returning to law, or are you definitely bound for a political career?

A: As far as career is concerned, I have one desire and that is to go on fighting for the liberation of black people throughout the world, and in particular black people here in America. I would like to relate to the Black Panther Party and our political stand that black people must arm themselves. I think that this has been misinterpreted in a number of ways many times. We make the statement, quoting it from Chairman Mao, that Political Power comes through the Barrel of a Gun. The Black Panther Party has analyzed the statement and comes up with a clear realization that any time a people are unarmed and that the administrators of that country maintain a regular police force and a regular military, and the people of that country are unarmed, they are either slaves or subject to slavery at any given moment that that administration desires to inflict the force of that military or police upon the people. So we say that as long as the military or police force is armed, then black people should arm themselves. Many people have spoken of violence or of our advocating violence. Well, we're not advocating violence. We're advocating that we defend ourselves from the aggression. That if America is armed, and if it's right for America to arm herself and even commit violence throughout the world, then it's right for black people to arm themselves. If it's wrong for black people to commit this violence in self-defense, then it's wrong for America to commit this violence against people in America and throughout the world. This reminds me of a statement that Ronald Reagan made shortly after our appearance at the capital. He said something to the effect of, "In these enlightened times people cannot and should not influence other people by the use of physical force and the gun." But at the same time we see throughout America that the police are being heavily armed, not only being armed but are escalating the war against black people in our black communities by ordering heavy military equipment. Now we think Reagan should take a look at what he's doing and what the American government is doing before he criticizes black people for arming themselves to defend themselves against the aggression of America.

Q: Do you see yourself as playing a part, say things go through an orderly process now towards reform, playing a part in the political scene through the present political structures?

A: I think that the present political structure is bankrupt and this is what the game is all about. The present political structure has perpetuated and protected and inflicted racism, so we say there has to be a drastic change in the political structure. As far as my running for office. I would only serve one purpose there—as a spokesman to articulate the grievances of the black community. And as far as playing the game that some black politicians have traditionally played, the day has come for this kind of action to stop. This is one of the reasons that we feel it's necessary for us to arm ourselves in a political fashion. It's a very important thing. For instance, when any candidate is going up for political office in the white power structure, he always has political power behind him. You can find political power in a number of areas; you have feudal power, or the farmers who own much land, and of course, they will put a candidate up who will serve their welfare and speak in their behalf. And his political colleagues, the people he has to work with understand that he has this political power behind him. If the farmers don't get what they want, if they don't get the price that they want for the crop, then they'll let the crop rot in the field. And then you have big business power, or economic power, where the people who own big businesses will get behind a candidate and this candidate will simply relay the message of these people who are big business. And it goes on, you have the cattle owners and so forth. We see that black people don't have this political power, they don't have economic power, they don't have land power—we've been robbed. For instance, our black politicians have been ineffective. Much of the time it's not their fault, it's simply because they don't have the grass roots political organization behind them. Even if we can vote for black people, simply to have the vote isn't political power. In the political arena, a thing is not political unless the people can inflict a political consequence if they don't get what they want. And black people in the past haven't been able to inflict this consequence. For instance, according to John Hope Franklin, the reason that Black Reconstruction failed where you had many black candidates holding office in the South wasn't because these black politicians were ignorant or inefficient. Many of the black representatives had been educated in France and in Canada and in

England and they were very efficient. The reason that it failed was because black people did not have economic or military power. After they put their man in office, he was still subject to those people who owned the land, he was still subject to these people who owned the military. So Black Reconstruction failed. We say now that we can develop political power by being a potentially destructive force. That if black people arm themselves in a political fashion, and the aggression is continued against us, we'll be able to offer a political consequence, very similar to Detroit.

Q: There's quite a phenomenon going on in the black community these days. It's quite clear that while you were out, there were a lot of groups and people who opposed your program and refused to approve of the Black Panther Party. But since you've been in jail a lot of people who opposed you have turned over and are now members of your party. Also, it's becoming necessary for people to take a public stand on this issue because the Black community is demanding that. One thing it's demanding is that Willie Brown, in particular, and all other black elected and appointed officials take a public stand. We're asking ones who're members of the Legislature to stand on the floor of the Legislature and speak out in your defense, they're demanding that. It's having a political effect because this is an election year. Byron Rumford and John Miller are trying to run for the same office in the 17th Assembly District. Willie Brown is running again, and John George is seeking to be elected to Congress. And all these people have before them the whole question of where they stand on Huey Newton, and not a meeting goes down without that coming up, and I thought you might be interested in knowing that. Would you expect that to happen?

A: Well, no. I'm very surprised that it did happen. But, after it happened, in retrospect, I understand what's going on. For instance, the black community is now forcing these political candidates into a direction that they want. They realize that they depend on black people to vote for them and black people identify with the Black Panther Party. They identify with the

Party more so now than they did in the past. And the reason for this, in my opinion, is that black people are always impressed by a reality. You could talk all day and articulate all sorts of beautiful things on how things could be and how things are and describing to the point. And you won't get the response that you would when a reality is put before them. Black people have understood what I've talked about and now that I'm being subjected to these very things that I've criticized, they can sympathize with the Party on this. And also, it makes them look around and observe, it brings to their consciousness many things that are happening in the Black community that are wrong. Many things that people have spoken about and many things that people have suggested be changed, and they haven't responded in the magnitude that they're responding now simply because now it's a reality. You cannot deny a reality. Anything that I've said in the past if it didn't relate to the situation, then it was my fault and it wasn't the situation's fault. So black people now are only relating to the reality of their existence. They realize that it's not only Huey Newton who's being persecuted, but it's the black community throughout America. And they are responding in their own defense.

Q: There's been a lot of talk about the generational gap in white families between the young people who are disillusioned with their parents and alienated from them. Is there a certain amount of this among black families, and is this part of the problem you have in bringing more adult black people into the movement?

A: I think that the older black people have realized for a very long time the problems, but they've been wanting in solutions, because in the past, the black political representatives have been somewhat misleading to the black community. In other words, we thought in the past that if we put a representative into office, we automatically got justice. But now its being realized that to have a black man in office doesn't necessarily mean that you're going to get political justice.

Q: Was the reason you dropped your studies of law that you got disgusted with the system of law here?

A: Of course, I'm disgusted with the judicial system, but more than that, I can only do so much, I can only be so many places at a certain time. And I felt it was more important to work to organize within the community than to continue law school.

Q: Are you allowed to have any contact with other prisoners in this courthouse here?

A: No, I'm kept in what's called the H tank. It's used as a hospital tank when someone is hurt. But I've recovered very well, and I've noticed that I haven't been moved away from the hospital cell. And I don't think the deputies here have any intention of moving me because it's been rumored that they don't want me to mix with the other prisoners. Although I've converted many black people, I shouldn't say converted because black people are Panthers by definition, but many people have joined the Party who have come through here simply by screaming back to my cell and I will define the Party and give them some understanding of the political direction of the Party. I haven't been abused here primarily for the reason that the department has been admonished by the black people to keep their hands off. For instance, when I first came here, this was a rumor again, from a reliable source, that the captain notified the deputies not to treat me any differently than other prisoners. So I haven't suffered any brutality here. The attitude of the deputies is somewhat hostile and just yesterday, for instance, I got into somewhat of an argument with one of the deputies for a very petty reason. The reason was this: the deputies here demand that when any of the prisoners addresses them, he must address them as sir or mister, and of course, they address the prisoners by the prisoners' first or last name. I was asking one of the deputies something yesterday and he kept walking; then he abruptly turned around and he came back and said, "Whenever you address me, you call me mister or you call me sir." And I told him, very fine, that I would do that, but in return I would demand equal respect and that he would speak to me as sir or as mister. He got very upset and he stormed out and approached the lieutenant and told the lieutenant his problem—that a prisoner wouldn't call him sir—and gave some indication that he wanted to put me in the punishment cell, where the—incidentally, I was asking him if I could shave, because we don't have the facilities within our tank to shave. We have to be taken to the barber shop; so, the lieutenant then told him, and this is heresay, that don't shave him until he says sir. Fortunately, another deputy came around and gave me a shave because if he hadn't I would be forced to grow a beard down to my knees before I would say sir if I wasn't getting equal respect. This is only to relate an attitude, but as far as physical brutality goes, I don't receive that.

Q: While you're here, what can you do?

A: Well occasionally, I get the paper about a day late. I have a few books that I have been reading. It's pretty difficult to get reading materials in, but I have received a few books, so I spend most of my time reading, and doing some writing.

Q: I wonder if you'd comment on something that struck me. Now some young white people, especially from the middle class, have dropped out from the middle class way of life but also from the activist role. This hasn't happened among young black people, they've sort of more or less shunned the drift into the drop-outs, marijuana, and everything.

A: Yes, among the dropouts I may infer that you're speaking of the hippies in Haight-Ashbury and if you analyze the Hippie movement you'll find that most of them were middle class, members of a middle-class family, upper or lower middle-class. These families have had just about every material thing that they could desire. Also, this class has had the opportunity to become well educated. And through this they realized how bankrupt the American system is, the governmental system, and as far as participating in it, they've chosen not to participate after their enlightenment, after their education and after they've analyzed the system. So because they're in a state of dismay about change, because the tremendous technology of this country sort of broke their spirits and they dropped out. Because the country has a great military and economic power, so they've concluded that they can make very little change, so they've dropped out. Black people, in general, are not middle class, we're socially and economically of the lower class. We haven't received the basic things that we want because of the system. Because of a tremendous spirit, because of a great revolutionary fervor that we've had and we've kept ever since we were brought here to this country from Africa. We have not been broken, we're still striving. We say that our spirit is greater than the technological developments and we can and will make changes. So we don't have time for anyone who has dropped out of the struggle for freedom.

Q: There are a lot of people interested in the Executive Mandate No. 3 that you've issued to the Black Panther Party. Would you care to comment on that?

A: Yes. Mandate No. 3 is this demand from the Black Panther Party speaking for the black community. Within the mandate we admonish the racist police force that if they continue to break down our doors and be aggressive towards us and inflict brutality upon us, that we will be forced to protect our homes from them. Party Members have experienced, Bobby Seale, the Chairman, in particular, the police breaking down the door and coming into his house without a warrant and acting in a criminal fashion. We maintain the right to protect ourselves from criminals. When the police come into our house acting as a criminal, he should be brought to justice by the occupants of that house. In the Mandate, we relate the St. Valentine's Day Massacre that gangsters dressed up in police uniforms under the leadership of Al Capone and because they were dressed up in police uniforms they were admitted into the house of the individuals who turned out to be their victims. So, in other words, just because a man has on a police uniform, doesn't make him a representative of justice or a representative of a peace officer. He could be a wolf dressed in sheep's clothing. We realize this and we would like the police to know that anytime they break down our doors unjustly, without a warrant and without any provocation whatsoever, that we're going to defend ourselves against them.

Q: Are you and the other Black Panthers working out a concept of what you'd like this country to be like, the specifics of what will replace this system one day?

A: Yes, the Black Panther Party, you'll note, has demanded full employment, we've demanded decent housing, we've demanded good education, and justice, and we feel that this system as it is, cannot give this to us. The American capitalistic Imperialist system has never been able to employ all of its people, particularly because of the greed of the private owner, and his so-called private enterprise. We know that when the American white people speak of free enterprise that goes along with the idea of capitalism. They assume that everyone has had the freedom of competition to compete with the next fellow, and it turns out the man who works hardest will reap more. This doesn't hold true for black people. When we move to the west where this free enterprise is working fairly well for white people. They were staking out land and the ones that would till the soil the hardest, would benefit the most. Well, at this period we were slaves, as we are now. We've never been given a chance to participate in this so-called free enterprise. We built this country, for the industrial system was built up on slave labor in the South. We made it possible for this country to industrialize. And we say since we have never benefited from free-enterprise and private ownership, this is not a good goal for us. And we say that every man that is born on the soil, he has a right to live. And to live, he's going to have to work. If he can't work because of some physical reason, then it's up to the administrators of that country to support the individual because of his right to live. If the administration says well, we can't possibly employ our people, then we say that system has to be changed, and we say that we'll put in new administrators who are really interested in the welfare of the people in the country. And as far as the means of production go, we say that if the way that the means of production are being handled now is not working, then it has to be changed. If we can't get full employment, then we say the means of production must be taken away from them and put in the people's hands, and we'll have managers or administrators to run our production for the welfare of the people in general of the country. You say that this is the richest country in the world, and we're sure the country can give us full employment if it wanted to. If you didn't have the greed of profit and racism in this country, tomorrow you could have full employment.

Q: Mr. Carmichael recently said that Socialism doesn't fit black people and Communism doesn't fit black people, and here you say that Capitalism doesn't fit black people. Do you think that is significant, from what you've said you don't think Capitalism done good for the black people?

A: Prime Minister of the Black Panther Party, Stokely Carmichael said Communism had no answers to the problems of black people because it didn't relate to racism. I remember him saying that Capitalism didn't answer the question either. Perhaps I'm wrong on that, but as I read it he said that Capitalism didn't answer the needs of black people. What I want to point out is this: Say you had a Communist structure without relating to racism. Communism relates to an economic system, in which the means of production are in the hands of the people, and the people put up administrators to run their production material so there will be no profit, there will only be wages which will go back into the community for the general welfare of the people. Now if you just treat it per se as Communism in this country, I would say that it wouldn't work, I would say that until you get rid of racism—racism is a psychological thing that stems all the way back to England and Europe in general—no matter what kind of economic system you have, black people will still be oppressed. Racism began when the Europeans met the Africans, and I have my own conclusions as to what happened during that time, some conclusions that I've drawn about it, and I think that it goes so deeply psychologically, it goes into the difference in the culture of the European and the culture of the African and particularly in how the European worships. The European had this one god that he defined as all good. He was created in the image of this god. And, of course, god can do no wrong, and since he was like god, he could do no wrong. As far as sexual drives and so forth, this had no place in god's mind, so therefore it should have no place in the European's mind. But this was a big deviation from human nature, discounting sex drives. So he looked for witches and everything else to blame his own human nature on. Since he couldn't fall beneath the grace of god, he had to be able to say, No, I'm not causing this within myself, so someone else must be. Then you have the contact with Africans who always had a god who was both good and bad. In Africa the religious system is called Dualism, in Europe you had Absolutism. And in Africa South of the Sahara where most black people came from you had Dualism, where the god had two or more heads, one good head and one bad head, and the Africans were created in god's own image. When he was out of the grace of the good head, he would try to manipulate to get back in so that the bad head couldn't do him any wrong. But, the African recognized himself as both bad and good. He had self acceptance. He didn't need to put his human drives off on other people. When the European met the African this was a good person for him to say these people are vulgar, these people are pagans, and every other kind of derogatory word. It had nothing to do at that present moment with anything economical, it was simply a difference of culture and a sick mentality in the Europeans. And I think you have the European coming to America and creating the American colony and bringing this psychological sickness with him. As far as an economical structure changing his sick mind, I doubt if this would happen. He needs a psychiatrist or some mental therapy. And I say economically black people cannot profit through Capitalism within the structure, and as far as Socialism solving the problems per se, and all together, I doubt very seriously whether it can. I believe that it can solve the economic problem, but as far as the mental attitude—who is to say that after we choose these representatives that if everyone is profiting, or is supposed to profit by the wealth or the materials that are in the country, who is to say that even this is not going to be handled in a discriminatory way? So, I say that any time we talk about a political or economic thing, we can't just dismiss the psychological part.

Q: You're looking for a more complete, fuller ideology, a more advanced one?

A: That's right.

Q: It's true, is it not, Huey, that racism got its birth through economic reasons so that one group could superimpose its economic power over another?

A: I would agree with that. I think the prime thing was the economic rape of Africa. But at the same time, why did Europeans choose the Africans South of the Sahara to enslave? Now, some accounts I read by Basil Davidson and Melville J. Herskovits stated that the priests in Spain said don't enslave those Africans North of the Sahara because they worship one god But it's all right to enslave Africans South of the Sahara because they are pagans and not human as they lack a soul. So, what happened? They needed this justification to condone their economic exploitation, but this sort of ran haywire. Afterwards, it starts being imbedded so that the economic structure can go on and black people don't have souls and now you run into a problem where people who don't understand the economic situation still have been imbedded with the value system that black is bad, black is evil.

77. DRUM: "DARE TO FIGHT! DARE TO WIN!"

I. Preamble

We the super-exploited black workers of Chrysler's Hamtramck Assembly Plant recognize the historic role that we must play and the grave responsibility that is ours in the struggle for the liberation of black people in racist U.S.A. and people of color around the world from the yoke of oppression that holds all of us in the chains of slavery to this country's racist exploitative system. Because we recognize the magnitude of the prob-

Constitution of the Dodge Revolutionary Union Movement (Detroit, Mich., 1968), mimeographed.

lem and the dire predicament of our people, we do here proclaim our solemn duty to take this the first step on the road to final victory over the great common enemy of humanity; i.e. the monstrous U.S.A. and the aforementioned system of exploitation and degradation.

We fully understand after 5 centuries under this fiendish system and the heinous savages that it serves, namely the white racist owners and operators of the means of production. We further understand that there have been previous attempts by our people in this country to throw off this degrading yoke of brutal oppression, which have ended in failure. Throughout our history, black workers, first slaves and later as pseudo-freedmen, have been in the vanguard of potentially successful revolutionary struggles both in all black movements as well as in integrated efforts. As examples of these we would cite: Toussaint L'Ouverture and the beautiful Haitian Revolution; the slave revolts led by Nat Turner; Denmark Vesey and Gabriel Prosser; the Populist Movement, and the labor movement of the 30's in this country. Common to all of these movements were two things, their failure and the reason why they failed. These movements failed because they were betrayed from within or in the case of the integrated movements by the white leadership exploiting the racist nature of the white workers they led. We, of course, must avoid this pitfall and purge our ranks of any traitors and lackeys that may succeed in penetrating this organization. At this point we loudly proclaim that we have learned our lesson from history and we shall not fail. So it is that we who are the hope of black people and oppressed people everywhere dedicate ourselves to the cause of liberation to build the world anew, realizing that only a struggle led by black workers can triumph our powerful reactionary enemy.

II. Purpose and objective

Our purpose is to come together as black workers to relieve the long suffering of our people under this demon system of racist exploitation. Our sole objective is to break the bonds of white racist control over the lives and destiny of black workers with the full understanding that when we successfully carry out this mammoth task, relief will be brought to people all over the world oppressed by our common enemy. With stakes so high the enemy will undoubtedly resist with great ferocity, this tide of change that will sweep over him and his system like a mighty storm.

We must gear ourselves in the days ahead toward getting rid of the racist, tyrannical, and unrepresentative UAW as representation for black workers, so that with this enemy out of the way we can deal directly with our main adversary, the white racist management of Chrysler Corporation. In this way we will be able to overcome the obstacle that the enemy has erected between himself and black workers that denies us the necessary confrontation in order to bring down this racist exploitative system.

III. Procedure

To reach our objectives, DRUM shall be a democratic organization demanding the full participation of all members. Our concept of democracy being, of course, different from the pseudo-democracy of the UAW and other so-called democratic institutions in this dictatorial land. Each member is required to prepare himself for full participation in the activities and discussions of DRUM through study and understanding the problems we face in carrying out our program. In our discussion, all relevant ideas should be raised and deliberated upon. And in our activities, great care must be exercised in planning and carrying them out to ensure their success. Meetings shall be chaired by an appointed chairman and an agenda will be circulated prior to meetings. Members will be required to exercise discipline over themselves to ensure an orderly meeting.

IV. Rules governing membership

Membership in DRUM will be contingent upon a member's ability to commit himself to the DRUM program and discharge his responsibilities to this organization. These responsibilities are: (1) Acceptance of the DRUM program which means full and resolute participation in activities and organizational affairs. (2) A member should be subject to evaluation and criticism of the members of the committee that he serves on. (3) The individual committees should set the criterion whereby membership is democratically granted, denied or withdrawn. (4) Membership is denied to all honkies due to the fact that said honkey has been the historic enemy, betrayer, and exploiter of black people. Any relationship that we enter into with honkies will be only on the basis of coalition over issues. (5) Members should pay their dues on a weekly or monthly basis. Each individual unit will have responsibility of collecting dues as well as deciding when a member is sufficiently delinquent to warrant disciplinary measures.

V. Duties of officers

The duties of officers has been outlined in the discussion of structure. It should be further added that all officers are accountable to the membership and should be constantly scrutinized, evaluated, and subjected to constructive criticism in open discussion by his committee. Officers can be removed by a democratic vote within his compartment with recourse to the membership at large if so desired.

We recognize our struggle is not an isolated one and that we have common cause with other black workers in this racist nation and throughout the world. For this reason it is incumbent upon us to foster, join with, initiate and lead other black workers in our common struggle. By being in the forefront of this revolutionary struggle we must act swiftly to help organize DRUM-type organizations wherever there are black workers, be it in Lynn Townsend's kitchen, the White House, White Castle, Ford Rouge, the Mississippi Delta, the plains of Wyoming, the tin mines of Bolivia, the rubber plantation of Indonesia, the oil fields of Biafra, or the Chrysler Plants in South Africa.

Needless to say, our line is the hard line. We are in a life and death struggle that has been raging savagely for 5 centuries. A struggle between master and slave, rich and poor, black and white, beast and prey, management and worker. A struggle which has shown no quarter to the black man and which we now wage and give no quarter. The ruthless and vicious nature of our enemy has brought us to a point where we are now prepared to be as ruthless and vicious, if not more so. All that the honkey has acquired, has been acquired through his exploitation of our people with his brutal tactics of murder, enslavement, mayhem, and rape. Our line is one of consistent struggle in which we support everything the enemy opposes and oppose everything the honkey supports.

DARE TO FIGHT! DARE TO WIN!

Fight, Fail, Fight again, Fail again—Fight on to Victory!
Long Live Black People in This Racist Land! Death to Their Enemies!
Long Live the Heroic Black Workers Struggle!
Long Live DRUM!

Index